b

c

Trade & Travel
Publications
and
MEED

The Gulf Handbook
1978

Uniform with this volume:

The South American Handbook, 1978

Edited by John Brooks, the 54th annual edition of The South
American Handbook is the pre-eminent guide for travellers to
that fascinating Continent.

Press Comment:

. . ."The South American Handbook goes a long way to bringing
Latin America into the light. . . . Its thousand-odd pages of small
and busy print clamour for the attention of anyone who is keen
on armchair travel or is thirsty for sheer information. . . . The
Handbook moves pyramidally from the general to the particular:
from geographical and historical summations to regions, cities,
towns, and even villages, from current economic reports to a
concluding section of brisk practical information on matters
like money, travel, documents, food, dress, and national habits,
sufficient to allay the anxieties of even the most timorous."

. . . "The pleasure one takes in reading the South American
Handbook is that of feeling the huge, unwieldy abstractions of
Latin-American countries reduced to a sharply observed
particularity, as though they had been trudged through by
someone in no hurry at all, and taken in by a kindly, unjudging,
sympathetic eye. . . . Soaked in attention, the little crowded
capsule of the Handbook swells into a whole continent of
information."

> Alastair Reid, in his 2,500-word encomium,
> *The New Yorker.*

Over 1,000 pages, with 8-pages sectional coloured maps,
full bound with tough, plastic-laminated four-colour case.

Write to the Publishers for prospectus:
Trade & Travel Publications Ltd.
Bath, England

ISBN 0 900751 10 X

SECOND, REVISED, EDITION

A Guide for Businessmen and Visitors

The Gulf Handbook 1978

General Editors

> **PETER KILNER**
> Editor, 'Arab Report & Record'
>
> **JONATHAN WALLACE**
> Editor, 'Middle East Economic Digest'

> *Editor*
>
> **SEAN MILMO**

**Trade & Travel Publications, Bath
and MEED, London**

TRADE & TRAVEL PUBLICATIONS LTD
THE MENDIP PRESS, PARSONAGE LANE
WESTGATE STREET, BATH, ENGLAND
Tel. 0225 64156   TELEX 44600 SOWPAL G

MIDDLE EAST ECONOMIC DIGEST LTD
21 JOHN STREET
LONDON, WC1N 2BP
Tel. 01 404 5513   TELEX LONDON 21879 MEEDARR

DS
326
G83
1978

First published 1976

ISBN 0 900751 09 6

Distributed in the United States by
Garrett Park Press, Maryland, 20766

Printed in Great Britain by
Dawson & Goodall Ltd, Bath BA1 1EN, England

Contents

Introduction p. 3—Religion/Culture p. 7—Women in the Gulf p. 13—Doing Business in the Gulf p. 16—General Information p. 21 (*Travel (to the Gulf)—Inter-Gulf and domestic travel—Visas and travel restrictions—Travelling expenses—Hotel facilities—Alcohol*)—Health Precautions p. 25

The Guide section in each country contains detailed information about hotels, restaurants, night clubs, taxis, car hire firms, airline offices, post offices and useful phone numbers, shops and souks, social clubs and leisure facilities, hospitals and pharmacies, banks, ministries and government departments, embassies, newspapers and the media, and major companies.

The General Information sections list details on how to get to each country, visas, hours of business, public holidays, health precautions, posts and telecommunications, customs and currency regulations, alcohol restrictions, useful advice on clothing and social customs, further reading and members of the government.

Guide p. 59—General Information p. 78

Guide p. 130—General Information p. 157

Guide p. 213—General Information p. 232

Guide p. 279—General Information p. 292

MAPS

Cover picture: *U.A.E. Earth Satellite Station at Dubai.*

Editorial

For this second edition, *The Gulf Handbook* has not only been brought up-to-date but the whole structure of the book has been revised. Although the first edition proved even more popular than we had anticipated, we felt that for the growing number of visitors to the area, especially to the newer, fast-changing countries, there was need of more information concerning the places likely to be visited, the facilities available in them, and the difficulties to be faced both by visitors and residents. The background articles on the history and economy of the eight countries covered have, therefore, been curtailed, while the guide sections have been greatly expanded. For the new introductory section on the region as a whole, special articles have been commissioned to provide the reader with a wider view of the cultural context in which he will be moving.

To achieve this revision, Sean Milmo, our Executive Editor, has travelled widely in The Gulf in order to obtain on-the-spot that accurate and factual information which is not available in other publications, and to add that personal flavour which cannot be obtained from the distance of London. He has had the support of correspondents working in each of the main cities of the region, as well as many friends of MEED who have provided him with additional material from their personal experience. It is, however, due to him that this revision has been so thoroughly carried out and it is thanks to the tolerance of our co-publishers and printers in Bath that we have been able to include in the book changes which have taken place up to mid-September 1977.

The Gulf, as understood in this book, has seen steady changes in the past year. Apart from the great strides in construction, industrialisation and general development which accompany the influx of sudden wealth, there has been, at the political level, an ever-closening understanding of mutual problems. The meeting of Gulf Foreign Ministers in Muscat was a first step towards regional cohesion. The compromise on oil prices, after the short-lived two-tier system, showed a willingness among the big producers to stand together. The tour by Iraqi leaders indicated, if previously it was in doubt, that that country could no longer be thought of as peripheral to The Gulf. It may be some years before that sought-after economic and financial unity is achieved but politically the leaders of all eight countries are dedicated to thinking 'regional'. This book sets out to provide the background and paint in the details of that fabric of society against which these changes are taking place.

PETER KILNER
JONATHAN WALLACE

Acknowledgements

In the compilation of this second edition, we have had the assistance of many people and organisations, apart from those already mentioned or identified as contributors of individual articles. In particular we would like to thank the following who helped us and the Editor with the Region and the country sections: *Bahrain*, Gerda Azmeh, Youssef Azmeh, Alan Grimwood, Salma Kronfli, and The Ministry of Information; *Iran*, Antony Adie, Nicholas Cumming-Bruce, Robert Graham, Mrs Johnson, Jean-Marie Lebon, Liz Thurgood, and the Iran National Tourist Office; *Iraq*, Patrick Cockburn, Naji Hadithi, the Association of Hotels and Restaurants, the British Council, the Commercial Section of the British Embassy, the Ministry of Information and the National Tourist Organisation; *Kuwait*, Alan Mackie, Imtiaz Muqbil, and Ralph Shaw; *Oman*, Hilary Brown, and Jill Brown; *Qatar*, Christopher Barrett, Jill Brown, Michael Prest, and the Qatar Embassy, London; *Saudi Arabia*, David Farrow, Jihad Khazen, Bob Leibling, Ahmad Rashad, the Commercial Section of the British Embassy, Jeddah, and the Embassy of Saudi Arabia, London; *United Arab Emirates*, Tim Edgar, Helen Evans, Joe Harris, Carole Hassan, John Whelan, the Commercial Section of the British Embassy at Abu Dhabi, and the Embassy of the UAE, London.

One contributor, Trevor Mostyn, FRGS, deserves special mention. A frequent visitor to the Arab world and to Iran, he has, through his experience of the people and the places, together with his knowledge of their languages and their way of life, come near to being classed in this less romantic age with the great travellers of an Arabia now fast disappearing. In London, we would also mention the special help we have had from our editorial assistant, Miss Georgina Watkins.

It has also been of great help to the editorial team working on this second edition to have had the comments and candid criticisms of many users of the first edition, whose suggestions have been incorporated in the revised text.

We are especially grateful to Cable & Wireless for the photograph which, well illustrating the new surge in telecommunications on the Gulf, appears on the front cover of this second edition.

Our main office is just down the street from these buildings.

In each country where we operate, we regard the local office as important as the headoffice back in Holland.

All our 200 banking offices and affiliates in 40 countries are staffed by carefully selected qualified banking experts.

They know the people, the language, the market and they are backed by a thorough international organisation, which means they can draw on main office help whenever necessary for your specific banking needs.

You see, wherever you are, we want to get main office treatment. That's how ABN works.

ABN Bank

Amsterdam, Vijzelstraat 32, The Netherlands.

Our offices are located in: The Netherlands, Ireland, Great Britain, Belgium, **France,** Federal Republic of Germany, Switzerland, Gibraltar, Italy, Greece, Turkey, **Lebanon,** Saudi Arabia, United Arab Emirates, Bahrain, Iran, Pakistan, India, Malaysia, Singapore, Indonesia, Hongkong, Japan, Morocco, Kenya, U.S.A., Canada, Netherlands Antilles, Suriname, Argentina, Uruguay, Paraguay, Brazil, Perú, Ecuador, Colombia, Venezuela, Panama, Australia, Mexico.

THE REGION

THE REGION

"The Gulf" is used in this book as the name for a region of the Middle East stretching from northern Iran to the Red Sea coast of Saudi Arabia. This region is centred on a stretch of water, separating Iran from the Arabian Peninsula, which the Iranians call the Persian Gulf and the Arabs the Arabian Gulf. Westerners, wanting to remain neutral, prefer to call it just the Gulf and have extended the name to describe the whole region.

The Gulf Region comprises eight countries—Iran, Iraq, Kuwait, Saudi Arabia, Bahrain, Qatar, The United Arab Emirates and Oman. Even though all these states have a shoreline or an outlet on the Gulf coast, they do not form a compact geographical unit. Iraq, traditionally considered part of the Levant, hardly has any land on the Gulf and Oman merely has a tiny stretch of territory on the tip of the Musandam Peninsula. The region is more an economic conglomeration of neighbouring states which are at present using substantial oil revenues to develop their economies at a remarkably rapid pace. Hence the region does not include either North or South Yemen, both poor countries without oil, which are part of the Arabian Peninsula.

Geographical features   The region is bounded in the north by the Elburz Mountains which run along the southern shores of the Caspian Sea in northern Iran. East of these mountains are the Eastern Iranian Highlands both of which are on the periphery of a large central plateau, much of it desert. Between the Gulf and this plateau rise the Zagros Mountains which extend from the Mount Ararat massif in eastern Turkey. West of the northern section of the Zagros Mountains lie the Tigris-Euphrates lowlands of Iraq.

Both of these great rivers rise in the Armenian highlands of Asia Minor, emerging on the lower plateau uplands of northern Syria and Kurdistan before making their way southeastwards towards the Gulf coast. The Euphrates takes a course across the hot plains of Iraq losing large amounts of water through evaporation. The Tigris lies closer to the Zagros range, fed by many

3

tributaries which give it a larger volume of water, often causing it to flood.

South of the Iraqi lowlands and east of the Red Sea is the Arabian Peninsula, the largest single land unit in the Middle East, which consists mainly of the kingdom of Saudi Arabia. In the east it is bounded by the Hijaz-Asir mountains, from which a massive area of desert and lowlands stretches downwards towards the Gulf coast. In the south is the Rub al-Khali, the Empty Quarter, one of the largest deserts in the world. Further east is the United Arab Emirates, which in the north-east is divided by the Hajar Mountains, the only other high range in the peninsula. They extend into northern Oman which has a smaller range of mountains in its southern province of Dhofar. Further up the western Gulf coast from the UAE are three Gulf coastal states—Qatar, the island of Bahrain and, to the north, Kuwait.

The peninsula is one of the driest and hottest areas in the world. In most places the average annual rainfall is rarely more than a few inches. In the summer months temperatures can soar above 120°F. Most of the peninsula is by-passed by the two major sources of rain in the Middle East, the Atlantic westerlies and the monsoons of the Indian Ocean. The westerlies pass over the Levant and across the Zagros and Elburz mountains in Iran. The monsoons only penetrate Yemen and the Asir mountains of Saudi Arabia, and the southern parts of Oman. Much of the rain that does fall in the central peninsula comes in quick cloud bursts, resulting from disturbances among continental air masses.

Geological origins The geological structure of the region has been determined by two major faults. One, called the Great Rift, started in the lake country of East Africa and ran along the Red Sea northwards beyond the Gulf of Aqaba. It thrust up the Hijaz-Asir Mountains. Another fault raised up the Zagros Mountains in Iran, causing the highly resistant basement rock of the Arabian Peninsula to tilt eastwards. This bedrock had previously been covered by sea water rich with organic life like plankton and algae. The silt on top of this bedrock turned into sandstone and limestone holding in these organisms. When the tilt occurred this organic material became trapped and concentrated between rock strata. Slowly it changed into oil with impermeable rock forming a lid over it. Hence the origin of the region's oil wealth which was later to change its history so dramatically.

Historical highlights For most of its history the Gulf region's vast tracts of arid land have been inhabited only by nomadic tribes eking out a living in merciless conditions. Its main centres of population have been present-day Iraq and the western half of Iran. But despite its generally low population, it has been the cradle of ancient civilisations and the birthplace of one of the world's greatest religions. Mesopotamia was the home of the first literate civilisation—that of the Sumerians, dating from well before 3000 B.C., who, by inventing writing, surpassed perhaps even their contemporaries along the Nile.

It was in the flourishing commercial city of Mecca, which stood on the caravan route between the Levant and the frankincense lands of the Hadhramaut on the Indian Ocean, that the Prophet Mohammad was born around A.D. 570. Forty years later he started to spread the message of a new religion and within 50 years Islam was sweeping across the Arabian Peninsula and the rest of the Middle East.

Over the last few centuries the region's history has been one of domination by colonial powers. Portuguese forces arrived in the Gulf of Oman in 1507 and within a few years had taken over much of the Gulf coast up as far as Kuwait Bay. They were soon followed by the Dutch, French and British who competed with each other for control of the region. They all wanted to ensure control of their trading routes between Europe and India and the Far East.

By the end of the 18th century the British reigned supreme in the Gulf virtually unopposed by their European rivals. For two centuries they were able to wield considerable influence over the region. They never imposed direct rule anywhere. Instead they acted as protectors and peacemakers to a string of shaikhdoms stretching from Kuwait to Ras al-Khaimah. Further north the Turks kept a tight grip on Iraq and for a period controlled the western part of present-day Saudi Arabia.

It is only comparatively recently that the Gulf region has been able to free itself fully from the colonial yoke. British power began to fade in the area only in the 1960s when the British

Government finally announced a total withdrawal of its forces. Kuwait, Bahrain, Qatar and the United Arab Emirates became fully independent countries in their own right.

It was no mere coincidence that at the same time the Gulf states were beginning to exploit the huge reservoirs of oil lying beneath their territories. Within a few years, the wheel had gone full circle. With oil wealth behind them, the Gulf countries no longer had to bow to their former Western masters and began to have a powerful influence on world events.

Oil wealth The Gulf's first barrel of oil was exported by Iran just before the First World War. It was the area's only commercial producer until the late 1920s and 30s when Iraq and Bahrain started exporting oil. But oil production on a large scale in the region did not really start until after the Second World War, which had delayed the exploitation of many oil fields. In the 1950s Saudi Arabia and Kuwait began to export oil and soon they were joined by the United Arab Emirates, Qatar and Oman. In September 1960 four Gulf countries—Iran, Iraq, Kuwait, Saudi Arabia—decided at a meeting in Baghdad, attended also by Venezuela, to form the Organisation of Petroleum Exporting Countries (OPEC). A year later Qater joined the new organisation, followed in 1967 by Abu Dhabi, which in 1974 transferred its membership to the United Arab Emirates. Both Bahrain and Oman have decided to remain non-members. Now Gulf states make up six of the 13 members of OPEC.

The formation of this cartel has enabled the oil exporters, among whom the Gulf oil producers form the biggest bloc, to end the artificial pricing of oil which for years had been in the hands of the seven big Western oil companies. They had calculated the Gulf price on the basis of the cost of a barrel of oil in the Gulf of Mexico. OPEC soon put an end to this and in 1973/74 the price of its oil was quadrupled.

Development boom The result has been a rapid accumulation of wealth by Gulf countries and a development boom unprecedented in world economic history. Saudi Arabia's Gross National Product (GNP) has jumped from $3,000 million in 1970 to $52,000 million in 1976. Iran's GNP has gone up from $11,500 million to $62,000 million and Kuwait's from $2,500 million to $16,000 million. In the ten years between 1976 to 1986, it has been estimated that Saudi Arabia's GNP will grow by an annual 21 per cent, Iran's by 22 per cent and Iraq's by 18 per cent—a much higher level than any likely to be achieved by most other countries in the world. Furthermore, countries like Saudi Arabia and Kuwait have been unable to spend all their oil revenues, notching up large trade surpluses with the rest of the world. By December 1976 Saudi Arabia had accumulated a surplus of $23,000 million and Kuwait $6,500 million.

Throughout the Gulf the last few years have been a period of frenetic building activity, turning parts of the region into vast construction sites. Countries have had the money to do everything at once, taking a big leap forward into industrialisation. Whereas developed countries had taken several generations to build up their infrastructures and industries, the Gulf countries are doing it in a matter of years.

Roads, ports, airports, hospitals, schools, universities, stadiums, power stations, telecommunication networks and housing estates are all being built at a remarkable speed. These are being followed by the machinery of industrialisation—refineries, gas processing plants, petrochemical plants, steel works, aluminium smelters and a plethora of light industries. Most of the work is being done by migrant workers from elsewhere in the Middle East, the Indian sub-continent, the Far East and Europe and North America. Countries which for centuries have remained among the most isolated in the world have suddenly been engulfed by an influx of expatriates of a wide variety of cultures. The social impact of this invasion is still difficult to calculate. Its creations in concrete and asphalt are there for the eye to see but the social revolution it has undoubtedly precipitated has yet to run its full course.

RELIGION/CULTURE

Tradition has always played an important role in the Gulf states and it still flourishes amid the new skyscrapers, gleaming offices and Cadillac showrooms. But the understanding of local culture by the foreigners who flock to Saudi Arabia, Iran and the smaller Gulf states is often minimal. If anything, the lack of comprehension among expatriates has worsened the more development has progressed.

The importance of Islam The manners and customs of the Gulf are rooted in Islam (literally "submission" to God) and in its Holy Book, the Koran, which comprises the words of God as revealed to the Prophet Mohammad in Western Arabia in the 7th century A.D. Islam was not a new religion but a correction of Judaeism and Christianity. Mohammad maintained that the Jews and Christians had adulterated their Holy Books. Jews and Christians have never been labelled as infidels. Instead they are recognised and tolerated as "the people of the book". The basis of Islam is found in the opening words of the *Shahada*, the Muslim profession of the faith: "There is no God but God and Mohammad is the Prophet of God". Mohammad was the "seal" of the Prophets of whom Jesus, for whom great reverence is shown, was the penultimate. Christ was a holy figure but was not The Son of God.

Islam is based upon five Pillars of the Faith:

      1. Prayer
      2. Alms
      3. Fasting
      4. Ablution before prayer
      5. The Shahada or Profession of the Faith.

Although the pilgrimage (*Haj*) is a religious obligation it is not absolute and takes into account the difficulties of getting to Mecca. The *Jihad* ("striving" in the Way of God) against non-believers, while not a pillar of the faith, is also considered important.

Splits and schisms A brief knowledge of the history of Islam and the schisms that grew up during the period of its expansion is necessary to understand fully the cultures and the diversities of the Gulf countries. The Arab armies that toppled the Byzantine and Persian empires in the 7th century offered only the Koran and the discipline and purity which it taught. They had defeated empires rooted in millenia of brilliant civilisation. While the Persians embraced Islam with energy, they quickly brought their own cultural influences to bear upon the religion. The Abbasid Empire, established in the 8th century with strong Persian support, soon reflected the glories of the earlier Sasanian empire rather than the austere culture of the desert Arabs. Moreover the Abbasids supported the *Shia* schism which, although originating in a dispute among Arab theologians in Iraq, became the banner of Persian religious identity. It also absorbed Sufism, the mysticism that was for the masses of the people a closer, more emotional association with God than the abstract, transcendant religion of the Arabians.

Arabia was little influenced by Persia and Islam in the peninsula remained to a large extent the simple religion of the Prophet. It was threatened more by the apostasy of the bedouin in the 18th century, who became religiously lax and anarchistic. At the same time the Holy City of Mecca lapsed into decadence. The inevitable puritanical reaction against this degeneration came with the Wahhabi reformation of 200 years ago which still has a profound influence on modern Saudi Arabia and its neighbouring Gulf states.

The influence of Wahhabism Wahhabism began in the largely bedouin village of Dariya near Riyadh. The alliance of the reformer, Abdul Wahhab, and the warrior, Ibn Saud, was to lead to the unification of the greater part of the peninsula and the establishment of a theocratic state, based on the literal interpretation of the Koran. The reformation lost its momentum for a period but was revived by Abdul Aziz al-Saud at the beginning of the 20th century. Alcohol, dancing and gambling were forbidden. Women were obliged to wear the veil. Praying was enforced by the muttawas, the religious "police", five times a day. Saint worship was forbidden, statues and elaborate mosques were destroyed and replaced by buildings of the utmost simplicity.

Capital penalties for murder, theft and adultery were carried out in public on the strength of the testimony of three witnesses. While in the Arab littoral states which adopted Wahhabism these obligations have become largely theoretical today, in Saudi Arabia they are preserved, specifically by the religious lobby that remains a powerful force in politics. It is also seen to be a means of preserving a culture threatened by massive injections of Westerners and Western technology. For the old buildings of Riyadh and Jeddah are being swept away and the poetry of the bedouin is being forgotten in the advance of materialism. But wealth must not be allowed to lead to the abandonment of the Wahhabi revolution.

Wahhabism is the most literal interpretation of the *Sunna* (the path), the original form of Islam which predominates in the Arab world. Followers of the *Sunna* (Sunnis) are distinguished from the *Shia* who predominate in Iran and form a large section of the population in Iraq. The Shia culture is more ornate and emotional and reflects the grandeur of Iran's pre-Islamic imperial past. In Manama, Bahrain, which has a substantial Shia minority, a Sunni and a Shia mosque stand side by side. From the simple minaret of the austere Sunni mosque comes the rasping call of the *mueddhin* ("he who calls" the faithful to prayer) while from the flowery mosque of the Shia floats a beautiful elaborate chant verging on song. Saint-worship is forbidden by the Wahhabi Sunnis while nothing could be more emotive than the processions of weeping Shia on the feast day of Husain, the son of the Prophet's nephew, who was martyred at Kerbala in Iraq in A.D. 680.

Cultural differences Contrasts in religious outlook and culture are evident in the day-to-day behaviour of the people of the Gulf. While the Iranians are sophisticated, the Arabians remain nomadic in spirit. A prince in his office in Saudi Arabia today will be indistinguishable in dress and superficial manner from the shopkeeper in the nearby souk. He will treat the tea boy with the same deep respect he shows a foreign visitor. Initially the conversation is about anything except business. In Dubai, the office may be filled with bedu with falcons on their gloved wrists.

On the other hand, a bank director in Tehran will work in grand surroundings, massive rooms glimmering with chandeliers reflected in walls and ceilings of cut glass. Sitting behind an expansive desk, he will want to talk business at once, concisely and competitively. Here the culture of desert society is replaced by an elegance inherited from the glories of the Sassanian Empire.

The style of officialdom differs among Gulf states. Officials tend to be more readily available than in the West. Even in Iran the most senior people are accessible and most visitors will manage to see a Minister if they are prepared to make an appointment and wait. You should dress well in Iran for all functions, never discarding a tie and jacket. Meetings will normally be in private and may well be short. Although great courtesy will be shown, greetings will be succinct and you will not be expected to make "empty talk". Nothing could be more different in Saudi Arabia. Instead of making an appointment to see a Minister, you can simply wait in a crowd in a lobby. A businessman visiting a senior official in the Ministry of Agriculture may find himself ushered in with 20 bedu bringing grievances over grazing rights. Half an hour may be spent exchanging greetings. The official will probably know the name of each man and ask for specific details such as the health of the farmer's mother. Up to three cups of coffee or tea will be drunk. Each man will be careful to keep his feet on the ground, for in Arabia it is a great discourtesy to point the sole of the foot. No business will be discussed until the very end and then, however important, it may be slipped in at the moment of departure as an afterthought. Eloquence is common and the official may present a theatrical soliloquy praising the King and the Minister and God.

Common courtesies Every businessman visiting the Gulf today obviously wonders how much of the local culture he needs to know for success in his work. The answer is that although he is not obliged to know more than the formal greetings in Arabic and Farsi, it is essential that he understand the courtesies of life, as it is for a foreigner in Europe. While time is tight in the West, for example, the ability to make social small talk before setting down to business is vital in the Arab countries. He should make polite conversation, never refuse the tea that is offered him and should never show impatience however much of a hurry he is in. He should never eat or drink with his left hand. In Saudi Arabia he should wear a long-sleeved shirt, for among the Wahhabis it is considered indecent to bare the arms or legs—even for a man. While in Iran it is always obligatory to wear a jacket and tie, with most Saudi clients it is not. In the smaller Gulf states, however, where Western influence is stronger, it is always safer to wear a tie.

For the foreigner, however, a superficial understanding of the Gulf can be deceptive. From a first class hotel, he will see massive new building complexes and then Arabian men in their traditional dress and their women veiled and unapproachable. The truth is that the visitor needs to understand the local cultures far more than is immediately apparent. In Saudi Arabia and the smaller Gulf states, most concrete buildings are only a few years old and development has far outpaced changes in the local way of life. The old and the new live side by side, some would say on a collision course. The Saudi business contractor sits in his office surrounded by relaxed visitors as though he were in a desert tent. He has little desire to sacrifice his own background in favour of the fast, business-like attitudes of the West. The peoples of the Gulf expect foreigners to know something about their past, to comply with local customs and to belie the current suspicion that they have only come for the money.

WOMEN IN THE GULF

By Doreen Ingrams

Islam has played a dominant role in determining a woman's place in Arab society, and its laws—the *Sharia*—governing marriage, divorce, inheritance and property are nearly everywhere in force, but generalising about women in the Gulf may be misleading, as their position varies not only from country to country but between townswomen, bedouin women, and village women.

In traditional countries the seclusion of girls takes place at an early age and their marriages are arranged, although the girl may be consulted as to her feelings on the choice of her husband. As she will have little opportunity for finding one for herself, she is likely to be quite content with the one chosen for her. The marriage covenant provides a bride-price, which is a safe-guard for the bride in case of divorce. Polygamy, which is legal, is becoming less practised as public opinion grows increasingly against it. However, it is sometimes considered preferable to a divorce as, if a woman is divorced, her husband ceases to have financial responsibility for her. It is more difficult for a woman to obtain a divorce than for her husband to do so, as she will have to prove serious misconduct on his part, whereas a man can divorce his wife by simple repudiation, but this is rarely done today. The *Sharia* lays down provisions for children of the marriage after divorce. Custody of sons goes to the mother until the child is about seven years old, and the custody of a daughter until she is about nine. The father can then take them from her. This does not necessarily happen, but the fact that a woman might lose her children can deter her from seeking a divorce or add to her fears of being divorced.

Property laws The laws on marriage and divorce are surely weighted against women, but those regarding property and inheritance are not so discriminatory. A woman may control or dispose of her own property without reference to her husband

13

or father, and there are women in the Gulf who run their own businesses. The laws of inheritance oblige a man to leave a certain proportion of his assets to his widow and daughters, and though a daughter receives less than a son this is because it is the son's duty to take on financial care of the women in his family.

The custom of seclusion and veiling was not laid down in the Koran nor in the *Sharia*, but it came to be observed because of the great importance placed on protecting a woman's chastity. The more influential the man, the more his women were secluded, so that seclusion became a status symbol, but it inevitably led to a denial of education to girls and it emphasised the dependence of women upon their menfolk. It is only in recent years that schools for girls have become totally accepted in the Gulf and now that more and more girls are going on to secondary and higher education, this is bound to have an effect on their attitude to their position in society. Not that there is likely to be any vociferous movement for reform, nor is there likely to be any immediate desire to do away with the veil, which is often seen not as a sign of woman's inferiority but of man's respect for woman.

In Saudi Arabia and in most of the Gulf it is difficult for a woman to take up a career which may bring her into contact with men. She is, therefore, largely restricted to teaching in a girls' school or becoming a doctor or nurse in a women's hospital. There are some states in the Gulf where the women work in government offices, or in business, in radio or television, but such work is more often undertaken by women from other parts of the Arab world. Today the secluded life has been greatly broadened by the telephone, which enables a woman to keep in close contact with relatives and friends, and by the local television and the radio which have made her more aware of the world outside. Also, women are increasingly travelling abroad with their families.

Women in rural communities may often be much 'freer' than women in the towns. They work in the fields, fetch water and firewood, herd the goats and sheep—in fact it has been said that the Arab woman's role in agriculture gives rural women an economic activity and usefulness that contrasts with the secluded life of many townswomen.

Opportunities in Iraq The position of women in Iraq is different to that in other Gulf Arab states, notably in their opportunities for employment. They form a high percentage of doctors, teachers and university lecturers. They are employed in industry and in Government departments, where they receive equal pay with men. Iraq was the first Arab country to send women delegates to the United Nations. It has to be remembered that education for girls has been established in Iraq for far longer than in Saudi Arabia or the other Arab states of the Gulf, with the exception of Bahrain.

Foreign women going to the traditional states of the Gulf for the first time will feel that they have stepped into a man's world, and they may find it difficult to make contact with the veiled and cloaked women going by in cars or walking in the streets. Many of the Arab women will not speak English so that, unless the foreigner learns at least a smattering of Arabic, there will be little communication between them even if they do meet. On the other hand foreigners may meet women who are well acquainted with London, Paris or Washington, and who do speak fluent English, but the fact that they lead secluded lives in their own country will seem strange unless there is some appreciation of their religious and cultural background.

The role of women in Iran may differ from that in the Arab states of the Gulf region and will be considered separately in the third edition of this handbook.

DOING BUSINESS IN THE GULF

By Miles Reinhold, of the Middle East Association, London

Inevitably, many visitors to the Gulf region will be business men or women, but it is a poor traveller who cannot make a working visit pleasurable and venture further afield than office, hotel or factory site. Increasing opportunities and facilities present themselves and are being developed for leisure activities. The inhabitants of the countries this handbook covers are becoming more sophisticated, more cosmopolitan and, through wider education, are more demanding in ways and means of spending their leisure hours as well as their surplus revenue.

The general economy There can be few who are not by now at least well aware of the riches with which this area is blessed, based as they are on a product which is not only essential in its basic form, but of vital necessity in its many derivatives to the needs of Western industry. The growth potential, with highest theoretical *per capita* income and massive development expenditure literally running into thousands of millions of dollars each year has naturally attracted a steady stream of visitors of all nationalities. Boom markets, however, contain the seeds of the two main dangers of inflation and exploitation. Already overspending and over-ambitious plans have shown up deficiencies in the absorptive capacity of a number of the countries, causing them to cut back on expenditure. However, these matters are the affair of those who own the riches of these countries: they are not the primary concern of the visiting businessman. In his dealings, the importance of trust, fair dealing and personal contact always has been and always will be the best basis on which to construct any relationship.

Preparation for a visit For a visitor to the Gulf, be it his first trip or his twenty-first, there are some basic guidelines. You are going to visit countries with quite a different culture, historical background, religion and climate from your own, so do not complain of dissimilarities. You expect foreigners to your country to adapt to your ways, and logically you must accept theirs—doing the best you can to understand them.

It is normal to want to enjoy a visit, as well as make it commercially profitable if business is your aim, and so it is worthwhile preparing oneself as thoroughly as possible; indeed that is what this handbook (as well as much besides that is available) is designed to facilitate. Apart from increasing understanding of the country and its inhabitants, this preparatory homework will prevent some of the more appalling gaffes and expensive mistakes which the innocent abroad is prone to make. Every traveller has his favourite story of the stupidity or ignorance of others.

Corporate or individual progress? It is a common misapprehension that all Gulf states have infinitely elastic revenues derived from oil and that all the inhabitants of the area are of similar background, upbringing and general education. A realisation that this is far from the case, that poverty exists alongside luxury and that great strides are still required to bring standards up to anything approaching a total Western concept of modern living, is perhaps the first lesson that any traveller must learn. The people of the area have generally different standards of living, speak different dialects and are often of different Muslim sects. Iran is, of course, a non-Arab country with its own native tongue of Farsi.

Each state also often includes minority religious groups, and in at least two cases the nationals of the country uneasily find themselves in a minority position with immigrant workers of all grades out-numbering them. To balance this there are, of course, numerous common interests and interlocking economic and political factors which serve to bind the area loosely together, though as yet there are not any well-defined groups or major common policy declarations, except OPEC and OAPEC and the various bodies derived from these two organisations. Plans and discussions abound on such obvious points of mutual interest as regional defence, shipping, communications, banking and currency, planned industrial development and the like, but as yet these are relatively unspecific. What, of course, have emerged as shining examples of co-operation are the many funds which have been established by the fortunate rich to help their less-endowed brothers. These serve to finance development projects, support ailing economies and generally recycle oil surpluses through investments, both in the Middle East and further afield in Western countries. Many banking and financial institutions have thus grown up and today certain areas in the Gulf, such as Bahrain and the UAE, have become major financial centres.

Industrial diversification As will be seen in greater detail in this handbook, the countries in our study produce a major part of world oil resources. It should not, however, be forgotten that many of these countries have other mineral resources—some as yet unexploited, and in the case of Iraq and Iran a substantial agricultural industry capable of considerable expansion. The waters of the Gulf and the Caspian Sea too provide rich fishing grounds.

The finite nature of oil resources and the constant search and development elsewhere of alternative energy sources are the main reasons for the Gulf states' diversification plans being pressed on apace, while the going is good. And they do not overlook the necessity for finding work and an outlet for human energy too—for the countless thousands who through higher education and wider horizons are being introduced to modern life and its economic pressures, such as the Western world takes for granted. The properly planned future of these citizens will largely determine the stable progress of these states and the region as a whole. One way of building up this management and technician class so vital to a balanced community is through joint ventures. Such ventures are now a familiar pattern in varying forms throughout the region and in general represent a profitable and sensible way for East and West to develop hand in hand. Even in public sector tenders there is often a training clause inserted to ensure that not just a monument is left behind at the end of the contract.

Here too one can only repeat the advice given to the visitor; define your objective and its attendant problems and carry out a careful market research using every source to check. In this area the old military maxim is more than usually apposite: 'Time spent in reconnaissance is never wasted.' Be patient and prepared to go back again and again. Only this way will a business partner be properly selected and the market properly covered.

Where can I find out?   What are the sources of information available and where can the intending visitor go to brief himself properly? Each individual will naturally have to judge for himself what is appropriate to his needs and indeed what is possible to digest in the time he can spare. In this brief introduction one can only generalise, and the best advice is to seek guidance from those with previous experience and the many competent organisations that exist for this purpose. These include Government trade and export departments, information media of all sorts such as reputable newspapers and magazines. Embassies of the countries concerned, and commercial and industrial bodies such as Chambers of Commerce, Trade Associations, banks and certain educational establishments. Additionally there are numerous conferences and seminars, which not only provide specialist advice but also an opportunity to meet and mix with men and women with practical knowledge of the region.

There can be few companies or business men of any consequence who have not considered doing business in or with the Gulf states. Their senses will have been battered with exhortations to export and seize the opportunities that exist. Their offices will be full of literature covering every aspect of interest, and much that is not. To their credit, very many business men have taken the plunge, the majority with profit, usually developing in the process close friendly relations and continuing business. The influx of Gulf visitors to Europe and the UK in the last year or two has served further to reduce the areas of ignorance the one has of the other and to stimulate personal as well as commercial relationships. Business, like travel, is a two-way affair.

Everyone is an ambassador   The politeness and hospitality that one finds in the Gulf countries has been much remarked upon. It is often shown in quite different forms from Western conventions, but is nonetheless genuine, and understandably our Gulf friends expect reciprocal treatment. This is not to say that one need match customs exactly, for many of us have neither the means nor time so to do, nor is it expected. However, a courteous approach is *de rigeur*, aided, if possible, by a few standard greetings, and naturally care should be taken that behaviour and dress should not give offence. Calling on a business man in

19

bizarre clothing will not gain respect in the Gulf, any more than giving him ten minutes of your time. It is important to plan enough flexibility into your visit to allow for unpunctuality, longer than usual discussions and time to negotiate. Invite your agent to visit your office or factory (and family too) when next he visits your own country. Many journeys and meetings may be necessary before you get close to the business in hand and certainly before establishing continuity. Expect the unexpected, for it will always happen.

It is fairly true to say that most Gulf business companies or government departments are usually short on middle management and administration, though increasingly one meets European managers or advisers. Letters are an unreliable means of communication, although the greater urgency inspired by the telex is improving matters greatly. A deal is still often concluded with a handshake and personal guarantee, but must always be more conventionally confirmed as a formal contract, drawn up preferably with professional advice. One thing is certain, no Gulf businessman likes to do business by remote control for very long. Sooner rather than later, personal contact must be made and from then on the business relationship may well prosper or founder on the basis of that relationship. It is not uncommon for the foreign firm of whatever size to be identified by its Gulf representative who may well be of junior rank. This underlines the importance of selecting your company's ambassador carefully and briefing him well; technical brilliance and enthusiasm is not enough, admirable qualities though they are. His face may be your fortune.

Not once but many times have I met travellers back from a Middle East trip who when, recounting their exploits have said 'If only I had known.' This handbook will certainly help some avoid this confession.

GENERAL INFORMATION

Travel (outside Gulf)   Air links with the Gulf have inevitably improved considerably in recent years. Now there are regular flights from the main Western European capitals to the major centres in the Gulf. London provides the best connections with several flights a day leaving for most Gulf capitals. There are only a few direct flights from North America to the region. Dubai, Bahrain, Kuwait and Tehran have direct flights from New York—the only North American city with regular connections each way. Tehran is the only city with a daily service to and from New York.

Connections between the Indian sub-continent and the Gulf are good, with cities like Karachi and Bombay running several flights a day to many Gulf cities. Flights from the Far East are not so numerous. Tokyo, for example, has a relatively small number of daily flights to the region, considering the high level of business between Japan and the Gulf. Australia's main airlink to the region is through Bahrain which receives daily flights from Sydney and Melbourne.

Some cargo shipping lines serving Gulf ports take paying passengers. Otherwise, a major means of travelling to the Gulf is overland through Europe, either by rail or road. Both Iraq and Iran have rail connections with Europe through Turkey. It is now possible to drive all the way by tarmac road as far as Qatar in the Arabian Peninsula. Soon the completion of a road between Qatar and Abu Dhabi will make it possible to drive straight through to the United Arab Emirates and Oman. By the 1980s Bahrain should also be linked by highway to Europe when a causeway between the island and the Saudi mainland is built.

Inter-Gulf and domestic travel   Air travel between Gulf states can at times be difficult. Some countries have poor connections with other Gulf states. Sometimes it is not easy to get to Iran, for example, from a Gulf Arab state. Passengers wanting to travel to Tehran from a lower Gulf state have to go to Shiraz or Bandar Abbas first and then take a domestic flight.

Air travel in the Gulf can be more arduous than long-haul flights. Frequently it is essential to turn up at the airport a few hours before the flight time to be certain of a seat. Airlines have tended to overbook and often passengers have been left behind even though they have made a reservation. A simple trip from the departure lounge to the aircraft can degenerate into a frantic scramble with people vying for seats. On one of the busiest inter-Gulf routes, between Bahrain and Dhahran, a shuttle service has recently been introduced which could at least eliminate the problem of overbooking.

Domestic flights can be much easier and less crowded. Iran and Saudi Arabia—the region's two biggest countries—both operate reasonably efficient domestic services covering all major centres. *Saudia*, Saudi Arabia's national airline, runs a shuttle service on its two busiest routes, between Jeddah and Riyadh and between Riyadh and Dhahran. The major problem with these routes remains booking which can involve a long session in a queue at the airline's sales offices.

Visas and travel restrictions With a few exceptions, all Gulf countries require visas from non-Arab visitors. Iran however allows in passengers from most Western European countries without visas. British subjects can also enter Bahrain and Qatar without visas. Otherwise in most cases visas must be obtained from the embassies of the countries concerned beforehand.

Some embassies take one to two months to vet visa applications. Businessmen are usually required to send a letter from their company with the application and in some cases a letter from a sponsor in the Gulf. Generally visas can be obtained without much difficulty, though Iraq and Oman can be strict about issuing them. Any passenger whose passport shows that a visit has been made to Israel will be barred from entry. Iraq and Saudi Arabia will only admit Jewish visitors in special circumstances.

Travelling expenses The Gulf is one of the most expensive places in the world for a visitor. An international survey on business expenses by the *Financial Times* of London in late 1976 put Abu Dhabi top of a list of 60 places just in front of New York. Bahrain came fourth. The survey compiled a price index using London as a base. Abu Dhabi was found to be 132 per cent more expensive than London, Bahrain 119 per cent, Oman 85 per cent, and Tehran 56 per cent.

The Brussels-based Management Information Consulting Services conducted a similar survey about the same time on the living costs of Western expatriate contract workers in the Gulf. It also used London as a base for a price index. Bahrain was found to be 40 per cent more expensive, Dubai 55 per cent, Jeddah 62 per cent and Kuwait 64 per cent. The *Financial Times'* price index tended to be more inflated because it included the price of a top class hotel room and alcohol. But both surveys give a rough guide of the differences in costs between the Gulf and Western Europe. By the end of 1977 the gap should have widened because inflation in the Gulf, running at an annual rate of between 30 and 40 per cent, is at least three times higher than the average rate in Western Europe and North America.

During the first half of 1977 an average daily expenditure figure of $85–100 (excluding the price of the air fare) was adequate for a business trip in the Gulf. In the more expensive countries like Saudi Arabia and the United Arab Emirates (mainly Abu Dhabi and Dubai) the figure rose to $100–120, depending on the class of hotel. In Tehran daily expenses would have averaged around $70–85 and in Baghdad $50–70. By late 1977 and early 1978 these average rates should have gone up by at least 20 per cent, perhaps with the exception of Iraq where hotel and restaurant prices are kept relatively low.

Most prices quoted in this book were those prevailing in mid-1977. All hotel and restaurant prices will almost certainly be raised by late 1977, going up by anything between 10 and 50 per cent.

Hotel facilities All Gulf countries have a shortage of hotel rooms. They have been unable to build enough new hotels to keep up with the large numbers of businessmen visiting the region. But now supply is beginning to meet demand and by the 1980s many countries could have a surplus of hotel rooms. So many new hotels are being built in Abu Dhabi that the emirate is refusing to issue any more hotel building licences. Neighbouring Dubai is adding 4,000 more hotel rooms in the next five years. Tehran will have an extra 3,000 rooms within three years.

But even though hotel rooms are no longer so scarce it is still necessary to book to be sure of a bed, particularly during the peak season from October to April. If possible hotels should be contacted directly either by letter or telex (or even telephone if possible). Bookings should be confirmed in writing. Frequently businessmen have found themselves without a room because they are unable to produce written confirmation of their booking. Travel agencies and airlines often refuse to handle bookings in places like Abu Dhabi, Saudi Arabia and Kuwait because so many hotels are fully booked.

Visitors who have not booked or who have to make a sudden trip out to the area can usually count on finding a bed somewhere. Big cities have many modest hotels which can at least provide a bed until a room is found in a better class hotel. Some quality hotels will put additional beds into rooms to accommodate extra visitors during busy times and even turn conference halls into dormitories.

Most hotels in the Gulf have been built during the last five years. Some—like the Hiltons, Inter-Continentals, Sheratons— maintain a standard which is equal to any top class hotel in the world. But the majority in the higher price range are little better than medium-standard hotels in the West. Exorbitant prices can sometimes mislead the visitor into expecting far more comfort than is available. A large number of hotels has been built hurriedly in a speculative spree and do not comply to Western building standards. Already they may show signs of premature decay.

Alcohol Alcohol is only readily available in Iran, Iraq and Bahrain. In other countries it is either banned completely or can be bought only by expatriate residents with special permits. In the United Arab Emirates and Oman drinks can be bought in most hotels and restaurants, though in Abu Dhabi the authorities have recently clamped down on drinking in restaurants. In Saudi Arabia, Kuwait and Qatar drinks are not publicly available in hotels or restaurants. In countries where alcohol is banned, liquor may, however, be available privately and in Kuwait City and Doha, for example, there are hotels where residents may be served drinks. But visitors are advised not to try to break the rules themselves. Don't for example try to smuggle liquor through the customs. The penalties are too severe to make it worthwhile.

More detailed general information about each Gulf state can be found at the end of each country section.

HEALTH PRECAUTIONS

By Dr Anthony Turner, Senior Overseas Medical Officer, British Airways. Author of 'The Traveller's Health Guide' and 'Travel Medicine'

For the visitor to the Gulf there are certain basic principles which need to be followed to avoid the sort of medical problems found in the area. In general they are a matter of common sense. But some background knowledge helps. The principles cover five points: (1) vaccinations prior to travel; (2) advice for the journey; (3) how to acclimatise and avoid heat disorders; (4) avoidance of diseases of insanitation, including travellers' diarrhoea; (5) avoidance of insect-borne diseases, including malaria.

Vaccinations Vaccinations should be carried out as well in advance of travel as is possible. They can be divided into two groups. First those required by International Health Regulations, without which you may not be able to enter a country, and, second, those which are strongly recommended medically but which are not obligatory.

The first group consists of vaccinations against smallpox, cholera and yellow fever. Vaccination against smallpox is required for visitors to all Gulf states. Remember that women should not be vaccinated during pregnancy. Vaccination certificates are valid for three years starting eight days after a successful primary vaccination and immediately after revaccination. Cholera vaccination is required for all visitors to Oman and the United Arab Emirates. Saudi Arabia requires it during the period of the *Haj* (pilgrimage). With Iran, Kuwait, Qatar and Saudi Arabia (outside the *Haj*) it is required for travellers from infected areas. Bahrain and Iraq do not require it. Vaccination certificates are valid for six months and travellers should be immunised at least six days before they leave. Yellow fever immunisation is only required if the passenger has been in the yellow fever areas of Central Africa and Central America in the six days prior to arrival in the Gulf. Immunisation lasts for ten years. Remember certificates must be on the special International Certificate and unless done in special centres, your own doctor's signature must be countersigned by the local public health authority. Immunisation should be given at least 10 days before departure. Certificates are valid for 10 years.

Certain other vaccinations or inoculations are even more important health safeguards. People visiting the Gulf should be inoculated against typhoid, tetanus and poliomyelitis. All these injections can be given to you by your general practitioner. Typhoid and tetanus vaccinations, which can be given combined or separately, consist of three injections given six weeks and six months apart and boosters every three to five years. Poliomyelitis is given orally with three doses at monthly intervals and boosters every five years. Plague and typhus inoculations are NOT necessary for the Gulf area. Prophylactic rabies is not recommended other than for veterinarians but anyone bitten by a stray dog must seek medical advice at once. Immune gamma globulin injections are given to prevent infective hepatitis which is fairly common in the developing countries in the tropics including parts of the Gulf. Protection is fairly brief, with smaller doses giving protection for about two months and large doses for four to six months. Your own doctor would advise you on this.

Air travel   Modern jets fly well above patches of bad weather so there is little risk of motion sickness. However because of this high flying and for engineering reasons, cabin altitude cannot be pressurised to sea level and is usually fixed at about 6,000 feet. This causes some expansion of the gases in the body and a slight decrease in the amount of oxygen available. Hence cut down your smoking before and during the flight; do not eat to excess so preventing distension; wear loose fitting clothing and shoes; avoid fizzy drinks, and drink only moderate amounts of alcohol because it later hinders your ability to acclimatise to the heat. There is in general a three-hour time change between the Gulf and Western Europe. Take it easy for the first 24 hours after arrival and do not go rushing into important meetings.

Heat disorders   It is important to know how we keep cool in the heat, especially during the summer months. You need to perspire more easily, without the sweat glands getting fatigued too quickly. Sweat is a weak salt solution. To encourage this sweating, you must first drink enough fluids, maintain your salt level and wear suitable clothes which will help sweat to evaporate and so encourage you to sweat more.

In intense heat, severe dehydration can be avoided by drinking plenty of liquids. Every 24 hours try to drink one pint of fluid for every 10° of Fahrenheit temperature. In other words when the temperature is around 100°F drink ten pints of water in 24 hours and so on. With the Centigrade system, it is a basic two litres plus one litre for every 10°C. So at 20°C you drink four litres and at 30°C you drink five litres in 24 hours. If your urine turns a strong yellow, you are dehydrated. Normally it should be nearly colourless.

In temperate climates, you need 10–15 grammes of salt every 24 hours. In the tropics, depending on your work and the temperature, you need 15–25 grammes. So you really want to double your salt intake. It is far better to do this by adding extra salt to your food rather than by taking pills. You absorb it better. Once you have fully acclimatised in about six weeks your need for fluid and salt decreases slightly.

Cotton clothing is the best material to wear in the tropics. It absorbs half its weight of water. Man-made fibres can only absorb from three to 12 per cent instead of 50 per cent. If your clothes do not absorb the sweat then your skin remains bathed in moisture and you will develop "prickly heat". Loose-fitting clothes allow a layer of air between the clothes and the skin which also assists evaporation. Sunglasses of a good make are advisable. Hats are best avoided as the head makes up 25 per cent of the sweating area but may be necessary to wear when the glare is particularly strong.

If you must sunbathe, whether intentionally or by going out sailing in the Gulf or lying by a swimming pool, remember the sun is very hot especially in a clear sky. A quarter of an hour exposure the first day is advisable, half an hour the second, and one hour the third and then double up daily. Use good quality sun lotions or creams, not oils. A lot of people have found that taking two tablets of Sylvasun, a vitamin A calcium carbonate preparation, for the first two weeks is very effective in preventing pain.

Intestinal upsets A large percentage of travellers suffer from brief attacks of diarrhoea lasting up to about three days. Despite their briefness, they can be completely incapacitating. There are the more serious outbreaks of diarrhoea, resulting from dysentery and typhoid. The chances of suffering from any of these complaints can be greatly diminished by abiding by simple food hygiene principles and, for the short-term traveller, taking an anti-infective agent. Many anti-diarrhoea tablets, like *Enterovioform* and *Mexoform*, which are bought over the chemist's counter, have been proved by clinical trials to be of little preventive value. A tablet proven to be effective is *Streptotriad*, with one being taken twice daily for up to one month. Many professional sportsmen use it with great effect but it is usually only available on a doctor's prescription. General food hygiene is highly important in preventing intestinal infections. Unless you are certain it is safe, tap water should be boiled before drinking. There are several proprietary sterilising tablets such as *Halozone* and *Steritabs* which are very effective. Milk should also be boiled if it is not known to have been satisfactorily pasteurised. Great care should be taken with shellfish. It is better to see them alive first and to look carefully at their cleaning. All cooked food should be well cooked and recently cooked. All fruit including tomatoes should be peeled. Fruit that cannot be peeled and lettuce should be well washed in chlorinated water. Foods from street hawkers and vendors must be avoided. Keep away from fly-infested restaurants, particularly those with dirty lavatories.

Malaria prevention Malaria is a serious disease which can be fatal. The visiting European or American with no acquired immunity is far more likely to be very ill and even die from malaria than the local who has been infected throughout his life and has acquired immunity. Malaria is very prevalent in Oman, and the United Arab Emirates. It also occurs in Bahrain, Iran, Iraq and Saudi Arabia.

The disease is spread by the anopheline mosquito. It is most important to keep yourself well covered with clothes after dark in malarious areas. Long sleeves and long trousers or skirts should be worn. If necessary, use an insect repellent on exposed skin areas such as *Skeet-o-Stik* or *Flypel*. One application lasts 3–4 hours, less when sweating. An insecticidal aerosol spray is effective in the bedroom. If the room is not satisfactorily air conditioned with tight fitting fixtures, a mosquito net should be fitted in the window framework or over the bed.

However the most efficient prevention is an antimalarial tablet, which should be taken while in a malarious area and for a minimum of 28 days after leaving it. A tablet called proguanil (*Paludrine*) is among the most effective. In the US doctors recommend chloroquine taken once or twice a week. But it is easier to remember a daily tablet rather than a weekly or twice weekly one. The incubation period of malaria is 10–12 days. To miss a daily tablet leaves a two day gap; to miss a weekly tablet leaves 14 days without protection which could be a disaster. But chloroquine is the best drug for treatment, rather than prevention.

Ten rules   In the Gulf there are ten commandments to follow:

(1) Rest for 24 hours after a five-hour time change.
(2) See that your foods are well cooked.
(3) Peel all fruit and be careful with salads and ices.
(4) Take two tablets of *Streptotriad* daily for up to four weeks.
(5) Be very careful with sunbathing at first and use good quality creams and lotions.
(6) Drink an adequate amount of fluids and maintain your salt level.
(7) Take anti-malarial tablets daily in the malarious area and for 28 days after leaving.
(8) Boil drinking water and milk.
(9) Never wear nylon in the heat.
(10) Do not bathe in rivers, lakes or harbours where the water is unclean.

There are two non-medical points worth noting. Firstly, if you are not covered by a company sickness scheme take out an insurance policy for at least $2,000, preferably more. It is very cheap. Secondly, if you fall sick at home within a few weeks of your return tell your doctor exactly where you have been.

BAHRAIN

THE AMIR OF BAHRAIN

THE AMIR OF BAHRAIN
His Highness Shaikh Isa Bin-Sulman al-Khalifa

Shaikh Isa succeeded to the Amirship on the death of his father, Shaikh Sulman Bin-Hamad, on 16 December 1961. Born in 1933 as Shaikh Sulman's eldest son, he became the tenth member of the Al-Khalifa family to rule in Bahrain since it was conquered by his ancestor Shaikh Ahmad in 1782. When Shaikh Isa succeeded his father at the age of 28 he had already acquired considerable experience in public life. In 1953 he had been appointed to the Council of Regency which administered the state during Shaikh Sulman's absence. Shaikh Isa subsequently became President of the Manama Municipal Council and also served with distinction on the Council of Administration. Shaikh Isa was appointed Heir Apparent in 1958. In the following year, because of the illness of his father, he was called upon to play an increasingly active role in the affairs of Bahrain.

Bahrain

Area 231 square miles
Population 266,078 (August 1975 estimate)
Chief towns Manama (capital) 150,000; Muharraq 37,732
Gross National Product $630 million (1975 estimate)
GNP per caput $2,440

GEOGRAPHY

Bahrain is an archipelago of 33 islands covering 255 square miles, situated about 15 miles off Saudi Arabia's eastern coast. Only six have a population of any significant size, the largest being Bahrain Island, 30 miles long and 10 miles wide, on which the capital—Manama—is located. The others are Muharraq, which is linked by a causeway to the main island, and on which the airport is sited, Sitra and Nibih Salih to the east and Jidda and Umm al-Nasan to the west.

The country's only large cultivatable area is a narrow strip of land three miles wide on the northern coast of Bahrain Island. Fresh water springs and artesian wells here help produce a variety of vegetables and fruits.

South of this cultivated area the land is lined with low, undulating hills, a few rocky cliffs and dry wadis. In many places the hard limestone rock is covered with sand dunes. The highest land on the island is in the centre, from where the ground slopes southwards into a basin bordered by steep cliffs. Near the middle of the basin rises a rocky hill called Jebal al-Dukhan ('Mountain of Smoke'), which is often surrounded by mist at the base, making it look larger than it is.

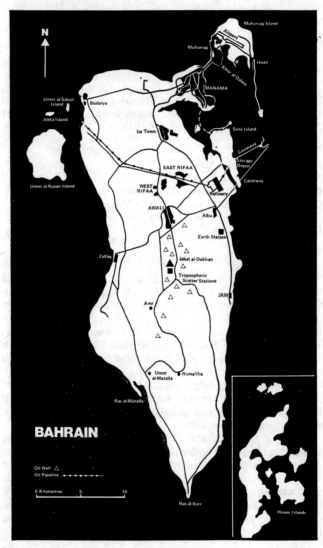

BAHRAIN

N

Muharraq Island
Airport
Muharraq
Hedd
Khor al-Qalta
MANAMA
Umm al-Saban Island
Budaiya
Jidda Island
Isa Town
Sitra Island
Umm al-Nasan Island
EAST RIFAA
Causeway
Storage Depot
Cableway
WEST RIFAA
Refinery
AWALI
Alba
Earth Station
Zellaq
Jabal al-Dukhan
Tropospheric Scatter Stations
JAW
Amr
Umm al-Matalla
Rumaitha
Ras al-Matalla

Oil Well △
Oil Pipeline ●●●●●●●

0 Kilometres   5   10

Ras al-Barr

Hawar Islands

Bahrain lies in bright green and blue waters clarified by fresh water from submarine springs. For centuries they have provided the population with fish, coral for buildings, and pearls.

CLIMATE

The climate can be harsh. In the summer months, extending from May to October, it can become extremely hot and humid. From July to September the temperature can reach 120°F. inland with 80 per cent humidity. The most pleasant time of year lasts from December to March, when a wind blows from the north and west and the temperature averages around 63°F. Sometimes frost even occurs. In April and May, and October and November the temperature hovers usually between 80°F. and 90°F. In June the heat is kept in check by a cool north wind called the 'Bara'. Annual rainfall averages between three to four inches.

PLANTS AND WILDLIFE

Date, almond, pomegranate, banana and fig trees and a variety of other vegetation grow on the fertile strip of north Bahrain. The remainder of the country is mainly restricted to desert flora and shrubs. Though there is relatively little wildlife it has been meticulously studied by expatriate enthusiasts who have taken advantage of the country's smallness to search out the rarest of species. The gazelle can sometimes be sighted in the evenings in the desert when it emerges from its daytime shelter. It was once hunted by packs of saluqi dogs but the animal is now so scarce that this practice has been stopped. Hares also used to be hunted and about 20 years ago four or five would be caught during an evening's coursing. But now they can only occasionally be seen in the south of the island. Both the jerboa and mongoose can be found in the desert.

Over 14 species of lizard and four types of snake have been reported in Bahrain. The most spectacular is the Dhab which can grow up to 21 inches long and live up to 15 years. It dwells in tunnels in the desert up to eight feet in length and four feet below the surface. The Dhab is a common sight in the desert, its head stretched high in the air looking like a miniature dragon. The Khawsi lizard, seven inches long with shiny skin, roams round gardens and cultivated land. It moves so quickly it is sometimes mistaken for a snake. The pink geckoe frequents old houses and buildings, living off flies and insects. The sand snake, which is rarely seen, is the only Bahrain snake which is poisonous. Scorpions and the massive camel spider have been found in the desert.

Bahrain has a relatively large number of birds, many of which are merely winter visitors. These include sparrows, larks, wagtails, warblers, thrushes and swallows. More rare are migrants like the kingfisher. The native Bahrain birds include the desert lark, the white-cheeked bulbul, the Graceful Warbler, the Green Bee-eater, the hoopoe, the parrakeet, the mallard and the sandgrouse and the snipe both of which are hunted. Close to the sea cormorants are fairly common, as well as plovers and terns. Ravens, barn owls, ospreys, flamingoes, and bustards have all been sighted but are considered rare. Falcons are still used as a traditional method of hunting.

COMMUNICATIONS

Bahrain has for many years been a main stopover point for flights between Europe and the Far East. As a result its airport is one of the busiest in the Gulf. It is now used by nearly 20 leading airlines on scheduled international flights. Bahrain's geographical position and the good facilities at its airport was a major reason why British Airways chose the island as the first destination for commercial flights of its *Concorde*.

The country is also the headquarters of Gulf Air, which has been a pioneer of civil aviation in the region. It is jointly owned by the governments of Bahrain, Qatar, Abu Dhabi and Oman and has grown rapidly in the wake of the Gulf economic boom. It now runs direct flights to several parts of Europe and covers numerous routes within the Gulf itself.

Bahrain's road network will soon be extended to the mainland. Both Saudi Arabia and Bahrain are building a causeway between the northwest of the island and the Saudi coast. It will link Bahrain with the trans-Arabian highway system and will ultimately provide an overland connection with Europe. Traffic congestion in Manama is being eased by the building of a double-lane ring road on land reclaimed from the sea.

Mina Sulman, the country's commercial port, to the south of

Manama, is being expanded to deal with the increased sea traffic. A two mile causeway has also been built to connect the port with Sitra and the industrial area on Bahrain's east coast. A massive dry dock, north of Muharraq, financed by the Organisation of Arab Oil Exporting Countries (OAPEC), has recently been completed.

Bahrain's international telecommunications are considered the best in the Gulf. The country's viability as a regional commercial and financial centre depends on their efficiency. The Gulf's first satellite earth station was opened in Bahrain in 1969 providing direct links with the major centres of the world. There is also a good internal telephone network.

SOCIAL BACKGROUND

Bahrain has proportionately one of the highest indigenous populations in the Gulf. Eighty per cent of the 280,000 population are Bahraini. The remainder consists of Arabs from Saudi Arabia, Oman and North Yemen (around 10 per cent), and Iranians, Indians, Pakistanis and British. About 55 per cent of the people live in completely urban districts with only about 22 per cent residing in totally rural areas.

The original inhabitants of the islands are thought to have been descended from Arabs taken by Nebuchadnezzar into Iraq who later fled to Bahrain. Religiously the Bahrainis are divided fairly equally between Sunni Muslims, who predominate in the urban areas and who, with the ruling al-Khalifa family, came to the country in the 18th century, and the Shia Muslims, who live mostly in the villages. There is also a number of descendants of freed slaves who found sanctuary on Bahrain.

Bahrain's population is among the most sophisticated in the Gulf. For over 50 years the country has provided free education for both boys and girls at all levels and as a result Bahrainis are relatively well educated. Power is less concentrated than in other Gulf states. Though the Khalifas have supreme authority in Bahrain, there are some business families who hold considerable sway in the community. There is also a relatively strong, active group of Bahraini intellectuals. The Government is planning to legalise trade unions through which to channel the growing power of labour.

The country is one of the few states in the lower Gulf to have a well-established industrial labour force in its own population. Most of the force work in the BAPCO refinery and the Alba aluminium smelter and live in Isa Town which has been built on the lines of a European new town. Bahraini skilled manpower is growing steadily and soon it will be displacing many non-Bahraini workers.

Women are less restricted than in most other neighbouring countries. Less and less Bahraini women cover their faces with a veil in public. In the villages even, women wear colourful shawls in contrast to the traditional black. Most girls now go to school and the number of women with jobs has doubled in four years.

CONSTITUTION

Bahrain's present Constitution will remain in force until 1979, after which the Amir will decide on any changes. The present Constitution provides that all citizens, regardless of sex, are equal before the law. Though guaranteed by the Constitution, the right to vote remains vague and so far has been withheld from women. It also guarantees freedom of speech and expression and allows public gatherings and processions as long as they do not endanger peace or security.

The state of Bahrain is ruled by Shaikh Isa Bin-Sulman al-Khalifa, who took over power on his father's death in 1961. In January 1970 he delegated executive authority to a council of ministers but retained sovereign power. Up till August 1975, the country had a National Assembly with legislative authority consisting of 30 members elected by male suffrage and 12 ministers. But after a period of dissent between its elected members and the Government, it was dissolved. The Government has since promised to form a new elected assembly but with different powers.

Eight ministers are members of the ruling al-Khalifa family—the Prime Minister, and the Ministers of Defence, Housing, Education, Justice, Labour and Social Affairs, Interior and Foreign Affairs. The Ministries more closely related to the economy and development are headed by Bahrainis outside the ruling family.

Bahrain.
Over 4,000 years of trade and development.

2,300 B.C. Sargon of Akkad wrote a stone tablet about the trading activities of vessels from "Dilmun" (Bahrain) in his harbours.
1977 Bahrain prepares to open its OAPEC supertanker dry dock, taking ships up to 500,000 tons deadweight for repair and overhaul.

2,400 B.C. Steatite stamp seals from Mesopotamia and Mohenjodaro (now in Pakistan) used in furthering regional commerce during the Copper Age, all over Bahrain.
1977 1½ years after the Amir of Bahrain put his seal to the launching of Bahrain's offshore banking operation, over 10 billion dollars of assets are being traded by 32 international financial institutions.

2,200 B.C. Tablets of the Second Dynasty of Ur of the Chaldees (2,200 - 2,100 B.C.) record copper, diorite, gold and ivory being traded out of Bahrain.
1977 Latest 12-months figures of the Aluminium Bahrain (Alba) smelter show exports of high purity ingot worldwide stand at 125,651 metric tonnes.

323 B.C. Alexander the Great's admirals, anchored off Bahrain, took nine weeks to send messengers to his armies in Asia.
1977 A direct dial call to London from Bahrain takes 16 seconds.

For further information please contact:
Ministry of Information   **The Embassy of the State of Bahrain**
P.O. Box 253   **98 Gloucester Road**
State of Bahrain   **London SW7 4AU**

Lloyds Bank Group in the Middle East.

Lloyds Bank International, the international bank in the Lloyds Bank Group, is established in four important centres of the Middle East.

Bahrain: Our offshore branch is engaged in active development of the international business of the Group in Bahrain, Saudi Arabia, Kuwait, Qatar and Oman.
Manager: Graham M. Harris, Almoayyed Building No. 1, Government Road, Manama, Bahrain. Telephone: 50069.

Dubai: We have a full commercial branch which is responsible for Group operations in the United Arab Emirates.
Manager: M. Kent Atkinson, P.O. Box 3766, Dubai, United Arab Emirates. Telephone: 24151. Telex: 6450 LBI DB.

Cairo: A foreign currency branch handles international Egyptian business.
Manager: G. H. Clayton, 44 Mohamed Mazhar Street, Zamalek, Cairo. Telephone: 809046.

Tehran: Our Representative Office is responsible for the Bank's Iranian operations and relationships.
Representative: J-L. Mesnil, 199 Bisto Panj-e-Shahrivar Avenue, Abbasabad, Tehran 15. Telephone: 85 14 87.

This network of offices enables Lloyds Bank International to play an increasingly active role in this vital area of the world.

LLOYDS BANK INTERNATIONAL

40/66 Queen Victoria St., London EC4P 4EL. Tel: 01-248 9822
A member of the Lloyds Bank Group

Fellow subsidiaries of the Lloyds Bank Group:
Lloyds Bank California, The National Bank of New Zealand.

LBI, the Bank of London & South America and their subsidiaries have offices in: Argentina, Australia, Bahamas, Bahrain, Belgium, Brazil, Canada, Cayman Islands, Chile, Colombia, Costa Rica, Ecuador, Egypt, El Salvador, France, Federal Republic of Germany, Guatemala, Guernsey, Honduras, Hong Kong, Iran, Japan, Jersey, Malaysia, Mexico, Monaco, Netherlands, Nicaragua, Panama, Paraguay, Peru, Philippines, Portugal, Singapore, Spain, Switzerland, United Arab Emirates, United Kingdom, U.S.A., U.S.S.R., Uruguay, Venezuela.

HISTORY

Bahrain's long history has mainly been one of different rulers vying for control of the wealth of its islands. From earliest times the islands' fresh water springs, pearling industry and prosperous trading activities have made Bahrain an obvious prize for the territorial ambitions of outside powers. Bahrain has rarely been able to enjoy the sort of independence it holds now.

Because Bahrain's history stretches back to the earliest days of mankind, it has aroused considerable interest among archaeologists. Detailed evidence about a series of civilisations lies waiting to be dug up and all this archaeological richness is contained within a small, easily accessible area.

Fabled Dilmun There is plenty of evidence that Bahrain was inhabited by primitive man. Numerous flint tools can be picked up quite readily in central parts of the island, where early nomads probably settled in temporary villages. These tools show some similarity to instruments of the same age discovered in North Iraq and Palestine and even northern India.

Long ago archaeologists discovered the vital links Bahrain had with the Sumerians in south Mesopotamia four or five thousand years ago and that it was Dilmun; the Sumerian land of immortality and enchantment. But besides having a mythological importance, Bahrain was also then a trading entrepôt between the cities of Mesopotamia and of the Indus.

The city of Dilmun was built in the north of the island, near what is now the ruins of the Portuguese fort. It first appears to have been destroyed by the Mesopotamian Ruler Sargon of Akkad who in about 2300 B.C. claimed sovereignty over the city. The inhabitants then built a well fortified city and for several centuries it was a wealthy entrepôt base for trade between the city states of Mesopotamia and the Indus Valley. Copper and diorite from Oman and gold and ivory from the Indus were shipped to Bahrain where they were exchanged for woollen goods from Mesopotamia. Groups of Indian and Mesopotamian merchants are likely to have settled in Bahrain and there is definite evidence that Bahraini businessmen lived in the seaports of Mesopotamia.

The people of Bahrain at this time buried their dead in burial mounds, 100,000 of which can be seen scattered throughout the northern half of Bahrain. So far only a relatively small number have been excavated. But there is enough evidence to show similarities between the burials and those uncovered in Mesopotamia in the third millennium B.C.

These graves are unique because in contrast to ancient burial mounds in the Mediterranean areas, Egypt and Mesopotamia, they were for ordinary people. In other regions only royalty were given elaborate burials but in Bahrain even the ordinary person was entombed in relative splendour and magnificence. Clearly society on the island was wealthy enough to afford expensive funerals on a mass scale. But a special burial was reserved for the élite who had exceptionally large tombs.

In the second half of the second millennium Bahrain seemed to have suffered a slump after the Indus cities began to decline, as a result of invasions by Aryan tribes, and the Sumerians were taken over by the Babylonians. Trading in copper and diorite from Oman continued for a while but on a much smaller scale. Around 1350 B.C. there is evidence of the island falling back on its own resources and doing fairly widespread trading in locally harvested dates.

Prosperity began to return at the time of the rise of the Assyrian Empire in Mesopotamia and the eclipse of Babylonia around the end of the second millennium. From about 750 B.C. onwards the Assyrian kings continually claimed sovereignty over Dilmun though it is doubtful if the kings of Dilmun took these claims seriously. By 700 B.C. Bahrainis were trading again with the copper producers of Oman and were importing spices, perfumes and rare woods from the Indus where the Aryans were establishing a new civilisation. The city at Qalaat was partially rebuilt and a third city of Dilmun began to thrive. Traces of the city's new wealth were found in burial spots in the city area. Earthenware coffins, shaped like bath tubs in the Mesopotamian style with bronze ornaments inside, have been unearthed.

Babylonian control Dilmun was made part of the neo-Babylonian empire in the sixth century B.C. During this time and in the succeeding years when Babylonia was part of the Persian Empire—the fourth historical period of the city at Qalaat—the city's inhabitants seemed to have become even richer. Large amounts of finely glazed and burnished pottery in ordinary homes indicate prosperity reached all social levels.

After the decline of the Mesopotamian empires, Bahrain appears to have gone through a period when it was free from the incursions of foreign powers. At the time of Alexander the Great, the Greeks sent an expedition of three ships down the Gulf, two of which reached Bahrain (known to the Greeks as Tylos). The Greeks appeared to have stayed there for a while and excavators of the Greek level at Qalaat have found a large number of silver coins virtually in mint condition. Most of them bear the portrait of Alexander "The Two Horned", wearing the Ammon diadem of rams' horns assumed after the proclamation of his divinity as King of Egypt. Several pieces of Attic Greek pottery of the later fourth and early third century B.C. have also been found.

The city's prosperity probably continued for two to three centuries into the present era but after that the reign of the ancient city appears to have finally come to an end.

In the fourth century A.D. the Persian Sassanid king Shapur II went to war against Arab tribes that had crossed the Gulf and sacked Persian cities. He landed on the Arabian coast and annexed Eastern Arabia, including Bahrain.

Caliphate rule Three hundred years later, with the rise of Islam, the Muslims found Bahrain under the rule of a Persian governor who was a Christian Arab. He and his court accepted Islam without much opposition, and for the next 350 years Bahrain and eastern Arabia were ruled by governors appointed by the Caliphs. But there were many revolts against the Caliph's authority, as various religious splinter groups used the islands as a rebels' sanctuary. Both Shia and Kharajite dissidents took refuge on Bahrain.

At the beginning of the tenth century Bahrain and much of eastern Arabia were finally detached from the Caliph's sovereignty when the Karmathian sect took control of the region. The Karmathians appear to have used Bahrain as a place to which exiles could be banished. But they also established a customs station on the islands, from which they levied taxes on Gulf shipping. Bahrain's tribute to the Karmathian rulers was half the proceeds of its pearling industry.

In 1058 the Bahrainis rebelled against the Karmathians and defeated an army sent to quell the revolt. But by then the power of the Karmathians was dwindling and Bahrain soon fell under the control of rulers of eastern Arabian cities who rose up to take their place. However by the 13th century it had become a dependency of the island of Qishm on the northern shores of the Gulf, and for over 200 years it changed hands many times, as rulers on the Arabian mainland and Persian island leaders competed for its control.

Pearling wealth By now Bahrain's major attraction was the wealth of its pearling industry. In the early 14th century it was described as the centre of the pearl fisheries of the region with over 300 villages on its islands. Its rich vegetation and abundance of dates were also noticed by contemporary writers. In 1485 Duarte Barbosa, a Portuguese explorer, wrote that around Bahrain 'grows much seed pearl, also large pearls of good quality. The merchants of the island itself fish for these pearls and have therefrom great profits'.

Knowledge of its pearling wealth made Bahrain the focus of interest of Portuguese expeditionary forces during the early 16th century. In 1521 the Portuguese attacked the islands, becoming the first Europeans to invade Bahrain, which was then ruled by Mukarraam, King of Hasa and son-in-law of the Shaikh of Mecca. He was driven onto the mainland and a Portuguese governor installed.

Portuguese conquest During almost 80 years of insecure Portuguese rule Bahrain was attacked by Arab forces and a Turkish fleet sent by Sultan Suleiman the Magnificent. Finally, the Prince of Shiraz seized the islands from the Portuguese in the name of the Shah of Persia. A series of Persian governors controlled Bahrain until the end of the 17th century, when the Omanis invaded the island, causing a great deal of suffering. The Omanis were members of the Kharijite sect, who bitterly opposed the Shia inhabitants of Bahrain, driving them onto the mainland. But the Omanis were not interested in permanent control of Bahrain and, in 1720, handed it back to the Persians in return for a large sum of money.

For much of the 18th century Bahrain was ruled by a variety

of Arab tribal leaders. At the same time the Persians made attempts to regain sovereignty. The islands also suffered another savage invasion by the Omanis in 1738 which resulted in more refugees fleeing to mainland ports. The incessant pillaging of Bahrain during this period caused villages to become deserted and ruined and a contemporary writer stated that Bahrain's 360 towns and settlements were reduced to 60 'wretched' villages.

Al-Khalifas arrive   The last successful invaders of Bahrain were the al-Khalifas in 1783 who have remained in control ever since, though for most of the time under the supervision of the British. The al-Khalifa family had come down the Gulf from Kuwait and settled in the little village of Zubara on the west coast of Qatar. They had already done some trading in pearls and wanted to be nearer the Bahrain pearling industry. They expanded Zubara to the size of a town, adding a large fort. The Persians, by then in control of Bahrain again, became worried about the growing power of the al-Khalifa family and the Governor of Shiraz sent a force to attack Zubara. But they were defeated in a battle beneath the high walls of the town and soon afterwards the family, under Shaikh Ahmed al-Khalifa, occupied Bahrain.

The al-Khalifas took some years to consolidate their hold on Bahrain. In 1799 the Omanis, under the Imam of Muscat, once again sent a fleet to the islands and the al-Khalifas were forced to return to Zubara. In 1809 the Wahhabis on the mainland drove the Omanis out and took over the islands. But soon, with the help of the Persians, the al-Khalifas were back in control again. A few years later they made contact with the British and so began an era of about 150 years during which the British exercised immense influence in Bahrain. They helped assure that al-Khalifa rule remained supreme on the islands and over the next 70 years they intervened several times to prevent attempts by the Omanis, Wahhabis, Turkey and Persia to assume sovereignty of the islands. Any fighting that took place on Bahrain was usually between warring al-Khalifa factions.

Treaties with Britain   The first treaty between Britain and a ruler of Bahrain was signed in 1820 and was mainly concerned with stopping piracy. The Shaikh of Bahrain agreed not to allow the sale of any goods obtained 'by means of plunder and piracy'. In

1856, at a time when the Wahhabis were having claims to sovereignty in Bahrain rejected by the British, Shaikh Mohammad al-Khalifa entered into an agreement with Britain to stop slave-trading vessels using the islands.

But in 1861 the British extended their influence beyond matters of slavery and piracy by signing a 'perpetual treaty of peace and friendship' with Shaikh Mohammad. The Shaikh agreed not to go to war against any adversary without the permission of the British, who in return promised to protect Bahrain against any outside aggression. The treaty also allowed the British to trade in Bahrain with their goods being subject to a minimal excise duty.

In 1867 the Qataris invaded Bahrain. But after Shaikh Mohammad had asked for military help from Persia for a counter-attack against Qatar, the British intervened, stopping the Persians taking any action and sending a man-of-war to Bahrain, which destroyed the Bahraini fleet. The British accused Shaikh Mohammad not only of violating the 1861 treaty by his action against Qatar but also of soliciting aid from both Persia and Turkey. They deposed him and put his brother Shaikh Ali in his place. Two years later Shaikh Mohammad returned with a force, killing his brother and again taking control. The British sent another man-of-war, and exiled Mohammad and his supporters to Bombay.

Shaikh Ali was succeeded by his son Shaikh Isa, who became Bahrain's longest reigning ruler in modern history, being in command for 54 years until he himself was forced to abdicate in 1923. He had little sympathy with either Turkey or Persia and signed two further agreements with Britain, mainly with the objective of extending British protection over Bahrain. In 1880 he undertook not to make virtually any agreement with any other state without the consent of the British Government. Another agreement in 1892 confirmed that in effect Britain was responsible for Bahrain's defence and foreign policy. The Shaikh promised not to correspond with any other power except Britain, nor 'to cede, sell, mortgage or otherwise give for occupation any part of my territory save to the British Government'. In 1914 Shaikh Isa gave the British ultimate control over any future oil industry by agreeing not to exploit any oil deposits without the approval of the British Government.

Shaikh Hamed's reign Shaikh Isa was deposed in 1923 as a result of an internal feud. But his exit from power was assisted by the British who sent two warships to the islands to permit a peaceful succession for his eldest son, Shaikh Hamed. He had a progressive outlook and during his 19 years as ruler helped transform Bahrain into a modern state. Municipalities, education and health services were established and, after the discovery and production of oil in the 1930s, money began to be channelled into the country's economic development.

After his death in 1942, his son Shaikh Sulman continued pressing ahead with the country's economic and social advancement. During the 1950s Bahrain's public and social services in particular showed big progress. In 1958 Shaikh Sulman arranged a meeting with King Saud of Saudi Arabia during which both agreed to share the profits from oil produced from a disputed area of the sea between the two states. This was eventually to provide a significant source of income for Bahrain and also helped cement a close relationship between the two neighbours.

During this time, however, British influence still remained strong. Sir Charles Belgrave, the Ruler's Adviser in Bahrain from 1926 to 1956, was a powerful figure who played an important role in the country's affairs. At the same time the British had set up a sizeable military base on Bahrain. But by the 1950s British power had begun to wane. In 1956 a visit by British Foreign Secretary Selwyn Lloyd was met by large anti-British demonstrations. The British began to hand over responsibilities they had previously undertaken to the Bahrain Government and, by the time Shaikh Isa, Bahrain's present ruler, took over from Shaikh Sulman in 1961, the Bahrain Government was able to participate in international organisations as an independent state in its own right.

British withdrawal When British troops pulled out of Aden in 1967, Bahrain briefly became the centre of Britain's Middle East military command. A year later the British Government announced that its forces were withdrawing from east of Suez by the end of 1971. Bahrain, along with other British-protected emirates in the Gulf, started preparations for the assumption of full independence.

Britain proposed the establishment of a federation of nine

states, consisting of Bahrain, Qatar and the seven emirates making up the present United Arab Emirates. However from the beginning of negotiations with its suggested partners, Bahrain met with difficulties. It wanted, for example, its share of the seats on the ruling body of the federation to reflect its 40 per cent share of the total population of the proposed new state. This met immediate opposition. In the end Bahrain decided to remain a single entity.

The Shah of Iran then put forward a claim to Bahrain based on Persia's sovereignty over the islands during the 17th and 18th centuries. But this matter was resolved when a United Nations special envoy, sent to Bahrain in 1970 to sound out public opinion on the claim, reported that the majority did not want to become part of Iran. A year later, on 15 August 1971, Shaikh Isa formally declared Bahrain to be independent and soon afterwards the new state joined the United Nations. In December 1972 elections were held for an assembly to draw up a constitution, which was promulgated in June 1973. Six months later elections were held for a National Assembly.

Recent Events

The National Assembly lasted only two years. In August 1975 it was dissolved, somewhat denting Bahrain's image as one of the most socially progressive states in the region. Social problems, such as a severe housing shortage and rising inflation, had precipitated bitter criticism of Government ministers in the Assembly. Finally the Government lost patience with the growing belligerence of the Assembly's outspoken members and dissolved it. Instead it promised to establish a new-style democratic legislative body in the near future.

The Government has since shown its concern over left-wing political activity and has clamped down hard on any signs of labour unrest. The murder of the right-wing newspaper editor Abdullah Madani in late 1976 was blamed on subversive left-wing groups and three men were later executed. The executions were the first in the country since 1954.

Even though nearly three-quarters of its income has come from oil, the country has become a major commercial centre in the Gulf. The establishment of offshore banking units (OBUs) on the island in early 1976 has helped it form an embryo regional financial market. At the same time it has further diversified its economy by setting up an aluminium smelter and drydock and developing light ancillary industries.

The country has also been forging closer links with Saudi Arabia. First the Saudis helped to reduce the island's budget deficit by financing relatively small development projects in the public sector. Then both countries announced they would be building a causeway between Bahrain and the Saudi mainland to bring the two economies together. Saudi Arabia has agreed to put up the money for the mammoth project estimated to be costing around $1,000 million.

ECONOMY

Traditionally Bahrain's wealth has come from its pearling industry. In ancient Mesopotamia, Greece and Rome, Bahrain was renowned for its pearls, and this fame remained until at least the 19th century. Then a decline began to set in. In 1833 around 1,500 boats were collecting pearls from the islands' pearl banks. By 1896 there were only 900 and by 1930 only 590 boats were being used, manned by 19,300 men. The great depression in the West pushed the industry into a slump from which it was never really to recover. Westerners could no longer afford the luxury of natural pearls and instead started buying cultured pearls which the Japanese were just starting to produce on a large scale.

Oil

However, Bahrain's economy was rescued by the discovery of oil. A New Zealander, Major Frank Holmes, who worked for a British prospecting company, predicted in the 1920s that oil in commercial quantities could be produced after drilling a number of test wells. British oil companies refused to believe him. But the Americans were more interested and after protracted negotiations between the British Foreign Office, then acting on Bahrain's behalf, and the US State Department, a concession was granted to Standard Oil Company of California. Through its associate, Caltex, the Bahrain Petroleum Company (Bapco) was set up.

Crude oil was first shipped from Bahrain in 1934 and two years later a small refinery built by Caltex was producing 10,000 barrels a day. Crude oil output reached a peak in 1972 at 76,000 barrels a day, but had fallen to a daily average of around 60,000 by 1977. But the refinery had continued to expand and was, for some time, one of the biggest in the Middle East. It now produces 30,000 barrels a day, with more than three-quarters of its throughput being pumped across the sea from Saudi Arabia. Bahrain also owns, in a 50/50 partnership with Saudi Arabia, the small offshore oil field of Abu Saafa which produces around 60,000 barrels a day.

Oil revenue is expected to reach $380 million in 1977, almost two-thirds of the total budget revenue. Over the last three decades oil has provided most of Bahrain's wealth. But its oil reserves are limited and are expected to run out before the end of the century. Already oil income is beginning to take up a smaller share of the country's earnings.

The Government set up a state oil company in 1976—the Bahrain National Oil Company (Banoco)—with the aim of taking over downstream oil facilities. By early 1977 it had acquired responsibility for local marketing and distribution of refined oil products from the Bahrain Petroleum Company (Bapco) in which Banoco already had a 60 per cent stake. The company also plans to collect and process associated gas at present being flared at the country's oil fields. But the Government announced in January, 1977, that at present it did not intend to take over the island's refinery operated by Caltex.

Industry

Bahrain has begun to diversify its economy to make it less dependent on oil. It has been helped in this task by the experience gained over a 30-year period from the refinery, which has generated a small but significant pool of skilled labour. The British military base also expanded the country's supply of trained workers. Besides having the manpower available to set up non-oil industries, Bahrain also has large reserves of gas to power them.

New industries In 1971 an aluminium smelter was set up by Aluminium Bahrain Company (Alba) in which the Bahrain Government owned 17 per cent of the shares, the remainder being taken by six Western companies. The smelter was the biggest industrial project, unrelated to oil, in the Gulf and, despite much scepticism about the viability of such a scheme in this area of the Middle East, it has been a major success. The smelter has been producing more than its rated capacity of 120,000 tons a year. But at a time of depression in the aluminium market the original shareholders have found it difficult to maintain the arrangement of marketing their share of the output. As a result, most have sold their holdings to the Government, which now owns 77.9 per cent of the company. Its remaining partners are Kaiser of the US (17 per cent) and Breton Investments of West Germany (5.1 per cent).

With the help of an intensive training programme, Alba has been able to ensure that the majority of its workforce is Bahraini. Around 2,300 nationals are now employed by the smelter, assisted by 300 expatriates. These Bahrainis have now attained a high degree of skill in the working techniques of the industry, and the smelter has one of the world's best safety records for such a plant.

Drydock opens At about the same time as Alba started production, the Organisation of Arab Petroleum Exporting Countries (OAPEC) chose Bahrain as a site for a drydock. The scheme, named the Arab Shipbuilding & Repair Yard (ASRY), suffered delays during the planning stages, and land reclamation and dredging work did not begin until August 1974. In 1975 the Hyundai group of South Korea started construction work with its own Korean labour force, and completed it on schedule in summer 1977. The yard was due to take its first ship in October. The project has one drydock for vessels of up to 500,000 dwt and two finger jetties providing four repair berths. Initially work is likely to be limited to routine inspection and repair jobs. But, after about four years, it will be able to undertake major maintenance and repair tasks. During the first few years Bahrainis will make up around 40 per cent of the yard's workforce.

The refinery, the smelter and the drydock are about all Bahrain can absorb at present in terms of large-scale industrial projects. Instead the Government intends to concentrate on building up ancillary industries, developing an infrastructure large enough to allow the island to expand as a services and banking centre and to exploit its tourist potential.

The establishment of new light industries will be mainly

53

c

centred around Alba and the drydock. An aluminium extrusion plant, employing around 200 people, is to manufacture aluminium sections, like doors and window frames, for the Gulf's construction market. The ASRY project is expected to provide business worth around $10 to $15 million for ancillary and service firms.

Bahrain already has a small nucleus of light industries built up with government encouragement. An eight million square foot free zone has been established at Mina Sulman port, where firms are exempted from import duties on raw materials and most capital goods. Three or four other estates are likely to be set up to accommodate the expected growth in light industries. Two will be situated on reclaimed land around Sitra and Manama and a third may also be placed near Mina Sulman port on a 14.5 million square foot site.

Infrastructure

The country's broad industrial base has also assisted its growth as a major commercial centre. In recent years it has become a commercial base for companies active in the Gulf and is even being used by some as their Middle East headquarters. It is a major stopover point on international air routes and has good telecommunication facilities. Its forty years of steady economic development has also made it better equipped than other Gulf countries to provide the sort of services required by foreign companies.

Power generation facilities are being expanded so that in future Bahrain will be able to get through its summers without power cuts. In March 1977, a West German company was awarded a $58 million contract to build a 200-MW power station at Rifaa. The first 100-MW phase is due to come into operation by the summer, 1978. In addition to the main power station at Sitra, this will be the island's third station. The station at Sitra is to be linked to a desalination plant with a daily capacity of five million gallons which, by 1982, will be raised to 20 million.

Bahrain's international airport is regarded as one of the best equipped and managed in the Middle East. Its passenger terminal is being expanded and plans have been drawn up for an air-freight terminal which would serve the whole Gulf. The airport serves as the headquarters of Gulf Air, which is jointly owned by

56

Bahrain, Qatar, Oman and the UAE. In 1976 it added four TriStars to its fleet of aircraft. Mina Sulman, the country's main port, has been doubling its present capacity of six berths, with more transit and storage sheds being built.

Causeway project   At present Bahrain's biggest communications project is the building of a 16-mile causeway linking Bahrain with Saudi Arabia. It will run from Jasra across Umm Nasan Island to a point between Al-Khobar and Al-Azizivah on the mainland. It will have four high-span bridges and is due to be completed by 1981. The cost, estimated to be around $1,000 million, will be met entirely by Saudi Arabia. The causeway will give Bahrain a road connection through the Arabian Peninsula to Europe but more important it will bring the economies of Bahrain and Saudi Arabia's oil-rich Eastern Province together. Bahrain could return to its traditional role as an entrepôt for the Gulf mainland.

Bahrain has one of the most advanced telecommunications systems in the Gulf. Its earth satellite station, built in 1969, enables it to maintain direct telephone contact with most parts of the world. Over the next few years there are plans to improve the international link-up and double the capacity of the domestic network.

In recent years government expenditure on development has been rising steadily. The 1977 budget shows a deficit of $35 million with expenditure totalling $624 million and revenue only $589 million. In the previous year for the first time in the state's history capital expenditure exceeded ordinary expenditure. The Government is anxiously looking round for outside sources of finance and its richer neighbours in the Gulf are starting to give financial help. Saudi Arabia is not only financing the causeway but also housing schemes and a $56 million sports complex. Abu Dhabi had loaned $400 million for development projects.

Trade and finance

The country's balance of trade has also been showing deficits for some years. Provisional estimates for 1976 put imports at $890 million and exports at only $330 million leaving a deficit of $530 million. However, Bahrain's large re-export business and earnings from commercial services have helped to provide a healthier balance of payments picture with annual surpluses being recorded over the last few years.

In the immediate term, one of Bahrain's major objectives is to keep down inflation. In mid-1977 the annual rate of inflation was estimated unofficially to be around 40 per cent. Rents have risen by as much as 60 per cent in two years. But a surplus in office and accommodation space may soon precipitate a fall in rents. A Government survey has shown that nearly half of an average family's budget is spent on food, despite the existence of large food subsidies.

Offshore banking Bahrain's economy was given a major boost in early 1976 when it became an offshore banking centre, with the object of operating as an embryo regional money market. By March 1977, 32 offshore banks (OBUs) had accumulated assets of $8,500 million, nearly three-quarters of it in US dollars. The OBUs looked well set to meet a target figure of $10,000 million within 18 months starting operations. At the same time money and insurance brokers and bond dealers have been setting up on the island.

The Government aims to make Bahrain a major international banking base like Singapore by using Arab oil surpluses as a source for short- and medium-term loans. The banks also help to bolster Bahrain's role as a commercial centre. They operate completely outside the domestic banking system and have no tax levied on their accounts, merely having to pay an annual fee of $25,000. During 1976 the offshore banks are estimated to have pushed up the country's invisible earnings from banking to $25 million.

Agriculture & Social Services

The country's relatively small agriculture and fishing sectors provided incomes for 4,000 of the 60,000 economically active population at the time of the island's last census in 1971. A declining water table with rising salinity and the movement of labour into the towns has increased the difficulties of agricultural production. Agricultural officials estimate that the general water table is falling by up to four inches a year and that by the end of the century all water for Bahrain's farms could be saline. Only about 45 per cent of potentially cultivable land is at present in use.

Dwindling fish stocks has reduced the fishing industry and there are only about 20 fishing dhows still operating. But the Government is anxious to revive both sectors. The Food and Agriculture Organisation is working on pilot projects covering livestock breeding and trawling experiments. An Agricultural Credit Fund is being introduced to provide interest-free loans.

Social services   Education on a wide scale has long been well established in Bahrain, producing a high proportion of educated Bahrainis. The first schools for boys were set up in 1919 and for girls in 1928. The country also has a health service stretching back to the 1920s. For many years expenditure on education and health absorbed over half of the state's budget. Social and educational services now include free universal education between the ages of six and 12 and selective secondary and higher education, free medical care and subsidised housing. State-run hospitals and clinics provide a comprehensive free health service covering both hospital treatment and primary health care. There are also doctors and dentists in private practice. In 1976 the Government announced an earnings-related pensions scheme.

GUIDE

MANAMA   Bahrain's capital, with around 150,000 inhabitants, is located on the north-east corner of the main Bahrain island. Around one third of the town's total area has been reclaimed from the sea and reclamation work is still going on.

The town's oldest buildings date back to the eighteenth century. Two examples are the tomb of Shaikh Ahmad al-Fatih near the Awal Cinema and the Fort that serves as the headquarters of the State Police. But Manama is known to have been in existence since at least the fifteenth century, when it was featured in the travelogues of a number of Portuguese writers.

Manama's centre point is Shaikh Sulman Square, around which are found all the main banks, travel agencies and business offices. The town's main streets are Government Road, Al-Khalifa Road, Tijar Road, Shaikh Abdullah Road and the narrow Bab al-Bahrain Road. In these streets are found all the main stores and shops. The main markets lie adjacent to Bab

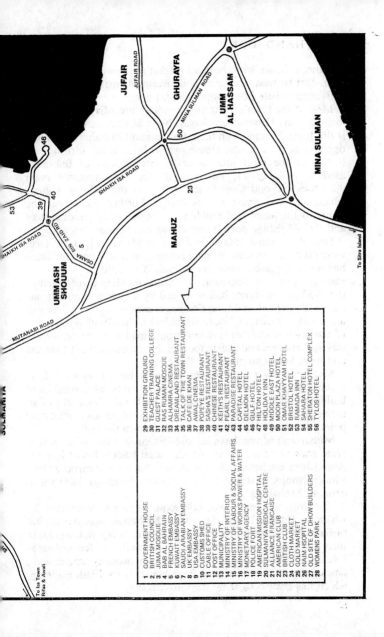

1 GOVERNMENT HOUSE
2 BRITISH COUNCIL
3 JUMA MOSQUE
4 BAB AL BAHRAIN
5 FRENCH EMBASSY
6 KUWAIT EMBASSY
7 SAUDI ARABIAN EMBASSY
8 UK EMBASSY
9 USA EMBASSY
10 CUSTOMS SHED
11 CABLE OFFICE
12 POST OFFICE
13 MUNICIPALITY
14 MINISTRY OF INTERIOR
15 MINISTRY OF LABOUR & SOCIAL AFFAIRS
16 MINISTRY OF WORKS POWER & WATER
17 MONETARY AGENCY
18 POLICE FORT
19 AMERICAN MISSION HOSPITAL
20 SULMANIYA MEDICAL CENTRE
21 ALLIANCE FRANCAISE
22 AMERICAN CLUB
23 BRITISH CLUB
24 CLOTH MARKET
25 GOLD MARKET
26 NAIM HSOPITAL
27 OLD SITE OF DHOW BUILDERS
28 WOMENS PARK
29 EXHIBITION GROUND
30 TEACHER TRAINING COLLEGE
31 GUEST PALACE
32 RAS RUMAN MOSQUE
33 ALHAMRA CINEMA
34 DREAMLAND RESTAURANT
35 TALK OF THE TOWN RESTAURANT
36 EDGE DE KHAN
37 AWAL CINEMA
38 POPEYE RESTAURANT
39 SASHA'S RESTAURANT
40 CHINESE RESTAURANT
41 KEITH'S RESTAURANT
42 PEARL RESTAURANT
43 PARADISE RESTAURANT
44 CAPITAL HOTEL
45 DELMON HOTEL
46 GULF HOTEL
47 HILTON HOTEL
48 HOLIDAY INN
49 MIDDLE EAST HOTEL
50 MOON PLAZA HOTEL
51 OMAR KHAYYAM HOTEL
52 BRISTOL HOTEL
53 RAMADA INN
54 SAHARA HOTEL
55 SHERATON HOTEL COMPLEX
56 TYLOS HOTEL

al-Bahrain Road, with the cloth market to the west, and running from east to west, the spice and sweetmeat markets and small workshops where iron, copper and tin goods are made.

Most of the town's interesting buildings are adjacent to, or are located near, Government Road. Near Shaikh Sulman Square is the Juma Mosque with the tallest minaret in Bahrain. Almost opposite is Government House, whose honeycomb form makes it one of the most architecturally adventurous of Bahrain's modern buildings. It contains all the Government's main ministries. Beyond Government House is the Bahrain Hilton, which has won praise for its design. Further back, near the centre, is the Municipal Building, the State Police Headquarters and the old fishing port, where dhows can be seen unloading.

One of the most notable buildings in Manama is the Palace, which is now a teacher-training college but is still used for State banquets. Situated near the Ghudaibia Garden, Manama's main park, it is an imposing 'U' shaped building constructed in the 1930s. Its entrance hall is topped by a copper dome. It has a giant dining hall and reception room each with chandeliers and a musicians' gallery. Close to the palace is the Ghudaibia district of the town where there are numerous small restaurants, mostly serving Lebanese and Indian food, clubs and cinemas. The newest and most luxurious cinema is the Awal.

Muharraq town is linked to Manama by a causeway. It is much older than the capital and contains many more traditional buildings, giving it more character than its neighbour. It has an active boat-building industry and is a loading and unloading point for dhows shipping cargo up and down the Gulf.

Muharraq's shops have an old-fashioned look, with neither plate glass nor fixed prices. All the usual traders found in most Arab towns are here, including antique dealers and carpet sellers. Modern shops, in streets of contemporary buildings, have yet to come to Muharraq.

The town has many old, tall houses with pretty courtyards, which hark back to the days when Muharraq was the capital of Bahrain and the centre of the pearling industry. Some contain three or more courtyards, and have high walls and few outward-looking windows, as if to emphasise their wealthy detachment. One of the most attractive of these houses is the Siadi Building, which has been bought by the Government.

MEED SPECIAL REPORTS

As well as providing weekly news, analysis and forecasts essential for conducting business in the Middle East, Middle East Economic Digest also produces surveys of the countries of the region.

Designed to keep you informed in depth, these surveys review central subjects such as banking and finance, industry, infrastructure, oil and gas, agriculture, education and foreign policy of each country. Usually of 36 pages in length, they are generously illustrated with photographs.

The following reports are available: —

Jordan (June 1976)	£3.50
Oman (June 1976)	£3.50
Saudi Arabia (December 1976)	£3.50
Libya (February 1977)	£1.50
Iran (February 1977)	£3.50
Qatar (April 1977)	£3.50
Iraq (June 1977)	£1.50
UAE (July 1977)	£3.50
Morocco (July 1977)	£2.50
Sudan (August 1977)	£1.50
Kuwait (August 1977)	£3.50

To obtain any, or all, of the above reports please write, enclosing the appropriate remittance to: —
Middle East Economic Digest
Dept F7, 21 John Street, London WC1N 2BP, England.

Hedd, Bahrain's fifth largest town, is built on a narrow strip jutting out into the sea at the south-east end of Muharraq Island. Houses are bunched together extending right to the edge of the sea. One narrow street runs through the centre of the town with alley-ways leading to the shore on each side. Hedd was an important pearling town and it contains some large houses built by pearl merchants. The town has also been famous for its prawns. Qasari is a fresh water pool near Manama which is large but too shallow for swimming. A garden overlooks the pool and is popular with picnickers. Turtles can be seen in the pool and sometimes come to the edge looking for food. Bilad Al-Qadim was the capital of Bahrain in the Middle Ages, but a large area of it is now in ruins. To the west is the Masjid al-Rafia mosque which contains an ancient Kufic inscription. Also nearby are the ruins of the Suq al-Khamis mosque, whose twin minarets were once landmarks for navigators. It is one of the most ancient Islamic relics in the Gulf, having been built between the tenth and eleventh centuries A.D. It has two rare Qibla stones with long inscriptions.

Adari is one of the most beautiful of Bahrain's freshwater pools, with deep cool water which makes it ideal for swimming. It has the largest natural spring in Bahrain which helps to irrigate many acres of gardens. One of Bahrain's largest villages and centre of the country's traditional pottery industry is Aali. Craftsmen can be seen making pots of all shapes and sizes. Lime is also produced here by the traditional method of firing limestone on top of layers of wood. Bahrain's 'new town', Isa Town, lying a few miles outside Manama, was designed by the British on the lines of new towns in Britain. It has two attractive mosques with blue tiled domes and slim minarets and a monumental gateway which has become one of the country's main landmarks. Awali, south of Isa Town, was built by the Bahrain Petroleum Company (Bapco) to provide housing, shops and leisure facilities for its expatriate staff. It has its own cinema, swimming pools, restaurants and library.

Hotels

Bahrain Hilton, King Faisal Road. P.O.B. 1090. Tel: 5000. Telex: 8288. 178 Rooms. Single room BD 29, double BD 38. 15 per cent service charge. Conference/banqueting facilities. Restaurant. Coffee-shop. Bar. Swimming pool.

Gulf Hotel, off New Palace Road. P.O.B. 580. Tel: 71288. Telex: 8241. 250 rooms. Single room BD 25, double BD 28, suites BD 35–65. 15 per cent service charge. Large conference room. Restaurant. Bars. Coffee shop (open 24 hours). Swimming pool. Tennis courts. Recreation room for snooker, table-tennis and darts. New 320-room extension due to open shortly.

Delmon Hotel, Government Road. P.O.B. 26. Tel: 54761. Telex: 8224. 92 rooms. Single room BD 26, double BD 30, suites BD 70–100. 15 per cent service charge. Two restaurants. Bar. Coffee-shop (open 24 hours). Reuter ticker-tape service. Conference and banqueting facilities. Discotheque. Swimming pool.

Delmon Hotel Habara Annexe, near Umm al-Hasam. P.O.B./Tel No., same as Delmon Hotel. 26 rooms. Single room without bath BD 18 including service, double without bath BD 22, double with bath BD 24 (private sitting room, dining room and kitchen BD 12 extra). Apartment containing three bedrooms, two bathrooms, sitting room, dining room and kitchen BD 70. The annexe is located some way out of Manama, close to the sea. Free, regular transport provided to Delmon Hotel, where annexe guests are entitled to use all facilities. The annexe, itself, has its own games room for American pool, table tennis and darts. Coffee-shop (open 24 hours).

Tylos Hotel, Government Road. P.O.B. 1086. Tel: 52600. Telex: 8349. 72 rooms. Single room BD 25, double BD 33. 15 per cent service charge. Restaurant. Coffee-shop. Bar.

Middle East Hotel, Shaikh Isa Road. P.O.B. 575. Tel: 54733. Telex: 8296. 52 rooms. Single room BD 20 (including service), double BD 25. Restaurant. Bar.

Omar Khayyam Hotel, off Shaikh Duaji Road. P.O.B. 771. Tel: 713941. Telex: 8401. 85 rooms. Single room BD 17–20, double BD 23–24, suites BD 25–30. 10 per cent service charge. Restaurant. Bar.

Sahara Hotel, Shaikh Abdulla Road. P.O.B. 839. Tel: 50850. Telex: 8345. 40 rooms. Single room BD 16, double BD 25–35. 15 per cent service charge. Bar. Restaurant.

Bristol Hotel, Shaikh Isa Road, P.O.B. 832. Tel: 58989. Telex: 8504. 80 rooms. Single room BD 10–14, double BD 15–17, suites BD 25–40. 10 per cent service charge. Restaurant. Coffee-shop. Two bars.

Capital Hotel, Tujjar Road, P.O.B. 153. Tel: 55955. Telex: 8296. 40 rooms. Single room BD 9.9, double BD 14.4. 10 per cent service charge. Restaurant. Bar. Conference and banqueting facilities.

Moon Plaza Hotel, Umm al-Hasam, P.O.B. 247. Tel: 8263. Telex: 8308. 106 rooms, single room BD 22, double BD 34, suites BD 36–70. 10 per cent service charge. Restaurant. Two bars.

Restaurants Dining out is a major part of social life in Bahrain. As a result there is a large number of restaurants. It is advisable to book in advance for an evening meal, especially at the hotel restaurants. Most of the main restaurants have live music. The majority of restaurants are run by Indians, Lebanese or expatriate Europeans. Most do not attempt to specialise in any type of cuisine and menus are fairly comprehensive and varied, usually including a selection of continental and Indian dishes. The larger hotels, whose restaurants tend to be the most expensive, mostly serve French-style food, with at least one kebab and curry dish.

HOTEL RESTAURANTS

Falcon Restaurant, Gulf Hotel, off New Palace Road. Tel: 712881. Open from 1900–2315 with dancing and entertainment. Buffet 'family' lunch served on Fridays from 1230–1445 (reasonable price).

Bazaar Grill, Hilton Hotel, King Faisal Road. Tel: 52843. Open in the evenings from 1930–2330 for dining and dancing. Daily buffet lunch every day from 1230–1530.

Alf Laila (*1,000 Nights*) *Supper Room*, Delmon Hotel. Government Road. Tel: 54761. High standard of French cooking. One of the few places with *Machboos* on the menu. Open from 1930–2300 for dining and dancing. Buffet lunch served daily from 1200–1430.

Alexander Room, Tylos Hotel, Government Road. Tel: 52600. Buffet lunch from 1200–1500. Dining with dancing from 1930–0100. Closed all day Monday.

OTHER RESTAURANTS (higher price-range):

Keith's, Quadibiya Road. Tel: 713163. Run by a British expatriate, serving French food. Very expensive but good place for impressive expense-account entertainment. Serves only evening meals. Open from 1930 until clients leave. No dancing.

The Pearl, Al-Khalifa Road. Tel: 52852. Lebanese and French food, which, though adequate, does not measure up to the price. Only non-hotel restaurant in the middle of town open during lunch hours. Open from 1200–1500, and from 2000–0130. Live music, dancing and show in the evenings.

OTHER RESTAURANTS (less expensive):

The Talk of the Town, off Shaikh Isa Road. Tel: 50728. Good food at very reasonable prices. No dancing. Lunch 1200–1500, dinner 1900–0100.

Popeye Restaurant, Old Palace Road. Tel: 714054. Good value with reasonable prices. Food good and varied. Atmosphere informal. Downstairs dining-room serves men only, but women welcome in the upstairs 'family' room. No live music or dancing.

Dreamland, Isa al-Kabir Road. Tel: 50128. Continental, Chinese and Indian food. Mexican dishes on Monday nights. Live music and dancing on Thursday nights. Meals served from 1200–1500, and 1800–2400.

Saasha's, New Palace Road, Quadibiya. Tel: 714364. Continental and Indian food. Show on Thursday and Sunday nights. Open from 1200–1500, and 1930–2400.

Paradise Restaurant, Old Palace Road. Tel: 51271. Wide variety of Indian food. Take-away meals.

Chinese Restaurant, New Palace Road, Quadibiya. Tel: 713603. Chinese cuisine.

Discotheques

Juliana's, Delmon Hotel, Government Road. Used to operate as an expensive private club for members and hotel residents, but has now relaxed its entrance restrictions. From 1800–2200 it is a glorified snack and drinks bar open to all-comers. From 2200 the discotheque proper takes over. Drinks become more expensive and membership rules come into effect. Non-member couples allowed in on payment of an entrance fee, and unaccompanied ladies can enter free of charge. Members can bring in one unaccompanied male or an unlimited number of couples.

Zartaj, near the Bristol Hotel, Shaikh Isa Road. Tel: 58552. Discotheque and restaurant with a separate bar for light snacks. Restaurant tables must be booked in advance. Food is mainly Indian. Jeans not permitted.

Bars

The Cavalry Club Bar, Hilton Hotel, King Faisal Road. Popular with expatriates. Dark wood-panelled walls decorated with antique military regalia.

The Huntsman Bar, Tylos Hotel, Government Road. Pleasant atmosphere. Panelled walls with hunting prints.

The Palm Grove Bar, Gulf Hotel, off New Palace Road. Serves a 'pub' lunch every day from 1230–1500. Ties must be worn except on Fridays.

Airport Bahrain International Airport is on Muharraq Island. One of the largest, best-equipped and most modern in the Gulf. A new terminal was built along the lines of London Heathrow Airport in 1971 and expanded in 1973. It is the main stopping point for Jumbo jets flying between Europe and the Far East.

The Airport Restaurant is reputed to be one of the best in Bahrain. The terminal building has a snack bar. The departure lounge includes a bar and a snack bar, as well as a very well-stocked (and relatively cheap) duty-free shop and book and magazine stand.

Taxis   Easily recognisable by their orange-painted mudguards. Each taxi driver carries a booklet issued by the Government which lists fare rates. The average fares for a short journey within Manama is 400 fils, for longer ones between the town centre and the residential sectors 500 fils. The official fare from the airport to Manama is BD 1. But the usual charge is BD 2–3 if there is a lot of luggage.

Buses   Buses connect Manama to all outlying areas. Though regular, they are few with a frequency of about one every hour. But with a flat rate fare of 50 fils they are a very cheap way of travelling around the island.

Car Hire Firms   *Husain Ali Slaibikh*. Tel: 52570. *Gulf Car Hiring Co.*, P.O.B. 5165. Tel: 713288. *Capital Establishment*, P.O.B. 90. Tel: 55317. For *Avis* cars contact *Bahrain International Travel*, Tareq Building, Government Road. P.O.B. 1044. Tel: 53315/6.

It is advisable to inspect a car personally before hiring. Average daily rates are BD 5 inclusive of everything except petrol.

Travel Agencies   *Al-Gusaibi Travel Agency*, Al-Khalifa Road. P.O.B. 540. Tel: 51827/55357/22398 (Airport). Telex: 8498. *Bahrain International Travel*, Tareq Building, Government Road. P.O.B. 1044. Tel: 5315/22340, 21431 (Airport). *Delmon Travel*, Al-Khalifa Road, P.O.B. 540. Tel: 53149. *Gray Mackenzie & Co. Ltd* (IATA Agents), Al-Khalifa Road, P.O.B. 210. Tel: 53901. *Jalal Travel Agency*, Al-Khalifa Road, P.O.B. 113. Tel: 53336. *Kanoo Travel Agency*, Kanoo Building, Al-Khalifa Road. P.O.B. 45. Tel: 54081/21455 (Airport), 53666 (Air Cargo). *United Travel*, Al-Khalifa Road. P.O.B. 45. Tel: 51447. *World Travel Service*, Government Road. P.O.B. 830. Tel: 52414/21520 (Airport).

Shipping Agencies   *A.K. Al-Moayed*, Al-Moayed Building, Al-Khalifa Road. P.O.B. 363. Tel: 51212. Telex: 8267. *Beirut Express* (Bahrain). P.O.B. 113. Tel: 53992/51259. Telex: 8233. *Gray Mackenzie & Co. Ltd*, Government Road. P.O.B. 210. Tel: 53536. Telex: 8212. *Gulf Agency Co. (Bahrain) Ltd*, Awal Building, Government Road, P.O.B. 412. Tel: 54228. Telex: 8211. *Yusuf Bin-Ahmad Kanoo*, P.O.B. 45. Tel: 54081. Telex: 8215. *National Shipping Agency*. P.O.B. 762. Tel: 55005/56117/55542. Telex: 8341. *Universal Shipping Agencies*. P.O.B. 5249. Tel: 53830. Telex: 8476.

Airline offices   *Air France*, c/o United Travel Agency, P.O.B. 45. Tel: 51447. *Air India*, c/o Kanoo Travel Agency, P.O.B. 45. Tel: 54081. *Alia*, c/o Bahrain International Travel, P.O.B. 1044. Tel: 53315. *British Airways*, P.O.B. 22. Telex: 8221. Tel: 54621 (Reservations), 53503. General sales agents: Kanoo Travel Agency, Al-Khalifa Road. Tel: 54081. *British Caledonian Airways*. Tel: 21235 (Airport). General sales agents: Kanoo Travel Agency. Tel: 54081. *Egyptair*, c/o United Travel, P.O.B. 45. Tel: 51447. *Ethiopian Airlines*, c/o Bahrain International Travel, Government Road. P.O.B. 1044. Tel: 53315.

Gulf Air. P.O.B. 138 Tel: 22200 (Administration), 22234 (Reservations), 21248 (Airport Reservation and Ticketing Office). Telex: 8255. General sales agents: United Travel (International Routes). Tel: 55856. Kanoo Travel Agency (other routes). Tel: 54081. *Iran Air*, Gulf Regional Head Office, P.O.B. 902. Tel: 54897/21444 (Airport). General sales agents: Bahrain International Travel, P.O.B. 1044. Tel: 53315. *Iraqi Airways*, Tareq Building, Government Road. Tel: 54458. *Japan Airline*, c/o Bahrain International Travel. P.O.B. 1044. Tel: 53315. *KLM*, 14–16 Awal Building, Government Road. P.O.B. 565. Tel: 53243/21538 (Airport). Reservations and Enquiries, Tel: 54275/50833. General sales agents: International Travel Bureau, Al-Khalifa Road. P.O.B. 584. Tel: 50833. *Korean Airlines*, c/o Al-Gusaibi Travel Agency. P.O.B. 540. Tel: 51827/55357.

Kuwait Airways, c/o Delmon Travel, P.O.B. 540. Tel: 55560/53419 (Sales Office). *Lufthansa*, United Travel Agency, P.O.B. 45. Tel: 51447. *Middle East Airlines*, Kanoo Building, Al-Khalifa Road. Tel: 55273 (ext 23213). Also c/o Kanoo Travel Agency. P.O.B. 45. Tel: 54081. *Pakistan International Airlines*, 30 Awal Buildings, Government Road. P.O.B. 817. Tel: 55069. General sales agents: United Travel. P.O.B. 45. Tel: 51447/54081. *Qantas Airways*, Al-Moayyed Building. Tel: 54774/55375 (Reservations) 21444 (Airport Flight Information). General sales agent: Kanoo Travel Agency. P.O.B. 45. Tel: 54081. *Sabena*, c/o Al-Gusaibi Travel Agency. P.O.B. 540. Tel: 51827/55357/22398 (Airport).

Saudia, c/o Al-Gusaibi Travel Agency. P.O.B. 540. Tel: 51827/55357/22398 (Airport). *Singapore Airlines*. P.O.B. 850, Government Road. Tel: 53314. General sales agent: Bahrain International Travel. Tel: 53315. *Sudan Airways*, c/o United Travel, P.O.B. 45. Tel: 51447. *Trans World Airlines*, c/o Bahrain International Travel. P.O.B. 1044. Tel: 53315. *UTA French Airlines*, c/o World Travel Service. P.O.B. 830. Tel: 52414/21520 (Airport).

Post Offices Head Post Office, Al-Khalifa Road (opposite Bab al-Bahrain). Tel: 53206/53782 (for enquiries). Branch post offices at Muharraq, Awali and Isa Town.

Telephones International calls are quick and reliable. Free public telephones are available in the lobbies of most of the main hotels and at the Cable and Wireless offices, Al-Khalifa Road.

Useful phone nos. *Directory enquiries* 181. *International Telephone Bookings* 151. *International Telephone Enquiries* 191. *Telegrams* 131. *Speaking Clock (English)* 140. *Speaking Clock (Arabic)* 141. *Fire, Police, Ambulance* 999.

Telex Most large hotels have telex facilities. A public telex service is available at the Cable & Wireless Building, Al-Khalifa Road.

Shops The main shopping thoroughfares are Al-Khalifa Road and Government Road and the adjacent souks. The Bahrain equivalent to London's Harrods or New York's Macy's is *Jashanmal's Department Store*, Al-Khalifa Road, where everything can be found but prices are high. Another big department store is *Ashraf's*, a little farther away from the centre of town, on Shaikh Isa Road.

Souks Close to Al-Khalifa Road and Government Road. Brass and copper objects are good buys, although most are made in Iran or India. Pottery goods, however, are usually made in Bahrain at the potteries at Aali. The clay is not very hard and easily disintegrates. The cloth market and the jewellery market both lead off the main souk. Though garish, the jewellery does provide bargains, especially as the gold content is often above 18 carat. It is priced according to weight without regard to the amount of craftsmanship involved. Good souvenirs are gold discs or pendants in the shape of Dilmun seals. Bahraini pearls, of course, are world famous, and jewellery made from seed pearls is unusual and interesting.

The fish market is worth a visit giving the visitor an idea of the wide variety of fish found in Gulf waters. It is advisable, however, to wear shoes with thick soles as the market floor becomes slimy and muddy. On a good day, enormous Gulf prawns can be bought at a reasonable price. Another well-known Gulf fish is the *hamour* which can be cut into large fillets of tender, white meat.

In the covered part of the vegetable market are the bird sellers with a wide variety of species ranging from budgerigars to mynah birds. Very good bargains are offered by village women congregating on a platform in the vegetable market selling hand-embroidered kaftans. An Indian shop on Tijjar Road sells cheesecloth kaftans, blouses, and skirts and Indian prints. An Iranian shop in the covered arcade leading off Al-Khalifa Road sells silver, brass and copper objects, as well as Persian carpets and jade and coral jewellery.

Social clubs The two main expatriate social clubs are the *British Club* (Tel: 8245) in Mutanabi Road, Mahouz (near the power station), and the *American Club* at the end of Quadibiya Road (Tel: 712212). The *Alliance Française*, Old Palace Road (Tel: 713111), is mainly a French cultural organisation but it organises a wide variety of social activities. Temporary membership for visitors is usually available at

73

these clubs. The *Rotary Club* meets at 1230 on Sundays at the Gulf Hotel.

Leisure/sports Swimming is the most popular leisure activity. The major hotels have swimming pools for the use of guests. The *Delmon*, *Gulf* and *Hilton* Hotels also run 'swimming clubs' so that, on payment of a fee, non-residents can use their pools. Shaikh Isa's private beach at Zellaq is open to all non-Bahrainis. Visitors are allowed in free but photography is strictly prohibited and all photographic equipment must be handed over to the guards at the gate. On Fridays it gets very crowded. For those who prefer less-crowded beaches, there are some lovely unspoilt stretches of sand at the southernmost tip of the island at Ras al-Barr. Bahrainis, themselves, swim at the Sobh beach at Budaiya. Another popular swimming-place is the fresh-water Ain Adari (Virgin's pool), but, in spite of its name, it is not advisable for women to swim there. The *Bahrain Petroleum Company* has its own beach at Zellaq for the use of Bapco employees and their guests.

Golf is a popular sport in Bahrain although the courses are on sand. There are two courses, the main one being the 18-hole course at the *Awali Golf Club*. The club, owned by the Bahrain Petroleum Company, is mainly for the use of the company's employees but visitors are permitted to play on payment of a 'green' fee. Another course has been built at Rifaa, mainly by young Bahrainis who learned the game while serving as caddies at Awali.

Camel and horse races are held at the race course at Saafra on the Awali Road, south of the Amir's Palace at West Rifaa. Informal races are sometimes held in the evenings and on Fridays the Amir himself often attends races. Riding facilities are also available at Budaia and Zellaq (for information telephone 54414).

There are two sailing clubs—the *Manama Sailing Association*, Quadibiya jetty (Tel: 712133), and the *Zellaq Sailing Club*. Temporary membership is available.

The *British Club*, off the Mutanabi Road (Tel: 8245), and the *American Club*, at the end of the Quadibiya Road (Tel: 712212), have swimming, tennis and other sports facilities. Their membership is not restricted to Americans and Britons and arrangements can be made for temporary membership. The *Alliance Française*, Old Palace Road (Tel: 713111), shows French films, and organises excursions, and dances.

For those interested in archaeology it would be worth contacting the *Bahrain Historical and Archaeological Society* (Tel: 51323), which arranges visits to the island's tumuli and other sites.

Bahrain has seven cinemas, most of which show Arabic and Indian films. The *Delmon* cinema in Awali, however, screens only American and European films. The *Awal* is the largest cinema in Bahrain.

Hospitals The main hospital is the *Sulmaniya Hospital*, off Sulmaniya Road (Tel: 52761). The oldest hospital in Bahrain is the *American Mission Hospital*, Shaikh Isa al-Kabir Road (Tel: 53449 for men, 53447 for women). Both provide emergency treatment.

Pharmacies *Al-Jishi Pharmacy*, Al-Khalifa Road. Tel: 54524/55602. *Ruyan Pharmacy*. Tel: 53751. Open 24 hours.

Bookshops *Family Bookshop*, Shaikh Isa al-Kabir Road (Tel: 54288). Large stock of English books and magazines. *Al-Hilal Bookshop*, Al-Tijjar Road (in the souk). Tel: 53836. *Jashanmal's Department Store* (Books Department), Al-Khalifa Road. *Awal Stationery Shop*, Al-Khalifa Road.

Banks Central Bank Authority: *Bahrain Monetary Agency*, Shaikh Daij Road. P.O.B. 27. Tel: 712657/71401. Telex: 8295.

Commercial Banks (main offices): *Algemene Bank Nederland NV*, Government Road. P.O.B. 350. Tel: 50123. Telex: 8614. *Arab Bank*, Government Road. P.O.B. 395. Tel: 55988. Telex: 8232. *Bank of Bahrain and Kuwait*, Government Road. P.O.B. 597. Tel: 53388. Telex: 8284. *Bank Melli Iran*, Government Road. P.O.B. 785. Tel: 51421/3. Telex: 8266. *Banque de Paris et de Pays Bas*, Al-Khalifa Road. P.O.B. 5241. Telex: 8458. *British Bank of the Middle East*, Al-Khalifa Road. P.O.B. 57. Tel: 55933/7. Telex: 8230. *Chartered Bank*, Government Road. P.O.B. 29. Tel: 51845/55946. Telex: 8229. *Continental Bank*, Government Road. P.O.B. 5237. Tel: 56228. Telex: 8373.

Grindlays Bank, Government Road. P.O.B. 793. Tel: 54707. Telex: 8220. *Habib Bank*, Government Road. P.O.B. 566. Tel: 54889/55062. Telex: 8240. *National Bank of Abu Dhabi*, off Al-Khalifa Road (near Al-Fateh Building). P.O.B. 5247. Tel: 51398/51689. Telex: 8483. *National Bank of Bahrain*, Government Road. P.O.B. 106. Tel: 55973/5. Telex: 8242. *Rafidain Bank*, Al-Khalifa Road. P.O.B. 607. Tel: 55656. Telex: 8332.

Offshore Banks: *Algemene Bank Nederland NV*, Government Road. P.O.B. 350. Tel: 52821. Telex: 8433. *American Express International Banking Corp.* P.O.B. 93. Tel: 53660. Telex: 8537. *BAII (Middle East) Incorporated*, Government Road. P.O.B. 5333. Tel: 54964/5. Telex: 8542. *Banco do Brasil*. P.O.B. 5489. Tel: 50133. Telex: 8710. *Bank of America NT & SA*, P.O.B. 5280. Tel: 50559/53180. Telex: 8616. *Bank of Bahrain and Kuwait*, Government Road. P.O.B. 597. Tel: 53388. Telex: 8284. *Bank Saderat Iran*, Government Road, P.O.B. 825. Tel: 50809. Telex: 8363.

Banque Nationale de Paris, Government Road, P.O.B. 5235. Tel: 50321. Telex: 8245/8595/6. *Bank of Nova Scotia*. P.O.B. 5260. Tel: 55522. Telex: 8690. *Canadian Imperial Bank of Commerce*, Government

Road. P.O.B. 7740. Tel: 50551. Telex: 8593. *Chartered Bank*, Government Road. P.O.B. 29. Tel: 55949. Telex: 8229. *Chase Manhattan Bank*, Government Road. P.O.B. 368. Tel: 50799. Telex: 8487. *Chemical Bank*. P.O.B. 5492. Tel: 52619. Telex: 8562. *Citibank*, Government Road, P.O. Box 548. Tel: 54755. Telex: 8575. *Grindlays Bank*, Government Road, P.O.B. 793. Tel: 51825 Telex: 8220.

Hong Kong and Shanghai Banking Corp., Al-Fateh Building, Al-Khalifa Road. P.O.B. 5497. Tel: 55947. Telex: 8230. *Kredietbank NV*, Room 302, Salaheddin Building. P.O.B. 5456. Tel: 54284. Telex: 8633/8635. *Gulf International Bank*, Government Road, P.O.B. 1017. Tel: 56245. Telex: 8766/8755. *Lloyds Bank International*, Government Road. P.O.B. 5500. Tel: 50069/50453. Telex: 8641. *Manufacturers' Hanover Trust*, Government Road. P.O.B. 5471. Tel: 54375. Telex: 8556. *Midland Bank*, Government Road. Tel: 57100. P.O.B. 5675. Telex: 8561. *National Westminster Bank*, Salaheddin Building. P.O.B. 820. Tel: 55412. Telex: 8294.

Scandinavian Bank, Government Road. P.O.B. 5345. Tel: 51068/51207. Telex: 8750/1. *Société Générale*, Government Road. P.O.B. 5275. Tel: 53641. Telex: 8568/9. *Swiss Bank Corporation*, off Al-Khalifa Road. P.O.B. 5560. Tel: 57222. Telex: 8812/4. *Union de Banques Arabes et Françaises*, Al-Khalifa Road. P.O.B. 5595. Tel: 57393. Telex: 8840. *United Bank of Kuwait*, Government Road. P.O.B. 5494. Tel: 56774. Telex: 8651. *Canadian Imperial Bank of Commerce*, Government Road, P.O.B. 5484. Tel: 54385. Telex: 8593.

Ministries/Government departments Government House (between King Faisal Road and Government Road) accommodates the following ministries. *Foreign Affairs*, P.O.B. 547. Tel: 53361. Telex: 8228. *Commerce, Agriculture & Economy*. Tel: 50813. *Oil Affairs Dept*. Tel: 53361. *Development & Industry*. P.O.B. 235. Tel: 53361. Telex: 8344. *Justice & Islamic Affairs*. Tel. 53339. *Cabinet Affairs*. Tel: 53361. *Finance*. Tel: 53361. *Council of Ministers*. Tel: 53361.

Other ministries: *Defence*, Rifaa. P.O.B. 245. Tel: 66743. Telex: 8429. *Communications*, Muharraq. Tel: 22800. *Education*, Al-Maarif Road. Tel: 713011. *Health*, Shaikh Sulman Road. P.O.B. 12. Tel: 50834. Telex: 8511. *Interior*, Mutanabi Road. P.O.B. 13. Tel: 51030. Telex: 8333. *Labour & Social Affairs*, Shaikh Isa Road, Quadibiya. Tel: 712891. *Housing*, Shaikh Isa Road, Quadibiya. P.O.B. 802. Tel: 712891. Telex: 8599. *Works, Power & Water*, Old Palace Road. P.O.B. 5. Tel: 55941. Telex: 8525. *Information*, Jufair Road. P.O.B. 253. Tel: 8711 Telex: 8399. *Amiri Court*. Tel: 66451. *Guest Palace*, Quadibiya. Tel: 712821.

Embassies *Australia* (Consulate-General), Al-Fateh Building, Al-Khalifa Road. P.O.B. 252. Tel: 55011. Telex: 8236. Trade Commission:

Al-Moayyed Building, Government Road. *Britain*, Al-Mathaf Square, Jisr Road. P.O.B. 114. Tel: 54002. Telex: 8213. *Egypt*, 3105/7 Adliya. P.O.B. 818. Tel: 712011. Telex: 8248 GJ. *France*, 1785/7 Mahouz, P.O.B. 1034. Tel: 712595. Telex: 8323. *India*, Shaikh Isa Road, Adliya. Tel: 712785. *Iran*, 1018 Shaikh Isa Road. Tel: 712151/712065. Telex: 8238. *Iraq*, Mutanabi Road, 911/8 Mahouz. Tel: 712837. Telex: 8325. *Jordan*, Shaikh Isa Road. Tel: 714287/714391. *Kuwait*, Bin-Otba Road, 2105 Quadibiya. P.O.B. 787. Tel: 713487. *Libya*, Mahouz. P.O.B. 5240. Tel: 714162. Telex: 8443. *Pakistan*, Shaikh Isa Road. P.O.B. 563. Tel: 713273. *Saudi Arabia*, Dilmun Road, off Sulmaniyya Road. P.O.B. 1092. Tel: 713406. Telex: 8411. *United States*, Shaikh Isa Road. P.O.B. 431. Tel: 8331. *Palestine Liberation Organisation* (Representative Office), Shaikh Daij Road, Quadibiya. Tel: 714369.

Newspapers/periodicals

Dailies: *Akhbar al-Khalij*. P.O.B. 224.
Weeklies/periodicals: *Gulf Weekly Mirror*, Al-Moayyed Building, Government Road. P.O.B. 455. Tel: 54324/51008. English weekly. *Al-Bahrain Al-Youm*, Arabic weekly published by the Ministry of Information. *Al-Adhwaa*. P.O.B. 250. Arabic weekly. *Al-Mawakef*. P.O.B. 1083. Arabic weekly. *Sada Al-Usbou*. P.O.B. 549. Arabic weekly. *Al-Jarida Al-Rasmiya* (Official Gazette). Arabic weekly published by Ministry of Information. *Al-Riyadha*. Arabic sports weekly. *Al-Najma Al-Usbou*. Arabic weekly published by The Bahrain Petroleum Company. *Al-Hiya Al-Tijariya* (Commerce Review). Arabic Monthly published by the Bahrain Chamber of Commerce and Industry. *Al-Murshid*. Arabic/English monthly includes 'What's on in Bahrain'.

Media The only English-language newspaper published in Bahrain is the *Gulf Weekly Mirror*, which comes out on Sundays covering events in the whole Gulf area. It includes information on radio and television programmes. On radio it is possible to listen to English-language programmes almost around-the-clock in Bahrain. In addition to the *BBC World Service*, there are four radio channels transmitted by Aramco from Dhahran which can be received on FM sets. The channels play popular, classical, country and western, and light music. On the country and western channel, a 15-minute *United Press International* news bulletin is broadcast daily at 1200 and 1800 Bahrain time. *Bahrain Radio* also has an English channel which broadcasts for a few hours each day in the afternoon and evening. Both the English and Arabic services of *Kuwait Radio* can also be clearly received in Bahrain.

Bahrain Television programmes (in colour) begin at 1730 and end at about 2330. It broadcasts an English-language news summary every day at 1900, as well as several English-language serials and occasionally films. *Aramco Television*, which can be received in Bahrain, begins transmissions at 1530 Saturday to Wednesday, and 1430 on Thursdays and Fridays, and broadcasts most of the well-known programmes from US and British television.

Churches *Sacred Heart of Jesus* (Roman Catholic), Shaikh Isa al-Kabir Road. Tel: 53598. Sunday Mass 0630, 0900, 1800 and 1900. Daily Mass 0620 and 1830. *St. Christopher's* (Anglican), Mutanabi Road. Tel: 53866. Sunday Services: Holy Communion 0700, Matins 0900, Evensong 1745. *National Evangelical Church* (Interdenominational), Shaikh Isa al-Kabir Road. Tel: 54508. Services: Sunday 1015, 1830; Tuesday 1900; Wednesday 0800. *Awali Community Church* (Interdenominational), Awali. Services: Friday 1030; Sunday School 0930. This church serves congregations of most other churches in Bahrain. *Syrian Orthodox Church*, near Sulmaniya Hospital. Tel: 52980.

Major companies *A. A. Al-Zayani*, Delmon Hotel Building, Government Road. P.O.B. 932. Tel: 51411/55921. Telex: 8367/8305. *A. K. Al-Moayyed*, Al-Moayyed Bldg., Al-Khalifa Road. P.O.B. 363. Tel: 51212. Telex: 8267. *Yousef Bin-Ahmad Kanoo*, Kanoo Building, Al-Khalifa Road. P.O.B. 45. Tel: 54081/52454. Telex: 8215. *A. E. Al-Mannai & Sons*, Government Road. P.O.B. 295. Tel: 53176. *Gray Mackenzie & Co. Ltd.* P.O.B. 210. Tel: 53536/53640. Telex: 8212. *Bahrain Petroleum Company* (*Bapco*), Awali Office, Awali. Tel: 910005. Telex: 8214. Sitra Shipping Office. Telex: 8218. *Aluminium Bahrain* (*Alba*). P.O.B. 570. Tel: 66751. Telex: 8253.

Useful addresses *Bahrain Chamber of Commerce & Industry*, Al-Khalifa Road. Tel. 50678. *Cable & Wireless*, Mercury House, Al-Khalifa Road, P.O.B. 14. Tel: 56655. Telex: 8201 (Administration), 8310 (Auto Telex Exchange). *Crown Agents*. P.O.B. 531. Tel: 54672. Telex: 8307.

GENERAL INFORMATION

How to get there BY AIR (outside Gulf): Bahrain has one of the longest established international airports in the Gulf, so its best connections tend to be along the traditional air routes (in particular between London, the Far East and Australia). There are usually around half a dozen flights a day from London, many of them using the island as a stop-over point. There is also virtually a flight a day from Paris, Amsterdam and Paris and several flights a week from Athens and Rome. Weekly flights go to Bahrain from Geneva, Vienna and Zurich.

Bahrain has the Gulf's best links with Australia. There are two to three flights a day from Melbourne and Sydney and a weekly flight from Perth. A number of flights each day go from Singapore to Bahrain and there are several flights a week from Bangkok, Kuala Lumpur, Bombay, Hong Kong, Seoul and Karachi. There are weekly flights also from Auckland, Calcutta, Colombo, Delhi and Manila.

From other Middle East centres outside the Gulf, there are daily flights from Beirut and several flights a week from Cairo and Amman. There are flights at least once a week from Addis Ababa, Larnaca, Taiz, and Sanaa.

BY AIR (Inter-Gulf): Bahrain has one of the best airports for inter-Gulf connections. There are around four flights daily to and from Abu Dhabi, Dubai, Muscat, Doha, Dhahran and Kuwait. There are several flights a week to and from Baghdad, Riyadh, Shiraz, and Sharjah, and less frequent weekly flights to and from Jeddah and Abha.

Visas Visas are required by all except nationals of Kuwait, Qatar, Saudi Arabia, United Arab Emirates, and British subjects, being 'Citizens of the United Kingdom and Colonies' born or resident in the UK. Visitors holding onward or return tickets may, on arrival at Bahrain Airport, obtain a 72-hour temporary visa. Extensions of this visa can be obtained on application and payment of a fee at the Department of Immigration, Al-Khalifa Road, near Bab al-Bahrain.

Language The official language is Arabic. But English is widely spoken, especially in business circles. It is often easier for a foreigner to make himself understood in English than in a non-Bahraini Arab dialect. The spoken Arabic of Bahrain resembles that of other Gulf states, especially that of Iraq.

Religion Bahrain is a Muslim State. About half the population belong to the Shia sect, the remainder are Sunnis.

Hours of business Friday is the weekly holiday when all offices and most shops are closed. Shops in the souk, however, remain open on Friday mornings. Some offices also shut on Thursday afternoons.

Government offices work from 0700 to 1300 Saturday to Thursday. Other offices open from 0730 to 1230 and from 1500 to 1800 Saturday to Thursday. Shops open from 0830 to 1230 and from 1530 to 1830 Saturday to Thursday. Banks open from 0730 to 1200 Saturday to Wednesday and 0730 to 1100 Thursday.

Official holidays The Islamic holidays are dependent on the Muslim lunar calendar and may differ by one or two days from the dates

79

given. The Muslim year has only 354 or 355 days, so Muslim dates and holidays fall 10 to 11 days earlier each year on the Gregorian calendar. Businessmen are advised to avoid visiting Bahrain during the month of Ramadan which ends with a three-day holiday (Id al-Fitr).

	1977/78
Id al-Adha	11-15 November
National Day	16 December
Al-Hijra	12 December
Ashura	21–22 December
New Year's Day	1 January 1978
Prophet's birthday	25 February
Id al-Fitr (end of Ramadan)	3–6 September

Time GMT + 3.

Electric current The electricity supply is 230 volts, 50 cycles, AC in Bahrain. But in Awali it is 120 volts, 60 cycles AC.

Health All visitors must produce an up-to-date international certificate of vaccination against smallpox. They must be immunized against yellow fever if arriving within 6 days from an infected area. Precautions should be taken against malaria which is sometimes prevalent on the island.

Water Tap water is not safe to drink. There is a good local brand of bottled water for drinking purposes but many residents prefer to buy purified 'sweet' water from local water sellers. This water is kept in special buckets fitted with spigots, and is perfectly safe and considerably cheaper than bottled water.

Post Bahrain's postal services are efficient. Airmail letters to Europe take, on average, 3 to 4 days and airmail parcels between 5 days and a week. Letters to Europe cost 80 fils for each 10 grammes, postcards 60 fils each. To North America the rate is 200 fils per 10 grammes.

Telecommunications Bahrain has the best international telecommunications links in the Gulf. There is direct dialling to Europe and also to Qatar, and the United Arab Emirates (Abu Dhabi, Dubai and Sharjah).

Currency The Bahraini unit of currency is the Bahraini dinar (BD) which is divided into 1,000 fils. Notes: 100 fils; ¼, ½, 1, 5, and 10 dinars. Coins: 5, 10, 25, 50, 100 and 500 fils.

Currency regulations There are no restrictions on the import or export of currency.

Customs regulations Visitors are allowed to bring in 400 cigarettes or 50 cigars or half a pound of tobacco, and a reasonable amount of perfume. Non-Muslim passengers are permitted to bring in two bottles of wine and spirits. The import of obscene, indecent or seditious literature or pictures is prohibited.

Alcohol Alcohol is freely available. Outside Iraq, Bahrain is the only country in the Gulf where people can buy it in retail shops without the need of a permit. Spirits can in fact be bought in bottles of ¼-gallon, ½-gallon and 1-gallon sizes, in addition to the usual sizes. Most well-known brands of both spirits and beer are sold at relatively low prices. Wine is expensive. It is often affected by the extremely hot weather, and in the summer it is advisable to buy only refrigerated wines.

The main and most easily accessible liquor stores in Manama are the *Gulf Cellar* in Al-Khalifa Road and the alcohol department on the ground floor of *Jashanmal's Department Store* also in Al-Khalifa Road.

Further reading *The Living Treasures of Bahrain*, Dara Al-Khalifa. Bahrain, 1971. *Welcome to Bahrain*, James Belgrave. The Augustan Press Ltd, Manama, 1975. *Bahrain*, James Belgrave and Bernard Gerard. Paris, Editions Delroisse, 1974. *The Pirate Coast*, Sir Charles Belgrave. Beirut, 1972. *Personal Column*, Sir Charles Belgrave, Beirut, 1972. *Looking for Dilmun*, T. G. Bibby. New York, 1970. Penguin Books, 1970. *The Bahrain Islands*, A. Faroughi. Verry & Fisher, New York, 1951. *The Amphibians and Reptiles of Bahrain*, Michael Gallagher. Bahrain, 1971. *A Guide to the Birds of Bahrain*, Michael Gallagher and M. J. Strickland. Muharraq ROAC Press, 1969. *Les Princes de L'Or Noir*, Ali Humaidan. Futuribles, Paris, 1968. *Bahrain, Qatar and the UAE*, M. T. Sadik and W. F. Snaveley. Lexington, 1972.

Government

Prime Minister	...	...	Shaikh Khalifa Bin-Sulman al-Khalifa
Defence	...	...	Shaikh Hamad Bin-Isa al-Khalifa
Foreign Affairs	...	...	Shaikh Mohammad Bin-Mubarak al-Khalifa
Finance	...	...	Ibrahim Abdel-Karim
Interior	...	...	Shaikh Mohammad Bin-Khalifa Bin-Hamad al-Khalifa
Education	...	...	Shaikh Abdel-Aziz Bin-Mohammad al-Khalifa
Health	...	...	Dr. Ali Mohammad Fakhrou
Information	...	...	Tareq Abder-Rahman al-Moayyed

Transport	Ibrahim Mohammad Hasan Humaidan
Housing	Shaikh Khaled Bin-Abdullah al-Khalifa
Public Works, Electricity & Water	Majid al-Jishi
Development & Industry ...	Youssef Ahmad Shirawi
Labour & Social Affairs ...	Shaikh Isa Bin-Mohammad al-Khalifa
Justice & Islamic Affairs ...	Shaikh Abdullah Bin-Khaled al-Khalifa
National Economy, Commerce & Agriculture ...	Habib Qassem
Minister of State for Cabinet Affairs	Jawad Salem al-Arayyed
Minister of State for Legal Affairs	Husain al-Baharna

IRAN

THE SHAH OF IRAN

THE SHAH OF IRAN

His Imperial Majesty Mohammad Reza Pahlavi,
Shahanshah Aryamehr

The Shah acceded to the throne on 25 August 1941
on the abdication of his father Reza Shah the Great.
The Shah was born in Tehran in 1919 and was
officially proclaimed Crown Prince on the
coronation of his father, who founded the Pahlavi
dynasty, in April 1925. The Shah was educated in
Iran and Switzerland before training at the Staff
College from which he graduated in 1938. Soon
after he was appointed Inspector of the Iranian
Armed Forces.

Iran

Area 628,000 square miles

Population 34,100,000 (1975)

Chief Towns Tehran (capital) 4.5 million; Isfahan 680,000; Mashad 620,000; Tabriz 545,000; Shiraz 400,000; Abadan 335,000

Gross National Product $65,507 (1976 estimate)

GNP per caput $1,950

GEOGRAPHY

Iran is a country of sharply contrasting scenery and extremes of climate. It is also very large, covering about 629,000 square miles—an area over half the size of India, or approximately the size of Britain, France, Germany, Switzerland, Belgium and Denmark added together. It is bordered in the north by the Soviet Union and the Caspian Sea, in the east by Afghanistan and Pakistan, in the west by Iraq and Turkey and in the south by the waters of the Gulf and the Gulf of Oman.

A large area of the country consists of a central plateau, which lies between 3,000 and 5,000 feet above sea level. This plateau is enclosed on most sides by high mountains, the largest group being the Zagros range which stretches from the north-west border with Turkey down the Gulf Coast before veering to the East. Several peaks in the Zagros mountains are over 10,000 feet, and some are as high as 14,000 feet. The other main group of mountains is the Northern Elburz range which, in places, is as high as the Zagros, but is much narrower. In fact, the Elburz

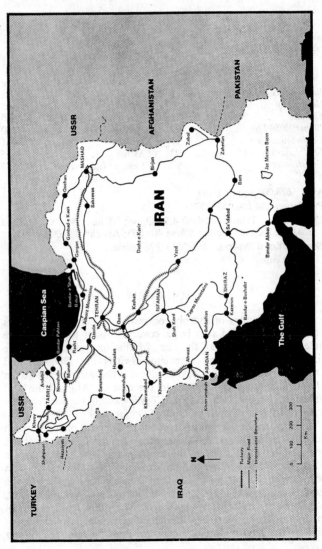

contains the highest peak in Iran, Mt. Damavand, an extinct volcano rising to 18,700 feet. These mountains drop away sharply to a flat plain near the Caspian Sea. Much of the country's agricultural produce comes from this area, as well as from the mountain foothills.

Most of the people of the central plateau live on its periphery because the centre is mainly desert. There is the large salt desert of Dasht-i-Kavir and the vast sand desert of Dasht-i-Lut to the south-east. Further east lie the swamps of Nainaq Sar.

The Gulf coast in the south of the country has sandy shores. But the climate there can be extremely hot and humid. Since ancient times silt has made the creation of ports difficult and most of the old harbours were established far inland.

Iran has few large rivers. In the west the Karun, which flows from the Zagros mountains into the Gulf, is about the only one which is navigable. The Caspian basin has four rivers, the Safid Rud, the Chalus, the Talar and the Gurgan.

But the country does have a number of sizeable lakes. The largest is lake Rezaieh, close to the Turkish border.

CLIMATE

The climate in Iran reflects the extremes of the landscape. Generally in the summer it is very hot and dry, but in the winter, because of the high altitudes, temperatures of −18°C. (0°F.) are common. Temperatures in Tehran range from a maximum of around 38°C. (100°F.) in summer to a minimum of −14°C. (7°F.) in winter. In January the average is around 3°C. (38°F.) and in July about 29°C. (84°F.). Humidity is low. In the Zagros mountains, the temperature can drop as low as −29°C. (−20°F.), while the deserts in the south experience some of the hottest and driest weather in the world: a temperature of over 51°C. (130°F.) is common in the summer.

Average rainfall is about 10 inches a year, although the interior and the east of the country get less than five inches on average. However, along the Caspian coast the rainfall is much greater— up to 80 inches in some parts—producing rich, almost tropical plant growth. After the rains, a few rivers flow from the mountains down into the central plateau, but they soon dry up.

Occasionally parts of Iran experiences earthquakes, causing widespread damage and loss of life. In the autumn of 1968 the province of Khorasan was hit by a severe quake which left many thousands dead and caused considerable destruction.

PLANTS AND WILD LIFE

Iran has a great variety of vegetation and animals. It has more than 10,000 different plants, 100 types of mammal and in the Caspian lowland alone 320 species of bird. The country is famous for some plants. The lilac and the water lily is reputed to have originated from Persia.

There are two main forest areas—on the Caspian Coast and in the Zagros mountains. The Caspian has a virtually tropical jungle in which abundant rainfall generates tall trees covered in creeper. Further up the slopes of the Elburz mountains the oriental beech, oak, hornbeam, maple, ash and elm are conspicuous. The yew can also be seen here. In the Zagros ranges the oak and maple predominate. In the Fars the forests have ceased to flourish and have turned into moors.

In the Iranian steppes below the mountain ranges a rich variety of herbs can be found, including giant fennel. There are also many shrubs traditionally used for making dyes and paint. Near the desert grasses give way to camel's thorn, with tamarisk replacing the poplar and willow along the dried-up riverbeds.

The lion, Iran's national emblem, is now extinct in the country. However, tigers still roam the Caspian jungles, where panthers and wild cats can also be found. Cheetahs, jackals, foxes, hyenas, brown bears and wild boars are scattered throughout the country. Marauding wolf packs are a danger in the Zagros mountains. The jerboa, mongoose, Persian squirrel and Indian-crested porcupine are fairly common in certain areas. Large numbers of wild sheep and the ibex live in the mountains, while the Persian gazelle can be seen in the steppes.

Among the country's more distinct birds are the flamingoes and the pelicans, which breed on the southern lakes and Gulf coast, and its birds of prey. Eagles can often be sighted in the mountains as well as falcons, buzzards and kestrels. Game birds like the partridge, sand grouse and snipe are hunted in some parts.

Iran's most renowned fish is the Caspian sturgeon from which caviar is extracted and then exported. Salmon and trout breed in the Elburz rivers and carp live in some southern rivers. The agamids are the country's main species of lizard, with some reaching three feet in length. Snakes and vipers are common.

COMMUNICATIONS

In recent years Iran has made a big effort to build up an efficient network of roads, railways, ports and airports which will adequately serve an industrialised nation. But the country has developed so fast that the expansion of new communications has not been able to keep pace. As a result ports have become clogged, roads overcrowded and the railway services severely stretched.

The country will soon have nearly 12,427 miles of main road linking the major cities and towns with about the same length of gravel and feeder road. A large number of roads is also being regraded. Around 1,056 miles of motorway are being built, some of which are being used to speed up traffic going in and out of the big cities. In Tehran dense traffic has become a serious problem.

It is now possible to travel by train from Europe through Turkey to Iran. The line runs via Tabriz to Tehran where it extends to Mashad in the north-east of the country. There are plans to link Mashad by rail to Afghanistan. Tehran is also connected by rail to Bandar Shahpur in the south-west and Isfahan and Kerman in the south-east. Kerman may shortly be linked to the Pakistan railway system at Zahedan. There are also plans to join Bandar Abbas and Kerman by rail.

Over 20 airports provide a well-distributed domestic air service. Internal flights are always heavily booked. Iran Air, which has a domestic monopoly, is one of the world's fastest growing airlines. In 1976 it started non-stop flights to North America and opened a Tehran–Cairo–Paris–New York route covering four continents.

Iran has seven major ports, some of which in recent years have become extremely congested because of the country's economic boom. But big strides have been made in easing the flow of goods through the ports. Khorramshahr has been the busiest port, closely followed by nearby Bandar Shahpour. Within a few years Bandar Shahpour should however have outstripped its neighbour, becoming the country's biggest port. A large new port is being constructed at Bandar Abbas so that vessels can bypass the heavy shipping traffic in the Gulf. Bandar Pahlavi on the Caspian is also being expanded.

Telecommunications have been expanding rapidly. Over 50 towns are now linked by an automatic microwave system. The number of telex subscribers has risen from 500 to near 10,000 in seven years. Two earth satellite stations give an automatic international service.

SOCIAL BACKGROUND

There are more than 34 million people living in Iran, and the population is growing at the rate of about 3 per cent a year. Well over half the population lives in villages, and by far the biggest concentration of people (over 4 million) is in the capital, Tehran.

The majority of indigenous 'Iranians' are descended from the Indo-European tribes that invaded the central plateau in the second millenium B.C. However, there have been many contacts with other races and cultures through wars and trade, and a number of other peoples have intermarried with the Iranians. Among these are Turks, Baluchis, Afghanis and Arabs, as well as some Armenians, Jews and Christians.

The Iranian language (Farsi) is also Indo-European in origin, and is spoken (according to official figures) by over 60 per cent of the population; it is the official language. It contains a number of Arabic words and derivatives and, in recent years, more and more English and French words have come to be heard in everyday speech. However, this trend is frowned upon, and efforts are made from time to time by the Language Academy, with only a certain amount of success, to expunge foreign influences from the language by finding Farsi equivalents. The script is derived from the Arabic script and, like Arabic, is written from right to left.

In the north of Iran several distinct dialects of Farsi and Kurdish are spoken (e.g. Gilaki, Tabri) while Baluchi can be heard in the south-east. It is estimated that about 200,000 people speak Turkoman, while around five million people speak a form of Turkish. Most of these live in east and west Azerbaijan. Arabic is spoken by some communities living near the Gulf coast. But with the spread of education and broadcasting, all of which is conducted in Farsi, the regional languages and dialects are becoming less common. The Ministry of Culture is, however, making an effort to record for posterity many of the regional dialects, as well as the customs that went with them.

Iran's rapid economic development over the past few decades has resulted in large numbers of foreigners coming to work in the country. Many of these have been Americans and Europeans, and their influence, together with the emergence of English and French as the accepted international languages for commerce and diplomacy, has resulted in the two languages becoming increasingly important. Most educated Iranians are able to speak either English or French.

Culture and religion Iranian culture is one of the world's richest. The country is famous for its miniature paintings. It was the advent of Islam that sparked off the golden years of Persian literature. The best known poet in the West is the Sufi mystic and astronomer of the twelfth century, Omar Khayyám, whose 'Rubaiyat' was translated into English by Edward Fitzgerald in the nineteenth century. Other great names from Persian literature are Ferdowsi (Abul Kasim Mansur) who lived in the last half of the tenth century, the twelfth and fourteenth century poets Saadi and Hafiz, and the philosopher, Abu Nasr Farabi.

The vast majority of Iranians are Muslims, following the Shia rather than the Sunni sect. The Shia differ from the Sunnis in believing that the true successor of the Prophet Mohammad was his cousin and son-in-law Ali, rather than the first three Caliphs of Islam, Omar, Abu Bakr and Uthman.

Because of the big foreign influences in Iran over the centuries, several different religions have been followed, and some still survive. Official figures show that 97 per cent of the total population are Muslims (only 7 per cent of whom are Sunnis). Other religious groups are the Christians, Jews and Zoroastrians.

CONSTITUTION

Iran is a constitutional monarchy, with the Shah holding executive power. The first step towards democracy came in

August 1906, when, by Imperial decree, a constituent assembly was set up. In December of that year, the assembly adopted the Iranian Constitution.

The Constitution upholds the rights of equality of individuals, security of their lives, property, homes and honour; it also upholds the right to bring legal actions in competent courts, the right of personal freedom to write and to assemble, and freedom of ownership. Foreign nationals in Iran enjoy the same rights.

Legislative power rests with the Senate (the upper house of parliament) and the Majlis (the lower house). According to the Constitution, only the Majlis has the right to debate and take a vote on the Budget and other financial bills, while the Senate remains a consultative body. In other matters, both houses are free to debate and vote on bills. The Majlis has 268 members and the Senate has 60, of whom 30 are appointed by the Shah, 15 are elected from Tehran, and 15 from the provinces. The Shah appoints the Prime Minister, who must be approved by the Majlis. An amendment to the Constitution in 1949 gave the Shah power to dissolve the Majlis and to call a new election.

The country is divided into 14 Ostans (provinces) and eight Farmandari-kiols (Chief Governors' Regions). The Ostans are divided into Farmandaris (Governors' Regions), which are subdivided into Shahrestans (Townships) and Bakhshdaris (Districts).

Rastakhiz Party In March 1975 the Shah dissolved the two-party system, urging existing political parties to join a new single organisation, the Rastakhiz (National Resurrection) Party. It was to have the Prime Minister, Amir Abbas Hoveyda, as its Secretary-General for at least two years. The ideology of the new party would be based on three cardinal principles of support for the Constitution, the Monarch and the White Revolution.

The Shah said that the aim of the single party was that 'everyone of voting age should establish their national position'. All those supporting the principles of the party should join, and those who did not subscribe to the three principles were traitors and should leave the country. People who opposed the principles should openly declare their position. If they were not communists or 'anti-nationalist', they would be left free. The Shah pointed out that 'playing the role of a loyal opposition is very difficult in this country'. Although Iran had free elections, freedom was needed in a wider sense 'because despite the existence of free elections, it was very difficult for those who did not belong to the majority party to succeed'. The Rastakhiz Party would make 'free and proper' political activity possible for everyone.

All members of the Cabinet and high-ranking Iranians are required to become members of the Rastakhiz Party, and several prominent figures, including the Minister of the Economy and Finance and the Minister of the Interior, were made members by the Shah's decree.

Before the formation of the new single party, the Iran Novin Party had been in office for 12 years. In March 1975 they had 229 representatives in the Majlis and the opposition Mardom Party had 37. The other two opposition groups, the Iranians' Party and the Pan-Iranist Party each held only one seat.

Elections for the 24th term of the Majlis and the seventh term of the Senate were held on 20 June 1975, the first with candidates from the Rastakhiz Party. It was reported that about 80 per cent of the Majlis and half the Senate were elected members for the first time.

A communist Tudeh Party used to exist in Iran but was declared illegal by the Shah. However, some support for the party remains, and it manages to operate a clandestine radio station ('National Voice of Iran'), as well as to distribute literature in Iran. Much of the support comes from Iranians living abroad. Over recent years there have been several guerrilla attacks by people opposed to the Shah's regime, and many of those caught have been executed. Iran's secret police (*Savak*) is one of the most efficient in the area and also tries to monitor the operations of Iranian activists in foreign countries.

HISTORY

Archaeological investigations have shown that Iran is the site of some of the oldest settlements in the world—some dating back to about 8000 B.C. However, the information is not complete and little is known of the people or of their way of life. It was in the second millenium B.C. that a number of Indo-European tribes migrated from central Asia to settle on the Iranian plateau. These people referred to themselves by the generic term 'Arya', from which the name 'Iran' derives. The name 'Persia' became more popular in Europe because the ancient Greeks came into contact with Iran when it was dominated by the Persians, a tribe living in the south-western province of Fars (or Persis), the home of the Archaemenid dynasty.

Cyrus the Great The first dynasty to rule Iran after the arrival of the Aryans was that of the Medes, who gained power in the western and northern parts of the plateau in the eighth century B.C. In 708 B.C. they founded the Median empire—the first government in Iranian history—based at what is now called Hamadan. The Medes and the Persians, both Indo-Europeans, became united through royal marriage, and in 550 B.C. Cyrus the Great revolted against the Median empire. He defeated his grandfather in battle and the Archaemenid empire began to take shape. The most striking reminder of this period is the city of Persepolis, near Shiraz, the ruins of which can still be seen today. Cyrus the Great began the conquests that were to be continued by his successors, conquests noted for the compassion and tolerance shown to the defeated peoples. Under Cambyses Egypt was taken, and further conquests were carried out by Darius and Xerxes (who burned down the Acropolis in Athens), until the empire extended as far as the Danube in the west and Afghanistan and India in the east. With such a large empire the Archaemenids developed a sophisticated network of land and sea communications. They also encouraged arts, science and culture, and set up efficient agricultural and monetary systems. The defeat of Darius III by Alexander the Great, in about 330 B.C., marked the end of the Archaemenid empire. Some Greek temples were built in Iran, but Greek influence was soon challenged by the Parthians, who came from the north-eastern regions of Iran and ruled for about 500 years. During this time trade flourished with countries as far away as China, but there was a number of military encounters with the Romans.

In A.D. 224 Ardashir I, from Fars, founded the Sassanian empire. The next 400 years are among the most distinguished in Iranian history. The Sassanians used their considerable wealth to set up an efficient administration, providing education and social care for their people. Their religion was Zoroastrianism, and science, art and architecture flourished throughout the empire.

The coming of Islam The Sassanians had to contend with invading nomads from central Asia, and also fought the Romans. These campaigns gradually weakened their armies, and they were able to put up little resistance when the Arab invasions began in the seventh century. And with the Arabs came the new religion, Islam.

Most of the inhabitants of Iran became Muslims, although several Sassanian dynasties survived around the southern coast of the Caspian Sea, and much of the local administration and many of the local customs carried on as before.

The conquest of Iran had been carried out by forces under the Ummayad Caliphs, who were Sunni Muslims, but they were followed by the Abbasids in the middle of the eighth century. The Abbasids, who held power for more than 500 years, were Shia—supporting the Prophet Mohammad's cousin and son-in-law Ali as his true successor. The Shiite sect of Islam is dominant in Iran to this day. Despite the Abbasid domination, many independent dynasties survived.

The Mongols In the eleventh century, Iran was taken over by the Seljuq Turks from Turkestan. Iran became part of an empire stretching from Syria to China, and in this period many buildings of outstanding architectural beauty were constructed. It was also a golden age for literature, science and the arts. But this golden age ended suddenly, when the Mongols under Genghis Khan arrived from the East in 1218, followed by a second Mongol invasion under Hulagu Khan about 40 years later. It was a time of destruction and bloodshed, with many of the outstanding memorials to the preceding centuries being razed to the ground.

Fortunes in Iran revived for a while in the fourteenth century under the Timurid dynasty founded by Tamurlaine. He came from central Asia, defeating the Mongols and providing a period of relative stability during which the arts and culture were allowed to blossom. But there was much turmoil ahead: the Ottoman Turks were just emerging, and, after a lot of fighting, the Safavids won the day in Iran. In 1502 their first king, Shah Ismail, was crowned and, for a while, the Persian empire regained something of its former glory.

Safavid dynasty The best known of the Safavid rulers is Shah Abbas I (the Great) who ruled from 1587 to 1629. He recovered much of the Persian empire that had been lost by his predecessors, and he has become famous for his construction of roads and, more especially, bridges. He transferred the capital from Kazvin to Isfahan and strengthened the spirit of Shiism by developing Mashad, the shrine of the eighth Imam, and encouraging its importance as a centre of pilgrimage. A large number of mosques and other buildings went up during his reign, and he gave every encouragement to the arts. In addition, he developed a number of political and trading links with Europe and other parts of the world. Merchants flourished, much of the trade being in silk, muslin and linen.

But the period of prosperity was not to last; after the death of Shah Abbas, wars broke out, and the Safavids were effectively swept away by an invasion of Afghan tribes, having also had to contend with the Uzbegs in the east, the Russians in the north and the Turks in the east. The end of the Safavid dynasty came in about 1722, and shortly after that a new figure appeared on the scene, Nadir Quli. He was the son of a shepherd from Khorasan who had turned into a brilliant soldier and military commander; he managed to seize power, and was crowned in 1736. Nadir is often hailed as the last of the great Persian warriors, and it is certainly true that in his 11 years in power he achieved remarkable military feats: not only did he defeat the Turks, but he also waged successful campaigns in India. Finally, he was assassinated by a member of his own household.

The Qajars Nadir's death produced a bitter struggle for power, with Karim Khan, a leading member of the Kurdish Zand tribe, emerging as victor. He made Shiraz his capital and gave the country 25 years of peace and stability. On his death in 1779, fighting broke out once more, until finally Agha Mohammad was proclaimed Shah. He was a leader of the Qajar tribe, and the Qajars were to remain in power in Iran until 1925.

The remainder of the nineteenth century was a period of relative stability, but Iran lost a lot of its territory to the Russians in the north and to the British, through Afghanistan, in the east. This was the beginning of European interest in Iran, which was to last for many years with the Russians, the British and later the French trying to gain supremacy. In this struggle the British made a major breakthrough in 1901 when W K D'Arcy secured a concession lasting for 60 years to search for oil; seven years later oil was found, and in 1909 the Anglo-Persian Oil Company was formed. Three years later the British built a refinery at Abadan, and a new era had begun.

Majlis established   This was also a time of great political change in Iran. Opposition to Qajar oppression was building up, and finally took shape in the form of civil unrest and demands for a constitution. In 1906 the Shah gave in and signed a proclamation for the setting-up of a National Assembly (Majlis) which, later that year, approved a constitution. But this was not the end of the trouble. In 1907 Shah Muzaffar died, to be succeeded by the despotic Shah Mohammad Ali Shah. He tried to reverse the liberal policies of his predecessor, and violence erupted, with Russia backing the Shah and Britain on the side of the constitutionalists, who wanted the Majlis to survive. The constitutionalists won the day.

In 1914, at the outbreak of the First World War, Britain and Russia declared war on Turkey, while Iran remained neutral. However, the neutrality was respected neither by Britain nor Russia. Much fighting took place on Iranian soil, and the general turmoil of war added to the disintegration of normal life that was being caused by oppressive Qajari rule, so that when the First World War ended, the atmosphere was right for a major change in Iran.

Pahlavi rule   In 1925 the last Qajar, Ahmad Shah, was deposed by the National Assembly and power was handed to the Commander-in-Chief, General Reza Khan. In December of that year, he was crowned Shah Reza, the first of the Pahlavi dynasty. The major task facing the new leader was to start bringing the country into line with the progress and developments of the twentieth century, after the many years of political instability when economic and social reforms had been largely ignored. Also he wanted to lessen his country's dependence on Russia and Britain.

During his years in office Shah Reza improved communications within Iran, building the Trans-Iranian railway, as well as a network of roads. A number of industrial schemes was started, and the exploitation of the country's rich oil reserves began in earnest. In 1932, the Shah demanded a revision of the concession agreement with the Anglo-Persian Oil Company, and, when this was not forthcoming, he cancelled the agreement. However, the matter was referred to the League of Nations and a new concession (to run to 1993) was agreed, under which royalty payments to the Iranian Government were greatly increased.

Social reforms Shah Reza also inaugurated many important social reforms, apart from building schools and hospitals. One of the biggest involved changes in dress. In 1928 it became illegal to wear traditional dress, and in 1936 it was announced that women would no longer be allowed to wear the veil. In addition, much was done to improve the legal status of women, who, in this period, gained the right to seek a divorce and were encouraged to go out to work and be educated.

Iran declared itself neutral at the outbreak of the Second World War in 1939—a stand that displeased Britain and its allies because of the presence of a large number of Germans in the country. Consequently, the Allies demanded that these Germans should be expelled, but the Shah did not comply with this request, and, in August 1941, joint Anglo-Russian forces invaded Azerbaijan and Kermanshah. In the following month, Shah Reza abdicated in favour of his son, Shah Mohammad Reza Pahlavi.

In 1942 the new Shah signed a Treaty of Alliance with Britain and Russia under which the two foreign powers guaranteed to defend Iran from attack, while respecting the country's sovereignty and political independence. This was to last until the war ended, and, in March 1946, the British and US forces left Iran; the Soviet forces left two months later. The countries continued, however, to maintain their influence in Iran, and, in October 1947, a United States Military Mission was set up in Tehran to help to modernise the Iranian armed forces.

Oil nationalized In the post-war years there were spectacular economic and social developments, and one of the most important events was the nationalisation of the oil industry in April 1951. Britain appealed to the International Court and UN Security Council, but without success, and in October 1951 the Anglo-Persian Oil Company pulled out of the country. The US

Government played a major part in trying to mediate in the dispute, threatening to stop financial aid unless the oil started flowing again. Towards the end of 1954 an agreement was reached under which eight companies would form a consortium to exploit the oil. The profits were to be shared equally between the Iranian Government and the consortium, and the agreement was to last for 25 years.

During this time the Shah encountered considerable opposition, especially from the communist Tudeh party, and was forced to flee the country for a while in 1953. However, the Shah gradually restored order, banning the Tudeh party and taking a number of stern measures to halt the economic decline that had been precipitated by the nationalisation crisis. Large amounts of aid were received from the US to bolster the country.

White Revolution But much of the Shah's energy was always directed towards social reform. He began to distribute his personal land among peasants and did a lot to break down the power of the thousands of absentee landlords, and to break up the large estates. In 1963 he proclaimed his now famous 'White Revolution', which included plans to redistribute land in favour of the peasants, nationalisation of all forest land, the sale of government shares in industry to raise money for land reform, the distribution of industrial profits among the workers, the entitlement of women to vote, and the creation of the Literacy Corps.

In March 1958 the Shah divorced his second wife Queen Soraya (his first marriage to Princess Fawzia of Egypt was dissolved in 1948), and in December 1959 he married Farah Diba. In October 1960 his son and heir, Reza Kurush, was born. The couple also have a younger daughter and a second son. Queen Farah plays an active part in Iranian affairs, particularly in supervising social reforms and encouraging the education of women. She also encourages them to play a bigger part in all aspects of modern Iranian society.

In 1967 the Shah and Queen Farah were crowned, over 20 years after the Shah's accession to the throne. The Shah believed that the coronation was the continuation of a process that had been started in Iran 2,500 years earlier. However, the coronation of Queen Farah, the first woman in Iran ever to receive the honour, symbolised the new direction that Iran is now taking with a confidence that it lacked for many years.

Recent Events

When Britain announced in 1968 that it was withdrawing its forces from the Gulf, Iran decided to adopt the role of guardian of security in the area. The Shah was watching with alarm the expansion of the Soviet Navy and the increased presence of Soviet ships in the Indian Ocean and the approaches to the Gulf. If there was to be a power vacuum when the British left the Gulf, Iran was not going to sit back and watch who filled it.

However, initially, the Shah's apparent desire to act as the new protector of the area merely served to revive the traditional rivalry between Arabs and Persians. In particular the Iranian Government's reiteration of its claim to Bahrain in 1968 aroused strong Arab opposition. Iran eventually withdrew its claim to the island in 1970 after a United Nations mission found that the majority of Bahrainis preferred full independence to being formally associated with Iran. In June 1970 Iran pressed its claim to a group of disputed islands off Sharjah—Abu Musa and the Greater and Lesser Tumbs. An agreement on joint ownership of Abu Musa was concluded with Sharjah, while the Tumbs (claimed by Ras al-Khaimah) were taken by force. Military bases were set up on these islands to strengthen Iran's watch over the vital Straits of Hormuz at the entrance to the Gulf. Iran regards freedom of passage through the Straits of Hormuz as vital to its strategic and economic interests.

This was the major reason behind Iran's decision to send troops to Oman to help put down the left-wing rebellion in Dhofar. The Shah saw the rising, supported by South Yemen with money and equipment from left-wing countries, as a potential threat to Oman, and therefore a threat to the control of the entrance to the Gulf. When the Sultan of Oman asked for help at the end of 1971 Iran agreed to send equipment and several thousand troops. With the help of these, and of forces from Britain and Jordan, the Sultan's army managed to defeat the guerrillas at the end of 1975, after a 10-year campaign, achieving what he claimed was the first total victory over international communism by an Arab state.

Iraq dispute ends Iran's relations with the Arab world had for a long time been undermined by a long-standing dispute with Iraq, which had resulted in a number of border skirmishes. The disagreement was over the control of the Shatt Al-Arab waterway. Also, Iran was giving military support to the Kurds in north-eastern Iraq, who were fighting for more autonomy from the central Government in Baghdad. In addition, Iran had long accused Iraq of harbouring Soviet interests in the area, and the prospect of the two countries settling their differences amicably seemed unlikely. But, in March 1975, it suddenly happened. Iraq conceded the division of the Shatt al-Arab along the centre of the waterway, while Iran accepted the demarcation of the land border according to the Constantinople Protocol of 1913. Later, Iran withdrew its support for the Kurds, and overnight the sting had been taken out of what was potentially an area of serious conflict.

The agreement with Iraq helped Iran to form closer ties with other Arab states. In 1975, the Shah visited Egypt, after which he said that Israel should withdraw from the territory that it took in 1967. This was the first sign that the Shah might play a part in resolving the Arab-Israeli conflict, which he obviously sees as a considerable threat to stability in the Middle East. Both President Sadat and President Assad of Syria visited Iran in 1976.

The Shah also visited Saudi Arabia in 1975, for talks with King Khaled who in turn visited Tehran in 1976. Relations with Saudi Arabia, the other big economic power in the region and a partner in OPEC, had been cool for many years. The Shah realised that two such powers had to co-operate, not only to ensure stability in the Gulf, but also to put up a joint front as oil producers in the face of disputes over the prices to be paid by the consuming nations.

Iran has been keen that the problems of the Gulf should be worked out at a conference attended by countries in the area, and by them alone. The Shah said during a visit to Iraq after the 1975 agreement that he wanted any American presence removed from the Gulf. At the same time he expected Iraq to agree to the exclusion of Soviet bases in the area. 'We want to keep third parties out', he added.

Internal opposition While Iran has been winning friends abroad, the Shah's regime has had to take steps to counter growing opposition at home. Many of the Shah's opponents were angered by the lavishness of the celebrations for the 2,500th anniversary of the Persian monarchy in October 1971, and the stringent security precautions accompanying them. Up to 1,000 people were detained in the months leading up to the celebrations. A series of guerrilla attacks was carried out by underground movements, culminating in the assassination of the Chief of Military Justice, Zia Farsiou. The Government responded with a massive clampdown on its opponents. In October 1973 the Government security authority *Savak* carried out further purges after discovering an alleged attempt to kidnap or kill the Shah, Queen Farah and Crown Prince Reza. In recent years *Savak* has been particularly active in controlling internal opposition.

In March 1975 the Shah turned the country into a one-party state. He announced the formation of the Iran National Resurgence Party (Rastakhiz), with the Prime Minister, Amir Abbas Hoveyda, as Secretary-General. The new party was to be based on the three cardinal principles of support for the Constitution, for the Monarch, and for the 'White Revolution'. The Shah said that all those supporting the principles of the party should join and those who opposed them were traitors and should leave the country. New elections to the Majlis were held in June 1975, giving an 80-per-cent new membership to the 268-seat parliament. But it contained more women and more representatives of the professional and workers' guilds than the old Majlis.

Economic problems While the country was going through a political reorganisation, its economy was beginning to show the strains of rapid development following the quadrupling of oil prices in 1973–74. By mid-1975 the Government had had to put a squeeze on the economy, as a result of diminishing oil exports, shortages of manpower and an inadequate infrastructure. Projects were delayed and development programmes cut back. Loans had to be negotiated from abroad. In an effort to contain inflation the Government started an anti-profiteering campaign which led to the fining and imprisonment of many businessmen.

Oil revenues started to pick up again in 1976 and some of the pressure on the economy began to ease. The Government was able to steer clear of what would have been its first budget deficit for six years. Iran was also able to show some economic muscle abroad. The Shah purchased a 25 per cent stake in the prestigious West German firm Freidrich Krupp in 1976, at an estimated cost of $200 million. The move caused a stir in Western Europe where people were suddenly made aware of Iran's growing economic power. At the end of the year Iran joined the more militant members of OPEC in calling for a large increase in oil prices. Along with the majority of OPEC countries, it decided to raise its oil prices by 10 per cent, even though Saudi Arabia and the United Arab Emirates insisted on restricting the increase to five per cent. A compromise, in which Iran joined, was, however, reached by the majority of OPEC member-states in July, 1977, and Iran agreed to forego its proposed mid-year increase of a further five per cent.

ECONOMY

The economy of Iran, like that of many of its neighbours, is tied closely to income from its oil industry. The Shah has spoken often about Iran becoming the 'Japan of the Middle East', but forecasts of this kind have been made possible only because of the existence of vast revenues from oil. Oil money has provided the vital catalyst in Iran's spectacular development over the past decade, and the money set aside for development each year has reflected the fluctuations in the price being paid by the oil-consuming nations.

These fluctuations can be traced in Iran's five-year development plans, the main vehicles for the country's economic planning. Total spending in the Fourth Plan (ending in March 1973) was estimated at IR 480,000 million ($7,000 million), while preliminary figures for the next five years put expenditure at IR 2,461,100 million ($35,500 million). In October 1973, however, the price of oil rose dramatically in a matter of a few months. The promise of increased oil revenues gave an enormous boost to the targets that could be achieved in the Fifth Plan, and consequently the estimates were revised. Investment in the public and private sectors was raised to IR 4,634,000 million ($69,000 million).

Development immediately progressed at a rapid speed. But soon it became apparent that the country could not press ahead as fast as it wished. During 1975 there was a steadily increasing awareness that Iran would not be able to advance at the pace originally envisaged at the end of 1973. The obstacles had come in the form of diminished oil exports and the uncertain future of oil income, the growing limitations imposed by inadequate infrastructure, shortage of trained manpower and the inflationary effects of rapid growth.

Economic squeeze By early 1976 the Government found itself overspending, at a time when oil revenues were falling. A squeeze was put on the economy and the Government imposed a slow-down on its payments for work on projects either in progress or completed. The Shah told ministries to avoid "showcase" schemes. He set up a top-level commission to check on wastage and called for higher productivity among workers. The Government's 1976/77 budget looked likely to be heading for a substantial deficit but in fact an upturn in oil revenues later in the year helped the Government to balance its books.

However, the country's continued vulnerability to fluctuations in oil exports was underlined in early 1977 when output slumped alarmingly after the introduction of a two-tier price system by the Organisation of Petroleum Exporting Countries (OPEC). Along with 10 other OPEC countries Iran opted for a 10 per cent increase while Saudi Arabia and United Arab Emirates insisted on keeping their price rise down to five per cent. But after falling to five million barrels a day (b/d) in January, output rose to six million b/d in February. Exports averaged 5.6 million b/d, over a third higher than in February the previous year. The Government was able to breathe a sigh of relief but nonetheless much of the economy still showed signs of strain from the imbalance between the country's commitments and its income.

Planning

Of the total fixed investments of IR 4,634,000 million (about $690,000 million) envisaged by the Fifth Development Plan, the public sector was to provide 66 per cent (IR 3,064,000 million). Total fixed investment by the public sector was composed of IR 2,619,000 million directly to be invested by the Government and a further IR 445,000 million to be invested by state-owned public enterprises.

Allocations for the oil sector were to be increased by 156 per cent, for natural gas by 112.5 per cent and for industry by over 95 per cent. Other major increases in allocations included those for electricity generation, which were more than tripled, for port, railway, road and other infrastructure projects, up by 128 per cent and for agriculture up by nearly 100 per cent.

The revised Fifth Five-Year Plan, launched in March 1973, called for a 51.5 per cent growth rate in oil and gas, 18 per cent for industry, 16.4 per cent for services and seven per cent for agriculture. Real GNP would rise from $17,300 million in 1973 to $54,600 million at the end of the plan period. In the same period, per caput income was expected to rise from $556 to $1,521. Growth rate for the oil sector was projected under the original Plan at only 11.8 per cent. Average annual growth rates for the other sectors in the first plan were: industries and mines, 15 per cent; services, 11.5 per cent; agriculture, 5.5 per cent.

Sixth Plan   Over the last few years the country's planners have been busy drawing up a Sixth Development Plan to run from 1978 to 1983. A total of 61 committees, including 36 sectoral and 23 regional study teams, have been examining current policy and programmes under the supervision of the Plan & Budget Organisation (PBO). The PBO was due to publish the Plan in October, 1977.

Like with the Fifth Plan, rapid industrialisation will be the first priority of the new Plan. Industry is expected to grow at around 16 per cent a year over the five-year period, while services will grow by 16–20 per cent. Agriculture should take second place to industrial development. At the same time priority will be given to the creation of a sound economic infrastructure. Health, welfare and education schemes will be co-ordinated in an attempt to stem the migration of manpower to Tehran and to achieve a more even balance between rural and urban incomes. More emphasis is likely to be put on decentralisation, with provincial organisations given a greater say in the planning of development.

Behind the planners' thinking is the stark realisation that in 12 years the country's oil production will start to decline. By the end of the Plan period there will be an urgent need for the non-oil sectors of the economy to be providing a higher share of the country's income. Certain fundamental ills in the economy will have to be remedied. Without doubt the Sixth Plan will have to be much more of a success in economic planning than its predecessors.

Budget for 1977/78 The 1977/78 budget indicated that the Government intended to tread carefully for a while and showed a shift in priorities. The general budget was increased by 12 per cent and current expenditure was raised by a mere five per cent. But investment expenditure went up by 40 per cent. Oil and gas revenues in 1977/78 were estimated to be $19,500 million, compared with $20,500 million in 1976/77. The forecast was based on an assumed average oil output of 4.6 million b/d, which was considered by some experts to be pessimistically low.

One of the budget's priorities was the elimination of bottlenecks in communications, power generation and manpower supply. Spending on power was raised by 66 per cent compared with a 30 per cent increase in credits for industry. Transport was allocated 60 per cent more than in the previous budget. Expenditure on housing and education was raised by 37 per cent, with education being given 10 per cent of the total general budget spending. Public affairs spending was actually cut by 20 per cent, resulting in a reduction of the Government's construction programme.

Iran's General Budget for 2536 (1977/78)

	IR '000 million	$ million
Revenues	2,188.6	30,740
Taxes	420.8	5,910
Oil and Gas	1,372.7	19,279
Government monopolies	30.3	425
Goods and Services	27.9	393
Miscellaneous	66.5	934
Loans	250.0	3,511
Interest on Loans and Investment Abroad	20.3	285

Expenditure				2,341.0	32,879
Public affairs	..	..	..	200.6	2,817
Defence	..	..	..	561.1	7,881
Social affairs	..	..	..	544.0	7,640
Economic affairs	..	..	..	874.7	12,285
Miscellaneous ..	..	..	..	35.8	503
Repayment of Loans ..	..	..	58.5	822
Loan Servicing	..	..	..	66.3	931

Oil and Gas

Iran has always been a pioneer among the Middle East oil states. It was the first country in the region to produce oil for the international market, the first to nationalise its oil industry, and the first to set up a national oil company and conclude joint-venture contracts with foreign companies.

The story of Iranian oil stretches back to the beginning of this century, when Persia was squeezed between British and Russian spheres of influence, but still maintained a nominal independence. Persia's oil seepages and the 'eternal fires' of Azerbaijan had been curiosities for centuries in the West. But it was only in May 1901 that William Knox D'Arcy, recently returned to his native England after making his fortune from Australian gold, obtained exclusive 60-year oil exploration rights over the whole of Persia, except the five northern provinces under Russian influence. Drilling started in 1902, but oil was not struck in commercial quantities until 1908, when the whole costly exploration venture was on the point of being abandoned through lack of funds.

First oil strike The first commercial oil strike was made at Masjid-i-Sulaiman (the Mosque of Solomon), the site of an ancient fire temple in the Zagros Mountains of southwest Persia. This timely discovery led to the formation in April 1909 of the Anglo-Persian Oil Company (APOC), with an initial capital of £2 million. Further development up to the First World War proved the existence of a great oil field. The Abadan refinery was built at the head of the Gulf and, in 1912, Persia became one of the world's oil-producing countries, with an output that year of 43,000 tons. By 1914, when output reached 273,000 tons, the British Government was persuaded by Winston Churchill, as First Lord of the Admiralty, of the need for more oil-fuelled

111

warships, and accordingly bought a voting interest of just over 50 per cent in APOC, and awarded it a contract to supply fuel oil to the Royal Navy.

Over the next 20 years more oil fields and at least one gas field were discovered. Total production rose from just over 7 million tons a year in 1933 to just over 10 million in 1938. Following a slump in production in the early years of the Second World War, new, but as yet untapped fields, found in the 1930s, were brought on stream to help fuel the Allied war effort, and by 1945 Iranian output had reached 17 million tons a year.

The years after the Second World War were a time of consolidation. There were no spectacular new finds, but in response to reviving world economic activity production rose from 19 million tons in 1946 to nearly 32 million in 1950. By 1946, Abadan refinery capacity was 17 million tons a year (double the 1939 figure), and over 24 million tons by 1950, making it the largest export refinery in the world.

Nationalisation In the early 50s the National Iranian Oil Company (NIOC) was formed and the country's oil reserves were nationalised. In 1954 a consortium of foreign oil companies agreed to produce oil on behalf of NIOC, which retained ownership of the oil and sold it to the individual consortium members, sharing profits equally with them. The main shareholder in the consortium (40 per cent) was British Petroleum (BP). Other members were Royal Dutch Shell (14 per cent), Compagnie Française des Petroles (6 per cent), while 8 per cent each was held by the five major American oil companies—Esso, Mobil, Standard Oil of California, Texaco and Gulf. In 1955 each of the American companies gave up one-eighth of their holdings so that a 5 per cent share in the consortium could be allotted to eight American independent operators in varying proportions.

Over 90 per cent of Iranian oil is still produced by the consortium. Since 1967 oil production targets in Iran have been decided largely in accordance with Government wishes. In practice, however, targets may not be met if demand for Iranian oil happens to be slack, as in 1975. This is still a source of friction between the consortium and the Government.

In July 1973 the entire operation of the Iranian oil industry was taken over by NIOC, which guaranteed to sell oil to the consortium members under a 20-year supply agreement and at a cost governed by OPEC posted prices. The 1973 agreement allowed NIOC to take over full ownership and control of the consortium's oil facilities, operations and reserves, with the consortium companies continuing to act as chief marketers of Iranian oil world-wide, with guaranteed security of supply. In addition to crude oil needed for internal consumption, NIOC retained stated volumes of oil for export—200,000 barrels a day (b/d) in 1973, rising to 1.5 million b/d by 1981. The agreement also called for a capital development programme, largely financed by the companies, to increase production.

NIOC is 10 years older than any other state oil company in the Middle East, and has pioneered most of the current practices of national oil companies in the area. NIOC was, for instance, the first national company to take over the internal marketing and distribution of oil products, the first to sell oil abroad and the first to establish its own tanker fleet. It has also set a trend in the use of natural gas, both for internal consumption and for exports. NIOC can rightly claim to be the most experienced of all the state-owned oil concerns in the Gulf, both in terms of time and in diversity of operation.

NIOC differs from some other state oil companies in being less interested in selling crude oil abroad than in using it for the industrial development of Iran, and in taking part in the so-called 'downstream' operations in other countries—transport, refining and marketing. NIOC acts as an oil producer and refiner in its own right, supplying oil products to a domestic market which is expected to increase its demand from a current rate of around 300,000 b/d to 700,000 b/d in the 1980s and to 1.5 million b/d by 1990.

Oil running out Within a comparatively short time Iran will have run out of oil. In about 12 years oil production will start to fall with the average output beginning to show a steady decrease. In early 1977 daily production was averaging around six million barrels, but the Government budgeted for an average daily output of 4.6 million barrels during 1977/78. Secondary recovery techniques have had to be applied as natural outflow in a number of major oil fields slows. During the Fifth Plan up to $2,500 million has been invested in the secondary recovery effort. The aim is to raise recoverable reserves of oil to about 40 per cent. Between 8–13,000 million cubic feet a day of natural gas will be needed to complete the programme. Water injection will also be used in some fields.

With oil exports providing over 70 per cent of Government income and 40 per cent of Gross Domestic Product, the country still needs to sell as much as it can abroad. But at times this has not been easy. Iranian crude oil has often cost more than its competitors' because it has been highly priced. After OPEC introduced a two-tier price system in December 1976, Iranian heavy crude cost $12.52 a barrel while a barrel of a comparable grade of crude from Kuwait cost $12.37. Both countries had applied the higher 10 per cent OPEC price rise. Iranian heavy crude was costing even more than the higher quality Saudi oil costing $12.48 a barrel.

The Iranian Government has tried to increase oil sales by resorting to barter deals with foreign companies. In 1976 the British Aircraft Corporation traded $660 million Rapier missile systems for 17–20,000 b/d over six years at a 22 cents-a-barrel discount. A group of Italian companies constructing a direct reduction steel mill at Bandar Abbas also agreed to a barter deal. But most countries have seemed reluctant to indulge in this type of trading.

Gas wealth While Iran may be running short of oil, it has massive gas reserves to fall back on. In fact the country's still largely untapped gas reserves are exceeded only by those of the Soviet Union. Natural gas promises to be Iran's main natural resource of the future, both for exports and to fuel a rapidly expanding economy. Iran's proven reserves were put at 375 million million cubic feet in early 1977, but with exploration this was expected to rise to almost 600 million million cubic feet. Among the big fields are the Sarakhs fields, with about three million million cubic feet of sweet and 18 million million cubic feet of sour gas. The largest reserves are on- and offshore Kangan Province. Offshore reserves are estimated at 75 million million cubic feet and onshore ones at 175 million million cubic feet.

At present Iran's plans for using its huge amounts of natural gas are unsettled. Planners are still uncertain about how exploitation of natural gas should fit into the country's long-term energy strategy. Nonetheless the National Iranian Gas Company (NIGC), which has responsibility for the development of the Iranian gas industry, hopes that all the country's associated gas, which for years has been flared, will be usefully employed in one way or another by the 1980s, probably mainly as an energy source for industry.

The most ambitious plans for exploitation of gas has been on the export side. In 1965 NIGC reached an agreement to export large quantities of natural gas to the Soviet Union, to be paid for in part by Soviet help in establishing a new steel plant in Iran. The 680-mile Iranian gas trunkline from the southern Agha Jari and Marun fields to Astara on the Soviet frontier was completed in 1970 with an initial capacity of 1,000 million cubic feet a day. Now it supplies 8–10,000 million cubic metres a year to the Soviet Union.

A much more ambitious gas export project was agreed at the end of 1975. The agreement is due to start operating in 1981, building up to a full flow in 1983 and continuing for 20 years. It provides for the export of 473,000 million cubic feet a year of gas from southern Iran by a new 680-mile pipeline to the Soviet Union for industrial consumption. In turn, the Soviet Union will supply 388,000 million cubic feet a year of its own gas to Czechoslovakia for onward transmission to West Germany, Austria and France, after in effect retaining some of the Iranian gas for its own use.

There are also plans to export liquefied natural gas (LNG). One of the biggest projects involves a US, Japanese and Spanish consortium which aims to exploit the gas fields offshore of Kangan Province. The scheme should yield annual exports of 5–7 million tons of LNG. Two other LNG projects have been postponed by NIGC because of differences with foreign partners over costs and doubts about access to markets abroad.

Nuclear energy Despite its massive gas reserves, Iran is pressing ahead with an ambitious nuclear energy programme. By the end of the century it aims to have about 20 reactors generating about 23,000 MW, or half the country's electricity. Kraftwerk Union of West Germany is building two nuclear power plants at Bushehr with a capacity of 1,200 MW each. In June 1977, it was reported that the German company was negotiating to construct two more plants at Isfahan. Framatome of France was due to start work shortly on two plants of 900 MW capacity near the Karun River, just north of Ahwaz. Iran has signed an agreement with France for six more plants to be constructed over the next 20 years.

The Shah has also been negotiating with the US for eight reactors. But the US Government, worried about nuclear weapons proliferation, has been insisting on stringent safeguards which the Shah has not been prepared to accept. The US has also been opposing the Shah's wish for a nuclear fuel reprocessing plant which he had hoped to obtain from France. The Iranian Government's nuclear programme has also been criticised by foreign nuclear experts for being too costly and unsafe. Many of the plants will be located in earthquake prone areas in the west of the country. The plants will necessitate as well the setting up of a hugely expensive transmission network across the country.

Industry

Most of the oil-producing states in the Middle East are realising the need to broaden their economies in order to lessen their dependence on oil, and most are making a big effort to develop other industries. In this respect Iran is much further advanced than many of its neighbours. Industry is already making a considerable contribution to the economy. It accounted for over 22 per cent of the GDP in 1972, compared with 21.3 per cent in 1967, while its contribution to the GNP in 1973–74 was 23 per cent (16 per cent in 1971–72). In 1976–77 it was expecting to show a growth rate of 18–20 per cent, giving a likely average of 19 per cent a year for the whole of the Fifth Plan. A growth rate of 18 per cent for the industrial sector had originally been envisaged at the beginning of the Plan in 1973. In the three years up to 1975–76 a total of $6,200 million has been invested in industry, making it the single biggest area for investment.

Total investment in industry in 1976–77 is estimated to have been about IR 280,000 million ($3,900 million), of which about two thirds was provided by the private sector. This represented an increase of over 30 per cent compared with the previous year. The total value of industrial products in that year was expected to reach IR 1,350,000 million ($19,000 million), compared with IR 1,100,000 million ($15,500 million) the previous year.

Another indicator of the growth of industry in Iran is the fact that the export of industrial products rose by 27 per cent in 1975 and has been increasing at a similarly high rate since then. There were signs that output from several thousand factories outside the oil industry was beginning to make an important contribution to Iran's economy.

Steel production The Iranian steel industry is receiving considerable attention in development programmes. The country's total steel consumption is expected to reach about 18 million tons a year by 1983, and it is hoped that, by then, Iranian steel mills will be producing around 15 million tons annually. Iran's first hot metal production came at the end of 1971, and the first steel production began in March 1973.

Investment in the iron and steel industry is coming from the state as well as from the private sector. Some experts believe that Iran's estimates for the expansion of the industry are over-optimistic, but a vast amount of technology and equipment is being brought in from abroad. The Soviet Union has agreed to help in expanding the Arymehr Steel Complex which it built near Isfahan. Its capacity is being tripled to an annual output of nearly two million tons of steel, possibly rising later to six million tons. This plant is owned by the National Iranian Steel Company. Coal, iron ore, oil and gas needed for the complex, which uses the conventional blast furnace process, are all plentiful in Iran. The further long-term expansion of the Isfahan complex will depend on what further quantities of these raw materials are found in the country.

The integrated plant at Isfahan was part of a deal involving the supply of gas to the Soviet Union. The plant now meets some, but nothing like all, domestic demand. When the decision was taken to build the complex, the Iranians followed a course, common in many developing countries, of integrating 'backwards', that is, beginning with the final stages of an integrated iron and steel plant, in this case a cold rolling mill, and buying the material for it—hot rolled coil—from elsewhere until it can be manufactured locally. In this way the market for the precision products is established before heavy investment is made in the rest of the iron and steel making process.

Most of Iran's steel will be produced by the direct reduction method, taking advantage of the country's gas reserves. By 1981 the state-owned National Iranian Steel Company (NISIC) aims to have about 6.7 million tons of installed liquid steel capacity. About 2.5 million tons of it will come from a three-plant complex being built at Ahwaz. A $1,000 million direct reduction plant is being set up with the help of the British Steel Corporation in Isfahan and the Italian group Finsider is assisting with the construction of a $3,000 plant at Bandar Abbas with a capacity of three million tons a year. Creusot Loire of France is helping to set up a special steels plant.

Manufacturing industries The Soviet Union financed the construction of a machine-tools and heavy engineering plant at Arak. It produces about 9,000 tons of agricultural equipment, boilers, transport equipment and other machinery. Around 8,000 tons a year of drilling equipment, pumps and other machines are produced at the Tabriz machine-tool plant, which was built with aid from Czechoslovakia. The plant is run by the Government's Development & Renovation Organisation (IDRO).

Iran is a major importer of cars in the Middle East, but it has been assembling passenger cars and commercial light vehicles, with the parts imported, for several years. It has already reached the stage of exporting vehicles to other Middle Eastern countries and to Eastern Europe. Iranian assembly plants produce passenger cars, buses, small vans and trucks and tankers.

The assembly of vehicles in Iran began in the early sixties with Jeeps and Land Rovers, and later with a version of the Fiat. Iran's biggest vehicle manufacturer is Iran National Manufacturing Company, which produces a version of Chrysler's British-made Hillman Hunter, known as the *Paykan*. About 87,000 cars for assembly were supplied to Iran in 1975/76. Iran National is hoping to produce 200,000 *Paykans* in 1978 and is working on plans for a second model. The components to meet the expansion programme are being supplied from Chrysler factories in the US, UK, and France. General Motors is producing 6-cylinder *Chevrolets*, and Citroen is manufacturing its *Diane* model while Renault is coming into production with its *Renault-5*.

Other important manufacturing industries include the making of Persian carpets for which the world market is growing fast.

By the end of the Fifth Plan in 1978 it has been estimated that exports will be worth $540 million a year. There is also a growing export market for traditional Iranian handicrafts and the textile industry is expanding fast with total investment expected to top $1,000 million during the Fifth Plan. Smaller manufacturing industries include sugar, canned food, cigarettes, footwear, pharmaceuticals and chemicals, cement and telephone equipment.

Minerals exploitation Although Iran is thought of primarily as being an oil state, it is also rich in other minerals. Copper, lead, zinc, iron, coal, chromite, manganese, sulphur, salt and even gold have been mined successfully in different areas of the country, particularly in the north-western region bordering the Caspian Sea. The mining industry has not in the past received as much attention as other sectors, but of late it has been growing fast. Exports of minerals have been rising by an annual rate of around 20 per cent. The Government's main mining agency—the Mining & Metal Smelting Company of Iran—has predicted big increases in production.

About IR 10,000 million ($144 million) is being invested in the exploitation of Iran's biggest iron ore mines in Golgohar, where, it is estimated, deposits run to about 200 million tons. A Swedish firm is working with the National Iranian Steel Company on various projects in this region. Soviet experts working with the Aryamehr Steel Mill Company in Isfahan have found four new coal deposits with reserves of around 100 million tons in the Kerman area. Full-scale mining is to begin in the Shahrud region shortly, and new deposits have been discovered in various parts of the country.

New discoveries of chromite have been made at Minab, Bafq and Shahrud, and Iran is now thought to own some of the largest reserves in the world. Deposits of uranium have also been found, discoveries which will help Iran in the development of nuclear power. In March 1976, Iran's Atomic Energy Organisation announced the discovery of rich uranium deposits at Shahroud, Dameghan and Semnan, north-east of Tehran, as well as in the eastern provinces of Sistan and Baluchistan.

Copper could soon become one of the country's major exports when large deposits at Sar Cheshmeh start to be exploited within the next few years. Facilities for processing around 200,000 tons of blister copper a year are being set up. The National Copper Company also intends to exploit other reserves of copper near Yazd. Altogether the country has copper reserves of over 1,000 million tons.

Petrochemicals   Iran's most ambitious industrial plans are for the manufacture of petrochemicals in which it hopes to become one of the world's leading producers. In 1976 about 40 per cent of Fifth Plan disbursements were allocated to new petrochemical industries. The National Petrochemical Company (NPC) aims to commission $3,000 million worth of new facilities by early 1980. By then the petrochemical industry will have grown from nothing 15 years ago to a production capacity of three million tons a year earning the country $1,000–1,500 annually.

In early 1977 Iran's annual petrochemical output totalled around 1.5 million tons, consisting mainly of ammonia products and other fertilisers, sulphur and polyvinyl chloride. Work has recently started on the building of a massive $2,500 million olefins and aromatics plant at Bandar Shahpour which is reputed to be the biggest venture undertaken by the world's petrochemical industry. The plant will have a total capacity of 1.4 million tons, divided up among 14 different products. It is being built with the assistance of a consortium of five Japanese companies.

Transport problems   Industrial expansion in Iran has and is likely to continue to be hampered for some time by an inadequate infrastructure. Two to three years ago ships were waiting five months at the port of Korramshahr to unload their cargoes. The country's roads could not cope with the sudden increase in traffic of goods. Inevitably projects fell behind schedule because of delays in the arrivals of materials. During the boom years of 1974–75 in particular there was a dearth of construction materials and other essential commodities.

However, since 1976 a lot of progress has been made in easing the country's transport problems. By the end of the year ships were waiting only 10 days at Korramshahr. At Bandar Abbas and Bushehr waiting times had been cut to 10–15 days. At the same time transport was being given extra priority by the Government. The actual handling capacity of the country's ports should be raised to 26 million tons a year in 1978, compared with 11 million in 1973. During the Sixth Plan the capacity target will be 71 million tons.

The biggest challenge has been to achieve a smooth movement of freight inland. A substantial proportion of the Government's road construction programme is being concentrated on the building of expressways linking the major industrial and commercial centres. The Government has been importing a large amount of trucks and trailers to offset an acute shortage of transportation equipment and has offered attractive credit terms to private companies. But there has been a scarcity of drivers and mechanics capable of servicing the vehicles.

A massive effort is also being made to expand the country's railways. The main aim is to electrify and double-track the lines between Tehran and the main ports and the country's western frontiers. The Tehran–Tabriz line is in most urgent need of modernisation. The Government plans to raise the railways present share of total freight from 12 per cent to 40–45 per cent by the end of the Sixth Plan. On some major routes such as between Bandar Abbas and Bandar Shahpour and Tehran that share should rise to 70–80 per cent.

Price controls   Poor infrastructure is not the only obstacle to fast industrial development. The Government's own economic policies have been criticised for their failure to encourage private and foreign investment in industry. In particular its imposition of price controls and plans for worker shares in industry have come under attack. The Government has maintained strict price controls on industry in an effort to keep down inflation, which unofficially is estimated to have ranged between 20 and 30 per cent in recent years. A campaign has been launched against price-rigging using youths from the ruling Rastakhiz Party as unofficial price inspectors.

A directive from the Shah in April, 1975, that all private companies should hand over 49 per cent of their shares to their workers and the general public has aroused much opposition among industrialists. By October, 1978, 320 companies with a registered capital of $1,500 million are supposed to have completed the transfer of shares. At the same time foreign shareholders are being limited to a maximum stake of 25 per cent in any single company, though this ceiling is being lifted to 35 per cent in firms using high technology.

Shortages of manpower have caused immense difficulties in the country's burgeoning industry. The Government has estimated that the country is short of 600,000 workers, a high proportion of them skilled and semi-skilled. One of the Government's solutions has been a campaign against laziness and illiteracy. But the main answer has been the recruitment of highly qualified labour from abroad, much of it from the rest of Asia. Labour scarcities have helped to push up wages and in 1976 some companies were increasing salaries by as much as 70 per cent. With demand for skilled manpower exceeding the supply, many companies have also suffered a high turnover in staff which has not helped to raise efficiency.

Agriculture

The aim of Iran's agricultural policy is to make the country self-sufficient in food, and although agriculture is one of the oldest industries in Iran, there is still a long way to go before this target is reached. Domestic production has been meeting around 80 per cent of the country's requirements. By the end of the Sixth Plan in 1983 it is expected to provide 90 per cent of Iran's total needs. The general policy of industrialisation has led to a movement towards the towns and agriculture has been largely overlooked. In development planning, agriculture fell well behind other sectors of the economy. When estimates for Iran's Fifth Plan (ending in 1978) were made in 1974, the growth rate set for agriculture was raised from 5.5 per cent to 7 per cent, compared with increases from 11.8 to 51.5 per cent for oil and gas, from 15 to 18 per cent for industry and from 11.5 to 16.4 per cent for services. Estimates of the actual growth rate in recent years range from seven to 10 per cent. But whatever the precise rate, rises in output have been falling short of increases in consumption, now reaching an annual rate of over 12 per cent. At the same time food imports have soared. During 1975/76 food imports reached $1,555 million, 82.5 per cent higher than the previous year. According to some forecasts, Iran will be spending around $4,000 million a year on food imports by the middle of the next decade.

Land reform   One of the most important events in the development and modernisation of agriculture in Iran was the decision by the Shah in 1963 to divide up the country's land, about 70 per cent of which had traditionally been controlled by a small number of powerful landlords. Ownership was in this way transferred to a larger number of people, and co-operatives were set up in many villages. The big change in ownership created many problems, but the main obstacle to agricultural development became a shortage of water and proper irrigation, as well as a lack of infrastructure.

These difficulties should be eased by the measures now being adopted for promoted planning on a regional basis. In addition, the Government has introduced a scheme for the provision of credits to agriculture. This should help develop infrastructure, particularly the construction of irrigation networks, the setting up of co-operatives and marketing facilities and land reclamation. For some projects, notably irrigation, the Government is prepared to meet up to 85 per cent of the cost.

With the land ownership reorganised and the substantial official funds available to farmers, the Government hopes at least to attain self-sufficiency in staple food items, such as wheat, sugar, pulses, oil bearing seeds, fruit and vegetables. It also expects the country's farmers to meet at least one third of domestic demand for meat. There have been some impressive increases in the output of grains. Wheat production has been rising by nearly 20 per cent and barley by over 50 per cent during good farming years.

Consolidation of farms   One major constraint to the introduction of efficient farming techniques is the large number of small farms in the country. Eighty per cent of farms have less than 10 hectares of land. The Government as a result has been anxious to consolidate farms as fast as possible. Originally the emphasis was on the development of rural co-operatives by merging farms and pooling machinery and equipment. But now the impetus has shifted to the setting up of large-scale agro-industries and farm corporations where instead of pooling resources, farmers surrender the title deeds of their land in return for shares in the collective enterprise. Inevitably this move has aroused opposition among farmers but the Government hopes to speed up the formation of large farming units by bringing some of the country's richest farming land under the supervision of its Regional Agricultural Development Organisation.

The Fifth Plan gave agriculture a high priority in investment, allocating IR 239,000 million to the sector with a further IR 160,000 million set aside for the development of water resources. But much of the funds set aside have failed to be taken up. During the first three years of the Plan only 33 per cent of the allocation had actually been used. Spending on water resources only reached 41 per cent of funds made available, Part of the problem was difficulties with poor infrastructure but a major cause of the shortfall seemed to be the concentration of the country's efforts on industrialisation and more prestigious development projects.

Agro-industrial schemes Inevitably as a result the Government has been keen on what it calls 'the industrialisation of agriculture'. Among the many agro-industrial schemes, the Haft Tappeh sugar cane project has proved the most successful. Its average yield of 12 tons per hectare is one of the highest in the world for sugar cane output. Hawaiian Agronomics, the project's US operators, is also involved with the Ministry of Agriculture in an agro-industrial development over a 1,500-square-mile area in the Moghan area of northwest Azerbaijan.

But some agro-industrial schemes have proved a total financial failure. Three large ventures in Khuzestan have collapsed. In one 15,000-hectare project involving Shell International, the Government's Agricultural Development Bank took over after allegations of mismanagement. But Shell and other concerns involved in the scheme blamed unexpectedly high development costs and misleading data on land and cropping potential supplied by a Government research station.

The fishing industry in Iran is one that has yet to be fully developed. Iranian caviar from the Caspian Sea has justly acquired a world-wide reputation, and just under 200 tons is exported each year. Caviar accounts for over 90 per cent of all fish exports. A large variety of fish is to be found in the Gulf, and Iran has declared a 50-mile fishing zone along its coasts. The development of the shrimp and prawn industry also has considerable potential, which has not yet been fully exploited.

However, fishing fleets are being expanded and plans are in hand for new fish meal plants, as well as plants for processing and canning tuna fish.

Banking and Finance

The oil boom has inevitably swollen the country's finance sector, pumping billions of dollars into Iran's relatively well developed banking system. Total domestic credit expanded from $4,945 million in 1970/71 to $16,951 million in 1974/75 and continued this strong upward trend in 1976 when the credit level topped the $20,000 million mark during the first quarter. Deposits displayed an even stronger growth, rising from $3,292 million in 1970/71 to $13,000 million in March 1977. Quasi-money—reflecting the high rate of domestic savings—has been rising at annual rates of around 50 per cent.

Strain on banks   The rapid economic expansion over the last five years has not surprisingly caused some inefficiency in the banking sector. One of the most serious defects is the inability of the banks to re-cycle petrodollars into long-term investments because of the profitability and extravagant demand for shorter-term funding. Some of this demand has been provoked by the Government's cash-flow crisis caused by soaring development expenditure and falling oil revenues. At times, budgetary spending has outstripped revenues. The domestic banking system has been tapped for short-term public funds. The Government and its agencies have also embarked on a mammoth import programme, the financing for which is met by credits from local banks. Loans from the banking system to the public sector more than doubled over three years to $9,000 million by March, 1976. Loans to the Government, which have accounted for about 40 per cent of total internal debt, went up by 32 per cent to $4,700 million during the same period.

Private sector import demand has been even more voracious and import financing has proved to be the largest item in loans to the private sector. Accordingly, both the public and private sector have reacted in such a way to the oil boom that the demand for short-term funds, especially for import financing, has swamped the banking sector's ability and willingness to provide long-term capital for productive investments.

Central Bank's role   At the apex of the banking structure is the Bank Markazi, or Central Bank, which issues currency, licences and regulates commercial banks and determines credit policy. Some of the usual regulatory powers, especially those which concern credit and investment policy, are also exercised by other central government institutions, such as the Ministry of Finance and National Economy—which favours an active expansionist policy—and the Plan Organisation. Since 1975, the Central Bank has assumed a more active role in order to create a more diversified banking system which will be more able to recycle savings into long-term capital.

The Central Bank has tried to keep down the rise in credits to 35 per cent a year by a series of measures. These have included a requirement that 45 per cent of increases in deposits should be used to purchase Government bonds and an across-the-board rise of nine per cent in rediscount rates in November, 1976. The smaller commercial banks have complained that these constraints on lending have seriously reduced their profits and have helped to prop up the privileged position of the larger commercial and specialised banks.

Commercial banking is dominated by four banks, which are thought to account for at least 70 per cent of all commercial banks' assets. They are Bank Melli, Bank Sepah, Bank Saderat and Bank Bazargani Iran. Bank Melli, which used to act as the country's Central Bank until 1960, is Government-owned and is by far the biggest. By March 1976 its total desposits had risen to around $5,500 million. Bank Saderat, the second largest, has deposits of around $3,400 million. Together the two banks accounted for over half the number of bank branches in the country and about one-third of employees in the banking sector.

Specialised banks   The burden of investment financing falls on nine specialised banks which now occupy a strategic position within the Iranian economy and fill much of the gap made by the commercial banks' inability to recycle savings into productive investments. The Agricultural Co-operative Bank and the Agricultural Development Bank accounted for 81 per cent of loans to the agriculture sector in 1975/76. The largest specialised bank is the Industrial Mining & Development Bank of Iran which has a private Iranian stake of 85 per cent and a 15 per cent share by foreign banks. In 1975/76 its total disbursement almost trebled to $660 million. As part of the process of decentralisation the specialised banks play a leading role in the establishment of regional development banks. They also have access to loans raised abroad.

The insurance sector has benefited almost as much from the economic boom. The amount of premiums collected rose from $49 million in 1970/71 to $245 million in 1974/75, an annual average increase of almost 90 per cent with an even faster pace— 100 per cent—recorded since then. The 15 insurance companies operate in a closed market to which only three foreign companies have been allowed entry—the Yorkshire Insurance Company (UK), Ingrostrakh (USSR) and Gras Savoye (France).

Social Services

Iran's rapid internal development over the past few years has created an urgent need for skilled labour and foreigners are having to be brought in to meet the shortage. Considerable importance is therefore attached to the development of education and vocational training, and the educational system is in the process of being overhauled. In the Fifth Plan IR 130,000 million ($1,900 million) was set aside for education. As a matter of urgency the Shah has instructed the Government to take over complete control of primary education, which is now free. Vocational training is also free, and secondary and university education can be obtained free in return for a period of service with the Government. The Government is offering to pay for a student to study for three years at a foreign university, provided he comes back to Iran to work for the state.

A big breakthrough in the development of education in Iran came with the establishment of the Literacy Corps in 1963. Under this scheme, young people doing national service are sent out to rural areas to teach children and adults how to read and write. This has done much to stamp out illiteracy, which nonetheless still remains a major problem. Education has a long history in Iran, but it was not until recent years that it has become anything like adequate to cope with the enormous demand.

Educational expansion It is hoped that by the end of 1978 all children of school age in urban areas and about 80 per cent of those in rural areas will be receiving education. At the beginning of the 1974/75 academic year it was estimated that about seven million children were going to school. A number of kindergartens exist in cities and the larger towns. According to government figures about 40,000 children in 1974 were receiving this level of education. In the same year there were about 3.6 million primary school children, a figure which, according to Plan estimates, should reach 5.5 million by 1978. It is estimated that there will be around 2.5 million people attending secondary schools by 1978. From secondary school, students have an opportunity of continuing their education at technical and vocational schools or teacher-training colleges. The other option is to go to one of the country's eight universities. A large number travel abroad to complete their education, a large proportion going to the US.

The enormous expansion of primary and secondary education in Iran will begin to reap its benefits in a few years. But such is the urgent need for skilled labour that much effort is now being concentrated on the development of vocational training. The Government is working out ways of eventually training about 100,000 people each year. The Government recruits trainees from companies through its Vocational Training Board, which was established in 1971 and now provides about 20,000 people each year with instruction in such subjects as electronics, car mechanics, woodwork, architecture and welding. The main training centres (in Tehran, Isfahan and Karaj) are being expanded to cater for a much bigger intake, and mobile training centres are being sent out to the smaller towns and villages.

The Vocational Training Board is also recruiting a team of university graduates to boost its efforts in tapping the considerable resources in rural areas, but, at the moment, over half its teaching staff are foreigners. A number of foreign countries are involved in training projects in Iran. The Soviet Union has agreed to provide mobile training units. The US is also playing a big part in vocational training. In 1975 the two countries signed an agreement for the implementation of a training programme costing around $280 million. Under the agreement 350 training offices were to be set up. In addition the US would supply mobile training centres.

Health care Health facilities in Iran have expanded rapidly over the past few years, with an emphasis on providing services to the outlying regions. The expansion of these services is considered of great importance to Iran's long-term planning, and an allocation of IR 43,000 million ($621 million) was made during the Fifth Plan.

The chief aim is to provide a free and comprehensive health service to all its citizens. Considerable steps have been made in achieving this aim, particularly in the major towns and cities, but there is still a long way to go because of the shortage of facilities, and, more important, because of the shortage of trained manpower. At the beginning of 1976 it was estimated that there was a shortage of 22,000 doctors in Iran. Medical schools were training some 700–800 doctors a year, but this fell well short of the 1,000 new doctors required to keep pace with an increase in the population of about one million people a year.

The shortage in trained medical staff in Iran has been aggravated by the fact that many Iranians training in medicine in foreign countries are not returning to work in Iran. However, even if the emigration of Iranian doctors ceased and all those abroad returned home, there would still be a shortage in rural areas. According to some estimates, the doctor-patient ratio in Tehran is about 1:600, whereas in certain rural areas it is still as high as 1:1200. Of the 15,000 or so doctors and dentists in the country, over a third have their practices in the capital. To man the increasing number of health facilities throughout the country, doctors and nurses from East and West European countries, as well as from India and other Asian countries, have had to be employed.

Official figures for 1975/76 showed there were about 550 hospitals and 2,800 clinics in the country, in addition to 250 medical centres. However, the majority of the facilities were centred around Tehran and the other major towns. The Government is aiming to raise the total hospital capacity from 54,000 beds to 140,000 beds, or one bed for every 250 people. There has been a programme for the construction of 13 new hospitals ranging in capacity from 300 to 600 beds. Many will include facilities for psychiatric treatment, the disabled, tuberculosis patients or drug addicts, as well as amenities for training nurses.

GUIDE

TEHRAN Tehran is not particularly oriental in personality. Nor is it a cultural microcosm of Iran. To the first-time visitor its sheer immensity, its crawling rush-hour traffic and its lack of either social centrepoints or visible places of entertainment are its most striking features. Central Tehran is a web of boulevards, named either after kings—Pahlavi, Shah, Shahreza, Shahabbas —or after poets and writers—Sa'adi, Hafez, and Khosrow. Some are several miles long and the taxi driver will insist on being given a number. But most buildings have no numbers, so it is important to remember the exact location of the building you are visiting.

With a population of four and half million, Tehran has become during the recent boom years a bustling city sprawling over the hills to the north—through the elegant residential districts of Shemiran and Vanak and up the fertile slopes of the Elburz Mountains. You need skill to understand the transport system. Private taxis tend only to serve the hotels. The incongruous British double-decker buses are liable to arrive three in a row. Most of the population travels in packed orange communal taxis which ply a set route. At dusk the corners of Pahlavi Avenue are dotted with groups of young people who run out from the trees beside the open, flowing drainage ducts to shout 'mostaqim' (straight on) through the taxi windows.

During the Lebanese civil war it was suggested that Tehran would replace Beirut as the playground of the Middle East. But its total absence of café life and central parks or pedestrian squares makes this unlikely. A high level of urban pollution helps to lessen its attraction even further. Most Tehranis treat the heart of the city merely as a place of work and depart to distant residential areas for their entertainment. But in the rush-hour even the suburb of Shemiran can be an hour's drive.

Tehran's charm, if any, lies in its liveliness and variety. It has a wide range of restaurants specialising in cuisines from many nations. Its nightclubs are among the best in the Middle East. It has many thriving social and sporting clubs. There is the Imperial Club which the Shah frequents, the Tehran Club which was and still remains to a certain extent the British Club and the French cultural Club, Les Amitiés Française. The city's main cultural centre, the Rudaki Hall, puts on operas, ballets and holds Iranian folk-singing concerts. Theatre is fairly popular, though not of a particularly high standard. The city has several interesting museums, including the Ethnological Museum (beside the Gulestan Palace), the Handicraft Museum and the Archaeological Museum.

The biggest contrast is between the city's northern periphery, where the land is over 4,000 feet above sea level, and the working class areas in the south. In the north the air is clean, and mountain fresh. In the winter, people living there can be on the ski slopes of the Elburz mountains after a short drive. In the south the air pollution is at its worst. It also has sewage problems. Tehran has no public sewage system. Instead the sewage goes into septic tanks or straight into the ground, and since the city lies on a slope, it tends to drain into the south.

To the businessman, however, one of Tehran's greatest defects is its lack of an administrative and commercial centre. Ministries and Government departments are scattered throughout the city. Even banks and financial institutions are not concentrated in one specific area. As a result the visitor can spend a disproportionate amount of time travelling through traffic jams from one business meeting to another. The Government hopes to change

Key to Tehran map on pages 132 and 133. 1. Archaeological Museum; 2. Crown Jewels; 3. Decorative Arts Museum; 4. Ethnological Museum; 5. Golestan Palace; 6. National Arts Museum; 7. Pahlavi Museum; 8. Municipality; 9. City Theatre; 10. Majlis; 11. The Senate; 12. Roudaki Hall; 13. Tehran Bazaar; 14. Sepahsalar Mosque; 15. Tehran University; 16. Park -e Shahr; 17. Canadian Embassy; 18. French Embassy; 19. West German Embassy; 20. Italian Embassy; 21. Japanese Embassy; 22. Saudi Arabian Embassy; 23. United Kingdom Embassy; 24. United States Embassy; 25. Foreign Ministry; 26. Central Police Department; 27. Customs Office; 28. Posts & Telegraph Office; 29. Parcel and Post Office; 30. Banks and Exchanges; 31. Railway Station; 32. Park Hotel; 33. Royal Tehran Hilton; 34. Tehran International Hotel; 35. Arya-Sheraton Hotel; 36. Inter-Continental Hotel; 37. Commodore Hotel; 38. Imperial Hotel; 39. Kings Hotel; 40. Marmar Hotel; 41. Semiramis Hotel; 42. Sina Hotel; 43. Vanak Hotel; 44. Victoria Hotel; 45. Versailles Hotel; 46. National Iranian Oil Company (NIOC); 47. Iranian National Tourist Office; 48. Pahlavi Hospital; 49. Marmar Palace.

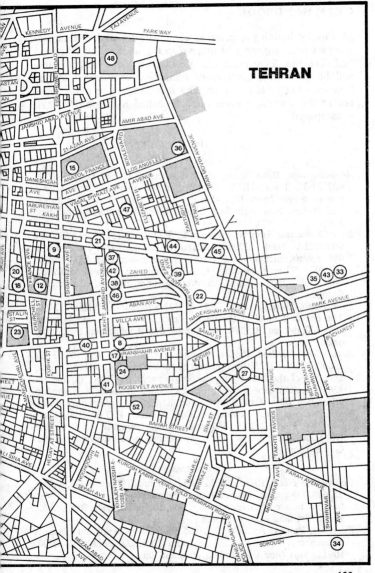

TEHRAN

all this by building a massive administrative and commercial complex in a large area of undeveloped land north of Abbassabad. The site, three times the size of New York Central Park, will be filled with government ministries, commercial offices, hotels, and cultural amenities. But it is likely to be many years before this ambitious scheme, to be called Shahestan Pahlavi, is completed.

Hotels

DE LUXE

Arya-Sheraton, Bijan Street, Pahlavi Avenue. P.O.B. 11/1961. Tel: 683021-31. Telex: 212798. Situated in the north of the city. 204 rooms. Single room IR 3,450, double IR 3,900. Two restaurants. Coffee-shop. Nightclub. Bars. Swimming pool. Conference facilities. Shops.

Inter-Continental, Iran-Novin Avenue. P.O.B. 12/1517. Tel: 656021-9/655021-9. Telex: 212300. Located in the corner of Farah Park. 416 rooms, including 36 suites. Single room IR 3,450, double IR 3,900. Three restaurants (*Rotiserie Française, Nanakdoon, Tiara*). Nightclub. Bars. Shops. Swimming pool. Sauna. Conference facilities.

Park Hotel, Hafez Avenue. Tel: 644121-5/649101-5. Telex: 212466. The cheapest hotel in the de luxe class. 270 rooms. Single room IR 2,300, double IR 3,000. Restaurant. Bar. Roof garden. Swimming pool.

Royal Tehran Hilton, Pahlavi Avenue. P.O.B. 1526. Tel: 290031-9/290021. Telex: 212510. At present about the biggest hotel in Tehran, and one of the best equipped. Single room IR 3,450, double IR 3,900. Restaurants (*Persian Garden, Chez Maurice*). Nightclub (*The Club*). Bars. Bank. Shops. Swimming pool. Conference facilities.

Tehran International, Kourosh-Kabir Avenue. P.O.B. 3446. Tel: 840081-9. Telex: 212700. 340 rooms. Single rooms IR 2,530, double IR 3,000. Restaurants. Bars. Swimming pool. Cinema. Sauna. Games room.

FOUR STAR

Commodore Hotel, 10 Takhte Jamshid Avenue. Tel: 669611-5. Telex: 212630. 138 rooms. Tatty, but often can make room for visitors who have not booked. Single room IR 2,000, double IR 2,600. Restaurant. Bar. Swimming pool. Ballroom.

Excelsior, Pahlavi Avenue. Tel: 665596/665997. Small but pleasant atmosphere. 50 rooms. Single room IR 1,800, double IR 2,300. Restaurants (one with Indian cuisine). Bar.

Imperial, Takhte Jamshid Avenue. Tel: 649310-2/644073. Telex: 212521. 86 rooms. Single room IR 2,000, double IR 2,600. Restaurant. Bar. Swimming pool.

Kings, Khosrokhavar Street, Pahlavi Avenue. Tel: 298661-5/298371-5. Telex: 212675. 86 rooms. Single room IR 2,200, double IR 2,900. Restaurant. Bar. Swimming pool.

Marmar, Sepahbod-Zahedi Avenue. Tel: 830083-7. Telex: 212475. 72 rooms. Single room IR 2,000, double IR 2,600. Restaurant. Bar.

New Naderi, Naderi Avenue. Tel: 312056/313160. Telex: 212704. 100 rooms. Single room IR 1,800, double IR 2,300. Restaurant. Bar. Swimming pool.

Semiramis, Roosevelt Avenue. Tel: 825145. Telex: 212331. 82 rooms. Single room IR 2,200, double IR 2,900. Restaurant. Swimming pool.

Sina, 50 Takhte Jamshid Avenue. Tel: 663291-5. Telex: 212599. 200 rooms. Single room IR 1,800, double IR 2,300. Restaurant. Bar. Swimming pool. Nightclub.

Royal Garden Hotel, 50 Takhte Jamshid Avenue. Tel: 663291-5. Telex: 212047. A new multi-storey hotel which has been serving as an annexe to the Sina. Single room IR 2,200, double IR 2,900. Restaurants. Bars. Swimming pool.

Tehran Palma, Shahreza Avenue. Tel: 661851-6. 200 rooms. Single room IR 2,000, double IR 2,600. Restaurant. Bar. Swimming pool.

Tehran Tower, Villa Avenue. Tel: 835051-6. Telex: 212832. 72 rooms. Single room IR 2,000, double IR 2,600. Restaurant. Nightclub. Swimming pool.

Versailles, Pahlavi Avenue. Tel: 295661-5/295710. Telex: 212877. 95 rooms. Single room IR 2,000, double IR 2,600. Restaurant.

Victoria, Pahlavi Avenue. Tel: 290051-8. Telex: 212710. 88 rooms. Single room IR 2,000, double IR 2,600. Restaurant.

THREE STAR

Ambassador, Villa Avenue. Tel: 294966. 24 rooms. Single room IR 1,350, double IR 1,700. Restaurant.

Atlantic, Takhte Jamshid Avenue. Tel: 290286. Telex: 212455. 40 rooms. Single room IR 1350, double IR 1700.

Caspian, Takhte Jamshid Avenue. Tel: 834066. 48 rooms. Single room IR 1,350, double IR 1,700. Restaurant.

Continental, Sepand Avenue, Villa Avenue. Tel: 291184-5. 35 rooms. Single room IR 1,350, double IR 1,700. Restaurant.

Elizabeth, Elizabeth II Boulevard. Tel: 650533. Telex: 212845. 65 rooms. Single room IR 1,350, double IR 1,700. Restaurant.

Evin, Parkway. Tel: 291021. Telex: 212845. 160 rooms. Single room IR 1,700, double IR 2,200. Restaurant. Nightclub.

Kian, Zartosht Avenue. Tel: 653236. 36 rooms. Single room IR 1,350, double IR 1,700. Restaurant. Swimming pool.

Miami, Pahlavi Avenue. Tel: 625670. 106 rooms. Single room IR 1,350, double IR 1,700. Restaurant. Nightclub.

Naderi, Naderi Avenue. Tel: 313610. 25 rooms. Single room IR 1,350, double IR 1,700. Restaurant. Nightclub.

Rudaki, Arfa Avenue. Tel: 666314. 50 rooms. Single room IR 1,700, double IR 2,200. Restaurant.

At least five top-class hotels are being built in Tehran, including a new de luxe-class *Evin Hotel* (with 500 rooms) due to open in early 1978. A 42-storey new *Arya-Sheraton* with 600 rooms and a revolving roof-top restaurant should be open in late 1979. Hyatts of the US are constructing a big hotel and a new 500-room hotel is being built on the site of the old Vanak Hotel in Vanak Square.

Restaurants

IRANIAN CUISINE

Namakdoon, Inter-Continental Hotel, Iran Novin Street. Tel: 655021-9. Top class food but can be expensive. Iranian music.

Persian Garden, Royal Tehran Hilton, Pahlavi Avenue. Tel. 290011. Specialises in buffet lunches.

Ali Qapou, Gandi Avenue (near Vanak Square). Tel: 685535. Over IR 1,000 per person.

Khansalar, Jordan Avenue, Argentine Square. Tel: 685765. Around IR 1,000 per person.

Sarbad, 25 Chahrivar Avenue, Abbasabad (near Pahlavi Corner). Tel: 629792. Inexpensive. Interesting old specialities.

Hattam, upper Pahlavi Avenue (Zafar Street corner). Tel: 222232. Good Jujeh Kekab. Around IR 400 per person.

Howzkhaneh, upper Pahlavi Avenue (before Tajrish). Tel: 270390. Around IR 800 per person.

Hotel Cristal Restaurant, Lalehzar. Tel: 393796. Not particularly comfortable but good atmosphere with lots of music. In the bazaar area.

Farid, Villa Avenue and Khabir Street. Tel: 294104. Iranian buffet. Around IR 600 per person.

FRENCH CUISINE

Rotisserie Française, Inter-Continental Hotel, Iran Novin Avenue. Tel: 655021-9. Considered by many to be the best restaurant in Tehran. Expensive (meal for one person with wine costs IR 4,000–5,000).

Chez Maurice, Royal Tehran Hilton, Pahlavi Avenue. Tel: 290011. French dishes but Persian décor.

138

Xanadou, Bahrami Avenue, Mehbod Street (behind Roudaki Hall). Tel: 640812. Small, bistro-type restaurant. Inexpensive but good authentic food.

La Fourchette D'Or (formerly Bavaria), Arak Street, Sepahbod Zahedi. Tel: 295246. Popular but food unpredictable. Around IR 1,000 per person.

Lautrec, Pahlavi Avenue, under Chattanooga (opposite Shahanshahi Park). Tel: 222596. Over IR 1,000 per person.

Restaurant Suisse, Forsat Street. Tel: 828518. Around IR 1,000 per person. Specialises in quick lunches.

Mirabelle, 100 Villa Avenue. Tel: 824774.

ITALIAN CUISINE

Piccola Roma, 212 Villa Avenue. Tel: 836592. Around IR 600 per person.

Ray's Pizza 2, 37 Villa Avenue. Tel: 829694. Between IR 400–500 per person.

WESTERN/STEAKS

Epicure, 148 Sanai Avenue (below Takhte Tavoos). Tel: 828420. American style steaks around IR 500–800 per person.

Cellar, Kakh Street (just before Elizabeth II Boulevard). Tel: 297379. Specialises in grilled meat dishes. Around IR 1,000 per person.

RUSSIAN FOOD

Leon's Grill Room, Hotel Leon, 306 Shahreza Avenue. Tel: 820605.

CHINESE CUISINE

Chinese Paxy's, 392 Takhte Tavoos. Tel: 297253. Around IR 1,000 per person.

Golden Dragon, Pahlavi Avenue (opposite Hilton Hotel). Tel: 290508. Informal atmosphere. Inexpensive.

Chinese Restaurant, 3 Abdoh (opposite Aryamehr). Tel: 90714. Good service. Around IR 500 per person.

Chinese Pam Pam, Shahreza Avenue (between Hafez and Villa Avenues). Tel: 661272. Good reputation, around IR 1,000 per person.

POLYNESIAN

Tiare, Inter-Continental Hotel, Iran Novin Avenue. Tel: 655021. Large generous dishes. Over IR 1,000 per person.

INDIAN CUISINE

Maharaja, Excelsior Hotel, Pahlavi Avenue (close to Takhte Jamshid corner). Tel: 665596. Pleasant atmosphere. Inexpensive.

INTERNATIONAL FOOD

Paprika, 91 Villa Avenue. Tel: 821136. Hungarian chef. Around IR 400 per person.

Inner Room Piano Restaurant, Takhte Tavoos Avenue (near Roosevelt). Mixed American/French menu. Piano music.

Nightclubs

Baccara, Pahlavi Road (next to Atlantic Cinema). Tel: 628208. Flashy and highly expensive. Shows and dancing.

Shecoufeh-Now, Simetri Avenue. Tel: 543033/544044. Large floor shows twice a night. International stars.

Cabaret Continental, Sepand Street, Villa Avenue. Tel: 891186. Western artistes. Dinner plus show IR 800.

Miami, Miami Hotel, Pahlavi Road. Tel: 620200. Cabaret and dancing.

Vanak Night Club, Vanak Square. Tel: 682557/684775. Dancing to live music.

La Bohème, Old Shemiran Road. Tel: 265600. International shows in nice atmosphere.

Peacock Rooftop, Arya-Sheraton Hotel, Bijan Street, Pahlavi Avenue. Tel: 683021-8. Top class Western artistes in restaurant with sweeping view of the city.

The Club, Royal Tehran Hilton, Pahlavi Avenue. Tel: 290011. High class disco.

La Cheminée, 529 Old Shemiran Road. Tel: 291260. Disco.

Cave d'Argent, Pahlavi Road, Vanak Square. Tel: 627589. Dark, cavernous disco.

Airport Tehran's Mehrabad International Airport is about seven miles from the city centre. A functional building with few facilities. Refreshment bars, bookstall, bank in departure lounge. The tourist information desk can sometimes find hotel rooms for visitors who have not booked. Small duty-free shop. All departing passengers are charged a IR 250 airport tax.

Taxis Tehran has three kinds of taxis—shared, radio and telephone. The shared taxis (orange) cost each passenger a basic IR 10 plus around IR 3–5 for each kilometre. Drivers try to overcharge foreigners. Watch the meter, but even if the fare is inflated, these taxis are still remarkably cheap. Most of them ply a certain route. It is customary to stand close to an intersection and shout your destination to get a driver to stop.

Radio and telephone taxis (usually coloured yellow) charge a fare on an hourly basis—generally around IR 300 for the first hour and then IR 250 after that. But the rate is higher for large cars and at night time it can more than double. Telephone taxis can be ordered on 840011-20. The normal fare to and from the airport in a single taxi is IR 300.

Buses The city has a complex bus system which can be puzzling to foreigners. There are no route maps available and tickets have to be bought at kiosks near certain bus stops. But bus travelling is cheap, with flat rate tickets for green double-deckers costing IR 2.

Car hire firms *Avis Rent-a-Car*, 245 Hafez Shomali. Tel: 824778. *Hertz*, Nahid Street, Takhte Tavoos Avenue (between Roosevelt and Farah). Tel: 827182/838720. Also has offices at Arya-Sheraton and Park Hotels. *Tehran Taxi*, Villa Avenue. 214 Sepand Street, Tel: 827255/837255. *Iran Cab Service*, Takhte Tavoos Avenue (between Farah and Roosevelt). Tel: 845501/843801. *Auto-Speed*, Takhte Tavoos Avenue, Amir-Atabak 55. Tel: 835038. *Kian Taxi*, Roosevelt Avenue, Diba Street. Tel: 833387.

Self-drive cars cost between IR 500 to IR 1,000 per day depending on the size of the car. An extra IR 4–6 is charged per kilometre. Chauffeur-driven cars cost a minimum of IR 200–250 an hour. Visitors can generally use a licence from their home country but it is advisable to have an international driving licence.

Travel agencies *Mandy International Travel Agency*, Vesal-Shirazi. Tel: 657807. Telex: 215176. *Galaxi International Travel Agency*, 70 Sepahbod Zahedi Avenue. Tel: 8172729/826774. *Levan Tour & Air Travel*, 349 Shahreza Avenue. Tel: 312554. *United Express*, Villa Avenue. Tel: 822860/838107. *Mondial*, 15 Villa Avenue. Tel: 821990. *Persepolis Travel Agency*, 72 Villa Avenue. Tel: 831011. *Skyways*, 139 Ferdowsi Avenue. Tel: 312001.

Airline offices Head office: *Iran Air*, Mehrabad Airport. Tel: 9111/911565. Telex: 212795.

Sales offices: *Iran Air*, 44 Villa Avenue. Tel: 979011-17/911578. Ferdowsi Avenue, Forsat Avenue. Tel: 911575/911591. Arya-Sheraton Hotel. Tel: 911580/925064. *Aeroflot*, 19 Villa Avenue. Tel: 829118/836164. *Air France*, 307 Shahreza Avenue. Tel: 666252-4/669801/667962. *Air India*, 37 Hafez Avenue. Tel: 669810, 93208. *Alia*, 33 Iranshahr Avenue. Tel: 833272. *Alitalia*, 251 Shahreza Avenue. Tel: 669811/649171, 669819 (Airport). *Ariana*, 34 Iranshahr Avenue. Tel: 827397/660224 (Airport). *British Airways*, 323 Shahreza Avenue. Tel.: 301625-9. *CSA*, 21 Villa Avenue. Tel: 829930/836754/661482 (Airport).

JAL, 5/7 Villa Avenue. Tel: 833067-69/661461 (airport). *K.L.M.*, 2 Avenue Mir-Emad, Takhte Tavoos. Tel: 858061-6/645722 (Airport). *Kuwait Airways*, 21/37 Villa Avenue. Tel: 835860/838997/838262.

Lufthansa, 311 Takhte Jamshid Avenue. Tel: 822071-8/640200 (Airport). *Loftleidir*, 67 Ferdowsi Avenue. Tel: 835860/838994/835057. *Pakistan International Airlines*, 56–58 Villa Avenue. Tel: 824095-9. *Pan American*, 1 Villa Avenue. Tel: 832051-5. *Qantas*, 323 Shahreza Avenue. Tel: 312325-9.

S.A.S., Assemi Building, Sepahbod Zahed Avenue. Tel: 895581/ 892227/660337 (Airport). *Sabena*, 48 Villa Avenue. Tel: 824026-9. *Saudia*, 63 Villa Avenue. Tel: 827865/820840. *Swissair*, 100 Villa Avenue. Tel: 835081. *Syrian Airlines*, 67 Ferdowsi Avenue. Tel: 312833/83507-9. *Yugoslavian Airlines*, 67 Ferdowsi Avenue. Tel: 312833/835057.

Airline offices are open from 8.30 to 17.00 from Saturday to Wednesday, and 8.30 to 1400 Thursday. Closed Fridays.

Shipping agencies *Alco*, South Iranshahr Avenue. Tel: 820186. *American Eastern Co.*, 76 Bahar Avenue. Tel: 825543. *Arya National Lines*, Karim Khan Zand Avenue. Tel: 310111. *Babco*, Berlin Street, Ferdowsi Avenue. Tel: 833061-5. *Gray Mackenzie Co.*, Amini Building, Ferdowsi Avenue. Tel: 314156-9. *Gulf Agency Co.*, 501 Bahar Square, Takhte Jamshid Avenue. Tel: 754073. *Hansa Line Co.*, Aftab Shargh Building, Ferdowsi Avenue. Tel: 311806. *Nahaee & Bros. Co.*, Habibollah, 5 Amir Kabir Avenue. Tel: 311543. *Press Express Co.*, South Saadi Avenue. Tel: 391291. *Sea Man Pak*, 130 Sorayya Avenue. Tel: 825086. *Trans Marine*, 337 Villa Avenue. Tel: 826009.

Post Office The *Central Post Office* is in Sepah Avenue, opposite the intersection with Khayyam Avenue. There is also a fairly large post office in Valiadh Square. But generally there is a dearth of post offices in Tehran.

Airmail letters to Europe take about five days. But delays are frequent and many expatriates use private courier services to ensure speedy delivery abroad.

Telephone The booking of international calls is highly unpredictable. Sometimes operators put calls through in ten minutes, at other times in three hours. It is usually best to book calls early in the day or after 7 p.m. in the evening when operators change shifts. Often a new shift fails to take up bookings made by the previous one.

Tehran is one of the few cities in the Gulf to have phone kiosks in the street. One short call cost IR 2. Local calls can be confusing because phone numbers change frequently without much notice. For example, many numbers starting with 8 have been changed to 2. There is also no official phone directory. Two privately printed directories—the *Yellow* and *Blue Books*—are very scarce. A new edition of the *Blue Book* was published in mid-1977, costing $60 (available from The Blue Book Company. Tel: 392900).

Useful phone nos. *Airport information*—43013-4. *Airport Switchboard* —41171. *Ambulance* (Private)—393666/315126. *Ambulance* (Public)— 23000. *Enquiries*—118. *Fire*—44444. *Medical Emergency* (24 hours)— 21726. *Pharmacy* (24 hours)—40386. *Police*—3201/112. *Post Office*— 312081. *Railway Station*—530993/531051. *Tehran Clinic*—622931-4/ 623013-6. *Telegraph*—301121. *Telephone Repairs*—17. *Time*—19. *Tourist Information*—657985/651983/657554. *Weather*—662740.

Telex Most large hotels have telexes. There is a public telex service at the *PTT Office*, Toopkhaneh, Sepah Square. A short telex to Western Europe costs around IR 1,000.

Shops Tehran is about the best city in the Gulf for shopping, parti-cularly for antiques and handicraft work and most of all carpets. The upper end of Ferdowsi Avenue, and the adjacent side streets (between Ferdowsi Square and Istanbul Avenue) is the main centre for carpets. There are even shops here managed by Westerners who can offer useful advice to foreigners. Bargains in carpets can be found in the bazaar and down Khayyam Avenue. The Armenian quarter centred around Manouchehri Street, off Ferdowsi Avenue, has a fascinating range of antique shops selling everything from guns and knives, to coins, ancient manuscripts, paintings, lacquer work, orna-mental metal objects and old textiles. There are more antique shops in other streets around Ferdowsi Avenue and Lalezar Street.

Government handicraft shops sell inexpensive items of high stand-ard, reflecting the rich variety of handicraft work in rural Iran. Jewellery, textiles, ceramics and pottery provide some of the best bargains. The city's two main shops are at 381 Takhte Jamshid Avenue (opposite the US Embassy) and at 226 Villa Avenue. Both are open from 09.00–20.00, except Fridays.

Tehran has some large departmental stores. The main ones include: *Forroshgahe Bozorg Iran* (Branch), Pahlavi Avenue. Tel: 892348-9. *Forroshgahe Bozorg Iran*, Shah Avenue. Tel: 660711-7. *Forroshgahe Kourosh*, Pahlavi Avenue. Tel: 662253. *Kourosh*, Pahlavi Avenue. Tel: 629058. *Sepah*, Sepah Street. Tel: 669827-9.

Bazaars The main bazaar is a maze of alleyways in a triangular area between Khayyam Avenue and Buzarjpmehri Avenue. It is a remarkable emporium selling an amazing variety of goods. But its lay-out is extremely complex and visitors should reconcile themselves to getting lost, unless accompanied by someone who knows the place well. Off the lower end of Ferdowsi Avenue there is an area of small shops, equivalent to a modern bazaar.

Social clubs Most social clubs are centred around national associations and societies, some of which are fairly active holding frequent meetings. They welcome visitors from their home countries. Some of the main ones are: *American Officers Club*, Shahrzad Street, Old Shemiran Road. Tel: 231477. *American Institute of Iranian Studies*, Kakhe Jonoobi Avenue (near Shahreza). Tel: 642488. *Austrian Cultural Club*, 276 Villa Avenue. Tel: 83741. *Armenian Club*, 69 Khark Avenue. Tel: 642117. *French Institute*, 58 Chahpour Ali Reza Avenue, Ariapad Street. Tel: 644202. *French Club*, 22 Sepahbod Zahedi. Tel: 824760. *German Cultural Institute* (*Goethe*), Vozara Avenue. Tel: 627336. *Italian Cultural Institute*, Hatef Street. Tel: 664349. *Iran American Society*, Abassabad, Park Avenue. Tel: 625545. *Iran-India Cultural Association*, 18 Sefidan Street, Jam Avenue, Shah Abbas Avenue. Tel: 825188. *British Council*, 38 Ferdowsi Avenue. Tel: 303346.

Other social clubs open to expatriates include—*Lions International*, Old Shemiran Road. Tel: 274282. *Tehran Club*, Ferdowsi Avenue, Kooshk Street. Tel: 305596. *Touring and Automobile Club*, 37 Varesh Avenue. Tel: 648342.

Leisure/sport Tehran and its surroundings has a wide range of sporting and leisure facilities which should satisfy most tastes. Some clubs specialise in sport and leisure activities, and are open to visitors (though usually they have to be accompanied by members). The main ones are: *Imperial Country Club*, Pahlavi Avenue. Tel: 293101. Telex: 212443. *Tehran Club*, Ferdowsi Avenue, Kooshk Street. Tel: 305596. *Pars American Club*, Old Shemiran Road, Shahrzad Street. Tel: 771477.

Swimming: Some hotels and clubs have swimming pools open to non-residents and non-members. There are indoor pools at the *Ice Palace* (Tel: 628391) and *Bowling Club*, City Recreation Centre (Tel: 263031).

Tennis: Public courts at Amjadieh Stadium, off Roosevelt Avenue. The *Imperial Country Club*, Maziar Club (north of Darrous in Tchizar—tel: 281910), *Taj Club* (north of Vanak Square), *NIOC Club* (Tel: 770607) and *Darrous Club* (end of Yakhchal), all have courts. Bowling: *Bowling Club*, Old Shemiran Road (Tel: 263031). 12 alleys. Golf: *Imperial Country Club*. Mini-Golf: Vanak Square, Pahlavi Road.

Horse riding: *Imperial Country Club*. *Tehran Riding School*, off Old Shemiran Road (above Mirdamad Street). Horse racing: *Iran Race Course*, 14 kilometres out on Karaj Road.

Skiing: Ski slopes are at *Ab-e-Ali*, one hour's drive east of Tehran and *Shemshak*, one hour's drive to the northeast. The best skiing is at *Dezin* where there are also good facilities but it is two and a half hours' drive from the city. Water Skiing: *Karaj Dam Lake*, 50 miles from the city. A 9-mile long artificial lake, also ideal for boating and fishing. Water-skiing club has good equipment.

Hunting/Fishing: Plenty of opportunities but restricted by conservation regulations. Contact *Fish and Game Department*, Shah Abbas Kabir (Tel: 821777).

Mountain climbing: There are some high peaks close to Tehran. Contact *Mountaineering Federation*, Sepahbod Zahedi Avenue (Tel: 822053). Flying/Gliding: The *Tehran Gliding Club* is at Doshantapeh Airport (Tel: 792858). *Civil Aviation Club* can hire small planes for visitors with valid pilot licences.

Soccer: Popular sport in Iran. Main stadiums are 100,000-seat *Aryamehr*, west of the city, and *Amjadieh*, off Roosevelt Avenue.

Athletics: Zurkhaneh, the art of ancient Iranian athletics, can be fascinating for visitors. Contact *Jafar Athletic Club*, Park Shahr, Varzesh Avenue (Tel: 666885).

Squash: Most courts are in private sports clubs, like *Bank Melli Sports Club, NIOC Club, Tehran Club*. Ice Skating: *Ice Palace*, Pahlavi Avenue. Tel: 685011. Snooker: *Midtown Club*, 1,000 Shah Avenue. Chess: Extremely popular in Iran. *Chess Club*, Kakh Street (between Takhte Jamshid and Shahreza Avenue) is open to everyone.

There are at least three large recreations centres with good facilities for indoor sports. *City Recreation Centre*, Old Shemiran Road. Tel: 263031. *Ice Palace*, Pahlavi Avenue. Tel: 685011. *Youth Palace*, Old Shemiran Road.

The *City Rrecreation Centre* and *Ice Palace* show undubbed English-language films. *Cinema Goldis*, Mohammad Reza Shah Avenue (Tel: 628713), specialises in English language films as well. There are also frequent film shows at some national cultural societies.

Bookshops *Keyvan Bookshop* (Central Branch), 307 Takhte Jamshid Avenue (near Villa Avenue). Tel: 820324. One of the best in the city. Has a large stock of foreign books, magazines and periodicals (ranging from *Farmer's Weekly* to *Playboy*), and newspapers.

Other Keyvan bookshops: *Takhte Tavous Bookshop*, Takhte Tavous Avenue (between Nader Shah and Shah Abbas); *Shahrzad Bookshop*, Old Shemiran Road, Zafar Avenue; *Jordan Bookshop*, Jordan Avenue, Nahid Boulevard.

There are two French bookshops: *Larousse*, Karimkhan Zand Boulevard. Tel: 826483. *Librairie de Paris*, Avenue Darya-e-Nour. Tel. 629308.

Hospitals The best hospitals for obtaining emergency treatment are *American Hospital*, Elizabeth II Boulevard; *US Army Hospital*, Old Shemiran Road (Tel: 861761/861967); *Reza Pahlavi*, Tajrish

(Tel: 870022/870023); *Sina Hospital*, Sepah Avenue (Tel: 663984/
649017). *Tehran Clinic*, Avenue Shah Abbas Shomali, Avenue Takhte
Tavous (Tel: 622931).

Pharmacies (after hours) *Americaie*, Shahreza Avenue (Pahlavi
Avenue crossing). Tel: 645290. *Takhte Jamshid Drug Store*, Takhte
Jamshid Avenue (Hafez Avenue intersection). Tel: 640386. *Takhte
Tavous Drug Store*, Takhte Tavous Avenue (Sanai corner). Tel:
827240.

Banks Head offices: *Bank Markazi Iran* (Central Bank of Iran),
Ferdowsi Avenue. Tel: 310100-9/311321. Telex: 212359/213119. *Bank
Melli Iran*, Ferdowsi Avenue. Tel: 3231. Telex: 212481/212890.
Bank of Iran & the Middle East, Ferdowsi Avenue, Koucheh Berlin.
Tel: 314355. Telex: 212656. *Iranians' Bank*, Takhte Jamshid Avenue.
Tel: 892070. Telex: 212418. *Bank Pars*, 193 Takhte Jamshid Avenue.
Tel: 645795/645731. Telex: 212520. *International Bank of Iran &
Japan*, 750 Saadi Avenue. Tel: 304981. *Bank Russo-Iran*, Jonoobe
Iran Shahr, Behesht Avenue. Tel: 532112. Telex: 212750. *Bank
Omran*, Istanbul Avenue. Tel: 30012/30018.

Bank Bazargani, Maydan Sepah. Tel: 315041. Telex: 212471. *Bank
Beinomelaly Iran*, Pahlavi Avenue, Dameshq Street. P.O.B. 41-1852.
Tel: 891020. Telex: 215228. *Bank Bimeh Iran*, Saadi North Avenue.
Tel: 304604. Telex: 212619. *Bank Dariush*, corner of Karimkhan
Zand and Roosevelt Avenues. P.O.B. 841. Tel: 821086. Telex: 212307.
Bank Etebarate Iran, 50 Avenue Sevom Esfand. P.O.B. 1639/1460.
Tel: 304231. Telex: 212593. *Bank Etebarate Taavonye Towzi*, 37 Fer-
dowsi Avenue. Tel: 312264. Telex: 212361. *Bank Iranshahr*, Baharestan
Square. Tel: 301255. *Iran Arab Bank*, Sorayya Avenue, Raghaii
Building. Tel: 824325. Telex: 213210. *Irano-British Bank*, Saadi
Avenue. P.O.B. 1584. Tel: 305504-8. Telex: 212542.

Bank Kar, Hafez Avenue. Tel: 669001. *Bank Refah Kargaran*,
125 Roosevelt Avenue. Tel: 825001-9. *Bank Saderat Iran*, 124 Shah
Avenue. P.O.B. 2751. Tel: 660561. Telex: 212352. *Industrial Bank*,
106 Sepahbod Zahedi. Tel: 837210. Telex: 212372. *Bank Sepah*,
Sepah Avenue. Tel: 311091-9. Telex: 212462. *Bank Shahryar*, Sepahbod
Zahedi. Tel: 839631. Telex: 212821. *Bank of Tehran*, 25 Pahlavi
Avenue. Tel: 660870-9. Telex: 212483. *Bank Tejaret Khareji Iran*,
Saadi Avenue. Tel: 304631-8. Telex: 212468.

Mercantile Bank of Iran and Holland, Saadi Avenue (North). Tel:
30041. Telex: 212534. *Tosseeh va Sarmayeh Gozari Iran*, Sepahbod
Zahedi Avenue. Tel: 83454. *Agricultural Co-operative Bank of Iran*,
Varzesh Avenue, Parke Shahr. Tel: 311011. *Bank Rahni Iran*, Ferdowsi
Avenue. Tel: 310171. *Mortgage Bank*, Ferdowsi Avenue. Tel. 311351.
Bank Khuzistan, Naderi Avenue. P.O.B. 968. Tel: 25184. *Bank Khazar*,

356 Pahlavi Avenue. P.O.B. 341. Tel: 20095/20093. *Bank Etebarate Sanati*, Ateshkadeh Avenue. Tel: 301434-9. *Agricultural Development Bank*, Takhte Jamshid Avenue. Tel: 669211-15.

Ministries *Agriculture*, Elizabeth II Boulevard (near Farah Park). Tel: 922460/920282. *Commerce*, Meidan-e Ark. Tel: 530043-9. *Culture and Art*, Baharestan Square. Kamalelmolk Street. Tel: 303581-5/ 311251. *Economy and Finance:* Naser Khosrow Street. Tel: 3251-9. *Education*, Ekbatan Street. Tel: 317316/304207-9. *Energy*, Sevom-Esfand Street. Tel: 312251-6/311051. *Foreign Affairs*, Foroughi Street. Tel: 3211. *Health and Welfare*, Shah Avenue. Tel: 667267-9. *Housing and Urban Planning*, Varzesh Street. Tel: 317201-9. *Interior and Civil Service Affairs*, Parkeshahr Avenue. Tel: 538840-5/524020-9. *Industry and Mines*, Meidane Ark. Tel: 533991-9. *Information and Tourism* (Administrative), Corner Shah Reza and Kakh Streets. Tel: 668860-5. *Justice*, Sepahbod Zahedi and Takhte Jamshid, Davar Street. Tel: 3221. *Labour and Social Affairs*, Eisenhower Avenue. Tel: 930031-9. *Post, Telegraph and Telephone*, Old Shemiran Road. Tel: 840875-9. *Roads*, Sepahbod Zahedi Street. Tel: 893070-9. *Science and Higher Education*, Villa Avenue, above Takhte Jamshid. Tel: 8141. *Plan and Budget Organisation*, PBO Building, Bahrestan Square. Tel: 3271.

Embassies *Afghanistan*, 16 Ebne-Sina Street, Pahlavi Avenue. Tel: 626739/626159. *Algeria*, N. Roosevelt Avenue. Tel: 857222. *Argentina*, 47 Pahlavi, Nahid Boulevard. Tel: 292384-5. *Australia*, Sepahbod Zahedi Avenue, Arak Street. Tel: 890080-5. *Austria*, Takhte Jamshid, Forsat Street. Tel: 828431. *Bahrain*, Vozara Avenue, 31 Street No. 16. Tel: 683383. *Bangladesh*, 352 Kakh Street. Tel: 665971. *Belgium*, 41 Takhte Tavoos, Daryay-e Noor Street. Tel: 626712/626689.

Brazil, Zafar Avenue, Alam Street 22. Tel: 223986-9. *Bulgaria*, Iran Novin Avenue, 23 Shabnam. Tel: 659199. *Canada*, Takhte Tavous Avenue, 19 Darya-e Noor Street. Tel: 622623-5. *Czechoslovakia*, Shahreza Avenue, 16 Sarshar. Tel: 828168/820339. *Denmark*, Lalezar-Now, 13 Kopenhagen Street. Tel: 316540/315832/391281. *Egypt*, Abbasabad Avenue, 123 Park Avenue. Tel: 627506/621286. *Finland*, 101 Gandi Street. Tel: 681085-6/684985-7.

France, 85 France Avenue. Tel: 665321/640097-8. *West Germany*, Ferdowsi Avenue (opp. Melli Bank). Tel: 314111-5. *East Germany*, Shah Abbas Avenue, 15 Afshin Alley. Tel: 626720/628909/627858. *Greece*, South Kheradmand Avenue, 43 Salem Alley. Tel: 827654/ 826980. *Hungary*, Park Avenue, 13th Alley, No. 7. Tel: 626899/ 622800. *India*, 166 North Saba Avenue. Tel: 898814/895654/894554. *Indonesia*, Shah Abbas Avenue, Magnolia Alley No. 1. Tel: 824992/ 824761. *Iraq*, Pahlavi Avenue, Valiahd Square, No. 180. Tel: 644461/

641031. *Italy*, 81 France Avenue. Tel: 662091/642023-4. *Japan*, Takhte Jamshid Avenue, North Saba Street, No. 53. Tel: 640909/ 649828.

Jordan, Bokharest Avenue, 16th Street, No. 55. Tel: 625650/ 624880. *North Korea*, 87 Tavanir Avenue. Tel: 680626. *South Korea*, South Kakh Avenue, Heshmatdowleh Crossroads, No. 427. Tel: 663913/662888. *Kuwait*, Meykadeh Avenue, Sazeman Ab Street, Nos. 31–38. Tel: 656712, 656311. *Lebanon*, Bokharest Avenue, 16th Street, No. 43. Tel. 629829/620052. *Lesotho*, Gandi Avenue, 11th Street, No. 11. Tel: 681396.

Malaysia, Abbasabad Avenue, Bokharest Street, No. 8. Tel: 629523/620406. *Morocco*, Mohammad Reza Shah Avenue, 5th Alley, No. 15. Tel: 622257/626566. *Netherlands*, Takhte Tavous Avenue, Mooazami Street. Jahansooz Alley No. 36. Tel: 896011-2/896207/ 892318. *New Zealand*, Shah Abbas Avenue, K. Afshin. Tel: 625061. *Norway*, Takhte Jamshid Avenue, South Aban Street, No. 3. Tel: 828819/831187. *Oman*, Bokharest Avenue, 17th Street, No. 10. Tel: 628359. *Pakistan*, Aryamehr Avenue (next to Garrison Jamshidabada, No. 1). Tel: 934331-2. *Philippines*, Amirabad Avenue, Bahman Alley. Tel: 653425, 650979.

Poland, 140 Takhte Jamshid Avenue. Tel: 645052/645090/646008. *Portugal*, Rudsar Street. Tel. 643589. *Qatar*, Vozara Avenue, Television Street, 2nd Street, No. 16. Tel: 629942/623997. *Rumania*, 12 Fakhrabad Street. Tel: 759841/759309. *Saudi Arabia*, 59 Bucharest Avenue. Tel. 624297-9/624604. *Senegal*, Vozara Avenue, 8th Street, No. 4. Tel: 620099/614142. *South Africa*, Park Avenue, 20th Street, No. 21. Tel: 621836-7. *Spain*, Fisherabad Avenue, Khoshbin Street, No. 29. Tel: 820432/825441.

Sudan, Vozara Avenue, 23rd Street, No. 3. Tel: 685739. *Sweden*, Takhte Jamshid Avenue, Forsat Street. Tel: 828305/829458. *Switzerland*, 18 Pasteur Street. Tel: 647319/644063/646036. *Syria*, Mohammad Reza Shah 34th Street, No. 9. Tel: 620460/624168. *Thailand*, Baharestan Avenue, No. 4. Tel: 301433. *Tunisia*, Abbasabad Avenue, 131 Park Avenue. Tel: 627616/624087. *Turkey*, 314 Ferdowsi Avenue. Tel: 315299/318997.

United Kingdom, Ferdowsi Avenue. Tel: 662394/45011-4/646017. *United Arab Emirates*, Abbasabad Avenue, Television Street, 8th Street. Tel: 625027-8. *United Nations*, 12 Bandar Pahlavi Street, Takhte Jamshid Avenue. Tel: 649281-9. *United States of America*, Takhte Jamshid Avenue (near Roosevelt). Tel: 820091-9/825091-9/ 824001-9. *U.S.S.R.*, Churchill Avenue. Tel: 313901/312428/312455/ 644946.

Vatican, France Avenue, Razi Crossroads, No. 97. Tel: 643574. *Venezuela*, South Aban Street, No. 90. Tel: 895226. *Vietnam*, 61 Shahpour Alireza Avenue. Tel: 645800. *North Yemen*, Bokharest Avenue, 6th Street. Tel: 625761. *Yugoslavia*, Villa Avenue, Arak Street, Shahrivar Alley, No. 6. Tel: 825280. *Zaire*, Vozara Avenue, 3rd Avenue, No. 38. Tel: 626822.

Newspapers/periodicals

Dailies: *Kayhan International*, Ferdowsi Avenue, Kuche Atabak. English. 15,000 circ. *Tehran Journal*, Ettelaat Building, Khayyam Avenue. English. 10,000 circ. *Le Journal de Tehran*, Ettelaat Building, Khayyam Avenue. French. *Alik*, Naderi Avenue. Armenian. 10,000 circ. *Bourse*, Sevom Esfand, Moharshakat Street. Financial. *Echo of Iran*. P.O.B. 2008. Economic. English. *Ettelaat*, Ettelaat Building, Khayyam Avenue. Evening. 100,000 circ. *Peyghame Emrouz*, Qavam Saltaneh Avenue. Evening. *Kayhan*, Ferdowsi Avenue. Evening. 100,000 circ. *Ayandegan*, Shah Avenue. 20,000 circ. *Rastakhiz*, 142 Villa Avenue. Organ of Iranian Resurgence Party.

Periodicals: *Al-Akha*, Khayyam Avenue. Arabic weekly. *Ettelaat Savanan*, Ettelaat Building, Khayyam Avenue. Youth magazine. *Ettelaat Banovan*, Ettelaat Building, Khayyam Avenue. Women's weekly. 80,000 circ. *Tamasha*, Takhte Tavous Avenue. Radio and TV weekly. *Donya-e Varzeshe*, Khayyam Avenue. Sports weekly. *Rastakhize Kargaran*, Vesale Shirazi Avenue, Bozorgmehr Square. Workers' magazine. *Rastakhize Rusta*, Bozorgmehre Gharbi. Farmers' monthly. *Kayhan-e Varzeshi*, Ferdowsi Avenue. Sports weekly. 60,000 circ. *Zane Ruz*, Ferdowsi Avenue. Women's weekly. 150,000 circ. *Die Post*, Baghe Saba Avenue, Danesh Rue. German economic/political weekly. *Tehran Economist*, 99 Sevom Esfand Avenue. Economic weekly in Farsi and English. Circ. 20,000. *Iran Economic Service*, Hafez Avenue, Behjatabad, 4 Kucheh Hurtab. P.O.B. 2008. Economic weekly.

Media Tehran has two English-language dailies—*Kayhan International* and *Tehran Journal*—which give a relatively good coverage of both Iranian and world news. There is also a French daily—*Le Journal de Tehran*—published by the same company as the Tehran Journal.

The national TV network has an 'International' channel (No. 3). It caters mainly for the 50,000 Americans in Iran so most of its programmes are in English. There are occasional news bulletins in German and French. Sometimes Channel 1 (NIRT Network) shows dubbed English language films with the original dialogue transmitted on radio (FM 98 MHz). The national radio also has an international programme, again most of it in English (AM 1,555 kHz, FM 106 MHz).

Churches *Armenian Gregorian Church*, 1 Stalin Street. Tel: 311853. *Assyrian St. Thomas*, 152 Amirabad Avenue, Rostam Street. Tel:

630135. *Catholic Mission*, Kouroshe-e Kabir Street. Tel: 866577. Masses in English, French and Latin. *Church of Christ*, Laleh Street. Tel: 883652. Services in English. *Community Church*, Saltanabad Road (next to AFRTS tower). Tel: 882464. Services in English. *Consolata Church*, 78 France Street. Tel. 43210. Masses in Latin, French, Italian, English. *Ecole Jeanne d'Arc*, Ferdowsi Avenue, Manouchehri Street. Tel: 335721. Masses in French.

Evangelical Church, Nadershah, 4th Street. Tel: 623058. Services in German. *Filadelfia* (Assemblies of God), West Takhte Jamshid (near Tehran University). Tel: 662898. Services in English and Persian. *Greek Orthodox*, Takhte Jamshid Avenue (near Roosevelt). Tel: 832288. *Pentecostal Church*, Simetri Street. Services in English. *Russian Greek Orthodox*, Takhte Jamshid Avenue. (opp. US Embassy.) Tel: 826640. Services in Russian. *St. Abraham's*, 100 Amirabad-e Shomali Street. Tel: 929203. Masses in English. *St. Paul's Episcopal*, Nadershah Avenue, Elahi Street. Tel: 628075. Services in English and Persian. *St. Sarkis Cathedral*, Karim Khan Zand, Villa Avenue. Tel: 831604. Services in Armenian.

Major companies/Government organizations *Central Organization of Companies*, 210 Sepand Square, Zahedi Avenue. Tel: 823912-4. *Civil Aviation*, Mehrabad Airport. Tel: 641171-6. *Cotton and Oil Seeds Organization*, Pahlavi Avenue. Tel: 40903/42205. *Fishery Co.*, Zardosht Avenue. Tel: 624100/624150. *Foreign Transactions Co.*, (next to Alborz High School), Shahreza Avenue. Tel: 640923/663329. *Hunting Organization*, Shah Abbass Avenue. Tel: 832791-5. *Industrial Development and Renovation Organization*, 435 Edalat Building, Takhte Jamshid Avenue. Tel: 820074-7. *Industrial Management Organization*, Takhte Jamshid Avenue. Tel: 820074-7. *Institute of Standards and Industrial Research of Iran*, Heravi Street, Pahlavi Avenue. Tel: 622202/451624. *Iran Carpet Co.*, 160 Ferdowsi Avenue. Tel: 317072. *Iran State Railway*, Rah Ahan Square. Tel: 25121-8. *Iran Tobacco Co.*, Iranshahr Avenue. Tel: 820081-9. *Mining and Metallorgical Corporation of Iran*, 467 Takhte Jamshid Avenue. Tel: 820147-9. *National Iranian Oil Co. (NIOC)*, Takhte Jamshid Avenue. Tel: 6151. *National Iranian Steel Corp.*, Pahlavi Avenue, Takhte Jamshid Square. Tel: 660802-4. *Ports and Shipping Organization*, Simorgh Street, Shah Avenue. Tel: 665911. *Social Insurance Organization*, 453 Eisenhower Avenue. Tel: 931018-27. *State Meat Organization*, 80 Takhte Jamshid Avenue. Tel: 663839/662037. *Sugar Organization*, Davar Avenue. Tel: 310041-5.

Useful addresses

Iran Chamber of Commerce, Industries & Mines, 254 Takhte Jamshid Avenue. Tel: 836031. Telex: 212398.

Regional Co-operation for Development (RCD), 254 Takhte Jamshid Avenue. Tel: 836031.

Iran Junior Chambers, 254 Takhte Jamshid Avenue. Tel: 836031.

International Chambers of Commerce (ICC), 254 Takhte Jamshid Avenue. Tel: 836031.

Iran American Chamber of Commerce, Takhte Jamshid Avenue (opposite Villa Avenue). Tel: 891168.

Tourist Information (main office), Ministry of Information & Tourism, Elizabeth II Boulevard. Tel: 651984/651986.

ISFAHAN Probably Iran's most splendid city. Situated on an oasis, the site of the city has been inhabited from earliest times. Its old Persian name derives from 'Sepahan' or 'armies', because the plain of Isfahan was used to assemble the armies of the Sassanians in the 3rd and 4th centuries A.D. The city of Isfahan, however, did not attain great prominence until the Safavid dynasty. In 1598, Shah Abbas I, the most powerful of the Safavid monarchs, captured the town and adopted it as his capital.

The Safavid era was the golden age of Persian art and under the patronage of Shah Abbas it flourished in Isfahan. Today this prolific epoch is reflected in the city's numerous architectural masterpieces, the most magnificent of which is the famous Meidan-e Shah and its adjacent buildings. This vast enclosed square, now usually crammed with traffic, was once a polo field (the stone goalposts are still there). The Shah would watch the games from a balcony in the Ali Qapu pavilion, overlooking the square. Behind the pavilion is a royal palace complex which includes the Chehel Soutoun ('forty pillars'). There is a museum here with a unique collection of the miniature paintings for which Isfahan is famous. Opposite Ali Qapu stands the yellow domed Shaik-e Lutfullah Mosque, built by Shah Abbas in honour of his learned father-in-law of that name. Behind the vaulted archways lining the square is a small but interesting bazaar where peasant rugs, copperware and other local craftwork are sold. A tumbledown caravanserai behind the bazaar houses the workshops of small textile merchants. Their woven cloth is covered with rich patterns of natural vegetable dyes, printed with hand blocks. This colourful material is usually made up into garments and bedspreads and then sold cheaply in the bazaar. The entrance to the main bazaar itself is at the north end of the

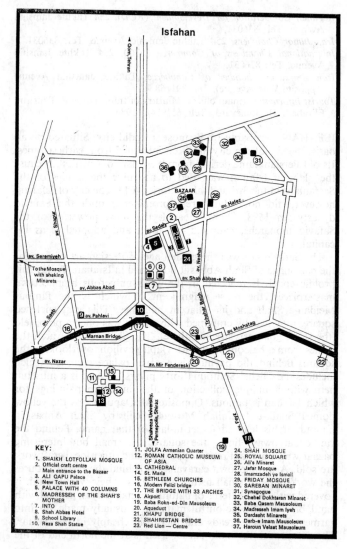

Isfahan

KEY:

1. SHAIKH LOTFOLLAH MOSQUE
2. Official craft centre
   Main entrance to the Bazaar
3. ALI QAPU Palace
4. New Town Hall
5. PALACE WITH 40 COLUMNS
6. MADRESSEH OF THE SHAH'S MOTHER
7. INTO
8. Shah Abbas Hotel
9. School Library
10. Reza Shah Statue

11. JOLFA Armenian Quarter
12. ROMAN CATHOLIC MUSEUM OF ASIA
13. CATHEDRAL
14. St. Maria
15. BETHLEEM CHURCHES
16. Modern Felizi bridge
17. THE BRIDGE WITH 33 ARCHES
18. Airport
19. Baba Rokn-ed-Din Mausoleum
20. Aqueduct
21. KHAPU BRIDGE
22. SHAHRESTAN BRIDGE
23. Red Lion — Centre

24. SHAH MOSQUE
25. ROYAL SQUARE
26. Ali's Minaret
27. Jafar Mosque
28. Imamzadeh ye Ismail
29. FRIDAY MOSQUE
30. SAREBAN MINARET
31. Synagogue
32. Chehel Dokhtaran Minaret
33. Baba Qasem Mausoleum
34. Madresseh Imam Iyeh
35. Dardasht Minarets
36. Darb-e Imam Mausoleum
37. Haroun Velaat Mausoleum

Meidan. It rivals the bazaars of Tehran and Shiraz, and, indeed, many articles can be bought here, which are otherwise sold by Government handicraft shops often at higher prices.

The most impressive sight on the Meidan is the Shah Abbas mosque, which dominates the southern side of the square. Its glazed tilework of clear, bright colours is unique. Commissioned by Ahah Abbas I in 1612, it took nearly 20 years to complete, which is understandable considering the complexity of the building and intricacy of its decoration. The mosque is out of line with the sides of the square because of the need to face in the direction of Mecca. This creates a highly unusual architectural feature, lending refreshing eccentricity to the mosque's otherwise classic Islamic symmetry.

Isfahan's main street, the broad Chahar Bagh ('Four Gardens') Avenue, is reached via Sepah Avenue at the north-west corner of the Meidan. Here are the city's main commercial offices, travel agencies, airline offices, and main shops. Across the Si-o-se Pol ('Bridge of the Thirty-three Arches') is the Armenian quarter, Jolfa, with its wine shops and cathedral, a strange hybrid of Islamic design and Christian iconography. Isafahan's Armenian community owes its existence to Shah Abbas. He transported them south from Azerbaijan in North West Iran to prevent their valued craftsmanship and business acumen from coming under the control of the Ottoman Turks.

Isfahan's Masjed-e Jami mosque is particularly interesting for its varied architecture. Parts of the building date from the 11th century Seljuk dynasty, but subsequent Turkish, Mongol and Afghan domination have also left their mark. The mosque has the biggest arch in Asia. The building's simplicity contrasts with the richness of the Shah Abbas mosque and its ornate brickwork and interior mosaic tiles are unusual.

As a modern city Isfahan seems to be returning to its traditional role as an international meeting place. It has a large university, a thriving Christian community and a growing number of expatriate workers, many of them Americans, who are helping with local development projects. The old axiom '*Isfahan nesfe-e jahan!*' (Isfahan is half the world) is now repeated gleefully to visitors by the owners of the city's Chai Khaneh (tea houses). These are as much a part of Isfahan's life as the pavement cafés are to Paris. A relaxing half-hour can be spent over a glass of tea and perhaps a hubble-bubble studying passers-by, while backgammon, the national game, is played noisily in the background.

Hotels

DE LUXE

Shah Abbas, Shah Abbas Avenue. Tel: 26010-7. One of Iran's plushest hotels. A restored 18th century caravanserai. Elaborate décor based on the nearby Chehel Soutoun Palace. 134 rooms. Three restaurants. Four bars. Swimming pool. Squash and tennis courts. Mini-golf. Sauna. Disco. Conference facilities.

Kourosh International, Bolvare Farah. P.O.B. 16. Tel: 40230-39. Managed by Sheraton Hotels. 138 rooms. Two restaurants (*Damavand, Zarin*). Bars (*Alvand, Khayyam*). Swimming pool. Conference facilities.

THREE STAR

Alighapou, Chahar Bagh Avenue. Tel: 31282. 46 rooms. Restaurant. Bar.

Pol, Bolvare Ayenehkaneh. Tel: 43950. 36 rooms. Restaurant. Swimming Pool.

Iran Tour, Abbasabad Avenue. Tel: 35976/32724. 65 rooms. Restaurant. Swimming pool.

Restaurants

Shah Abbas, Shah Abbas Hotel, Shah Abbas Avenue. Tel: 26010. Excellent Iranian/European food but very expensive. Meals can be served in the hotel's Persian garden.

Canary, Chahar Bagh Avenue. Tel: 31867. European food. Iranian décor. Limited menu.

Shahrzad, Abbasabad Avenue. Tel: 34474. Good Iranian food in traditional Persian surroundings.

Soltani, Chahar Bagh Avenue. Tel: 32239. Iranian cuisine.

Taxis Shared (yellow) taxis cost IR 20–30 for a short trip. Single taxis are sometimes difficult to hail in the street but can be found outside hotels.

Car hire firms *Sasan Tourist Transportation*, Kamal Esmail Avenue. Tel: 28054. *Airport Car Union*, Ferdowsi Avenue. Tel: 22307.

Travel agencies *Persian Express*, Ferdowsi Avenue. Tel: 28005. *Iran Travel*, Chahar Bagh Avenue. Tel: 23010/26363.

Airline offices *Iran Air*, Chahar Bagh Avenue. Tel: 28200/28292.

Post Office   The main post office is on the corner of Faiz and Abadana Avenue.

Bazaars   The main bazaar is the Qaisarieh at the north end of the Meidan-e Shah. There is another one just off Shah Abbas Avenue (opposite the Shah Abbas Hotel). Some of the best bargains are in ceramics, mosaics, glassware, and engraved silver.

Hospitals   *British Christian Hospital*, Pars Street. *Isfahan Clinic*, Shaikh Bahai Avenue (Tel: 30016) and *Soraya Hospital*, Sepahbod Zahedi Avenue (Tel: 32114), are the best hospitals for emergency treatment.

Useful addresses   *Tourist Information Office*, Shah Abbas Avenue. Tel: 27667/31212.

SHIRAZ   Shiraz has been traditionally considered the jewel of Persia. It stands in a fertile valley, surrounded by gardens of trees and flowers. To the traveller the streams and groves in and around the city were a refuge from the torment of the desert and the nearby arid hills. But today it is a flourishing modern city where some of the major developments outside Tehran are taking place. Its gardens of Hafez, blue-mosaic mosques and Bazaar Vakil with its corridors of interlacing cupolas are nostalgic gems. In Shiraz, as elsewhere in the country, the city's heritage is preserved as a symbol of its present renaissance. The old and the new stand side by side without seeming incongruous. Karim Khan Zand Avenue, the principal axis of the city, with its lines of orange trees, is now daily jammed with rush-hour traffic. Car repair shops are nearly as prolific as grocers. Shiraz today is the new industrial centre of Iran and the visitor who has read about the old-world magic of the city can be disappointed.

In the midst of the oil-boom world, old Shiraz lives quietly with its shrines kept with meticulous care. Goats mill about the massive arch of the Masjid-e-Vakil (Regent's Mosque) with its dome of blue and white faience and elaborate calligraphy above the gate. Tourists, Baluchi and Qashgai tribesmen, and soldiers and students in Levi jeans, roam among the 48 cupolas of the bazaar.

Close to the University in the west of the city are the sprawling gardens of Hafez, surrounded by their decaying walls. The courtyard and central pavilion are as elegant as they were in the

14th Century and the bulbuls (the Iranian poet's equivalent to the nightingale) still sing from the cypresses. Trees and flowers of all kinds are scattered in apparent disorder but overall harmony. The gardens fascinated Western writers, like Vita Sackville West, because they were built not just to be looked at. They represented freedom and luxury and were to be enjoyed by the mind and the body, not merely the eye. There are tens of thousands of gardens in and around Shiraz but many are decaying because their owners have been unable to maintain them properly.

The River Khoshk, which divides the city in two, would be called a stream in a fertile country but it is the life-blood of Shiraz. Its tributaries are carefully exploited to irrigate expanding agricultural land whose greenness contrasts with the starkness of surrounding desert. Shiraz stands 1,600 feet above sea level and for most of the year the climate is pleasantly temperate. The air is dry and pure and even in August the temperature remains moderate.

Hotels

Kourosh Hotel, Park Farah. P.O.B. 528. Tel: 28000-14. De luxe class. 152 rooms. Restaurant. Coffee shop. Bar. Swimming pool. Tennis court. Conference facilities.

Park Hotel, Chahar Rahe Zand. Tel: 21426. Four star. 31 rooms. Restaurant.

International, Ghasredasht Avenue. Tel: 38780. Four star. 106 rooms. Restaurant.

Restaurants

Saray Mochir, main Bazaar. Persian cuisine in traditional atmosphere. Huge domed room with octagonal fountain in the centre. Recitals of Iranian poetry.

Car hire firms *Avis Cars*, Anahita Tourist Agency, Park Valiahd. Tel: 26333/26496.

Travel agencies *Anahita Tourist Agency*, Park Valiahd. Tel: 26333/264 96.

Airline Offices *Iran Air*, Zand Avenue (opposite Saadi Hospital). Tel: 30045/30046/7.

Saudia, Moshir Building, 63 Zand Avenue. Tel: 34679.

Useful phone nos. *Tourist Office*—7044/3907. *Telephone information* —118. *Fire*—111. *Emergency/Police*—112.

Bazaars. The main bazaars are around Zand Avenue. The Bazaar Vakil is the best. Shiraz is famous for its rugs and carpets. Some of the finest are made by the Qashgai tribe, a nomadic people who usually pass through the city in the winter. Another Shiraz speciality is marquetry (inlaid wood). The bazaars are highly picturesque, being a focal point for colourfully dressed tribal people from outlying areas.

Hospitals *Namazi Hospital*, north end of Karim Khan Zand Avenue. Tel: 2223.

Banks *Bank Melli*, Zand Avenue. *Bank Saderat*, Zand Avenue.

GENERAL INFORMATION

How to get there BY AIR (outside Gulf): Tehran's Mehrabad International Airport has the most wide ranging connections of all airports in the Gulf. It is the only airport with daily flights to and from North America. There are several flights a day from New York, most of them operated by *Iran Air*, the country's national carrier. From Western Europe, several flights a day go to Tehran from London and there are also daily flights from Rome (half a dozen a day on average), Frankfurt, Munich, Paris, Zurich and Athens. Several flights a week leave from Amsterdam and Geneva and there are less frequent weekly flights from Prague, Moscow, Nice, Barcelona, Madrid, Bucharest, Brussels and Vienna.

Between Tehran and the Far East and Indian sub-continent, there are daily flights to and from Bangkok, Hong Kong, Tokyo (up to four flights daily on average), and Delhi. Several flights a week go to and from Singapore, Karachi, Kabul, and Bombay. There are at least two flights a week to and from Peking and a number of weekly flights from Sydney and Melbourne.

Connections with Middle East countries outside the Gulf are fairly limited. There is a daily service between Tehran and Istanbul and several flights a week to and from Tel Aviv, with less frequent flights to Ankara. But from the Arab countries there are weekly flights only from Cairo, Beirut, Amman and Damascus. There are at least two direct flights a week to Abadan from London, Amsterdam and Athens.

BY AIR (inter-Gulf): Direct connections between the rest of the Gulf and Iran still remain limited, particularly to and from Tehran. But the number of flights is increasing. There are several flights a week between Tehran and Kuwait and Baghdad and a weekly flight to and from Jeddah. Shiraz is the busiest airport with inter-Gulf flights. There are around half a dozen flights a week to and from Bahrain, Dhahran, Doha, and Dubai and less frequent weekly flights from Abu Dhabi, Jeddah, Riyadh, Kuwait and Muscat. Bandar Abbas has a regular service to and from Dubai (sometimes flights six days each week) and a weekly flight to and from Abu Dhabi. There is a daily service between Abadan and Kuwait.

BY AIR (domestic): All Iran's main towns and cities are covered by a good domestic air service operated by *Iran Air*. Besides Tehran, Abadan, Shiraz and Bandar Abbas, there are airports at Rezayieh, Tabriz, Rasht, Ramsar, Mashad, Sanandaj, Hamadan, Kermanshah, Ahwaz, Isfahan, Yazd, Kerman, Lengeh, Bushehr, Khark Island, Zahedan. Most of these are served by daily flights from Tehran, with Shiraz, Isfahan, Mashad and Abadan having several flights each way a day.

BY RAIL: Weekly trains from Western Europe go through Turkey to Tabriz and Tehran. There is also a service from Russia. *Iranian State Railway* has daily services between Tehran, Tabriz, Ahwaz, Khorramshahr, Gorgan and Mashad, Isfahan and Zarand.

BY BUS: There are international bus services to Western Europe. Private bus companies provide a daily service connecting most big towns in Iran. Buses leave Tehran daily for Isfahan, Shiraz, Tabriz, Mashad, Hamadan and other large centres. Most are reasonably comfortable and a good, inexpensive way of seeing the country if there is time to spare. From Tehran, the fare to Isfahan is, for example, around IR 250 maximum, to Shiraz around IR 500, and Abadan IR 600. The main bus companies in Tehran are: *Iran Peyma*, Amir Kabir Street. Tel: 312171. *Levan Tour*, Villa Street. Tel: 822444. *PMT*, Amirkabir Street. Tel: 313678. *Mihan Tour*, Ferdowsi Avenue. Tel: 301622.

Visas Visas are required by all visitors, with the exception of the following nationals (for visits not exceeding three months): British subjects being 'Citizens of the United Kingdom and Colonies' (not applicable to holders of British passports prefixed C or D and issued to passengers of Indian origin from Kenya, Tanzania or Uganda); Belgium, Denmark, Finland, France, West Germany, Greece, Italy, Japan, Luxembourg, Morocco, Netherlands, Norway, Saudi Arabia, Spain, Sweden, Tunisia, Turkey and Yugoslavia.

Passengers are recommended to obtain visas in advance. Passengers stopping over in Tehran, Abadan or Shiraz must have confirmed onward but not return reservations. Otherwise a transit visa is required. All foreign nationals remaining in Iran more than three months must obtain a resident permit.

Citizens of all countries may obtain a 15 day Tourist Visa on arrival if coming from countries where there is no Iranian Consul. Valid tickets must be held for onward transportation. Tourist visas can be obtained at Tehran, Abadan and Shiraz only.

Transit without visa is available for all passengers in direct transit by the same service, or transferring to another service provided they hold reservations for an onward (not return) within 72 hours of their arrival.

Nationals of Albania, Bulgaria, Cuba, Czechoslovakia, Egypt, East Germany, Hungary, Israel, Korea (North), Mongolia, China, Poland, Rumania, Syria, U.S.S.R., Vietnam and Chinese residents of Taiwan require transit visas unless they transit by the same aircraft.

An exit permit is required by all whose stay in Iran exceeds 3 months. But citizens of Belgium, Denmark, France, West Germany, Luxembourg, Netherlands, Norway and Spain, do not require Exit Visas but must present resident permits to the Immigration Office at the airport of departure.

Religion The main religion is Islam but there are minority communities of Assyrians, Armenians, Jews, and Zoroastrians.

Language Persian (Farsi) is the most widely spoken language. Turkish is more common in the north-west around Tabriz and Arabic is spoken in Khuzistan in the south-west. Most businessmen and government officials speak English or French and some speak German.

Hours of business It is government policy to implement a five-day working week (Saturday to Wednesday: usually 0800–1630 hours). All Ministries and government offices are closed on Fridays. Banks work from Saturday to Wednesday 0730–1300, Saturday to Wednesday 1700–1900, and Thursday 0730–1130 (summer); from Saturday to Thursday 0800–1300, Saturday to Wednesday 1600–1800 (winter). Shops open from 0800–2000 Saturday to Thursday, 0800–1200 Friday (winter); 0800–1300 and 1700–2100 Saturday to Thursday, 0800–1200 Friday (summer). Offices work from 0800–1300 in winter, with variable afternoon hours. Many offices work a standard 0800–1700 day, while more traditional firms may close from 1300–1700 and open again from 1700–1900. In summer offices work 0800–1300 and 1800–2000. Many offices are closed on Thursday afternoon and most on Friday.

Official holidays The Iranian year starts on 21 March. During the New Year holiday, which runs from 21 to 25 March, all Government offices and most business firms are closed. In addition, it would be as well for business visitors to allow four or five days before and 11 days after the holiday when business may be slacker than usual. The following are public holidays in Iran in 1977–78 (some of religious holidays have approximate dates):

Death of Imam Jafar Sadeq	...	...	...	9 October
Birthday of Imam Reza	...	...	...	25 October
Birthday of HIM The Shah	...	...	...	26 October
Id al-Qurban	...	...	...	22 November
Id al-Ghadir	...	...	...	30 November
Al-Ashura... ...	...	...	...	25 December
Death of the Prophet ...	...	...	...	7 February 1978
Prophet's Birthday ...	...	...	...	25 February
Nowruz (Iranian New Year)	...	...	...	21–22 March
13th Nowruz	...	...	...	2 April
Prophet's Call to Mission	...	...	...	3 July
Birthday of 12th Imam ...	...	...	...	21 July
Constitution Day ...	...	...	...	5 August
Death of Imam Ali ...	...	...	...	27 August
Id al-Fitr	...	...	...	5 September.

Time GMT + 3½.

Calendar The dating system in Iran is based on the Islamic Lunar Calendar, which started in A.D. 622, the year that the Prophet Mohammad fled from Mecca to Medina soon after the birth of Islam. The Iranian New Year (Nowruz) begins on 21 or 22 March, and the year beginning in March 1976 was the equivalent to 1355 in the Islamic calendar. However, at the beginning of 1976, a joint session of parliament in Tehran decided that the calendar would in future be based on the year 533 B.C., the year that Cyrus the Great established the first Persian empire under the Archemaenian dynasty. Under the new system the year beginning 21st March 1976 would be 2535. When the announcement was made about the new calendar the Prime Minister, Amir Abbas Hoveyda, said Iran wanted to show the world that its history was already 12 centuries old when it embraced Islam. He then went on to say that the country would continue to observe the Islamic calendar. It was reported, however, that all official correspondence, records and birth certificates signed after 21st March 1976 would be dated 2535, but it is not clear yet which calendar will remain in popular use.

Electric current 220 volts, 50 cycles AC.

Health International certificates of smallpox vaccination are required by all visitors. Cholera immunisation is necessary for passengers arriving within 5 days after leaving or transiting an infected area and Afghanistan, Bahrain, Bangladesh, Burma, India, Iraq, Malawi, Malaysia, Pakistan, Philippines, Saudi Arabia, Singapore, Thailand, Vietnam Socialist Rep. Yellow fever vaccination is required if arriving within 6 days after leaving or transiting endemic zones.

Some visitors should take precautions against malaria. Risks exist between July and November at altitudes below 1,500 metres, except in the regions of Azarbaijan (East), Azarbaijan (West), Bushehr, Guihan, Hamedan, Isfahan, Khorasan, Khuzestan (excluding provinces of Behbehan, Izeh, Masjed Soleyman), Kordestan, Markazi, Mazandaran and Yazd. Also in the provinces of Abadeh, Estahban, Neyriz and Shiraz in Fars. Kerman, Rafsanjan and Sirjan in Kerman. Borujerd in Lorestan. Zabol and Zahedan in Baluchistan. There are no risks in urban areas, except Minab Bandar Abbas, Jiroft, Chahbahar and Iranshahr.

Water In Tehran and other large cities, tap water is reasonably safe but it is heavily chlorinated. Elsewhere it is advisable to purify the water before drinking.

Post Iran's postal service is not particularly reliable. People sending mail abroad often use private courier services, especially with packages. Posting parcels is a laborious process involving the completion of many customs forms. Mail being sent into Iran from abroad should be typed and give as much detail of the address as possible.

Telecommunications The country's telephone system is improving fairly rapidly. There is now automatic dialling in major cities and STD links between 54 towns. But international calls can still have difficulty getting through.

Currency The monetary unit is the Iranian Rial (IR). Notes in circulation: 20, 50, 100, 200, 500, 1,000, 5,000 and 10,000; coins: 1, 2, 5, 10 and 20 rials.

Currency regulations There are now no restrictions on the import or export of currency.

Customs regulations Visitors can bring in 200 cigarettes or equivalent in tobacco products, and a bottle of alcohol and a reasonable amount of perfume.

Local dishes Iran's most famous dish is *caviar* (eggs of the Caspian sturgeon). But most Iranians have never tasted it. So the bulk of Iranian caviar is exported. It is available at large hotels and expensive restaurants, where it can be as dear as in any Western European city.

For Iranians the most common national dish is *chelo kabab*. It mainly consists of pieces of grilled lamb placed on rice (*katteh*), served with slices of raw onion, herbs, radishes, and butter. Some people break a raw egg (*tokme*) over it. Often the rice is covered with rich sauces of plums, spinach, mushrooms, celery, peach, orange, and rhubarb and mangoe. The dish is a meal in itself.

Iranians are also fond of numerous appetizers being served altogether before a main course. In restaurants these are laid out like a buffet and make a fine, colourful spread. The most popular hors d'ouevres consists of sliced tomato (*goje farangi*), lettuce leaves, fresh cheese (*panir*), and cucumber, accompanied by a dish of yogurt (*mast*) in which the lettuce leaves are dipped. Sometimes fresh vegetable soup mixed with sour milk is served before the appetisers. The Iranians also like meat stews, mixed with rich, spiced sauces.

Alcohol   Alcohol is freely available in most large cities, though the average Iranian does not drink much. There are liquor stores and bars, mostly selling draught beer. In Tehran, a large glass of draught beer costs about IR 250–300. In the stores a bottle of whisky costs IR 850–1,350, gin IR 850, brandy IR 1,400–3,000, champagne IR 1,800. Iranian wine (*sharab*) is strong and fruity. The main wine-growing districts are Rezaiyeh, Qazvin and Shiraz. With foreign wines costing up to IR 3,000 a bottle in a restaurant, it is relatively inexpensive with prices normally IR 200–300 a bottle.

Visitors to Tehran are advised to drink with care because the high altitude makes alcohol metabolise very quickly in the body.

Useful advice   The Iranians are an open and friendly people. But they are also proud and sensitive. Dealing with them requires tact and diplomacy. They are wary of foreigners, sometimes almost hostile. To the uninitiated visitor they can appear to be arrogant and obstinate. But frequently they are merely showing a desire not to be pushed around by outsiders. They will react frankly when they feel slighted and are not used to turning the other cheek. Business meetings are usually brisk and to the point. However, in ordinary conversation Iranians can be meticulously polite. They like formal gestures, small talk and minor items of etiquette. It is sometimes customary, for example, for a visitor to an Iranian household to bring small presents. For foreigners, souvenirs from home usually go down well.

Iranians attach great importance to dress. The better dressed a person is the higher his status and respectability. An untidy appearance is a sign of weakness and lack of authority. So businessmen should take care to look smart and a jacket and tie is generally essential, even during hot weather. Otherwise visitors should bring both light and heavy clothing. The weather in Iran can produce sharp changes in temperature. So even, during relatively warm months visitors should bring both light and heavy clothing.

Further reading *Area Handbook for Iran*. Foreign Area Studies, The American University, Washington DC. 1971. *Iran Almanac and Book of Facts*. Annual editions. Echo of Iran, Tehran. *Iran, Past and Present*, by Donald N. Wilber. Princeton University Press. 1975. *A History of Persia*, by Sir Percy Sykes. London. 1969. *Cambridge History of Iran*. Cambridge University Press. 1968.

Modern Iran, by Peter Avery. London. 1967. *The Modernisation of Iran, 1921–1941*, by Amin Banani. Stanford University Press. 1961. *The Foreign Relations of Iran*, by Shahram Chubin and Sepehr Zabih. University of California Press. 1975.

The Legacy of Persia, by Arthur Arberry. Oxford: Clarendon Press. 1953. *The Heritage of Persia*, by Richard Frye. Weidenfeld and Nicolson. 1963. *The Politics of Iran*, by James Bill. Merrill, Ohio. 1972. *Economic Development in Iran, 1900–1970*, by Julian Bharier. Oxford University Press. 1971. *Iran—A Business Opportunity*, by Patrick Sinnott and Melvyn Else. Metra Consulting Group, London. 1974. *Iran*. The Chase World Information Series, New York. 1976.

Twentieth Century Iran, edited by Hossein Amirsadeghi. Heinemann. 1977. *Persia: An Archaeological Guide*, by Sylvia Matheson. Noyes Press/Faber. 1973.

Government

Head of State	Mohammad Reza Pahlavi Shahanshah, Aryamehr
Prime Minister	Jamshid Amouzegar
Court Minister	Amir Abbas Hoveyda
Economy & Finance	Hushang Ansary
Foreign Affairs	Abbas Ali Khalatbari
Industry & Mines	Mohammad Reza Amin
Agriculture	Ahmad Ali Ahmadi
Energy	Taqi Tavakoli
Commerce	Kazem Khosrowshahi
War	General Reza Azimi
Interior	Assadollah Nasr-Isfanhani
Roads & Transport	Morteza Salehi
Posts & Telecommunications	Karim Motamedi
Housing & Town Planning	Firouz Towfiq
Education	Manuchehr Ganji
Health & Social Welfare	Shojaeddin Shaikholeslami-zadeh
Justice	Gholam Reza Khianpour
Information & Tourism	Darius Homayun
Arts & Culture	Merdad Pahlbod
Labour & Social Affairs	Amir Qassem Moini

Ministers of State:

Director of the Plan & Budget Organisation	... ...	...	Mohammad Yeganeh
Assistant to Prime Minister in Economic Affairs	... ...	...	Safi Asfia
Assistant to Prime Minister, Parliamentary Affairs	...	...	Mohammad Kashefi
Women's Affairs	... ...	...	Mahnaz Afkami
Administrative Affairs	...	...	Manuchehr Agah

IRAQ

THE PRESIDENT OF IRAQ

THE PRESIDENT OF IRAQ
Field Marshal Ahmad Hassan al-Bakr

Field Marshal Bakr was elected President and Prime Minister in 1968 and assumed the portfolio of Defence Minister and Commander in Chief of the Armed Forces in 1973. President Bakr was born in Tikrit in 1914. He was educated at teachers' training college and the Military Academy. He commanded the First Infantry Brigade in 1957, but was forced to retire from the army in 1958 because of his participation in revolutionary activities. He took part in the Fourteenth Ramadan Revolution and was appointed Prime Minister and a member of the Revolution Command Council in 1963. He held the post of Vice-President between November 1963 and January 1964. He took part in the Revolution of July 1968 and was promoted to the rank of Field Marshal in 1969.

Iraq

Area   168,134 square miles

Population   11.1 million (1975 estimate)

Chief Towns   Baghdad (capital) 2.8 million; Basra 915,000; Mosul 857,000; Kirkuk 559,000; Sulaimaniya 504,000

Gross National Product $13,200 million (1976 estimate)

GNP per caput $1.160

GEOGRAPHY

Iraq is 'Mesopotamia', the land between the two rivers. The Tigris and the Euphrates flow through the entire length of the country—first in almost parallel course and then, from Qurna to the Gulf, in joint passage in the great river highway of the Shatt al-Arab. Along with their extensive networks of tributaries, they impose a distinct geographical unity. This river system, bringing fertility with it, is perhaps the only common denominator which, geographically, the country enjoys. Indeed, with the exception of the Tigris and Euphrates, Iraq is characterised more by the clearly-defined differences of its various zones.

The country incorporates almost every type of scenery and condition—desert, steppe, alluvial plain, marshland, upland and mountains. The most unfamiliar area is the mountainous region of north-eastern Iraq of which the highest point is Hasarost Peak (12,227 feet). Covering 35,500 square miles, principally in the governorates of Dhok, Arbil, Sulaimanaiya and parts of Kirkuk, this region has a population of around 1.5 million (14 per cent of the total population). It is characterised by ranges of scrub- or forest-covered mountains, enclosed

valleys and innumerable water courses. To the west the mountains give way to the rolling hills of ancient Assyria.

Westward across the Tigris, the undulating uplands dissolve into an almost desert zone that extends down the entire western flank of Iraq (roughly corresponding to the governorates of Anbar, Muthanna and parts of Nineveh and Basra) and on into Syria, Jordan and Saudi Arabia. With the exception of the extremely fertile strip along the Tigris and Euphrates, this desert zone is sparsely populated.

The great alluvial plain of central Iraq (roughly, the Governorates of Baghdad, Diala, Waset, Babylon, Qadissiya, Thi-Qar,

Maysan and parts of Basra, Kerbaela and Kirkuk) lies amid the stark contrasts of the mountains to the north and the desert to the west and south. It covers 51,000 square miles and accounts for 85 per cent of the total population. It is extremely flat and relatively fertile. The northern area of this zone is marked by extensive irrigation canals and networks supporting an abundant cultivation of wheat, barley, cotton, vegetables and fruits.

In the southern areas of the plain marshland and desert alternate. In the irrigated and drained zones, however, there is a flourishing cultivation of dates, citrus fruits, summer grains, corn, cotton and rice (although here, as in the rest of the central plain, bad drainage and consequent soil salinity are severe problems).

CLIMATE

The main feature of the climate in most of Iraq is a dry and extremely hot summer which is intensified by high humidity near the rivers. Over the years many of the richer Iraqis have built underground rooms or cellars (*sirdab*) which act as a cool refuge from the summer heat.

Summer starts around May when an area of low atmospheric pressure starts to build up over the Gulf drawing in air from the northwest. This produces a persistent, dry northwest wind (*shamal*) over much of the country. For several weeks or months the sun beats down relentlessly with temperatures soaring to between 38°C. (100°F.) and 49°C. (120°F.) in July and August. In Baghdad the temperature tends to drop at night but in Basra the nights are hot and humid. The winds generate dust or sand storms, July being the worst month with Baghdad averaging about one storm a week.

The summer ends in October when the first rainfalls occur. Winter lasts from December to March and is relatively cool and humid. But often the weather is very variable. Cool damp winds from the southeast bring rain. Sometimes cold air masses from the interior of Asia penetrate the country producing frost as far south as Basra. By contrast hot air masses can come up from the south giving January temperatures of over 27°C. (80°F.).

The mountainous northeast has a different climate from the rest of the country. The summers are cooler and the winters can be severe. Up to 30 to 40 inches of rain fall each year on the highest mountains with 15 to 25 inches in the Assyrian hills. The damper weather helps crop growing. In some parts snow covers the ground for as long as three months in the winter.

PLANTS AND WILD LIFE

Over much of the north and east, the landscape is covered by steppe vegetation consisting of perennial bushes, low shrubs and grasses. In the arid areas of the south and west thorns and salt-resistant shrubs, like rhanterium and papposum, are about the only plants. Poplar, willow and licorice are common near the rivers and in the marshland below Qurnah reeds, tall grasses and sedge flourish. The southern delta region is scattered with millions of date palms which provide one of Iraq's major agricultural exports. The northeast mountains used to be covered by oak forest but land reclamation and unrestricted grazing have now reduced a lot of it to scrub. In the upper reaches alpine plants, similar to those found in Europe, grow.

Such distinguished wild animals as the lion, oryx, ostrich and wild ass could once be found in Iraq. But now they are extinct, the last lion reputedly being shot in 1910. The most common mammals are rats, bats, jackals and wildcats. The wild pig and gazelle roam around some isolated areas. Lizards and snakes are numerous. The cobra is now rare but poisonous horned and blunt-nosed vipers are still a danger. The Tigris breeds salmon reaching up to seven feet in length. The marshlands and delta area of the south is a favourite spot for migrant birds.

COMMUNICATIONS

The waterways of Iraq have traditionally been its main means of communication. But both the Euphrates and Tigris are difficult to navigate. Strong currents, flooding and sudden rises in the water level can make travelling by boat hazardous. The building of dams and barrages has helped to make the rivers easier for boats in places. North of Baghdad most boat trips can still only be made downstream. However, between Baghdad and Basra there is a fairly heavy two-way traffic on the River Tigris. In the southern marshes everyone travels by water with the population spending most of their day-to-day life on boats or rafts.

Over the last few decades the country's railways have provided an important transportation system. It used to have an inconvenient mixture of standards- and metre-gauge lines. But now a standard-gauge line runs from the Syrian border through Mosul onto Baghdad from where it extends via Kut to Basra. Other lines, not all standard-gauge, link Baghdad with most of the country's major cities. New lines are planned and by the 1980s total track length should have doubled in five years to 1,864 miles.

Road building and maintenance has always posed a problem because of extensive flooding. But over the last few years the country's road network has been undergoing major reconstruction with World Bank assistance. Now good roads connect all the main cities and towns. One of the more ambitious new road-building schemes aims to link Kirkuk with Rutbah on the main road between Baghdad and the Jordanian border.

Basra is the country's main port. But within a few years it should be overtaken in size by Umm Qasr, a new port being built near the Kuwait border at the head of a lagoon. Control of the approaches to the lagoon is a matter of dispute between Kuwait and Iraq and until this is settled the new port's future will not be secure. The country's main oil terminals on the Gulf are at Fao and Khor al-Amaya.

Iraq has international airports at Baghdad and Basra and smaller ones at Mosul and Kirkuk. The airport at Baghdad is being expanded and facilities at the others improved. *Iraqi Airways* runs regular services to most other Arab countries and to Europe and the Indian sub-continent.

Telecommunications are still being modernised and telephone calls are sometimes delayed, particularly on the international circuit. Subscriber trunk dialling is being introduced in many parts of the country and the main centres linked by a micro-wave system.

SOCIAL BACKGROUND

The main social divisions in Iraq are not so much based on urban and rural differences but on religion, race, tribe and language. Not unsurprisingly, religion has been the cause of frictions and tensions which have plagued Iraq throughout much of its history. Although 95 per cent of the population is Muslim, Islam in Iraq, unlike other Islamic states, does not serve as a unifying force. Half the Muslim population adheres to the orthodox Sunni sect—and is drawn by this adherence to the other Sunni societies in the Arab heartland; the other half follow the 'schismatic' dogmas of the Shia sect, whose single most important representative is the Shah of Iran. The differences of dogma— and, in many respects, of culture and outlook—are reinforced by the neat geographical divisions, with most of the Sunnis living in the north and central sections of the country and most of the Shiites in the central and south sections. This historical cleavage within Iraqi society has resulted in an antipathy, now diminishing, and an unresolved competition for dominance between Sunni and Shia and, thus, between north and south. The Sunnis, moreover, tend to be more prosperous, better educated and firmly established in the higher echelons of society and politics.

The Christian–Muslim distinction, though certainly less important than the Sunni–Shia divide, is still significant, especially in social life. There is, for example, very little intermarriage between Muslims and Christians. The Christians, numbering about 400,000, are themselves fragmented into various sects— Chaldeans (Nestorians converted to Catholicism), Syrian Catholics, Syrian Orthodox, Greek Catholics, Greek Orthodox, Armenian Orthodox and Protestants. With the exception of the Armenian Orthodox, these Christian groups are Arab in language and race.

Kurds and other groups Ethnic differences present another problem. About 80 per cent of the population is Arab, although only a small proportion have an unmixed ancestry like the Arabs of Saudi Arabia or Jordan. The largest non-Arab ethnic group is the Kurds who account for about 14 to 16 per cent of the total population and who are concentrated in the mountainous region of north-eastern Iraq. Linked with other sizeable Kurdish minorities in Iran and Turkey, the Kurds are ethnically Aryan and have their own language, which is similar to Persian. Farmers and herders by occupation, the Kurds are renowned for their warrior ferocity and have pursued aspirations of an independent Kurdistan for centuries.

Racially akin to the Kurds are the Yazidis, settled in the Jebel Sinjar area of northern Iraq. Numbering about 65,000, they form tightly-knit and isolated communities, distinct from their Kurdish and Arab neighbours because of their language and unique religion which incorporates pagan (for example, subservience to the devil), Christian and Islamic elements. Only recently have the Yazidis begun to integrate themselves into the mainstream of Iraqi life.

The Assyrians are concentrated around 'Amadiya and Rowanduz and probably number about 40,000. The majority, organised in clans and led by village priests, are farmers, but a significant number has now drifted away to the cities and the oil fields. They follow a Nestorian or Monophysite version of Christianity and speak a form of Syriac. Isolated by their culture, religion and language, the Assyrians have historically resisted domination by the central Government. Even today there are indications that this resistance has not ceased.

The 100,000-strong Turcoman minority has succeeded in integrating much more easily. Dispersed in an arc in the mountains from Diala to Mosul, they are descended from pre-Ottoman Turkish invaders and still speak a Turkish dialect. Like most groups in northern Iraq, they adhere to the Sunni Muslim sect. Only half are rural dwellers, living off smallholdings in the mountains. The other, town-living half is relatively advanced and progressive; it is noted for its craftsmen and some have risen to important provincial posts, especially in Kirkuk.

Attracted by the Shia holy places at Najaf, Kerbala, Khadimain and Samarra, a large number of Persians has also settled in Iraq. Until recently they formed an important element in Iraqi religious and political life. Their influence and numbers have gradually diminished with the secularisation of society and with the onset of Irano–Iraqi border disputes in the early 1970's. Numbering about 60,000 in the 1960's, an unknown number now remains as a result of mass expulsions in the 1970's. The remainder is probably relatively Arabised and will be easily absorbed into full participation in the Iraqi state.

The Armenians, who are scattered throughout Iraq, are exceptionally successful merchants and craftsmen with a high level of education and of integration into Iraqi life. Avoiding politics, they do have an almost unshakeable cultural nationalism represented by their strict loyalty to the Armenian Orthodox Church and to their own language.

CONSTITUTION

Baathist dogma is enshrined in Iraq's Constitution as providing the main framework of government. Socialism has been declared the official ideology. The Constitution lays down a number of basic liberties: freedom of religion, of speech, of opinion, of the press, to hold public meetings and to join trade unions. Discrimination on account of race, religion and language is also forbidden and the rights of minorities, especially the Kurds, are recognised.

Supreme authority is invested in a Revolutionary Command Council (RCC) of up to 15 members who are in practice drawn solely from the leadership of the Baath Party. The President, as Supreme Commander of the Armed Forces and President of the RCC, has powers to increase the membership of the RCC at his discretion. He must be elected by a two-thirds majority of the RCC and is directly responsible to the RCC. In turn, all ministers are responsible to the President.

In 1971, a National Charter was announced, which called for the creation of a National Assembly, popular councils in each district and a permanent Constitution. None of the major provisions of the charter has yet been implemented.

Although the constitutional framework seems to emphasise the importance of the President, real power is still exercised by the RCC and its committees. The nature of the Council of Ministers makes the RCC even more important and powerful: ministers have executive power only within their own departments and rarely meet with their colleagues in cabinet. All co-ordination is carried out by the RCC (whose members are also the heads of the important ministries such as defence, interior, industry and communications). Thus, the RCC has assumed in effect all executive and legislative functions of government in promulgating laws and ratifying decrees.

The President, despite his wide constitutional powers, is probably not the most important member of the RCC. The paramount role has probably been assumed by Saddam Hussain al-Takriti, the actual leader of the 1968 revolution, who wields power and influence far in excess of that which his official position as Vice-President of the RCC would seem to warrant. His support comes from various sections within the army and from the more radical majority faction in the leadership of the Baath Party.

Administratively the country is divided into 16 governorates or liwa, which in turn comprise between three and 10 qadhas. Each governorate is headed by a governor appointed by the central government. Throughout the country all civil legal cases are heard by Courts of First Instance which also have penal and religious courts. Litigants can appeal to Regional Courts of Appeal and the Supreme Court in Baghdad.

HISTORY

Iraq has been one of the cradles of civilisation, harbouring a succession and complexity of cultures for the last 6,000 years. The first advanced society—dating from well before 3000 B.C.— was that of the Sumerians who, by inventing writing, surpassed perhaps even their contemporaries along the Nile. Formed in a system of city states—Ur, Lagash, Eridu, Agade, Kish, Larsa and others—and supported by an efficient and complex irrigated agriculture, the Sumerians were absorbed by the short-lived Akkadian empire under Sargon of Agade in 2400 B.C. The collapse of this Semitic empire heralded a period of confusion promoted by the successive invasions of the Guti, the Semitic Amorites and the Iranian Elamites and broken only by a brief flourishing of Sumerian culture under the dominion of Ur around 2100 B.C. However, it did make possible the fusion of Akkadians and Amorites, both Semitic in language and race, which resulted in the formation of a vigorous Amorite state centred on Babylon.

Assyrian Empire Under Hammurabi in the 18th century B.C., the Amorite empire reached the peak of its power, imposing written laws and a single administration on a territory that included most of present-day Iraq. It was unable, however, to withstand the thrusts from the Hittites of Asia Minor and the Aryan Kassites (or Mitanni) from Persia and had disappeared by 1700 B.C. For the next 300 years, most of Iraq was dominated by the Kassites and threatened by the Hittites. The same period also witnessed the growth of a small Semitic-speaking state on the upper Tigris, Ashur, which eventually replaced both the Hittites and Mitanni as the leading power of the area.

This Assyrian empire covered at its height a vast area stretching from Persia to Egypt, uniting an enormous diversity of peoples under a harsh and autocratic regime which, by ordering the mass movements of ethnic groups and tribes, profoundly altered Iraq's racial balance. It collapsed beneath the burden of its own auto-cracy, of constant confrontation with Egypt and the Scythians and, finally, of assaults by the Medes from Persia who captured Nineveh and northern Iraq in 612 B.C.

The Babylonians The Chaldeans, another Semitic and perhaps Arab people who had taken over Babylonia, emerged as the dominant power in southern Iraq and created a new Babylonian empire which, under Nebuchadnezzar II, reached an almost unparalleled wealth. Lasting less than a century, it was captured in 538 B.C. by the Persians under Cyrus the Great and remained part of the Persian Achaemenid empire until Persia itself was conquered by Alexander the Great in 327 B.C. For the next 150 years, Iraq was a part of the Hellenic Seleucid empire, ruled in an autocratic manner from Antioch in Syria. The always turbulent Seleucid empire was finally replaced in Iraq by the Parthians, a war-like people from the Caspian steppes who carved out a considerable kingdom in Persia in the 3rd century B.C.

The Parthians operated Iraq as a buffer to the expanding Roman empire and were able to withstand periodic Roman assaults until the short-lived conquests of Trajan, who even captured the Parthian capital at Ctesiphon, and the longer-lasting successes of Marcus Aurelius, who seized most of nor-thern Iraq. The Sasanids, who overthrew their Parthian over-lords and created an invigorated Persian state, were, however, able to push back the Romans to the Levant. Moreover, their empire achieved a remarkable brilliance and promoted a dramatic resurgence of Persian culture and religion that was oftentime in conflict with the Christianised and Semitic societies of their subject people in Iraq.

All vestiges of the valuable Hellenic heritage were eradicated by the self-conscious Persianism and intolerant Zoroastrianism of the Sassanids. Though invaded by Romans or Byzantines for short periods, the country remained a part of this Persian empire for 400 years. At the end of this period—in the 7th century—Iraq presented a complex and complicated society made up of Persian, Greek, Syrian and Arab elements speaking Persian, Greek, and Arabic and practising orthodox Christianity, Nestorianism, Manicheanism, Zoroastrianism and paganism.

The coming of Islam The rise of Islam had profound consequences in Iraq. After the defeat of the Sassanid army at Kirkuk in 641, Persian control was destroyed for ever. A huge Arab Muslim army based at the garrison towns of Basra and Kufa ensured the rapid Islamisation and Arabisation of this new and crucial conquest. The concentration of Arab forces in Iraq, as well as the successful conversion of the area into an Arab and Muslim territory, made it an obvious focus of power in the rivalries that followed the first flush of victory.

After the murder of Caliph Uthman in 656, this competition among rival Arab factions burst out into civil war between Ali, Uthman's successor and son-in-law of the Prophet, and Mu'a-wiya, Uthman's kinsman and governor of Syria, in which the Iraqi forces were mobilised in support of the former and the Syrian armies on behalf of the latter. With the assassination of Ali at Kufa, Mu'awiya was named Caliph, moved the Caliphate to Damascus and firmly established the ascendancy of his Umayyad dynasty. There were, however, frequent confrontations between pro-Ali armies, basically drawn from Iraq and Persia, and Umayyad forces which lasted until the death of Ali's son, Husain, at the battle of Kerbala in 680. At the same time, the Ali faction was being transformed into a viable religious expression which, on theological grounds, refused the orthodox authority of the Umayyad Caliphate and gradually formed the distinct Islamic sect of the Shi'a which, in turn, attracted other anti-Umayyad dissidents, especially from among the newly-converted in Iraq and Persia.

Abbasid dynasty This political and religious opposition to the Umayyads was successfully mobilised by a Quraishi (the tribe of Muhammed) claimant to the Caliphate, Muhammed ibn Ali bin al-Abbas, who was also a descendant of the Prophet's uncle. Supported by a large Iraqi and Persian army, he established his capital at Kufa in 749 and, after a series of engagements, captured Damascus in 750.

The ensuing Abbasid dynasty removed the Caliphate from Damascus to the virtually new city of Baghdad, promoted a remarkable development of Islamic culture, especially under Haroun al-Rashid, and formulated a distinct Islamic civilisation. Its decline, marked by the ascendancy of Turkish mercenaries and Persian functionaries, was unfortunately rapid. The empire as a whole fragmented into independent or autonomous kingdoms—Spain in 756, Morocco in 788, Tunisia in 800, Egypt in 868 and Persia in the 9th century. Iraq itself experienced rioting, religious conflicts and army rivalries which, in 836, resulted in the abandonment of Baghdad as the seat of government in favour of Samarra. Small kingdoms, such as that of the Hamdanids in Mosul, of the Negro slaves at Basra or the Qarmati sect at al-Hasa, were carved out of Iraqi territory and, from 945 to 1055, the entire area was in the hands of the Shi'ite Buwaihid tribe from the Caspian littoral.

Seljuks and Mongols Unity was restored by the invasion of Seljuk Turks from Turkestan who rapidly conquered Persia, Iraq and, eventually, the greater part of western Asia. From 1055, all temporal power was in the hands of the Seljuk Sultan, normally resident at Isfahan, while the Abbasids were allowed to continue as Caliphs, exercising only spiritual authority from their seat at Baghdad. The decline of Seljuk power in the 12th century allowed the Abbasids to re-assume an independent political role, at least in Baghdad and central Iraq, despite recurring inroads made by the Kurds under Salah al-Din and by various Seljuk principalities in the north.

The eradication of both Seljuk and Abbasid power came with the devastating invasion by the Mongols in 1258. The Caliph and his family were executed, Baghdad looted, its population slaughtered and the ancient irrigation system on which the prosperity of the country depended was destroyed. The Mongol occupation, except for 50 years of peace and progress in the middle of the 14th century under the relatively enlightened and Persianised Jala'ir Amirs, witnessed the growing impoverishment of Iraq. The devastation was made final by the second Mongol invasion, led by Timur the Lame in 1401. The death of Timur in 1405 was followed first by the resurgence of the Jala'ir Amirs and then by the uncontrolled rivalries of Turcoman tribes in Iraq and finally by the re-appearance of a strong Persian kingdom which subdued the Turcoman factions and conquered Iraq by 1524.

Ottoman-Persian rivalry The hegemony of the Persian-Shi'a Safavid empire confronted almost immediately the expansive force of the Sunni-Turkish Ottoman Empire. Persian territories in Iraq were quickly acquired, first by Sultan Selim I and then by Sultan Sulaiman the Magnificent in the first half of the 16th century. The Ottoman-Persian competition, despite the initially overwhelming successes of the Turkish forces, continued for the next 200 years and, in Iraq, was marked by the Persian occupation of Baghdad from 1621 to 1638 and by intermittent invasions by the Persians during the reign of Shah Nadir in the early 18th century. But, basically, Iraq remained a poor, neglected and often ignored province of the vast and inefficient Ottoman Empire until it fell apart in the 1914–18 war.

At the beginning of Ottoman rule, Iraq was a country devastated by the Mongol invasions and by the misrule of a succession of foreign conquerors. Four hundred years later, the impoverishment and backwardness had hardly lessened. During this period, the Ottoman administration was mainly concerned with collection of taxes and tribute and not with the re-creation of Iraq's once flourishing commercial life. Its backwardness, unhealthy climate and distance from Istanbul gradually isolated it from the central administration which, more and more, had difficulties in maintaining a loyal local government and provincial army in an area so far removed from the centre of power. Consequently, autonomous governorates evolved, controlled by local families in the Baghdad, Basra and Mosul provinces and tolerated by the Sublime Porte as long as the imperial treasury received its share of taxes. Indeed, from 1704 to 1831, governors were invariably self-appointed local notables or administrators who relied on their ability and support from local factions and garrisons rather than on the Sultan's approval.

Baghdad supremacy Under Hassan Pasha (1704–1723), the Baghdad governorate began to dominate the other Iraqi vilayets and this supremacy was partially consolidated by his son, Ahmed Pasha. The Persian invasions from 1727 to 1747 prevented further improvements in economic and political life but some advances were made under the governorships of a succession of Mamluk rulers (former Circassian slaves) who followed Ahmed Pasha. The slackening of central Ottoman control also meant that Iraq was open to internal rebellion and external attacks. Basra and Baghdad suffered from regular raids by the Nejdi Wahhabis and from other encroachments by neighbouring Arabs, while Mosul was constantly weakened by Kurdish feuds and the hostility of the Yazidis. And the country as a whole was burdened with the ever-constant threats of Persian attacks.

The modernisation of the Ottoman Empire under Selim III and Mahmoud II saw the re-assertion of central control over Iraq and the deposition of the last Mamluk pasha in 1831. After a period of military consolidation, reforms which had already been carried out in Istanbul were applied to Iraq by the Ottoman governor Midhat Pasha. A modern system of communications was created, public services introduced, military conscription applied, municipal and provincial councils promoted and troublesome Arab and Kurdish tribes pacified. With the development of a modern infrastructure came a strong European interest in the area, especially German and British, which continued unabated until the outbreak of the First World War.

British Mandate The war smashed the Ottoman Empire. One of the first areas to be taken was Iraq, captured by British forces in 1914 to protect vital oil supplies in Persia. Despite a dramatic defeat at Kut in 1916, the British steadily advanced northward and, by 1918, almost all of Iraq was dominated by Allied forces. The prospect of independence offered to the growing number of Arab nationalists in return for their military support against the Turks was replaced by the reality of a British military occupation and, from 1920 onwards, by a British Mandate, confirmed by the conference at San Remo in 1920. Local rebellions in the south followed the announcement of the Mandate but could only marginally retard the establishment of a secure British administration and the coronation of Amir Faisal, nominated by the British, as King of Iraq.

The basis of British administration was codified by the Anglo-Iraqi Treaty of 1922 which specified the rights and privileges of the British and other foreign nationalities in Iraq. The Treaty excited substantial opposition and was only ratified by a newly-created Constituent Assembly in 1924. The same Constituent Assembly also promulgated the British-designed Organic Law which constitutionally defined Iraq's sovereignity, representative form of government and hereditary monarchy. The growing problem of Turkish claims to Mosul was also resolved by the tripartite treaty of 1925, by which Britain, Turkey and Iraq formally agreed to the incorporation of Mosul into the Kingdom of Iraq. Having established a certain geographical security and constitutional basis, the British-advised central government consolidated its domestic authority by creating local agencies of government ministries and provincial judiciary, and by forming a disciplined national army and police force.

Independence British control was gradually relaxed in favour of Iraqi administration. In 1930, a new Anglo-Iraqi Treaty entrusted all domestic government to Baghdad. The provisions of this treaty, which required obligatory consultation on foreign affairs and enshrined British responsibility for defence, provoked the usual nationalist outcry but, nonetheless, heralded the creation of an independent sovereign nation which, in 1932, was finally admitted to the League of Nations.

Independence was bedevilled by racial and religious animosity, further aggravated by the failure of political parties to become truly national. The only encouraging development was the expansion of the oil industry which, by 1934, was exporting oil from Kirkuk to Mediterranean ports in large quantities. Although economic prospects may have seemed brighter, political realities darkened.

A massacre by the army of members of the Assyrian minority took place in 1933, a tribal revolt broke out along the Euphrates in 1935–36 and in 1936 the first coup d'état occurred. The coup, managed by the army and reformist politicians, was led by General Bakr Sidqi, who succeeded in exaggerating domestic tensions even more until his assassination in 1937.

The trauma of Palestine began to affect Iraq in the late 1930's, when British policy became more and more pro-Zionist. German influence, on the other hand, became more apparent, especially in the army. Finally, a coup, led nominally by Rashid Ali al-Gaylani, toppled the pro-ally government in 1941 and resulted in the new regime's declaration of non-belligerency. In turn, the British occupied Basra and Baghdad later in the same year and secured the right of passage for British troops through Iraq.

Domestic politics were severely curtailed and the vociferous Arab nationalists muzzled. The basic anti-British sentiments and the aspirations of Arab nationalists again came to the fore with even greater vigour with the resumption of normal political life at the war's end. A period of instability followed with a number of governments—including that of Salih Jabr who was the first Shi'ite to hold the office of Prime Minister—alternating between repression and nationalist fervour. The new Anglo-Iraqi Treaty of 1948, which called for the evacuation of the British bases at Habbaniya and Shuaiba but still enshrined the British a special role in defence and foreign affairs, provided a focus for the now suppressed left-wing opposition groups. Riots in Baghdad forced the resignation of the Jabr Government and the new government's repudiation of the treaty. The new Prime Minister, Muhammed al Sadr, who was also a Shi'ite, was, however, forced to resign six months later as a result of continued disturbances and of the first Arab-Israeli war. His successor, Muzahim al-Pachachi, lasted a similar period and was followed by the year-long administration of the omnipresent Nuri al-Said.

King Faisal II The failure in Palestine of the Arab armies, including an Iraqi force of 8,000, radicalised Iraqi politics as no single event had ever before done. Martial law and repression which followed the 1948 war prevented all outbursts of violent opposition until the riots of 1952. But the new nationalism had taken hold. The dominance of the moderate parties—the Constitutional Union Party under the leadership of Nuri al-Said, the Socialist Party of the Nation under Salih Jabr and the United Popular Front of senior politicians—restricted any real expression of this nationalism. The riots of 1952, ostensibly provoked by a new oil agreement concluded by the Umari cabinet and by student agitation, reflected the dangerous tensions and confusions of post-1948 Iraq. The assumption of full executive powers by

King Faisal II on his coming of age in 1953 resulted in the formation of a more progressive government under the consistently pan-Arab and Shi'ite statesman, Fadhil al-Jamali. The liberal policies of the Jamali Government briefly reduced tensions but its pro-Western complexion eventually excited substantial opposition. Jamali resigned as a direct result of the devastating Tigris floods in 1954 and was succeeded by Arshad Umari who, a few months later in August 1954, was replaced by General Nuri al-Said.

Baghdad Pact The Said Government, which lasted until 1957, benefited in many ways from Iraq's new prosperity which the oil profit-sharing agreement of 1952 had promoted. Substantial funds were available for development and rapid improvements in irrigation and flood control were especially made possible. The great strides in economic development were, unfortunately, accompanied by a certain political retrogression. Said disbanded all political parties, tightened press laws and outlawed communists. Disregarding the anti-Western sentiment that had marked Iraqi politics since 1918, he brought Iraq into a close partnership with Britain, Turkey and Pakistan in the Baghdad Pact in an effort to balance the assumed Soviet penetration of the Middle East. The Pact, formulated in 1955, effectively isolated Iraq from the aggressively Arab regimes in Syria and Egypt and hardened the moderate-nationalist divisions in Iraq itself.

The dangers of Nuri al-Said's Western connections became more apparent with the Anglo-French invasion of Egypt in 1956 and the subsequent anti-Western vehemence of Arab nationalists. Faced with riots in Baghdad, Najaf and Mosul, the Said Government imposed martial law and effectively repressed all nationalist opposition. The improvement of relations with Egypt and Syria in the following years and the resumption of prosperity reduced the almost catastrophic tensions of 1956; but two years later Iraq, responding to the example of the 'radical' United Arab Republic of Egypt and Syria in 1958, produced the federation of the two Hashemite kingdoms of Jordan and Iraq, both bastions of conservative monarchy.

14 July coup On 14 July 1958 the monarchy was overthrown in a coup d'état led by Brigadier Abdel-Karim Qassem, in which the

King, the Crown Prince and Nuri al-Said were killed. Iraq was declared a Republic and supreme authority vested in a command council headed by Qassem. The new regime was plagued by troubles, including the inevitable power struggles—between Qassem and the pro-Egyptian, pro-Baathist Deputy Prime Minister, Colonel Aref—ethnic riots between Kurds and Turcomans in 1959, the suppression of communist organisations, an assassination attempt on the life of Qassem and, more intractably, a full-fledged Kurdish uprising under the leadership of Mustafa Barzani. The Kurds, from the beginning of the rebellion in 1961, progressively consolidated their gains in northern Iraq, pushing government forces back to the larger towns. In 1964, a ceasefire was arranged in return for the central government's recognition of Kurdish rights and the promise of a new provisional constitution.

Baathists take over   Mainly as a result of the Kurdish war and the infiltration of the army by the Baath Party, Qassem was overthrown in a coup d'état in February 1963 and his arch-rival, Colonel Aref, installed as President with the help of nationalist and Baathist elements in the army. The Aref regime purged the army and civil service of its pro-Qassem members and put Iraq on a pan-Arab and pro-Egyptian course. The severe divisions in the Baath Party between pro-Nasserites and anti-Nasserites, between moderates and radicals, presented the new regime with immediate problems, the most serious of which was an attempted coup by Baathist extremists in November 1963. The discredited radical Baathists, despite their entrenched position in the National Guard, were excluded from the next government formed immediately after the coup.

The downfall of the extremists allowed President Aref to pursue his pan-Arab ambitions. A union between Iraq and the United Arab Republic, first agreed upon in April 1963, proceeded with the announcement of a Joint Presidency Council and a unified political command in 1964. Domestically, the envisaged union was anticipated by the creation of the Iraqi Arab Socialist Union along the lines of the one-party system promoted by President Nasser in Egypt and by the nationalisation of all financial institutions and 32 large industrial organisations. The visions of Iraqi-UAR unity were brought to an end

Choose MEA for frequency

MEA offers you a wide choice of timings and destinations — we serve every major centre in the Middle East and many key cities in Europe, including London, Paris, Rome, Athens and Frankfurt. At every destination there are MEA people ready to help in any way they can. We know that in-flight service is important too. We take great care in training our cabin staff and they're keen to make every journey a pleasant one. There are so many reasons for choosing MEA. With 30 years experience behind us we've built up a reputation for service and reliability.

MEA
the natural
choice airline

by the attempted coups of the reputedly pro-Nasserite Brigadier al-Razzaq against President Aref in September 1965 and again in June 1966 against the new President, Abdel-Rahman Aref, the brother of the previous president, who was killed in a helicopter crash in April 1966.

The Kurdish war, which had flared up again after the short ceasefire of 1964, continued to bedevil the Aref regimes and, in 1966, caused severe tensions between Iran and Iraq after a series of border infringements. Prime Minister Abdel-Rahman Bazzaz succeeded, however, in gaining Mustafa Barzani's support for a ceasefire settlement that would ensure a degree of Kurdish autonomy. At the same time, relations with Iran improved, heralded by an official visit by President Aref to Tehran in March 1967 and by the later agreement to settle the Shatt al-Arab border dispute and to regularise the position of Iranian nationals in Iraq.

The 1967 June War in the Middle East, because of its brevity, involved Iraq less than was to be expected. Relations were severed with the United States and Britain and oil to pro-Israel countries embargoed. This led to a reduction in oil revenues, which in any case had been diminished during the oil pipeline dispute between the western-owned Iraq Petroleum Company and Syria over transit fees during 1966 and 1967. Iraq was, however, anxious to increase its oil exports and, accordingly, resumed diplomatic relations with Britain in 1968. In the same year, President Aref entered into wider economic co-operation with France.

President Aref was overthrown in July 1968 by a group of radical army officers led by General Ahmed Hassan al-Bakr and General Hardan Takriti. The new government was first composed of moderates and included, significantly, two Kurdish ministers but it was soon dismissed by President al-Bakr and replaced by an avowedly extreme Baathist cabinet.

Kurdish settlement   To the Baathist regime of President Bakr the Kurds were its most difficult problem. The 1966 ceasefire was abandoned by the Kurds in 1968 and full-scale fighting continued until 1970. In March that year, a new settlement was negotiated which guaranteed Kurdish participation in the government, the creation of Kurdish areas where Kurdish would be one of the official languages and the constitutional right of the Kurdish minority. The 15,000 Kurdish irregulars were transformed into an official frontier force. However, relations with Baghdad became increasingly strained in 1971 and 1972. Demands by the Kurdish parties for participation in the Revolutionary Command Council were refused, as were claims that the census of northern areas agreed upon in 1970 should be undertaken. There were also two attempts on the life of the Kurdish leader, Mustafa Barzani, which again radicalised the Kurdish minority against Baghdad. Finally, fighting broke out in 1973 but soon subsided in anticipation of the central government's willingness to honour the 1970 settlement.

In March 1974—the deadline agreed for the implementation of the 1970 provisions—Vice-president Saddam Hussain announced the establishment of Kurdish autonomy. An autonomous Kurdistan, which did not include Mosul and Kirkuk, was far less than the Kurds considered as their rightful homeland. Nor were the Kurds invited to provide a representative on the Revolutionary Command Council. Barzani immediately rejected the offer and fighting resumed. The Iraqi army, well equipped with Russian arms and relying on armour and air attacks, succeeded in driving back the main body of the Kurdish forces to the Iranian border. The final victory, when it came in 1975, was, however, less military than a result of the Iran-Iraq treaty in March which included guarantees for the withdrawal of Iranian support for the Kurds. The Kurdish war was finally over.

Domestic purges The radical Baathist regime dealt with its own internal opponents with a firm hand. Former leaders like ex-Premier Abdel-Rahman al-Bazzaz were imprisoned; purges were mounted against both communists and reactionaries; and press freedom was curtailed. In 1969, more than 50 Zionist spies and anti-Baathists were publicly executed. Following an abortive coup, another 20 executions took place in January 1970. Even the Revolutionary Command Council was purged of possible opponents: in 1971, Samar Ali Umar and Hardan Takriti were removed and, following a reported coup in September 1971, two more members were dismissed. In July 1973, Nazem Kazzar, the Director of Security, led a coup attempt in which the Minister of Defence was killed and the Interior Minister wounded. The other coup leaders were all from the extremist Baathist faction and the purge of their supporters following the coup had the effect of pushing the regime into a more moderate position. This new and visible tone of domestic moderation, which has continued during the last four years, is also reflected in the growing pragmatism of the regime and its concentration on the development of the economy and, particularly, the oil industry.

Nationalised industries were re-organised and rationalised, development promoted with the help of Soviet and East European aid and insistent attempts made to expand oil exports. The oil boom in 1974 provided the development funds that, with the financial demands of the Kurdish war and with the confrontation with the Iraq Petroleum Company, had been so scarce since the 1960's. The new explosion of development has also been accompanied by a visual relaxation of government restrictions, partly in order to attract foreign investment and expertise and partly as a result of the government's own sense of internal security. Consequently, the atmosphere of suspicion which characterised the first few years of the Bakr regime has almost disappeared, replaced by a tolerable level of authoritarian and central control of political and economic activity.

Belligerence abroad   A new tone of radicalism was initially reflected in external policy. The Bakr regime expounded an inflexible hard line on the question of Palestine, full financial support was initially given to the Palestinian commandos and the various peace proposals put forward by the United States. Partly as a result of this extremism, Iraq became increasingly isolated from the rest of the Arab world and, in the case of Egypt, conducted a 'cold war'.

Relations with Iran proved to be the most severe external test for the Baathist regime. The traditional hostility between the two countries reached dangerous levels of confrontation over a number of problems. The most intractable was, of course, the conflict with the Kurds, who were given military aid and refuge by the Iranian Government. In reaction, Iraq expelled a large part of its substantial Iranian community and periodically closed its borders to Iranian pilgrims coming to visit the Shi'ite holy places at Najaf and Kerbala. The continuing crisis over the Kurdish war was aggravated by the sharp confrontation over the sovereignty of the Shatt al-Arab waterway. The refusal of the Iraqi Government to re-negotiate the 1937 treaty which gave Iraq full control was met by an example of 'gunship diplomacy' in April 1969 when Iranian warships were sent, unchallenged, up the Shatt al-Arab. Relations deteriorated even more with attempted coups, in Iraq in January 1970 which the Baathist regime insisted was supported by Tehran, and in Iran in December 1970 to which the Iranian Government alleged Iraqi sponsorship.

Peace with Iran The seizure by Iran of the Tumb islands in the lower Gulf in November 1971 brought a sharp reaction and provided another example of Iraq's deep hostility towards Iran. It was followed by even more deportations of Iranian nationals from Iraq. In 1975, the long-standing hostility was abruptly and dramatically ended by the announcement, at the OPEC summit conference in Algiers, of an Iraqi-Iranian settlement. It called for the cessation of Iranian aid to the Kurds, the internationalisation of the Shatt-al Arab waterway and the regulation of other border disputes.

As relations with Iran improved, those with Syria worsened. A continuing row erupted over the use of the waters of the Euphrates, on which Syria was constructing a massive dam. Underlying this conflict was, however, the omnipresent rivalry between the Iraqi and Syrian versions of Baathism and the equally wide differences over a Palestinian settlement. More generally, Iraq began to detach itself from the extremist position which, since 1968, had isolated it in the scheme of Arab politics. Subsidies to the extreme Palestinian organisations and to the Omani rebels evaporated completely in 1975 and successful overtures were made to the other oil-producing countries of the Arabian peninsula. The poorer states in the Arab world were provided with aid either on a government-to-government basis or through the Iraqi External Development Fund set up in 1975.

Recent Events

Since 1975 Iraq has managed to forge closer links with some of its neighbours, with other Gulf states and even with the United States, without changing its radical foreign policies. In particular it has been striking up a deeper friendship with its northern neighbour Turkey. The inauguration of the Kirkuk-Dortyol pipeline in January 1977 provided Iraq with an additional outlet for its oil exports and in turn gave Turkey access to a new source of oil supplies at preferential rates. Relations with Iran, which had improved immeasurably since the border disputes settlement of April 1975, were further consolidated by a visit to Tehran by Foreign Minister Saadoun Hamadi in early 1977. In 1975 a co-operation agreement was concluded with Bahrain and moves made towards an aid deal with Qatar and the United Arab Emirates. In April 1977, a high-level Government delegation visited all the Arab states of the Gulf, including Oman, which for many years had been hostile to Iraq because of its support for left-wing guerrillas in Dhofar.

Relations with Kuwait however have been soured by Iraq's persistent claims to the Kuwaiti islands of Bubiyan and Warba at the head of the Gulf. In September 1976, Iraqi troops were reported to have crossed into Kuwaiti territory. At the same time the Iraqi Government started a propaganda war against Kuwait's leaders. But tension between the two countries eased considerably when both countries agreed to set up a joint ministerial committee in July 1977 to settle the border dispute.

Iraq has had increasingly angry confrontations with Syria. In April a long-standing financial dispute over the price of Iraqi oil pumped to the Banias refinery in Syria culminated with Iraq closing the trans-Syria oil pipeline. Iraq was also extremely hostile to Syria's involvement in the civil war in Lebanon, accusing Syria of pursuing expansionist policies. In June 1976 Iraq massed troops on the Iraqi-Syrian border and later in the year Iraqi soldiers were reported to be fighting alongside leftist forces in Lebanon. Iraq blamed a bomb explosion at Baghdad airport on Syrian agents and accused Syria of fermenting riots among pilgrims to the Shia shrine of Kerbala in February 1977.

US overtures Outside the Middle East, Iraq made tentative steps towards normalisation of relations with the USA, with whom it had broken off diplomatic links in 1967. In May 1977, a US State Department official visited Baghdad for talks with Foreign Minister Saadoun Hamadi. This was believed to be the first bilateral meeting between officials of the two countries since the diplomatic break. At the same time, however, Iraq continued to maintain close ties with the Soviet Union. A delegation led by Vice-President Saddam Husain visited Moscow in early 1977 and the Government also stepped up its economic contacts with Eastern Europe.

Internally, the Kurds have still remained the Iraqi Government's main political problem. In 1976 Kurdish guerrilla groups claimed that widespread fighting was still going on despite the settlement which followed the Shatt al-Arab agreement with Iran in 1975. The armed wing of the Kurdish Democratic Party (KDP) was reported to have made several guerrilla attacks against the Iraqi army. The revival of guerrilla action was linked to the Government's policy of dispersing Kurds into the Arab areas of the Mesopotamian plains which aroused intense hostility in Kurdistan. At one time it was thought that up to one million Kurds might be uprooted from their villages. But by early 1977 the Government was reported to have softened its dispersal policies because of strong opposition.

Iraq's Arab population also showed signs of deep discontent when riots broke out during a Shia pilgrimage at Kerbala in February 1977. The Government blamed the troubles on Syrian agents who, it claimed, had infiltrated a pilgrim's march. But the disturbances showed a continued underlying friction between the country's mainly Sunni ruling group and the Shia minority in the south.

ECONOMY

Iraq's economy has bright prospects. The country's oil reserves are estimated to be the second highest in the Middle East. Only a quarter of its 24 million hectares of cultivable land is at present being farmed. By 1980 its population should exceed 13 million, large enough to provide an indigenous labour force for its industries and farms. Nonetheless the country has a long way to go before its potentials are fully realised. Its infrastructure is still inadequate and with the majority of the population under 20 years of age, there is going to be a serious shortage of skilled manpower for many years.

Oil

Oil revenues provided 98 per cent of Iraq's export earnings in 1976 and 92 per cent of the 1977 $8,100 million investment programme came from oil incomes. The country is almost fully dependent on its oil earnings for the realisation of its development plans. As a result it is highly exposed to fluctuations in oil sales. The introduction of a two-tier price system by the Organisation of Petroleum Exporting Countries (OPEC) in December, 1976, under which Iraq raised its prices by 10 per cent compared with Saudi Arabia's and the United Arab Emirates' five per cent increase, led to an immediate 30 per cent fall in exports. Temporary slumps like these are constantly forcing the Government to make cutbacks and to postpone projects.

Iraq is chronologically the second major Middle East producer, after Iran. Its oil history dates back to the late 19th century when a contract awarded to Germany allowed for preliminary surveys in the areas around Mosul and Baghdad, then provinces of the Ottoman Empire. In 1914 the Turkish Petroleum Company (owned by Britain through the Royal Dutch Shell group and the Anglo-Persian Oil Company and by Germany through the Deutsche Bank) was promised an oil concession covering Mosul and Baghdad by the Ottoman Government. The outbreak of the First World War prevented ratification of the agreement, however, and it was not until the post-war territorial settlements of 1920 that the concession question was revived. That year the 25 per cent German holding in the Turkish Petroleum Company was assigned to France. In return France, having been promised Mosul as part of its 'sphere of influence' in the Middle East under the May 1916 Sykes-Picot Agreement, agreed to cede Mosul to Britain. In March 1925 the company obtained the concession it had first set out to win some 10 years earlier. For the next 45 years British, French, Dutch and American interests controlled Iraq's oil industry.

IPC formed The Americans entered the scene in 1928, when the Anglo-Persian Oil Company (now British Petroleum) handed over part of its 50 per cent share in the venture to the Standard Oil Company of New Jersey and the Socony-Mobil Oil Company. Represented by their common affiliate, the Near East Development Corporation, the two US firms together held 23.75 per cent of the shares. The new international group then changed its name to the Iraq Petroleum Company (IPC) and, in March 1931, obtained a new and larger concession including areas east of the Tigris. Its subsidiaries, the Basrah Petroleum Company (BPC) and the Mosul Petroleum Company (MPC) took over areas southwest and northwest of the Tigris in 1938 and 1942 respectively. By 1932, after five years of drilling, 26 wells had been completed, whose rate of production gave some indication of the country's enormous oil wealth. Twelve-inch pipelines to the Mediterranean terminals of Tripoli and Haifa were finished in 1934 and, when pumping to Haifa was disrupted by the Palestine War in 1948, a third, 30-inch pipeline was built, linking Kirkuk with Banias on the Syrian coast.

After a long and protracted dispute IPC was nationalised in 1972 and in December 1975 BPC was also taken over. The only foreign oil companies now operating in Iraq have service contracts with the Iraq National Oil Company (INOC). Elf-Iraq, a French-Japanese group, helped bring the Buzurgan and Abu Ghuraib fields on stream in October 1976 and Braspetro, the exploration subsidiary of the Brazilian national oil company Petrobras, has discovered a new oil field near Basra which is expected to yield 350,000 barrels a day (b/d).

Large reserves In the Iraqi oil industry today the emphasis is on exploration, as well as maintaining a steady flow of exports. The question of establishing the size of oil reserves is considered sufficiently urgent to warrant expenditure of $1,500 million on a five-year exploration programme due to end in 1979. For a long time Iraq, with proven reserves of 35,000 million barrels, was thought to have the fourth largest reserves in the Middle East—although IPC's failure to develop more than a minor part of its concession area left room for doubt on this score. In mid-1973 new surveys were said to indicate a figure more than double the old one, of around 75,000 million barrels. But now it is thought that Iraq's reserves could be second only to those of Saudi Arabia at 95,000 million barrels. Of this total some 80,000 million are thought to lie to the south, where the two most important oil fields at present are at Rumaila and Zubair.

Though Iraq is anxious to assess its reserves and expand its production capacity, the targets for actual production set in 1972 before the OPEC oil prices quadrupled in 1973–74 have since been scaled down. From a daily production level of 71,000 barrels in 1935, output had risen to 1.4 million barrels by 1962 where it remained virtually static until the sudden 35 per cent growth which followed nationalisation, bringing output to a level of just over two million barrels a day (b/d) in 1973. In 1976 production averaged 2.3 million b/d. It had been scheduled to reach 6.5 million barrels (325 million tons a year) by 1980. Now however the aim is to produce just four million b/d (200 million tons a year) by 1982 while nonetheless installing the extra production and transport facilities to allow for 'market flexibility'.

Outlet problems This concern for flexibility, a key point in Iraqi oil policy, results from the country's geographical position. Having only one maritime outlet, onto the Gulf, and having to rely on Mediterranean ports as outlets for all northern crudes, the Government began, from early 1973, arranging for alternatives to the established Syrian and Lebanese routes. The first of these, inaugurated in December 1975, is the 42-inch 44–48 million ton-a-year 'strategic pipeline', so-called because of its capacity either to pump southern oil northwards or northern oil southwards to Gulf terminals. The second, completed at the end of 1976, is the 40-inch pipeline from Kirkuk to the Turkish port of Dortyol. This has an initial capacity of 25 million tons a year rising later to 35 million.

No sooner had the strategic pipeline been opened than its potential became clear. Early in 1976, following the collapse of talks with Syria on a new scale of dues for the transit of Iraqi oil through to Banias, Iraq closed the pipeline and notified its major customers that they should make arrangements to lift their requirements of Kirkuk crude from Basra instead of the East Mediterranean. Export capacity through the two southern terminals of Khor al-Amaya (raised to 80 million tons a year in 1976) and Mina al-Bakr (completed in 1975 with a capacity of 50 million tons a year) was adequate to handle all Iraqi oil exports, though for a while flow had to be reduced because of initial technical problems.

The increase in Iraq's oil revenues over the years has been spectacular. The first sudden leap—from $15 million in 1950 to $110 million in 1952—resulted from the new profit-sharing agreement with IPC. The next upsurge came in 1974, when, from an income of $1,900 million in 1973, the Government suddenly found itself with revenues totalling some $6,900 million. The severe production cutbacks endured by virtually every other major oil producer in the area during the Western recession and oil glut of 1975 were unheard of in Iraq, where output increased by 21 per cent over 1974. But oil revenues have recently begun to show a less spectacular increase. In 1976 they totalled $8,800 million, a 4.6 per cent increase over the previous year's.

Industry

Motivated by the desire to establish an industrial base which will quickly transform Iraq into a developed country and by the continual need to keep one step ahead of the inflation which has been doubling and tripling project-cost estimates, the Government is forging ahead with an industrialisation programme at some speed. Industrial development schemes launched during 1975 were estimated to be costing at well over ID 1,000 million ($3,390 million). During 1977 38 projects costing $1,035 million were due to be completed. Industry was taking 41 per cent of the country's $8,100 million investment programme in 1977. In future investment programmes, industry is likely to continue to take 40 per cent and between 1976–80 its total allocation should amount to $21,000 million. The emphasis is on the exploitation of locally available raw materials with export potential, diversification away from dependence on oil and a complete revitalisation of the mostly small-scale manufacturing industries which have dominated the non-oil sector in recent years.

New industries Until the huge programme of industrial expansion began to take shape in 1974–75, non-oil industry was oriented mainly towards simple consumer goods—manufacturing building materials such as bricks and cement, packing dates and processing food, drink and agro-industrial products such as cotton, wool and silk textiles, clothing, footwear, paper, vegetable oils, soap, sugar and cigarettes. The few large plants still in private hands were nationalised in 1964 and taken over by the state-owned General Industrial Organisation. By that time many industrial innovations, including sulphur extraction, a steel rolling mill and rayon, fertiliser and plastics factories, had been planned for almost 10 years, but were nowhere near implementation. It was not until some years later that these began to get under way—the Hindiya rayon plant opening in 1968 and the Kirkuk sulphur extraction plant reaching full capacity in mid-1973.

Most of the heavy industrial projects now under construction are oil-based or dependent on gas and tend, therefore, to be concentrated mainly to the south, in the Basra area. Total oil refining capacity was estimated to have reached about 10.5 million tons a year by late 1974, with the completion of a 30,000 b/d refinery in Mosul and another of 80,000 b/d in Basra. Basra's oil refinery is being expanded to a capacity of four million tons a year by 1979. A 15-million-ton-a-year export refinery is being built south west of Basra at Khor al-Zubair by a Japanese consortium.

Petrochemicals Petrochemicals, another important element in Iraq's industrial plans, have a ready market in such neighbouring countries as Jordan, Syria and Lebanon, where traditional textile industries can absorb synthetic fibres and dyestuffs, and where fertilisers and plastics are also in demand. The largest project is a $1,000 million complex at Basra which is being built by a West German/US joint venture. Scheduled to begin production by 1981, the complex will produce 90,000 tons a year of polyethylene, 60,000 tons of polyvinyl chloride (PVC) and 40,000 tons of caustic soda. Plans for a second complex in the Basra area costing around $2,300 million with a capacity of 170,000 tons a year of ethylene, polyethylene and PVC, have been postponed. A Japanese consortium has been favourites to win the contract. There have also been plans for a third plant, the largest of the three, with a projected capacity of 400,000 tons a year of ethylene and other derivatives. As these complexes develop it is hoped to install plants to produce intermediary and finished products, including acrylic and polyester fibres and plastic containers.

Mitsubishi of Japan is building a 1,600-ton-a-year urea plant at Khor al-Zubair, due for completion in 1979. Another similar sized plant will be added in 1980. A fertilizer plant at Basra was expanded in early 1977 to a capacity of 300,000 tons of nitrogenous fertilizer and 500,000 tons of urea.

By-product gas from crude oil production in southern Iraq will be used to fuel the first Basra petrochemical complex, as efforts are made to increase utilization of the country's gas reserves. These are estimated at 27 million million cubic feet, of which 18 million million cubic feet is associated gas, most of which is flared off. A liquefied petroleum gas plant, with a capacity of 3.3 million tons a year, is due to be built by the Japanese at Rumaila in the south. A second plant, to produce 200,000 tons a year, is being built by Italians in Kirkuk.

Heavy industry   Many other major plants will rely on natural gas reserves. The Khor al-Zubair steelworks under construction by a French company was due to begin operating by the end of 1977 with an output of 400,000 tons a year. It will comprise four 70-ton furnaces, two six-line cooling machines, two rolling mills and a technical training centre for 400 students. An aluminium factory at Nassiriya has just started turning out sheets, foils, sections and wires. But a 200,000-ton-a-year aluminium smelter planned for Basra has been deferred.

Iraq's construction materials industry is expanding fast. Though formerly able to export cement to the rest of the Gulf and East Africa, Iraq banned cement exports in April 1974 in order to meet the rapid increase in local demand. Cement output in 1976 was scheduled to reach 2.8 million tons. This figure is being raised to seven million tons in 1978 by the opening of seven new cement factories. By 1980 output could rise to 10 million tons a year, of which a high proportion could be exported. Brick production should reach 960 million bricks in 1978.

Minerals output   Minerals other than oil appear to be plentiful and varied. Iron ore, chromite, copper, lead, limestone, gypsum, salt and dolomite have all been located, although the commercial viability of these deposits has yet to be determined. Exploitation of sulphur and phosphates is so far the most advanced. Commercial production of sulphur at the Mishraq mines began in January 1972 and was boosted several months later with the discovery, also in northern Iraq, of useful quantities of bentonite, an important ingredient in sulphur refining which had, until then, been imported at considerable cost from West Germany. The Mishraq mines, developed in co-operation with Poland, yielded an initial 250,000 tons a year, with 1.5 million tons a year as the long-term target. New port facilities designed for handling liquid sulphur have been installed at Umm Qasr, allowing for sulphur exports to be doubled.

The development of phosphate mining is even more recent. Initial negotiations with the Soviet Union on the implementation of a mining project at Akashat in the Western Desert began in April 1972. Studies started the following June, pointing to an annual production level of around 900,000 tons, but this figure has since been drastically revised. A three-year contract, won by a Belgian consortium in September 1975, specified a production target of 3.4 million tons a year. The mines' output will be used by a chemical fertiliser complex at Al-Qaim due to be completed by 1979. It will produce 1,100 tons a day of phosphoric acid, 4,500 tons a day of sulphuric acid and a total 1.1 million tons of phosphate-based fertiliser a year. About 85 per cent of production will be exported.

Other industries based on local raw materials and showing rapid progress include the manufacture of paper, glass and associated chemicals. Two paper mills, one in Basra and the other in Maisan, are being built by a Swiss and a number of West German firms under agreements signed in May 1974 and December 1975. The scheduled annual capacity of new units at the Basra plant, due to be finished by the end of 1977, is 36,000 tons a year of bleached pulp and 30,000 tons of paper. That of the Maisan mill, costing around $185 million and due to be ready in 1978, stands at 95,000 tons of paper bags and cardboard, manufactured from sugar cane waste provided by the governorate's sugar refinery and reeds from the southern marshes.

Motor industry In the Iraqi motor industry the biggest step to be achieved during the Five-Year Plan is the shift from vehicle assembly to complete manufacture. Most of the new motor plants are to be grouped in a complex at Suwaira, served by a central foundry. The complex is expected to assemble 50,000 cars, 15,000 trucks, 5,000 other vehicles and 36,000 diesel motors a year. The country already has two truck assembly plants. Two tyre plants are due to be opened by the end of 1977. One at Duwaniya was being built by Pirelli of Italy with a capacity of 300,000 sets a year.

Huge additional supplies of power are needed for these schemes and there are numerous projects both to increase industrial power supplies and electrify villages. It was announced in March 1976 that ID 76 million ($258 million) had been earmarked for rural electrification over the five years to 1980. Electricity output capacity by 1977 was 1,000 MW. Among future projects are a 800 MW power station at Haritha near Basra and a 840 MW plant at Nassiriya.

Land communications are being improved to help both industrial and general economic development. Construction work on a six-lane highway between Basra and Baghdad should start in 1978. At least 15 major bridges are being built, mainly across the Tigris and Euphrates rivers, including two large ones over the Tigris in Baghdad. Railways are being improved, with the two largest projects being the building of a standard gauge line between Baghdad and Umm Qasr and Baghdad and Al-Qaim.

Trade

Iraq's trade has grown at a staggering rate in recent years. Between 1973 and 1975 imports rose by 400 per cent to $4,221 million. But in 1976 they fell slightly to $4,200 million, possibly because of port congestion. Waiting times at Basra had risen to 90 days.

The country has ceased to rely on the Soviet Union and the Eastern Bloc for its goods. The Soviet Union is no longer the country's main supplier. The US, however, with no official diplomatic representation in Baghdad since 1967, has come to rank with West Germany, France, Italy and Japan as one of Iraq's leading customers, building hotels, vital port installations and petrochemical plants, and providing aircraft, airline management assistance and ever increasing quantities of food. US exports during 1976 totalled $382 million, a rise of 19 per cent on the previous year. In 1975 Iraq became West Germany's biggest Arab customer, with purchases increasing almost 170 per cent to no less than $1,025 million.

Bilateral deals An important feature of Iraq's trading policy with the industrialised world has been its readiness to conclude big bilateral package deals of the oil-for-technology and oil-for-credit kind. Three of these were signed during 1974 while the oil shortages which had followed the 1973 embargo were still a major preoccupation of the industrialised world. Italy signed a 10-year deal providing for increased supplies of Iraqi crude to the state firm ENI in proportion to the extent of increased Italian investment in Iraq. The tentative figure set for the investment was $3,000 million.

In August 1974, lengthy negotiations with Japan on a similar agreement were concluded. This time it was decided that Iraq should supply Japan with 160 million tons of crude oil, liquefied petroleum gas (LPG) and other petroleum products over a period of 10 years. In return Japan agreed to extend a $1,000 million line of credit (of which almost a quarter is thought to have been offered on development aid terms) to help cover the cost of Japanese-built LPG, fertiliser, cement and other industrial plants. The Japanese agreement was not an immediate success. By the end of 1974 oil stocks were no longer a problem to Japan and it was unable to take delivery of Iraqi oil at anything like the rate foreseen. Some of the industrial contracts listed went to non-Japanese firms instead. But relations remained good and in early 1977 another $1,000 million credit was agreed.

A third major economic co-operation deal, worth $2,800 million, was concluded with France in December 1974. France agreed to sell fighter aircraft to Iraq and build a steel works and aluminium plant. Subsequent attempts to reach a deal with West Germany have failed, however, apparently due to West German reluctance to provide financial assistance in any form. Iraqi requests for low interest rates and guarantees against inflation on West-German-supplied goods, and for help in meeting the cost of industrial training programmes, have all been refused.

Iraqi exports, still almost exclusively oil, are for the most part directed to Western Europe. Iraq's non-oil exports, though providing only 4 per cent of export income, are not to be ignored, however. The world's largest exporter of dates, Iraq earns some ID 10–11 million ($34–$37 million) a year from this commodity, with China, the Soviet Union and India among its biggest customers. Exports of sulphur are also on the increase, to India, China, Indonesia, Pakistan and a number of Arab and African states and, as the various chemical fertiliser projects get under way they, too, will add to non-oil earnings.

Agriculture

Though endowed with abundant water resources and a centuries-old agricultural tradition, Iraq today, as in the past, still faces the basic agricultural problem of controlling these assets and exploiting them to the best advantage. The two rivers, the Tigris and Euphrates, which with their many tributaries traverse the length of the country from the southern marshes to the Turkish and Syrian borders, are a mixed blessing. Often rising without warning and causing flood damage to irrigation works, plants and property, their water is slightly saline. When it is spread on the central and southern plains, rapid evaporation and the high water table lead to salination of the soil. The time of flooding does not naturally coincide beneficially with the growing seasons. At a maximum flow both rivers are too late for winter crops and too early for summer ones. Annual variations in the water supply are considerable and though the rivers are relatively manageable, because of their bifurcating nature which allows small amounts to be dammed, the more the water supply is increased, the worse the salt problem becomes. Salinity of the soil at present affects about 60 per cent of all irrigated land, and, although about 55 per cent of the total land area is potentially cultivable, only 25 per cent is actually being farmed.

Flood control The main requirements, then, for any agricultural development plan must be flood control and drainage. Realising this, the Development Board, shortly after its establishment in 1950, launched two major schemes which are still focal points in the ongoing development programme. The first involved the construction of a dam at Samara about 60 miles north of Baghdad to harness and divert the waters of the Tigris river to the depression known as the Wadi Tharthar. Completed in 1956 the dam was designed both for irrigation and to prevent flooding in and around the capital. Today another stage of this project is nearing completion—a Soviet-built, 25-mile canal to link the Wadi Tharthar with the Euphrates, making it possible to transfer surplus water from the Tigris to the Euphrates basin and flush away the salt. The second was the Habbaniya project, comprising a dam at Ramadi on the Euphrates which took five years to build. It was intended to divert flood water to the Western

Desert through the Habbaniya lake. The lake is now to be extended.

Over the next decade 36 major irrigation and dam schemes should give Iraq an additional four million hectares of irrigated land. Twenty projects will be on the Tigris, 13 on the Euphrates, and three on the Shatt al-Arab. Among the large schemes are the Upper and Lower Khalis projects on the Diyala River, the 225,000-hectare Abu-Ghuraib scheme on the Euphrates, and and 100,000-acre Kirkuk-Adhaim project.

Agricultural investment During the period of the 1976–80 Development Plan about 30 per cent of total expenditure of $49,000 million had been expected to be allocated to agriculture. But agriculture received only 16.5 per cent of the 1977 total investment allocation of $8,100 million.

The Government's aim is self-sufficiency in food production and the targets set for output in each of the major crops are, for the most part, well ahead of the levels attained in previous years. Wheat, for example, a crop particularly vulnerable to salinity, has gradually given way to barley. The most successful cereal crop in recent years was in 1972 when 2.6 million tons of wheat and 980,000 tons of barley were produced. Target output for both crops by 1980 stands at 2.26 million tons and 1,785,000 tons respectively, but violent fluctuations in production each year, resulting from weather changes, make these seem slightly optimistic. Production of barley in 1973 was down to half that of the previous year, while wheat was down to one-third.

Iraq's other major food crop, rice, shows signs of progressive decline, falling from 306,000 tons in 1971 to just 69,000 tons in 1974. Iraqi cotton likewise, a product once prized on the world cotton market, now occupies a less important place, with 1974 output standing at 40,000 tons. Other crops, including tobacco and vegetables, are grown but the most consistent of these is, of course, dates. The world's largest producer and exporter of dates, Iraq grows an average 350,000 tons a year. The problem here has more often been in surplus produce, which is now processed to provide natural vinegar, industrial alcohol, date syrup and fodder yeast. Research is also in progress on the possible use of the sucrose content in dates as a sugar substitute, as the chances of great improvement in the local sugar cane and sugar beet crops are not good. At present two-thirds of the sugar processed at the Mosul, Maisan and Sulaimaniya refineries has to be imported raw.

Livestock schemes Large sums are being spent on livestock raising on integrated farming complexes, the largest of which are to be found at Abu-Ghuraib, Al-Ishaqi, Dujaila and Nahr Saad. But not all the funds allocated to agriculture are being invested inside Iraq. Joint ventures in oil-seed plantations and livestock farming with Sudan, fruit farming with Chad and cattle breeding and fishing in Somalia, under discussion since 1974–75, have all reached various stages of implementation. Another more novel joint venture is that undertaken with Egypt to develop farm lands south of Baghdad. Five hundred Egyptian farmers and their families have been recruited to settle in Iraq, where they have been given land, livestock and equipment in an effort to channel their skills into the cultivation of Iraqi soil.

It can be said that agriculture in Iraq has more than 40 years to make up. Lack of security in rural areas dates back at least to the 1932 land registration programme which transferred communal and tribal land into private hands, quickly creating a large landowner class on the one hand and landless peasants on the other. Agrarian reform following the 1958 revolution has been hampered by administrative difficulties and has had only partial success. Unrest, especially during fighting in the Kurdish area of the fertile north, has further prevented the application of advanced farming techniques. By the end of 1975, agricultural co-operatives were to have been set up to cover all areas affected by the land redistribution. But the agricultural sector remains a weak point in the Iraqi economy. It contributed 22 per cent to the 1973 GNP, but employed 54 per cent of the population. Its development is imperative if costly food imports are to be eliminated. As one Iraqi planning official has said, 'it is ridiculous to suggest that the Tigris and Euphrates, which fed 10 million in biblical times, cannot feed 10 million now'.

Social services

The level of literacy has registered remarkable improvements since 1958. Then, the literacy rate was 20 per cent but improved consistently under the various republican regimes—50 per cent in 1970 and perhaps 60 per cent in 1975. Almost all the population under the age of 20 has benefited from these strides although there are serious anomalies remaining. For instance, 37 per cent of the adult male population and 71 per cent of females are still illiterate. The Government is attempting to reduce these intolerably high levels of illiteracy to 13 per cent for men and 45 per cent for women by 1980.

Education spending Education, always important in a developing country, has become crucial in Iraq. Demographic strains— almost 60 per cent of the population is below the age of 20—as well as the manpower needs made necessary by the dramatic pace of development since 1974, have severely strained existing educational resources. Consequently, expenditures by the Ministry of Education under the ordinary state budget have leapt from $54 million in 1972 to an annual equivalent of $139 million in 1975. Education and research was allocated $275 million under the 1977 investment programme, an increase of 84 per cent on the previous year. Such increases should continue into the 1980's since the current Five-Year Development Plan envisages a total outlay on education of $3,560 million.

Elementary education is free and compulsory. A significant proportion of the female population of primary-school age does not, however, seem to benefit from this educational system. Out of a total of 1.5 million pupils, only 425,000 are girls. There is, as well, the usual Muslim bias towards segregated schooling: there are a total of 6,731 primary schools of which 4,848 are for boys, 1,501 for girls and 382 mixed. Surprisingly, there is a significant number of private primary schools, mostly denominational, which account for 18,000 pupils and which have higher proportions of mixed classes and of girl pupils. In both sectors teaching staff totals 58,000.

Elementary education is expected to increase enormously over the next few years. By 1980, there will probably be about 219,000 pupils (with another 88,000 in nursery schools) which will necessitate the construction of a thousand new schools. Already, the Government has begun to set up 700 new, low-cost primary schools throughout the country.

Secondary education, also free, is expected to expand even more rapidly in order to satisfy the manpower requirements of

Iraq's rapidly developing economy. Currently, there are 450,000 pupils in secondary schools. The total number of schools is over 1,000 (of which 99 per cent are single sex establishments) staffed by about 15,000 teachers.

By 1980, the number of intermediate pupils alone will probably reach 501,000 with a corresponding increase in the number of new schools and teachers. More importantly, this quantitative increase will be accompanied by a qualitative improvement and all new schools will most likely incorporate many of the most advanced teaching and audio-visual aids. With an extraordinarily high failure rate of 49 per cent for all male arts students and 37 per cent for science students, such improvements are indeed necessary.

Vocational training Much emphasis has been placed on vocational training in an effort to plug the technical gap apparent in Iraqi society. Vocational enrolment now stands at over 20,000—the most popular courses being agriculture, commerce and technical training. Until recently, the number of students completing their vocational courses has, in fact, been dropping but such wastage will probably be overcome by the anticipated re-organisation of vocational training during the current Five-Year Plan. Programmed instruction packages and modern apparatus will probably be included in this re-organisation. Thirty new technical schools for the petrochemical, iron and steel, textile, printing and automobile industries are now being constructed.

University education is also being promoted at a fast pace, judging from the estimated increase in student enrolment anticipated by the Five-Year Plan—from 22,000 in 1975 to 90,000 in 1980. In recent years the budget of the Ministry of Higher Education and Scientific Research has been raised by over 200 per cent. Iraq has five main universities where the overall student-teacher ratio is about 34 to one. About 800 university teachers come from abroad. Some students are also sent to foreign universities, but their numbers are being reduced.

Health provision Until recently, Iraq had a long, miserable history of endemic and epidemic diseases which, in most cases, reflected the geographical and social conditions of the country. For instance, marshlands and the bad drainage typical to almost

MEED SPECIAL REPORTS

As well as providing weekly news, analysis and forecasts essential for conducting business in the Middle East, Middle East Economic Digest also produces surveys of the countries of the region.

Designed to keep you informed in depth, these surveys review central subjects such as banking and finance, industry, infrastructure, oil and gas, agriculture, education and foreign policy of each country. Usually of 36 pages in length, they are generously illustrated with photographs.

The following reports are available:—

Jordan (June 1976)	£3.50
Oman (June 1976)	£3.50
Saudi Arabia (December 1976)	£3.50
Libya (February 1977)	£1.50
Iran (February 1977)	£3.50
Qatar (April 1977)	£3.50
Iraq (June 1977)	£1.50
UAE (July 1977)	£3.50
Morocco (July 1977)	£2.50
Sudan (August 1977)	£1.50
Kuwait (August 1977)	£3.50

To obtain any, or all, of the above reports please write, enclosing the appropriate remittance to:—
Middle East Economic Digest
Dept F7, 21 John Street, London WC1N 2BP, England.

will you
help us?

We do all we can to get our facts right in *The Gulf Handbook.* Each chapter will be thoroughly revised year by year by people living in each country. When revision is not enough whole sections will be rewritten. But the territory covered by the Handbook is enormous. New hotels and restaurants are springing up all the time. A new cabaret is born, a street is renamed. Names and addresses of good hotels and restaurants for businessmen are always very welcome.

Due possibly to a recent visit, you may have information more up-to-date than ours, or perhaps a suggestion for information to be included in future editions. Please write and tell us about it; your letters will be most welcome.

—Thank you

**Trade & Travel Publications Ltd
Middle East Economic Digest Ltd**
The Mendip Press, Parsonage Lane, Westgate St., Bath BA1 1EN England

all parts of Iraq encouraged the spread of malaria and bilharzia. Equally, poverty and deprivation promoted communicable diseases such as smallpox, typhus, cholera and dysentery.

Now the general health of the nation has much improved. The Ministry of Health, first elevated to cabinet rank in 1952, has imposed a preventative and curative service in all governorates which has resulted in the elimination of smallpox and reductions in cases of diphtheria, typhoid fever, dysentery, malaria, hookworm and bilharzia. Malaria and bilharzia are still somewhat common in rural areas and eye diseases, such as trachoma and acute ophthalmia (whose incidence is actually increasing and which now account for around 250,000 new cases a year) are devastatingly prevalent. Improvements should also be made in the levels of infant mortality, low by Asian standards but still intolerably high at about 90 deaths per 1,000 live births.

The health infrastructure is relatively well developed. Around 180 hospitals provide over 20,000 beds, and are staffed by around 2,200 doctors, 130 dentists and 7,000 ancillary staff. The number of out-patient and in-patient treatments, although decreasing over the last five years, averages each year about 10 million and 600,000 respectively. Despite the reduction in the number of patients, the increase in hospital facilities has kept pace with the rise in population. The ratio of inhabitants per hospital bed stands at a constant 500 and will be improved even more with the completion of the Government's current hospital building programme.

Disparities in care Urban areas are far better served with hospitals than rural regions in both quantity and quality. Baghdad, for instance, which accounts for 35 per cent of total population, has 45 per cent of total hospital beds and 100 per cent of hospital beds for mental and nervous diseases, ophthalmia, radio-therapy and neuro-surgery and almost 50 per cent of all maternity beds. In contrast, Sulaimaniya with more than 5 per cent of total population has less than three per cent of all hospital beds and only one specialist hospital (for children). Similarly, Dhok has two per cent of total population, only half per cent of all hospital beds and no specialist hospitals.

Attempts have been made to overcome the disparities in the hospital system by promoting non-hospital health centres in rural areas. These health institutions, providing a wide range of treatment, have doctors and dentists as well as nursing and ancillary staff. But the reliance on para-medical staff is much more pronounced than in the hospital service.

There are over 4,500 doctors, or nearly one doctor for every 2,500 inhabitants. Again, the Baghdad governorate has attracted the majority (almost 50 per cent) of all doctors at the expense of the poorer and more rural districts. In Dhok and Sulaimaniya, for example, the ratio of doctors to population is one to 4,000 and one to 7,000 respectively. Most doctors are foreign trained although an increasing proportion of the younger doctors are from Iraqi universities, notably the University of Baghdad which has a large and well-equipped medical school with 1,600 students. Dentists number over 700 (one dentist for every 16,000 inhabitants) and have favoured the Baghdad area at the expense of the other governorates. Indeed, there is only one dentist for every 60,000 inhabitants in Sulaimaniya. Most are educated abroad but a substantial number are now being trained at home. Para-medical staff have increased dramatically over the last few years—from 9,820 in 1972 to about 14,000 in 1975. They are much more evenly distributed throughout the country since they are heavily relied on to operate the rural health schemes and non-hospital health institutions.

The increase in facilities and staff is a direct result of the consistent government emphasis on the development of the health sector. For example, the total expenditure on health rose by 200 per cent between 1970 and 1975. During the same period, the total expenditures by the ordinary budget increased by 170 per cent. A new 1,600-bed military hospital near Baghdad is under construction. An ultra-modern Medical City at Baghdad, complete with clinics, hospitals, laboratories, teaching halls, accommodation and nursing home, is also being built.

GUIDE

BAGHDAD Iraq's capital belongs historically and culturally to the urban sophistication of the Levant rather than the desert austerity of the other Arab states in the Gulf. Baghdad was originally founded by the Caliph Al-Mansour in A.D. 762 on the west bank of the River Tigris. It was planned and built within a few years in the form of a circle within which were three concentric enclosures. The ruler lived in the inner enclosure, the army within the second and the people within the outer one.

Now Baghdad has grown to a large sprawling city, covering both banks of the river with a population of nearly three million. The inhabitants are predominantly Arab Muslim, with sizeable Christian and Kurdish minorities. The population and the country's recent high oil earnings help to make it a city of contrasts. The white-robed desert Arab rubs shoulders with the brightly-clothed Kurd with chequered turban. Minarets and church spires poke up into the sky. Oil money is financing a renovation programme. Large modern structures stand adjacent to old crumbling buildings. But much of the new architecture is of a high standard. At the same time attempts are being made to preserve some of the old houses. So in time the city should show in its architecture a reasonable balance between the historic past and contemporary prosperity.

Key to Baghdad map, pages 214 and 215. 1. Ministry of Health; 2. Ministry of Planning; 3. Ministry of Municipalities; 4. Ministry of Information; 5. Government Press; 6. Parliament Building; 7. Directorate General of Summer Resorts and Tourism; 8. Republic Palace; 9. College of Sciences; 10. Fine Arts Institute; 11. Presidency of Baghdad University; 12. Al-Khuld Hall; 13. Iraqi Museum; 14. Al-Shaab Hall; 15. Iraqi Academy; 16. Modern Art Museum; 17. Baghdad Exhibition; 18. Abbasid Palace; 19. International Railway Station; 20. Nidhal Post Office; 21. Kindi Square; 22. British Embassy; 23. French Embassy; 24. Dar al-Salam Hotel; 25. Moulin Rouge Nightclub; 26. Embassy Nightclub; 27. New British Club; 28. Alwiyah Club; 29. Al-Naman Gardens; 30. Armenian Quarter; 31. Opera Park 32. Marjan Mosque; 33. Al-Masbah; 34. Saadoun Park; 35. Al-Umma Gardens; 36. 14th July Park; 37. Copper and silver souks; 38. Medical City; 39. Al-Sayid Soltan Ali Mosque; 40. Al-Khallani Square; 41. Unknown Soldier Square; 42. Ali Baba Square.

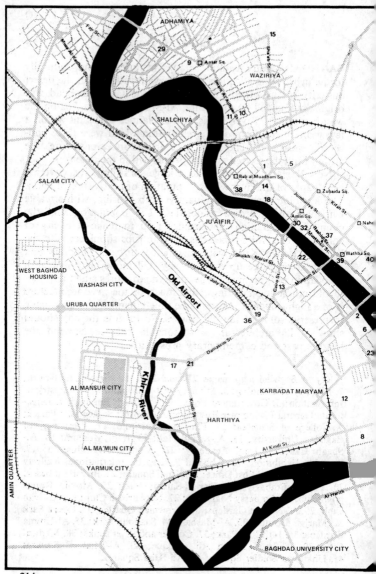

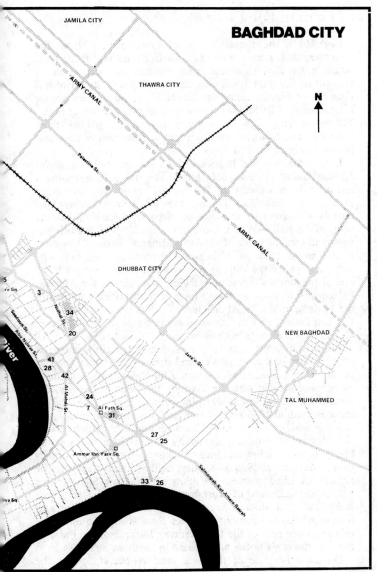

BAGHDAD CITY

JAMILA CITY

ARMY CANAL

THAWRA CITY

N

Palestine St.

ARMY CANAL

DHUBBAT CITY

NEW BAGHDAD

Tahrir Sq.

3

Nidhal St.

34

20

Saadoun St.

Abu Nuwas St.

River

41

28

42

Jaza'ir St.

TAL MUHAMMED

Al Mahdi St.

24

7   Al Fath Sq.

31

27

25

Ammar Ibn Yasir Sq.

Salhawak, Kut Amara Basrah

33   26

...ya Sq.

Baghdad is the country's seat of government, with all the ministries and major state organisations having their head offices in the city. Its recent expansion has also been given an impetus by the establishment of new industries on its periphery. One of the biggest industrial plants is the oil refinery whose bright flame of flaring gas can be seen all over the city at night. There are also light and heavy engineering plants, three breweries and factories whose output ranges from cement and bricks, to cigarettes and shoes.

Little remains of the Baghdad of the 8th century when, under Abbasid Caliph Haroun al-Rashid, its libraries, palaces, mosques and schools embodied early Islamic civilisation. The exceptions perhaps are 'Zubaida's Tomb', popularly, but probably mistakenly attributed to the wife of Haroun al-Rashid, and the ruins of the Bab al-Wastani, the last of the city's twelve original gates and now the home of the Arms Museum. There is, however, a number of relics of 12th and 13th century Baghdad. The Mustansiriya college with its spacious courtyard (thought to be one of the world's oldest universities), the ruins of the Abbasid Palace with its stone archways (once a citadel, now a museum), the Mosque of Shaikh Abdel-Qader Gailani (its dome unique in size and design) and the towering white shrine of Shaikh Omar al-Sahrawardi all date back to between 1179 and 1234.

These and other sites and museums are mainly clustered around seven of the capital's central streets—Mustansir, Rashid, Jumhouriya, Kifah, Shaikh Omar, Abu Nawas and Saadoun—all running parallel with the Tigris in the heart of the city. On Rashid Street, the main shopping centre, there is the Marjan mosque, built in 1356 and notable for its ornamental brickwork, together with the Museum of Costumes and Ethnography. Near the Marjan Mosque are Baghdad's two antique bazaars, the Shorja Market, selling all kinds of merchandise, and the Coppersmith Market, or 'Suq al-Safafir', selling hand made copper articles. A third market, the 'Suq al-Sagha' or Silversmith's bazaar, lies at the end of Mustansir Street. On Kifah Street there is the Gallery of Modern Art, displaying contemporary Iraqi and foreign works. On Jumhuriya Street there is the Suq al-Ghazil minaret, once part of the tenth-century Mosque of the Caliphs. Most of the city's hotels are situated in Saadoun Street.

On the other side of the river, near Al-Mataf Square, the

Iraqi Museum houses relics of the many civilisations which predated the Islamic era. But for a glimpse of the ancient sites it is necessary to leave the old city. Tel Harmal, for instance, in what is now called New Baghdad, is the site of a provincial capital of 4,000 years ago which reached the peak of its development in the Babylonian period around 1850 B.C. Archaeological excavations here and in nearby Tel al-Dhibai have produced cuneiform tablets analysing algebraic and geometrical problems. At Aqarquf, 12 miles west of Baghdad, is the one remaining landmark of Dur Kurigalzu, capital city of the Kassite Kingdom (1585–1171 B.C.)—the 57-metre-high ziggurat (temple) with the traces of the palaces and houses which once surrounded it. Twenty-two miles south of Baghdad the Arch of Ctesiphon may be seen—the 1,700-year-old relic of a Sassanid castle, originally a Parthian military camp, remarkable for its huge single-span vault of unreinforced brickwork. Opposite the Arch, on the right bank of the river, are traces of the town of Seleucia, built by Seleucus Nicator, an army commander under Alexander the Great and founder of the dynasty which ruled Syria, Iraq and Persia from 324 to 135 B.C.

The attractions of Baghdad and its environs are not exclusively historical. Fifty-three miles from the capital is the **Habbaniya Lake**—the 'beach' of Baghdad. Hidden behind a chain of low hills to the west of the Euphrates, this resort has facilities for swimming, boating and water-skiing. Work on a de luxe hotel and a tourist village of chalets providing accommodation for 2,000 people is nearing completion.

Many historical sites south of Baghdad may be reached from various points on the 311-mile railway that links the capital with Basra. **Babylon,** some 59 miles south of Baghdad, lies adjacent to the station at Hilla. Babylon, whose Hanging Gardens were considered by the Greeks to be one of the seven wonders of the world, flourished as a centre of culture and government for fifteen centuries, from the arrival of the Amorites in about 1850 B.C. to the time of Alexander the Great. It reached its first peak of greatness under the Amorite King Hammurabi (1792–1750 B.C.) who was famous for his legal code. Eleven centuries later it was completely destroyed, only to be reconstructed by the Chaldeans and rise to its second golden age under Nebuchadnezzar (604–562 B.C.). What remains of Babylon today belongs to Nebuchadnezzar's reign. The Ishtar Gate, its lion, bull and dragon symbols still visible, cuts across Procession Street, once paved with colourful enamelled tiles. This leads on to the ziggurat, the seven-storey tower which the Babylonians called 'Etemen-an-ki', the foundation of heaven and earth—its topmost storey the sanctuary of the god Marduch. This may well have been the Biblical Tower of Babel. Three palaces are still distinguishable among the ruins of the city, as is the site of the Hanging Gardens at the northeast corner of the Summer Palace. Comprising 14 rooms balanced one on top of the other either side of a passageway, the gardens are said to have been built by Nebuchadnezzar to remind his queen of her homeland. The ponderous basalt Lion of Babylon still stands, overlooking the once magnificent scene.

From **Hilla,** the station next to Babylon, the golden mosques of Kerbala, Najaf and Kufa may also be reached. **Najaf,** some 37 miles from Hilla, houses the mosque of Imam Ali, cousin of the Prophet Muhammed and the last of the first four Caliphs of Islam. From **Kerbala** one may continue 31 miles southwest to the eighth-century fortress at **Ukaidhar,** one of the oldest buildings still sufficiently intact to give an idea of early Islamic construction. Beyond Hilla the next stop is **Samawa,** providing access to Uruk, the 7,000-year-old settlement which grew to prominence under the Sumerians. South of that, 10 miles from Nasiriya and next to the station known as Ur Junction, lie the remains of the centre of Sumerian civilisation at **Ur.** Here the ziggurat built in 2000 B.C. may still be seen with the royal tombs whose rich and beautiful contents are now on display at the Iraqi Museum in Baghdad. About 15 minutes' drive from Ur one may also visit what the Sumerians themselves thought to be the first city in the history of mankind at **Eirdu.**

Seventy-five miles north-west of Baghdad is **Samarra.** Excavations here have shown signs of settlements dating back to 6000–7000 B.C. Under the ninth-century Caliph al-Mutassim, Samarra replaced Baghdad as the seat of Government and the Caliphs' Palace, the Grand and Abu-Dulaf mosques were built. The Grand Mosque or Mosque of Al-Mutawakkil is the largest Mosque ever built.

Hotels

Baghdad Hotel, Saadoun Street. Tel: 8889031–50. Telex: 2200. Cables: Bagotel. At present Baghdad's largest hotel. Overlooks the Tigris River. 200 rooms. Restaurant. Bar. Bank. Car rental.

Dar Al-Salam, Alwiyah, Saadoun Street. P.O.B. 123. Tel: 90506/90714/96151. Telex: 2318. Good reputation for comfort and service. Used by the Government to accommodate official delegations. 107 rooms. Restaurant. Bar. Egyptian staff.

Andalus Palace Hotel, Alwiyah, just off Saadoun Street. Tel: 91069/98827. Telex: 2172. Cable: Andalustel. Opened spring 1977. 106 rooms. Restaurant. Bar.

Ali Baba, Saadoun Street (near Ali Baba Square). Tel: 92395/92396. Restaurant. Bar.

Al-Abbasi Palace Hotel, Alwiyah, Saadoun Street. P.O.B. 123. Tel: 91521/94384–6/93938. Telex: 2318. 77 rooms. Restaurant. Bar. Casino.

Khayam, Alwiyah, Saadoun Street. Tel: 96176. Telex: 2429. Restaurant. Bar.

Diwan, Saadoun Street (near Nasr Square). Tel: 8889961. Close to city centre. Restaurant. Bar.

Babylon Palace Hotel, Alwiyah, Nidhal Street (next to the Italian Embassy). Tel: 94146/93579. Used to be the Italian Ambassador's residence. 24 rooms. Restaurant (Italian cuisine).

Ramses, Betaween, off Saadoun Street. A newly-built small hotel tucked away in a back street near Tahrir Square. Restaurant.

Park Hotel, adjacent to the Opera Park, Al-Fath Square. Just opened. Restaurant.

Orient Palace, close to Al-Fath Square. Just opened. Restaurant.

Aghadir Hotel, Alwiyah, Saadoun Street. Due to open end of 1977 or early 1978. Between 70–100 rooms. Restaurant.

Baghdad International Hotel, close to British Embassy on west side of the river. De luxe class hotel being built by the State Organisation for Tourism. Due to open sometime in 1978. 300 rooms.

All First Class 'A' hotels charge ID 8 for a single person in a double room (including breakfast), ID 9 for two people, and ID 6 for a single person in a single room. Lunches and dinner cost just under ID 2 each. Ten per cent service charge.

Ambassador, Abu-Nawas Street. Tel: 8886105. Cable: Ambotel. Overlooks garden cafes skirting the Tigris. 65 rooms. Restaurant, Car rental. Conference room.

Adam, Saadoun Street. Tel: 92381. Cable: Admotel. 45 rooms.
   Restaurant.
Sahara, Andalus Square, Nidhal Street. Tel: 90003. 40 rooms.
   Restaurant.
Rumailah, Saadoun Street. Tel: 92963. Cable: Lacaldo. 35 rooms.
Carlton, Aqaba Bin-Nafi Square. Tel: 96091. Cable: Carlhotel. 60
   rooms.
Guilgamish, Alwiyah, Saadoun Street. Tel: 96051. Cable: Khurisbad.
   45 rooms. Restaurant.

First Class 'B' hotels charge ID 6.5 for a single person in a single
room (including breakfast), ID 7.5 for two people and ID 5 for one
person in a single room. Meals are slightly cheaper than in First Class
'A' hotels.

SECOND CLASS

Akad Hotel, Nidhal Street (close to Al-Fath Square). Tel: 92376.
Saint George, Nidhal Street (close to Al-Fath Square). Tel: 95121.
Roosha, Abu-Nawas.

Second Class hotels charge ID 5 for a single person and ID 6 for
two people.
The State Organisation for Tourism is building several hotels in
Baghdad which will be managed by Western hotel companies. They
are likely to include Sheraton, Inter-Continental and Meridien hotels
all located close to Unknown Soldier Square, all with around 400
rooms each. A Novotel hotel is due to be built in Nidhal Street. All
are scheduled for completion in the early 1980s. Until then Baghdad
will have a shortage of hotel beds.

Restaurants

All restaurant prices are fixed by the Government. In the following
restaurants a meal costs between ID 2 and ID 5. The price of wine is
between 500 fils (Iraqi) and ID 4 (French).

Fawanis (*Lantern*), Saadoun Street (opposite Babylon cinema).
   Tel: 90522. Popular with expatriates. Good European food.
Pine Palace, off Al-Fath Square. European cuisine.
Strand, on the corner of Saadoun Street and Al-Fath Square. Tel:
   92788. European cuisine.
Candles, Alwiyah, Saadoun Street. Run by the State Organisation for
   Tourism. Mixed European/Iraqi food.
Farouk, Damascus Street (near site of Baghdad International Fair).
   Tel: 32475. European food.
Taj Mahal, Masbah (opposite West German Embassy). Tel: 94479.
Hamurabi, Nidhal Street (behind Dar Al-Salam Hotel). Tel: 90559.
   Iraqi/European food.

Pearl, Zawra Park (opposite Baghdad International Fair site).

Mat'malmata'm, Saadoun Street (close to Ali Baba Square). Arab cuisine.

Babylon Palace Hotel, Nidhal Street (adjacent to Italian Embassy). Italian cuisine.

Al-Rashid Palace, Saadoun Street (opposite Dar Al Salam Hotel). Tel: 92800. European/Arab cuisine.

Garden cafes on the Tigris River along Abu-Nawas Avenue serve fresh *masgouf*. Fish, caught in the river, are cooked right on the river bank on fires fuelled by specially selected wood. Usually the fish is laid out on a slab so that customers can make their own choice.

Night clubs

FIRST CLASS 'A'

Embassy, Al-Masbah (close to Sudan Embassy). Tel: 95971. Faces the Tigris River. International artistes. Restaurant has a good reputation. Bar. Entrance ID 2–5.

Moulin Rouge, on the Rashid Camp road, close to Aqaba Square. Tel: 90809. Mainly Egyptian artistes. Can get a bit rowdy.

FIRST CLASS 'B'

Baghdad Cabaret, adjacent to Aqaba Square. Tel: 97945. Mixed Western/Oriental programme. Restaurant. Bar.

1001 Nights, close to Ali Baba Square.

Airport Baghdad International Airport is a 20-minute drive from the city. Facilities are minimal. Small refreshment bar. Bank. The terminal is being rebuilt and expanded.

Taxis Taxi drivers are supposed to charge official fares, based on a rate per kilometre. But they rarely keep to them, leaving their metres switched off. Fares are instead agreed before each ride. Most drivers charge a minimum 500 fils for a short journey within the city. Usually the fare is ID 1. Trips over the river cost 600 fils minimum. Fares are often doubled after midnight. Fares between the airport and the city (usually ID 2, ID 1.50 if shared) are collected by an airport official who gives the driver a refundable chit. But some visitors are caught unawares and pay both the official and the driver.

Buses Baghdad has a reasonably good public transport system. Main routes are served by a regular double-decker bus service. Tickets, costing 20 fils flat rate, are bought either at kiosks at the main stopping points or on the buses themselves. No. 13 bus serves the

221

whole of Saadoun Street. Buses are supplemented by privately-run minibuses which can be flagged down at green 'Taxi Stops'. Fares range from around ID 30–50.

Car Hire   *Sumer Cars*, Alwiyah, Saadoun Street (opposite Khayam Hotel). Tel: 92143. *Nineveh Car Hire*, Alwiyah, Saadoun Street. *Baghdad Cars*, Al-Assaf Building, Masbah Square (behind West German Embassy). Tel: 97721, 90628.

A self-drive car costs around ID 7 a day, plus 30 fils per kilometre. The daily rate for a car with a driver is about ID 12. Petrols costs between 35–40 fils per litre.

Travel agencies   *Semiramis*, Saadoun Street (opposite Tigris Palace Hotel). Tel: 888114. *Sahara*, Saadoun Street. Tel: 8882451. *Al-Mansour Travel*, Saadoun Street. Tel: 8884316. *Baghdad Tours*, Saadoun Street. Tel: 8888764.

Airlines   Main office: *Iraqi Airways*, Saadoun Street. Tel: 5519999. Telex: 28906. Sales Tel: 8880051.

Most sales offices of other airlines are in the lower end of Saadoun Street: *Aeroflot* (Tel: 8881250), *Air France* (96014), *Air India* (99686), *Alitalia* (8889741), *Austrian Airlines* (96014), *British Airways* (8886446), *Balkan Air* (8888978), *CSA* (94920), *Egyptair* (8885128), *Interflug* (8889789), *Iran Air* (8886567), *KLM* (92397), *Kuwait Air* (8886337), *Lufthansa* (8889721), *Middle East Airlines* (95128), *Pakistan International Airlines* (8887181), *Saudia* (8881269), *Scandinavian Airlines* (95592), *Swissair* (92344), *Syrian Arab Airlines* (96503), *LOT* (90077), *Japan Air* (96503).

Shipping forwarding agencies   *Al-Iktisad Transport*, Salihiya, Karkh. Tel: 33126. *Levant Express Transport*, P.O.B. 3002, Kubba Building, Saadoun Street. Tel: 96014. *Saadoun Transport*, Pachachi Building, South Gate. Tel: 8886035. *United Transport*, Karima Building, Khullani Square, Jumhouriya Street. Tel: 8882206/8880925. *State Company for Land Transport*, Al-Baghdadi Building, Jumhouriya Street, Tel: 68341, *Al-Manar Transport*, Nabeel Al-Dahan, Nidhal Street (opposite Zwaini Showroom).

Post Offices   The main post office is in Rashid Street. Branch offices are in Nidhal Street (opposite Seventh Day Adventists Church), at Alwiyah in Saadoun Street, and off lower Saadoun Street (adjacent to Baghdad Hotel). Poste Restante is in the Nidhal Street office.

Useful phone numbers   *Emergency police* 104. *Ambulance* 122. *Baghdad International Airport* 5518888.

Telex Some hotels have telexes. There is a public telex service at the PTT Office in Rashid Street. A short telex to Western Europe costs around ID 3.

Shops Handicraft: *Rural Crafts* (Ministry of Agriculture), Saadoun Street (close to Ali Baba Square). *Education Ministry Handicrafts Shop*, Saadoun Street (round the corner from Baghdad Hotel). *Centre for Folkloric Handicrafts*, Ali Baba Square. Departmental Store: Orosdi Back, Rashid Street.

Souks Baghdad has two antique bazaars both near the Marjan Mosque—the *Shorja* market, selling all kinds of merchandise, and the Coppersmith market or *Suq al-Safafir*, selling hand-made copper articles. Some high class silver work is sold in a third market—the *Suq al-Sagha* or Silversmiths bazaar at the end of Mustansir Street, close to the Rafidain Bank building. The bazaar is famous for the unique black engravings on silver done by the Sabaen sect which believes that John the Baptist was the last prophet. Adjacent to the bazaar is the gold souk. There is also a silk and textiles market close to the coppersmith market.

Social clubs *Alwiyah Club*, Unknown Soldier Square. Tel: 95115. Used to be the British Club before being taken over by the Iraqis. Mixed Iraqi/expatriate membership. Visitors can be admitted as guests of members. Has good facilities—restaurant, bar, swimming pools, squash court, tennis courts. *New British Club*, Rashid Camp Street (adjacent to the Moulin Rouge night club). P.O.B. 2180. Tel: 93127. Open only to British and Commonwealth citizens. Temporary membership is available from ID 1 a day, but visitors must be signed in by a member. Swimming pool, bar, billiard room, library, film shows. Meals served. Five bedrooms are available to visitors, but they are usually booked up well in advance.

Leisure/sport Baghdad has two public halls—*Shab Hall*, Bab al-Muadham Square, and *Al-Khuld Hall*, Karradat Mariam (Tel: 34022)—where Western musicians and artistes give concerts, as well as the Iraqi National Symphony Orchestra. The Russian-run *School of Music and Ballet* sometimes gives public performances. The city has several art galleries, the biggest of which is the *National Gallery of Modern Art*. The *Iraqi Museum* (close to the railway station) has an excellent collection of relics from the ancient Mesopotamian civilisations. Most cinemas show Arabic or dubbed films. But both the *New British Club* and the *British Council* (7/2/9 Waziriya, behind Saudi and Turkish embassies. Tel: 20091/3) regularly show films in English.

The most popular spectator sports in Baghdad are soccer and horse racing. Internationally, Iraqi football has now reached a high standard. Soccer matches are played regularly at the *Malaab Al-Saab* stadium, near Dhubbat City. During the cooler months, race meetings with betting facilities are held every Sunday, Wednesday and Friday at *Baghdad Race Course* in Al-Mansour City.

The State Organisation for Tourism is building a leisure resort for bathing and water sports on the southern shores of Habbaniya Lake, 53 miles from Baghdad. It will have a 2,000-bed tourist village and Iraq's first de luxe hotel is due to be opened there in February, 1978, with 360 rooms.

Bookshops   Foreign language books are difficult to find in Baghdad. But the following have a selection of books in English and foreign magazines (usually out-of-date): *White House Book Shop*, 26 Nidhal Street (opposite Saadoun Park). *New Book House*, Tahrir Square. *Alwiyah Book Shop*, Alwiyah, Saadoun Street.

Hospitals   *Medical City*, North Gate. Tel: 8889001. The city's main general hospital. *Emergency Hospital*, Alwiyah. Tel: 96971. *Ibn Sina Hospital*, Karradat Mariam-Haifa Street. Tel: 32134. Private hospital with British medical staff.

Pharmacies (24-hour)   Pharmacies on 24-hour duty are announced in the *Baghdad Observer*. Many Western drugs are difficult to obtain because Iraq is trying to build up its own drugs industry.

Banks   Head Offices: *Central Bank of Iraq*, Rashid Street, Shorja. Tel: 8889051. *Rafidain Bank*, Rashid Street, Shorja. Tel: 8889051. *Industrial Bank of Iraq*, Industrial Bank Building, Khullani Square, Tel: 8889761. *Real Estate Bank*, Eqari Bank Building, Al-Sarai (opposite Directorate General of Police). Tel: 8889091. *Agricultural Co-operative Bank*, Rashid Street, Sinak. Tel: 8884191.

Rafidain Bank, the only bank in the country dealing with normal business and commercial transactions, has numerous branches throughout the city.

Ministries   *Ministry of Information*, Tahrir Square. Tel: 69181. *Ministry of Foreign Affairs*, Karradat Mariam. Tel: 300091. *Ministry of Interior*, Karradat Mariam (close to Shawaf Square). Tel: 30030.

Government organisations/departments   *State Organisation for Agricultural Development*, Naji Jewad Building, Saadoun Street (Tel: 92371). *State Organisation for Engineering Industries*, Ismail Al-Tamimi Building, Saadoun Street, close to Unknown Soldier Square. P.O.B. 3093 (96191. Telex: 22261). *State Organisation for Construction Industries*, Ismail Al-Tamimi Building, Saadoun Street, close to

Unknown Soldier Square (96191. Telex: 2236). *State Organisation for Textile Industries*, Rafidain Bank Building, Samawal Street (8889121). *State Organisation for Electricity*, Jumhouriya Street, Nafoora Square P.O.B. 5796. (69771. Telex: 2220).

State Organisation for Chemicals Industries, Khullani Square, Jumhouriya Street (69061. Telex: 2205). *State Organisation for Food Industries*, Camp Sara, Rashid Camp Road. P.O.B. 2301 (7715713. Telex: 2205). *State Organisation for Grains*, Baghdad Chamber of Commerce Building, Mustansir Street (8887146). *State Organisation for Insurance*, Iraq Re-Insurance Building, Khullani Square, Jumhouriya Street (8889981). *State Organisation for Industrial Design & Construction*, Industrial Bank Building, Khullani Street, Sinak (8885191).

General Establishment for Drugs, Mansour City (39171/39010). *State Organisation for Broadcasting & Television*, Karkh, Salihiya (31151). *State Organisation for Exports*, over African–Iraqi Trading Showroom, South Gate, near Jumhouriya Bridge (8884115). *State Organisation for Soil & Land Reclamation*, Abdul Sattar Al-Janabi Building, Orfaliya, Saadoun Street (8880066). *State Organisation for Industrial Development*, Khullani Square (8881990). *State Organisation for Animal Slaughtery*, Kifah Street, Fadhwat Arab, Bab al-Shaikh (60144).

Administration of Traffic Locations Affairs, Shaikh Omar Street, near Thawra Square (61020). *State Organisation for Tharthar Project*, End of 14 Ramadhan Street, Mansour (5517541). *State Organisation of Excavation & Agricultural Stations*, Abu Nawas Street (96101). *State Organisation for Cinema & Theatre*, Karradat Mariam, opposite National Assembly (3136134). *General Trade Establishment for Consumer Materials*, Turaihi Building, Jumhouriya Street, Khullani Square (8888768).

General Trade Establishment for Capital Goods, Dhaman Al-Ajtimaie Building, Jumhouriya Street, Kullani Square (8889703). *State Organisation for Minerals*, opposite Unknown Soldier Square Filling Station, Saadoun Street. P.O.B. 2330 (92361. Telex: 2292). *State Organisation for Technical Industries*, 52nd Street. *Foundation of Scientific Research*, Jadiriya, near University of Baghdad Building, (96747). *State Organisation for Housing*, near the Arab Child's Hospital, Karradat Miriam, Karkh (33161).

State Organisation for Land Transport, near Garage Maslaha No. 5, opposite Mustansiriya University, Waziriya (69191). *State Organisation for Iraqi Water Transport*, Alwiyah, Saadoun Street (95011). *General Organisation for Iraqi Railways*, Damascus Square, Karkh (30011. Telex: 2270). *State Organisation for Distribution of Oil Products & Gas*, Khayam Cinema Street, South Gate (8889911. Telex: 2247).

225

Embassies *Afghanistan*, Wasiriya, Maghrib Street (Tel: 29986). *Algeria*, Karradat Mariam (32181). *Austria*, Masbah, Aqaba Bin-Nafi Square (99032). *Brazil*, Alwiyah, Wathiq Square, 52nd Street (98746). *Britain*, Karkh, Sharia Ud-Din (32121). British Commercial Section, Shaheen Building, Saadoun Street, Kard al-Pasha (99001–3). *Belgium*, Saadoun Park (69301). *Bulgaria*, Al-Harthiya Kindi Street (31212). *Bangladesh*, Masbah (90063). *People's Republic of China*, Karradat Mariam-Haifa Street (33770). *Czechoslovakia*, Karradat Mariam-Haifa Street (37890). *Cuba*, Masbah 19/B/36 (95048). *Denmark*, Alwiyah (93058). *Egypt*, Karradat Mariam (34127). *Finland*, Masbah (96172). *France*, Karrada Dakhil-Kard Al-Pasha (96061). *Germany (East)*, Masbah (90071). *Germany (West)*, Masbah (92037). *Greece*, 52nd Street, near Al-Wathiq Market (96729). *Hungary*, Karradat Mariam (357790). *Iran*, Karradat Mariam-Haifa Street (33095). *India*, Adhamiyah-Taha Street, Najeed Pasha (22014). *Indonesia*, Alwiyah, Wathiq Street (98677).

Italy, Alwiyah, Nidhal Street (95143). *Japan*, Masbah (95156). *Jordan*, Karradat Mariam (33185). *Korea (North)*, Karrada Al-Sharkiya, Al-Fath Square (98021). *Kuwait*, Karradat Mariam-Haifa Street (33151). *Lebanon*, Masbah-Hussam Al-Din Street (99019). *Libya*, Mansour, Main Mansour Street (5518590). *Morocco*, Karradat Mariam (38151). *Netherlands*, Saadoun Park, Nidhal Street (8887175). *Pakistan*, Karradat Mariam (35191). *Poland*, Masbah (90296). *Qatar*, Masbah (96144). *Rumania*, Masbah (98644).

Republic of Central Africa, Mansour, Zaitoun Street (5516520). *Saudi Arabia*, Waziriya-Safi Al-Din Al-Hilly Street (20036). *Sri Lanka*, Alwiyah (93040). *Spain*, Masbah (92851). *Sweden*, Nidhal Street (95391). *Switzerland*, Karradah Al-Sharkiah (98170). *Syria*, Masbah Square (95130). *Sudan*, Masbah (99007). *United Arab Emirates*, Mansour (5515206). *Somalia*, Masbah (90077).

Tunisia, Mansour (5517786). *Turkey*, Waziriya-Safi Al-Din Al-Hilly Street (20021). *U.S.S.R.* Karradat Mariam-Haifa Street (34350). *Vietnam*, Al-Mansour Daoudi (511388). *Yemen (North)*, Masbah (98420). *Yemen (South)*, Masbah (96027). *Yugoslavia*, Bustan Kabba, Saadoun Street (95913).

Media Most foreign newspapers are banned in Iraq and Western papers are virtually impossible to buy. Some bookshops sell a few Western general and specialist magazines and occasionally copies of *Newsweek* and *Paris Match* are allowed in. The *British Council Library* (7/2/9 Waziriya) has a fairly wide selection of English-language weekly and monthly periodicals.

Baghdad Observer, the city's only English language daily paper, has little foreign news. Iraqi TV and radio has a nightly news bulletin in English, usually around 10 o'clock.

Newspapers/periodicals

Dailies: *Baghdad Observer*. English. P.O. Box 257, Karantina (Tel: 69721). *Al-Jumhuriya*. Arabic. Karantina. 30,000 circulation. *Al-Riyadhi*. Published by the Ministry of Youth. 30,000 circ. *Al-Iraq*. Kurdish. P.O. Box 5717. 30,000 circ. *Al-Thawra*. Arabic. Aqaba Bin-Nafi Square, P.O. Box 2009 (Organ of the Baath Party). 50,000 circ. *Tarik al-Shaab*. Saadoun (Organ of the Iraqi Communist Party). *Al-Mou Laeib*. 8,000 circ.

Periodicals: *Al-Fikr al-Jadid*. Weekly. 25,000 circ. *Alif Ba*. Weekly. Karantina, 6,000 circ. *Al-Mutafarrij*. Weekly. P.O. Box 409, Rashid Street. *Al-Iqtisad al-Iraqi*. Monthly. 12,000 circ. *Al-Amal al-Shaabi*. Arabic monthly. Directorate of People's Work. *Al-Naft Wal Aalam* (Oil and the World). Monthly. Published by Iraq National Oil Company. *Al-Thaqafat al-Jadida*. Arabic monthly. Published by Ministry of Culture & Information. 6,000 circ. *Commerce*. Quarterly. Chamber of Commerce. (Also weekly bulletin dealing in commodity prices/market conditions.) *Iraq Government Gazette*. Arabic and English editions weekly. Published by Ministry of Information. *L'Opinion de Baghdad*. Bi-monthly. French. Dar el-Jamaheer de Presse, P.O. Box 4074. *Al-Sinai*. Arabic and English quarterly. Published by Iraqi Federation of Industries, P.O. Box 5665. *Saut al-Fallah*. Weekly. Organ of General Federation of Peasant Societies. *Waal Ummal*. Weekly. Iraq Trades Union organ. General Federation of Trade Unions in Iraq, Gialani Street, Sinak. P.O. Box 2307. 30,000 circ. *Iraq Today*. Fortnightly. English. Published by Ministry of Information.

Churches A few of Baghdad's churches are still located in the old Christian quarter of the city called Agd Al-Nasara (Christians Alley), off Rashid Street, south of Marjan Square. But several modern churches have since been built in various parts of Baghdad. *Armenian Catholic Church*, Christians Alley. *Armenian Orthodox Church*, Tayaran Square. *Chaldean Church*, Christians Alley. *St. Fatima's Church* (Catholic), Karradat Mariam. *Iraqi Protestant Church*, Nidhal Street. *St. George's Church* (Anglican), Baghdad West (Karradat Mariam). *St. Joseph's Church* (Catholic), Rekhaita–Inner Karradah. *Syriac Orthodox Church*, Tunis Street. *Syriac Catholic Church*, Alwiyah. *Seventh Day Adventists Church*, Nidhal Street. *Greek Orthodox Church*, Gailani Camp.

Useful addresses

Baghdad Chamber of Commerce, Mustansir Street. Tel: 8886111.
Federation of Iraqi Chambers of Commerce, Baghdad Chamber of Commerce Building, Mustansir Street. Tel: 8888819.
Federation of Iraqi Industries, Khullani Square.

Iraqi Fairs Administration, Baghdad International Fair, Damascus Street, Al-Mansour. Tel: 37130/31. Cable: ALMAARIDH.

Directorate General of Police, Al Sarai. Tel: 8885111.

Directorate General of Customs, Karradat Mariam. Tel: 34161.

Directorate of Residence, 52nd Street. Tel: 92377.

State Organisation for Tourism, Alwiyah, Saadoun Street, Tel (Enquiries): 99306. Telex: 2265.

Interpreter/translation services: *Albert Nisan*, Gharibjan Building, Shorja. P.O.B. 11034. Tel: 8886888. *Khayam Advertising Bureau*, Mubjir Jassim Building, Al-Fath Square. P.O.B. 5681. Tel: 99215. *Khalid al-Ani*, Paiha Building, Jumhouriya Street. P.O.B. 3119. Tel: 8887835/66544.

BASRA Iraq's second largest city 345 miles south of Baghdad. Estimated population 915,000. It is situated on the west bank of the Shatt al-Arab in the date growing region of south Iraq and is the country's only general port. Traditionally it has been known as the 'Venice of the East' because of its many waterways and bridges, and it is linked with the legend of Sindbad the Sailor of *A Thousand and One Nights*. Over the last decade it has become the country's industrial centre and among Iraqis it is known as the nation's 'work shop'. Basra lies close to the country's biggest oil fields and oil is the main industry in the area. The city has an oil refinery. Other industries in the area include paper and flour milling, date packing, boat building, pressing and baling of liquorice and the manufacture of bricks, soft drinks and artificial fertilisers. An industrial complex, including petrochemical plants and a steel mill, is being built 25 miles south of the city at Khor al-Zubair. A new port is being constructed further south at Umm Qasr.

Though the city dates back to A.D. 636, Basra is about the most modern of Iraq's large cities with a prevalence of contemporary buildings. A lot of construction work is still going on. But relics of the city's long history are still evident, especially of the time when it served as the Ummayyad capital of Iraq and of the Abbasid period when it was a flourishing centre of trade and literature. The city is divided into three areas—Basra town, Ashar (the business centre) and Maaqal (the port). Basra town still has some old houses standing which are fine examples of Islamic architecture. Sindbad Island, legendary base of Sindbad, is in Maaqal. Within the city there are some interesting shrines dating back to the early Islamic period. These include the shrines of Talha Bin Sirin and Al-Zubair, both companions of the Prophet.

Among the extensive date groves surrounding Basra there are several historic places. Nine miles from the present city lies the site of Old Basra which contains the ruins of the Imam Ali mosque. To the north of Basra is Al-Qurna, where the Tigris joins the Euphrates. This is the legendery spot of the Garden of Eden and even has a tree called Adam's Tree.

North of the city also are the marshes of the three south eastern governorates of Thiqar, Basra and Maisan. Intense heat and humidity from April to September and strong winter winds make March and October the best months for a visit to this attractive area. The inhabitants live in reed huts and use reed canoes—the only mode of transport through the narrow waterways. It is also well-known for its wild life, especially water birds. Not far from Nasiriya, is the town of Chebayish, built on a multitude of small islands linked by bridges.

Hotels

Shatt Al-Arab Hotel, Maaqil, Built around 30 years ago but still Basra's main hotel. Located in the port area overlooking the Shatt al-Arab. Foyer tends to get crowded because the hotel is used as a terminal for Basra airport. Room for single person costs ID 5–7. Restaurant. Bar.

Ur Hotel, Istiklal Street, Ashar. Newer and more centrally located than the Shatt al-Arab. Single person ID 5–7. Restaurant. Bar.

A Sheraton hotel with 150 rooms and a Novotel hotel are due to be built in Basra but unlikely to be completed before 1980.

Restaurants

Ali-Baba, Watany Street. Arab/European food.
Koremana, Watany Street. Arab/European cuisine.
Restaurant Governorate Recreation Centre, Dinar Street.

The waterfront along the Shatt al-Arab has numerous small cafes which serve snacks with beer. Some have small casinos.

Airport Conveniently located close to the Maaqal area of the city.

Travel agencies *Basrah World Tours*, Istiklal Street, Ashar. Tel: 4444.

Souks Handicraft work by the people of the nearby marshes can be bought in the main souk.

Social clubs Some foreign and Iraqi companies have social clubs which visitors, accompanied by a member, can use.

Leisure/sports Basra University has a public hall where concerts are sometimes held. There is a race course 12 miles outside the city.

MOSUL Northern Iraq's largest city with a population of around 900,000. Lies about 250 miles north of Baghdad on the west bank of the River Tigris in an agriculturally rich region which relies mainly on natural rainfall. It is known as the 'City of the two springs' because its moderate climate makes autumn similar to a second spring. Mosul is a communications centre linking the country with Syria, Turkey and Europe by road and rail.

The city has many fine old buildings reflecting its long history stretching back to 410 B.C., when it was first mentioned by the Greek traveller Xenophon. It was predominantly Christian until Islamic forces captured it in A.D. 640. But it still has a large Christian population. Under the Ummayyads and Abbasids it was an important strategic city in which trade and industry flourished.

Some of the more imposing buildings include two 12th century mosques—Al-Kabeer Mosque (The Great Mosque) with a leaning minaret, and Al-Mujahidi Mosque with its ornamented dome. The 13th century Mausoleum of Imam Yayha Abul Qasim has some remarkable arabesque decorations in plaster and blue marble. There are also ancient churches and monasteries. The Mar Gurgis monastery, to the north of the city, was probably built in the 7th century and Mar Behnam monastery 21 miles southeast of Mosul was built beside a 4th century tomb which is reputed to contain the remains of a son of an Assyrian king.

Traditionally Mosul has been famous for its textiles, copper articles and inlaid craftworks. The word 'muslin' is derived from "mosulian". Today textiles are still an important industry in the city. But it also produces cement, leather, bricks and refined sugar.

The city is close to the summer resorts of the northern mountains and to the sites of several famous ancient cities.

These include the Assyrian cities of Ashur (62 miles to the south), Khorsabad (16 miles to the north), Nimrud (22 miles southeast of the city), and Nineveh opposite Mosul on the other side of the river.

At **Nimrud,** founded in 883 B.C., stand the remains of the seven-storey ziggurat, the temples and palaces with their strange lion symbols, human-headed and eagle-winged, and the canal which once brought water from the Greater Zab river. **Nineveh** had its golden age in the seventh century B.C., when King Sennacherib embellished it with zoological and botanical gardens. Excavations at what is today called Tel-Kuyunjik have recovered a library of 35,000 cuneiform tablets on religious, literary and scientific subjects, some of them Assyrian translations of Sumerian and Babylonian works. The most clearly visible relics of **Nineveh** are the walls and what is left of their 15 gates, dedicated to the gods of the age. Some are still guarded by enormous statues of winged bulls.

Around 56 miles east of Mosul is **Arbil** whose history can be traced back to 2,000 B.C. It is considered to be one of the oldest continually inhabited cities in the world. Near Arbil are the mountain resorts of Salahuddin and Shaqlawa which contain tourist villages of chalets, restaurants and night clubs.

Hotels

Station Hotel, Railway Station. Tel: 3083. Located right in the railway station. 31 rooms. Single person around ID 4–5. Restaurant.

Al-Hidara Al-Mahaliya Hotel, Cornish Street. Tel: 71151. Faces onto the Tigris River. Run by the local governorate. 71 rooms. Single person around ID 5–7. Restaurant. Bar.

Rafidain Hotel, Wadi Hajar. Tel: 71121. Small modest hotel of 10 rooms.

Souks   Main bargains in the city's souks are the locally-made carpets and textiles.

KIRKUK   One of the main centres of Iraq's oil industry. Though originally an Assyrian ancient city, it had little importance until oil was discovered nearby in 1927. It is surrounded by giant gas flares which light up the oil wells at night. The city is 114 miles southeast of Mosul and 180 miles directly north of Baghdad. Over the last few decades Kirkuk's population has grown rapidly and now totals around 600,000. About the only historical attraction is the city's old castle which used to serve as a garrison for Ottoman troops.

About 43 miles east of Kirkuk in the Kurdish region, is the mountainous city of **Sulaimaniya,** which has a population of 540,000. It stands in an area of forests and fruit orchards which has made it a popular holiday resort. The surrounding mountains have a rich green vegetation in the summer but are usually covered with snow in the winter.

Hotels

Kirkuk Hotel, City Centre. Tel: 6614. Recently taken over by the State Organisation for Tourism. 61 rooms. Single room ID 5, single person in double room ID 7. Restaurant. Bar. Casino.

Station Hotel, Railway Station. Tel: 2566. 13 rooms.

GENERAL INFORMATION

How to get there BY AIR: *Iraqi Airways* runs four flights a week to and from Baghdad and London, three to and from Paris, two to and from Copenhagen, Athens and Geneva and weekly flights to and from Belgrade, Rome, Madrid, Vienna, Munich, Frankfurt, Amsterdam and Brussels. It also has three flights a week to and from Beirut and Cairo, and regular flights between Baghdad and Damascus, Amman, Khartoum, Tripoli, Tunis, Algiers and Casablanca. Flights go regularly to Eastern European capitals and to India and the Far East.

Other airlines give Baghdad additional direct connections with most European and Far East capitals. There are only indirect air links with North America.

OVERLAND/SEA: Iraq is accessible by road from Kuwait, Saudi Arabia, Jordan, Syria, Turkey and Iran. The Baghdad–Kotchek railway line can provide connections with Aleppo, Beirut, Ankara and Istanbul from where trains can be taken into Europe. The *P & O/ Strick Line* operates a passenger/cargo service to Basra.

INTER-GULF/DOMESTIC SERVICES: There are daily flights between Baghdad and Kuwait. *Iraqi Airways* and other airlines provide several flights a week between Baghdad and Bahrain, Abu Dhabi, Dubai and Tehran. There are flights at least twice a week to and from Jeddah, Dhahran and Doha.

Iraqi Airways operates a daily service between Baghdad and Basra and Mosul. *Iraqi Railways* run trains from Baghdad to Basra, Mosul and Kirkuk. A branch line on the Baghdad–Basra route goes to Kerbala. The rail journey to Basra can take up to 10 hours and costs around ID 14.

Visas Visas are required by all visitors except nationals of Iraq, Algeria, Bahrain, Egypt, Jordan, Kuwait, Lebanon (with passports issued after March 31, 1975), Libya, Mauritania, Morocco, Oman, Qatar, Saudi Arabia, Somalia, Sudan, Syria, Tunisia, United Arab Emirates, North Yemen, South Yemen, and Yugoslavia. Applications for visas should be made well in advance of travelling and usually should be accompanied by a written invitation to visit Iraq from an official organisation. Admission and transit is refused to all holders of Israeli passports, of passports containing a declaration that it is valid for Israel and/or a visa for Israel or any data that a passenger has been to Israel.

Visitors must register for stays exceeding 14 days and exit visas are required for visits exceeding 30 days. Registration is made with the Directorate of Residence, 52nd Street. Tel: 92377.

Languages Arabic is the official language. Minority groups in the north speak Turkish and Kurdish and Farsi is spoken in the East. Most well-educated Iraqis speak English which is the main foreign language. French and German are becoming more widely used as second languages.

Hours of business Friday is the weekly holiday when government offices and business concerns are closed. A few Christian firms are closed on Sunday. Government offices work from 0800–1400 Saturday to Wednesday and from 0800–1300 on Thursday in summer; in winter they work from 0830–1430 Saturday to Wednesday and 0830–1330 on Thursday. Shops and business firms open from 0800–1400 and 1700–1900 from Saturday to Wednesday, from 0800–1300 on Thursday in summer; in winter they work from 0830–1430 and 1700–1900 from Saturday to Wednesday and 0830–1330 Thursday. Banks open in summer 0800–1200 Saturday to Wednesday, 0800–1100 Thursday; in winter they work from 0900–1200 on Thursday.

Official holidays In the list below the Muslim holidays, marked with an asterisk, are only approximate since they depend upon sightings of the moon. As a result they may differ by one or more days from the dates given. Usually Muslim holidays occur 10 to 11 days earlier than the previous year.

233

				1977/78
Id al-Adha*	... ...	...	...	22–26 November
Al-Hijra (Muslim New Year)*	...	...	...	12 December
Al-Ashura*	... ...	...	...	21 December
New Year's Day ...	... ...	...	...	1 January 1978
Army Day	... ...	...	...	6 January
Anniversary of 1963 Revolution		...	...	8 February
Prophet's Birthday*	... ...	...	...	25 February
Nairuz ...	... ...	...	...	21 March
Labour Day	... ...	...	...	1 May
National Day	... ...	...	...	14 July
Baath Revolution Day	...	...	...	17 July
Id al-Fitr (end of Ramadan)*	...	...	...	3–6 September

Time GMT+3.

Electricity 220V, AC50 cycles.

Health International certificates of vaccination are required for smallpox for visitors who have left or transited infected areas. Though cholera immunisation is only required for visitors from infected areas, a cholera jab is advisable as well as vaccination against typhoid.

Water In Baghdad and large towns tap water is generally safe to drink, even though it can be cloudy and have deposits.

Post Air mail letters between Iraq and Western Europe usually take between four and nine days. Surface mail is subject to lengthy delays, with parcels taking over two months to arrive.

Telecommunications Local calls in Baghdad and other large cities can usually be made reasonably quickly but calls between cities can be difficult. International links are good and calls are not generally delayed for long. It is advisable to make them during the day. Calls to Western Europe cost around ID 5 for the first minute and ID 1 for every minute after that.

Currency The basic unit is the Iraqi Dinar (ID) which is divided into 1,000 fils. The following denominations are in circulation: Notes; $\frac{1}{4}$, $\frac{1}{2}$, 1, 5 and 10 Dinars. Coins; 1, 5, 10, 25, 50 and 100 fils.

Currency regulations Local currency up to ID 25 and unlimited amounts of foreign (except Israeli) currency can be brought in, as long as it is declared on arrival. Export of local currency is restricted to ID 5 and to the amount of foreign currency imported and declared.

Customs regulations Visitors are allowed to bring in duty-free 100 cigarettes or 50 cigars or 250 grammes of tobacco, one litre of wine or spirits, and half a litre of perfume. The import of most foreign newspapers and magazines is banned and they will be confiscated on arrival. Typewriters are also liable to be confiscated and only returned to the owner on departure. Customs officials also tend to be suspicious of cameras.

Local dishes *Kubba* is a popular northern dish, made from *borghul* or crushed boiled wheat. Borghul is mixed with minced meat and then flattened before being shaped into a round ball. This is stuffed with nuts, sultanas, spices, parsley and onion before being cooked. *Dolma* is made from stuffed vine leaves, cabbage, lettuce, onions, eggplants, marrow or cucumbers with a stuffing of rice, and spiced meat. *Qouzi* consists of a small lamb boiled whole and then grilled with a stuffing of rice, minced meat and spices.

In Baghdad fish from the River Tigris is cooked right on the river bank and served as a dish called *masgouf*. The fires are fuelled by specially selected wood which helps to make the fish extra tasty. It is served crisp at the edges and succulent in the middle. Throughout Iraq traditional Arab dishes like *kebab* and *shawarma* (sometimes called *guss*) are popular.

Alcohol Alcohol is freely available in the main cities. In Baghdad a large glass of locally brewed draught beer costs around 300 fils. Bottled beer is slightly higher in price. In liquor stores Mosul wine costs around 550 fils and a bottle of whisky about ID 5. Restaurants serve Iraqi, Russian and French wines.

Useful advice Iraq is very security conscious. Visitors are advised to carry their passports at all times. Be careful when taking photographs, especially in the vicinity of public buildings.

It is generally considered polite to wear a jacket and tie when visiting Government officials. Dark lounge suits are worn on formal social occasions. Dinner jackets are rarely needed.

From the end of October to mid-April, most people wear medium-weight clothing. A raincoat or light top coat is a useful precaution as well as a pullover for cold spells. In summer months light-weight clothes are essential, preferably tropical clothing with cotton shirts and underwear.

Further reading *Area Handbook for Iraq*. Foreign Area Studies, The American University. Washington D.C. 1971. *Iraq: Its People, Its Society, Its Culture*, by George Harris. Connecticut. 1958. *Four Centuries of Modern Iraq*, by Stephen Longrigg. Beirut. 1968.

Independent Iraq, by Majid Khadduri. Oxford University Press. 1960. *Republican Iraq* (since 1958), by Majid Khadduri. Oxford University Press. 1969. *A Modern History of Iraq*, by Phebe Marr. Praeger, New York. 1975.

Guests of the Sheikh: An Ethnology of an Iraqi Village, by Elizabeth Fernea. Robert Hale, London. 1968. *The Marsh Arabs*, by Wilfrid Thesiger. Longmans. 1964.

The Role of Government in the Industrialization of Iraq, 1950–1965. Frank Cass. London. 1972. *Progress and Planning*, by Professor B. Zaremba. Baghdad. 1975. *Iraq.* Chase World Information Series. New York (in preparation).

Revolution Command Council

Chairman	Ahmad Hasan Bakr
Deputy Chairman	Saddam Husain Takriti
Members	Saadoun Ghaidan
	Izzat Ibrahim Douri
	Taha Yasin Ramadan
Secretary-General (non-member)	Muhyi Abdel-Husain

Government

President, Prime Minister, and Minister of Defence ...	Ahmad Hasan Bakr
Deputy Chairman of the RCC	Saddam Husain Takriti
Vice-President	Taha Muhieddin Maarouf
Interior	Izzat Ibrahim Douri
Oil	Tayeh Abdel-Karim
Communications	Saadoun Ghaidan
Foreign Affairs	Saadoun Hamadi
Public Works & Housing ...	Taha Yasin Ramadan
Transport	Aziz Rashid Aqrawi
Information	Tareq Aziz
Finance	Fauzi Qaisi
Agriculture & Agrarian Reform	Latif Nasif Qassem
Industry & Minerals	Najib Muhammad Khalil
Health	Riyad Ibrahim Husain
Justice	Munzer Ibrahim Shawi
Labour & Social Affairs ...	Bakr Mahmoud Rasoul
Trade	Hasan Ali Amri
Planning	Adnan Husain Hamdani
Youth	Karim Mahmoud Husain
Higher Education & Scientific Research	Mohammad Sadeq Mashat

Education	Mohammad Mahjoub
Waqfs (Religious Endowments)	Ahmad Abdes-Sattar Jawari
Irrigation	Mukarram Jamal Talbani
Minister of State for Foreign Affairs	Hamed Alwan Jebouri
Head of the Office of the RCC Deputy Chairman	Ghanem Abdel-Jalil
Minister of State, Kurdish Affairs	Burhaneddin Abder-Rahman
Ministers of State	Ubaidalla Mustafa Barzani
	Abdullah Ismail Ahmad
	Amer Abdullah
	Naim Haddad
	Taher Taufiq
	Abdel-Fattah Muhammad Amin
	Saadoun Shaker
	Jaafar Qassem Hammoudi
	Abdullah Fadl
	Adnan Khairullah
	Hikmat Azzawi
	Muhammad Ayesh
	Muhyi Abdel-Husain

237

KINDLY MENTION

The Gulf Handbook

WHEN WRITING TO OUR ADVERTISERS

KUWAIT

THE AMIR OF KUWAIT

THE AMIR OF KUWAIT

His Highness Shaikh Sabah al-Salim al-Sabah

Shaikh Sabah succeeded and assumed power on the death of his brother, Shaikh Abdullah al-Salim al-Sabah, on 24 November 1965. Shaikh Sabah was born in 1915. After extensive studies, particularly in subjects related to religion, law and Islamic literature, he was appointed successively Chief of Police and Head of the Department of Public Security in 1938. He occupied these offices for 21 years during which he also held a variety of other public responsibilities, including Director of the Foreign Affairs Department, before it became a Ministry, on 3 October 1961. Shaikh Sabah was appointed Minister of Foreign Affairs on 17 January 1962. Later that year he was appointed Deputy Prime Minister. On 27 January 1963 Shaikh Sabah was given the responsibility of forming the first Government. Shaikh Sabah was appointed Head of State in 1965 after having been chosen as Heir Apparent on 29 October 1962.

Kuwait

Area   6,880 square miles

Population   1,055,000 (1976 census)

Chief towns   Kuwait City (capital) 80,405; Hawalli 106,542

Gross National Product $12,826 million (1976 estimate)

GNP per caput $12,565

GEOGRAPHY

The mainland state of Kuwait covers an area of 10,000 square miles, to which must be added 625 square miles of islands, including Failaka, located just to the east of Kuwait Bay, and the group of eight islands at the mouth of the Shatt al-Arab waterway dividing Iraq and Iran, of which Bubiyan is the biggest. Kuwait also administers half of the 3,500 square mile Neutral or Partitioned Zone, on its southern border, the other half being administered by Saudi Arabia.

The country consists primarily of flat desert. It lacks any permanent source of natural irrigation in the form of rivers or streams, although it is dotted with a number of oases, the largest of which is Al-Jahra, 18 miles west of Kuwait city. The land slopes gently from east to west. Much of the surface is flat but there are a few rocky hills varying in height from 180 to 300 metres above sea level. Some parts of the desert have shallow depressions.

Kuwait city lies at the southern entrance to the bay of Kuwait which is 20 miles long and 10 miles wide. It provides one of the few natural harbours in the north of the Gulf and its deep-water inlet has been a traditional anchorage for boats.

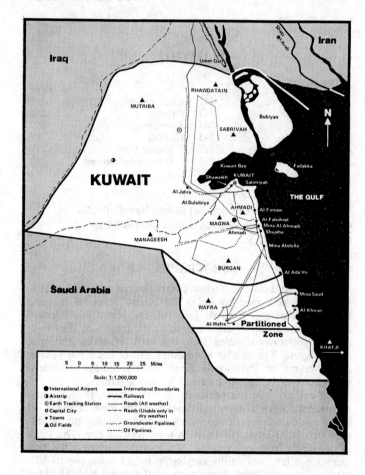

Scale: 1:1,000,000

● International Airport — International Boundaries
◑ Airstrip ▭▭▭ Railways
⊕ Earth Tracking Station —— Roads (All weather)
○ Capital City – – – Roads (Usable only in dry weather)
● Towns ······ Groundwater Pipelines
▲ Oil Fields – – – – Oil Pipelines

CLIMATE

Summers in Kuwait can be extremely harsh. Between May and October the average maximum shade temperature is around 38°C (100°F). In July temperatures in the shade can go up to 50°C (122°F) or even higher. At the same time humidity is high,

244

sometimes rising to 90 per cent during July and August because of the increased evaporation of water from the Gulf. The winters are generally pleasant. In January the maximum shade temperatures range between 7°C and 20°C (45° to 60°F). But the nights can be cold, and occasionally there is a frost.

Throughout the year Kuwait is affected by winds. In the winter a cold north wind brings rain. But it alternates with a south wind blowing from the Indian Ocean which is warm though often sandy. In the summer, this wind raises the humidity. The most irritating wind comes from the southwest bringing with it sandstorms which have originated in the deserts of central Saudi Arabia. The dust can cloud the air for long periods. Kuwait has a rainy season stretching from November to March. Rainfall averages around six inches annually and most of it tends to fall in the early spring.

PLANTS AND WILDLIFE

Kuwait's plant- and wildlife has been copiously documented by interested expatriates and Kuwaitis and what was once regarded as being scarce has now been shown to be relatively abundant. A natural history group in the oil centre of Ahmadi has, for example, recorded no less than 373 desert flowers and has even had a new discovery verified by the Royal Botanical Gardens of London and Edinburgh. The group has also listed more than 260 species or sub-species of birds.

The country's arid parts seem to be far more receptive to flora and shrubs than other desert areas. The flowers bloom during Kuwait's short spring season when the rains suddenly turn the desert into a colourful panorama. Springtime annuals include the daisy, various species of thistle, vetches and the convolvulus. The moisture revives perennials like the tamarisk, the cornulaca and the anastatica. As soon as the rain arrives, they expand to release their seeds, and when the intense heat of the summer comes they adopt a form aimed at keeping water loss to a minimum. The leaves of some plants for example develop a felted or hairy surface to gain some insulation from the hot atmosphere.

Wildlife in Kuwait has to some extent been helped by the country's rapid development in recent years. The growing of gardens along the coast and further inland has provided more cover for birds and more plants for insects. Migrant birds which used to fly over Kuwait are now using it as a stopping-point.

Desert animals   But the country's economic expansion has also led to an upsurge in hunting. Several desert animals are now virtually extinct because of it. Gazelles used to roam the desert in hundreds but now there are few left. The oryx has disappeared and the ibex is rare. The badger-like ratel, the fox and civet cat are seen only in isolated parts. A few wolves have been left to prowl the deep desert. The Somali ostrich used to be common but it has not been seen since 1940. Its disappearance however may have been due to environmental influences rather than hunting.

The jackal is still a danger to the sheep and goats of Bedouin herdsmen. The desert also has hares and golden sand rabbits. Rodents like the jerboa, porcupine, mouse and rat are common. Small hedgehogs can sometimes be found scavenging among the rocks.

New greenery in the urban and industrial areas of Kuwait has made the country a favourite staging place for a wide variety of migratory birds. Some are even now staying to breed. The more spectacular migrants include the rose-ringed parakeet which moves between the southern end of the Arabian Peninsula and the Levant and the golden oriole which flies to and from East Africa and Europe. An osprey was spotted once but did not stay for long.

Of the numerous species recorded by the Ahmadi natural history group, about 85 are considered common, the majority being migratory. The average Kuwaiti garden would have robins, warblers, song thrushes and sparrows. Swallows, swifts, hoopoes, kestrels and crested larks, bulbuls and collared doves are frequent sights. In the coastal areas flamingoes, crab plovers and terns are found. Other birds considered less common include the parakeet, pied flycatcher, peregrine falcon, and the moorhen. The imperial eagle, the ring ouzel and the hubara bustard, once the ornithological symbol of the Arabian Peninsula, are among 60 types listed as being very rare.

In the desert, insects like mosquitos, roaches, ants, beetles and mantids are common. Also a variety of butterflies and moths breed there, as well as the scorpion and its enemy the sapulgid.

Lizards include large types like the Dabh and the monitor both of which can grow up to three feet in length. The most dangerous snakes are the sand cobra and the viper which usually moves around only at night time.

COMMUNICATIONS

Kuwait has one of the highest ratios in the Middle East for vehicles per head of population. There are over 300,000 vehicles, three-quarters of them passenger cars. The Government's major problem has been to prevent such a large number of vehicles clogging up the country's roads.

With the great majority of the population living in and around Kuwait city, the main objective of the country's road construction programme has been the building up of an efficient urban network. A ring road has been constructed on the outskirts of the city. A four-lane highway on reclaimed land on the shore line aims to syphon off commuter traffic between the residential and business centres. Generally new roads within the city area have helped to reduce traffic congestion which is now mainly confined to the inevitable rush-hour crawl. But Kuwait city has become dominated by the motor car and the pedestrian tends to be forgotten with some new roads lacking pavements.

Motorways link the city with the country's main oil fields, in particular Ahmadi, the headquarters of Kuwait Oil Company. Iraq and Saudi Arabia are both connected to the country by highways.

Kuwait has a relatively large international airport which can not only handle the world's biggest jets but also service them. The airport has a mammoth hangar-workshop which can strip, repair and reassemble most aircraft. The Kuwait Airways Corporation (KAC) runs regular flights to Europe and the Indian sub-continent.

There are two ports, the largest being Shuwaikh, one mile west of Kuwait city. The second port of Shuaiba, 30 miles south of the city, has a commercial harbour and a smaller one for service vessels and fishing trawlers. A 3,280-feet pier at the harbour approach is used to load shipments from the nearby refinery of the Kuwait National Petroleum Company. A few miles north is Mina al-Ahmadi, the country's main oil terminal.

Kuwait has a reasonably efficient local and international tele-communications service, though there has been a shortage of new lines and equipment. An earth satellite station in the middle of the desert at Umm Al-Aish, 55 miles north of Kuwait city, gives the country direct links with most of Europe. Another station, which is about to come into operation, will provide a direct connection with North America.

SOCIAL BACKGROUND

The population of Kuwait has shown extremely rapid growth in recent years, reaching 1,055,000 by 1976. Eleven years earlier the population had numbered only 467,339, rising to 738,662 by 1970. The increase is largely attributable to an influx of foreign workers to Kuwait, drawn by its need for expatriate labour and the relatively high salaries available. By 1975 foreign residents were estimated to have reached 521,169, representing 53.6 per cent of the population and some 70–75 per cent of the workforce. The proportion of non-Kuwaitis in the total population is also rising as a result of a growth rate of about seven per cent a year, while that of the Kuwaiti population is put at about 2.3 per cent a year. This poses a number of serious political questions, especially concerning the rights of non-Kuwaitis. At present non-Kuwaitis, however long they have resided in the country, are not even allowed to own property, homes or places of work, while also being deprived of free education, although they do benefit from the free health service. Senior appointments are also restricted to Kuwaitis, keeping the incomes available to non-Kuwaitis at a lower level. There is a strong fear among some Kuwaitis that they may lose ultimate political control to outsiders.

Of the foreign communities in Kuwait, much the biggest is Jordanian and Palestinian, which rose by 90 per cent between 1965 and 1970 to number 147,696, representing 20 per cent of the total population. Iraqi and Iranian communities each account for a further five per cent of the population, although their rate of growth has been less rapid and the demand for labour in their country of origin has been making Iranian labour harder to find. The Egyptian community rose in size from 11,021 to 30,421 between 1965 and 1970, becoming the fourth biggest foreign community, but there are also substantial numbers of Syrians, Lebanese, Omanis, Saudis and Yemenis from both the North and the South. There are, in addition, large numbers of Indians and Pakistanis, who represent the biggest non-Arab communities. Most of the Palestinians, Egyptians and Lebanese have white collar jobs. Other non-Kuwaiti Arabs, Iranians, Indians and Pakistanis do most of the industrial work. Many workers from the Indian sub-continent come to Kuwait on short-term contracts.

Emerging liberalism The Kuwaiti population still displays a sharp contrast between the old and the new, between traditionalism and a Western-orientated liberalism. These two opposing elements are mainly represented by the old desert tribal culture and the modern urban population which has absorbed Western ideas.

The strong traditionalism is reflected in a spartan austerity inherited from the desert Arab and in a lingering puritanism which is similar to the Wahhabism of Saudi Arabia. But the country's trading history and long experience of commerce has made it highly adaptable to new economic forces and technological advances.

The patriarchal system, in which all authority is entrusted to the Amir and his family, is still supremely powerful. The establishment of the National Assembly in 1961 created a form of constitutional monarchy but when it clashed too strongly with the Amir and his Government it was dissolved. Until fairly recently all the top Government posts were held by the Sabah family. Now members of Kuwait's newly emerging technocracy are being appointed to ministerial positions.

Slowly the country's power structure is beginning to change. For a long time the Sabah family ruled with the backing of the merchant class and together the two groups dominated the country. In recent years the merchant class has had to compete with the new industrialists, financiers and bureaucrats who have grown in strength as Kuwait has developed into a modern state.

Advantages for Kuwaitis Around 50 per cent of all workers in Kuwait are employed by the Government and most Kuwaiti workers have Government jobs. Many of these, with some

Government encouragement, run businesses. So Government officials will also tend to be entrepreneurs as well, either in commerce or industry. There are big opportunities for any Kuwaiti wanting to enter business because of restrictions on foreigners owning property or commercial premises.

In addition to their earnings from outside businesses, Kuwaiti workers also tend to be better paid than expatriates which can cause friction. But the younger Kuwaitis in particular are determined to take full advantage of their relatively privileged position to achieve as much advancement as possible within the existing system. This has created an indigenous force which is demanding an increasing say in the formation of national policy.

Women now have more influence than before. Many still go around veiled and attired in the traditional black but the younger generation follow Western fashion. Girl students are at present in a majority at Kuwait University and women are prominent in the country's commercial life and in the civil service. Some are openly agitating for a relaxation of social restrictions on females, more women's rights and an increase in job opportunities.

CONSTITUTION

Kuwait's Constitution, promulgated on 16 November 1962, defined the state as a sovereign, independent and a hereditary Amirate in which succession is restricted to the heirs of the late Mubarak al-Sabah (died 1915). Government was based on the principle of the separation of powers, with executive authority vested in the Amir and exercised through the Council of Ministers, and legislative authority shared by the Amir and a unicameral National Assembly. The Amir now rules by decree following the abolition of the National Assembly in 1976. He appoints and dismisses the Prime Minister 'after the traditional consultations' and further appoints or dismisses ministers on the recommendation of the Prime Minister.

The Constitution lays down a strong basis for the individual rights and freedom of Kuwaiti citizens, who are equal 'in human dignity, and in public rights and duties before the law'. Personal liberty is guaranteed, freedom of belief and religious practice is assured, provided it does not conflict with public policy or morals. Freedom of opinion is guaranteed within the conditions and procedures specified by the law. Freedom to form national associations and unions is also assured within the conditions of the law.

The Constitution also gives the state responsibility for providing social amenities in order to promote social justice. Education is therefore a right guaranteed by the state, and is both compulsory and free in its preliminary stages. The state also ensures aid for citizens in old age, sickness or inability to work. The rights of non-Kuwaiti residents are more obscure. The Constitution bars them from holding public office, except in cases specified by the law. At the same time, non-Kuwaitis are not allowed to own property, including either homes or business premises and do not have full access to health and education facilities.

HISTORY

Kuwait's long history has lengthy periods of which little is known. This is partly explained by the fact that until the 18th century it was a territory of shifting communities and for many centuries few people appeared to have been living there. Kuwait has tended historically to belong to the nomadic traditions of the Arabian desert rather than the urban culture of the Fertile Crescent.

Ancient Failaka During its early history, however, the country was in fact linked to the city states of Mesopotamia and its satellites. From 3000 B.C. to 1200 B.C. there was a flourishing community on the island of Failaka. Archaeologists have unearthed an abundance of evidence which shows that the island had close connections with the cities of the Tigris and Euphrates and with Dilmun, a civilisation centred on Bahrain which served as an entrepôt for trade between Mesopotamia and the Indus Valley.

Ancient seals found on the island give a clear indication that trade links and political alliances were first established by the people of Failaka with the thriving communities of Mesopotamia. Then it appeared to have come under the sway of Dilmun, probably being used as a trading outpost.

Between the end of the Bronze Age in the early second millenium and the fourth century B.C., the history of Failaka and mainland Kuwait remains virtually unknown. The next major recorded event is the arrival of Greek forces just before the death of Alexander the Great in 323 B.C. The Greeks built a Hellenistic temple, dedicated to Artemis and renamed the island Ikaros and called the mainland Larissa. Archaeological discoveries of stone inscriptions and coins on the island show that at the time Kuwait was a strategic centre on the land route to the Arabian hinterland.

During the third century B.C. Failaka became part of the Seleucid empire which stretched from Syria, through Arabia and Persia to India. A silver coin, dug up near the site of the Greek temple, bears a face similar to that of the Syrian King Antiochus, who ruled the Seleucid empire from 223 B.C. to 187 B.C.

Portuguese occupation The Greek colony on Failaka finally seems to have disappeared after the Romans conquered parts of the Middle East and for centuries the island and the Kuwaiti mainland was only sparsely populated by nomadic tribes. After the coming of Islam the area probably came under the control of the Abbasids who reigned in Baghdad and later after the 13th century the Mongols. During the 16th and 17th centuries Dutch and English sailors appeared to have stayed in Kuwait for a while, probably attracted by its long, landlocked bay which provided the only sheltered anchorage on the south side of the Gulf.

After the Portuguese arrived in the Gulf in the early 16th century, they built a fort where Kuwait city now stands along with several others on the Gulf coast and in Bahrain. They were unlikely to have met any opposition because probably few people lived in Kuwait at the time. They might have used the territory as a base from which to make incursions further north. In 1550 the Ottomans attacked the Portuguese, seizing Basra and then moving down the coast to take Qatif. Later the Portuguese counter-attacked, pushing the Turks out of Qatif, but appeared not to have marched much further north, leaving Kuwait under at least nominal Ottoman control.

Sabahs arrive Around 1710 a group of Arab settlers arrived in Kuwait, from whom the modern state of Kuwait was later to emerge. It has been suggested that the name Kuwait, which is the

Arabic diminutive of *kut* (a fortress), may stem from the presence of a Portuguese fort there. It is more likely that the name was associated with a fort built for the protection of these migrants.

The newcomers were families of the Aniza tribe who came from the interior of the Peninsula to escape drought, settling on the southern shore of Kuwait Bay where there was, at that time, sufficient fresh water. Among the families that settled there were the Khalifa, later to become the ruling dynasty in Bahrain, the Al-Sabah and families from which the Al-Ghanim, Shemlan and other families prominent in contemporary affairs trace their origin. This applies notably to the ruling Al-Sabah, from which the first Amir, Sabah I, was selected in 1756. His name had cropped up earlier as a member of a delegation that visited Basra to discuss relations with the Turks.

Nine years after the selection of Sabah I, Kuwait was visited by the Danish explorer Carsten Niebur, who estimated the population at 10,000. 'The inhabitants live by the fishery of pearls and fishes,' he wrote. 'They are said to employ in this species of naval industry more than 800 boats. In the favourable season of the year this town is left almost desolate, everybody going out either to the fishing or upon some commercial venture.' A little under a hundred years later, Kuwait was described by the British Resident in the Gulf, Colonel Lewis Pelly, as a 'clean, active town, with a broad and open main bazaar and numerous solid stone dwelling-houses containing some 20,000 inhabitants and attracting Arab and Persian merchants from all quarters by the equity of its rule'.

Outside interference This initial prosperity was not, however, entirely secure from outside interference from either Turks to the north, pirates in the Gulf or warring tribes in the hinterland. Kuwait's attractions as a trading centre were greatly enhanced by the Persian occupation of Basra between 1755 and 1759 and drew many merchants from Basra during this period. Disagreement with the Turkish authorities in Basra also led the British East India Company to move its staff and factory to Kuwait in 1793 and the company helped fend off attacks by Wahhabi tribes. But, by 1795, retaliatory attacks by Wahhabis on the mail service led the company to move its southern terminal back to Zubair.

It was this insecurity that led Shaikh Abdullah, Kuwait's Amir, who had taken over in 1866, to make contact with the British in the hope of receiving a guaranteed safe retreat in Bahrain. At this stage, however, the British were concerned with remaining uninvolved in local politics and the idea was quashed.

For much of the 19th century Kuwait went through a peaceful period during which it consolidated its position as a busy trading centre and seaport. Kuwait became the most important port in the northern part of the Gulf. At the same time the ruling family maintained its traditional links with the Bedouin tribes of the Kuwait desert.

But the country fell into difficulties after the accession to power of Shaikh Mohammad in 1893. He lacked the authority to keep order in his territory, which increasingly fell prey to raids from neighbouring tribes, with deleterious effects on trade. On internal affairs, Mohammad was strongly influenced by an Iraqi, Yusuf Bin-Abdullah al-Ibrahim, whose ambition was to undermine the position of the ruling family and have himself appointed Governor by the Turks.

British protectorate The decline in the state's fortunes led to the murder of Mohammad by his half-brother Mubarak, a forceful personality who after seizing power declared that Kuwait owed no allegiance to the Turks. Fear that the Turks might try to occupy Kuwait led Mubarak to ask Britain for protection in 1897. Britain's initial disinterest altered in 1899 however, when Germany won a concession from the Turks to build a Constantinople-Baghdad railway with a possible extension to the Gulf. Suspicion of Germany's motives led Britain in 1899 to conclude an agreement under which Kuwait would receive protection and, in return, would conclude no other special agreement with any other country or admit foreign agents without British consent. This was the start of a relationship which led Britain to appoint its first Political Agent, Colonel G. S. Knox, in 1904, and in October 1913 to an agreement by Kuwait not to grant oil concessions without British permission. By this stage Kuwait's autonomy had been recognised by Britain. An agreement between Britain and Turkey was concluded in 1913 defining Kuwait's borders, although ratification was prevented by the outbreak of the First World War.

Although Shaikh Mubarak was therefore successful in getting round the Turkish threat and in fostering the identity of an autonomous state of Kuwait, the next few years were to prove extremely testing and brought much hardship. Kuwait was threatened by the revival of Wahhabism in the Ikhwan movement spreading throughout the Arabian peninsula. In addition, the close relations with Ibn Saud resulting from the support provided by Shaikh Mubarak during the Saudi recovery of the Nejd were ruptured in 1915 by Mubarak's second son Salim. The only influence which might have restored them was lost when Shaikh Mubarak died the same year.

Ikhwan invasion   Shaikh Mubarak's eldest son, Jaber, ruled for two years but died in 1917 and was succeeded by Salim. A belief that Turkish supplies were going through Kuwait led Britain to impose a blockade on the country in 1918, disrupting the trade on which a large section of the community had come to depend for its livelihood. Then, in 1920, the Ikhwan forces launched an attack on Jahra on the road linking Kuwait with Basra, greatly outnumbering the Kuwaiti defenders.   The ensuing battle ended in defeat for the Ikhwan, but Shaikh Salim still had to make a plea for help from Britain.

Shaikh Salim died in 1921 and was succeeded by Shaikh Ahmad al-Jaber, and Ibn Saud immediately declared that he had no quarrel with Kuwait. However, in an attempt to remove areas of dispute and to fix internationally recognised boundaries, a conference was called by Sir Percy Cox, Britain's Political Resident in the Gulf. At this conference Kuwait's present boundaries were defined and the Neutral Zone between Kuwait and Saudi Arabia established. The Ikhwan forces under Faisal al-Duwish, who defied Ibn Saud's authority, continued however to make raids across the border. Despite the defeat of one raiding party in Kuwaiti territory in 1928, it was not until the surrender of Faisal al-Duwish in 1930 that the threat of invasion ended.

Kuwait, nonetheless, faced further problems. In 1923 Ibn Saud had applied a boycott on trade between the tribes of the Nejd and Kuwait, which thus lost a major traditional trading relationship. The slump that resulted was apparent from the much-reduced imports of such staple commodities as tea and sugar, which, by 1929, were running at only a quarter of the level maintained before the boycott was applied. In addition, world conditions had by 1930 brought a slump in the other valuable source of income, the pearl trade.

First oil strike By the early 1930s, however, the seeds of Kuwait's future prosperity were being sown. An oil concession was granted by Shaikh Ahmad to Kuwait Oil Company (KOC), a joint venture established by British Petroleum (BP) and Gulf Oil of the US. Drilling commenced in 1936, the first oil being struck in 1938, but exploitation was delayed by the outbreak of the Second World War, as a result of which the wells were plugged in 1942. Rapid development of the oil facilities after the war meant that, by the death of Shaikh Ahmad in 1950, the wealth derived from this source had already substantially altered the character of Kuwait. Under Shaikh Abdullah al-Salim, Kuwait's oil revenues began to be systematically deployed for the development of public utilities, health and education programmes.

Full independence Kuwait's full independence came in June 1961, when the 1899 treaty giving Britain control of foreign policy was ended. A military assistance agreement, though, was retained, and it was under this that Britain supplied troops at the request of the Amir following an Iraqi claim to Kuwait's sovereignty in 1961. There was criticism of this move elsewhere in the Arab world and, by September 1961, an agreement was reached to substitute British solders with an Arab League force comprising units from Saudi Arabia, Jordan, Egypt and Sudan. The Egyptian troops were pulled out by the end of that year and the remainder early in 1963. Two months later, in May 1963, Kuwait became the 111th member of the United Nations and, in October 1963, Iraq, in the hands of a new regime, recognised Kuwait's independence.

By the end of 1962 a Constitution had been promulgated providing for the establishment of a 50-man National Assembly, the first of which was elected and in operation by the end of January 1963. This development had been building up for many years. The first moves to establish government by council had come in the early 1920s under Shaikh Ahmad when, under pressure from merchants led by Hamad bin-Abdullah al-Saqar, a council of 12 was appointed with Al-Saqar as President. The foundation of the council had been intended to produce regular consultations on the external affairs of Kuwait town, but meetings were infrequent and Government continued on much the same basis as before. In 1961 Kuwait's first election took place for a 20-man Constituent Assembly which prepared the constitution. The first elections to the National Assembly were not free from influence of the Government and, with a large bedu component, was innately conservative. But debates in the Assembly were lively and often critical and as early as January 1965 disagreement between the ruling family and a democratically-inclined Assembly produced a constitutional crisis leading to the formation of a stronger cabinet by the Crown Prince, Shaikh Sabah al-Salim. But, later the same year, another reshuffle took place when, on the death of Shaikh Abdullah in November, Shaikh Sabah became Amir and his place as Crown Prince and Prime Minister was taken by Shaikh Jaber al-Ahmad in May 1966.

When the Arab-Israeli war of June 1967 broke out, Kuwait was one of the countries to respond with financial assistance for the war effort, amounting to KD 25 million ($85 million), and also with aid for reconstruction amounting to KD 55 million ($186 million) a year under the terms of an agreement at the Khartoum Conference of September. The closer alignment of Kuwait's foreign policy with that of other Arab countries was consolidated by the announcement in 1968 that the military assistance agreement with Britain would be allowed to expire in 1971. Kuwait also gave its support to the idea of Britain withdrawing its presence from the Gulf altogether and to the formation in 1971 of the United Arab Emirates from what, under British administration, had been the Trucial States.

Dispute with Iraq Kuwait's foreign ties were marred, however, by the revival of its dispute with Iraq in March 1973, when Iraqi forces occupied a border post. The withdrawal of the forces later in the same year did not end the disagreement. Iraq's interest, in fact, is focused on possession of the Bubiyan islands and the improved access Iraq would have to the Gulf as a result. The border dispute gave momentum to a programme of buying arms to build up Kuwaiti defences.

In 1973 ample evidence of the Assembly's ability to act independently was provided over the Government's negotiations to acquire an interest in the KOC. Independent elements in the Assembly had been strengthened by the elections two years earlier in which the Assembly's 50 seats had been contested by 184 candidates and an independent group led by Ahmad al-Khatib was elected, which has subsequently assumed the role of a main opposition party. The participation agreement concluded by the Government with KOC provided for a state interest of 25 per cent in the company rising to 51 per cent by 1982. The agreement was never ratified by the National Assembly, whose strong opposition to the agreement obliged the Government to renegotiate it. The agreement settled on by the Government in January of the following year, providing for the state's acquisition of an immediate 60 per cent stake with an option on the remaining 40 per cent in 1979, did not forestall pressure from some deputies for full nationalisation, but it was finally accepted by the Assembly in May.

Oil embargo　In October 1973 the Middle East was embroiled in another Arab–Israeli war. Apart from providing substantial financial assistance, Kuwait also had troops stationed on the Suez front. And it was at a meeting of the Organisation of Arab Petroleum Exporting Countries (OAPEC) held in Kuwait that the decision was taken to impose cutbacks in oil production rising by 5 per cent each month to pressure the West into calling for an Israeli withdrawal from occupied Arab territories. At the same time some countries, including Kuwait, applied a total embargo on all crude supplies to the US and the Netherlands. Before the year was out two major oil price increases had also been announced. The first, declared unilaterally by the six Gulf members of OPEC on 16 October, amounted to 70 per cent, taking effect from 1 November 1973 and the second raised market prices a further 130 per cent from 1 January 1974.

In 1974 negotiations commenced with Gulf Oil and BP for the takeover of their remaining 40 per cent holding in KOC. An agreement was not announced till December. Backdated to 1 March, it gave full ownership of KOC to the Government, although the companies continue to operate KOC facilities in return for a discount of 15 cents a barrel on their crude liftings. Additional compensation of some $60 million was agreed.

Recent Events

In August 1976 the Kuwaiti Government prorogued the National Assembly and suspended the Constitution. The decision surprised the outside world, for it meant the closure of the last democratic assembly in the Gulf. Bahrain had dissolved its own assembly during the previous year. The Government said that the National Assembly had abused its functions by obstructing vital legislation. But its action seemed to be linked to the civil war in Lebanon amid fears that unrestricted political activity could unleash similar social unrest in Kuwait. At the same time the Government imposed tough new restrictions on the country's press.

By the end of 1977 a team of Egyptian lawyers was due to finish work on draft reforms of Kuwaiti law incorporating some aspects of Islamic *Sharia* law. A constitutional committee was then scheduled to start work on drafting a new constitution which would attempt to redefine the essential Islamic character of the state. The National Assembly will probably be transformed into a *majlis al-Shura*—the traditional consultative assembly found in the more conservative Islamic states—which would be comprised of some Government appointees and some elected members.

Abroad, Kuwait has continued to have a moderating influence in Arab affairs. It played an influential role in healing the rift between Syria and Egypt in September 1976. Relations with its northern neighbour, Iraq, which had earlier been strained over border questions, showed a distinct improvement in July 1977 when, following the visit of the Interior & Defence Minister to Baghdad, it was agreed to set up a joint ministerial committee to settle any matters still in dispute.

ECONOMY

On the basis of per capita income, Kuwait is by far the richest country in the world. In 1976 the country's income per head of population amounted to $12,565, compared with $9,320 in

Switzerland, the nation with the second highest figures. Kuwait is earning more money from its oil than it needs. and one of its economic problems is finding suitable investments for its huge surplus funds. Its easily acquired wealth has lessened the pressure to industrialise quickly, even though the country's oil is running out. Industry still only provides four per cent of its Gross National Product.

One major reason for the comparative lack of enthusiasm for industrialisation is the deep seated concern among Kuwaitis about the number of non-Kuwaitis in the population. A census in 1976 confirmed that Kuwaitis were a minority in their own country—48 per cent of a total population of 1,055,000. Many economic decisions are now dictated by a desire to keep the number of non-Kuwaitis as low as possible. As a result all new industrial projects will be highly capital intensive rather than labour intensive.

Oil

The economy of modern Kuwait has been and will remain for the foreseeable future dependent on its one natural resource, oil and associated natural gas. In 1975/76 oil accounted for 90 per cent of Government revenues, and 95 per cent of export earnings. In 1976 oil revenues were estimated to have totalled around $8,500 million from an average production of just over two million barrels a day (b/d). Kuwait is the sixth largest producer of oil in the world.

The country's oil reserves have been estimated around 71,000 million barrels (40–50,000 million of which is in the Burgan field alone). There is little likelihood of further discoveries of significant quantities of crude although the level of recoverable reserves may rise with improvement in secondary and tertiary recovery techniques. If production is kept at a level of two million b/d, Kuwait's reserves would last 70–80 years. Crude oil production has fallen substantially since reaching a peak in 1972 as a result of conservation policies. In recent years the Government has tended to favour keeping production at a relatively low level in order to preserve the country's oil for as long as possible. Output in the 1950s showed the fastest growth rate in the world at 17 per cent a year, climbing from 17 million tons in 1950 to 53.9 million tons in 1955 and 80.5 million tons in 1960. By 1970 it amounted to 148.3 million tons and in 1972 it reached its peak of 163.4 million tons, falling to 126.6 million tons in 1974 and about 105 million tons or an average two million b/d in 1975. In the first quarter of 1977 output fell to an average 1.7 million b/d and Finance Minister Abdel-Rahman Salem al-Atiqi said in May, 1977, that he favoured a new production ceiling of 1.5 million b/d.

The rapid growth of the 1950s reflected the ease of production of Kuwaiti crude. The oilfields are close to good export loading facilities. In the Burgan field the oil rises under its own pressure. Production costs are, as a result, among the lowest in the world, so production can be raised or lowered at little more than a turn of the tap.

Gas Reserves Kuwait's gas reserves are estimated at 32.5 million million cubic feet. Commercial exploitation of a significant proportion of natural gas output is, however, comparatively recent. Of 643.7 million cubic feet produced in 1972, 61.7 per cent was flared. By 1974 only 46.1 per cent of the production was flared and two years later the proportion had fallen to as low as 30 per cent. About 37 per cent of gas produced is used by industrial companies, 18 per cent is injected in oil fields mainly to maintain pressure and the remainder is used by State utilities.

All Kuwait's gas is associated gas, which poses problems. Until substantial reserves of natural gas are found, gas output is tied to oil production. The Government hopes that drilling in the Burgan field may reveal natural gas and that it may be possible to extract natural gas from the Dorra field offshore of the Neutral Zone shared with Saudi Arabia. But for the moment a drop in oil production means a fall in gas supplies to industry and power and desalination plants. Experts estimate that oil output can decline to 600,000–800,000 b/d in the winter and one million b/d in the summer before cuts in present gas consumption would have to be made. An official of the Kuwait Oil Company (KOC) has estimated that an oil output of 350,000 b/d would be sufficient to fuel electricity and desalination plants. Pressure on oil supplies could increase substantially when the country's major liquefied petroleum gas (LPG) project starts operating in 1978.

The Gas Utilization Project

The Government of Kuwait are concerned that the oil/gas wealth of the country should be conserved and that all aspects of energy production and consumption should be controlled and planned, to ensure maximum safeguards for their oilfield resources. A similar control emphasis, is to be exercised to protect the environment from organic, inorganic and noise pollution.

In pursuance of this policy a project was launched in April last year when a contract was signed for the construction and commissioning of an LPG (liquid petroleum gas) fractionation plant, a storage tank farm for LPG products, LPG loading facilities and an acid removal plant.

A three-train LPG plant and a gas-gathering system are under construction and these will gather the gas produced with the oil at well-heads, remove LPG components and natural gasoline, treat them to conform to international standards and distribute them to fuel-users and to pressure-maintenance facilities.

As part of the project, a major contract was awarded to the Kuwait Metal Pipe Industries for the engineering, procurement and construction of a 300-mile network of gathering and transmission pipelines.

Completion of the gas-gathering centres, booster stations and pipelines is scheduled for 1978. The first process train is due to be completed in the first quarter of 1978 with the second and third trains completed afterward at three-month intervals.

Capacity of the plant will be 100,000 barrels per day of propane, 55,000 barrels daily of butane and 41,000 barrels daily of natural gasoline to give a total production of 196,000 barrels per day.

In his address at the opening ceremony the Minister
Oil, Mr. Abdul Muttaleb Al Kazemi, described the KOC
s Project as a memorable objective attained by the
ate and made possible by the country's takeover of its
resources. This had made it possible for Kuwaitis to
tiate and complete a programme of development
ojects which would enhance the well-being of the
untry in the future.

The Minister said he was proud to reveal that Kuwait
d started many ambitious projects in the oil sector,
rticularly in the areas of production, processing and
porting oil and its derivatives. A start had been made,
so, on creating a solid, by-products industry with the
m of building up the national economy. The cost of the
as Project represented about 24 per cent of the total
tlay allocated to the oil sector in the five-year plan.

He added that Kuwait had established the highest
as-utilisation record in the Middle East and the quantity
f gas utilised in proportion to the gas produced had
creased from 18 per cent in 1964 to 60 per cent in 1975.

Prime reason for the establishment of the Gas Project
ad been to stop the wastage of natural gas. The project
ould ensure that this target was reached and it would
stablish Kuwait as the first member of OPEC and Gulf-
rea country to take complete control of its natural-gas
sources.

The Minister said it was noteworthy that Kuwait was
he biggest exporter of natural gas in the Gulf region and
he present project would build an even stronger position
vhen it began operations about the beginning of 1978.

Kuwait Oil Company Kuwait's main oil producer is the state-owned Kuwait Oil Company which is responsible for over 95 per cent of output. It was fully nationalised in late 1975 when the Kuwait Government concluded a take-over agreement with its former minority shareholders, British Petroleum and Gulf Oil of the US. They agreed to lift 450,000 b/d and 500,000 b/d respectively and to use Kuwaiti tankers to ship their crude up to 1980. In return they received a 15 per cent discount a barrel on contracted liftings with a tolerance of 10 per cent either way over the year. The two companies remain KOC's major customers but the state firm has recently reached a deal with Anglo-Dutch Shell for sales of 310,000 b/d. The Kuwait National Petroleum Company (KNPC), which is also state owned, takes between 250,000–350,000 b/d for its refinery.

The history of Kuwaiti oil revolves round KOC. Originally competitors for the concession to search for and produce oil in Kuwait, Gulf and what was then the Anglo-Persian Oil Company agreed to combine forces and in February 1934 registered the Kuwait Oil Company with capital of $100,000. In December of the same year they concluded an agreement with the ruler Shaikh Ahmed, providing for payment on signature of 470,000 rupees (about $71,250), an annual rent of 95,000 rupees (about $14,250), royalty payments of three rupees a ton and, in place of duty, an additional payment of four annas a ton. The agreement was for 75 years and covered an area of 6,000 square miles. In 1951 the agreement was extended for 17 years to the year 2026.

KOC spudded its first well at Bahra in May 1936 without finding commercial quantities of oil and it was not until early 1938, after an extensive survey of the concession area, that the first major discovery of oil occurred in the Burgan area. Preparations for the production and export of oil were interrupted by World War II. Output started in 1947, when 800,000 tons of oil was produced. By the early 1950s, the Burgan field had become the biggest single known deposit in the world. The Magwa field just north of the Burgan and the Ahmadi field in the south-east were proved in 1952 and 1953 respectively and the first well was drilled in the important Raudhatain field in 1959.

In 1951 KOC agreed to pay 50 per cent of its realised profit to the Government. In 1955 a new system of royalty payments and income tax gave the Government over 50 per cent of actual per barrel revenue. The company, however, was still free to determine the posted price. In May 1967 the Government's share was increased from 50 to 56¼ per cent of the posted price and the profits from oil sales divided on a 70/30 basis. The first stage towards the state takeover of KOC was accomplished by an agreement signed in January 1974 under which a 60 per cent Government participation was settled.

Foreign Companies Two small foreign oil companies still operate in Kuwait—the American Independent Oil Company (Aminoil) and Arabian Oil Company (AOC). Jointly owned by eight US companies, Aminoil was granted a 60-year concession in 1948 covering Kuwait's onshore share of the Neutral Zone. It maintains a joint operating agreement with Getty Oil under which they share certain expenses. It has established a refinery (Mina Abdullah) in Kuwait where it refines all its offtake of 80,000 b/d. In mid-1977 the Government announced its intention to take over Aminoil, following a failure to agree on higher taxation rates.

AOC has a concession covering offshore areas of the Neutral Zone shared with Saudi Arabia. The company is a subsidiary of the Japan Trading Company, itself a consortium of 60 Japanese companies, including the Mitsui and Mitsubishi groups. During 1976 its output averaged around 158,000 b/d.

Kuwait's oil industry has a complicated administrative structure. KOC is the main organisation within the industry. But the two foreign oil companies—Aminoil and AOC—deal solely with the Oil Ministry. KOC is not even responsible for its own marketing. The Kuwait National Petroleum Company (KNPC), formed in the 1960s, runs all marketing activities concerned with Kuwait's own oil industry. It also operates Kuwait's most modern refinery. KOC has its own refinery, but its output is marketed by KNPC. In 1975 the Government talked about forming the Kuwait Oil, Gas & Energy Corporation (KOGEC) to take supervisory control of both KOC and KNPC as well as the state-owned petrochemicals concern Petrochemical Industries Company (PIC). But the idea was soon dropped because of fears that the industry might become overcentralised. Instead the day-to-day activities of the industry are co-ordinated by the Oil Industry.

Industry

Industrialisation has been considered since the last decade as playing an important part in Kuwait's strategy for diversifying its economy away from dependence on oil and gas resources. To date, however, progress has been limited. Since 1966, industrial output has been growing at a rate of 11 per cent a year, but by 1976 it still contributed only four per cent of Gross Domestic Product (GDP), of which a large proportion was from oil refining.

These constraints on industrial development have been the lack of any natural resources apart from oil and gas, necessitating the import of all other raw materials, the limited size of the domestic market, and the lack of manpower, which has resulted in Kuwait importing the bulk of its industrial work force. Reluctance to increase the proportion of foreign labour in Kuwait, which already makes up 70 per cent of the total working population, was an important factor in the decision not to proceed with a project for setting up a steelmill. This difficulty is not helped by the preference prevailing among Kuwaitis for white collar rather than industrial or manual employment.

Traditionally a trading community, there has also been a lack of commitment on the part of Kuwait's private sector to investing in industrial ventures where the return on funds is slow. In addition, the Government has not prepared any form of industrial plan, which might have provided a lead on this subject. Only in late 1974 was the Industrial Bank of Kuwait (IBK) set up, which has had the task of devising a long-term industrial strategy and initiating projects within its framework. All industrial schemes have also to be licensed by the Ministry of Trade and Industry which tends to hold up their implementation.

Petrochemical output The only heavy industry to emerge in Kuwait so far has therefore been in the manufacture of hydrocarbon products. The biggest single operator in oil- and gas-related industries is Petrochemical Industries Company (PIC), set up in 1963 to manufacture fertilisers. The Government has increased its initial 80 per cent shareholding and, in January 1976, announced its intention to take over the remaining six per cent owned by private interests.

PIC runs three plants, mostly producing fertilisers. One has a capacity of 900 tons of urea and 400 tons of ammonia. Another, owned by the PIC subsidiary, Kuwait Chemical Fertiliser Company (KCFC), has a daily capacity of 1,400 tons of urea, 1,600 tons of ammonia, 400 tons of sulphuric acid and 500 tons of ammonium sulphate. But since 1975 this plant has been running at only 75 per cent capacity. PIC's third plant is a salt and chloride plant at Shuwaikh, but mainly because of market conditions this has been operating at well below capacity.

For the future, PIC's major project and the centrepiece of Kuwait's industrial development is a liquefied petroleum gas (LPG) plant at Shuaiba which should come on stream in 1978. It will overshadow Kuwait's present LPG plant run by KOC which has a capacity of 300,000 b/d. The new project is being managed by Eastern Bechtel Corporation of the US and is being built by a combination of Japanese and US companies. The plant will consist of three trains, each with a capacity of 560 million cubic feet a day. The $1,100 million plant's eventual output is expected to reach five million tons a year of butane, propane and natural gasoline, to be exported by four gas-carriers ordered from Chantiers Navals de la Ciotat of France. One major difficulty confronting the project is the level of operation required to meet its full requirement for associated natural gas. Initial estimates put this at three million barrels a day b/d, compared with the current norm of around two million b/d. One mitigating factor is that each of the three trains can operate economically on its own.

The plant will provide feedstock for an expanded petro-chemicals industry. Output from the plant will feed a $800 million olefines complex which will produce ethylene from ethane gas for plastics factories. But by mid-1977 the Government had still not decided whether to go ahead with this plant. However the authorities have decided to press ahead with a $250 million aromatics complex, which would involve a foreign partner, as yet unselected. The plant would require some 37,000 b/d of naphtha as feedstock from the KNPC refinery, and would produce some 300,000 tons a year of para-xylene and benzene. Its output will be used as feedstock for a melamine plant of 15,000 tons capacity—one tenth of the world's production.

Kuwait's present oil refining capacity of 580,000 b/d is the second largest in the Middle East after Iran. The biggest plant is KOC's refinery at Mina al-Ahmadi which has a capacity of 300,000 b/d. But KNPC's refinery at Shuaiba with a capacity of 280,000 b/d is a more modern and sophisticated plant. However it has been running below capacity and doubts about the future market for refined oil products has led to the cancellation of a second KNPC refinery. Aminoil has a refinery at Mina al-Ahmadi with a capacity of 145,000 b/d. KOC's 100,000 tons a year bitumen plant is being supplemented by a second one of 250,000 tons capacity which will be operational by mid-1978.

Manufacturing industries Oil and gas based industries account for the bulk of Kuwait's industrial production and under the Kuwait Five Year Plan stretching from 1976/77–1980/81, the majority of funds for industry are going to refining, gas liquefaction and petrochemicals. According to one draft of the Plan, which has never been published, non-oil related industries were to receive only 15 per cent of a total outlay for industry of around $3,000 million. The draft plan predicted that by 1981 the total annual value of industrial output outside the oil sector would be around $900 million. Most of this would consist of food and beverages, clothing, footwear and leather products, construction materials and certain types of assembled and processed products.

Some of the longest established industries in Kuwait have been set up by the Government. In the early 60s it formed the Kuwait Flour Mills Company, and the National Industries Company, which has been producing asbestos cement pipes and itself created the Kuwait Metal Pipes Company. This firm exports a high proportion of its 70,000 tons annual output. The Government has also established two industrial zones at Shuwaikh and Shuaiba where land is provided for industrial use at a nominal rent.

However generally the Government wants to keep non-oil industries the preserve of the private sector. The Government's Industrial Bank of Kuwait (IBK) has been used to encourage private investment in industry. By the end of 1976 it had financed, through loans, 47 per cent of the $276 million total cost of 39 projects. It has been particularly active in granting funds for construction materials projects. By mid-1977 Kuwait was virtually producing all the cement it needs.

One of the advantages enjoyed by industry in Kuwait has been the availability of well-established infrastructural facilities. Water is supplied by desalination plants in Kuwait City and Shuaiba. Around 90 per cent of Kuwait's daily consumption of 60 million gallons of water comes from desalination plants. Total electricity stands at around 1,400 MW compared with 370 MW in the 1960s. It is being increased to 2,600 MW by 1980 and by the end of the century could rise to 3,000–4,000 MW, with the possible installation of a nuclear energy plant. Total electricity generated reached 4,092 million kWh in 1974.

Trade

Kuwait is assured of a surplus on its overall trade balance for many years to come, on the strength of its oil exports and the limited size of the market for imports. The surplus for 1974–75 was estimated to have risen 74 per cent over the previous year to KD 2,496.5 million ($8,463 million), exports having risen by 70.6 per cent to KD 3,013 million ($10,214 million), of which non-oil goods accounted for only KD 130.5 million ($442 million). Imports were up by 56 per cent over the previous year to around KD 516.9 million ($1,752 million). In 1975 they increased to KD 693 million ($2,389 million) and in 1976 rose by another 30 per cent to an estimated KD 900 million ($3,103 million).

Non-oil exports are showing a faster rate of growth than imports. But about 40 per cent of goods passing through Shuwaikh port, Kuwait's main port, are re-exports. The re-exporting business is likely to remain a significant source of revenue for some time, with Saudi Arabia and Iraq being the main destinations of re-exported goods.

Much the most important non-oil export of Kuwaiti origin is chemicals, particularly chemical fertilisers, of which about 200,000 tons is supplied to both China and Sudan and a further 150,000 tons to India under three-year contracts. A further 200,000 tons is supplied to Sudan on a concessional basis. Kuwait is also, however, building up markets in the Middle

East, notably Saudi Arabia and other Gulf states. Iraq and Iran have also substantially raised their purchases of goods from Kuwait, although the value is still low.

Import bill If the size of the Kuwaiti market has been one factor in keeping the rise in its import bill below that of many other oil exporters, the lack of domestic manufacturing capacity has spread import requirements across the whole spectrum. These have, however, been concentrated in consumer goods, which has accounted for 45 per cent of the total, the largest single item being passenger cargo. During 1975 over 58,000 cars were imported, amounting to 8.5 per cent of imports. Capital goods have been accounting for about 25 per cent of imports, of which transport equipment made up the highest proportion.

Kuwait's major supplier is the European Economic Community, which raised its sales by some 64 per cent to around KD 151.1 million ($512 million) during 1974. But the Eastern Bloc's share of imports is rising. As far as individual countries are concerned, Japan has established itself as the leading supplier, with 20 per cent of the market in the first half of 1976. Apart from the sales of electrical goods and appliances, Japan is a leading contender in the car market, where it has been running second only to the US.

Overall, the US has been the second biggest individual supplier, closely followed by West Germany. Britain has been taking fourth place, after being Kuwait's main supplier during the 1960s. It has been struggling to hold onto its market even though it has been putting a lot of effort into its export drive. During 1975 its exports to Kuwait increased by 75 per cent and in 1976 by around 45 per cent.

Banking and Finance

The finance sector is a major and rapidly increasing sector within Kuwait's economy. Its importance to the economy as a whole is demonstrated by the steady expansion of credit to the private sector, which rose by 42 per cent to $1,212 million in 1974, and by 32 per cent to $1,621 million in 1975. Between September, 1975, and September, 1976, bank credits increased by 87 per cent to around $2,650 million. The money supply rising from $267 million in 1970 to $667 million in 1974 and then increasing by 46 per cent in 1975 to $970 million, has tended to keep pace with this credit expansion. Quasi-money, usually two or three times the amount of money in circulation, progressed from $747 million in 1970 to $1,862 million in 1975. Domestic savings rose by 32 per cent over a year to $1,800 million in September, 1976.

Bank credit is being increasingly dominated by trade financing which, in 1975, absorbed 36 per cent of total extended credit compared with 34 per cent in 1974 and 33 per cent in 1973. Construction, usually in the form of short-term financing, takes another 21 per cent although its share has been dropping. Credit to the finance and services sector has accounted for 20 per cent compared to a 13 per cent share in 1974. Personal credit, whose share fell from 22 per cent to 16 per cent in 1974–75, has reversed the previous downward trend and was responsible for 17 per cent of total credit in the first quarter of 1976. Loans to industry take another 5 per cent and agriculture and fisheries 2 per cent. In the year ending September, 1976, credit for financial and other services rose by 198 per cent, for personal loans by 119 per cent, for trade by 59 per cent and for construction by 46 per cent.

The predominance of short-term credit in bank loans reflects Kuwait's increasing commercial importance in the region and, unlike many other banking sectors of the Gulf, does not indicate the banking system's inability to indulge in long-term development financing since the Kuwaiti infrastructure, already one of the most advanced in the area, does not need the rapid development necessary in neighbouring countries. The banking system is, therefore, relatively free to indulge in the more profitable short-term financing at home and abroad.

Banking system The banking system is headed by the Central Bank which replaced the Currency Board in 1968. It regulates the money supply, determines credit policy, manages the banking industry and acts as the Government's banker. The commercial banks must be 100 per cent Kuwaiti-owned. However, the Bank of Bahrain and Kuwait, which only has a 50 per cent Kuwaiti holding, was given permission in 1976 to begin operations in Kuwait. There are five other commercial banks. Only one—the Bank of Kuwait and the Middle East—has a government stake.

The others are privately owned. All five banks have enormous assets and are among the biggest in the Arab world.

There is a growing number of investment companies. The largest, known as the three Ks—the Kuwait Investment Company (KIC), the Kuwait International Investment Company (KIIC) and the Kuwait Foreign Trading, Contracting and Investment Company (KFTCIC)—are designed to recycle Kuwait's surplus oil revenues into productive long-term investments at home and abroad. The Government has a 50 per cent stake in KIC and an 80 per cent share in KFTCIC. All three underwrite and manage bond issues. Other financial institutions include Arab Financial Consultants Company (AFCC), which has prominent foreign Arabs among its shareholders, and the Kuwait Financial Centre, whose majority share is held by Kuwaiti businessmen and the rest by the International Bank of Washington. Both are active in the retail bond market. The recently formed Arab Corporation for Trading Securities (ACTS) aims to build up a secondary market for international Kuwaiti dinar bonds. There is also the Kuwait International Finance Company which has foreign participation and provides local business and Middle East private institutions with development finance.

Kuwait also possesses a thriving equity market on which the stocks of around 40 companies are traded. The market is generally speculative, characterised by rapid stock appreciation—up to 100 per cent of stock over face value. Consequently, the volume of trading is hectic with 204 per cent rises registered in 1973 and another 239 per cent in 1974. In 1976 the market valuation of 31 tested Kuwaiti companies soared from about $3,300 million to $8,000 million. Real estate companies, insurance firms and banks were the focus of investors' interest. The turnover in 1976 was bigger than on most European stock exchanges and during one day in September, 1976, share transactions exceeded in value those in London. The volume is low but the sums being exchanged by a relatively small number of wealthy individuals can be colossal.

Surplus funds Kuwait's boom as a financial centre is a result of the massive surplus funds it has accumulated in recent years. By mid-1977 the Government's foreign holdings were estimated to have reached $16,000 million and private investment funds to have totalled around $6,000 million. A lot of the private money went abroad but a high proportion has stayed in the country, chasing a limited number of investment outlets. As a result equity speculation, particularly in real estate, has sometimes got out of hand. The Government has tried to mop up some of the excess liquidity by issuing bonds through its own agencies. The Industrial Bank of Kuwait (IBK) has floated at least two bonds even though it appeared not to need the extra money.

Abroad, private investment has gone into real estate and even equity shares. The Kuwaiti company Gulf International has, for example, a 23 per cent holding in the London-based trading conglomerate Lonrho. The Government formed the Kuwait Real Estate Investment Consortium (KREIC) in 1974 to channel private funds into specific projects abroad. It has invested $750 million into real estate in the Arab world, in particular Morocco, Tunisia, Jordan and Egypt.

The Government's own investment funds abroad are handled by special agents in the main financial centres—Citibank in the US, Deutsche Bank and Dresdner Bank in West Germany, the Swiss Bank Corporation, Credit Lyonnais in France and Kuwait Investment Office in London. The Government has said that it is aiming to find longer-term investments, particularly in the strong currency area. But a high proportion of the Government's overseas holdings are still held in short-term deposits, mainly in US banks. The Government likes its investments to remain secretive and has been deterred from taking many large equity holdings in foreign firms in some Western countries because of rules that shares above a certain percentage must be disclosed.

Some Government investment funds are diverted through KIC and KFTCIC, the two Kuwaiti investment companies in which it holds a controlling interest, into schemes in developing countries. It has also used other agencies to channel investments into Africa, Latin America and Asia. However much of official Kuwaiti finance for developing countries comes in the form of loans. Altogether eight per cent of Kuwait Gross Domestic Product is allocated to foreign aid. The Kuwait Fund for Arab Economic Development (KFAED)—the Government's main aid body—is now one of the world's major aid institutions. By

Kuwait's Foreign Aid

It is generally assumed that it is only in recent years that Kuwait has given aid to other countries, but Kuwait has, in fact been giving foreign aid almost since its inception as an independent State. Public recognition of this fact was not however given, until the establishmen of the Kuwait Fund for Arab Economic Development (KFAED) on December 31, 1961.

The KFAED is now firmly established as one of the world's leading national aid agencies, and is the main agent for providing official development assistance from Kuwait, operating independently of Government and depending solely on economic criteria for evaluating the viability of a particular project.

The capital of the KFAED was quintupled in 1974 from KD 200 m to KD 1 b.n. ($3.45 b.n.) and its field of activities extended to take in countries outside the Arab World. The year 1975/76 was the first in which loans to non-Arab States were made. In that year non-Arab State received loans worth KD 75 m while Arab States receive KD 84.3 m.

The Kuwait Fund concentrates mainly on infra-structural projects: 54 per cent of the loans to African an Asian countries in the period 1975/76 were for power projects, 22 per cent went to agriculture, 16 per cent to industry and 8 per cent to projects in transport and communications.

The KFAED co-operated with other aid agencies not only in co-financing but in the evaluation and general research of projects. In the 15 month 1975/76 fiscal year, eight out of 34 loan agreements concluded involved co-financing. One of the best examples of this co-operation is the Rahad irrigation project in Sudan where the

AED's loan is supplemented with assistance from the
A, AFESD, the Saudi Fund for Development and
S.AID. A project in Nepal is being co-financed by the
AED, IDA, UNDP and Japan, and one in Sri Lanka by
e KFAED, Asian Development Bank and Kreditanstalt
r Wiederaufbau of West Germany. Thus it can be seen
at Kuwait co-operates on a world wide basis.

Another aid agency located in Kuwait is the Arab
nd for Economic and Social Development (AFESD).
wait is the biggest contributor to this fund, in which it
ok the lead in establishing. The capital of the Arab Fund
ands at KD 400 m. (US$1.4 b.n.) of which Kuwait
ntributed KD75 m ($270 m). Kuwait is also a member of
e Arab Bank for Economic Development in Africa, with
$20 m. share, the Special Arab Fund for Africa,
signed to meet oil costs and in the Islamic Bank which
s been established to provide assistance bearing no
terest charges in accordance with Moslem precepts
ainst usury.

Another organ for the provision of aid from Kuwait is
e General Authority for the South and Arabian Gulf
ich specialises in social type projects such as the
ilding and operation of schools, clinics and hospitals of
e Arabian peninsula. The annual budget of the
thority for 1975/76 is about KD 10 million.

Kuwait is a regular contributor to the United Nations
d its regional agencies, to the United Nations
velopment Programme, to the U.N. Fund for
pulation Activities, the U.N. Industrial Development
ganisation, to the World Food Programme, to the U.N.
lief and Works Agency for Palestine Refugees, to the
N.H.C.R. and to the U.N. International Children's
ergency Fund. Kuwait's support for the World Bank
oup has also been a constant feature of its international
sistance policy.

1977 it had disbursed around $500 million and was committed to making loans of $1,000 million.

Social Services

On paper Kuwait's record on social services expenditure looks far from impressive. In 1960 the state spent KD 24 a head. By 1977 it was spending only KD 60 per head. Taking into account inflation, this has been a negligible increase. But these figures tend to be misleading. Kuwait's population has grown spectacularly since the early 60s because of an influx of foreign labour, many of whom are not eligible for all the state's social services. Education for example is only free to Kuwaitis and other Arabs. On the basis of the Kuwaiti population alone, per capita spending on social services has gone up considerably in recent years. Under the Five Year Plan ending in 1981, a total of $6,200 million is being spent on social services—40 per cent of all allocations.

At present the Government's main aim is to provide decent housing for its own population. Inflation and real estate speculation, which has sent rents rocketing, has made it difficult for the poorer Kuwaitis to find housing. This has caused widespread discontent which has forced the Government to give housing a high priority. By the end of 1981 it plans to eradicate the housing crisis by building 52,000 homes for low income groups. The total cost of this housing programme will be around $4,800 million, half of which will be met by the state itself and the other half by the private sector. At the same time the capital of the Credit & Savings Bank, which provides cheap home loans, has been more than doubled to over $1,100 million.

Education expansion Education has been representing the biggest single item on the budget for current expenditure. Expenditure has risen from the KD 54.5 million ($185 million) in the 1973–74 budget to KD 62.2 million ($210 million) in the following year and to KD 86.7 million ($294 million) for 1975–76. Under the budget estimates for 1976–77, a further rise of about 27 per cent to KD 110 million ($373 million) was envisaged.

The development has not, however, been confined to the level of spending, but spread across the whole range of education, which is free for Kuwaiti citizens. Free schooling has recently been extended to all Arab children in the country. A total of 118 new schools should have been built by the end of 1978.

Expansion in all areas of education has been rapid. The number of schools rose from 134 (with 1,475 classrooms) in 1960–61 to 230 (4,644) in 1970–71 and 309 (6,426) by the end of 1974–75. The number of students attending government schools had reached 182,778 by 1974–75, compared with 138,747 in 1970–71 and only 45,157 10 years earlier. Also by 1974–75, the number of teachers had reached 14,035, bringing the teacher-student ratio to 13:1.

But Kuwait relies heavily on teachers from abroad. Only around a third of teachers hold Kuwaiti citizenship, of which over half are involved with primary schools. In intermediate and secondary education the biggest group are Egyptian teachers, although Jordanians and Palestinians also make up a proportion of teachers at the intermediate level.

To ensure a future supply of teachers, there are around 45 teacher training colleges providing a two-year course with attendance close to 1,000. Teachers and school administrators are also sent abroad to attend postgraduate courses at foreign universities.

The University of Kuwait was established in 1966 with faculties of economic and political science, arts and natural sciences, commerce and law, statistics and insurance, although the number of departments is rapidly diversifying. A medical school has just been added. By 1976, the attendance at the university had reached 6,500, compared with 1,988 in 1970–71, of which well under half were Kuwaiti, with students from other Gulf and Arab countries accounting for about 60 per cent. The University has been due to move to a new $410 million site at Shuwaikh.

Kuwait has a free health service which has recently been put under strain by heavy demand. By the end of 1978 its hospital bed capacity will have been doubled to 6,000 beds. At least four new hospitals are being built, raising the country's total to around 15. Remarkable progress has been achieved since 1936 when the Ministry of Public Health (then known as the Ministry of Health) was established. At that time there was one hospital and one clinic. The Government, which employed four doctors in 1949, now employs around 850, giving a ratio of one doctor for every 1,200. In recent years the Government has been allocating around 11 per cent of its current expenditure to health.

But one of the health service's major problems is staff shortages. Kuwait relies heavily on Egyptian and Palestinian doctors and is trying to recruit doctors outside the Middle East. Nurses are being recruited from India and South Korea as well as Egypt and Sudan.

GUIDE

KUWAIT CITY In the early 1960s Kuwait town had one main street, Fahad al-Salem Street, which on a fine spring evening the population of a few thousand would use as a promenade. The area beyond Al-Sour Street was desert and most of the town's houses were made of mud with hollowed pieces of wood sticking out of the roofs to serve as drains. Now the town has been transformed into a extraordinarily wealthy city of high-rise buildings and tall office blocks, wide boulevards, and parks and gardens. At any given working hour the population is around 350,000, most of whom have their own cars, giving the country the highest number of cars per head of population in the world. The only remains of the older town are the three main gates, preserved when its walls were pulled down in 1957.

The focal point of the city is Safat Square, close to which can be found the former National Assembly building, the Telecommunications Building, and a distinguished construction housing the Kuwait Fund for Arab Economic Development. Between the square and the sea front lies the main banking area and the souk. Although a traditional feature of the city, and a place of enduring interest, the souk offers little in the way of traditional handicrafts. The most sophisticated shopping area is located in Fahad al-Salem Street, providing abundant evidence of the penetration of the Kuwaiti market by Western and Japanese radios, televisions, cameras, calculators and other consumer bric-à-brac. The main embassy quarter is in the eastern Sharq district, where the former Dasman palace is situated along with the British, US and Soviet Embassies, while many other embassies are close by in Hilali Street.

The city's road system has largely been laid out in a spider web's pattern, with six major roads leading out of the centre, criss-crossed by the four in-city ring roads. The Fourth Ring Road is normally considered the suburban border of the city. Arabian Gulf Street is perhaps the most handy road, running direct from Shuwaikh port to Salmiyah beach. It has less traffic than others and fewer traffic signals.

The city's most prominent landmark is the Kuwait Towers, opposite the TV station, which contain a revolving restaurant and a water storage facility. The towers have three pointed

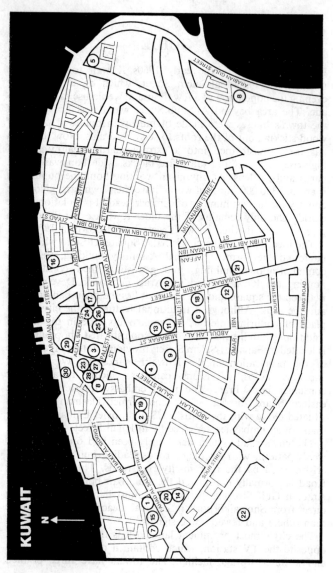

KUWAIT

N

pinnacles, two of them topped by large spherical structures. One of the oldest buildings in the city is the Seif Palace, the Amir's administrative headquarters, which has undergone extensive restoration work. It is a large fortress-like building on the sea-front with a massive clock-tower.

Outside Kuwait City, the country's two main centres are Fahaheel and Ahmadi, both virtually one-street towns. **Ahmadi,** a well-laid out town dotted with trees and single-storey buildings, is the headquarters of the Kuwait Oil Company (KOC) and the site of large oil-related development projects. **Fahaheel** serves mainly as a residential district for workers in the nearby **Shuwaiba** industrial area where most of the country's manufacturing projects are located. It is the site of the Petrochemicals Industries Company, oil refineries, gas liquefaction schemes and cement, plastic and light industrial plants. It is also the main industrial port and inevitably the most polluted area in the country.

Failaka Island, 20 miles east of Kuwait Bay, is becoming the country's main leisure centre. There are plans to turn it into a big tourist resort with amusement parks and wide range of recreational and sporting facilities. Dhows sail regularly to the island from the dhow port near the Sief Palace. It is also a place of great historical interest because of its archaeological sites. The remains of a Bronze Age community dating back to around 2500 B.C., have been found as well as the remains of a town dating back to the Seleucid empire and the site of a Greek temple dedicated to Artemis. Some of the items discovered on the sites are displayed in a museum on the island. But for those who do

Key to Kuwait City map, page 280. 1. General Post Office; 2. Bristol Hotel; 3. Souk area; 4. PTT; 5. British Embassy Chancery Offices; 6. British Embassy Commercial Offices; 7. Sheraton Hotel; 8. Hilton Hotel; 9. Bus Station; 10. Information Ministry; 11. Education Ministry; 12. Public Works Ministry; 13. Social Affairs & Labour Ministry; 14. Foreign Affairs Ministry; 15. Finance Ministry; 16. Public Health Ministry; 17. Justice Ministry; 18. Electricity & Water Ministry; 19. Oil Ministry; 20. Commerce & Industry Ministry; 21. Waqfs & Islamic Affairs; 22. Interior Ministry; 23. National Bank of Kuwait; 24. Commercial Bank; 25. Al-Ahli Bank; 26. Gulf Bank; 27. Bank of Kuwait & Middle East; 28. Kuwait Real Estate Bank; 29. Central Bank; 30. Industrial Bank.

not have the time, a selection of the antiquities recovered is on display in the former Dasman Palace, now the Kuwait Museum, in Arabian Gulf Street, Kuwait City. A large selection of seals dating back to around 2500 B.C. can be seen, together with pottery fragments, stone carvings from the Greek temple, and, of outstanding interest, the famous Ikaros stele dating back to about the third century B.C. The stele bears a message believed to come from the Seleucid monarch Selukos II Kallinikos. The museum also houses displays of dhows, costumes and other traditional features of life in Kuwait.

Hotels

Kuwait Hilton, Bnaid al-Gar Street. P.O.B. 5886. Tel: 530000. Telex: 2039. De luxe class. 212 rooms. Single person around KD 25–30. Restaurant (*Failaka Grill*). Night club (*Starlight Supper Club*). Coffee shop (afternoon buffet for KD 1 per head). Summer barbecues beside swimming pool with music (KD 5 per head). Bar in Terrace Room. Tennis courts. Bowling alley. Billiards. Gymnasium (lessons in Yoga, jiu-jitsu, karate). Closed-circuit TV (two films daily). Shopping arcade. Darkroom. Conference facilities.

Kuwait Sheraton, Fahad al-Salem Street. P.O.B. 5902. Tel: 422055. Telex: 2016. De luxe class. 263 rooms. Single person around KD 25–30. Two restaurants—*Hunt Room* and *Al-Hambra* (also night club). Coffee shop has good food and service (specialities Grilled Hamour and Zubeidi). Summer barbecue around swimming pool with music (KD 5 per head). Bank. Small shopping arcade. Bookshop. Barber shop. Airline office. Tennis/squash courts. Sauna. Conference facilities.

Messilah Beach Hotel, Messilah Roundabout. P.O.B. 3522. Tel: 613466. Telex: 2215. Good facilities but not of the same class as the Sheraton or Hilton. 14 miles from city centre (regular free bus service to and from city available). 400 rooms. Single person around KD 20–22. Restaurant (*Mubarakiyah*). Night club (*Jawarah*). Coffee shop (open 24 hours). Three swimming pools (one for children). Private beach. Tennis/volleyball courts. Closed circuit TV (two films daily). Shopping arcade. Bookshop. Sauna. Conference, banqueting facilities.

Golden Beach, Arabian Gulf Street. P.O.B. 3483. Tel: 439521. Telex: 2231. Four star. 44 rooms. Single person around KD 18. Restaurant. Swimming pool. Conference facilities.

Carlton, Fahad al-Salem Street. P.O.B. 3492. Tel: 423171. Telex: 2064. Four star. 75 rooms. Single person around KD 18. Restaurant. Conference facilities.

Bristol, Fahad al-Salem Street. P.O.B. 3531. Tel: 439281. Telex: 2061. 115 rooms. Single person around KD 18. Restaurant.

Universal. P.O.B. 5593. Tel: 425361/425361. Telex: 2347. Four star. Single person around KD 16. Two restaurants—one serving European, the other Chinese food. Coffee shop.

Phoenicia, Fahad al-Salem Street. P.O.B. 3666. Tel: 421051. Telex: 2062. 72 rooms. Single person around KD 16–18. Restaurant.

Sahara Hotel, Al-Sour Street. P.O.B. 20461. Tel: 424121. Telex: 2102. 52 rooms. Single person around KD 20. Restaurant.

Ambassador, Abdullah Al-Ahmed Street. P.O.B. 2813. Tel: 425288. 32 rooms. Single person around KD 14.

New Cedars, Sharq (near Hanra Cinema). P.O.B. 1793. Tel: 432938. 20 rooms. Single person around KD 12.

Restaurants

HOTEL RESTAURANTS

Failaka Grill, Kuwait Hilton, Bnaid al-Gar Street. Tel: 530000. Usually only open for lunch hours. Limited menu. Afternoon buffet at KD 3 per head.

Hunt Room, Kuwait Sheraton, Fahad al-Salem Street. Tel: 422055. Pleasant atmosphere. Limited menu but excellent food. KD 3–7.5 per person.

Al-Hambra, Kuwait Sheraton, Fahad al-Salem Street. Tel: 422055. Roof-top restaurant with a good view of city. Also serves as a nightclub in the evening with live music. Buffet lunch of European and Arab dishes (KD 2 per head). In the evening, meal per person from KD 2.

Mubarakiyah, Messilah Beach Hotel, Messilah Roundabout. Tel: 613466. Overlooks the sea. Buffet lunch at KD 3 per head. Dinner à la carte.

Mandarin, Universal Hotel. Tel: 425361. Chinese food. Around KD 1.5 per person.

OTHER RESTAURANTS

Adnan Jabri, Fahad al-Salem Street. Tel: 434676. Mainly Arab food. Also serves snacks (around KD 0.5 per head). Main course around KD 1.5 per head. Pleasant atmosphere but poor service.

Caesar's, behind Kuwait Sheraton Hotel. Also in Hamad al-Mubarak Street, Salmiyah. Tel. 634913/633044. Two restaurants considered to be among the best in Kuwait. Chinese and Western cuisine. Good food and service at reasonable prices. Soups around KD 0.300 per head, main course around KD 1 and dessert around KD 0.400. Intimate candlelit atmosphere.

Caesar's (Indian), Anwar al-Sabah Building, Hilali Street. Hot heavily-spiced dishes, otherwise good. Main course around KD 1

Golden Nest, near Old Traffic Department, Sharq. Chinese cuisine, also specialising in South-east Asian dishes. Expensive with meals per head from KD 2.

Kuwaitia Towers, KAC Building. Tel: 412400. Roof-top restaurant with excellent views. Afternoon buffet KD 2. Lavish atmosphere. Nightclub in evening.

Hubara Seafood, Salmiyah. Tel: 616827. Arab seafood dishes. Inexpensive.

Khyber, Fahad al-Salem Street. Tel: 425112. Indian cuisine. Specialises in Tikka cooking. Cheap.

Silver Star, Abdullah al-Mubarak Street, Salmiyah (on Hamad al-Mubarak crossing). Newly opened Chinese restaurant. Food served in abundance but expensive (over KD 7 for two persons). Dimly lit.

Nightclubs

Starlight Supper Club, Kuwait Hilton, Bnaid al-Gar Street. Tel: 530000. Floor shows and bands. Very expensive.

Al-Hambra, Kuwait Sheraton, Fahad al-Salem Street. Tel: 422055. Live music and dancing. Meal per person from KD 2.

Al-Jawharah, Messilah Beach Hotel, Messilah Roundabout. Tel: 613466. Band with occasional floor show. Expensive.

Marzouk Peal, Marzouk Pearl Building, Salmiyah beach road. Tel: 616073/616108. Dinner and dancing to live music.

Kuwaitia Towers, KAC Building. Tel: 412400. Band and floor show. Price plus meal KD 6-8 per person.

The *Sheraton* and *Hilton* hotels hold evening barbecues around their swimming pools during the summer. Dancing to live music. Sometimes a floor show. Breezy, informal atmosphere. KD 5 per head.

Airport Located about 10 miles from the outskirts of the city. Taxi service is available from the airport to the nearest hotel at a fixed charge of KD 3. The *Hilton* and the *Messilah Beach* hotels operate a regular private bus service to and from the airport. No duty-free shops. Refreshment bars. Bank. Bookstall.

Taxis There are two types of taxi—the shared 'common' taxi which plies a fixed route and the single 'private' taxi. Single taxi fares range from KD 1.5 for a ten-minute drive to KD 3 for a trip to the suburbs. Officially fares should not exceed KD 2 within the city area but drivers generally overcharge. Taxis between the airport and the city have a fixed charge of KD 3. Shared taxis are much cheaper. Taxi drivers do not understand directions easily and it is sometimes necessary to write down addresses for them. There is also a taxi-telephone service. The biggest operators are: *Ahmadi Taxi Hubara Club* (Tel: 980044/5), the *Carlton Hotel*, Fahad al-Salem Street (423171) and the *Gulf Taxi Company* which has a 24-hour home service (411450-411457). Charges are a standard KD 1.5–2, but can go higher depending on distance and waiting time.

Buses Kuwait city suburbs are well served by buses. The most convenient services are number 15 which goes from the centre, along Istiqlal Street, Salem al-Mubarak Street to the Salmiyah beach; number 18 which goes from the Centre, along Cairo Street and Tunis Street, down the Fourth Ring Road to Shuwaikh; and number 11 which goes from the Centre down Fahad al-Salem Street and Jamal Abdul Nasser Street to the Shuwaikh port and industrial area. Number 101 goes to Ahmadi and number 102 to Fahaheel and 103 to Jahra. Fares to the suburbs range from 40 to 70 fils. The fare to the outer towns is 100 fils. Many people make ample use of pick-up trucks or 'varnets'. These are double-seater trucks mainly for carrying heavy goods but their drivers make extra money by carrying passengers. Standard fare is around 500 fils, with overcharging it might come to 750 fils or a dinar. But they are fast and will take passengers to their doorstep.

Car hire firms *Al-Ghanim Company.* Tel: 423327. *Automobile Club.* Tel: 423008. *Jazeera & Quoraini Transport Company*, Ahmadi. Tel: 980554.
Visitors wishing to drive must obtain a permit from the Traffic section of the Police Department. Tel: 423111. It is issued on presentation of an International Drivers' Licence.

Travel Agencies *Al Athla*, Al-Sour Street (near Foreign Ministry). Tel: 425738. *Al Ghanim*, Fahad al-Salem Street. Tel: 432104. *Al Gharabally*, Fahad al-Salem Street. Tel: 420401. *Al Mulla*, Fahad al-Salem Street. Tel: 423231. *Globe Express*, Fahad al-Salem Street. Tel: 432969. *Kuwait Travel Bureau*, Fahad al-Salem Street. Tel: 434183. *Marafi Travel*, Mubarak al-Kabir Street. Tel: 425967. *Reem Travels*, Phoenicia Building, Hilali Street. Tel: 426504.

Airlines *Aeroflot*. P.O.B. 1316. Tel: 430227. *Air France.* P.O.B. 1316/153. Tel: 430224. *Air India.* P.O.B. 5997. Tel: 42033/438184. *Alia.* P.O.B. 576. Tel: 433141. *Alitalia.* P.O.B. 3172. Tel: 426868. *British Airways*, Al-Ghanian Travel Agencies. P.O.B. 81. Tel: 433206. *C.S.A.* P.O.B. 20062. Tel. 424662. *Cyprus Airways.* P.O.B. 81. Tel: 432104. *Egyptair.* P.O.B. 3697. Tel: 439586. *Garuda Airways.* P.O.B. 178. Tel: 432260. *Interflug.* P.O.B. 3539. Tel: 439298. *Iran Air.* P.O.B. 47. Tel: 424515. *Iraqi Airways.* P.O.B. 21965. Tel: 425721. *Japan Air*

Lines. P.O.B. 22423. Tel: 413454/433529. *Kuwait Airways Corp.* P.O.B. 394. Tel: 431821-10. *K.L.M.* P.O.B. 263. Tel: 433348.

Lufthansa. P.O.B. 21291. Tel: 422493/420362. *Malev Airlines.* P.O.B. 241. Tel: 433529/439771. *Middle East Airlines.* P.O.B. 310. Tel: 981046/423070. *Yemen Airlines.* P.O.B. 3539. Tel: 439298/423699. *Pakistan Airlines.* P.O.B. 3926. Tel: 421043. *Pan American.* P.O.B. 976. Tel: 420401.

Polish Airways. P.O.B. 3573. Tel: 433604. *Sabena.* P.O.B. 576. Tel: 434346. *Saudia.* P.O.B. 576. Tel: 434141/424741. *S.A.S.* P.O.B. 3488. Tel: 439561/62. *Swissair.* P.O.B. 3488. Tel: 439561. *Syrian Arab Airlines.* P.O.B. 3697. Tel: 425313/434313.

Shipping agencies *Abdel-Rehman al-Bahar.* P.O.B. 89. Tel: 438090. *Al-Ghanim Shipping Agencies.* P.O.B. 21708. Tel: 439296. *Al-Rashid Shipping Agencies.* Tel: 422022. *Arabian Seas Shipping Agency.* P.O.B. 856. Tel: 421303. *Ashkanani Shipping Agencies.* P.O.B. 4698. Tel: 435340. *International Shipping Agencies.* P.O.B. 2063. Tel: 422841. *Steamco Shipping Agencies.* P.O.B. 484. Tel: 439973. *United Shipper Services.* P.O.B. 403. Tel: 427029.

Post offices *General Post Office,* Fahad al-Salem Street (near Jahra Gate). Open from 0700–1900. *Central Post Office,* Hilali Street (opposite Planning Ministry). Opening hours from 0700–1900. Fridays from 0700 to 1000 hrs. For telegrams and registered letters. *Salmiyah Post Office,* Hamad al-Mubarak Street (near the Salmiyah co-operative society). Open from 0730–1330 and from 1600–1900 (winter), and 0700–1300 and 1630–1930 (summer). Closed Fridays.

Telephones Local telephone calls are free and visitors can walk into any shop and request the use of a telephone for local calls. International calls can be made from the telecommunications centre on Abdullah al-Salem Street.

Telephone numbers beginning with 2, 3, 4 cover Kuwait City; those with 5 Nogra, Nuzha and Hawalli; 6 Salmiyah; and 7 Farwaniyeh, Jebrieh and Sixth Ring Road.

Useful phone nos. *Flight Information*—710253. *Harbour*—427051. *Fire*—105. *Police*—109. *Ambulance*—422121. *Sabah Hospital*—812000. *Information*—101. *Trunk Calls* (Arab countries)—104. *Trunk Calls* (other countries)—102. *Enquiries & Complaints*—103. *Telegraphic Enquiries*—427033/358. *Postal Enquiries*—439091.

Telex Telexes can be sent from the telecommunications centre in Abdullah al-Salem Street (near Safat Square). Credit cards are accepted. Visitors may make use of a firm called *Teletex Services* which provides a 24-hour telex, telephone answering and secretarial service. It is located near the Kuwait Hilton (Tel: 445779/445788/445668).

Shops There are several large departmental stores in Fahad al-Salem Street. There is a shop (with two branches) specialising in antiques—*Saled Ismail Sayed Abdul Rasool*, at Ali al-Salem Street (Tel: 433765) and off First Ring Road, near Silver Towers Grocery (Tel: 422972).

Souks The main souk is in a mammoth building in Mubarak al-Kabeer Street, which is one of Kuwait's few modern commercial complexes. The shops are on the ground floor and mezzanine. The souk sells mainly modern imported goods. *Souk al-Kabir*, a smaller market, is in Fahad al-Salem Street.

Social clubs *The Gazelle Club*, on the Fahaheel Road in the Funtas area, is the most popular club among Western expatriates (Tel: 911911). It has facilities for water-skiing, boating, table tennis and badminton. It also has a swimming pool and cafeteria and puts on movie shows. A limited number of guests, accompanied by members, are allowed in for a charge of KD 1 per head. *Hunting and Equestrian Club* (Tel: 717271). Mainly Arab membership. Holds weekly horse races during winter. Also arranges hawking trips. Facilities for table tennis and volleyball. *Kuwait Sea Club* (Tel: 610131). Swimming, boating and water-skiing. Guests with members admitted on Thursdays and Fridays for KD 2.

Other clubs include the *Qadesiyah* (Tel: 514554), *Arabi*, *Kuwait*, *Salmiyah*—all of which have sporting facilities (swimming, squash, soccer, volleyball, table tennis). Guests must be accompanied by members.

Leisure/sport Kuwait's sporting facilities have mushroomed over the last few years from practically nothing. Most amenities are centred round private clubs and football stadiums. But the Government is setting up public recreational centres. One scheme involves turning Failaka Island into a grand amusement park and tourist resort.

The sea is excellent for swimming and fishing. Kuwait Bay has some fine beaches, some of which have already been taken over by private clubs. Riding is popular, with horses being provided by several stables. Horse races are held at the *Hunting and Equestrian Club* (every Thursday in the cooler months) and at the *Ahmadi Governorate Horsemen's Association*. The traditional sport of falconry still remains but it is expensive.

Soccer is now the national sport and has become increasingly popular since the national team's success in several big international tournaments. At least half a dozen football clubs have their own stadiums which also have facilities for basketball, handball, volleyball, tennis and gymnastics.

Kuwait has at least two museums worth visiting—the *Kuwait National Museum*, Arabian Gulf Street (Tel: 432020) and the *Science and Natural History Museum* in Abdullah Mubarak Street (Tel: 421268). *The British Council*, Mansouriyah (off Cairo Street), has a library and puts on regular film shows.

Bookshops *Family Bookshop*, Salem al-Mubarak Street, Salmiyah (Tel: 614340). *Khayat Bookstore*, Khaled Zaid Building, crossroads of Hilali Street and Fahad al-Salem Street (Tel: 437579). *Kuwait Bookshop*, Thunayan al-Ghanim Building, Sour Street (Tel: 434226). Large stock of Western books, newspapers and periodicals.

Hospitals The best hospitals for emergency treatment are *Sabah Hospital* (Tel: 812919), *Amiri Hospital* (Tel: 422121) and *Mowasat Hospital* (Tel: 610345), which is private.

Pharmacies *Al-Ghanim Pharmacy*, Fahad al-Salem Street. Tel: 422061. *Indian Medical Store*, Fahad al-Salem Street. Tel: 420034. *Sahara Pharmacy*, Salem al-Mubarak Street, Salmiyah. Tel: 611404. *Sima Pharmacy*, Baghdad Street, Salmiyah. Tel: 614183. All pharmacies are open from 0800–1230 and from 1600–2100. The English and Arabic daily newspapers publish a list of pharmacies on all night duty, along with addresses.

Banks Head offices: *Central Bank of Kuwait*, Abdullah al-Salem Street. P.O.B. 526. Tel: 427121. *Al-Ahli Bank*, Mubarak al-Kabeer Street (behind Gulf Bank). P.O.B. 1387. Tel: 411101. Telex: 2067. *Bank of Kuwait & The Middle East*, Ali al-Salem Street. P.O.B. 71. Tel: 421161. *Commercial Bank of Kuwait*, Mubarak al-Kabeer Street. P.O.B. 2861. Tel: 411001. Telex: 2004. *Credit & Savings Bank*, Muazi Street (off the Arabian Gulf Street). P.O.B. 1454. Tel: 420091. *Gulf Bank*, Mubarak al-Kabeer Street. P.O.B. 3200. Tel: 449501. Telex: 2001/2015. *National Bank of Kuwait*, Abdullah al-Salem Street. P.O.B. 95. Tel: 422011. *Kuwait Real Estate Bank*, P.O.B. 22822. Tel. 410110. *Industrial Bank of Kuwait*. Behind Gulf Bank Building. P.O.B. 3146. Tel: 442000. *Burgan Bank*, Ali al-Salem Street (opposite National Bank Building). Tel: 411992/411886. *United Trading Group*, Mubarak al-Kabeer Street (near Al-Ahli Bank). P.O.B. 8733. Tel: 420115. *Financial Group of Kuwait*, Kuwait Souk Building, Mubarak al-Kabeer Street. P.O.B. 23986. Tel: 444013/444023.

All head offices are open from 0800–1200 during May to October and from 0830–1230 from November to April. Closed Fridays.

Ministries/Government departments Ministries: *Commerce and Industry*, Fahad al-Salem Street. P.O.B. 2944. Tel: 422101. *Communications*, Jamal Abdul Nasser Street (near the Ports area). Tel. 439091.

Defence, Jahra Road. P.O.B. 1170. Tel: 819288. *Education*, Commercial Area 9, Hilali Street. P.O.B. 7. Tel: 427041. *Electricity and Water*, Mubarak al-Kabeer Street. P.O.B. 12 & 54. Tel. 433821. *Finance*, Fahad al-Salem Street, P.O.B. 9. Tel: 439001. *Foreign Affairs*, Al-Sour Street. P.O.B. 3. Tel: 422041. *Housing*, Arabian Gulf Street, Salmiyah. P.O.B. 23385. Tel: 617033.

Information, at cross roads of Hilali Street and Mubarak Al-Kabeer Street. P.O.B. 193. Tel: 427141. *Interior*, off First Ring Road, Shamiyah. P.O.B. 4 & 11. Tel: 816111. *Justice*, Abdullah al-Mubarak Street. P.O.B. 6. Tel: 435044. *Oil*, Fahad al-Salem Street. P.O.B. 5077. Tel: 415201. *Public Health*, Arabian Gulf Street (near Seif Palace). P.O.B. 5. Tel: 431911. *Public Works*, Mubarak al-Kabeer Street. P.O.B. 8. Tel: 435151.

Social Affairs and Labour, Abdullah al-Mubarak Street. P.O.B. 563. Tel: 427104. *Awqaf and Islamic Affairs*, Mubarak al-Kabeer Street. Tel: 433849. *Planning*, Hilali Street (opposite Central Post Office). P.O.B. 15. Tel: 423100. *Legal & Administrative Affairs*, Municipality Buildings, Hilali Street.

Government departments: *Auditing Bureau*, Kuwait Souk Building, Fahad al-Salem Street. Tel: 421036. *Civil Service Commission*, Shuwaikh. P.O.B. 1074. Tel: 817402. *Kuwait Fund for Arab Economic Development*, Mubarak al-Kabeer Street. P.O.B. 2921. Tel: 439261. *Kuwait Institute for Scientific Research*, Jamal Abdul Nasser Street, Shuwaikh. P.O.B. 12009. Tel: 816988. *Kuwait University*, Khalidiyah, Fourth Ring Road. P.O.B. 5969. Tel: 811188. *Municipality*, Hilali Street. P.O.B. 10. Tel: 439061. *Shuwaiba Area Authority*, Shuwaiba. P.O.B. 4690. Tel: 961760. *National Housing Authority*, Airport/Jahra Road. P.O.B. 23385. Tel: 817022. *Radio Stations*, Hilali Street (behind Kuwait Governorate). P.O.B. 193. Tel: 420181. *TV Station*, Arabian Gulf Street (near Kuwait Hilton Hotel). P.O.B. 193. Tel: 439041.

Embassies *Afghanistan*, Flat 3, 10 Shaikh Ahmed Jaber Building, Dasman. P.O.B. 22944. Tel: 442701. *Algeria*, Istiqlal Street, Daiyah. P.O.B. 578. Tel: 519987. *Bahrain*, Birjis Homoud Building, Riyadh Street, Dohai. P.O.B. 196. Tel: 513691/511172. *Bangladesh*, Istiqlal Street, Dasmah. P.O.B. 22344. Tel: 542205/542688. *Belgium*, Mohammed al-Ghunaim Villa, Damascus Street. P.O.B. 3280. Tel: 512455/514644. *Brazil*, Istiqlal Street, Dasman. P.O.B. 21370. Tel: 549600. *Bulgaria*, Street 11, Plot No. 1, Mansouriyah. P.O.B. 11141. Tel: 531181. *People's Republic of China*, Shaikh Ahmed Jaber Buildings 4 and 5, Dasman. P.O.B. 2346. Tel: 423871-423811.

Cyprus (Honorary Consulate), Office 22, Commercial Centre 3. P.O.B. 1447. Tel: 433075/440040. *Czechoslovakia*, Cairo Street,

Daiyah. P.O.B. 1151. Tel: 514451/514507. *Denmark*, Plot 175, Block 1, Abdullah al-Salem district. P.O.B. 5452. Tel: 544988/543166. *Egypt*, Istiqlal Street. P.O.B. 11252. Tel: 519955/519956. *France*, Qabazard Building, Istiqlal Street. P.O.B. 1037. Tel: 516144/516323. *Gabon*, House 15, Plot 4, Sayed al-Ali Street, Abdullah al-Salem district. P.O.B. 23956. Tel: 542032. *West Germany*, Al-Mamoun Street, Shamiya. P.O.B. 805. Tel: 814182/814055. *East Germany*, Ibrahim Fleij Building, Shuwaikh. Tel: 817055/817056. *Greece*, Al-Mansour Street, Shuwaikh. P.O.B. 23812. Tel: 814169.

Hungary, Villa 44, Plot 1, Daiyah. P.O.B. 23955 Safat. Tel: 516530-516420. *India*, 34 Istiqlal Street. P.O.B. 1450. Tel: 530600/530612. *Indonesia*, Nuzha Main Street, Block 3, Nuzha. P.O.B. 21560. Tel: 519923. *Iran*, 24 Istiqlal Street. Tel: 533220/533327/ 532236/531869. *Iraq*, Istiqlal Street, Plot 26, Daiyah. P.O.B. 5088. Tel: 533466/7/8. *Italy*, Mulla Buildings, Omar Bin-Khatab Street, Sharq. P.O.B. 4453. Tel: 445120/445121. *Japan*, Badr Salem Building, Al-Sour Street, P.O.B. 2304. Tel: 424051. *Jordan*, Istiqlal Street, Daiyah. Tel: 533500/1.

Lebanon, Shaikh Duaij Building, Istiqlal Street. P.O.B. 253. Tel: 519765/6. *Libya*, 27 Istiqlal Street. P.O.B. 21460. Tel: 518188/518278. *Malaysia*, Block 1, Parcel 2, Mansouriyah. P.O.B. 4105. Tel: 546022. *Mauritania*, Parcel 3, Street 34, Rawdah. P.O.B. 23784. Tel: 531424/ 512382. *Morocco*, Khaled al-Ghunaim Building, Street 46, Shuwaikh. P.O.B. 784. Tel: 813700/813912. *Netherlands*, Al-Saleh Building, 14 Sha'ab district. P.O.B. 21822. Tel: 547573/547471. *Oman*, Villa No. 3, Istiqlal Street. P.O.B. 21975. Tel: 514380/514177. *Pakistan*, Villa 29, Plot 4, Hamza Street, Daiyah. P.O.B. 988. Tel: 532101/531135.

Paraguay (Honorary Consulate), Kharafi Factories, Shuwaikh Industrial Area. P.O.B. 886. Tel: 814462. *Poland*, Block 4, 3rd Ring Road, Parcel 111. Rawdah. P.O.B. 5066. Tel: 510355/6. *Qatar*, Shaikh Duaij Buildings, Istiqlal Street. P.O.B. 1825. Tel: 513599/ 513606. *Rumania*, Shaikh Duaij Ibrahim Building, 16 Istiqlal Street. P.O.B. 11149. Tel: 548363/519640. *Saudi Arabia*, Istiqlal Street, Embassies Area. P.O.B. 20498. Tel: 531155/531206/531419. *Senegal*, House 9, Street 35, Parcel 3, Rawdah. P.O.B. 29832. *Somalia*, House 7, Nasir Street, Shuwaikh. P.O.B. 22766. Tel: 815788/815433. *Soviet Union*, Shaikh Ahmed Jaber Building No. 5, Dasman. P.O.B. 1765. Tel: 431422/415192.

Spain, Block 1, Parcel 395, Street 12, Abdullah al-Salem district. P.O.B. 22707. Tel: 512722. *Sudan*, Shaikh Duaij Ibrahim Building, Istiqlal Street. P.O.B. 1076. Tel: 519299/519382. *Sweden*, Uthman Building, Hilali Street, Salhieh. P.O.B. 21488. Tel: 415539/415548. *Switzerland*, Kuwait Souk Building, Oman Street. P.O.B. 23954. Tel: 444725. *Syria*, Street 46, Parcel 4, Daiyah district. Tel: 530163/4.

Tunisia, Shaikh Duaij Ibrahim Villa, Istiqlal Street. P.O.B. 5976. Tel: 542144/542215. *Turkey*, Bnaid al-Gar (near Hilton Hotel). P.O.B. 20627. Tel: 531466. *United Arab Emirates*, Abdulaziz al-Mutawa Building, Istiqlal Street. P.O.B. 1828. Tel: 518381/518569.

United Kingdom, Arabian Gulf Street. P.O.B. 2. Tel: 432047. UK Commercial Office, 6 Kuwait Investment Company Building. P.O.B. 300. Tel: 439220. *United States*, Bnaid al-Gar (opposite Hilton Hotel). P.O.B. 77. Tel: 424156. *North Yemen*, Abdullah al Mazidi Building, Abdullah al-Salem district. P.O.B. 4626. Tel: 518855. *South Yemen*, Building 19, Street 10. Mansouriyah district. P.O.B. 5174. Tel: 517898. *Yugoslavia*, Al-Mansour Street, No. 15, Shuwaikh 'B' district. P.O.B. 20511. Tel: 818872. *Zaire*, Street 34, Rawdah, Villa 24, Parcel 3. P.O.B. 3998. Tel: 518923.

Newspapers/periodicals Dailies: *Kuwait Times*, Fahad al-Salem Street. P.O.B. 1301. Tel: 813133. English. 6,000 circ. *Arab Times*, P.O.B. 2270. Tel: 813566. Telex: 2270. English. *Akhbar al-Kuwait*, Shuwaikh. P.O.B. 1747. Tel: 431767. 4,000 circ. *Al-Qabas*, Airport Road, Shuwaikh Industrial Area. Tel: 812820. 40,000 circ. *Al-Rai al-Am*, Airport Road, Shuwaikh Industrial Area. P.O.B. 695. Tel: 813133. 35,000 circ. *Al-Siyassah*. P.O.B. 2270. Tel: 813566. 19,000 circ. *Al-Watan*. Safat. P.O.B. 1142. Tel: 448123. 30,000 circ.

Periodicals: *Adwah al-Kuwait*. P.O.B. 1977. Weekly. Literature and arts. Circ. 5,000. *Al-Arabi*. P.O.B. 748. Monthly published by Ministry of Information. 125,000 circ. *Al-Hadaf*, Al-Sour Street. Weekly. Politics and culture. 35,000 circ. Also monthly supplement *Economic Review*. *Al-Nadha*, Airport Road, Shuwaikh Industrial Area. P.O.B. 695. Tel: 813133. Weekly. Social and political. 45,000 circ. *Al-Yaqza*, P.O.B. 6000. Tel: 428971. General weekly. 20,000 circ. *Usrati*. P.O.B. 2995. Tel: 810093. Fortnightly women's magazine. 10,000 circ.

Media Kuwait has two English language dailies—*Kuwait Times* and the recently launched *Arab Times*, both of which give a reasonably comprehensive coverage of Kuwaiti and world news.

Radio Kuwait's English Service runs from 0800–1100 and from 2000 –2300. News bulletins are broadcast at 0830 and 2030. An FM radio service runs daily from 0800–0200, broadcasting mainly classical/pop music. *Kuwait TV* station shows English-language films and cartoons and English news bulletins. An English movie is transmitted every Wednesday night at 2245 and serials every Friday at 2245. On average, the TV station devotes 180 minutes daily to English transmissions.

Churches *National Evangelical Church*. Tel: 433230. *Roman Catholic Church*. Tel. 434637. *Roman Catholic Church*, Ahmadi. Tel: 983647. *St. Paul's Anglican Church*, Ahmadi. Tel: 983203.

Useful addresses   *Chamber of Commerce and Industry*, Ali al-Salem Street. P.O.B. 775. Tel: 433864.

GENERAL INFORMATION

How to get there   BY AIR (outside Gulf): Kuwait has good direct connections with Europe and other Middle East countries outside the Gulf. There are daily flights from London (averaging twice a day) and several flights a week from Paris, Rome, Athens and Frankfurt. There are less frequent weekly flights from Amsterdam, Madrid, Belgrade, Skopje, Belgrade, Zurich, Prague, Geneva, Bucharest and Copenhagen. *Air India* has been operating two weekly flights from New York. There are virtually daily flights from Bombay and flights at least once a week from Bangkok, Delhi, Karachi, Tokyo, Kuala Lumpur, Rangoon and Singapore.

There are daily connections from Beirut, Damascus (averaging about two a day) and Cairo (twice a day). Several flights a week go to Kuwait from Amman and there is a less frequent weekly service from Aden, Tunis, Casablanca, Khartoum, Sanaa, Taiz, Tripoli and Larnaca.

BY AIR (Inter-Gulf): Daily flights connect Kuwait with Bahrain, Dubai and Abadan. There are also several weekly flights from Abu Dhabi, Baghdad, Riyadh, Dhahran, Jeddah, Muscat, Shiraz and Tehran. There is a weekly flight from Ras al-Khaimah.

Visas   Visas or entry permits are required by all except nationals of Kuwait, Bahrain, Qatar, Saudi Arabia, United Arab Emirates.

Transit visas are not required by passengers continuing their journey to a third country by the same aircraft, or by passengers transiting within 24 hours. But passengers must have tickets with reserved seats and valid documents for their onward journey.

With visas for a visit sponsored by a Kuwaiti resident a form in duplicate must be validated by the Minister of the Interior. For a visit without a sponsor, permits in duplicate can be obtained from a Kuwaiti consulate. Some nationals require a No Objection Certificate issued by Ministry of Interior. A personal cable from a contact address in Kuwait that N.O.C. will be available on arrival is sufficient for transportation. The cable must state number and validity of N.O.C. and flight number.

Holders of passports bearing on the cover the inscription British Passport at the top, and at the bottom the inscription United Kingdom of Great Britain and Northern Ireland or, Jersey or Guernsey and its dependencies do not require visas, if their national status is shown on page one as either British Subject, Citizen of the United Kingdom and Colonies, or British Subject, Citizen of the United Kingdom, Islands and Colonies and their place of birth or country of residence is shown on page two as being in the United Kingdom or Channel Islands. Instead they must have an entry permit, in duplicate, one to be handed to the immigration authorities on entering the country, the other on leaving. Visitors' permits may be obtained from a Kuwaiti consulate or any authorised Kuwaiti mission abroad. Alternatively, a visitor's card, in duplicate, may be obtained from the Passport, Nationality and Residence Department, Ministry of the Interior, through a sponsor resident in Kuwait.

Language The official language is Arabic. English is the second language and most businessmen either speak English or have an English-speaking person on their staff.

Hours of business The Muslim weekend is Thursday afternoon and all day Friday, Saturday and Sunday are normal working days. Banks work from 0830–1230 Saturday to Thursday (winter) and 0800–1200 Saturday to Thursday (summer), 0830–1230 Saturday to Thursday (Ramadan). Government offices work from 0730–1330 Saturday to Wednesday, 0730–1130 Thursday (winter) and 0700–1300 Saturday to Wednesday, 0700–1100 Thursday (summer). During Ramadan from 0830 or 0900–1230 or 1300 Saturday to Thursday.

Private offices work (in summer and winter) from 0830–1230 and from 1630–2000. Shopping hours are from 0830–1230 and from 1630 to 2100. American owned or affiliated companies work from 0900–1300 and from 1400–1700, and have Thursday and Friday off.

Fahaheel working hours are from 0800–1230 and from 1330–1700. Shops remain open till 1900, except for a break in the afternoon between 1330 and 1500. In Ahmadi, shopping hours are from 0900–1230 and from 1500–1800.

Official holidays In Kuwait the Muslim weekend is Thursday afternoon and all day Friday. Saturday and Sunday are normal working days.

		1977/78
Id-al-Adha*		22–26 November
Al-Hijra (Muslim New Year)*		12 December
New Year's Day		1 January, 1978
Kuwait National Day		25 February
Prophet's Birthday*		25 February
Ascension of the Prophet*		3 July
Id al-Fitr (end of Ramadan)*		3–6 September

293

The dates of the Muslim holidays, marked with an asterisk *, are only approximate as they depend upon sightings of the moon, hence there may be differences of one or more days from the dates given. In general, Muslim holidays recur 10 to 12 days earlier each year. When planning a visit to Kuwait, businessmen are advised to seek confirmation of these dates. It is advisable to avoid visiting Kuwait during the fasting month of Ramadan (the month preceding Id al-Fitr). During the month Muslims fast between sunrise and sunset. The consumption of food, drink and tobacco in public is prohibited; restaurants are closed and government departments work short hours. The month of Ramadan ends with a three-day holiday during which all businesses are closed.

Time   GMT + 3.

Electric current   Electricity is supplied at 240 volts, 50 cycles AC. Plug adaptors are available in hotels.

Health   International certificates of vaccination against smallpox required by all passengers. Cholera immunisation is necessary for visitors from infected countries. The certificate must show two injections of vaccine at one week's interval. Yellow fever vaccination is required if arriving within 6 days after leaving or transiting countries, any parts of which are infected.

Water   Tap water is not normally safe to drink. Imported mineral water is available from any grocery.

Currency   The unit of currency is the Kuwaiti Dinar (KD) divided into 1,000 fils. The following denominations are in circulation:
   Notes: ¼, ½, 1, 5 and 10 dinars
   Coins: 1, 5, 10, 20, 50 and 100 fils

Currency regulations   There are no restrictions on the import or export of currency.

Customs regulations   Visitors can bring in any amount of cigarettes, tobacco or perfume. But the import of alcohol is prohibited (see below).

Alcohol   Alcohol is banned in the country. But it is available in some hotels. The diplomatic corps is also allowed to import a certain amount. Customs men at the airport, borders and ports keep a strict lookout for liquor. They are particularly keen at checking bags of passengers coming in from Europe. Anyone caught bringing in bottles of alcohol will normally merely have them confiscated. Visitors frequently manage to bring in bottles for personal consumption but the official advice is: Don't risk it. People caught with liquor can spend anything from a month to a year in jail, especially if found with a large amount.

Useful advice Lightweight clothing is essential between April and September when it can be extremely hot. During the cooler months thicker clothes should be brought as a precaution against cold spells. Women should dress modestly. Men are advised not to wear shorts. At most times open necked shirts are acceptable but a jacket and tie (preferably a lounge suit) should be worn on formal occasions, particularly when meeting government officials.

Further reading *Kuwait*, by Ralph Shaw. Ministry of Information. Kuwait. 1976. *A Golden Dream: The Miracle of Kuwait*, by Ralph Hewins. W. H. Allen. 1963. *A New Look at Kuwait*, by Zahra Freeth. Allen and Unwin. 1972.
The Arab of the Desert: A Glimpse into Badawin Life in Kuwait and Saudi Arabia, by Harold Dickson. Allen and Unwin. 1959. *History of Eastern Arabia*, 1750–1800, by Ahmad Abu Hakimah. Beirut. 1965.
Kuwait. Chase World Information Series, New York (in preparation). *The Gulf States: Business Opportunities*. Metra Consulting Group, London. 1976.

Government

Head of State	Amir: Shaikh Sabah al-Salem al-Sabah
Prime Minister	Shaikh Jaber al-Ahmad al-Sabah
Deputy Premier and Minister of Information	Shaikh Jaber al-Ali al-Salem al-Sabah
Education	Jassem Khaled al-Marzuq
Housing	Hamad Mubarak al-Ayyar
Public Works	Hamad Youssef al-Nisf
Interior & Defence ...	Shaikh Saad al-Abdullah al-Salem al-Sabah
Social Affairs & Labour ...	Shaikh Salem al-Sabah al-Salem al-Sabah
Communication & Transports	Sulaiman Humud al-Zaid al-Khaled
Foreign Affairs	Shaikh Sabah al-Ahmad al-Jaber al-Sabah
Finance	Abdel-Rahman Salem al-Atiqi
Health	Abdel-Rahman Abdullah al-Awadi
State for Cabinet Affairs ...	Abdel-Aziz Hussain
Justice	Abdullah Ibrahim al-Muffarij

Electricity & Water	...	...	Abdullah Youssef al-Ghanim
Oil	... ...	...	Abdel-Muttaleb al-Kazimi
Trade & Industry	...	...	Abdel-Wahhab Youssef al-Nifisi
Planning	... ...	...	Mohammad Youssef al-Adasani
Waqfs (Religious Endowments)			Youssef Jassem al-Hijji
State for Legal & Administrative Affairs	... ...	...	Shaikh Salman al-Duaij al-Sabah

OMAN

THE SULTAN OF OMAN

THE SULTAN OF OMAN
His Majesty Sultan Qabous Bin-Said

Sultan Qabous assumed position as Sultan (after the abdication of his father Said Bin-Taimur) in July 1970. He was born in Salalah in 1940, educated privately in the UK and at the Royal Military Academy, Sandhurst. He lived in the UK between 1956 and 1966 during which time he also studied local government. His assumption of power ended a long period of feudal and repressive rule by his father. Sultan Qabous is the fifteenth descendant of the ruling dynasty of the Abousaid family. In early 1976 he married the younger daughter of Sayyid Tariq Bin-Tarmini al-Said.

Oman

Area   120,000 square miles

Population   1.5 million (official estimate 1976)

Chief towns   Capital Area (including Muscat, Muttrah and Ruwi) 80,000

Gross National Product $1,600 million (1975 estimate)

GNP per caput $2,070

GEOGRAPHY

Oman is a land of barren mountains, sand and gravel desert and comparatively fertile coastal plains. It has a thousand-mile coastline which for centuries gave it domination over the vital trade routes along the Arabian Sea and the Gulf of Oman.

The country lies between latitudes 16° 40′ north and 26° 20′ north and longitudes 51° 50′ east and 59° 40′ east. It has borders with the People's Democratic Republic of Yemen, with Saudi Arabia and with the United Arab Emirates. The northern tip of Oman, the Musandam Peninsula, is cut off from the main area of the Sultanate by the UAE. This Peninsula overlooks the Strait of Hormuz and has a commanding position at the entrance to the Gulf. The mountains fall with dramatic suddenness into the sea, forming a rugged, rocky background to seas that can be so dangerous to shipping that, from time immemorial, Musandam has been considered a hazard to navigators. In the first century A.D. a Greek merchant seaman wrote: 'All the Arabian ships take their departure from it with some ceremonies of superstition, imploring a blessing on their voyage and setting afloat a toy, like a vessel rigged and decorated which, if it is dashed to

301

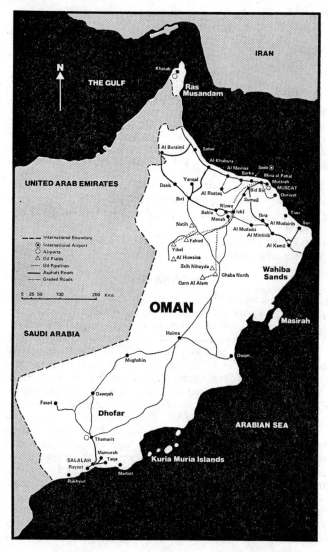

pieces by the rocks, is to be accepted by the ocean as an offering for the escape of their vessel'.

The backbone of the country is the Hajar Mountains which stretch from the Musandam Peninsula across the north of Oman almost to Ras al-Hadd on the extreme south-eastern tip of the Arabian Peninsula. The highest peak is the 10,000 foot Jabal Akhdar massif.

The Hajar range is divided by the Sumail Gap into two parts, the Western and Eastern Hajar. The area of the Eastern Hajar is known as the Sharqiya or Eastern Region. It is dominated by mountains, which form a barrier between Muscat and Sur, the principal town and port of the Sharqiya. Apart from some fishing settlements and a few date groves, the coastline of the Sharqiya is rugged with the mountains reaching the sea.

Muscat, the capital of Oman, was, in the past, reached with difficulty from the interior, because mountains form a wall round the town. They fall steeply into the sea, giving Muscat its name—*Masquat* meaning 'the place of falling'. Muscat and the neighbouring towns of Muttrah and Ruwi, form the Capital Area, with an estimated population of around 80,000. Although the Sultan has built a new palace in Muscat there is little room for expansion there, so that the main urban development is taking place outside that town, notably in Ruwi. Muttrah has always been the commercial centre of Oman.

North west of the Capital Area, between the mountains and the sea, lies the Batinah coastal plain which contains around 40 per cent of Oman's cultivated land. It is about 160 miles long with a width varying from $1\frac{1}{2}$ to 19 miles. Apart from some areas of mangrove swamp the coastline is virtually a continuous belt of cultivated land behind which is an expanse of gravel plain extending to the foothills of the Hajar mountains.

Northern Oman and the southern Dhofar province are divided by a large area of desert which consists of a mixture of stony plains and sand dunes. To the west is the vast Rub al-Khali, or Empty Quarter. Under the northern periphery of the deserts lie the country's oil fields. Masirah Island is situated off the desert's coastline.

Dhofar is divided by the Qara Mountains which form an escarpment cutting off a coastal plain, flanking both sides of the town of Salalah, from the gravel desert in the north. The mountains reach up to 3,600 feet in height and have a high plateau covered in sparse, stunted vegetation. The coastal plain is about 44 miles long with a width ranging from one to six miles. Off the north east coast of Dhofar lies the Kuria Muria Islands.

CLIMATE

Oman has a varied climate. In the north on the coast it is hot and humid during summer months from June to September. Temperatures average around 40° C (104°F) but can go as high as 50°C (122°F). Inland the heat is much more arid but can be more intense. In winter the temperature remains warm on the coast, seldom falling below 10°C (50°F). Inland it can be cold.

The north has an annual rainfall varying from less than one inch to four inches. Much of the rainfall comes in the winter or spring when the weather can be stormy. In the Hajar Mountains road travel can be hazardous during storms because the wadis can swell up and swamp the roads within a matter of minutes.

Dhofar has a sub-tropical climate. Most of the area receives the annual monsoon off the Indian Ocean, between mid-June and mid-September. As a result temperatures are more temperate. The monsoon brings rain to the coastal plain and penetrates over much of the Qara Mountains. For many weeks the upper reaches are covered in mist with a drizzle turning the dried vegetation into a rich green.

PLANTS AND WILDLIFE

Most vegetation in Oman is confined to the Batinah coast, various oases in and around the Hajar Mountains and the monsoon areas of Dhofar. The Batinah has numerous date palms, and papaya and mangoe trees. It is full of gardens, groves and smallholdings growing fruits and vegetables ranging from tomatoes and cabbages to limes and bananas. The bare Hajar Mountains are scattered with patches of greenery covered in lucerne, date palms and lime bushes. Some of these oases, well irrigated by a network of underground channels or *falajs*, have orchards of pomegranates, peaches, figs and even grapes. Beneath the Jebal Akhdar a few small villages have vines and walnut trees. Oleanders are frequently found lining the *falajs*.

In Dhofar the combination of the monsoon and the heat gives the coastal plain a luscious tropical vegetation which makes Salalah and its vicinity look more like part of East Africa than the Arabian Peninsula. On the plateau of the Qara Mountains the rains provide a grassland on which the local people feed their cattle.

There used to be a time when leopards were reputed to have lived in the Hajar Mountains and ostriches wandered in Oman's desert. But hunting and environmental influences have now forced the more spectacular examples of the country's wildlife into extinction. The Sultan has banned the hunting of rare species. As a result gazelles still roam parts of the desert and a few oryx are thought to be still living there. But now the most common inhabitants in the desert are the jerboa, the fennec fox, desert hare, a certain species of mouse and a variety of lizards. The fearful camel spider is found occasionally. In the mountains a wild goat of a similar variety to one in the Himalayas is reported to be still in existence. Rabbits are also fairly common in the Hajar range.

Indigenous birds Oman has a reasonably large population of indigenous and migrant birds. The Batinah coast is frequented by waders like the heron, flamingo and sandpiper. Sometimes a kingfisher can be spotted flitting among the greenery skirting the shore. In the Hajar oases bulbuls, roller birds and red-billed plovers are fairly common sights. Pigeons and crag martins can also be found. There used to be numerous bustard in the desert where they lived off the scattered vegetation and were the main prey for hawks. But now hawking has reduced them almost to extinction. Dhofar has a variety of tropical birds.

Oman's offshore waters are thought to be one of the richest fishing grounds in West Asia. The most common fish are tuna, sardines, mackerel, barracuda and jacks. There are a variety of sharks of which the hammer-head type is the most popular among the Omanis. Shark meat is considered to be a delicacy. Other dangerous fish are the sting-ray and sword-fish. Omani fishermen have caught the occasional dolphin. Green turtles are sometimes seen swimming close to the shore. Oysters breed in shallow waters off Muscat. On some beaches in northern Oman crabs can be a menace.

COMMUNICATIONS

In 1970 Oman had only five kilometres of tarmac road, no port and no civil airport. But within a few years it had built up a basic communications system good enough to support a rapidly expanding economy. The construction of roads has probably had the biggest economic and social impact. The country now has around 620 miles of asphalt road. Tarmac roads link the Capital Area with the main towns along the Batinah coast to Sohar and with Nizwa, the principal town in the interior. An asphalt road now cuts across the Dhofar Mountains, connecting Salalah with Thamarit. New roads also connect Buraimi with Sohar and Salalah with Raysut and Taqa. Sur will no longer be so isolated from the rest of the country when a new road linking it with Bid Bid and the Capital Area is completed.

Within the Capital Area itself the huge rocky escarpments separating Muscat from Muttrah have always made travelling between the two difficult and has recently led to severe traffic congestion. But the two towns are being linked more directly by the construction of a road being blasted through a rocky promontory.

New airports Oman's only airport used to be a military airstrip just south of Muttrah. Then in the early '70s an international airport was built 30 miles away at Seeb, the nearest suitable patch of land. This now provides regular flights to Europe and the Indian sub-continent. The country's national carrier is Gulf Air which it owns jointly with Bahrain, Qatar and Abu Dhabi. Gulf Air runs domestic flights between Seeb and Salalah where the airport is being improved to international standards. There is a third airport at Thamarit which is reputed to have one of the longest runways in the Middle East.

The country now has a new port at Muttrah called Mina Qabous which is large enough to meet most of the country's needs. A small harbour has also been built at Raysut to serve Dhofar. Sur has a fishing harbour.

The nation's telephone system used to be restricted to Muscat and Muttrah. Now it extends through the Ruwi Valley to Seeb and up the Batinah coast and into the interior. Salalah has a small network which is linked to the north by radio. Cable & Wireless of the UK has been replaced as the operator of the system by a new national company called Omantel which is run with help from the US.

With the completion of a 60-circuit earth satellite station in the Hajar Mountains the nation's telephones can be linked directly to the international circuit. International calls have been relying on a small 24-circuit booster station at Wattiyah, which relays calls via Bahrain.

SOCIAL BACKGROUND

A census of the whole population of Oman has never been carried out. The Government estimated it to be 1.5 million in 1976. But unofficial estimates put it closer to 500,000. In 1974 the United Nations calculated the population to be 750,000, but some expatriate observers considered this to be too high. Various surveys by foreign consultants in recent years have put the population of the Capital Area at 50,000 (now thought to be at least 80,000), the Batinah coast and nearby foothill at 130,000, the mountains and inland foothills at 150,000, and Dhofar at 50,000. In addition the desert, Musandam Peninsula and Sur areas have been thought to hold 20,000, 15,000 and 11,500 respectively.

The people of Oman come from varied backgrounds. A high proportion of the population of the Capital Area consists of Baluchis, Somalis, Indians and Pakistanis, and expatriate Arabs, Europeans and North Americans. Many have come to the country as immigrant workers during the development boom of the last few years. In 1976 an estimated 60,000 people from the Indian sub-continent were working in Oman, most of them under short-term contracts in the construction industry in and around the Capital Area.

Former immigrants But for many centuries groups from the Indian sub-continent and Africa have been coming to Oman. Baluchis from the Makran coast of Baluchistan and the port of

Gwadur, which was part of Oman until 1958, have settled on the Batinah coast. In Muttrah trade and commerce has for a long time been dominated by the Khoja or Lothis, a community of Hindus who migrated to Oman several generations ago. They are Omani citizens but have retained their own customs and language.

There are also substantial numbers of black Omanis, particularly in Dhofar, who are descendants of slaves from Zanzibar, the East African island which was controlled by Oman when its sea power was at its peak. Since the Zanzibar revolution of the 1960s when Arabs were expelled from the island, many Omanis have returned from there to the land of their forefathers. Many are now playing an important part in administration and the running of the social services.

Nomadic tribes still roam the deserts and mountains, herding camels, goats and sheep. A large proportion of the settled people in the interior are small farmers, cultivating date groves and cash crops. A lot of rural people are however leaving the land and migrating into the Capital Area looking for jobs to boost their income.

In the Musandam Peninsula there is a little-known tribe of fishermen and herdsmen called the Shihuh who speak their own dialect. They may be descendants of the original inhabitants of northern Oman, pushed into the mountains by successive invaders. The same is perhaps true of the Bayasirah community found in central Oman. Another small community is the group known as Zatut (singular Zutti), who might be described as tinkers, and who carry out specific jobs such as circumcision. They have a language of their own and seldom marry outside their group.

Variety of dress The ethnic variety of the Omani people is evident in their dress. Almost without exception Omani men and boys wear the long shirt known as a *dishdasha*. If it is cold he may wear a Western-type short coat, but on official or ceremonial occasions he wears a *bisht* or cloak and his decorated dagger, the *khanjar*. Omanis do not wear the *aqal* and *kafia* worn in Saudi Arabia and the Gulf States, but instead they wear a turban of Kashmir wool or white cotton, either meticulously pleated or wound loosely round the head.

Here to serve you.

ABU DHABI
    PO Box 278, Sheikh Hamdan Road. Tel: 23661
BAHRAIN
    PO Box 540, Manama. Tel: 55357/51827
DAMMAM
    King Street. Al-Fahd Bldg. Tel: 26460
DHAHRAN
    Booking and Sales Office, Alkhobar. Tel: 42000
DOHA
    PO Box 3668. Tel: 323165
DUBAI
    PO Box 1810. Tel: 25944, 22885
KUWAIT
    Fahad al-Salem Street. Tel: 415401, 415481
MUSCAT
    Maqbool Hameed Bldg, PO Box 392. Tel: 734863

saudia
SAUDI ARABIAN AIRLINES Member of IATA
Key to the heart of the Middle East.

a

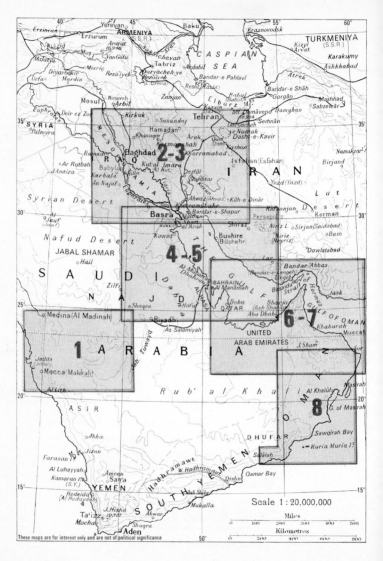

Scale 1 : 20,000,000

Miles
0   100   200   300   400   500

Kilometres
0   200   400   600   800

These maps are for interest only and are not of political significance

b

Al Ḥulayyrah

Ad Dawādimī

Abū Shaʿrāʾ

Shubrānīyah

J. Dhaḥlān

Ar-Rumādīyah

Ar-Ruwaydah

Ṣanāʿ

Nufayyid Sablah

Arwā

Ḥalaban

Bīr Ghuwaib

Surrah

Jibāl

W. ar. al Ḥawshah

Immi Wazīr

J. Khidā

Jabal Zāin

Jabal Jizlug

Bīr Jizlug

As Qaṣrab

Al Qaṣrab

Bīr Malīyah

Al Khaṣirah

as Nafūd

J. al Yanūfi

Bīr eṣ Sukhīs

Budayyiʿah

ʿIrq Subay

Ad-Dablat Shabab

Ar-Ruwaidah

Ash ʿarīyah

Shubramīyah

Afīf

Baqarah

Bīr Hudūf

Al Haqbah

Ẓaim

J. Ghurūb

J. Ḥasan

J. al Gharāmīl

Bīr Ḥaraqī

Jabal Ḥawzah

J. Kursh

J. Raṣen

Bīr Wurshah

W. Bishāh

W. Aslam

Shubramīyah

Al Khurmah

Al Ghārith

Ranyah

ʿAmāʿir

Al Amlaḥ

Bīr al Jahilīyah

Ar-Rawidah

J. Ḥimā Ḍarīyah

Bīr Hudūf

Al Mowayh

Bīr Khawārah

Bīr Haroym

Ḥarrat Ḥaḍan

Turabah

Ḥarrat Nawāṣif

Harrat al buqūm

ʿAmiu

As-Suwayrqīyah

Ad-Dafina

Mahd adh Dhahab

Khabra al ʿArn

Ḥadhah

Al Ḥawīyah

Usheyrah

As Seyl al Kabīr

Ḥarrat

Kulakh

Medina (Al-Madīnah)

Harrat Kuramā

J. Murayr

J. Abhā

W. al Aṭig

Bīr al Mashī

Abū Ruḍayy

Al Khafrīn

Sugaynah

Harrat Rahat

Bīr ʿal Arn

Abū Burmah

Wadi Ḥamnah

Madrakah

Rowyān

Shadād

Nejdi

Baqʿān

Al Madam

Sūq ar Rubā

Al Aqit

Alʿuyūn

Abyār Aṭi

Siaq Stowqg

Al Muṣeyya

Abū Ḍibā

Al Bīrān

ʿUmm Sama

Mirwaniyah

Maʿgadabah

J. Abū Shidād

J. Abū Shidād

Yanbuʿ

Suq Stowqg

Waṣṭah

Ḥuṣayr Ṣubḥ

Umm al Bīrak

Ir Mubeyth

Ḥajaʾr

Rabigh

Kuleys

Dahabān

Jiddah (Jedda)

MECCA MAKKAH

Arafat

At Ṭāʾif

Shadād

Ar Rakh

J. Qarnayt

Mastābah

Ḥāddā

Khumrah

ʿBakrah

Ar Raʾīs al Aswad

Niʿs Ḥāẓibah

7206

2

0 20 40 60 80 Kilometres
0 10 20 30 40 50 Miles

J. Qarachoq
Altün Köprü
Tāqtāq
Maʿāna Gaviheh
Kūh-e Chehel Chashineh
Chwārtā Penywin
Sarshive Zāgheh
KURDISTAN
KORDEST
Il Hadr
Ash Sharqāt
Ashur
Chamchamāl
Jarmo
Sulaymāniyah
Dezh Shāhpūr
Hoseynābād
Khosr
Arbat Owrāmān
Kirkūk
Hassara
Nuzi
Tāzoh Khurmātū
Tārjīl Lāylān
Qādin Karam
Dānūq Jambur Darbandikhān
Arandān
Zhivār
Sarvabad
Aliābād
Sanan (Sinneh)
Dehgolā
Gaveh
Halabja
Dam Dehe Sheykh
Pāveh
Qeshlāq
Yūzīdar
Kāmyārān
Kal Sā
Al Fathan
K-2
Bāiji
Parapāra
Tuz Khurmātū
Sulaymān Beg
Kifrī
Kalār
Maydān
Chāh-i Surkh
Zobeyr
Kānī Sur
Jabal Hamrin
Tikrīt
BAGHDAD
Daur
Qasr-e-Shirīn
QaraTappah
Zohāb
Tairūj
Sare-Pol-e Zehāb
Gahvāreh
Ravansar
KERMANSHAHAN
Tāqe B
Istabulāt
Sāmarrā'
Nahr al-ʿUzaim
Sunbula Kūh
Gilan Garb
Kermānshāh
Karand
PāytākP
Kaseh
Garon
Shāhabad
Tharthar Basin
Hit
Balad
Ruins of Opis
Daltawa
Al Mansūrīyah
Al Miqdādiyah (Shahrābān)
Al Khanaqīn
Jalūlā
Naft-e Shāh
Sūmār
Mandalī
Soltangoli
Zarneh
Manisht Kūh 2712
Chavār
Chardāvol
Hulūl
Ilam
Sarne
Al Khalis
Khān al Mashāhida
Baʿqūbah
Kaʿān
Imām Hāmid
Shandrukh
Tursāq
Shirwān
ILAM VA
Kūshke
Salehābad
POSHTKUH
Tarhān
Sim
BAGHDAD
Kadhimain
Habbanīyah
Lake Habbanīyah
R. Euphrates Barrage
Ar Ramadī
Al Mahmūdīyah
Ctesiphon
Old Nahrwān Canal
Zurbātīyah
Mehrān
Badrah
Jassān
Wārab
Meymeh
Qalʿeh Safid
Posht-e
Rahhalīyah
Bahr al Milh
Hindīyah Barrage
As Suwayrah
Al Iskandarīyah
Al Musayyib
Al ʿAzīzīyah
Hawr as Suwayqiyah
Nasrīan-e Paīn
Emāmzādeh Nasrod Din
Ghudaf
Karbala
HILLA
Khān al Mahāwīl
An Numānīyah
Al Kūt
(Kut-al-Imāra)
Tigris
Jannāh
Shaykh Saʿd
Shithatha
Ukhaydir
Borsippa
Al Hillah
Al Hāshimīyah
Al Muwaffaqiyah
Shaykh Jūwi
Wāsit
Abi al Gharbi
Musaiu
Subail
Musallā
Al Kūfah
Al Kifl
Ishāqī
Al Dāghghārah
Nippur
Al Hayy
Hawr as Saʿdiyah
Marhaj Khalil
KARBALA
Khan Jadwal
Cheharīz
Al Kumayt
Abū Sukhayr
An Najaf
Al Chammas
Ad Diwānīyah
Issin
Shuruppak
Qalʿat Sikkar
Al Am
Khān Kuhābih
Imām al Hamzah
Umma
Ar Rifāʿī
Al Lussuf
Al Sanīt
DIWANIYA
Shanāfīya
Ar Kumaythah
Telloh
Hawr al Awdah
Gharab
Birkat Hamad
Erech (Uruk)
Ash Shatrah
Al ʿUzayr Ezraʾs Tomb
As Samāwah
Al Khidr
Batha
Hammam
Ar Rihāb
Ur
An Nāsiriyah
Kharfīya
Al ʿAshūrīyah
Ash Shabakah
SHAMIYA
Al Qusayr
Suq ash Shuyūkh
Hawr al
Al Maʿānīyah *Sharaf*
Wāqisah
As Salman
Jalibah
BASRA (Ash Shuʿu
Al Luṣayah
Athāmin
Birkat Athāmin
Sudayr
DESERT
Rushī
Sh
Qabr Bandar
Az Zafiri
Birkat al ʿAqabah
Qasr Shagra
Safay al Maqūf

© JOHN BARTHOLOMEW & SON LTD.

3

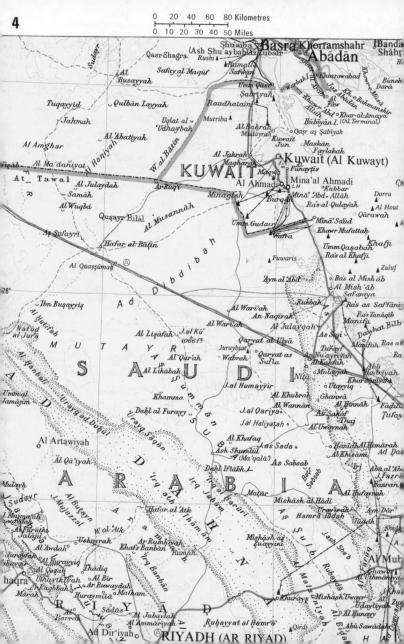

© JOHN BARTHOLOMEW & SON LTD.

5

Pazanan · Dishtar-e · Kūh-e · Ganjgān · 3,573 · Majnavā · Khowrjān · Abbāsābād · Mōrj
Cham-e · Khāiz · Bāsht · Nūrābād · Ardakān · Morghāb · Pasargadae · Kūpān · Sa'in
Zeydun · 3,188 · Gach Sārān · Kor · Qavāmābād · Shādatābād · Tājābād
Zohreh · Bābā Kalū · Gas Pipe Line · Sheykhi · Shūl · Rūdiān · Takht-e Jamshīd · Jashni · Khvānsār
Bandar-e Deylam · Sivand · (Persepolis) · Arsenajān · Tashk · Chāh · Shīr
Heṣār · Garangan · Kūh-e Tābask · Güyom · Kenāreh · Daryācheh-ye Tashk · Hāqq
Bibi Hakimeh · 3,218 · Chukāk · Qalāt · Zarqān · Sāvakān · Khērāmeh · Chāh Dar
Kāzerun · Kotal-e · **Shīrāz** · Dovon
Ganāveh · Kilur Karim · Chāh · Dokhtar · Daryācheh-ye · Tafihān · Daryācheh-ye · Daryācheh-ye · Ghowr
Rūstā'i · Kesht · Fāmūr · Mahārlū
Bandar-e Rīg · Deh Kohneh · Kōnar Takhteh · Kavār · Sarvestān · Bakhtigān · **Neyrīz**
Khārg Is. · **Borāzjān** · Dālakī · Bālādeh · 10,500 · Abādeh · Jang-e Karam · Rūnīz-e · Bālā
Khārk · Helleh · Jereh · Mūrjān · Mand · K-e Safīdār · Eṣṭahbānāt · (Savtanāt)
Ra's osh Shatt · Sa'dabad · Jazīreh-ye Shīf · Gardaneh · Sandalī · Khāniyak · 3188 · **Fasā** · Fedeshkūh
Darius · Khowr-e Soltāni · Choghādak · Farrāshband · Asemānjerd · Zāhedan · Dārākūyeh
Būshehr · Rīshahr · Ahram · K-e Khormūj · Dasht-e Palang · **Firūzābād** · Mādevān
(Bushire) · Bāshī · 1,960 · Rūdbār · Khafr · Sīar · Dowlatābād
Ra's Halīleh · **BŪSHEHR** · Khūrāb · Kord Sheykh · **Jahrom** · Khosiyel
Fereidoon · Bu ol Kheyr · Seng · Qīr · Mobārakābād · Hajjiābā
Faqīh Ahmadān · Darvīslu · Pasrūdak · Mākū · Harm · Gowd
Lāvar · E · Mand · Jūyom
Kabkan · Kaki · Zir-Rūd · Dowlatābād · Kūr Deh · Makiyeh · Dehkūyeh
Kuh-i-Mand · **KHALI-E FARS** · Garmosht · Kūrdeh · Ewīz · e Lār · Lā
Zir-Rūd · Ālamarvdasht-e · Haftvān · Khonj · Kūh-e Khonj · Gerāsh
Kangan · Jam · Kārez · Ālāmarvdasht · Hormūz-e Bāgh · Anve
Botkhāneh · Deyyer · Akhtar · Tāheri · Asīr · Dār · Khalīlī · Kūh-e Gāvbus
Parak · Gāleh · Varāvī · Khīārū Lamard · Kuhvār
Asalūyeh · Nakhl-e Taqī · Nāy Band · Beyram · Jonu
Gāvbandi · Eshkanān · Rostāq Mará
Ali Janā · Bandar-e Shīū · Heshnīz · Band-e · Band-e · Chārm
Al Jurayd · Bandar-e Māqām · Bāzeh · Nakhīlū · Chārū
Kurayn · Ra's · Sheykh Sho'eyb · Bandar-e
Jubayl · Abu Sa' Fah · Hendorābī · Qeys
Ra's al Qulay'ah · Najmah
Ras Tannurah · Tarūt
Al Qatif · Sayhāt · Bāni For
BAHRAIN · Ra's Rakan · 26
Al Khubar · Al Muharraq · Al Hadd
Al Budayyi · **Al Manamah** · Fuwayriṭ
Az Zallāq · Sitrah · Khuwayr · Ra's Laffān
Awālī · Al Ghuwayr · An · Rakhsh
Rumaythā · Nuqay'ah · Ra's · Rostam
Gulf of · Huwār I. · al Matbakh · LH · Hālūl · Maydan · Sassan
Bahrain · Al Jamāliyah · Al Khawr · Mahzam
Al Qarah · Al Wusayl · As Sakhāma · Idd el Sharqi
Jishshah · Dukhān · **QATAR**
Fudul · Dawhat Salwāh · Ar Rayyān · **Doha (Ad Dawhah)**
ofuf · Umm · Al · Al Bandaq · Dās
Bāb · Wakrah · Shirā'awh · Umm al Sheif
Al Kirānah · Al Wukayr · Qarnein · Zirkūh
Juh · Umm Sa'īd · Dayyina
ah · (Musay'īd) · Arzanah · Al-Zukum
Al Khisah · Salwāh · Khōr al 'Udeid · Al Qaffāy
As Sīkak

LEGEND

International boundary	
Administrative boundary	
Main road	
Other road	
Track	
Railway	
Canal	
Oil pipeline	
Oilfield	
Ancient site	Qabr Bandar∴
Pass	≍
Waterhole	⌣
International airport	Ⓐ
Airport, airfield	Ⓐ
Sand area	
Marsh	
Salt lake	
Salt swamp	
Salt desert	
Lava field	
Escarpment	
Wadi	
Tribal name	BALI
Height in metres	▲ 3,333

HELĪ-YE
Pathān
Khvorgū
Rīg Matī
Shamīl
Dozdān
Sārās
Kahn 'Alī
NADER-E
Kūhhā-ĕ
Hasan Langī
Rudān (Deh Barez)
Manūjān
71°ye Genū
Jalābi
Tamp-e Gīrān
BS VA
Abbās
OMAN
Hājjīābād
Jaghīn
uru Spit
Hormoz
Rīāb
Rāyang
Sar Ney
Qeshm
Mināb
Mināb
Mazār
Teleng
Sūzā
Lārak
Kūhestak
Shām
2,161
Kūh-e Kūhrān
ngām
Taherū'ī
Angohrān
TRAIT OF HORMUZ
Sīrī
Gānī
Parākiu
Musandam Pen.
LH
Kamsar
Ra's Qabr al Hindī
Gaza
Deh Bandan
Yamāsūr
Khasab
Elphinstone Inlet
Berizak
Mīr Shahdād 1,896
işa
Ghubbat al Ghazīra (Malcolm Inlet)
Tujak
Būdīng
Gūh Kūh
al Harim 2,08
Lima
Ra's-al-Kūh
Kangān
Sogar
Hasār
TO OMAN
Ra's Ḥaffah
Jāsk-e Kohneh
Gabrik
Ra'l
Dabā al- Bay'ah
Jāsk
Adhan 1,128
Dadnah
GULF
Khōr Fakkān
Al Qurayyah
Fujairah
OF
Kalbā
Khatmat al Malāha
Aswad
OMAN
Ash Shinas
Al Ḥusayfīn
Liwā
Mahdah
Sohār
atar
991
Sahm
NL
Dayl
Qaşbīyat al Burayk
Al Khābūrah
24°
Al
Wuqbah
Ghuzayn
Waqam-'Alwā
Mina al Fahal
As Siwayq
Al Masana'a
Sīb
Maṭrah
Dank
Yanqul
Mulaḋḋah
Barkā
Baushar
MUSCAT (MASQAT)
Fida
Miskīn
Hazm
Jummah
Fanjah
Ra's al Khayrān
Mazim
Muqniyāt
Ar Rustāq
Nakhl
Al
Bidbid
As Sīfah
Dubāi
Dārīz
Al Awābī
Sumāil
Al Ḥajar
Qurayat
Ibrī
J. Kawr 3,018
Hamrā
Al 'Ayn
Wabāl
Al Wāsiṭ
Daghmar
Kubārah
2,719 Al Akhḋar
Mutī
Izkī
Mazāra
Dibab
Al Ghāfat
Bahlā
Birkat al Mawz
BUWA SHAH
Fins
Wal 'Ayn
Nizwā
Samad
Samad
Ibrā
Tīwī
Bisyah
Ma'mūrah
Al Mudabī
Manāh
Mudairib
Qalhāt
Sur
Al Ḥadd
Adam
Sanāw
Ash Sharqiyah
Badiyah
J. Khadar 2,151
Ra's al Hadd
Al Aswad
Wāsiṭ
Mintirib
Fulayj
J.Fahūd
Natih
Al Kāmil
UB U
J.Salakh 1,055
Barzamān
Afar
Bilād Banī Bū Hasan
Al Waft
Ra's al Khabbah
Fahūd
Awaifī
Bilād Banī Bū 'Ali
As Suwayh
Yiba
W.Umaq
Al Huwaisah

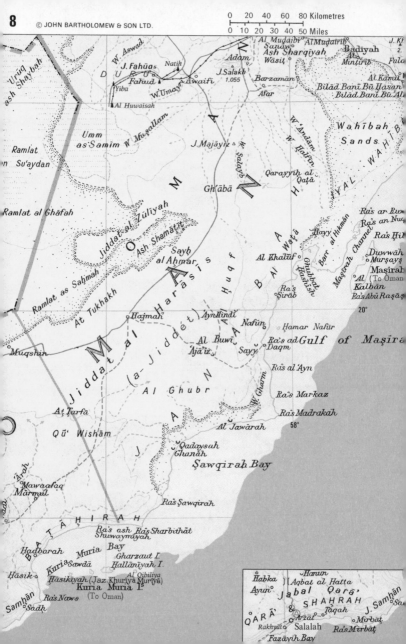

It's only natural...

that you want the most luxurious airliner in the world when flying **to the Gulf**

The longer the journey the more comfort counts – and our FiveStar TriStars will take you direct to the Gulf in comfort no other airline can surpass. There is a departure from London (Heathrow) at 10.00 every morning – and at least one other departure, direct to the Gulf, each evening. On the FiveStar TriStar, passengers enjoy more space . . . more individual attention . . . more beautiful service, including superb international cuisine and club-style bar . . . more luxury, including multi-channel stereo and businessman's library.

Luxurious Rolls-Royce powered comfort . . . beautiful service . . . the most convenient timetable . . . all reasons why Gulf Air is the natural choice to the Gulf. For further information contact your travel agent or Gulf Air.

London Gulf services in association with British Airways.

the most luxurious airliner the world has ever known

GULF AIR FiveStar TriStar

★★★★★

Corner of Piccadilly & Berkeley Street, London W1V 9HF.
Reservations: *Tel:* 01-409 1951 *Telex:* 28591 A/B GFRES G
Birmingham, 021-632 5931 • **Manchester,** 061-832 9677 **Glasgow,** 041-248 6381 • **and all offices of British Airways.**

c

d

In the coastal areas the Omani women wear the *abaya*, a long black cloak, out of doors, but they rarely veil their faces. Up-country the *abaya* is not usually worn but the women do tend to veil or wear a mask. The Baluchi women, in their brightly coloured cotton dresses and draperies, present a gay contrast to the black *abayas* and the white *dishdashas*.

Most Omanis on the coast are Sunni Muslim. But inland the majority of the people belong to the Ibadhi sect, which has emphasised the principle of an elected, rather than a hereditary, religious leader, or Imam. The first Imam of Oman was Julanda Bin-Masuud, elected about 750 A.D. as 'the first of the rightful Imams of Oman'. The Ibadhi creed became a rallying point for Omanis who were constantly under attack from neighbouring forces, like the Wahhabis of Saudi Arabia, who wanted them to change their beliefs. They have clung tenaciously to their creed, but nevertheless have shown toleration towards other sects.

CONSTITUTION

Oman has no written constitution. The Government is headed by Sultan Qabous, who appoints ministers responsible for the various functions of the Government. They meet under the chairmanship of the Sultan as a Council of Ministers.

Regional government follows a pattern largely unchanged for over a thousand years. The Sultan appoints *walis* or governors to represent the principal towns and districts, and each *wali* is assisted by a *qadhi*, or religious judge. Local government is being developed in the larger towns by the setting up of municipal councils.

The Sultan has absolute power. All legislation comes in the form of decrees issued by the Sultan who is under no obligation to consult anyone beforehand. But some tentative steps are being made towards institutionalising government, rather than leaving it totally dependent on personalities. The Council of Ministers has been able to take its own decisions in the absence of the Sultan. A series of planning and development councils has been established to co-ordinate decisions and to ensure that ministers comply with long-term plans. Until recently decisions on some major projects were taken without much investigation into their viability or cost effectiveness. Now a

309

L

reasonably efficient administrative structure is slowly taking shape which in time should become a smooth-working bureaucracy.

The legal system is based upon the Ibadhi interpretation of the *Sharia*, and jurisdiction is administered by the *qadhi* in conjunction with the *wali*. There is an appeal court, and final authority for appeals rests with the Sultan. Otherwise the country does not have an independent judiciary. Traffic offences and petty crimes are handled by the police with the offenders being brought before the local *wali* or governor for punishment.

HISTORY

Although little archaeological exploration has been carried out in Oman, flint artifacts discovered there indicate that a hunting people inhabited the fringes of the present desert 10,000 years ago. At the time the desert was probably covered in vegetation. Since earliest times Oman's position, at the junction of the Indian Ocean and the Gulf, also made it an important staging post and entrepôt on east–west trading routes. As a result the Omanis have for a long time been a seafaring people. In ancient times they not only ventured along the coasts of Oman and the Gulf but, taking advantage of the monsoons, they sailed across the Arabian Sea to India and beyond, or to the coast of East Africa. They carried cargoes from India up the Gulf to be offloaded and transported overland for the benefit of people of Mesopotamia, the Phoenicians, the Greeks and the Romans.

Oman could have been the country of the Magan people, a nation described on Sumerian tablets of 3000 B.C. as being sea-traders who brought cargoes of copper, alabaster, diorite, timber and even onions and garlic to Ur and other Mesopotamian centres. But archaeologists in the United Arab Emirates believe that Magan could have been located there. In the first millenium B.C. Dhofar exported frankincense to Mesopotamia where it was burnt in large quantities during religious ceremonies. The temple of Baal at Babylon used two and a half tons a year.

Islam embraced   Persian forces later invaded Oman at various times leaving the *falaj* irrigation system as a legacy. This network of underground channels and wells, still in use today, supported a thriving agricultural economy inland. Persian influence was gradually eroded by the settlement of two migratory waves of Arabs—from the north the Nizari, and from south-west Arabia, the Yemeni Azdites.

The Omanis embraced Islam before the Prophet died in 632 A.D. But they were one of the first to break away from the control of his successors. During the caliphate of Ali bin Abi Talib, the Prophet's son-in-law and fourth successor, a break-away sect, the Khawarij, was founded. Although many of the Khawarij were annihilated in battles with the Caliph's armies, their doctrine survived and was widely accepted in Oman, where the sect was named Ibadhi after one of the first Khawarij leaders.

The Ibadhi preferred to elect an Imam (one who sets an example) as spiritual and temporal leader, who could be dismissed, if proved unsuitable. Imams were elected as Omani leaders from 751 to 1620. But the Ibadhi had to fight to maintain their sectarianism against incursions by the Caliph's armies seeking loyalty in the form of payments of the *zakat* (tax) levied on all Muslims by the Caliphate. They also had to struggle to preserve their independence against subsequent attacks by Persians, Karmathians, Kirmani, Seljuks, Ghuz and Moghuls.

From the fourth to the tenth century, the Omanis widened their sea trade to places as far away as China, Indonesia, Madagascar and East Africa. Sohar became one of the most important ports in the Indian Ocean and Oman's shipbuilding started to gain fame.

Portuguese invasion   In the beginning of the 16th century Oman was one of the first to fall victim to European penetration into the region. The Europeans, led first by the Portuguese, wanted control of the coastal areas of the Arabian Peninsula in order to ensure their command of the trading routes between Europe and India and the Far East. In August, 1507, a Portuguese fleet commanded by Alfonso de Albuquerque anchored off Ras al-Hadd and soon afterwards the Portuguese took over Muscat and Sohar apparently without much difficulty and built massive forts in both places.

Albuquerque described Muscat as: 'a large and very populous

city, surrounded on the inner side with very large mountains, and on the seaboard it is close to the water's edge. . . . The harbour is small, shaped like a horseshoe, and sheltered from every wind; it is the principal entrepôt of the Kingdom of Ormuz, into which all the ships which navigate these parts must of necessity enter, to avoid the opposite coast, which contains many shallows. It is of old a market for carriage of horses and dates; it is a very elegant town, with very fine houses, and supplied from the interior with much wheat, maize, barley and dates, for loading as many vessels as come for them'.

At this time there were a number of petty chiefs in Oman, warring with each other. But when Nasir Bin-Murshid al-Yaarubi was elected Imam in 1624, he set out to unite the country and to end the internal strife. When he died in 1649 he had become the unchallenged ruler of Oman and his armies were attacking the Portuguese in Muscat. He was succeeded by his cousin, Sultan, who took Muscat and expelled the Portuguese in 1650, pursuing them to India and to the east coast of Africa and building up a considerable fleet from their captured ships. The seafaring trade flourished and with the wealth that this brought to the country agriculture was improved and many houses and forts built, among them the great fort at Nizwa. An Omani historian, Salil Bin-Razik, wrote of the Imam's reign: 'Oman revived during his Government and prospered; the people rested from their troubles, prices were low and roads were safe, the merchants made large profits and the crops were abundant. The Imam himself was humble. . . . He used to traverse the streets without an escort, would sit and talk familiarly with the people'.

Civil war Civil war broke out in 1718, resulting from the rivalry between two tribes, the Yamani and the Nizari. The former were led by a member of the Beni Hina tribe and thus became known as Hinawi. The latter were led by a member of the Beni Ghafir and so were called Ghafiri. Although the two leaders were killed during the fighting, the names of the factions are still remembered and every tribal child knows whether his tribe belongs to the Hinawi or Ghafiri. The war ended with the coming to power of Ahmad Bin Said, who was elected Imam in 1749 by both warring factions. He was the first in the long line of Al Bu Said rulers, ancestors of the present Sultan.

Towards the end of the 18th century the son of the then reigning Imam left his father in command at Rostaq and set himself up as ruler in Muscat. This was the beginning of the concept of 'Muscat and Oman', by which name the country was known to the West for many years. When Sultan Qabous assumed power in 1970 he changed the name from the Sultanate of Muscat and Oman to that of the Sultanate of Oman, thus emphasising the unity of the coastal community with the communities of the interior.

Treaties with Britain By now Britain was interested in Oman and the Gulf through the trading activities of the East India Company. The first treaty between Britain and Oman was concluded in 1798 when the East India Company wished to prevent the French from competing in Gulf trade and using Oman as a stepping stone to India. In Article 3 of the treaty the Imam stated: 'Whereas frequent applications have been made, and are still being made, by the French and Dutch people for a Factory . . . it is therefore written that, whilst warfare shall continue between the English Company and them, never shall from respect to the Company's friendship, be given to them throughout all my territories a place to fix or seat themselves in, nor shall they get even ground to stand upon within this state'.

Two years later a further treaty was negotiated in which the Imam agreed that 'an English gentleman of respectability' should reside at Muscat as agent of the East India Company in order that 'the friendship of the two states may remain unshook till the end of time, till the sun and moon have finished their revolving career'.

Later there were several treaties concluded for the suppression of the slave trade, a Treaty of Friendship, Commerce and Navigation signed in 1891, and an agreement in that same year by which the Sultan pledged himself not to cede, sell, mortgage or otherwise give for occupation, save to the British Government, the dominions of Muscat and Oman or any of their dependencies.

Zanzibar connection The son of the Imam who had signed the first treaty in 1798 became an outstanding figure in Omani history. He was Said Bin Sultan who, soon after his accession, had to resist attacks from the powerful Wahhabis based in central Arabia. With the aid of the British and the Iranians he was finally successful in keeping them at bay. He then became increasingly involved in expanding Omani influence in East Africa, spending most of his life in Zanzibar. When he died in 1857 his two sons, Majid and Thuwaini, quarrelled over who should rule in Oman and who in Zanzibar. Their dispute was referred to the Government of India and its Governor-General, Lord Canning, awarded Zanzibar to Majid, with an agreement that there should be an annual payment to Oman of 40,000 Maria Theresa dollars. Thuwaini became Sultan in Oman. Payment of the annual sum was made by India from 1871 after Zanzibar fell into arrears, and this arrangement continued until Indian independence in 1947, when the Foreign Office took on the responsibility. Payment finally ceased in 1956.

Said Bin Sultan never sought the title of Imam, possibly because he was primarily interested in foreign affairs and did not wish to make his capital in the interior, at Nizwa, Rostaq or Sohar, the three towns in which by custom the Imam could properly lead the Friday prayers. As a result Oman was without an Imam, and this led to several attempts being made by other leaders to claim the title. For most of the 19th century and the early part of the 20th there was unrest between Muscat and the interior.

Clashes with interior Discontent developed into open rebellion in 1915 two years after Sultan Taimur became Ruler. The rebels attacked Muscat, but the Government of India sent troops to aid the Sultan and the attack was repulsed. The revolt, however, was not settled until 1920 when a peace agreement was signed at Seeb between Isa Bin Salih, the leader of the rebels, and the Sultan. Under this agreement a measure of autonomy in local affairs was allowed to the interior tribes, but it did not allow for any abrogation of the Sultan's sovereignty over Oman as a whole, nor of his responsibility for external affairs.

In 1932 Sultan Taimur abdicated and was succeeded by his son Said, father of the present Sultan. For most of his reign there was still division between Muscat and the interior, with a claimant to the title of Imam exercising spiritual authority in Nizwa. To add to the Sultan's problems the Saudi Arabian

Government sent forces to occupy the Buraimi settlements in 1952, some of which were claimed by Oman and some by Abu Dhabi. The case was taken for arbitration to a Tribunal consisting of Belgium, Cuba, Pakistan, Saudi Arabia and Britain, but arbitration broke down and with British support the Saudis were expelled in 1955. The Sultan's forces then proceeded to occupy other parts of the country, taking Rostaq and Nizwa from the followers of the Imam. A revolt by tribesmen supporting the Imam broke out in the Jebel al-Akhdar region in 1957. The British again assisted the Sultan who finally defeated the rebels in 1959. From that date there has been peace in the hinterland of Muscat, but not in Dhofar.

Dhofar War In 1963 tribesmen in this southern mountainous area rebelled. When the Aden Protectorate became independent in 1967 they were aided by left-wingers from the newly-styled People's Democratic Republic of Yemen. The mountains of Dhofar are difficult terrain in which to carry on a war and it dragged on into the 70s, being a continual drain on manpower and oil revenues. The British supported the Sultan's forces, Iran sent in several thousand troops, and Jordan sent a contingent. Finally, at the beginning of 1976, the war came to an end. Sultan Qabous announced the defeat of the Popular Front for the Liberation of Oman (PFLO), and the destruction of the People's Liberation Army as a cohesive force on Omani territory. The only route through which the PFLO could bring their supplies from their bases in the People's Democratic Republic of Yemen was virtually sealed.

Meanwhile the country was beginning to benefit from oil production. The first concessions for exploration were granted in 1925 but it was not until 1967 that oil exporting began. Although there were plans for the development of the country Sultan Saaid Bin-Taimur was unwilling to allow education and other social and economic changes to alter the way of life of the Omani people. He lived the life of a recluse in Salalah until, in 1970, his son Qabous deposed him and became Sultan.

Over the next four years Oman's economy expanded at an unprecedented pace. Development expenditure went up more than sevenfold, most of it going on the building up of modern communications. Previously the country had virtually no surfaced roads and no ports or civil airport. But in late 1974 the Government suddenly had to put the brakes on its spending because it found it was running out of money despite a quadrupling in oil revenues. As a result over the past two years the country's expansion has slowed down considerably.

Recent Events

Despite Oman's victory over left-wing guerrillas in Dhofar in early 1976, there were still isolated outbreaks of hostility for a time. Pockets of PFLO guerrillas carried out intermittent raids in the province and in November 1976 an Iranian Phantom jet was shot down by South Yemenis near the South Yemen–Oman border. By early 1977, however, Iran decided that peace had at last been restored and withdrew most of the 3,200 Iranian troops stationed in Dhofar. Only Iranians operating radar installations and anti-aircraft units would remain. In March 1977 it was reported that Oman and South Yemen had reached a reconciliation but by mid-year Saudi Arabia and Kuwait were still mediating in an attempt to make reconciliation a reality.

The defeat of the PFLO allowed the Omani Government to launch a reconstruction programme in Dhofar which had been left behind in the country's drive towards modernisation. Iran and Saudi Arabia were expected to contribute funds for development projects, which mainly involved building up the province's infrastructure. Dhofar's economic future was also boosted by the discovery of oil in commercial quantities in the Amal area in 1976.

The return of peace to Dhofar helped Oman to strengthen its ties with other Arab states. In 1976 several Arab leaders, including King Khaled of Saudi Arabia and President Sadat of Egypt, visited Oman and in November that year Oman was the venue for the Gulf Foreign Ministers' Conference. The change in Oman's status in the Middle East was highlighted by a transformation in its relations with Iraq, which had formerly been a strong supporter of the PFLO. Iraq decided, at the last moment, to attend the Gulf Foreign Ministers' Conference and in May 1977 a high-level Iraqi delegation visited Oman for talks on strengthening bilateral relations.

317

ECONOMY

In recent years Oman has developed even more rapidly than its neighbours in the Gulf. In the 60s the ultra-conservative Sultan Said ensured that virtually no modern facilities were established in the country. So when his son Sultan Qabous succeeded him after his overthrow in 1970, Oman had no roads, port, or civil airport and only three small schools and one missionary hospital. The country had to start from scratch and by 1974 development expenditure had risen more than six times. In fact the country was spending money so fast that the Government found itself running out of cash in late 1974.

Since then the rate of expansion has slowed considerably. For about 18 months no new projects of any significance were initiated. Instead the Government concentrated on restoring some order to the country's finances. A Development Council was set up to establish some co-ordination between government departments. In 1976 a Five Year Plan was drawn up to ensure that the country progressed at a measured pace. The Plan, due to end in 1980, envisages a 12.6 per cent annual growth in Gross National Product (GNP) and provides for total investment of $2,800 million, most of which will come from government sources.

The basic aim of the Plan is to relieve the country of its dependence on oil by diversifying the economy. Priority has been given to industry and agriculture and fishing, which could become major earners of income. In the early 1970s 93 per cent of Government development expenditure was allocated to infrastructure. As a result the country's main centres are now linked by tarmac roads. There are two modern harbours, the principal one being Mina Qabous at Muttrah, an international airport at Seeb, a power and desalination plant, over 200 schools and around 15 hospitals. Under the Plan, however, spending on infrastructure will drop to 70 per cent.

Oil

Oil accounts for 95 per cent of government revenue. In 1976/77 it was expected to bring in some $1,360 million compared with $1,120 the previous year. In 1976 output averaged 365,000 barrels a day (b/d) and was expected to be about the same in 1977. Oman is not a member of the Organisation of Petroleum Exporting Countries (OPEC) but nonetheless it applies OPEC price rises.

Serious exploration for oil began only in the 1950s. The first successful discoveries were made between 1962 and 1964. The original four fields were in the Fahud region beyond Jebel al-Akhdar to the west of Muscat. The Ghaba fields to the south and southeast of Fahud came into production in 1975. Crude from both the Fahud and Ghaba fields is taken by a common pipeline to Mina al-Fahal. New fields came on stream in 1976.

The company responsible for the oil industry is Petroleum Development Oman (PDO). It is 60 per cent owned by the Government, along OPEC lines. The remaining shares are divided between Shell with 34 per cent, Compagnie Française des Petroles (CFP) with 4 per cent, and Partex with 2 per cent.

Oil finds Oman must discover more oil if it is to keep up a high level of development over the next decade. Production will start to fall within a few years unless new oil fields can be brought on stream soon. Prospects of new commercial finds have however been good. Sun Oil, a consortium of North American and German companies, has found a promising well offshore near Masira Island. One of the most hopeful finds has been by France's Elf-Aquitaine who have been drilling off the Musandan Peninsula in a concession which stretches into Iranian water. Any output would have to be shared with Iran. PDO itself has already found oil in Dhofar and in mid-1977 was reported to be going ahead with production there at a cost of $200–250 million. Initially, production was expected to reach 30,000 b/d. But the Government hopes that further discoveries in its southern province could boost Dhofar's oil output to as high as 200,000 b/d.

The Government is also anxious to discover more gas. Oman's reserves of associated and non-associated gas stand at around 40 million million cubic feet. But it needs more, particularly if its tentative long-term plans for petrochemical and fertiliser industries are to be realised. Nonetheless, there is enough there at the moment to power a few large projects. However there have been delays in setting up facilities to harness gas output. In 1974 the Government bought enough pipes to lay a 300-kilometre pipeline from the oil fields to the coast near the Capital Area. But the 1974 cash crisis forced it to delay the laying of the pipes. In late 1976 it was finally announced that SNAM Progetti, a subsidiary of the Italian state-owned ENI oil concern, would be constructing the pipeline. It will initially be used to power the electricity and desalination plant at Al-Ghubra.

Industry

Around $550 million is being invested in industry under the country's Five Year Plan extending to 1980. A relatively high proportion of this figure will come from the private sector. Priority is being given to the establishment of new industries under the Plan but industry is unlikely to start to make a significant contribution to the economy until well into the 1980s. In 1975 manufactured products provided less than one per cent of the Gross Domestic Product.

There was a time in the early 1970s when the Government was being highly ambitious with its industrial plans. Proposed projects included gas liquefaction and fertiliser plants, a steel mill and drydock. But the cash flow crisis of 1974 put an end to these projects. Now the Government is being much more cautious about its industrial programme. It is conscious of constraints on industrial expansion such as a limited domestic market and an acute shortage of local skilled labour. It has been especially aware of the need for industrial plans to be fitted into the overall development strategy of the country. No industrial project will now go ahead without some thorough groundwork being done.

Copper project The Government is looking for income-generating projects other than oil, such as the exploitation of the country's deposits of copper, asbestos, phosphates, coal, manganese and chrome. Of these, copper is at the moment by far the most important. The Government has been hoping that exploitation of 20 million tonnes of high grade copper ore near Sohar will start by the end of 1977. Around 3,000 tons of copper-rich ore a day could be produced initially. Prospecting has been carried out by Marshall Oman Exploration of the US and Prospection of Canada, which between them own 49 per cent of the 51 per cent Government-owned company, Oman Mining Company. The copper finds lie between Buraimi and Sohar, at the foot of the Hajar Mountains. There is already a road linking the two towns and it is planned to build a port at Sohar for copper exports. There are also plans to build a smelter close to the copper deposits.

Oman also plans to use its other mineral resources for industrial purposes. In April 1977 Sultan Qabous announced that the country was planning to exploit coal deposits of at least 10 million tonnes. These are thought to be located near Sur. There have been proposals for an asbestos fibre plant exploiting asbestos deposits and two companies are pressing ahead with manufacturing projects using Oman's high quality marble.

Within a short time the country should be able to go ahead with oil-related industrial projects which have been on the drawing boards for several years. These could include an oil refinery which there have been plans to build near the Mina al-Fahal oil terminal. Such a refinery would be particularly well placed to provide bunker fuel for ships going back and forth from the Gulf. The completion of a 300-kilometre gas pipeline from the oil fields to the coast should lead to the establishment of industries using gas as feedstock. Originally it had been proposed that the pipeline should provide an energy source for a 350,000-ton-a-year cement plant which a British and Swiss company were due to set up in a joint venture with the Government. But in late 1976 the British company—Associated Portland Cement (APC) —pulled out of what would have been Oman's largest industrial scheme after a disagreement over costs. As a result the original 1979 completion date was pushed back while the Government found another partner.

Agriculture and fisheries

Oman's agriculture and fisheries have great potential. Some agricultural experts believe that the country could become a major supplier of foods to the rest of the Gulf. A long-term study of Oman's fisheries has for example shown that they are among the richest in Asia. But there are major constraints to expansion of this promising sector of the country's economy. The biggest is probably shortage of manpower, but with agriculture availability of water is equally important.

Oman has only irregular rainfall, much of which falls in the mountains, runs down the wadis and into the ground. Most of the water for irrigation is therefore obtained from wells pumped up by diesel engines and channelled for distribution. The *falajs*, an ancient irrigation system of underground channels, are so extensive and efficient that they still supply much of the interior of Oman with its water. Western hydrologists have found relatively large supplies of water in tables close to the surface which remain unexploited. In some areas they calculate cultivable land could be increased by as much as 250 per cent if their reserves were fully exploited. But there are doubts whether there is enough manpower and money available to do this.

Rural migration has been one of the most severe problems facing agriculture. In the early 1970s it was estimated that 80 per cent of the population were engaged in agriculture and fishing, the majority of them in farming. But now it is thought that this proportion has dropped dramatically as large numbers of people have left the rural areas to earn higher incomes in the urban centres, in particular the Capital Area. In places the *falaj* system has been deteriorating because of a shortage of men to carry out repair work.

Agricultural plans   Under the the Five Year Plan, the Government aims to bring an additional 20,000 hectares under cultivation which would raise the country's cultivable area by over half. But it is thought unlikely that this target will be reached and that it would be a big achievement to add even 10,000 hectares of new farmland. The Government intends to invest heavily in maintaining the *falajs* and in the provision of other irrigation systems. Altogether $200 million could be invested in agriculture by 1980, and the Government has been setting growth targets in agricultural output of at least 50 per cent between 1976–80.

Since the early 70s the Government has taken various steps to help farmers. It has set up four agricultural co-operatives, three in the Jebel al-Akhdar area and one in Sharqiya. There is also a programme of research and marketing. There are several research centres but the area around Rumais, on the Batinah coast, has become one of the main centres. It was chosen because it is an area of poor soil near the sea, so that whatever can be grown there can be grown in other cultivable areas. Many varieties of vegetable and fruit are successfully grown at Rumais, including pumpkins, cabbage, spinach, cucumbers, sweet potatoes, mangoes, guavas and oranges.

There is also an Extension Service which helps farmers with cash loans, pumps, tractors, fertilisers, spraying and instruction. There are two date-processing plants and at demonstration farms new varieties of dates have been introduced to improve the local strain. It is proposed also to introduce new methods of cultivation and harvesting. Dates and limes are the principal agricultural exports, although many other crops are grown for home consumption, such as wheat, lucerne, citrus fruits, sugar cane, bananas, onions and coconuts.

The quality of livestock is being raised by crossing local cattle, sheep and goats with foreign breeds. The *jebalis*, or mountain people, of Dhofar grow crops in small quantities but their main support is from livestock, especially cattle. Their cattle are poor specimens, however, and as they are reared for milk many of their calves are slaughtered at birth. The Government is now not only improving the mountain strain by cross-breeding with imported Kenyan bulls, but it is also buying up bull calves to rear them for beef. This means that the *jebalis* are now aware that their calves have a market value. The aim is eventually to export beef from Dhofar to the rest of the Gulf.

Fishing potential Oman's main fish catch includes tuna, barracuda, sardine, shrimp and lobster. Shoals of sardine come close inshore and can be caught by the fishermen off the beaches with hand nets. The sardines are dried in the sun and sent to the interior as animal fodder, or they are drained for oil or fertiliser. Improved road conditions have made it possible for fresh fish to arrive at markets in the interior within a few hours, and there is a growing demand for fresh or frozen fish.

The Government has been expecting Oman to be self-sufficient in fish by the end of 1977. By 1980 its exports of fish should have increased considerably. A Japanese consortium was awarded a three-year concession in April, 1976, to fish a deep-water area off the country's desert region. The Japanese take 60 per cent of the catch and hand the remainder over to the Government. The project is the first venture in Oman involving the large scale exporting of fish from the country, and will increase the country's annual output of around 70,000 tons by as much as 20 per cent. Other foreign companies have shown interest in acquiring similar concessions, so there could be other agreements over the next few years.

With fisheries, the Government's main aim is however to build up the capacity of the country's own fishing industry. One objective has been the formation of an Omani trawling fleet. A New Zealand company has been training crews in trawling techniques. The Government has set up a fund which will enable fishermen to buy modern equipment with cheap loans. Onshore facilities are being improved with cold stores and fish processing plants being established at the main fishing centres. New fishing harbours are being built at Sur and Sohar.

Banking and Finance

The banking and finance sector has made enormous strides since 1970 when there was only one bank in operation; fiscal and monetary control was almost non-existent and economic policy primitive. By mid-1977 there were 17 commercial banks, around a dozen insurance companies, and a Central Bank with full regulatory powers and a rapidly expanding money supply. Between 1970–75 bank credits rose fortyfold to $442 million and the money supply from about $31 million to around $160 million.

Despite this rapid expansion, the banking sector still presents mixed prospects. The major burden has been cash flow problems which the Government has been experiencing in recent years brought about by the high rate of infrastructural spending and the financial demands of the Dhofari war. Consequently, the public sector has soaked up a substantial part of available credits. In 1974–76 the Government took 44 per cent of credits. In 1974 alone bank credits to the Government increased by 600 per cent, compared with a rise of 300 per cent registered by private sector credits.

There is also an extravagant private sector demand for short and medium-term capital. A significant part of this demand is due to government schemes which allow all Omani citizens access to three-to-five-year low-cost money to build houses or improve land. Consequently, 17 per cent of all credits extended in 1974–76 were used for short- and medium-term construction ventures. The high rate of import consumption by both private and public sectors has, however, made short-term import financing the most profitable and necessary form of lending activity and in 1974–76, 75 per cent of all bank loans were used for this purpose. As a result, there is little private money available for long-term productive investments. Almost all development investment is financed by the Government which itself ran short of funds in 1974 and 1975. A few import substitution manufacturing concerns have been locally financed by private capital but, generally, the banks are unable and unwilling to extend long-term credits for investment ventures. The Government has tried to solve this problem by setting up the Oman Development Bank in autumn 1976. It is 40 per cent owned by the Government with the remaining shares divided between foreign interests and the Oman private sector.

The fiscal strains apparent in 1974 prompted a complete re-organisation of the banking sector and, in November 1974, a new Banking Law was issued that specified tighter controls and created the Central Bank of Oman—in place of the Oman Currency Board set up in 1972 and basically concerned only with the insurance of currency. The Central Bank, which began operations in 1975, was given a broad mandate to supervise the finance sector as well as to monitor the economy as a whole. It issues currency, licences and regulates all banks, manages credit and determines interest rates and receives and distributes all government funds. Its regulatory powers are flexible but are increasingly applied to impose strict controls on the banking sector.

Social Services

Before 1970 Oman was isolated from the social development occurring in other Arab countries. Apart from Koranic schools there were only three primary schools for boys, and a religious institute. There was also a US mission school for girls. Because of this lack of educational facilities, Omani parents ambitious for their children and with the means to assist them sent them abroad to be educated. This was fortunate for the country because when Sultan Qabous came to power, he was able to call upon a nucleus of qualified Omanis to take on the responsibility of government posts.

Since then there has been a remarkable advance in the development of educational services. In 1970 there were some 700 boys and 30 teachers in the three schools. By mid-1976 there were around 58,000 pupils in 207 schools with some 2,000 teachers. Owing to the lack of qualified Omanis, many teachers have been brought from other Arab countries, notably Egypt and Jordan.

By the 1980s it is hoped that all children eligible for primary school education will be able to receive it. But it will be longer before universal secondary education is available. In 1976 only 200 pupils—or one per cent of the child population—were having secondary education but this was because of the total lack of education before 1970.

The Government is concentrating more of its educational resources on vocational training, reflecting the countries' desperate need for trained manpower. There has been a World Bank/United Nations scheme to set up two educational centres of over-age pupils, who will be able to take a mixture of vocational and academic courses. Qatar has expressed a desire to establish a college of agriculture in the country which would be the agriculture faculty of its own new university.

Health care In 1970 there was no government hospital. A US Mission hospital in Muttrah and its maternity wing in Muscat were the only sources of extended medical care. Altogether there were about a dozen doctors in the country. As soon as Sultan Qabous assumed power he set up a Ministry of Health which immediately began to develop a national health service. There are now more than 200 government and around 130 private doctors, and 1,200 hospital beds in 14 hospitals. There are over a dozen 24-bed health centres, each staffed by two doctors and 10 nurses. There are about 50 dispensaries staffed by health assistants. By 1980 there will be about 26 centres and 80 dispensaries.

Medical care is free of charge and, as was only to be expected, the people have been using the health facilities offered with alacrity, so that in effect the service is continually overburdened. Some hospitals see as many as a thousand out-patients a day. Omanis make up only 10 per cent of doctors, the remainder coming from India, Pakistan or Egypt. The nursing staff is almost entirely recruited from abroad, but doubtless the proportion of expatriates will gradually decrease as more and more qualified Omanis become available.

Initially, cure was given priority over prevention but now more attention is being given to public health. A community health system is slowly being created, particularly in the area of ante- and post-natal care. Around 70 midwives are employed to go into homes to assist at birth. Nonetheless, though the infant mortality rate is falling, it still remains high.

GUIDE

CAPITAL AREA The towns of Muscat, Muttrah and Ruwi make up what is now known as the Capital Area. The total population is thought to be around 80,000. The old towns of Muscat and Muttrah have been unable to expand because both are enclosed by rocky hills. So the area's main urban development has been in the Ruwi valley which opens out through the hinterland towards Qurum and Seeb.

Muscat, the traditional capital of Oman, sits in an amphitheatre of volcanic hills, topped by two large forts and small watchtowers. There are only two passes into Muscat, one leading west into Muttrah and the other south to the village of Sidab. The seafront is dominated by the Sultan's Indian-style palace which looks out over Muscat's small bay. Two forts guard the bay—Fort Mirani to the west and Fort Jelali (now a prison) to the east. Both were built in the 16th century by the Portuguese.

Within the walled town one of the few open spaces is in front of the Sultan's Palace. There is also a small square close to the British and American embassies. The rest is a mass of small alleyways, which have some fine old houses. Most consist of small rooms built round a courtyard. Each floor has a verandah opening onto the courtyard. The upper floors have a reception room or majlis. The walls are thick with deep recesses inside so that the houses remain cool in hot weather.

Muttrah has traditionally been Oman's commercial centre. Now it also has the country's main port—Mina Qabous. It is a busier town than Muscat with a large souk. Two roads lead out of the town into Ruwi, one a dual carriageway which goes straight through to Seeb and the interior. Beyond the Corniche is a narrow road which twists its way into Muscat. Most of the large houses facing onto the Corniche belong to Khojar Indians, most of whom are well-established merchants and businessmen. In the small streets and alleyways leading off the Corniche is the souk, which is the biggest in Oman.

A few years ago **Ruwi** consisted of little more than a small collection of burasti hamlets, a military airport and an old fort. Today it is a bustling sprawl of urban development which can look like a vast building site. It is a mixture of tall apartment

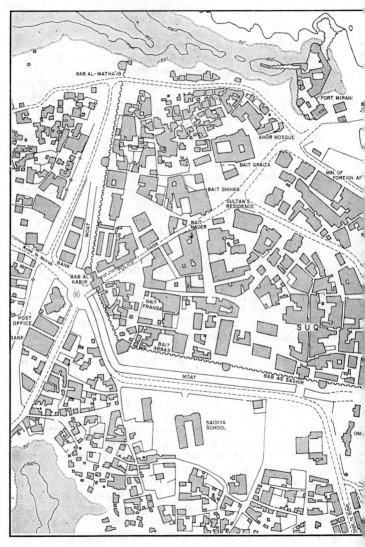

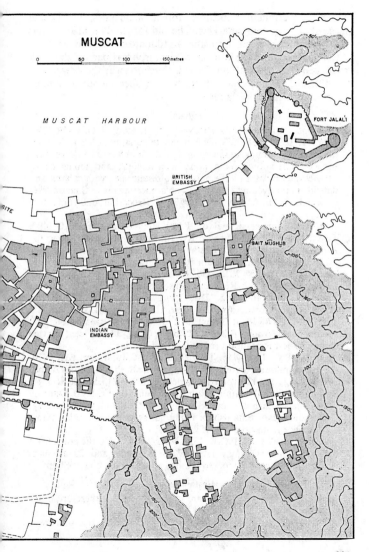

MUSCAT

0   50   100   150 metres

M U S C A T   H A R B O U R

FORT JALALI

BRITISH
EMBASSY

BAIT MUGHUB

INDIAN
EMBASSY

blocks, government ministries, foreign embassies, hotels and large shops and supermarkets. The old fort of Beit al-Falaj has now been converted into the headquarters of the Sultan's Armed Forces and the runway of the airport is part of the back road between Muttrah and Ruwi. Directions in the towns can be difficult, because few streets have proper names and most places are located by landmarks.

Hotels

The Al-Falaj, Ruwi (off main Ruwi-Muttrah road). P.O.B. 456. Tel: 70–2311. Telex: MB 3229. One of the first quality hotels to be built in Oman. 150 rooms. Single room RO 18, double RO 25. 15 per cent service charge. Swimming pool, squash court and tennis court. Movies once a week by the pool. Two restaurants, with cabaret and dancing in the evenings. Bar is a popular meeting place. Supermarket attached, and an Aspreys jewellery shop. Receptions and conference rooms.

The Al-Falaj Annexe, Ruwi (off Ruwi High Street). Tel: 70–1497. Telex: MB 3229. Single room RO 16. Built as an extension to the *Al-Falaj*. A lot less grand. Restaurant for guests only.

Ruwi Hotel, Ruwi (on the main Ruwi–Muttrah road). P.O.B. 5195. Tel: 70–2244. Telex: MB 3456. 100 rooms. Single room RO 18.50. Swimming pool. Bar. Restaurant has good reputation. Barbecue on Thursdays with dancing. Disco every night except Mondays.

Muttrah Hotel, Muttrah (on the outskirts of the town). P.O.B. 4525. Tel: 70–1711/70–1913. Telex: MB 3266. Quiet, small hotel. 40 rooms. Single room RO 14, double RO 20. 15 per cent service charge. Good Restaurant (mostly French cuisine).

Gulf Hotel, P.O. Box 4455. Tel: 60–0100/60–0810. Telex: MB 3416. About ten minutes drive from Ruwi, off the Seeb road. Built on hill overlooking sea. 120 rooms. Single room RO 23, double RO 28. Swimming pool. Restaurant (lunchtime buffet on Fridays). Dancing in evenings. Barbecue on Mondays by the pool with dancing. Coffee shop. Bar. Small shop. Hotel bus service into Capital Area. Taxi service from hotel but it is expensive.

Inter-Continental Hotel. P.O.B. 1398. Tel: 60-0500. Up the coast from the *Gulf Hotel*. Opening late 1977. 308 rooms and 20 cabanas. Restaurants. Bars. Disco. Swimming pool. Tennis court. Shops.

Restaurants

Most of the best restaurants are in the hotels. But there are other reasonably good ones.

The Palm Tree, Ruwi (on the main dual-carriageway out of Ruwi), Brightly lit by neon lights. Kebabs, homous. Unlicensed.

The Taj, Muttrah (near the Muttrah Hotel). Tel: 70–2532. At least RO 4 per person. Indian food.

The Muscateer (on dual-carriageway, near Darseit roundabout). RO 3–4 upwards per person. Mixed Western/Arab cuisine.

Alakeifak (near Family Bookshop). Reasonable prices. Indian and European food.

The Airport Restaurant (at Seeb airport). Tel: 61-0418. RO 4 upwards per person. Licensed. Mixed European/Arab cuisine. Service slow.

Airport Seeb International Airport is about 25 miles from Ruwi. Departure lounge has coffee bar. A few duty-free shops. Restaurant. Taxi into Capital Area costs around RO 5.

Buses Local bus system is mainly for people commuting into the Capital Area from surrounding villages. Not recommended.

Taxis Taxis are either single or shared. Shared taxis ply a fixed route between the three main towns. Fares are cheap (around 200 baizers for most journeys). In Muttrah the shared taxi ramp is close to the vegetable souk. With single taxis, fares are agreed beforehand. Examples of standard single fares are Ruwi–Muscat RO 1; Ruwi–Muttrah 500 biazers; Ruwi–Seeb Airport RO 5.

Car Hire Most hotels have their own car hire facilities, with some (like the *Al-Falaj* and the *Ruwi*) having their own cars. International driving licenses are not valid. Temporary driving licenses are not available for short visits. A car with driver from the *Al-Falaj Hotel* costs over RO 100 for a week's hire.

Travel agencies *Oman Shipping & Travel Agencies*. Tel: 72–2340. *S.M.G. Tours & Travel*, Muscat. P.O.B. 431. Tel: 70–1539 (will arrange journeys into the interior and dhow and fishing trips).

Airlines *Air France*, Muttrah. P.O.B. 282. Tel: 77–3251. *Air India*, Muscat. Tel: 70–1517, 70–1017. *British Airways*, Muscat. P.O.B. 70. Tel: 70–1291, 70–1299. Ruwi Office. P.O.B. 3985. Tel: 70–1362, 70–1434. *Gulf Air*, Muttrah (opposite *Muttrah Hotel*). Tel: 70–2612. Airport Tel: 610329. *Middle East Airlines*, Muscat. P.O.B. 70. Tel: 70–1482. *Pakistan International Airlines*, Muscat. P.O.B. 646. Tel: 77–2301. *KLM*, Muscat. P.O.B. 70. Tel: 70–1291. *Lufthansa*, Muscat. P.O.B. 629. *Iran Air*. Tel: 70–2165. *Saudia*, Tel: 70–2557. *Singapore Airlines*, Muscat. P.O.B. 269. Tel: 70–2330, 72–2719.

Shipping agencies *Oman United Agencies* (Gray Mackenzie & Co.), Muscat. P.O.B. 70. Tel: 70–1299 70–1362. *Gulf Agencies*, Muttrah. P.O.B. 1033. Tel: 70–1165. Telex: MB 3284. *Bagin Haji Al-Latif Fadhel*, Muscat. P.O.B. 51. Tel: 77–2501.

Post Offices There are three main post offices in the Capital Area. In Muscat, the post office is opposite the main gate next to the British Bank of the Middle East. In Muttrah it is on the Old Muttrah Road near the Wali's house, and in Ruwi opposite the main gate to Beit al-Falaj, adjacent to the Omantel building.

Telephone The headquarters of *Omantel*, the national telephone company, are adjacent to the main post office and Beit al-Falaj in Ruwi. The phone directory tends to get out of date quickly because of the rapid expansion of the Area's phone system.

Useful phone numbers Emergency numbers: *Police HQ*—60–0099. *Ruwi Police Station*—70–1770. *Muscat Police Station*—72–2611. *Muttrah Police Station*—77–2226. *Fire Station*—Darsait 70–2077 (or 999). *Fire Station*—Muscat 72–2666. *Water*—77–2724, 70–1721. *Electricity*—77–3144, 77–3140. *Overseas operator*—15. *Seeb Airport*—60–1470 (Flight information), 60–1456 (Departure lounge).

Telex Most hotels have telexes. A public telex service is available at the Omantel headquarters, adjacent to the main Post Office in Ruwi.

Shops The largest supermarket is the *Muttrah Cold Stores* (Tel: 70–2333), which is in fact in Ruwi (behind Grindlays Bank). Other useful shops include: *Sharikat Fanniya Omania*, Ruwi, (near Ruwi Hotel), tel: 70–2400 (cold store and liquor shop); *The Photocentre*, Ruwi, close to Ruwi Hotel, tel: 70–1415 (good for film and camera equipment).

Souks There are two main souks, one in Muttrah and the other in Muscat. The largest is in Muttrah—a mass of small streets and alleyways where you can buy almost everything from antique Omani silver to fishing rods and cameras. Some of the old silver is made from melted down Maria Theresa dollars. The designs are traditional, bold and spectacular. There is some good copper work on sale, as well as swords, cartridge belts, guns, camel sticks and hide shields. Gold jewellery is relatively cheap, even though a lot of it comes from Italy. The money changers sell interesting old coins. Some of the textiles from India, Pakistan and China are a bargain, especially the Khashmiri shawls which the Omanis often wear as turbans.

Leisure/sports Some hotels have swimming pools open to non-residents. The Armed Forces and large companies have private beaches. Otherwise everyone is free to bathe virtually where they like. Oman is good for fishing, its waters being particularly rich fishing grounds. Boats can be hired from local fishermen. Sailing is becoming popular, with some companies having their own sailing clubs.

There are no public tennis or squash courts. Some larger firms and the police and the Armed Forces have courts. The Al-Falaj Hotel has them but to use them non-residents must join a special club, which has a long waiting list. On religious and official holidays camel races are held on the Batinah coast beyond Seeb. The Ministry of Information has a small museum beside the TV station at Qurum.

Book shops Several small shops in Ruwi High Street sell foreign newspapers, magazines and books. The biggest stock is in the *The Family Bookshop* (near Muttrah Cold Store), tel: 70–2850.

Pharmacies *Al-Hashar Pharmacy*, tel: 73–4687. *Muscat Pharmacy*, Muscat, tel: 72–2297; Ruwi, tel: 70–2542; Muttrah, tel: 77–2782.

Hospitals *Al-Nahda Hospital*, Ruwi. Tel: 70–1255. *Al-Khoula Hospital*, near Mina Al-Fahal. Tel: 60–0455. *Arrahmah*, Muttrah. Tel: 77–2281.

Banks Head offices: *Central Bank of Oman*, Muscat. P.O.B. 534. Tel: 74–5021. Telex: 3288 MB.
Commercial banks (main offices): *Al-Bank Al-Ahli Al-Omani*, Ruwi. P.O.B. 3134. Tel: 70–1044. Telex: 3540 MB. *Arab African Bank*, Muttrah. P.O.B. 1117. Tel: 72–2796. Telex: 3364 MB. *Arab Bank*, Muscat. P.O.B. 991. Tel: 72–2831. Telex: 3285 MB. *Bank of Baroda*, Muttrah. P.O.B. 1231. Tel: 73–4556. *Bank of Credit & Commerce International*, Muscat. P.O.B. 410. Tel: 72–2222. Telex: 3317 MB. *Bank Melli Iran*, Muscat. P.O.B. 410. Tel: 72–2646. Telex: 3295 MB. *Bank of Oman, Bahrain & Kuwait*, Muscat. P.O.B. 920. Tel: 72–2966/72–2114/72–2104. Telex: 3290 MB. *Banque de Paris et des Pays Bas*, Muscat. P.O.B. 425. Tel: 72–2740. Telex: 3360 MB. *British Bank of the Middle East*, Muscat. P.O.B. 234. Tel: 77–2041/77–2043. Telex: 3213 MB. *Commercial Bank of Oman*, Ruwi. P.O.B. 4656. Tel: 73–4448. Telex: 3392 MB. *Citibank*, Muscat. P.O.B. 918. Tel: 72–2933. Telex: 3444 MB. *Grindlays Bank*, Muscat. P.O.B. 91. Tel: 77–2030. Telex: 3219 MB. *Habib Bank AG Zurich*, Muscat. P.O.B. 1338. Tel: 72–2686. Telex: 3331 MB. *Habib Bank Ltd.*, Muttrah. P.O.B. 1326. Tel: 72–2155. Telex: 3283 MB. *National Bank of Abu Dhabi*, Muscat. P.O.B. 303. Tel: 72–2355. Telex: 3452. *National Bank of Oman*, Ruwi. P.O.B. 3751. Tel: 70–1295. Telex: 3291 MB. *Union Bank of Oman*, Ruwi. P.O.B. 4565. Tel: 70–2444. Telex: 3434 MB.

Ministries *Interior*, Muscat. P.O.B. 297. Tel: 73–4966. *Justice*, Ruwi. P.O.B. 3354. Tel: 70–1248. *Communications*, Muscat. P.O.B. 303. Tel: 70–1249. *Public Works*, Muscat. P.O.B. 215. Tel: 72–2801. *Commerce & Industry*, Muscat. P.O.B. 550. Tel: 72–2036. *Agriculture, Fisheries, Oil & Minerals*, Muscat. P.O.B. 55. Tel: 70–2066/70–1432.

Health, Muscat. P.O.B. 393. Tel: 60–0847. *Education*, Muscat. P.O.B. 3. Tel: 70–1051. *Information & Culture*, Muscat. P.O.B. 600. Tel: 60–0022. *Lands & Municipalities*. Tel: 70–2230. *National Heritage*, Muscat. P.O.B. 668. Tel: 70–1066. *Al-Aqwaf & Islamic Affairs*, Muscat. P.O.B. 767. Tel: 70–2688. *Foreign Affairs*, Muscat. P.O.B. 252. Tel: 70–1211/70–1208. *Social Affairs & Labour*, Muscat. P.O.B. 560. Tel: 70–1242. *Diwan Affairs*, Muscat. Tel: 72–2621. *Finance*, Muscat. Tel: 72–2549.

Embassies *U.S.A.*, Muscat. P.O.B. 966. Tel: 72–2021. *Britain*, Muscat. P.O.B. 300. Tel: 72–2411/72–2415. *Egypt*, Muscat. P.O.B. 3969. Tel: 70–2426/70–2421. *France*, Muscat. P.O.B. 591. Tel: 72–2916/72–2927. *India*, Muscat. P.O.B. 177. Tel: 72–2488/72–2204. *Kuwait*, Muscat. P.O.B. 890. Tel: 70–1166. *Qatar*, Muscat. P.O.B. 802. Tel: 70–1802. *Saudi Arabia*, Muscat. P.O.B. 873. Tel: 70–1111. *United Arab Emirates*, Muscat. P.O.B. 335. Tel: 70–1372/70–1371. *Jordan*, Muscat. P.O.B. 990. Tel: 70–2255. *Iran*, Muscat. P.O.B. 702. Tel: 72–2668. *Pakistan*, Muttrah. P.O.B. 1005. Tel: 70–2526.

Newspapers/periodicals *Al-Watan*, Muscat. P.O.B. 445. Weekly. *Al-Aqida*, Muscat. P.O.B. 691. Weekly. *Al-Usra*, Muttrah. P.O.B. 1440. Weekly. *Al-Nahda*, Muscat. P.O.B. 979. Fortnightly. *Jund Oman*, Muscat. P.O.B. 114. Monthly. Published by the Department of Defence. *Oman*, Muscat. P.O.B. 600. Weekly. Produced by the Ministry of Education. *Tijarat Oman*, Muscat. P.O.B. 580 (Commerce of Oman). Quarterly trade magazine. *Times of Oman*, Muscat. P.O.B 183. English-language weekly.

Media Oman's only English-language paper is the weekly *Times of Oman* which covers mainly government news. The *Gulf Weekly Mirror*, published in Bahrain but containing news from Oman, circulates in the country. Oman radio broadcasts news bulletins in English at 1 p.m. and 2.30 p.m. Both Oman radio and TV have programmes in English.

Churches Ruwi has a Catholic and a Protestant church, adjacent to each other just off the Ruwi–Muttrah dual-carriageway. Sunday Mass is at 9, 10, and 11 a.m. and the Protestant church has evensong at 7.30 p.m. on Sundays.

Major companies Accountants: *Saba & Co*, Muscat. P.O.B. 790. Tel: 72–2145. *Whinney Murray & Co.*, Ruwi. P.O.B. 4750. Tel: 70–1461. Insurance: *Oman United Agencies*, Muscat (represents British insurance companies). P.O.B. 70. Tel: 70–1165 or 70–1362. *The Muttrah Trading Co.* (Royal Insurance). P.O.B. 1377. Tel: 77–3254. *Gulf Insurance*. Tel: 72–2991.

Consultants: *Cagdas Associates*, Muscat. P.O.B. 446. Tel: 70–1230. *Brian Colquhoun & Partners*, Muscat. P.O.B. 402. Tel: 77–5347. *Roy Lancaster Associates*, Muscat. P.O.B. 970. Tel: 70–1466. *Coopers & Lybrand*, Muscat. P.O.B. 633. Tel: 72–2176. *Gibb Petermuller & Partners*, Muscat. P.O.B. 592. Tel: 70–1811. Telex: MB 335. *W. A. Fairhurst & Partners*, Ruwi. P.O.B. 3528. *Sir William Halcrow & Partners*, Muscat. P.O.B. 220. Tel: 70–1347. Telex: MB 421. *H. G. Huckle & Partners*, Muscat. P.O.B. 75. Tel: 72–2475. *Whitehead Consulting Group*, Muscat. P.O.B. 699. Tel: 72–2806. *TEST*, Ruwi. P.O.B. 4688. Tel: 70–2710. *John R. Harris Associates*, Muscat. P.O.B. 214. Tel: 61–0511. *Hoare, Lea & Partners*, Seeb. P.O.B. 3037. Tel: 77–5346. *Jack & Letman Ass*, Muscat. P.O.B. 970. Tel: 73–4150. *D. G. Jones & Partners*, Muscat. P.O.B. 621. Tel: 62–0394. *Mantech Engineering*, Ruwi. P.O.B. 3166. Tel: 73–4064. *Scott Wilson Kirkpatrick & Partners*, Muscat. P.O.B. 214. Tel: 77–5346. *Triad Oman*, Ruwi. P.O.B. 4397. Tel: 77–2734. Telex: 332 MB. *Widnell & Trollope*, Muttrah. P.O.B. 1101. Tel: 77–5346. *Llewellyn Davies, Weeks, Forrester, Walker & Bor*, Ruwi. P.O.B. 5246. Tel: 70–1655.

Trading firms and contractors: *Abdul Aziz & Bros*, Muscat. P.O.B. 5. Tel: 72–2399. *Nasser Abdullatif & Co*, Muscat. P.O.B. 36. Tel: 77–2807. *Almulla Construction Co*, Muscat. P.O.B. 100. *Abdullah & Hussein Hamza al-Asfoor*, Muscat. P.O.B. 315. Tel: 72–2705/72–2359. *Suhail & Saud Bahwan*, Muscat. P.O.B. 169. Tel: 72–2293. *Darwish & Brothers*, Muscat. P.O.B. 75. Tel: 72–2826/77–3174. *Al-Darwish Enterprises*, Muscat. P.O.B. 135. Tel: 72–2821. *Ratanshi Gordhanda*, Muscat. P.O.B. 137. Tel: 77–2527. *Al-Hashar & Co*, Muscat, P.O.B. 1028. Tel: 77–2791/73–4011. *Moosa Abdul Rahman Hassan*, Muscat. P.O.B. 4. Tel: 70–1566/70–1486. *Mustafa Jawad Trading Co., Muscat Overseas Agencies*, Muscat. P.O.B. 1. Tel: 77–2035. *Khimji Ramdas*, Muscat. P.O,B. 19. Tel: 72–2225. *Taylor Woodrow Towell Co.*, Muscat. P.O.B. 253. Tel: 70–2861. *W. J. Towell & Co.*, Muttrah. P.O.B. 1061. Tel: 77–2131/77–2167. *Waleed Associates*, Muscat. P.O.B. 437. Tel: 72–2495. *Zawawi Trading Co.*, Muscat. P.O.B. 58. Tel: 72–2061. *Zubair Enterprises*, Muscat. P.O.B. 127. Tel: 72–2821. *Sharikat Fanniya Omanya*, Ruwi. P.O.B. 4949. Tel: 70–2400. *Muscat (Overseas)*, Muscat. P.O.B. 442. Tel: 70–2737/72–2348. Telex: 3323.

Useful address *Oman Chamber of Commerce*, Ruwi. P.O.B. 4400. Tel: 70–2259.

THE INTERIOR The Batinah coast, Oman's most fertile area, stretches west of the Capital Area beyond the fishing port of Sohar, 150 miles away. Until the 18th century **Sohar** used to be Oman's major port and a big trading centre. Some relics of its past prestige still remain. The town is at the end of a pass which comes through the Hajar mountains from Buraimi and the United Arab Emirates.

The Hajar mountains and the towns and villages in its foothills are known as the interior which has in the past tried to be independent of the rest of the country. The symbol of this independence has been the Imams, elected religious leaders who often emerged as rivals to the Sultans of Muscat. **Rostaq,** 30 miles south of the Batinah coast road and around 100 miles from Muscat, was once the home of the Imams. The town, sitting at the foot of the Hajar escarpments, has a large fort which can only be seen with the permission of the wali. Adjacent to the fort's high walls is the souk, once a selling centre for the work of coppersmiths. The town is surrounded by big date gardens where hot springs flow. **Al-Hazm,** five miles out of Rostaq, has a huge 18th-century fort built by Imam Sultan Bin Saif. Its battlements, dominating the country for miles around, still hold Portuguese cannons.

Nizwa, 110 miles from Muscat and the interior's largest town with 10,000 inhabitants, is divided into several walled sections. In the lower part of the town is a large bustling souk whose character probably has not changed for centuries. It is well stocked with traditional craftwork, in particular silver work, weaponry and armaments. The town's fort, which overlooks the souk, was built in the 17th century by Sultan Bin Said, the conqueror of the Portuguese. It has a 150 foot wide and 80 foot high tower, the lower part of which is solid rock. The 20 foot high walls have small storerooms inside them and below are a couple of dungeons.

Bahla, a small walled town 20 miles west of Nizwa shrouded by palm trees, is a pottery-making centre of 8,000 people. Despite its crumbling appearance, the town's fort, parts of which date back to the 12th century, serves as the home of the local wali. **Jibreen,** further west on the Ibri road, has one of the biggest forts in Oman, similar in design to the one at Al-Hazm. It has been recently repaired by an Italian specialist team and its main attraction is its painted ceilings and interior floral motifs. **Ibri,** 75 miles from Nizwa, is well-known for its silversmiths. But since a tarmac road from Buraimi was recently completed, an upsurge of business from the Emirates had made the price of silver in the town's souk excessive.

Buraimi, close to the border with the United Arab Emirates, is the traditional gateway to Oman. A strategically placed oasis, it has had a stormy history being taken forcibly by the Saudi Wahhabis several times in the last few hundred years. It used to be an important stopping point for camel trains between the north of Oman and the Gulf coast. Its dilapidated fort was built by the Wahhabis as a base for raids into Oman. Now the town is rather overshadowed by Al-Ain, just over the border in neighbouring Abu Dhabi.

About 220 miles southeast of Muscat, near the eastern tip of the Arabian Peninsula, is the town of **Sur,** at one time a slaving centre. Now fishing is its main source of income. The town is also renowned for its dhows, which are built in the port by the traditional methods, even if they are later installed with a motor rather than a sail. Many of the people of Sur are descended from slaves and some of the boat-building songs are in Swahili. **Kalhat,** about 20 miles north of Sur, is the site of a town believed to have been destroyed by an earthquake a few hundred years ago. It has a lot of archaeological interest and is scattered with many relics, including the remains of a mosque and several types of graves and tombs. It can be reached either by a hired dhow or by driving along a dirt track and then walking on cliff paths.

DHOFAR Oman's southern mountainous province, separated from the north by a large expanse of desert, is different climatically and ethnically from the rest of the country. Between June and September the Indian Ocean monsoon covers the mountains in a blanket of mist from which it emerges a brilliant green, providing abundant grass for the mountain people's cattle. The province, once the land of frankincense, is divided between a coastal plain on which most Dhofaris live and the wide Qara mountain range where an estimated 20,000 to 30,000 people eke out a semi-nomadic existence. Only a few years ago most of the mountains were under the control of left-wing guerrillas supported by neighbouring South Yemen. Now they have been driven out with British and Iranian military help and the

Government has started to build roads, schools and clinics to consolidate its hold over the area.

Salalah, Dhofar's capital, was described by the Venetian explorer Marco Polo as 'a great and noble city' 700 years ago when it was an important trading *entrepôt*. Today it has lost much of its old glamour and its main significance is as the commercial centre of Dhofar's coastal plain. Its only imposing feature is the Sultan's palace which in recent years has become the ruler's main home. But much of the building is hidden behind walls. East of Salalah is the fishing village of **Taqa** where sardines are spread out to dry on the beach before being transported into the mountains for camel and cattle fodder. Further east is the site of the old city of **Sumran** from where frankincense was once sent by caravan along the trade route across southern Arabia to the Levant.

Raysut, Dhofar's port, lies 10 miles to the west of the capital. A tarmac road runs northwards out of Salalah across the mountains to **Thamrit** (sometimes called Midway) which has an airbase with reputedly the longest runway in Asia.

Hotels

Al-Salalah Hotel, Salalah. A newly-built hotel on the outskirts of the town close to the sea. 100 rooms with 10 villas with three bedrooms each. Single person around RO 28. Villas cost RO 85 a night. Restaurant. Swimming pool. Conference facilities.

Dhofar Hotel, Salalah. Tel: 451. Formerly Dhofar's only hotel. Consists of villas with a total of 28 rooms. Single person around RO 20 including meals. Restaurant. TV room.

Airport Salalah airport lies close to the town. It is being upgraded to international standard and a terminal building is being constructed.

Taxis Fares are similar to those in the northern Capital Area.

Telephone/telex Salalah has a small local network. International calls and calls to the north can be made from the Omantel office in the centre of town. Telex messages can also be sent from here.

Souk Salalah's old souk has recently been pulled down and its traders have set up stalls in the main street, selling mainly modern imported goods.

Leisure/sport There are many good beaches close to Salalah. The area is also good for fishing. Boats can be hired locally. Thamrit has a relatively large expatriate community which has set up its own leisure and sporting facilities.

Hospitals Salalah's old district hospital is being replaced by a newly built hospital on the western outskirts of the town.

GENERAL INFORMATION

How to get there BY AIR: There are daily flights between London and Muscat (Seeb airport). There are also regular direct flights between Muscat and Paris, Amsterdam, Larnaca and Athens (usually on three or four days each week). Regular flights go to the Far East and Australia, with virtually a daily service to Karachi and Bombay. But North America has no direct connections and passengers from there generally travel via London. There are several flights a week to and from Middle East capitals like Cairo, Beirut and Amman.

BY SEA: Four London-based cargo shippers sometimes take passengers to Oman: *Eastern Liner Services, Killick Martin & Co., Fred Olsen Lines, P & O General Cargo Division.*

INTER-GULF/DOMESTIC AIR SERVICES: *Gulf Air*, which is partly owned by Oman, provides a regular service to other countries in the lower Gulf. There are daily flights between Muscat and Dubai, Abu Dhabi and Bahrain, and several flights a week to and from Kuwait and Doha. Three flights a week go to Shiraz and one a week to Riyadh and Dhahran. There is a daily service between Muscat and Salalah.

Visas Visas are required by all foreign visitors. They are issued in advance by the Omani Embassy in London (64, Ennismore Gardens, S.W.7). In all other cases, No Objection Certificates (NOC) must first be obtained from local sponsors and then a visitor will be issued with a visa on arrival at Seeb International Airport. Passengers resident in a country with an Omani Embassy must have the NOC endorsed in the passport before departure. NOCs are valid for three months. The Oman Embassy in London does issue one-week visas for visitors without local sponsors. Applications for these visas must be accompanied by three letters—one from the visitor's company, another from the local chamber of commerce and a third from the British Arab Chamber of Commerce.

Language Arabic is the official language. English is widely spoken.

Hours of business Government hours: 7.30 a.m.–2 p.m. Banks: 8.00 a.m.–12 a.m. Sat.–Wed., 8.00 a.m.–11.30 a.m. Thursdays. Business establishments: 8.00–12 a.m. and 4–7 p.m. Souks/shops: 8.00 a.m.–12 a.m. and 3–6 p.m. Post Offices: 8.00 a.m.–1 p.m.

M

Official holidays Friday is the weekly holiday; Saturday and Sunday are normal working days. Businessmen are advised to avoid visiting Oman during the month of Ramadan which ends with a four-day holiday, Id al-Fitr. The holidays marked with an asterisk * are dependent on the Muslim lunar calendar and may differ by one or two days from the dates given. The Muslim year has only 354 or 355 days, so Muslim dates and holidays fall 10 to 12 days earlier each year on the Gregorian calendar.

	1977/78
National Day	18 November
Birthday of Sultan Qabous	19 November
Id al-Adha*	21 November
Al-Hijra (Muslim New Year)*	12 December
Prophet's Birthday*	25 February 1978
Ascension of the Prophet*	3 July
Id al-Fitr (end of Ramadan)*	3–6 September

Times GMT + 4.

Electricity 220/240 V, AC 50 cycles.

Health Smallpox and cholera vaccination certificates required for all visitors. Yellow fever immunisation needed for travellers arriving within six days of leaving an infected area. All visitors are advised to protect themselves against malaria which is endemic in the country.

Water Do not drink tap water or water from the *falajs*. Keep to mineral water or boiled water.

Post Letters to Western Europe and North America take three to 10 days by air. Surface mail can take up to three months. An airmail letter to Western Europe costs 75 baizers and to North America and Japan 100 baizers.

Telecommunications The telephone system is run by the national phone company, *Omantel*. Local calls can be erratic, particularly between Dhofar and the north of the country which are connected by a radio link. International calls are subject to delays.

Currency The unit of currency is the Rial Omani (RO). There are 1000 baizers to one rial.

Currency regulations There are no restrictions on the import or export of local or foreign currency.

Customs regulations Visitors are allowed to bring in 50 cigarettes or four ounces of tobacco and eight ounces of perfume. The import of alcohol is prohibited.

Alcohol Alcohol is available but restricted. It is sold in hotel bars and restaurants. Otherwise it can be bought in bulk by foreign residents who have been issued with liquor licences by their embassies. Penalties for drunkenness in public are extremely severe.

Useful advice Women should not wear sleeveless dresses nor very short skirts nor trousers in public. Men should not go around without shirts nor with bare legs even in the hottest weather.

When eating with Omanis (without cutlery) use your right hand and sit with the soles of your feet hidden from the company. Do not take close-up photographs of people without asking their permission. Occasionally people will object to photos being taken of them, especially women. Three cups of coffee is the polite limit. Do not smoke inside people's houses unless you are offered a cigarette by your host.

Maps The Ministry of Defence in London issues maps of Oman of various scales. One, covering most of the northern area from just south of Sur to south of Sohar, is useful for trips into the interior. Its reference is 563 B, Series 1404, Edition 2 GSGS (scale 1:500,000). Maps of the three main towns of Muscat, Muttrah and Ruwi are available from the Ministry of Land Affairs in Oman. Shell have produced a good folding map of Oman usually on sale at *The Family Bookshop*, Ruwi.

Further Reading *Muscat and Oman*. Ian Skeet. Good general introduction to Oman (up until 1970). Faber & Faber, 1974. *Oman: a History*, Wendell Phillips. Longmans. *Unknown Oman*, Wendell Phillips. Longmans. *Arabian Sands*. Wilfred Thesiger. London, 1960. *Oman, the Making of a Modern State*. John Townsend. Croom Helm, 1977.

Government

Head of State	Sultan Qabous Bin-Said
Prime Minister, Defence and Foreign Affairs	Sultan Qabous Bin-Said
Minister of State for Foreign Affairs	Qais Abdel-Moneim al-Zawawi

Interior	Mohammad Bin-Ahmad
Justice	Hilal Bin-Hamad al-Sammar
Communications	Abdel-Hafez Salim Rajab
Public Works	Karim Ahmad Harami
Commerce & Industry ...	Mohammad Zubair
Agriculture, Fisheries, Petroleum & Minerals ...	Said Ahmad al-Shanfari
Health	Mubarak al-Khaddouri
Education	Ahmad Abdullah Ghazali
Information & Tourism ...	Fahd Bin-Mahmoud al-Said
Waqfs & Islamic Affairs ...	Shaikh Walid Bin-Zaher Hanawi
Labour & Social Affairs ...	Khalfan Bin-Nasser Wahabi
Land Affairs & Municipalities	Assem Ali Jamali
Youth Affairs	Fahar Bin-Taimour al-Said
National Heritage	Faisal Bin-Ali al-Said
Without Portfolio & Governor of Dhofar	Shaikh Braik Bin-Hamoud al-Ghafari
Diwan Affairs	Hamad Bin-Hamoud

Those who use this book should know. . .

. . . that it is to be revised continuously, right up to the day when the third edition closes for press. Facts no longer true must be deleted, new facts are to be added, maps will be augmented and changed for the better, and whole passages re-written. You may very well hand this book on to a friend about to visit the Gulf.

On second thoughts, make him a present of the current edition—yours may be out of date

QATAR

THE AMIR OF QATAR

THE AMIR OF QATAR
His Highness Shaikh Khalifa Bin-Hamad al-Thani

The Amir of Qatar, His Highness Shaikh Khalifa Bin-Hamad al-Thani acceded to the Amirship on 22 February 1932. Shaikh Khalifa was born in Rayyan in 1930. He is the fourth son of Shaikh Hamad Bin-Abdullah Bin-Jassim al-Thani, who died in 1947 after exercising—as Heir Apparent—rulership on behalf of his father for many years. On Shaikh Hamad's death Shaikh Khalifa succeeded him as Heir Apparent. He served as Deputy Ruler from 24 October 1960 before acceding to the Amirship.

Qatar

Area 4,000 sq. miles

Population 202,000 (1975 estimate)

Chief town Doha (capital) 130,000 (1975 estimate)

Gross National Product $1,680 million (1975 estimate)

GNP per caput $8,320

GEOGRAPHY

The Qatar peninsula, projecting north into the Gulf from the mainland, is approximately 100 miles long, has a maximum width of 55 miles and a total area of 4,000 square miles. In the north it is separated from the island of Bahrain by a 20-mile strait. The peninsula is flat, except for a range of low hills, the Dukhan anticline, on the west coast. This range, about 35 miles long and nowhere much more than 300 feet above sea level, rises gently from the east to a limestone plateau which is three-to-five miles wide and covers the country's deposits of oil. Most of the country is stony, sandy and barren, divided into salt flats, dune desert and arid plains. Salt flats across the neck of the peninsula suggest that, at some time in the past, Qatar may have been an island. Sand covers most of the south and much of the southeast consists of sand dunes. Such natural vegetation that exists is mainly in the north, around wells and small wadis. The area is very dry, with little fresh water for agriculture. Much of the drinking water is provided by desalination processes.

There are numerous small islands and coral reefs off the coast, and a few larger ones, belonging to Qatar, of which Halul, about 60 miles east of Doha, is of special importance. It is the collecting

QATAR

Al Ruwais
Madinat
al Shamal

Al Khor

N

Dukhan

Al Rayyan   DOHA

Umm Bab

Al Wakrah

Karana   Umm Said

THE GULF

Salwa

■ Capital
● Towns
—— Asphalted Roads
—·— Desert Roads
····· Oil or gas pipelines
▲ Oil Fields
■ Oil Wells

and storage point for the country's three offshore oilfields. Despite the Qataris traditional reliance on fishing and pearl diving for a living, the country's coastal waters can be extremely treacherous. Fast moving shallows and unpredictable coastal winds have always made navigation difficult. There are no natural harbours. The desert in the south and the sea conditions have helped to keep the Qataris relatively isolated.

Doha, the capital, on the east coast, is the only town of any real size and importance and about 80 per cent of Qatar's population is concentrated in and around it. Second in importance as a centre of population is Al-Khor, some 35 miles to the north and also on the east coast. In the past these were the two ports for the pearling fleet. To the south of Doha an industrial town is being created at Umm Said.

CLIMATE

Qatar is exceptionally hot and humid during the summer and mild in the winter. From June to September the heat is intense, with midday temperatures in July and August reaching 44°C (111°F) or even higher and humidity exceeding 85 per cent. Winters are warm and sunny and less humid with temperatures from December to March ranging between 10°C (50°F) and 20°C (68°F). But sometimes, particularly at night, it can be very chilly.

Rainfall is light, averaging from two to three inches a year, all of it coming during the winter months. A north-east wind (*shamal*) often blows across the peninsula. In the winter a gale force wind called the *naashi* occasionally sweeps in off the sea. Hot and dry breezes from the south sometimes bring sand clouds.

PLANTS AND WILDLIFE

Intensive cultivation in recent years, using the most advanced of agricultural techniques, has turned parts of Qatar's arid landscape into flourishing expanses of greenery. However not all plant life is confined to these new farming areas. At least 150 different plant specimens have been found in the country's desert. Most of these are shrubs which blossom briefly during the spring when rain falls. Some of the more common species are the Desert Hyacinth with its yellow and lilac sweet-scented flowers, the *Sidr* whose tiny star-like flowers are much prized by the Bedouin, and the Desert Apple (*cirtullus colocynthis*) with its large green and white striped fruits which turn bright yellow when ripe.

Qatar has little animal life. The gazelle is now extremely rare in the peninsula and only in the deserts of the south, close to the Saudi Arabian border, are camels kept in herds. The jerboa or desert rat is a fairly frequent sight in the interior.

The rapid expansion in farming and the growing of gardens in and around Doha has helped to increase the country's bird population. Migrant birds use the new greenery as a resting place. Flamingoes wade in the shallows on the coast and cormorants can often be seen near the shore. Among the species identified in recent years are the osprey, kestrel, plover, swift, lark, swallow, martin, pipit, wagtail, thrush, stonechat, warbler, sand grouse, curlew, bustard and hoopoe. Amphibians and reptiles include lizards and monitors, toads, sand boas, tortoises and turtles.

COMMUNICATIONS

Qatar is one of the few Gulf countries which appears to have more road space than its immediate needs. All the country's towns are linked by asphalt roads. A road runs *via* Salwa into Saudi Arabia and a direct connection is being built with the United Arab Emirates. Doha has a modern network of ring roads, interchanges and wide boulevards which should adequately serve the capital for many years.

The country's main port at Doha has suffered severely from congestion but an expansion to eight berths should help to ease the flow of goods considerably. The port's main problem is that ships must use a $3\frac{1}{2}$-mile narrow approach channel which was dredged when the port was built eight years ago. This means that the port is reaching its maximum size and any extra traffic will soon have to be transferred to a new port or the country's second port at Umm Said, 30 miles south of the capital. This has mainly been used as an industrial port, even though it is a less limited deepwater harbour than Doha.

Doha's international airport which has been operating since 1957 lies so close to the capital that it is now in danger of being engulfed by it. A new airport is being built 10 miles west of the town but it is unlikely to take over before the early 1980s. In the meantime facilities at the present airport are likely to come under increasing strain. *Gulf Air*, the state's national carrier, whose ownership is shared between Qatar, Bahrain, Abu Dhabi and Oman, runs regular direct flights between Doha and Europe.

The country has good telecommunications with an adequate supply of lines to meet demand. There are automatic connections with neighbouring countries and an earth station beamed on the Indian Ocean satellite provides 'multi-hop' links with most of the world.

SOCIAL BACKGROUND

The majority of the Qatari population of around 200,000 are immigrants. There has been no official census since 1970 but the indigenous population is estimated to number around 50,000. A Government survey has shown that in 1975/76 about 70 per cent of the 44,000 people in employment (outside the security and armed forces) were foreigners. Most manual work is done by labour imported from India and Pakistan and semi-skilled, skilled and managerial jobs are taken by Europeans and non-Qatari Arabs. There is also a fairly large number of Iranians who are mainly self-employed and have lived in Qatar for some time. The majority of Qataris in employment work for the Government.

The influx of foreign workers has placed a heavy strain on the traditional conservatism of the Qataris. Most of them follow the Wahhabi interpretation of Islam which gives Qatari life a strong streak of puritanism. But Qatar is not quite so strict as neighbouring Saudi Arabia where Wahhabism originated. Liquor can for example be sold under licence to non-Muslims. Nonetheless women seldom venture on to the streets and television was introduced only in the face of strong protests from religious leaders.

But economic necessity is beginning to give more freedom to women. A few years ago hardly any women had jobs. Now two per cent of the labour force is female and this proportion is likely to grow fairly rapidly. Girls account for nearly half the total school enrolment. Because of the dire need for Qatari workers an official manpower commission has recommended that more should be done to bring women into employment.

Immigrant restrictions Qatar has probably done more to come to grips with the problems of immigrant labour than most other Gulf states. For some years the Government appears to have recognised that the country could only safely absorb a limited number of foreign workers at a time and has paced its development accordingly. It has been implementing an unofficial quota system in order to achieve a balance of nationalities among immigrants.

However, the Government has yet to tackle the difficulty of how to assimilate non-Qataris into the indigenous population. It is still reluctant to grant nationality to foreigners who have been living in the country for many years, particularly if they are not Arab. Iranians, who have been resident in Qatar for a long time and have become virtually completely integrated with the local community, have still not been granted full citizenship rights.

Though the Ruler, Shaikh Khalifa bin Hamad Al-Thani, has supreme power, he aims to involve the native Qatari population much more in the decision-making process. But this could take many years. The present power structure is very firmly established. For such a small country, the royal al-Thani family is extremely large. It holds all the key ministries and other leading posts in the Government. However, Shaikh Khalifa has already taken steps to raise the Government above the confines of family or tribal loyalty. A large percentage of oil revenues are vested in the national treasury rather than the Ruler or his family. He is establishing a civil service to which authority is being delegated and an independent legal system. He intends to institutionalise power rather than let it remain personalised.

CONSTITUTION

The country's provisional constitution, promulgated on 2 April 1970, declares Qatar to be an independent, sovereign state with a democratic regime and that its people are a part of the 'Arab Nation'.

It requires the State to direct its efforts to the consolidation of a proper basis for the establishment of true democracy, and the creation of an administrative organisation that will ensure justice, tranquility and equality for its citizens and respect for public order.

Strong emphasis is laid on the brotherhood of all Arabs and the promotion of Arab causes and interests. Foreign policy should aim at strengthening ties of friendship with all Islamic states and peoples in particular, and with all peace-loving states and people in general. Also the State should adhere to the principles of the United Nations Charter.

The constitution gives the State the right to supervise the national economy although rights of intervention must be defined by law. In addition the State should aim to instil proper Islamic principles in society, to provide equal opportunity for all citizens, to care for their health and to maintain a social security system covering old age, sickness and other disabilities. Education should be the right of every citizen.

All persons are to have equal public rights and duties regardless of race, sex or religion. Retrospective legislation is not allowed and an accused person shall be considered innocent until proved guilty.

The office of Amir or Head of State is hereditary in the family of Al-Thani. The Head of State appoints the members of the Council of Ministers as well as the Prime Minister, and may act as his own Prime Minister. Only a citizen of Qatar 'by origin' may be appointed a minister.

Advisory Council The constitution also provides for an Advisory Council to discuss draft laws and general policy. The Council has the right to request statements from ministers and the Prime Minister. Membership is again restricted to Qataris by origin. The first Council, with 20 members, was established shortly after Shaikh Khalifa became Amir. In December 1975 the Council's membership was raised to 30 and it was given more explicit rights to question ministers on budgetary and administrative matters. The Amir has indicated that he wants to open the way as much as possible for the constructive participation of capable citizens in the management of the country's affairs.

There are two criminal courts, a civil court, a court of appeal and a labour court, all applying codified law. Sharia courts administer religious law in certain fields of litigation but non-Moslems are always handled by the appropriate court specialising in codified law. The independence of the judiciary is firmly guaranteed in the constitution.

Qataris by origin are those who were settled in Qatar before 1930 and who resided there and preserved their Qatari status until the first Nationality Law of 1961. Anyone born of a Qatari father in Qatar or abroad is Qatari.

Nationality may be granted to an adult male foreigner who has been resident in Qatar for 10 years if an Arab, or 15 years if non-Arab. Such applications are usually not successful unless the applicant has technical skills and qualifications. These conditions may be waived and nationality granted to any Arab who has rendered high service to the Government. A foreign woman married to a Qatari must inform the authorities of her wish for Qatari nationality which will be granted if the marriage continues for a further two years.

HISTORY

Recent excavations by archaeologists in Qatar show that the peninsula was inhabited as long ago as 4000 B.C. Relics have been found of the Old and New Stone Age. Also Sumerian-type pottery has been unearthed showing that the area had links with civilisations in Mesopotamia. The finds indicate that the early settlers in Qatar developed from a primitive life to a relatively sophisticated level at which they used tools to create items of excellent workmanship.

The coming of Islam The Greek historian Herodotus (484–425 B.C.) wrote that the first settlers in the peninsula and surrounding areas were members of the Canaanite tribes. Other early historians note that the inhabitants of the area were well known for their sailing skills. The people of Qatar were converted to Islam in 628 A.D. after the Persian governor of Bahrain embraced the new religion. Around the ninth century Qatar is described by Arab geographers as a point on Gulf sea routes. It was also mentioned in contemporary historical works because of the fame of the poet Qatari bin al-Fujaa who was born in Qatar.

At the beginning of the tenth century Qatar and other parts of the region came under the control of the Karmathian sect. After the Karmathian power dwindled towards the end of the 11th century, command of the area changed hands many times for a few centuries as Arab and Persian rulers vied for possession of the lower Gulf. At the beginning of the 16th, Portuguese vessels made the first European incursion into the area. They were quickly followed by the Dutch, French and British navies. But for a while Qatar seems to have remained unaffected by the European presence in the Gulf.

Migrants arrive Soon however Qatar became a big attraction to desert migrants, drawn to the peninsula by its good supply of water and its growing pearling and fishing industry. They came overland from central Arabia and by sea from neighbouring Gulf shores. The largest contingent arrived in the 1770s from Kuwait. They were members of the Aniza tribe which had been forced out of the Nejd by drought and had gone to Kuwait in search of water. A group broke away to seek a better settling ground in Bahrain and Qatar. They moved into the village of Zubara on the northwest coast of the peninsula, presumably to be within easy reach of the local pearling beds, and immediately clashed with the Musallim tribe which seems to have been in control of Qatar at the time.

Zubara was expanded into a large town and a big fort was built nearby at Qalat Marir. The Persians, who then governed Bahrain, viewed with increasing alarm the growth of Zubara and sent a fleet to take it over. An army collected from the Arab tribes in Qatar was there to meet the invaders. After hours of fierce fighting beneath the tall walls of the town the Persians fled back to their ships. At the time the town was dominated by the Al-Khalifa family which had its eyes on Bahrain and soon afterwards a Khalifa force occupied the island and have been in control there virtually ever since.

Clashes with Bahrain But for several years the Khalifas retained command over Zubara. The first Khalifa ruler of Bahrain, Shaikh Ahmed, spent his winters in the town. They were driven out by the Wahhabis who were spreading their power throughout the Arabian Peninsula. But after the Imam of Muscat expelled the Wahhabis from Zubara in 1809, the Khfilifas soon returned. They did not leave Qatar for good until later in the 19th century.

The Khalifa presence led to clashes between the Bahrainis and the Qataris among whom the Al-Thani family was beginning to emerge as the dominant force. In 1868 the British Resident in the Gulf, Colonel Lewis Pelly, visited Qatar to sort things out after a raid on the country by the shaikhs of Bahrain and Abu Dhabi and a retaliatory raid on Bahrain by the Qataris. Pelly made an agreement with Shaikh Mohammad bin Thani al-Thani, by then 'the most influential man in the whole promontory'. The Shaikh agreed that the Qataris would abstain from war at sea and would refer disputes with their neighbours to the British Resident.

A few years earlier the English traveller, William Gifford Palgrave, had written about his impressions of Qatar on a journey across Arabia to the Gulf coast. He described the country as consisting of 'miles and miles of low barren hills, bleak and sun-scorched, with hardly a single tree to vary their dry, monotonous outline'. The town of Al-Bida (present-day Doha) was dismissed as 'the miserable capital of a miserable province'. But Palgrave soon discovered another side to the country: the wealth from the sea. There were, he wrote, 'the most copious pearl fisheries of the Gulf and an abundance almost beyond belief of whatever other gifts the sea can offer or bring'. He learnt that the people of Qatar spent half the year searching for pearls and the other half in fishery or trade and that the real homes of the Qataris were their boats.

Al-Thani rule In 1878 the command of the Al-Thanis was formally acknowledged when Shaikh Gassem bin Mohammad al-Thani was made Amir. So began the reign of the present ruling Al-Thani dynasty in Qatar. At the time the Turks had pushed southwards from Iraq to al-Hasa and established a small Ottoman garrison in Doha. Shaikh Gassem managed to restrict Turkish influence by playing the Turks and British off against each other. In July 1889 the Turkish Governor of Al-Hasa came to Qatar with the object of setting up a Turkish administration and tax centre there. He was met by Shaikh Gassem at the head of a force of 700 armed men about 70 of whom were on horses or camels, carrying modern rifles. The Governor's proposals were firmly rejected and he was forced to return empty handed.

The Qataris were able to maintain a relative independence by taking advantage of the desert in the south of the peninsula which tended to act as a buffer between the Arabian hinterland and the northern inhabited areas of Qatar. They were also helped by a later agreement between Britain and the Turks which divided up parts of the Arabian Peninsula between the two powers and placed Qatar under nominal British control. But the British seemed content to give the country comparative freedom. In 1916 Shaikh Abdullah, the present ruler's grandfather, negotiated a treaty with Britain under which the British pledged to protect the country from outside attack. In return Qatar agreed not to enter into any relationship with a foreign government without British consent.

Oil found Oil was discovered at an opportune time in the 1930s because the pearl industry was then on the brink of collapse following the manufacture of artificial pearls by Japan. The country's first oil concession was granted to the Anglo-Iranian Oil Company. This was later transferred to the Petroleum Development (Qatar) Ltd, a subsidiary of Iraq Petroleum Company. But the Second World War delayed the exploitation of the nation's oil wealth and production did not begin on a commercial scale until 1949.

In his old age Shaikh Abdullah handed over power to his son, Hamad. However, in 1947 Shaikh Hamad died and, because his son Khalifa was too young to succeed, Shaikh Abdullah assumed once again his position as head of state until his death in 1949. A family council then decided that the young Khalifa's uncle, Ali, should rule and that Khalifa should become heir-apparent. But when Shaikh Ali abdicated in 1960, it was his own son, Ahmad, who became Amir. For the next 10 years or so Shaikh Khalifa, as Prime Minister, was the effective ruler of the country. He negotiated the end of the Treaty with Britain and full independence for Qatar in August and September 1971.

Finally, on 22 February 1972, Shaikh Khalifa assumed supreme authority of the country. In a radio broadcast he spoke about obstacles that had been put in the way of Qatar's development, and he immediately took measures to stamp out corruption, as well as to curb the privileges of certain members of the Al-Thani family which were resented by public opinion.

Recent Events

Qatar has been able to use its economic wealth to achieve a diplomatic status out of proportion to its small population. In

October 1975 the Amir visited France where he received a welcome of a kind normally reserved for the leader of a major country. The Amir has also been using his diplomatic weight to bring about a *rapprochement* among Gulf states. In June 1976 he showed foresight by calling for the establishment of a Gulf common market along the lines of the European Economic Community, an idea which was to receive increasing support among his fellow Gulf leaders. In December 1976 Doha was the venue for one of the most dramatic of conferences of the Organisation of Petroleum Exporting Countries (OPEC). The meeting produced a split in OPEC ranks which resulted in the introduction of a two-tier oil price system. Qatar showed itself to be independent of its stronger neighbours by opting for a 10 per cent rise while Saudi Arabia and the United Arab Emirates insisted on limiting their increase to five per cent.

At home, Qatar assumed complete control of its oil industry with the 100 per cent takeover of the Qatar Petroleum Company (QPC) and the Shell Company of Qatar (SCQ). Full ownership of QPC was announced in September 1976 after the Western consortium who were the Government's partners in the company agreed to compensation terms. In February 1977 Shell, the Government's partner in SCQ, signed an agreement providing for a takeover on similar terms. Three months later, however, the Government's economic development plans received a set-back when a gas liquids processing plant at Umm Said was destroyed by fire. The disaster inevitably delayed Qatar's gas export programme and caused other projects to be postponed.

ECONOMY

Qatar has huge energy resources, which include one of the biggest natural gas fields in the world. The country should remain extremely wealthy for many years to come, on the basis of its oil and gas reserves alone. It also has some of the most ambitious plans for industry in the Gulf. The Government has poured money into heavy industrial projects in an effort to give the nation an even stronger economic base.

Nonetheless doubts remain about some aspects of the country's economic future. About half of its 200,000 population are non-Qatari and foreigners make up an estimated 85 per cent of the labour force. Yet Qatar's industrial programme will necessitate the import of even more expatriate manpower, which could place a strain on the country's conservative social structure. Even immigrants who have been in the country for many years are not allowed to become Qatari citizens.

At the same time the future world markets of two products of Qatar's planned industries—steel and petrochemicals—are not assured. Even sales of liquefied natural gas (LNG), which will be one of the major products of Qatar's large gas reserves, are fraught with uncertainties. If the markets for these exports collapse, Qatar will have little to fall back on but depleted reserves of oil. The dangers of depending on gas as a main source of energy and feedstock were also highlighted in April, 1977, when the country's natural gas liquids (NGL) plant was destroyed by fire, upsetting Qatar's industrialisation plans.

Oil

Oil accounts for 97 per cent of Government income. In 1976 oil revenue amounted to $2,020 million and during 1977 it is expected to rise to $2,200 million. Output in 1977 has been expected to be about the same as the 1976 total of 23 million tons. From its oil income, the Government has been accumulating relatively large surplus funds. Between 1965–1975, budgets amounted to just 40 per cent of income, and in turn only an average three-quarters of each budget was actually spent.

The history of Qatar's oil started comparatively recently. In 1931 the Anglo-Persian Oil Company, now British Petroleum, started a geological survey of the Qatar Peninsula, at the same time that Standard of California was prospecting for oil in neighbouring Bahrain. Anglo-Persian was granted a concession in 1935 and the development contract was transferred to Petroleum Development (Qatar), associated with the Iraq Petroleum Company in which Anglo-Persian was a shareholder. Petroleum Development (Qatar), which later became the Qatar Petroleum Company (QPC) struck oil near the village of Dukkhan on the west coast in January 1940. Two more wells were drilled in the same structure but the war made it necessary to plug all three. Activity was resumed at the end of 1947. A pipeline was built across the peninsula because the shallow water of the Gulf of Salwah made it impossible for tankers to approach Dukkhan. The first shipment was made from the new terminal, at Umm Said, in December 1949.

Offshore discovery Also in 1949, offshore exploration started under American auspices but without success until 1952 when the concession went to Shell. The Shell Company of Qatar (SCQ) eventually struck oil at Idd al-Shargi, 60 miles east of the northern tip of the peninsula, in May 1960. Within a few months an even more promising find was made 11 miles to the north-east, at Maydan Mahzam. A third offshore field, Bul Hanine, was put on stream in 1972 after the demarcation, in 1969, of Qatar's maritime boundary with Abu Dhabi. All three offshore fields feed the storage tanks on Halul Island.

The Qater–Abu Dhabi maritime boundary cuts straight through an oil-bearing structure known as the Al-Bunduq field. It was agreed that the two states should benefit equally from this joint possession. Abu Dhabi Marine Areas (ADMA) was designated as the operator. British Petroleum sold half its interest in the company to a Japanese group, Qatar Oil Japan, and a new Al-Bunduq Company was formed to develop the field, owned equally by British Petroleum and Compagnie Française des Pétroles, the two former owners of Abu Dhabi Marine Areas, and Qatar Oil Japan. So far the field has been a relatively small producer.

When the principle of government participation in the equity of the operating companies was accepted, Qatar was one of the first Arab states to acquire, in 1973, a 25 per cent interest in the country's two oil companies. Qatar was also one of the first to go further and secure, in February 1974, a 60 per cent interest in them. In September 1976 the Government acquired the remaining 40 per cent of QPC and in February 1977 it took over the outstanding 40 per cent in SCQ.

Take-over terms The Government agreed to pay $30 million for the remaining QPC interests. Its former Western partners in the company still operate the Dukkhan field and provide the necessary expertise for a 15 cent-a-barrel service fee. The foreign companies have also undertaken to lift 130,000 barrels a day (b/d). Shell received $18 million for its holding in SCQ, and is thought also to be receiving a 15 cents-a-barrel service fee for continuing to operate the offshore fields. Its liftings have been restricted to 140,000 b/d.

Overall responsibility for the country's oil industry now lies with the Ministry of Finance & Petroleum. The day-to-day affairs of the oil, gas and petrochemical industries are controlled by the Qatar General Petroleum Corporation (QGPC), which in turn has delegated supervision of oil output to Qatar Petroleum Producing Authority (QPPA). It is divided into QPPA Onshore Operations and QPPA Offshore Operations.

Up to 1973 most of Qatar's oil came from the onshore Dukkhan field. But since then this field's output has been overtaken by offshore production. In 1975 SCQ pumped out 12.3 million tons and QPC eight million tons. The Dukkhan field produces good quality oil of low sulphur content. Its output from 60 oil wells averages around 225,000 b/d. Output from Qatar's three offshore oil fields averages about 330,000 b/d and tends to be of lower quality than onshore oil. Production from the Bunduq field, the revenues from which is shared equally with Abu Dhabi, total about 30,000 b/d. The field is still operated by ADMA, now called ADMA–OPOC.

Gas wealth Qatar has limited reserves of associated gas in the Dukkhan fields but its real gas wealth lies under its northwestern territorial waters. So far drillings have revealed a field of 80 million million cubic feet of natural gas. This makes it one of the biggest gas fields in the world, with a potential export capacity of 1,200 million cubic feet a day for 100 years. There could be other fields of similar size nearby, perhaps to the southeast along a geological formation known as the 'Qatar arch' which runs the length of the country like a spinal cord.

So far only the country's onshore associated gas has been harnessed to provide an energy source for power and desalination facilities and industrial plants. It has also been used as feedstock for a natural gas liquids (NGL) plant. But plans have been drawn up to tap the large offshore reserves with the objective of using them as feedstock for industrial and petrochemical plants.

Focus on Planning

Qatar's population has increased by 50 per cent since the beginning of this decade and this is reflected in the massive amount of construction going on in various parts of the peninsula. A quick drive through Doha, the east coast capital, shows that all this activity is not haphazard.

The skyline is as yet unspoiled by skyscrapers; much of the new architecture is in good taste; and the lines of traditional architectural styles can be seen either incorporated in modern designs or intact in restored traditional houses. The streets are wide, well-lit and lined with trees. These positive results in fact derive from the implementation of long-term development planning that is leaving as little as possible to chance.

Overall development policy is co-ordinated at the Office of HH the Emir (*al-Diwan al-Emiri*) in the office of Mr. Hisham Kaddoumi, Technical Adviser to the Emir. Two well-established Western companies are handling major development activities. The British architects and planners Llewelyn-Davies, Weeks, Forestier-Walker and Bor are mainly concerned with the implementation of planning and operate in conjunction with the existing municipal authorities in Doha, Khor, Wakrah and Rayyan; and American architects and planners William Pereira Associates are concerned with overall

The National Museum

364

planning—mainly in the West Bay development area
and at Umm Said, the country's industrial "capital."

The national concept of planning is based on future
growth patterns, social and economic. The population
by the end of the century is expected to be around
500,000—mainly centred on Doha and Khor, north of
the capital. The country's main natural resources—oil
and gas—are located around Dukhan, on the west coast,
and off-shore. The Umm Said industrial zone lies south
of Doha, on the east coast. Planners are concerned with
linking these areas as an integrated whole, backed by
an efficient transport and communications network.

WEST BAY

Perhaps the most exciting development scheme
being implemented at the moment is in the West Bay
area, where a large area of land, three kilometres in
diameter and forming a rough circle, has been reclaimed
at the north end of the wide sweep of corniche on the
capital's waterfront. It is already being referred to as
"new Doha".

It is estimated that 25 per cent of the total growth
of Doha over the next quarter of a century will be located
on the West Bay. So overall design philosophy
incorporates Middle East traditions adapted to local
social and environmental conditions. A major feature
of "new Doha" will be an "activity corridor"—a sort of
town centre wandering through the development,

The Emiri Palace

crossing major roads and housing blocks, with the result that everyone will be near shops, offices, government services, schools and so on. The corridor will link up with a planned "district centre", where major shopping facilities and prestigious office buildings will be located. Here also will rise, within the next few months, a major hotel-conference complex with a pyramid-like structure and an imposing view of the coast. To the north will be based a number of Arab and Western diplomatic quarters.

New premises for ministries are rising on either side of the *Diwan al-Emiri* along the waterfront, so that the *Diwan* will become the centre of operations in a physical as well as governmental sense. An architectural competition for a ministerial complex between the *Diwan* and the new Ministry of Information building is now in its preliminary stages. The Doha road network is to be expanded to provide the West Bay area with linear links with the university area to the north and the existing town to the south.

UMM SAID

Another hive of activity can be found at Umm Said, on the east coast 30 kilometres south of Doha, an area which the Government has decided to develop as a versatile industrial estate, fuelled by natural gas from the Dukhan field. Umm Said already groups some of the country's major industrial plants and the

Aerial View of Doha

development plans provide for the estate to be fully supported by an integrated infrastructural pattern of access and service roads, electric power generation and water distillation plant, and gas gathering and distribution pipeline systems.

The industrial area at Umm Said is located on the seafront, with the town proper behind. The development of the town, which will eventually have a population of 15,000, is following the same lines as those of the "new Doha" area. The town will be self-contained, with an "activity corridor" running through it.

Already in 1976 an allocation of QR 350 million was made towards the cost of a combined generation/distillation plant designed to produce 450mW of electricity and 8 million gallons of potable water daily. Other major allocations were for dredging and reclamation of coastal salt flats earmarked as sites for plant construction and four wharves—two mechanically equipped to handle bulk industrial products and the other two to handle general commercial cargo; for the self-contained township with a "mix" of high-rise and low-rise housing, a shopping centre, schools, hospitals and public services. In the 1977 budget specific allocations totalling QR 528 million were made for the construction of a 150-kilometre gas pipeline to the town, for a Doha-sourced water pipeline to supply the construction sites, and for more housing schemes.

Government House

Industry

Qatar's economic policy, like that of every other Gulf state, is aimed at diversification to reduce dependence on oil as the single source of income. Early in the 1970s the Government decided to develop heavy industries, on the grounds that they would be able to exploit fully the country's large reserves of cheap energy, in particular gas. Altogether the Government has allocated at least $1,500 million to the establishment of new industries. But the vulnerability of the country's dependence on gas as an energy source became clear in April, 1977, when its NGL plant at Umm Said, opened in 1975, was destroyed by fire. The accident appeared to have been caused by a fracture in one of the storage tanks and caused damage amounting to about $68 million.

The plant, which produced propane, butane and gasoline for export, was part of a scheme to use associated gas from the onshore Dukkhan oilfield. But it was also to form the base for a further gas liquefaction plant. A new processing unit was expected to be sited nearby so that it could share some of its facilities. The destruction of the plant will have almost certainly necessitated a replanning of Qatar's gas-based industrialisation plans. Some large projects will have to be put back.

Umm Said complex   Qatar's future industry will be centred at Umm Said about 30 miles south of Doha. Gas will be piped from the Dukkhan field on the west coast and from the new gas field off the northwest coast. Imported raw materials will be brought in through Umm Said port which is being expanded to serve the new plants.

It was originally planned that the second NGL plant to be built alongside the destroyed NGL plant would export propane, butane, and natural gasoline to Japan. Both plants would have provided feedstock for a petrochemicals complex, being set up at Umm Said, by the Qatar Petrochemicals Company (QAPCO) in which the state oil company QGPC has a 84 per cent share with the remainder held by CDF Chemie of France. The $500 million complex was due to become operational by 1978 but the destruction of the NGL plant has made this highly unlikely. The output was scheduled to be 280,000 tons a year of ethylene,

140,000 tons a year of polyethylene and 130,000 tons a year of unspecified products.

Gas will be the energy source for a $85 million iron and steel plant being built by Kobe Steel of Japan at Umm Said. Kobe will have a 15 per cent stake in the company running the plant, Tokyo Boeki 10 per cent with the remainder owned by the Government. The plant will produce 400,000 tons a year, the majority of which the Government hopes to export in the Gulf. The raw material for the plant will have to be imported. Perhaps as much as 600,000 tons a year of ore will have to be shipped from Australia and Brazil. Labour and managerial staff will also have to be brought in from abroad.

First industries Qatar's first industrial project, dating back to 1965, was the Qatar National Cement Company. The shareholding is 60 per cent public and 40 per cent government. Production started in 1969 with a daily output of 100,000 tons which has been raised to 200,000 tons. An expansion to the plant should raise daily capacity to about 600,000 tons. The cement works is at Umm Bab, on the western side of the peninsula and at the southern end of the Dukkhan oilfield.

The first industrial concern at Umm Said was the Qatar Fertiliser Company (QAFCO). The Government has a 70 per cent share in QAFCO which was formed in 1969 to build an ammonia and urea plant. Other shareholders are Hambros Bank, the British Power-Gas Corporation and Norsk Hydro, who both manage and market the production. The plant, powered and fed by gas from the Dukkhan field, was inaugurated in 1973. The plant has a daily capacity of 900 tons of ammonia, and 1,000 tons of urea. But it has never reached this capacity on average falling short by over 20 per cent. Nevertheless the Government has shown enough confidence in the fertiliser market to build an extension.

Close to the QAFCO plant at Umm Said is the Qatar Flour Mills Company, a project undertaken by a group of Doha merchants in 1969 and completed in 1972. It has storage for 8,000 tons of grain and initial output was 100 tons a day.

Infrastructural Development

The infrastructure for the future economy of Qatar is well organised, However, of all factors in the country's forward planning, water is the most critical. Rising population, agriculture and developing industry create huge demands for water in a hot and arid country. At present, daily water consumption is over 10 million gallons a day. Natural underground supplies from a rapidly falling water table can, at present, provide about three million gallons. The difference is made good by desalinated water from the power and desalination plant at Ras Abu Aboud which was installed in 1957 with a daily output of only 150,000 gallons. Within a relatively short time the country will have 32 million gallons a day (g/d) produced by desalination plants. The extra capacity will come from extensions and new plants at Ras Abu Aboud, Wakrah, and Umm Said. Each desalination plant is also being combined with a power plant.

As with electricity and water, roads and sewage disposal are constantly being improved to keep up with development. With the roads the emphasis is on improving the existing network rather than building new roads. Qatar is no longer an isolated peninsula but is linked to the Mediterranean and Europe by the trans-Arabian highway via Saudi Arabia. This overland route to Saudi Arabia has enabled Qater to handle goods destined for the Saudis which have been unloaded at Doha because of congestion at Dammam port.

However, with Qatar's own development speeding up, port expansion has become a priority as shipping bottlenecks could easily disorganise the whole programme. Ships in mid-1977 were having to wait around 40 days to unload their goods at Doha. At present five new berths are being added to the Doha jetty and long-term port requirements are the subject of a comprehensive study. Umm Said port is being expanded to serve the town's industrial complex and a proposal to build a new port at Jaziret al-Alyah north of the capital are under investigation by consultants. Increasing imports have also put strains on the airport facilities but, rather than improve the existing airport, it has been decided to build a completely new one for which the contract has been awarded to an Indian company. A site has been chosen 15 miles west of Doha.

Qatar's telecommunications system has been considerably improved in recent years and is now among the best in the Gulf. Altogether 11 out of 100 people in the country have telephones which is only slightly lower than the ratio of telephone subscribers in Kuwait. About 80 per cent of lines and telephone sets are concentrated in Doha, which makes the network easier to operate. Qatar now has its own earth satellite station which allows direct calls to other countries in the lower Gulf and to Egypt, Britain, France, Italy, India and Pakistan. There are tentative plans to lay direct cable links with other Gulf states because of the expense of making direct-calls over a relatively short distance via satellite.

Agriculture and Fishing

Agriculture does not come naturally to Qatar which has always been considered barren. Nevertheless, in the past 10 to 15 years, improved water supplies have enabled production of vegetables to be increased to meet the needs of the local market and provide small surpluses for export. Yields of fruit are also being steadily improved. Most remarkable of all, an area has been identified 40 miles north of Doha which is suitable for cereal production. This may enable Qater to become self-sufficient in wheat. In addition the Government owns a large poultry farm and the privately-owned Qatar Dairy Company produces 660 gallons of milk a day from a herd of Friesians imported from Australia. The Government aims to achieve self-sufficiency in basic foodstuffs by the 1980s. But food imports in 1975 totalled $51 million, suggesting that there is a long way to go before this target is reached.

Fishing has always been a source of food and wealth to Qatar and today the fishermen continue to provide fish for the local market. However a modernised fishing industry, especially dealing with shrimp, is in the hands of the Qatar National Fishing Company, one of the country's favoured joint ventures, formed in 1969 with the Government holding a 60 per cent share and Ross Group International 40 per cent. The company has a refrigerated storage and processing plant in Doha and, in 1976, exported nearly $1 million worth of shrimp, mainly to Japan. The company expected exports to be substantially higher in 1977.

Trade

Since the quadrupling of oil prices in 1973–74, Qatar's imports have soared. In 1974–75 they rose from $278.5 million to

$405 million and then in 1976 they more than doubled to $846 million. About 70 per cent of imported goods come by sea, but nonetheless Doha airport has been handling 30–40 tons of freight a day. A high percentage of the country's imports also come from Dubai which still acts as a re-exports entrepôt for Qatar, especially for high-value items like heavy duty transport equipment.

Qatar imports 1976

	Value ($ million)	per cent
Japan	239	29
UK	140	17
US	66	8
West Germany	65	8
France	37	4
Dubai	34	4
Italy	33	4
Kuwait	28	3
Others	204	23
Total	846	100

The composition of imports in 1975 reflected Qatar's total dependence on imported goods for its industrial development ambitions. Electrical machinery and appliances alone accounted for $76.3 million or 18.7 per cent of the total, supplied predominantly by the UK and Japan, with West Germany in third place. Non-electrical machinery accounted for $66.3 million. Iron and steel imports added a further $31.2 million to the overall import bill, most of these goods coming from the UK and Japan. The US also gained the biggest share of Qatar's booming transport equipment market, supplying some 36 per cent of the $42.6 million worth of imported passenger cars, with Japan hard on its heels. Japan, however, led in the import of trucks. Food imports have also absorbed a significant 12.5 per cent of spending on imports, amounting to $50.8 million.

Banking and Finance

Qatar has no proper central bank. The Qatar Monetary Agency (QMA) issues bank notes but has little control over the country's banking system. Banking licences are granted by the Amir who has decided to limit the country's commercial banks to 12. The Government mainly uses decrees and the existing commercial law to keep the banks in line, and bankers in the country say that as a result the Qatari lending market is more tightly controlled than in some other Gulf countries.

Up to 1970 there were only five banks in the country—the Qatar National Bank (QNB), the British Bank of the Middle East, Grindlay's Bank, Chartered Bank and the Arab Bank. Of the seven new banks which have since started business in Qatar only the Commercial Bank of Qatar (CBQ) is owned by locals. The CBQ is in fact the only bank in Qatar owned solely by private Qataris. The QNB is half-owned by the Government.

Banks' growth The QNB is the country's largest bank. It accounts for 40 per cent of all banking business and is used as a major channel for government funds, particularly when dealing with foreign companies. QNB in fact fulfils some of the functions of a central bank because of its access to government money. The CBQ, opened in April 1975, has grown at a spectacular pace. By September 1976 its balance sheet stood at $31 million, having more than doubled over the previous nine months. One of the reasons for the bank's rapid expansion was that it was the only commercial bank providing a full foreign exchange service.

In September 1976 total assets of the commercial banks stood at around $1,700 million compared with $770 million in March 1975. Between March and September 1976 assets increased by 18 per cent alone. Within the banking system interest rates are restricted to a minimum of 9½ per cent on loans and 4 per cent on savings accounts. A maximum 6½ per cent is paid on deposits. But most borrowing in the country is done through the use of overdrafts rather than loans. Personal credit standing is still important in Qatar's small community. At the same time banks tend to be regarded more as a source of credit than as a place to put your money. Private sector bank deposits in late 1976 amounted to a comparatively low $510 million. A lot of people tend to hold onto their cash and big denomination notes are in frequent use.

Qatar has accumulated large surplus funds from oil exports in recent years. The Government is thought to have foreign holdings totalling about $2,000 million. These are handled by the Qatar Investment Board, though the Qatar General Petroleum Company (QGPC) makes overseas investments and the QMA has certain holdings to back the Qatari riyal. The Investment Board uses at least 10 investment funds which are spread over the world's major currencies. A group of international bankers advises the board where to place funds, particularly with regard to secure long-term investments which the Government is beginning to favour.

Foreign loans Qatar has surprisingly low official foreign reserves. At one time during 1976, they only covered about three months imports. The low reserves may have been a reason for Qatar's first entrance into the European financial markets in April 1977. The Government announced to the surprise of some local bankers that it was raising a $530 million loan for four state-owned industrial companies. Around $230 million was for the country's planned petrochemical complex and $300 million for three other projects in steel, gas and fertilisers.

Outside the banking sector, financial business is mainly limited to the Qatar Insurance Company (QIC), founded in 1964. It is the only insurance company allowed to operate in the country and as a result has grown rapidly. Premium income is thought to have reached $13 million in 1976, a five-fold increase over three years. The Government has a 20 per cent stake in the company which has recently expanded into other areas of the Gulf. Offices have been opened in Dubai and Riyadh and the firm has participated in the insurance cover for the Bahrain drydock and Saudi Arabia's new port at Jubail.

Social Services

Medical services are provided free in Qatar to nationals and non-nationals alike. Already in hand is the building of a new 600-bed general hospital in Doha due for completion in 1978. It will replace the existing Rumaillah General Hospital which will specialise in obstretrics and gynaecology, chest complaints, and geriatric and psychiatric cases. The existing women's hospital will in turn be converted to a geriatric and long-stay centre. Also planned are 10 health centres which will each serve 20,500 people and provide the basis for a primary health care system.

In 1964 a 'popular housing' scheme was introduced and has become an important feature of the country's housing programme. Low-cost housing units are provided on the basis of long-term, interest-free government loans. Repayment is either related to the financial capacity of the recipient or completely waived. Over 650 units have been handed over free of charge. The home ownership scheme provides a 20-year loan of up to $33,000 either to build or to buy a house, a $6,000 furnishing grant, and a free site. A total of 1,500 low-cost houses have been built, mostly on estates and in 1977 $20 million was allocated by the Government to build 600 more houses.

For Umm Said there is a five-year plan for the creation of an entirely new and self-contained town to house the labour force of the industrial complex being developed there. The plan envisages a radial pattern of mixed high-rise and low-rise housing around a central commercial core. A longer-term scheme is for a new, self-contained, suburb on reclaimed land at the western extremity of Doha Bay. Here there will be a tower with restaurants and observation area, a shopping plaza and arcade, a hotel and conference complex, and housing for senior officials and diplomats.

Education growth   By 1982 the Government expects all children of primary school age to be receiving free compulsory education and two-thirds of secondary students. Total attendance currently exceeds 31,000 and plans to extend classroom accommodation to 600 units have high priority. The school population is now almost equally divided between boys and girls. Some 800 youngsters are attending Arab and non-Arab foreign higher education establishments.

Students attending existing teacher-training colleges for men and women will shortly transfer to buildings designed to serve as the nucleus of a university. The sexes will be taught separately but share common campus facilities. Qatar's University of the Lower Gulf is scheduled to open in five years with 2,000 students. At present higher education is also provided by the Doha Regional Training Centre which specialises in technical education.

GUIDE

DOHA Within a few years, Doha has been transformed from a sleepy fishing village into a spacious, well-planned modern city which has nonetheless kept its links with the past. Something of the old village atmosphere remains, and a sense of continuity with Arab and Islamic culture has been preserved. The new Doha has a refined look. The architecture of its public buildings is of a high standard. The ministries along the Corniche have been designed as a collective whole. None is high enough to break the sweep of the eye. Each attractively combines the modern with the traditional.

The new city is built around a series of ring roads which spread out in a half circle from the centre. They are wide double-carriageways with tree-lined central reservations which in turn are connected by a series of roads radiating out from the centre. Once this pattern has become familiar the city is easy to travel around. The heart of modern Doha is the pink and white Clock Tower and the vast new Emiri palace alongside. Behind is the Grand Mosque whose tall slim minaret serves as a useful landmark. From here, the wide boulevards lead to rows of enormous villas surrounded by purdah walls which the richer Qataris have built for themselves. The spaciousness of outer Doha contrasts with the narrow streets of the old centre which are not so well maintained and have many potholes. Traffic congestion is a problem in central Doha.

Key to Map of Doha Town opposite.

1. Central Bank; 2. Ministry of Interior; 3. British Bank of the Middle East; 4. Ministry of Education; 5. Chartered Bank; 6. Ministry of Municipal Affairs; 7. Traffic Police/Fire Dept.; 8. Arab Bank; 9. Ministry of Agriculture & Industry; 10. Grindlays Bank; 11. Qatar Chamber of Commerce; 12. Cable & Wireless; 13. Doha Palace Hotel; 14. Public Library; 15. Dental Clinic; 16. Museum; 17. Oasis Hotel; 18. Beach Club; 19. Gulf Hotel; 20. Power Station; 21 Qatar Fishing Co.; 22. Port & Customs Offices; 23. Government House; 24. Amir's Office; 25. First National City Bank; 26. Immigration Dept.; 27. British Embassy; 28. Rumaillah Hospital; 29. Guest Palace; 30. White Palace; 31. English-Speaking School; 32. Sudanese Embassy; 33. Lebanese Embassy; 34. French Embassy; 35. Jordanian Embassy; 36. Indian Embassy; 37. Syrian Embassy; 38. Kuwaiti Embassy; 39. Iraqi Embassy; 40. Saudi Arabian Embassy; 41. Banque de Paris; 42. Somalian Embassy; 43. Egyptian Embassy; 44. Water Dept.; 45. Electricity Dept.; 46. Youth Welfare Dept.; 47. Ministry of Commerce & Economy; 48. Women's Hospital; 49. Mechanical Equipment Dept.; 50. Engineering Services Dept.; 51. Ministry of Information; 52. Al-Hasr; 53. Al-Bahar; 54. Airport; 55. Pakistani Embassy.

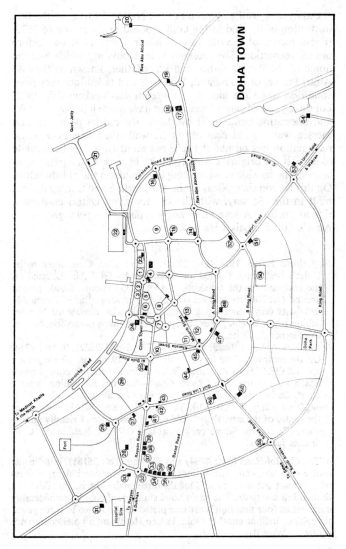

DOHA TOWN

Qataris are justifiably proud of the National Museum, the first institution of its kind in the Gulf, opened in the spring of 1975. It is a record of the old way of life in Qatar as it was before the oil revolution. The museum is in a building which was the home of the Amir's father and grandfather, known as the Old Amiri Palace, or the Salatah Palace. It had fallen into very poor condition when the idea of a museum was conceived in 1972, but three years of careful restoration have made it into a beautiful and interesting building. It overlooks the old harbour site, and the sea was a good deal nearer its walls than it is now. Land reclamation has pushed it back, but an attempt has been made to suggest the original close proximity by making a sort of pool-lagoon, the far side of which roughly simulates the old shoreline. On this lagoon six replicas of the old pearling and trading dhows, built in the old way, with the old tools, by Qatari craftsmen, ride at anchor. A seventh is not a replica, but belonged to the Amir's father, Shaikh Hamad.

Hotels

Gulf Hotel. P.O.B. 1911. Tel: 25251. Telex: 4250. Considered to be Doha's best hotel. Owned and managed by Gulf Air. Located on the seafront, on the outskirts of Doha. 350 rooms. Single person around QR 300. Restaurant (*Oryx*). Coffee shop. Bar in Room 501 (residents only). Swimming pool. Marina with dhows for hire for fishing trips. Bowling alley. Shops. Barber shop. Bookshop. Sauna. Conference facilities.

Oasis, Ras Abboud Road. P.O.B. 77. Tel: 26181/28221. Telex: 4214. On the seafront, close to the Gulf Hotel. 179 rooms. Single person around QR 275. Restaurant. Coffee shop. Swimming pool. Private beach with sports club (*Beach Club*)—facilities for sailing, squash court. Cinema. Barber shop. Conference facilities.

New Doha Place. P.O.B. 710. Tel: 26131. Telex: 4265. Located in the centre of the city. Doha's oldest top class hotel. Friendly atmosphere. 78 rooms. Single person around QR 250. Restaurant. Conference facilities.

The *Capital Hotel* (Tel: 4794) and *Carlton* (Tel: 25181), both in the centre of town, can provide inexpensive accommodation for visitors who cannot get a room at Doha's three main hotels. Facilities are limited but adequate. The city's hotel shortage should be considerably eased when four new hotels are completed in about two to three years' time. They include another Doha Palace Hotel and a hotel/conference centre on West Bay.

GULF HOTEL
DOHA

P.O. Box 1911, Doha, Qatar, Arabian Gulf
Telephone: Doha 25251
Telex: GLFHTL DH 4250
Cable: GLFHTL DOHA

Restaurants

Oryx Restaurant, Gulf Hotel. Tel: 25251. Provides the best food in Doha. Buffet lunch and à la carte menu in evening.

Oasis Hotel Restaurant. Tel: 26181. European/Oriental food. Buffet lunches.

Abu Nuwas, Kharaba Street. Tel: 322626. Good but unspectacular food.

Airport Restaurant, Doha Airport. Food much improved since management taken over by Gulf Hotel.

Muntazah Park Restaurant, Muntazah Park. Due to open by late 1977. Attractively designed.

Airport Now in danger of being enveloped by the rapidly expanding city. Has the second longest civil runway in the world. Small terminal building with limited facilities. Duty-free shop (often closed). A new terminal building is being constructed. Complete new airport is at the planning stage.

Taxis Taxis (identified by yellow number plate) have no meters and fares should be fixed with the driver beforehand. A short trip in the city costs QR 3–5. But taxis outside the *Gulf* and *Oasis Hotels* can cost a minimum QR 10. The official rate for a journey to and from the airport to the city centre is QR 15.

Car hire firms *Rent-a-Car*. P.O.B. 1316. Tel: 28100 (office), 5248/26697 (residence). *Khalaf Services*. P.O.B. 951. Tel: 24205 (office), 26534 (residence). *Pananghai Services*. P.O.B. 226. Tel: 25778.

The daily rate for a self-drive small saloon is around QR 100–150. International Driving Licences are not recognised. Instead, visitors require a special temporary licence issued by the Police Traffic Department, on presentation of a licence from their home country with four passport photos. Sometimes a test on knowledge of road signs has to be taken.

Travel agencies *Darwish Travel Bureau*, Clock Tower Square. P.O.B. 737. Tel: 22555. *Qatar Tours*, Karabah Street. P.O.B. 737. Tel: 23465. *Ali Bin-Ali Travel Agency*. P.O.B. 2197. Tel: 6393.

Airline offices Most airline sales are handled by the city's main travel agencies. *Air France*—Tel: 26788. *Air India*—27747. *Austrian Airlines*—22679. *British Airways*—25498. *Gulf Air*—22555-7. *Iran Air*—22555. *Alia*—27110. *Kuwait Airways*—23167. *MEA*—22288. *PIA*—4949/5959. *Singapore Airways*—6393/22679. *Saudia*—23465/23453. *Syrian Arab Airlines*—23910.

Shipping agencies *Kassem & Abdullah Darwish Fakhroo.* P.O.B. 71. Tel: 22343. *Qatar National Navigation & Transport Co.* P.O.B. 153. Tel: 29335.

Post Office The main post office is opposite Government House. Hotels will sell stamps. Air mail letters to Europe take 3–7 days. Surface mail should be avoided because of port delays. Mail delivery is generally quick and reliable.

Telephone International calls have to be booked but are not usually subject to much delay. All local calls are free.

Useful phone nos. *Emergency* (Police, Fire, Ambulance)—*999. Airport enquiries*—321400/328011. *International operator*—15. *Police headquarters*—28231. *Traffic & Licensing Office*—5266. *Customs*—22214. *Immigration*—23606.

Telex The main hotels have telexes. Telex messages can also be sent from the *Cable and Wireless Building* in Musarib Street.

Souks Close to the Clock Tower. The main souk mainly sells imported modern goods. The fish market has the traditional atmosphere of haggling and bargaining which has not changed for centuries. It is at its best in the early morning. Behind is an area of small shops selling copper pots, brass bowls and other small antiques.

Social clubs Several companies (like Shell and QAFCO in Umm Said) have social clubs which admit guests accompanied by members.

Leisure/sport Facilities are limited. The largest sporting amenity is the city's new Khalifa stadium, which is mainly reserved for soccer matches. Some companies have their own tennis courts. The *Beach Club* at the Oasis Hotel has facilities for sailing and a squash court. The marina at the *Gulf Hotel* hires out small boats and dhows mainly for people wanting to fish. Qatar has many fine beaches, giving ample opportunities for swimming. There is a race course and occasionally camel races are held privately.

Bookshops *The Family Bookshop*, Khabara Street, has the best selection of foreign newspapers, periodicals and books. *Arabian Library*, Abdullah Bin-Thani Street (Tel: 324416), also sells foreign newspapers and magazines.

Hospitals The *Rumailah Hospital* (Tel: 26251) is the main centre for emergency treatment.

Pharmacies *Al-Bakar Pharmacy*—Tel: 22837. *Cure Pharmacy*—Tel: 23918. Off-duty pharmacies are announced daily on TV and radio.

Banks Head offices: *Qatar Monetary Agency*. P.O.B. 1234. Tel: 5987. Telex: 4335. *Commercial Bank of Qatar*. P.O.B. 3232. Tel: 321010. *Qatar National Bank*. P.O.B. 1000. Tel: 23092.

Main offices: *Arab Bank*. P.O.B. 172. Tel: 324745. *Bank Al-Mashrek*. P.O.B. 388. Tel: 23981. *Al-Fardan Banking & Finance*. P.O.B. 339. Tel: 26544. *Bank of Oman*. P.O.B. 173. Tel: 26281. *Bank Saderat Iran*. P.O.B. 2256. Tel: 24447.

Bank de Paris et des Pays-Bas. P.O.B. 2636. Tel: 26291. *British Bank of the Middle East*. P.O.B. 57. Tel: 23124. *Chartered Bank*. P.O.B. 29. Tel: 23321. *Citibank*. P.O.B. 2309. Tel: 24416. *Grindlays Bank*. P.O.B. 2001. Tel: 26141. *United Bank*. P.O.B. 329. Tel: 321420.

Ministries/Government departments Ministries: *Agriculture & Industry*. P.O.B. 1966. Tel: 25221. *Communications & Transport*. P.O.B. 2633. Tel: 4098. Telex: 4378. *Economy & Commerce*. P.O.B. 1968. Tel: 5394. *Education*. P.O.B. Tel: 22791. Telex: 4316. *Electricity & Water*. P.O.B. 41. Tel: 23241. Telex: 4478. *Finance & Petroleum*. P.O.B. 83. Tel: 4054. Telex: 4233. *Foreign Affairs*. P.O.B. 250. Tel: 5759. Telex: 4252.

Information. P.O.B. 1836. Tel: 6273/5256. Telex: 4229. *Interior*. P.O.B. 2433. Tel: 26214. *Justice*. P.O.B. 893. Tel: 23181. *Labour & Welfare*. P.O.B. 201. Tel: 5418. *Municipal Affairs*. P.O.B. 2727. Tel: 4818. Telex: 4476. *Public Health*. P.O.B. 42. Tel: 23937. Telex: 4261. *Public Works*. P.O.B. 38. Tel: 24133.

Other departments: *Amir's Doha Palace*. Tel: 25241. *Industrial Development Centre*. Tel: 29211. *Government House*. Tel. 321444. *Department of Tourism*. Tel: 28535. *Department of Telecommunications*. P.O.B. 2633. Tel: 25446. Telex: 4468. *Petroleum Affairs*. P.O.B. 83. Tel: 21311. Telex: 4233. *Civil Aviation*. P.O.B. 3000. Tel: 28611. Telex: 4306.

Embassies *Britain*. P.O.B. 3. Tel: 23991/2. Telex: 4205. Commercial Secretary, P.O.B. 3. Tel: 22637. *Egypt*. P.O.B. 2899. Tel: 25136. *France*. P.O.B. 2669. Tel: 25216. *West Germany*. Tel: 29720. *India*. P.O.B. 2788. Tel: 26824. *Iran*. P.O.B. 1633. Tel: 5052. *Iraq*. P.O.B. 1526. Tel: 22894.

Japan. P.O.B. 26152. *Jordan*. P.O.B. 2366. Tel: 25146. *Kuwait*. P.O.B. 1177. Tel: 5227. *Lebanon*. Tel: 5193. *Morocco*. Tel: 29182. *Tunisia*. P.O.B. 2707. Tel: 21694. *Saudi Arabia*. P.O.B. 1255. Tel: 27144.

Somalia. Tel: 5758. *Sudan*. P.O.B. 2999. Tel: 25156. *Oman*. Tel: 29113. *Syria*. Tel: 21873. *U.S.A*. P.O.B. 2399. Tel: 87701.

Newspapers/Periodicals *Al-Doha Magazine*. P.O.B. 1836. Arabic monthly. *Al-Ouruba*. P.O.B. 633. Arabic weekly. Published by Arabian

Newspaper Printing and Publishing House. *Al-Arab*. P.O.B. 633. Arabic daily. Published by Arabian Newspaper Printing and Publishing House. *Al-Ahad*. P.O.B. 2531. Weekly. Published by Khalifa Abdullah al-Husaini. *Al-Fajr*. P.O.B. 2908. Weekly. Published by Qatar National Printing Press and Publishing Establishment.

Media. The *Gulf Weekly Mirror*, published in neighbouring Bahrain, is the only local English-language paper carrying news from Qatar. Qatar radio broadcasts English programmes between 6–9 a.m., noon–4 p.m., and from 8–midnight. There are news bulletins in between these times, the main one at 6 p.m. Qatar TV transmits programmes in English, with a news bulletin at 10 p.m.

Churches Interdenominational services are held regularly at the British Embassy.

Major companies *Qatar General Petroleum Corporation* (*QGPC*). P.O.B. 2233. Tel: 26241. Telex: 4343. *National Oil Distribution Co.* (*NODCO*). P.O.B. 2244. Tel: 4606. Telex: 4324. *Qatar Gas Company*. P.O.B. 2233. Tel: 77601. *Qatar Cement Co.* P.O.B. 1985. Tel: 77452. Telex: 4337. *Qatar Fertiliser Co.* P.O.B. 10001. Tel: 77252. Telex: 4215. *Qatar Insurance Co.* P.O.B. 666. Tel: 23819. Telex: 4216. *Qatar National Fishing Co.* P.O.B. 403. Tel: 24461. *Qatar Petrochemical Co.* P.O.B. 756. Tel: 28723. Telex: 4361. *Qatar Steel*. P.O.B. 689. Tel: 29001. Telex: 4362. *Darwish Trading Co.* P.O.B. 92. Tel: 22781. *Al-Nasr Trading Co.* P.O.B. 28. Tel: 22280. *Mannai Trading Co.* P.O.B. 76. Tel: 26251.

Useful addresses *Qatar Chamber of Commerce*. P.O.B. 402. Tel: 25131. *Director of Information*. P.O.B. 1836. Tel: 6355. Telex: 4229. *Qatar News Agency*. P.O.B. 1836. Tel: 4723. Telex: 4394. *Immigration Department*. P.O.B. 2433. Tel: 23606. Telex: 4345. *Qatar Petroleum Producing Authority* (*QPPA*). P.O.B. 70. Tel: 27674. Telex: 4253.

GENERAL INFORMATION

How to get there BY AIR (outside Gulf): With the exception of a good service to and from London, Qatar has poor air connections with Europe. There are daily flights from London (on average two daily). Otherwise there are only a few weekly flights from Paris and Amsterdam. There are weekly flights from Bombay (about three), Karachi (around four), Tokyo, Hong Kong, Delhi, Dacca, Colombo, and Brunei. Several flights a week go from Beirut and Cairo to Doha and less frequent ones from Amman, Damascus, Sanaa and Taiz.

Welcome to the world of alnasr . . .

OUR INDUSTRIAL MACHINERY CENTRE

It's worth a trip from anywhere!
We sell, we service, we demonstrate the latest ideas in mechanical equipment to help you move ahead—and stay ahead. See us for names like Rolls-Royce and Perkins Diesels, Seddon Trucks, Hyster Fork-lifts, Coles Cranes, Liner Concrete Plant, Aveling-Barford Heavy Earth Moving and Road Building Equipments, Brown-Boveri Heavy Electric Installation, CAV Fuel Equipment and more. All backed by our expert repair, overhaul and General Engineering Workshops.

OUR GENERAL MERCANTILE DIVISION

It now serves you in industrial and development projects!
We install N.E.C. and continental tele-communication and broadcasting equipment, Cumberland Electro Chlorination Plants, Kent Electro Chemical Oxygen and Analysers and Tely-Tone Audio Level Transmitters, cables, I.C.I. chemicals, paints, explosives, Firestone tyres, Bohler-Vienna, Borsig Berlin high pressure vessels, heat exchangers, compressors, petro chemical plants and allied equipment, building material and general orders supplier to the State of Qatar.

OUR AIR CONDITIONING & REFRIGERATION CENTRE

It's headquarters for fine brands!
While you're here, see us for colour TV's, radios, stereos and appliances, too. You'll get a great buy on a Siemens Colour TV, Prestair, Diakin and McQuay Room and Central Air Conditioning, Morris Passenger lifts and many more. Along with our customer satisfaction plan and our own dependable repair services.

OUR TOYLAND AND GIFT STORE

It's a full visit for everyone!
It's the first, and still the biggest and best-loved toystore in Doha! (Ask any youngster in town.) It's a gift shop filled with fabulous finds in housewares, decorator items, jewellery, watches, perfume, cosmetics, luggage and lots, lots more.

OUR ALNASR TRAVEL AGENCY

It's ready to serve you better!
Just tell us when and where you want to go. And we'll take care of the rest, quickly and efficiently. For information call our Travel Agents now. Tel. 6236 and 6167.

ALNASR TRADING ORGANIZATION, DOHA

Machinery Centre, Tel. 22284, 24452; General Mercantile, Tel. 22280, 25106 (5 lines); Air Conditioning & Refrigeration, Tel. 23271, 324102; Toyland, Tel. 22582; Carpentry, Tel. 23852. Telex; 4401 MACDIV DH & 4242 ALNASR DH

BY AIR (inter-Gulf): There are about four flights a day from Bahrain, which is the main transit point for passengers to Qatar. There are also daily flights from Abu Dhabi and Dubai (on average two a day).

Several flights a week go to and from Sharjah, Shiraz, and Muscat and there are less frequent weekly flights from Baghdad, Ras al-Khaimah, Riyadh, Kuwait and Dhahran.

Visas Visas are required by all except nationals of Qatar, Bahrain, Kuwait, Oman, Saudi Arabia, and the United Arab Emirates and holders of British passports in which their national status is described as 'British Subject' Citizen of the United Kingdom and their place of birth or country of residence as the United Kingdom (for a stay not exceeding 30 days).

Transit visas are not required by those who continue their journey to a third country by the same or first connecting aircraft within 24 hours. But they must hold tickets with reserved seats and documents for their onward journey. Business and company representatives may be issued with a 72 hour visa provided that their passports are endorsed for Qatar and they hold onward tickets with confirmed bookings. They must be in possession of valid proof of identity from their company and be met at the airport by a commercial representative of the company being dealt with. Nationals of Albania, Bulgaria, Czechoslovakia, East Germany, Hungary, North Korea, Pakistan, China, Poland, Rumania, U.S.S.R. and Vietnam require a visa at all times.

Language The official language is Arabic. English is widely spoken in business circles.

Religion Qatar is a Wahhabi Muslim state.

Official holidays The holidays marked with an asterisk * are dependent on the Moslem calendar and may differ by one or two days from the dates given. The Muslim year has 354 or 355 days, so Muslim dates and holidays fall 10 to 11 days earlier each year on the Gregorian calendar. Businessmen are advised to avoid visits to Qatar during the month of Ramadan which is the month preceding the Id al-Fitr.

	1977/78
Id al-Adha*	22–26 November
Independence Day	3 September 1978
Id al-Fitr (end of Ramadan)*	3–6 September 1978

Time GMT + 3.

Electric current 220–240 volts, 50 cycles AC.

Health Smallpox vaccination certificates are required by all visitors. Cholera immunisation is required if arriving within 5 days after leaving or transiting infected areas. A yellow fever vaccination certificate is required if arriving within 6 days from or via an infected area. Preventive precautions should be taken against malaria because risks exist in all places including urban areas.

Water It is generally unsafe to drink water from the tap, even though most of it is desalinated. The country still does not have a proper water distribution system and many homes rely on delivery by tanker. But the large hotels are served by mains.

Post Qatar's postal service is quick and reliable.

Telecommunications Links with other lower Gulf states are good. There is direct dialling to the United Arab Emirates and Bahrain. International calls usually can be made relatively quickly, but there are delays sometimes on calls to Saudi Arabia and to some Middle East capitals.

Currency The unit of currency is the Qatar Riyal (QR) divided into 100 dirhams. The following denominations are in circulation:
  Notes: Qatar Riyal 1, 5, 10, 100 and 500
  Coins: Dirhams 1, 5, 10, 25 and 50.

Currency regulations There are no restrictions on the import or export of currency.

Customs regulations Visitors are allowed to bring in 1 lb of tobacco and perfumes up to the value of QR 20. The import of alcohol is prohibited.

Alcohol Visitors may have difficulty in obtaining alcohol because of severe restrictions on its sale. The Gulf Hotel is about the only public place that has a bar but it is only open to hotel guests. Residents can obtain permits from their embassies allowing them to buy alcohol from a restricted number of licensed syndicates. Company clubs are also allowed to buy and sell liquor. With the exception of canned beer, alcohol bought with a permit tends to be cheaper than in Europe.

Useful advice During the hot and humid summer months between April and September, light cotton clothing is best for comfort. Qataris are strict Wahhabi Muslims, so women should dress very modestly with long-sleeved dresses. In December/January, sweaters may be needed as a protection against cold weather.

Further reading *Qatar Today*. Ministry of Information, Doha. 1976. *Qatar: a Forward Looking Country with Centuries Old Traditions*, by Bernard Gerard. Editions Delroisse, Paris. 1974. *The Gulf States: Business Opportunities*. Metra Consulting Group, London. 1976. *Bahrain, Qatar and the United Arab Emirates*, by Mohammad Sadik and William Snavely. Lexington, Mass. 1972. *Narrative of a Year's Journey through Central and Eastern Arabia* (1862–1863), by William Palgrave. Gregg International Publishers. 1969.

Government

Head of State	Shaikh Khalifah Bin-Hamad al-Thani
Foreign Affairs	Shaikh Suhaim Bin-Hamad al-Thani
Economy & Commerce ...	Shaikh Nasser Bin-Khaled al-Thani
Justice	*Vacant*
Water & Electricity ...	Shaikh Jassem Bin-Mohammad al-Thani
Interior	Shaikh Khaled Bin-Ahmad al-Thani
Industry & Agriculture ...	Shaikh Faisal Bin-Thani al-Thani
Municipal Affairs ...	Shaikh Mohammad Bin-Jaber al-Thani
Finance & Petroleum ...	Shaikh Abdel-Aziz Bin-Khalifah al-Thani
Public Works	Khaled Bin-Abdullah al-Atiya
Labour & Social Affairs ...	Ali Bin-Ahmad al-Ansari
Transport & Communications	Abdullah Bin-Nasser al-Suweidi
Public Health	Khaled Bin-Mohammad al-Manai
Information	Isa Ghanem al-Kawari
Education, Culture & Youth	*Vacant*

KINDLY MENTION

The Gulf Handbook

SAUDI ARABIA

THE KING OF SAUDI ARABIA

THE KING OF SAUDI ARABIA
His Majesty King Khaled Ibn-Abdel-Aziz

King Khaled succeeded to the throne on the death of his brother King Faisal Ibn-Abdel-Aziz on 25 March 1975. King Khaled was born in 1913 and educated traditionally at a number of religious schools. He was appointed assistant to his brother Prince Faisal in 1934 and represented Saudi Arabia at a number of international conferences. He became Vice-President of the Council of Ministers in 1962, a post he held until his succession. He was nominated Crown Prince in 1965. On his accession he also took on the Premiership—a post he still holds—and the Foreign Ministry portfolio; he relinquished the latter in October 1975.

Saudi Arabia

Area 830,000 square miles

Population 8.7 million (mid-1974 estimate)

Chief towns Riyadh (royal capital) 350,000; Jeddah (administrative capital) 300,000; Mecca 250,000; Medina 100,000

Gross National Product $42,000 million (1976 estimate)

GNP per caput $4,665

GEOGRAPHY

The Kingdom of Saudi Arabia covers four-fifths of the Arabian Peninsula. This is approximately the same area as the whole of Western Europe from Spain to the Eastern Bloc borders, including Britain and Ireland.

The country has two areas of desert, the Great Nefud in the north, and the Rub al-Khali, or Empty Quarter, in the south. The former covers about 22,000 square miles, while the latter covers more than ten times that area, approximately 250,000 square miles, an area the size of the state of Texas. These two great deserts are linked by what look on the map like two curving ribbons of sand. The eastern ribbon is known as the Dahna, and the western as the Nefud Dahi. These features have had a great influence on the political and demographic topography. To travel from Al-Hasa to the Nejd, the central plateau, it is necessary to cross the Dahna. Similarly, in the west the Nejd is divided from the Hejaz by the Nefud Dahi. The Nejd, therefore, can be thought of as an island surrounded by desert sand in the centre of Arabia.

In the past the routes across the peninsula were much influenced

395

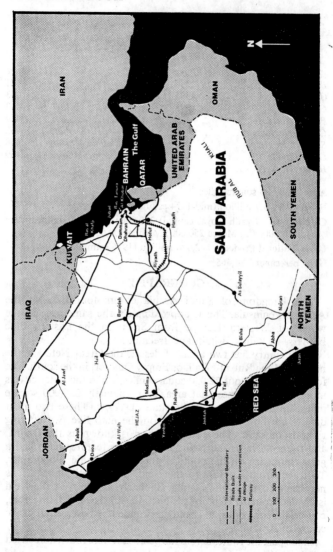

by the need to find the shortest crossings of the deep and shifting sand into and out of the Nejd. The old travellers crossed the Dahna at one of its narrowest points opposite Al-Kharj, afterwards swinging north-west to approach the capital, Riyadh. Similarly, they did not normally make their way to Taif and Mecca by striking due west from Riyadh. They first journeyed from Riyadh into the northern Nejd, to Anaiza or Buraida, from where they approached the Red Sea and Mecca in a southwards curve by way of Medina. This indirect route not only crossed the Nefud Dahi where it is narrow, west of Qasim, but had the advantage also of avoiding the formidable escarpment of the Tuwaiq Mountains. The eroded cliffs of this range facing the Nefud Dahi reinforce the impression of the Nejd as an island.

Western Province In the west of the country a virtually unbroken mountain chain stretches from the Gulf of Aqaba to North Yemen. The northern half down to a point 200 miles south of Mecca is called Hejaz and the remainder down to Najiran near the Yemen border is named Asir.

Hejaz contains the two holiest cities of Islam, Mecca and Medina, which non-Muslims are forbidden to enter. In places it widens into two parallel ranges separated by a plateau, with the lower range closer to the coast. In its northern section the peaks rise to as high as 9,500 feet. At the southern tip of Hejaz, 5,000 feet up in the mountains above Mecca, lies Taif, Saudi Arabia's traditional summer capital which is famous for its orchards and gardens.

In Asir the mountain peaks are closer and higher and some passes are particularly difficult to negotiate. Towards the south, the area catches the Indian Ocean monsoon and is more fertile than Hejaz. Abha, seated high in the mountains, is the capital of the district.

The Red Sea coastal plain (Tihamah) varies in width from nine to 31 miles. There are no natural harbours but modern ports have been built at Jeddah (the country's commercial and diplomatic capital), Yabu and at Jaizan in the south. There are numerous small islands along the southern coast and coral reefs.

Eastern Province East of the Dahna sands the country consists of the Summan Plateau, which varies between 50 and 100 miles in width, and has a low, rolling coastal plain. In the north the plain runs into gravel flats west of Kuwait and in the south it stretches into the Jafurah sands which merge with the Rub al-Khali desert. It has many salt flats formed by the evaporation of saline water in depressions. The plain's main landmark is the Al-Hasa oasis, the largest in the country. The water table lies close to the surface and in places like Qatif on the coast and Hofuf, the area's main city, water has seeped up to form large springs.

The main claim to fame of the Eastern Province (more frequently named merely Al-Hasa) is the oilfields underneath, some of the world's largest. It is the centre of the country's oil industry which has caused the rapid growth of such places as Damman on the Gulf, Al-Khobar and Dhahran. Ras Tanura has a big oil terminal and a large port complex is being built at Jubail, which a few years ago was only a fishing village.

CLIMATE

Most of Saudi Arabia has an extremely hot summer and a relatively cool winter. The exceptions are the coastal areas, particularly on the Red Sea coast. In Riyadh temperatures can reach 49°C (120°F) in the shade in June, July and August but humidity remains low. In the winter during December and January temperatures can drop to freezing point. In the eastern region the heat can be equally intense during the summer but because humidity is higher the weather is much more tiring. Winter temperatures do not tend to fall so low.

On the Red Sea the temperatures are more constant. Jeddah is relatively warm and humid for most of the year with the summer temperature seldom rising higher than 38°C (100°F). In September humidity can often exceed 90 per cent. In south Asir it is particularly temperate with monsoon rainfalls during summer providing an annual average of around 12 inches (compared with 2.7 inches in Jeddah and three inches at Dhahran in the east).

Saudi Arabia can be very windy during both summer and winter. A prevailing north-west wind blowing in off the sea helps to relieve the summer heat in Riyadh. In the east the *shamal*, a north wind, produces frequent dust storms. Occasional heavy rainstorms between November and April can sometimes disrupt air services. Torrential rains often flood streets and swamp wadis, making travelling by road dangerous.

PLANTS AND WILDLIFE

Traditionally the date palm has provided a major part of the staple diet of Saudi Arabia. Alfalfa was grown in between the palms to supply cattle fodder and in a few fertile areas grains were cultivated. But the recent introduction of modern agricultural techniques has made the growing of wheat, barley, maize and sorghum widespread and the production of dates has declined.

Wild flowers are fairly common in the spring and a welcome sight when found blossoming in the bleak landscape. Taif is famous for its roses and some flowers grow freely in the Asir mountains. The oleander thrives in parts of the desert. Besides the date palm, the country is devoid of trees. The tamarisk has traditionally been grown on the edge of the desert to stop the encroachment of drift sand. Several varieties of bushes in the desert are used as fodder for camels. One called the *hamd* has leaves containing enough salinity to satisfy the animals' need for salt.

Saudi Arabia has been a country where most animals have always been domesticated. The nomadic tribes have made the camel, sheep and goat their chief support. There have never been many wild animals and the ones that are left are rare. The oryx used to roam the Rub al-Khali but now there are very few, if any, left. The ibex has also become rare, and the gazelle has been sharply reduced in number by indiscriminate hunting.

The desert has poisonous snakes like the horned viper and an uncommon species of cobra, large lizards like the desert monitor, and birds like the sand grouse and lark. The eastern oasis is a stopping-point for migrating European birds—cuckoos, thrushes, swallows and warblers in particular—and is a habitat for a variety of indigenous Arabian birds as well.

The French film-maker Jacques Cousteau has made the underwater life of the Red Sea famous throughout the world. Its coral reefs make an ideal home for some fish. Fishermen catch amberjack, barracuda, tuna, red snapper, sea bass and sailfish. Off the Gulf coast groupers, mackerel and barracuda are common.

Locust swarms are a problem on the Red Sea coastal plain, particularly in the south where relatively frequent rains help the insect to breed. Insects like cockroaches and ants are numerous in the cities, as well as the mosquito. Scorpions can sometimes be seen in the desert.

COMMUNICATIONS

Over the last few years the Saudi Government has spent large sums of money linking up the scattered centres of population in its vast country. Now most major cities and towns are connected by asphalted roads and the present Five Year Plan aims to double the present total length of main road to 16,840 miles by the 1980s. For the moment major defects remain in the road network. The roads between Jeddah and Riyadh and Tabuk in the northwest are still inadequate. New roads are linking the towns of the Asir mountains with Mecca and Jeddah but there is no direct route between the southwest and Riyadh. Travelling between the northwest and southeast requires long detours. The streets of Jeddah, Riyadh and Dammam have become heavily congested with traffic because the city planners have been unable to keep up with the rapid increase in cars. But hopefully over the next few years the country's road building programme will be able to deal with some of the main shortcomings.

Saudi Arabia has the Arabian Peninsula's only railway— running between Riyadh and Dammam. It was built by the Arabian American Oil Company (Aramco) and is single track, 350 miles long, carrying about 200,000 passengers and 1.5 million tons of freight a year. From Riyadh the line runs south to Al-Kharj where it goes over the Dahna sands at the traditional crossing point before turning north to Hofuf through the Al-Hasa oasis to Dammam. For some time the Government has been considering building a multi-billion dollar line between Riyadh and Jeddah and there has been much talk about rebuilding the old Hejaz railway from Mecca to Amman.

The country has over 20 airports which could provide the basis for a comprehensive air service. But most internal traffic is confined to the Dhahran-Riyadh-Jeddah route. All three of these places have international airports. Jeddah's second international airport is nearing completion and the airports at Dhahran and Riyadh are being expanded. Medina, Jaizan, Khamis Mushayt, Qal al-Bishal and Hofuf have airports and one is planned at Tabuk.

Saudi Arabia's fast development has put tremendous pressure on the ports at Jeddah, Dammam and to a lesser extent Yanbu. For a time they did not have the capacity to deal with an incessant flow of goods. In the late summer of 1976 over 150 ships were waiting to unload their cargo at Jeddah's 13 berths. The Saudi Ports Authority was forced to take drastic action, like banning ships of 15 years or over with inadequate unloading gear and switching to roll-on, roll-off (ro-ro) vessels. The congestion eased considerably. Now the ports are operating much more efficiently and they are also being greatly expanded. New ports are also being constructed at Jaizan and at Jubail on the Gulf.

SOCIAL BACKGROUND

In the absence of any officially published census, estimates of the population in Saudi Arabia vary between four million and nine million, but the lower figure is likely to be closer to reality. The population is Arabic-speaking and was originally composed mainly of nomadic tribespeople, village agriculturalists in the oases, pearl fishers on the Gulf coast and traders on the Red Sea coast.

The nomadic tribes have been the dominant element in Saudi society. Among the main tribes are the Anaiza, the Shammar, the Mutayr, the Utaybah, the Murrah and the Manasir. They are divided into subtribes down to the level of extended families. Their day-to-day life is spent herding their camels in the desert, searching for grazing land. They regularly visit oases and villages, both to resupply themselves with basic necessities and to sell their own milk products and camels. Village and nomadic life are totally interdependent, despite the hostility nomads and settled people show for each other.

Under Abdel-Aziz al-Saud (1880–1953) the traditions of desert life were gradually eroded. He outlawed intertribal warfare and brought the entire area under his domination, thus attacking the basic structure of the traditional society. He was assisted by droughts which impaired the tribes' ability to survive without external aid, as well as by the pressures of outside powers. The discovery of oil also helped. From the 1940s onwards, the Arabian American Oil Company (Aramco) began to employ local labour, thus enticing people away from subsistence agriculture and nomadism.

A recent influx of large numbers of foreign workers and professionals has ended Saudi Arabia's isolation from the rest of the world. This isolation used to be interrupted only by the pilgrimage, an important feature of the Islamic faith. Foreign labour was brought in because of a general lack of education among the Saudis; hence the large numbers of doctors, teachers and engineers from Egypt, Palestine and Pakistan. The small population also made it necessary to import many unskilled and semi-skilled labourers, mainly Yemenis and Baluchis. There are reputedly over one million Yemenis in the country. These immigrants, as well as providing badly needed skills, also introduce new ideas into the society which will eventually affect social norms. Currently there are also significant numbers of Westerners working on major economic projects, many of whom live in relative isolation.

Modernisation of the country has also created an increasing trend towards urbanisation and corresponding depopulation of the countryside, resulting in great changes in family, social and economic life, as well as reducing tribal allegiance. It has also led to a slow relaxation of the puritanical Wahhabi code, which to this day forms the basis of social life in the Saudi state.

Wahhabism A branch of Sunni Islam, Wahhabism developed in the 18th century out of the alliance of Mohammad bin Abdel-Wahhab, a religious reformer, and the Al-Saud family. A very strict form of Islam, Wahhabism follows the Hanbalite legal school and calls for a return to the word of the Koran. The movement had a fluctuating success in the 18th and 19th centuries but was the first to reunite the country under a single political authority. Under Abdel-Aziz Al-Saud, the country was unified as a kingdom and Wahhabism formed the social and legal practices of Saudi Arabia. Prayers are compulsory and all other activity stops at prayer times; religious law is strictly applied, even to the amputation of limbs for theft. The *Ulema*, religious leaders, have the power to hinder or delay developments which they consider contrary to the principles of Islam. For example, they succeeded in preventing the opening of any public cinemas in the country, but failed to prevent TV and radio which have been successfully introduced, although programmes are kept within very strict limits. In the early 1960s they opposed the opening of girls' schools, but were overruled by King Faisal.

In the eastern region there is a large Shiite minority who refused to be converted to Wahhabism and were oppressed in the period of Wahhabi expansion. They are now allowed to practise Islam as they interpret it. No non-Islamic religion may be practised in the country. The yearly pilgrimage to Mecca is a very important part of social life in Saudi Arabia. It asserts the central role played by the country in Islam both politically and religiously. Pilgrim facilities have been considerably improved in recent years and, although the number of pilgrims increases every year, health amenities have improved.

Attitude to women Life for women is still extremely restricted. Since the 1960s women have had a right to education and increasing numbers of girls go to primary school. But their numbers diminish in later stages of education and very few reach university. The religious authorities still insist that Saudi women should not appear in public unveiled; that they may not drive cars or work except in all-female institutions. Women are supposed to remain in the home. This traditional view is increasingly being challenged by women who have studied in foreign countries, where they have discovered unheard-of freedom, and by Western-educated men who would prefer marriages based on free choice and mutual compatibility. Furthermore, changes in living conditions, such as the increased provision of nuclear family apartments, and the corresponding decrease of extended-family houses make the traditional restricted life of women more oppressive. Women can find themselves in total isolation. Finally, the country's desperate need for skilled labour is such that the authorities may soon find it necessary to allow women to work freely.

Although the religious authorites still keep a very tight control on social developments in Saudi Arabia, they are slowly losing their influence as the country is modernised and as a Western-educated middle-class emerges, demanding greater freedom.

CONSTITUTION

Saudi Arabia has no written constitution. It has been said that the constitution of Saudi Arabia is the Koran, and its law, the *sharia*, is derived from the same source. The word of God in the Koran, together with the *hadith*, the well-attested reports of the Prophet Mohammed's personal statements on social and political rights and duties, contain all the guidance that is needed by the good ruler and good citizen. Similarly, the *sharia*, the comprehensive system of law built up by the great Muslim jurists on the basis of the Koran and the *hadith*, is the key to justice in both civil and criminal matters.

In a society of this type, the idea that all men are equal before God does impose a form of democracy, exemplified in the practice of many Arabian rulers of sitting in *majlis* at regular times, when they are personally accessible to people who have a grievance. The ruler may have great power, but he is not regarded as absolute, or as being protected by divine right, even though he is Imam as well as King, the leader of the people in prayer and in religious matters, as well as supreme in secular affairs. His position depends on consent. This was clearly seen at the time of the deposition of King Saud in 1963. The three bodies which withdrew their consent were the Council of Ministers, the *Ulema* (the twelve leading theologians and religious juris-consults), and the Family Council of the House of Al-Saud.

Council of Ministers Nonetheless much is done within the framework of a formal organisation. King Abdel-Aziz's informal authority was replaced in 1958 by a Council of Ministers, with a Royal Decree defining the position and duties of the Prime Minister (the President of the Council of Ministers) and the Ministers. This is set out in 58 detailed articles. The King may appoint himself Prime Minister, but there is a very clear distinction drawn between the two posts, and the Prime Minister has real power, distinct from that of the King. In 1963 another law set out the organisation of the provinces and local government. Governors of Provinces ceased to be Emirs representing the King but became administrative officials responsible to the Minister of the Interior. In October 1975 the size of the Council of Ministers was greatly increased, by the creation of nine new ministries. The Council included 12 men who had not previously held full ministerial responsibility, creating a wider spread of responsibility in response to the challenge, and the administrative demands of the Second Five-Year Plan.

HISTORY

The earliest relics of civilisation found in Saudi Arabia date back to 5000 B.C. and show that settlements along the country's Gulf coast had links with the Ubaid culture in Mesopotamia—one of the world's first agricultural societies. Indeed, some archaeologists believe that the Ubaid culture could have had its roots in the Arabian Peninsula itself.

Around the third millenium B.C. the civilization of Dilmun grew up on the islands of Bahrain which became an entrepôt for trade between the Indus Valley and Mesopotamia. Dilmun's influence spread up the Gulf coast as far as Kuwait and seems to have brought some prosperity to areas like the oasis of Al-Hasa.

The Southern Kingdoms The empires of Mesopotamia continued to be the major power in the region until the kingdoms of southern Arabia emerged as a counterforce. They stretched from North Yemen, through South Yemen to the western parts of Oman. One of the most ancient was the Minaean kingdom which had its centre at Ma'in in northern Yemen and appeared to have reached a peak of power around the fourth to second centuries B.C. It was replaced by the kingdom of Saba (Sheba) with its capital at Ma'rib in eastern Yemen. In the first centuries A.D. the Sabaeans took control of the Hadhramaut, another centre of power in South Yemen. The Christian tribe of Himyar then became a powerful force and later Christians from Ethiopia conquered much of Yemen.

From the middle of the first millenium B.C. the desert tracts of Saudi Arabia acted as a buffer zone between the cultures of the

405

o

Fertile Crescent in the north and the kingdoms of southern Arabia. The area was merely an arena for warring Bedouin tribes.

The Hadhramaut soon became a trading centre for Indian goods such as spices, silk, swords and pearls and was itself a big producer of frankincense and myrrh. Hadhramaut traders began to transport their goods overland to the Levant using camel caravans. Trading routes became established and cities like Mecca and Medina were built up at important crossroads. Eventually these cities became even bigger trading stations than the entrepôts in the south.

Mecca established Mecca emerged as the most important city. It was half-way between the south and the markets of the Levant. An annual trading fair was held at Ukaz a few miles outside the city which had pagan shrines and altars. This helped to make Mecca a place of pilgrimage as well as a mercantile centre. The Meccans also ran a protection scheme under which, in return for a fee, merchants would be guaranteed safe passage through tribal areas outside the city.

It was in this flourishing city that Mohammad, the founder of Islam, was born around 570. Contrary to Western myth Islam did not originate among the tribes of the desert but the urban people of Mecca and Medina.

Mohammad founds Islam Mohammad (full name: Abdel-Qasim Mohammad bin Abdullah bin Abdel-Muttalib bin Hashim) came from a respected, though not wealthy, family of the Quraysh tribe. He was orphaned at the age of six and brought up by his grandfather and later by an uncle. At the age of 25 he married a rich widow, Khadija, who was older than himself and bore him six children, only four of whom—all daughters— survived. For a while Mohammad led a quiet life as a tradesman and became relatively prosperous.

Around 610 at the age of 40, he was walking in the mountains near Mecca when he had an overwhelming spiritual experience. The archangel Gabriel appeared before him revealing the word of God. Mohammad related later that he first heard a loud, commanding voice and then a luminous figure grasped him by the throat and ordered him to repeat the sacred words. Afterwards Mohammad did nothing except debate within his own mind the genuineness of his experience. Three years later he finally decided he had a message to spread and started preaching, first secretively to members of his family.

When he began preaching in public, the Meccan establishment showed immediate hostility. They saw his beliefs as a threat to the mercantile system of the city. Persecution soon followed. People were forbidden to marry or trade with Mohammad's followers.

Flight to Medina Some of his group took refuge in nearby Medina, then called Yathrib, which, unlike Mecca, had a large agricultural community living off the cultivation of date palms. It was also the focal point of hostile tribes, three of them Jewish. Finally after an unsuccessful assassination plot against his life, Mohammad himself fled to Medina in 622 with the rest of his followers. This journey is called the *hijrah* (or emigration) and marks the starting point of the Arab calendar.

Mohammad helped to establish himself in Medina by acting as an arbitrator among the feuding tribes. Soon he had won over the majority of them (except the Jews) to his beliefs. A community of the faithful began to form with Mohammad as its head. Now he was not only a religious leader but also a ruler, politician and later a general.

But exile at Medina was considered to be a temporary phenomenon. Mecca was the major place of worship. For seven years the two cities warred with each other. Finally in 630 the Meccan people capitulated to the incessant pressure of Mohammad and his forces. The city was taken without a blow being struck and nearly all its people agreed to accept Islam. The Ka'ba (or Black Stone) was established as the geographical centre of Islam.

Mohammad dies Mohammad'a authority was now firmly established and he created the framework for a government based at Mecca, before dying on June 8, 632. Abu Bakr, the newly elected caliph (successor), announced his death by saying: "If you are worshippers of Mohammad, know that he is dead. If you are worshippers of God know that God is living and does not die".

Tribes, which had shown only nominal adherence to Islam,

took the opportunity of Mohammad's death to rebel. They refused to pay the *zakat* tax imposed by Mohammad's government in Mecca. Tribes in Yemen, Hadhramaut, Oman and Bahrain turned their backs on the faith. But after waging a series of secession wars, Abu Bakr and his successor Omar I managed to bring them back into the fold again. The Peninsula was divided into ten provinces, each headed by a governor responsible to the caliph. At the same time the tribes were encouraged to use their warlike spirit to the advantage of the new religion, and tribal groups started to make crusading incursions into the Levant. With the help of armies fired by religious fervour, Islam began to spread rapidly throughout the Middle East.

Tribal strife But as a result the centres of Islamic power soon moved from Mecca to Damascus and afterwards to Baghdad. After Ali, Mohammad's first cousin and son-in-law, was elected fourth caliph in 656 he established his capital at Kufa and a long period of rivalry between Syria and Iraq began.

The unity of the tribes of the Arabian Peninsula again disintegrated and religious sects started to take hold. The turbulent Kharijites took control of eastern Arabia and Oman before being crushed by armies sent from Damascus and Baghdad.

In Medina the Alids rose up against Abbasid power in Baghdad in the eighth and ninth centuries. At the end of the ninth and in the tenth centuries Ismailism and the Fatimids held sway in southern Arabia and the Karmatians set up their own state in eastern Arabia centred on Al-Hasa. In 930 the Karmatian ruler Sulayman occupied Mecca and took away the Ka'ba stone. It was not returned until 20 years later.

In the 11th and 12th centuries the Peninsula was riven by tribal rivalries. Some order was restored by the Seljuk Turks under Saladin who invaded Arabia in 1174. The establishment of the Rasulid dynasty in Mecca whose rule was recognised by most tribes brought comparative peace for two centuries.

In the early 16th century the Mamelukes of Egypt invaded Arabia. They were soon swept aside by the Ottomans who under Suleiman the Magnificent established their authority over the Hejaz and the Yemen. But at the beginning of the 17th century the Turks started to lose their hold on the area and it soon reverted to a traditional pattern of tribal hostility and strife.

Advent of Wahhabism The events which culminated in the formation of modern Saudi Arabia can be traced to the first half of the 18th century. At that time the Al-Saud family, part of the Masalikh branch of the great Anaiza tribe, were not particularly important in the affairs of Arabia. Mohammad bin Saud was Shaikh of Dariya, a town about 10 miles from modern Riyadh. His importance lies in the compact he made around 1740, with the great religious reformer, Mohammad bin Abdel-Wahhab. This alliance between the Al-Saud family and the movement founded by Mohammad bin Abdel-Wahhab has continued to this day, and was to determine not only the history of what is now Saudi Arabia, but to have an influence far beyond its boundaries.

Abdel-Wahhab was born in 1703 in neighbouring Uyaina. As a young man he became obsessed by the need for a return to the basic truths and original simplicity of Islam, based only on the Holy Koran, and on those Traditions of the Prophet, the *hadith*, unanimously accepted by the Imams as indisputably true. He first preached publicly against current elaborations of belief and ritual in Basra, and was driven from the city. There was opposition in Uyaina when he returned home, and he sought refuge in Dariya, winning the support of Mohammad bin Saud. Their compact was that the man of religion would not seek the protection of any other ruler, Mohammad bin Saud being prepared to support Mohammad bin Abdel-Wahhab's movement with the sword, if the need should arise for *jihad*, or holy war. Thus it was that 'Wahhabi' teaching (the wahhabis are properly called 'unitarians', *muwahhidun*) became inextricably intertwined with Arabia's political development.

For the first decades after 1740 the story was one of confused local struggle between the protagonists and the enemies of the new doctrine. It was not until 1773 that the Wahhabis finally took Riyadh, which was Dariya's most determined local opponent, as well as closest neighbour. Even so, word of what was happening did reach the outside world. About 1760 Carsten Niebuhr, the greatest of the 18th century European travellers in that part of the world, heard in Basra that 'some time since a new religion sprang up in the district of al-Ared (southern Nejd). It has already produced a revolution in the government of Arabia, and will probably hereafter influence the state of the country still further'. He explains that he had not met any disciples of the new faith, but, as far as he could judge, 'the new religion of Abdel-Wahhab' was a reformation of Islam, 'reducing it back to its original simplicity'.

Wahhabi expansion Niebuhr was an accurate and prescient observer. In the time of Abdel-Aziz, Mohammad's son, and after Riyadh had been secured, expansion from central Arabia began, most notably in the direction of the Hejaz in the west to Al-Hasa on the Gulf coast, and southwards in the direction of Najran. In 1791 there was the first conflict with the forces of the Sharif of Mecca, and in 1792 Qatif on the Gulf coast was taken and its idols destroyed. Both were victories won by Saud bin Abdel-Aziz, who was his father's commander in chief, and who showed himself to be a man of immense energy and unquestionable military genius. In the year of the capture of Qatif, Mohammad bin Abdel-Wahhab, the man who had supplied the religious fervour which was inspiring the Wahhabi expansion, died at the age of 89.

Near the end of the century the Ottoman authorities in Southern Iraq decided to take the initiative against the growing Wahhabi menace. In reply, raiding parties were sent towards the Shia cities close to the Euphrates. Kerbala was sacked and many of its people massacred. The tomb of Hussain was desecrated and its treasure seized. At much the same time Wahhabi forces were operating far to the south, in the direction of Oman. In 1803 Saud took Mecca without opposition and held it long enough to destroy much that was offensive in Wahhabi eyes. A few months later Abdel-Aziz bin Mohammad was assassinated in the mosque at Dariya by a member of the Shia sect seeking revenge for the outrage at Kerbala. Saud succeeded his father and, with the help of his son Abdulla, continued his victorious career. Bahrain was taken, and the whole of the coast to Ras al-Khaimah came under Wahhabi influence. In 1806 Saud was in Mecca once again, and Medina also. Wahhabi practices were rigorously enforced in the places most closely associated with the life of the Prophet Mohammad. In a way the most striking exploit of all was the appearance in 1808 of a Wahhabi force outside Damascus. It did not have the strength to storm the city, but it pillaged the Ghuta, the famous, idyllic, orchards and gardens lying between Damascus and the desert.

Egyptian-Turkish invasion Between 1806 and 1811 Wahhabi power and influence rose to a new peak. The Ottoman Sultan, already worried by this manifestation in Arabia, was positively alarmed by the loss of the Holy Cities and the threat to Damascus. Mohammad Ali Pasha, the near-independent Governor of Egypt, was asked to take steps to crush the Wahhabi movement, and his first troops landed in the Hejaz in October 1811. He recovered Mecca and Medina, but on the whole the Turkish-Egyptian onslaught was well contained until Saud died in 1814. Abdulla bin Saud was unable to cope with the situation. By 1816 Mohammad Ali's son, Ibrahim Pasha, was ready for a march across Arabia to destroy the Wahhabi capital, and in April 1818 he laid siege to Dariya. He entered in triumph in September and razed the city. Abdulla was taken to Istanbul and publicly executed. Other members of his family scattered into obscurity. It seemed that the religious power of Wahhabism and the political power of the Al-Sauds had been broken forever.

A revival began, however, as early as 1822, made possible by the logistical problems of the Turkish-Egyptian army. Turki bin Abdulla, a cousin of the great Saud and an uncle of Abdulla, managed to establish himself with Riyadh as his capital, instead of the ruined Dariya. Over the years he won back Al-Hasa and a large part of the northern Nejd. With Ottoman approval he was assassinated by a distant relative in 1834. His son Faisal foiled the assassin's effort to seize power, and led the resistance to a new Turkish-Egyptian attack. He was captured and sent to Cairo. However, he escaped to Damascus. His supporters called him back to the Nejd in 1843, when the Turkish-Egyptian forces were again thin on the ground. The next 25 years were spent in reconquering and consolidating the lands which his father Turki had once controlled (northern Nejd and Al-Hasa).

Al-Sauds in exile Disaster followed Faisal's death in 1869 because of the reckless rivalry of his two eldest sons, Abdulla and Saud, and the rising fortunes of the Al-Rashid family of Hail, in the Jebel Shammar area of northern Nejd. Eventually in 1884 Mohammad bin Rashid of Hail also became master of Riyadh. The Al-Sauds had already lost Al-Hasa to the Turks. In 1891 the remnants of the family fled into exile in Kuwait, led by Abdel-Rahman, the last surviving son of Faisal, accompanied by his 11-year-old son, Abdel-Aziz.

The flight to Kuwait was, perhaps, a greater disaster even than the destruction of Dariya, in the sense that the rule of central Arabia had been wrested from the Al-Sauds by indigenous rivals, fighting and intriguing on the same terms and in the same style. There were no invaders from Cairo, whose powerful armament might explain defeat and against whom local resentment could easily be aroused. But in 1898 the ablest of the Rashidi rulers of Hail died, and within a year or two hostilities broke out between Kuwait and Hail, the Rashidi ruler acting as the instrument of the Turks, who had been offended by the policy of Shaikh Mubarak of Kuwait. In 1901 the main fighting went against the Kuwaitis, and the young Abdel-Aziz bin Abdel-Rahman al-Saud, who commanded a diversionary attack in the direction of Riyadh, had to withdraw.

Riyadh retaken   Late in the year Abdel-Aziz set out again with a raiding party, and in January 1902 was close to Riyadh with some 60 men. He took 30 picked men and made for the city, ordering the remainder to return to Kuwait. Of the 30, 20 were left in the palm groves outside Riyadh, as a reserve and a line of communication. The rest entered the city under cover of darkness and seized a house opposite the main gate of the Mismak fort where, it was known, the Rashidi governor always spent the night for safety's sake. At dawn the governor emerged to go to his private house. The Saudi party rushed him from their hiding place, cut him down and entered the fort before the gate could be swung to. An Al-Saud was once more master of Riyadh, and a new chapter had been opened in the story of Arabia. The young Abdel-Aziz was recognised as Emir by his father, the senior member of the family, who returned to Riyadh to live there with his son until his death in 1928.

Abdel-Aziz established his authority fairly quickly in the areas of central Arabia which had been held by his grandfather Faisal. But the Ottoman Sultan did not welcome the prospect of a Wahhabi revival and a repetition of the events of a century earlier. Prodded politically by the Ottoman authorities in Iraq and stiffened by Turkish troops, the Rashidis of Hail mounted a counter-offensive with several years of swaying fortune. Abdel-

Aziz had also to deal with sedition inside his own family, from a group known as the Araif. Nevertheless, in 1913, taking advantage of Turkish preoccupations in Libya, he was able to drive out the Ottoman troops from Al-Hasa and restore that important province to the Saudi domain.

Bedouin settlements He also embarked on his controversial policy of settling volunteers from the bedouin tribes as *ikhwan*—brothers—on agricultural colonies. The aim was partly social and economic, to provide a more stable and productive way of life than nomadic pastoralism and promote a transfer of loyalty from the tribe to the new state which he wanted to create. There was also a military purpose, to have the *ikhwan* settlements as sources of brave and fanatical manpower, warriors steeped in and ready to die for Wahhabi doctrine. The first of these colonies was at Artawiya, in the northern Nejd, and eventually there were scores of them. They fostered a religious and xenophobic fanaticism which Abdel-Aziz was at a later stage hard put to control.

When the First World War broke out Abdel-Aziz was clearly one of the two outstanding personalities of the Arabian Peninsula, his only rival being Sharif Hussain in Mecca. Britain's Middle Eastern experts, the Arab Bureau in Cairo, backed the latter as leader of an Arab revolt against the Ottoman Empire. Hussain was recognised as King of the Hejaz and referred to himself as 'King of the Arab Countries'. Sooner or later there was bound to be conflict between the two men, but for the time being Abdel-Aziz was persuaded to ignore Hussain's provocations, notably attacks on the oasis of Khurba, between the Hejaz and the Nejd.

Hail captured After the Allied victory in 1918, when the Middle East map was being redrawn, Abdel-Aziz's first concern was to secure control of Hail, especially after Hussain's son, Faisal, became King of Iraq. There was reason to suspect that Faisal was encouraging a sort of pincers movement against Wahhabi power by using his father in the Hejaz and the Al-Rashid ruler of Hail. Having been acclaimed in Riyadh as Sultan of Nejd and its Dependencies, Abdel-Aziz took Hail in November 1921 after a two-month siege, dealing magnanimously with the family which had opposed him for so many decades. This so greatly improved his strategic position that the next summer he was able to take the Jauf oasis, north of Hail, and the Great Nafud Desert. Shortly afterwards an incident occurred which showed that the cultivation of Wahhabi fanaticism in the *ikhwan* colonies was a two-edged weapon. A powerful Bedouin raiding party went close to Amman without Abdel-Aziz's authority and massacred all the inhabitants of a small village. The raiders were then attacked by R.A.F. aircraft and armoured cars, and were either slaughtered by machine-gun fire or driven into the waterless desert to die. It was a fearful display of the ancient and modern horrors of warfare.

Abdel-Aziz in Mecca Conflict between Sultan Abdel-Aziz of the Nejd and King Hussain of the Hejaz was precipitated by Turkey's abolition of the Caliphate in March 1924. Within days the ambitious Hussain, who was, indeed, of the Prophet's family, declared himself 'Prince of the Faithful and Descendant of the Prophet'. This presumption was galling for Abdel-Aziz personally, and infuriated Wahhabi opinion. A military offensive was launched during the summer, and Hussain abdicated in favour of his eldest son, Ali, in October. The Wahhabi forces entered Mecca when Ali retired to Jeddah, which was under desultory siege until the end of 1925. On 8 January 1926 Abdel-Aziz was proclaimed King of the Hejaz, as well as Sultan of Nejd, in the Great Mosque of Mecca.

Before this proclamation, Abdel-Aziz had already announced his intention to call a general conference representative of all Muslims to discuss the future administration of the sacred territory and the pilgrimage. All his statements and actions were designed to dispel any idea that he intended the Holy Cities to become Wahhabi preserves, and to show that he regarded himself as trustee for the whole of Islam. This tolerant attitude triggered off an extremist Wahhabi backlash, based on the *ikhwan* colonies, which became one of the severest crises of his career.

British recognition The Treaty of Jeddah with Britain in 1927 was for King Abdel-Aziz an important recognition of his achievements. Britain was the dominant 'great power' in the

Middle East. Therefore Britain's acknowledgement of the 'complete and absolute independence of the dominions' of the Saudi king gave a compelling lead to the rest of the world. The Treaty replaced an old agreement of 1915 which, on paper, could have limited Abdel-Aziz's freedom of action, though it never did in practice. Other clauses committed him to respecting Britain's treaties with the shaikhs and rulers of the Gulf, and to co-operate in the suppression of the slave trade.

A brief war with Yemen in 1934 resulted from Yemeni ambitions in the province of Asir and the oasis of Najran. After some years of fruitless negotiation, Abdel-Aziz decided to force the issue. A rapid advance put the Amir (later King) Faisal in possession of the port of Hodeida, and Yemen at the mercy of the Saudis. But no territory was seized, and today's frontier was drawn. There were still undefined frontiers elsewhere, but the new state was taking firm shape. Already in 1932 the Kingdom of Saudi Arabia had been proclaimed, uniting the Hejaz, the Nejd and Al-Hasa. Order was being introduced into the Arabian Peninsula. The country was being given a structure and an administration, becoming less of a kaleidoscope of shifting, warring tribes and rival princelings.

Oil struck The picturesque, heroic period of Saudi history, recorded in the warrior ballads and epics, began to fade in the early thirties. The first oil exploration concession was granted in 1933 to Standard Oil of California. Texas Oil joined with Standard of California on a 50/50 basis in 1936, and oil was struck in large quantities in 1938. The outbreak of the Second World War stopped oil development in Saudi Arabia, as elsewhere in the Middle East. When the ban was lifted in 1944 the two concessionaires formed the Arabian American Oil Company (Aramco). In 1947 two more partners were admitted, so that the final set-up was Standard of California, Texas Oil (Texaco) and Standard of New Jersey (Exxon) 30 per cent each, and Socony-Vacuum (Mobil), 10 per cent.

Oil was first struck on Jebal Dhahran, then more was found at Abqaiq, 37 miles to the south west. Abqaiq eventually proved to be near the northern end of a separate and still greater field, Ghawar. The first small refinery was built on Ras Tanura in the early post-war years, and work started on the 1000-mile trans-

Arabian pipeline (Tapline) to Sidon on the Mediterranean coast, which brought Saudi Arabian oil 3,500 miles nearer to the markets of western Europe. It was completed in less than four years. Welding of the pipes started on 16 January 1948. The first tanker was loaded at Sidon on 2 December 1950.

After Aramco there were two more operating concessions, both in the Partitioned Zone. The first went to Pacific Western Oil (later the Getty Oil Company) in 1949. Oil was struck in commercial quantities in 1957. In the same year the Japanese were successful in obtaining an offshore concession, also in the Partitioned Zone.

Abdel-Aziz dies   The last 20 years of King Abdel-Aziz's life were a period of steady consolidation and, from 1946, of rapidly growing oil wealth. It was also a period in which Saudi Arabia and its ruler began to figure in the outside world. The King's meeting with President Roosevelt on board a US warship moored in the Suez Canal in February 1945, after Roosevelt had attended the Yalta Conference with Churchill and Stalin, attracted much attention. The principal subject was growing Zionist pressure in Palestine. Abdel-Aziz's personality and arguments evidently made a strong impact on Roosevelt, a sophisticated politician not easily impressed. After the meeting Roosevelt said he wanted to re-examine America's policy on Palestine. He was now convinced, he added, that if nature took its course there would be bloodshed between Arabs and Jews. Some formula would have to be found to prevent this warfare.

Saudi Arabia was a founder-member of the United Nations and of the Arab League. When Abdel-Aziz died in 1953 the world was aware that a career of great achievement and colour, and of historic importance, had been brought to a close.

The reign of his eldest son, Saud, who was deposed after 11 years, saw at least two useful innovations, the establishment of a regular ministerial system, instead of Abdel-Aziz's informal groups of advisers and counsellors, and the setting up of a National Planning Council. How far the credit for these initiatives should go to him and how far to his brother Faisal is uncertain. He was not lacking in intelligence or ability. His fault may have been that he was too easy-going to relish the rigours of kingship.

417

Our background puts us in the foreground of Middle East Insurance.

At Lowndes Lambert Group we have been active throughout the Middle East for many years, matching our service to the speed and scale of development in that area and to the increasing demands it is making on the insurance market.

Our insurance broking expertise is allied to a detailed knowledge of local conditions and requirements. That's why we have been appointed to handle many of the Middle East's biggest and most difficult insurance problems – a recent example being the construction risks insurance for the billion-dollar industrial harbour at Jubail, Saudi Arabia.

Whatever the insurance cover required, Lowndes Lambert Group have the resources and experience to handle it economically and efficiently.

Lowndes Lambert Group

International Insurance and Reinsurance Brokers
53 Eastcheap, London EC3P 3HL Telephone 01-283 2000 Telex 887370/886994
And at Lloyd's and worldwide

Faisal in power Towards the end of Saud's reign, the financial affairs of the Kingdom fell into confusion. Faisal, who succeeded him in 1964, first set about restoring financial order. A devoutly religious man, with an instinct for statecraft and an immense capacity for work, Faisal inspired admiring respect. At the time of his assassination in March 1975, he was, partly because of his personal qualities and partly because of his country's wealth, the outstanding figure in the Arab and Islamic world. He was a reformer absolutely convinced of the compatibility of the Holy Koran and the *sharia* law on the one hand and modern material progress and scientific knowledge on the other. It is possible that the most important of all his decisions was the support he gave, when Prime Minister in 1960, to the first girls' school opened by the State in Riyadh. In the face of ultra-conservative opposition, he said no girl would be compelled to attend but the school would remain open to cater for those who came. This was the start of one of the most radical of all changes in Saudi Arabian life.

Islamic leader Under King Faisal's guidance Saudi Arabia kept pace administratively with the rapid increase in wealth, which was no mean achievement. In external affairs his primary concern in the earlier years of his reign was the civil war in Yemen and the involvement on the republican side of Nasser's Egypt. Saudi Arabia's line was that the Yemenis should settle their own affairs, without interference from outside the Peninsula. Republicanism triumphed in Yemen, but so also did King Faisal's policy. It was at the Khartoum Summit of Arab leaders, after the Israeli war with Egypt and Jordan in 1967, and the Rabat conference of Islamic leaders, after the fire at the al-Aqsa Mosque in Jerusalem in 1969, that King Faisal achieved his full stature as an Arab and Islamic leader. The al-Aqsa outrage caused him deep concern, so that his feelings on the subject of Palestine and Zionism became even more strongly held. Hence his warnings to the United States (a country with which Saudi Arabia had normally been on good terms) about the dangers of her bias towards Zionism. As a result Saudi Arabia supported the use of the oil weapon in the October war of 1973.

Like his father, King Faisal took his responsibility as custodian of the holy cities of Islam seriously. He travelled widely in the

Muslim world and did an enormous amount to improve the facilities for the pilgrims visiting Mecca every year. Indeed, this aspect of his duties may have been for him the most important of all.

When he died in March 1975, his brother, Prince Khaled, who had been appointed Crown Prince at the time of King Saud's deposition, succeeded him as King, and also took over the posts of Prime Minister and Foreign Minister, which Faisal had always kept in his own hands. Price Fahd was appointed Crown Price and Deputy Prime Minister, and continued in the post of Minister of the Interior, which he already held.

Recent Events

Over the last few years Saudi Arabia has begun to assume a role of immense power in the world. Not only has it used its massive oil wealth to advance the Arab cause and to bolster its own position in the Middle East, but also in support of world-wide moderation. Saudi Arabia's assumption of a world role became apparent in 1975 when it played a crucial part in reviving the 'dialogue' between the Third World and industrial countries on energy and commodities, with the objective of achieving a new international economic order. Saudi Arabia took advantage of its position as the biggest oil exporter within OPEC to urge restraint, overcoming pressure for a rise in oil prices in June 1976.

In December 1976 it refused to bow to the majority view within OPEC which wanted a 10 per cent price increase and together with the United Arab Emirates insisted on raising its prices by only five per cent. Crown Prince Fahd said later that the Saudi Government had wanted to prevent the world's economy from falling into further recession and to protect the economies of the developing countries. He also hoped that Saudi Arabia's stance for moderation would help bring about a just settlement of the Arab–Israeli issue. In fact the Saudis could now exert quiet pressure on the US, the main importer of Saudi oil.

Dominant force In the Middle East, Saudi Arabia has now become a dominant force. Its financial assistance helped to rescue Egypt from economic disaster and to provide much-needed finance for the other front-line Arab states. But also Saudi diplomacy was instrumental in creating more stability in the Arab world. In June 1976 Egypt and Syria reconciled their long-standing differences at a meeting in Riyadh and later in the year Saudi Arabia helped to bring an end to the civil war in Lebanon.

In the Arabian Peninsula and the Gulf, the Saudis have been an all-powerful but stabilising influence. In early 1976 they ended their nine-year hostility to the Marxist regime in Aden by agreeing to set up diplomatic relations with South Yemen. In return the hard-up South Yemenis were reported to have received a promise of $100 million in aid. In March of the same year, King Khaled made a tour of Arab states in the Gulf to emphasise the closer ties that had been forged with the country's neighbours. He also paid a four-day visit to Iran.

ECONOMY

Over the last two decades Saudi Arabia has emerged from comparative poverty to become one of the world's richest nations. It has accumulated vast financial assets with its official reserves second only to those of West Germany's. The country is earning more money than it can spend. This transformation is all due to the existence of giant reservoirs of oil in the country's Eastern Province which make up a quarter of non-Communist oil reserves.

Saudi Arabia's economic development went into top gear after 1973 when within a short period OPEC's oil prices quadrupled. By 1976 the country's Gross Domestic Product had risen ninefold in six years to SR156,000 million ($45,000 million) and in the same period revenue increased twelvefold. Between 1973 and 1976 imports went up almost five times to an estimated SR44,000 million ($12,500 million). The nation's new wealth was being poured into schemes for new ports, roads, power stations and other basic utilities which would enable the Saudis to build up a diversified economy freed from total dependence on oil.

Problems of expansion But rapid economic expansion has brought its own problems. New ports could not be built quickly enough to take in all the goods that Saudi money could buy. The existing ports became severely congested with ships waiting months to unload goods. At the same time inadequate roads made the distribution of goods from the ports painfully slow. An influx of foreign workers and businessmen put urban amenities in cities like Jeddah under tremendous strain. Water and electricity utilities were stretched to the limit. Hotels could hardly cope with the demand for beds. A serious housing shortage sent rents soaring. Some progress has been made in dealing with these difficulties. In particular waiting times at ports have been reduced to a minimum and power and water cuts are now much less frequent.

Inflation has instead become one of the Saudi Government's main preoccupations. Over the last two years consumer prices have risen by around 50 per cent annually, and, if rents are taken into account, the increase may have been as much as 70 per cent. The Government became alarmed about this trend which if allowed to continue would have made nonsense of its economic planning. A top level West German team was called in to advise on measures for tackling inflation, and soon the Government decided to slow down its own expenditure and to curb the cost of development projects. The first victims of the new anti-inflation policy were several large Western companies whose bids for big power and telecommunications contracts were angrily rejected by the Government in early 1977 because they were considered to be exorbitantly overpriced. At the same time food subsidies have been increased and rent controls imposed.

Besides the concern about the economic problems of fast development, there lies in the minds of many Saudis the much deeper worry about its effects on the country's culture and traditions. The nation's main objective remains the preservation of the religious and moral values of Islam. But some Saudis are already debating how this will be possible if the country is to maintain its remarkable economic growth. Out of an indigenous population of around four million there is a potential maximum workforce of 1.5 million which is barely enough to run defence and security, government administration and the private sector. If the country is to industrialise on a large scale, it will need as much as 800,000 foreign workers by the early 1980s. This massive inflow could undermine the strict moral code ruling Saudi society. This is a prospect which has put Saudi leaders in a dilemma as yet unresolved.

Oil

Oil was first struck in Saudi Arabia at Jebal Dhahran in 1938 by a consortium consisting of Standard Oil of California (Casoc) and Texas Oil (Texaco). But the Second World War delayed commercial production and the country did not export oil until 1950. By then two other companies, Standard of New Jersey (Exxon) and Socony-Vacuum (Mobil) had joined Casoc and Texaco to form the Arabian American Oil Company (Aramco). In 1957 Getty Oil found oil in the Partitioned Zone shared with Kuwait and Arabian Oil of Japan struck oil in the same area in 1961. But the great majority of Saudi Arabia's oil was and still is produced by Aramco.

Output by Aramco increased by an average of one million barrels a day (b/d) in 1958 to two million b/d by 1965 and 3.5 million b/d by 1970. After the OPEC price increases of 1973, production soared to 8.2 million b/d in the following year but world recession pushed output down to 6.8 million b/d in 1975. It went up again to 8.2 million b/d in 1976 and after the OPEC conference at Doha in December of that year, at which Saudi Arabia and the United Arab Emirates stuck out for an oil price rise of five per cent, a new ceiling of 11.8 million b/d was set for mid-1977.

The Saudi Government claims that after an expansion of production facilities, Aramco will soon have the capacity to push production up to 16 million b/d if necessary. But it is unlikely that such a high level could be maintained for long. The average would probably be around 13 million b/d. But oil experts believe that at this peak Aramco will have difficulty in keeping the quality of its present mixture of crudes. The Government could be using the knowledge of this high capacity as a weapon in its bid to keep down oil prices.

Giant oilfields The bulk of Aramco's production comes from four fields. The largest amount—around five million b/d—is contributed by Ghawar, south of Abqaiq, which measures 124 miles from north to south and is between 19 and 31 miles wide.

Saffaniyah, the largest offshore oil field in the world, produces one million b/d, Abqaiq over 750,000 b/d and Berri, another offshore field which has some of Saudi Arabia's highest quality oil, over 500,000 b/d. Less than half of the country's oil fields, now totalling nearly 40, are actually producing oil. Virtually all are in the Eastern Province or its offshore waters. The big exception is Shaybah which is in the Rub al-Khali or Empty Quarter.

At the end of 1976 Saudi Arabia's proven reserves stood at 110,200 million barrels and probable reserves at 177,500 million. The proven total includes Saudi Arabia's half share of the 6,300 million barrels of the Partitioned Zone. The Government believes that Aramco's figures are too cautious. Its own estimate of proven reserves was 151,400 million in December 1976. At present the lower figure is equivalent to 25 per cent of the world's proved oil reserves.

Aramco's discoveries of new reserves seems to be endless. Every year it has been able to find new oil reservoirs which are greater in volume than that year's actual production. In 1976 alone Aramco found three fields, though none of them were particularly large. It now seems unlikely that other vast fields of the size of Ghawar or Saffaniyah will be discovered.

Most of Saudi Arabia's gas resources is associated with oil and at present the bulk of it is flared. But there is a mammoth scheme to gather all this wasted gas and feed it to electric power stations, export terminals and heavy industrial plants. Altogether 5,000 million cubic feet of gas a day would be harnessed in an operation which would be the world's biggest ever industrial project (see **Industry**).

At present Aramco makes use of about 20 per cent of its gas output or around 1,000 million cubic feet. About two thirds of it is used by Aramco itself as fuel or is reinjected. The rest is exported as propane, butane or natural gasoline from a gas processing plant at Ras Tanura or fed to industrial schemes like the Hofuf cement plant and a fertiliser unit.

Aramco takeover Since 1973 the Saudi Government has embarked on a gradual takeover of Aramco. Initially it acquired a 25 per cent stake in the producer assets of the company. In 1974 that share was raised to 60 per cent, though it did not include the refinery at Ras Tanura. The Government then pressed for 100 per cent ownership, which plunged both sides into protracted secretive negotiations. By the end of 1976 it was assumed that the takeover was virtually complete with the only major point of dispute being the amount of compensation to be paid to the four US partners in the company. But Saudi ownership of the firm is unlikely to affect its personnel for a while, with day-to-day management remaining mostly in the hands of 4,500 expatriates over 1,500 of them Americans.

Saudi Arabia also has other mineral resources besides oil. Oil & Mineral Wealth Minister Shaikh Zaki Yamani has predicted that in 20 years the country will be exporting copper, gold, phosphates and perhaps even uranium. Several large exploration concessions have been granted to international mining companies. However, relatively few large mineral deposits have yet been found.

Nickel and copper-zinc deposits lie in the Asir mountains, south of Jeddah. Copper–zinc, gold and silver has been found north of the city. Between 1939 and 1954 a mine at Mahd al-Dhahab, northeast of Jeddah, produced 766,000 ounces of gold and just over one million ounces of silver before being closed down.

A Swedish company is exploring extensive phosphate deposits in the northwest of the country near the Jordanian border. The British Steel Corporation is evaluating the potential of iron ore deposits in the same area of the country which might be used as supplies for the country's future iron and steel industry. When exploitation of mineral deposits takes place, Petromin, the state oil and minerals company, has an option to take a 50 per cent interest in any mining operation.

Five-Year Plan

Saudi Arabia's Second Five Year Plan (1975–80) provides the basis for the country's transformation into a modern industrial state. It in fact looks beyond 1980 and provides a comprehensive picture of the Saudi Arabian economy and of Saudi economic thinking. It is a massive document of over 700 pages, in which the individual plans of ministries and other government agencies are fitted together into a coherent whole.

Altogether SR 498,000 million (about $142,000 million) has been set aside for the Plan, about six times more than was spent on the First Plan (1970–75).

For the planners finance is no problem. As the Plan says: 'The Kingdom's financial resources are more than ample for all programmes deemed feasible and economically rational. The problem is one of physically obtaining, moving and managing the raw materials, goods and human resources needed. . . .' They show anxiety on two major points—the adequacy of the labour force and the capacity of the construction industry. The enormous education programme will increase the efficiency of the work force at all levels, but at the same time it is planned to recruit growing numbers of non-Saudis. The Saudi workforce is expected to increase from 1,286,000 to 1,518,000 over the five years, while non-Saudis will more than double, from 314,000 to 812,000. The construction industry is the key to the Plan's success in all other fields. Long sections of the Plan document show that much thought has been devoted to ways and means of maximising the growth and efficiency of this particular industry. It estimates that construction would account for half proposed public expenditure and about 80 per cent of fixed capital investment.

Plan's goals The fundamental values and principles by which the planners have been guided are: 1) to maintain the religious and moral values of Islam; 2) to assure the defence and internal security of the Kingdom; 3) to maintain a high rate of economic growth by developing economic resources, maximising earnings from oil over the long term and conserving depletable resources; 4) to reduce economic dependence on the export of crude oil; 5) to develop human resources by education, training and raising standards of health; 6) to increase the well-being of all groups within the society and foster social stability under circumstances of rapid social change; 7) and to develop the physical infrastructure so that these goals can be achieved. It is the intention to achieve all this within a free economy, with the public sector playing a fundamental role. Shaikh Hisham Nazer, Minister of Planning, has called the Plan 'an experiment in social transformation'.

The Plan was issued in July 1975, since when the Government

has had to think again about some of its proposed projects. Within a short time, it became clear that several schemes could not be achieved by 1980. But Ministers insist that the Plan has not been revised nor its priorities changed. Merely it has been a matter of rescheduling projects so that time limits will be extended into the period of a probable Third Plan. No schemes would be axed though some might have to be trimmed in size.

The Government claims that when the Plan was drawn up, the probability that projects would have to be put back was kept in mind. Postponements would be inevitable since the workforce is being increased by 53 per cent and construction activity is growing by an annual rate of 60 per cent. At the same time physical constraints like bottlenecks in the country's infrastructure are unpredictable.

But some important factors were not fully taken into account by the Plan. It grossly underestimated spiralling costs within the Kingdom and as a result the price of projects has turned out to be far higher than expected. Also the Plan was unable to foresee that the Government would be forced to slow down its own expenditure in order to help curb inflation. Though Government spending accounts for the greater part of economic activity in the country, the private sector has also been growing faster than the Plan predicted.

The major victim of the rescheduling process has been the giant gas gathering project being carried out by Aramco. The scale of the scheme has been reduced and its completion is being pushed back well into the 1980s. This postponement means that gas-dependent projects like export refineries and petrochemical plants will be delayed.

The 1976/77 budget reflected the Government's desire to curb its spending. A total of SR 110,000 million ($31,400 million) was budgeted for expenditure which is the same amount for the previous financial year ending in June, 1976. But in fact during that year the Kingdom spent only SR 77,500 million ($21,800 million). Senior officials claim that 1976/77 figures for actual expenditure show a slowing down in the rate of increase in spending since 1973. Between 1973 and 1976 Government expenditure almost quadrupled. Government revenue, 90 per cent of which comes from oil, levelled out after the 1973/74 oil price rises at around SR 100,000 million ($28,600 million). But the five per cent price increase announced in December 1976 and a similar rise in mid-1977 will push revenue up again.

Infrastructure

The development of infrastructure has rather surprisingly been placed last in the order of goals of the Five-Year Plan. But it is doubtful whether the Government wanted to give such a vital part of the economy a subordinate role. The establishment of good communication and basic utilities must inevitably still remain a priority for a country whose economy continues to be relatively underdeveloped.

Ports cleared   Soon however Saudi Arabia should rid itself of the major problems of congested ports which has slowed economic growth. In 1976 up to 200 ships lay at anchor outside Jeddah, facing a four to six months' wait to unload their cargoes. At Dammam, the country's other main port, ships were waiting around three months for a berth. Within a period of six months big efforts were made to clear the congestions. Two British firms were called in to improve the management of both ports. Expatriate workers were recruited to work day-and-night shifts to move goods. Ex-military landing craft were used to unload ships at sea and helicopters introduced to lift cargoes of cement. Old vessels with out-of-date unloading gear were banned and much more use made of roll-on roll-off (ro-ro) ships. These measures quickly achieved success and by early 1977 waiting times at both ports had been reduced to a minimum.

At the same time the Government has embarked on massive plans for the expansion of existing ports and the building of new ones. Dammam's capacity is being increased from 22 to 38 berths by 1980, and its storage and handling facilities are being considerably extended. Twenty additional berths are being built at Jeddah and its throughput capacity is being raised to six million tons a year by 1978. A 16-berth commercial port is being constructed at Jubail with an adjacent deep-water industrial port. Yanbu on the Red Sea coast is being developed into a medium-sized commercial harbour which will have one of the biggest cement terminals in the world, capable of handling 700,000 tons a year.

Saudi Arabia's road network is unable to cope at present with the country's fast growing traffic. The roads on the east coast for example were built only as service roads for Aramco vehicles. The Five-Year Plan aims to ease the flow of cars and lorries in the cities and to make travelling between cities quicker. Altogether 8,000 miles of new road are scheduled to be built under the Plan, at an average of 1,250 to 1,900 miles a year. But this programme got off to a bad start in 1975 when less than 1,200 miles were constructed. However since then construction has been speeded up and by 1980 a large part of the proposed extended network should be built. A shorter route from Jeddah to Riyadh should be opened by then and a number of more direct links between the northwest and southeast should be completed.

Electricity generator   Installation of new electricity generation capacity has so far just managed to keep pace with soaring demand. This is quite an achievement because, unlike most other Gulf countries, private enterprise has been responsible for providing the bulk of the country's needs. Six major electricity companies are licensed to supply power to the main urban centres of Jeddah, Riyadh, Dammam–Dhahran–al-Khobar, Mecca–Taif and Al-Hasa. But they have been helped considerably by interest-free loans from the Government's Saudi Industrial Development Fund and Government subsidies on electricity prices which guarantees the firms a profit of between seven and 10 per cent.

In Jeddah additional units with a capacity of about 260 MW have been added in the past two years. The city has also been able to take electricity from a desalination plant which should be supplying 130 MW by the end of 1977. In Riyadh three emergency gas turbines with a total capacity of 76.5 MW have been brought into service while a large 300 MW station is being built, with a second of similar capacity also due for construction. The power company responsible for Dhahran and neighbouring towns, which has just installed two units with a total 100 MW capacity, has another unit of 150 MW scheduled to come into operation in 1978. Generation capacity is also being expanded at Mecca–Taif, Medina and Al-Hasa.

Over the period of the current Five-Year Plan the Government will play a much more direct role in the provision of electricity by helping to distribute it throughout rural areas and to establish a national grid system. The Government claims a national grid will save labour and would be about 30 per cent cheaper in terms of capital investment. Total investment for the whole system has been estimated at SR 7,800 million ($2,200 million). The reconstituted Ministry of Industry & Electricity has been given the task of developing the system with the recently created General Electricity Organisation put in immediate charge. The long-term plan is to interconnect within a national grid the regional networks consisting of central power stations using long-distance high-tension cables to distribute supplies. The short-term aim is to integrate towns and satellite villages into single networks.

Water desalination and natural gas are increasingly being used as a source of electrical power. Work has recently started on a second extension to the Jeddah desalination plant due to be completed in 1975/80. Other plants are being built at Al-Khobar, al-Wajh, Duba, Amlaj and Khafji, while several more are planned. Aramco is setting up an integrated supply system in the Eastern Province which will be fuelled by natural gas.

Water resources Saudi Arabia's low rainfall, which averages less than four inches in most areas except the southwest, has made the country dependent on underground aquifers and desalination plants for its water supplies. The country has a massive desalination programme which over the five years to 1980 is expected to cost SR 63,000 million ($18,000 million). By then desalination plants will be producing 212 million gallons daily and by the mid-1980s this capacity is expected to have risen to 418 million gallons daily, making Saudi Arabia the largest producer of desalinated water in the world. By late 1977 Jeddah's desalination plant should be the biggest in the country with a daily output of 10 million gallons. But the majority of the city's water will still come from wells in nearby Wadi Fatima and Wadi Khulays.

Riyadh is totally dependent on underground aquifers, some of them 60 miles from the city. Some of the world's deepest water wells have been bored to reach the vast aquifers which exist in the region. Hydrologists believe that there are enough aquifers within reach of the city to keep it supplied for the foreseeable future. But the salt-concentration in the water may soon become so high that it will need to be desalinated.

Decent homes   One of the objectives outlined in the Five-Year Plan is "to enable every household in the Kingdom to have a decent, safe and sanitary dwelling of a standard consistent with its level of income." But the Plan recognises that this aim might not be achieved until well into the 1980s. Nonetheless it has set a five-year target of 219,000 new housing units, excluding temporary accommodation for expatriate contract labour. About a quarter of these will be built by the Government and over a fifth by householders themselves under a self-help construction scheme. The remainder will come from the private sector.

The Government will concentrate on housing for low income groups who have been hit the hardest by the severe accommodation shortage in the country's cities. Families living off comparatively low salaries have been forced to live in make-shift dwellings in shanty towns. Around 42,000 units for poorer households are being built at Jeddah, Riyadh, Dammam, Al-Khobar, Mecca, Medina and Khafji.

Private business, which has been highly active in housing construction, at present looks likely to achieve the target fixed for it by the Plan. Jeddah in fact has been heading for a surplus in quality accommodation, helping to bring down rents which had soared to excessive levels between 1974 and 1976. The private sector has, however, been assisted considerably by the Saudi Real Estate Development Fund, established by the Government to finance the construction of houses. The Fund supplies cheap money for private developers—up to 70 per cent of the cost of houses for personal use and 50 per cent for investment purposes. Demand for the Fund's money has been so great that its capital was increased from SR 9,000 million ($2,600 million) to SR 12,000 million ($3,400 million) in 1976 when its total number of loans reached nearly 50,000.

A big pressure was taken off the housing market in March 1977 when a new law came into force obliging foreign companies on large projects to provide their own accommodation for their workers. The influx of expatriate contract labour has been a major factor behind the country's housing shortage. In the market for quality housing in particular, the accommodation needs of foreign managerial and professional staff had sent rents rocketing. By 1976 rents for reasonably spacious houses had reached $20–30,000 a year, before beginning to level off.

Telecommunications problems Saudi Arabia's telecommunications facilities have been lagging well behind demand. This is partly because the establishment of efficient telecommunications in such a vast country over a short period is a mammoth task for the world's telecommunications industry. The Saudi Government has also seriously underestimated its cost. The telecommunications budget for the first two years of the Five-Year Plan easily exceeded the total of SR 4,220 million ($1,190 million) set aside for this sector over the whole 1975-80 period. There have also been disputes between the Government and major contractors. A price put forward by Philips of Holland during direct negotiations for the bulk of the work on the Government's telecommunications programme was rejected in early 1977. Instead the project was put out to limited tender among 11 large international companies.

By 1980 the Government hopes to treble the number of telephones to 660,000. In Riyadh they should be increased from 50,000 to 170,000 and in Jeddah from 50,000 to 150,000. The service is also being substantially extended in the smaller towns. By the end of the decade the country should have at least 20 telephones for every 100 residents in the larger cities and five per 100 in the smaller towns.

The major task is the expansion of the microwave co-axial cable link between Jeddah, Riyadh, and Dammam to the northern and southern parts of the country. Also modern automatic telephone exchanges have to be established in the main centres. The present international communications system which relies on ground satellite stations and two earth stations is being extended with another satellite station being built near Jeddah.

There used to be a time recently when telex facilities were so scarce that foreign companies would exchange accommodation for a telex link. But since 1975 the provision of telexes has considerably improved. By mid-1977 the country was scheduled to have at least 5,000 telexes and a target of 15,000 has been set for 1980.

Industry

Saudi Arabia's programme for the setting up of heavy industries, which is vital to the country's long-term economic future, is dependent on the implementation of its giant gas gathering project. This aims to harness around 5,000 million cubic feet a day of associated gas for use as industrial fuels, and for the manufacture of natural gas liquids (NGL), and petrochemicals. But since 1975 when this scheme, the world's biggest industrial project, was first conceived, its realisation has been repeatedly delayed. Now it seems likely that it will not be completed until the latter half of the 1980s. And when the scheme is finally finished it will be smaller in scale than originally anticipated. The main problem has been spiralling costs, the total estimated price doubling to $10,000 million by the end of 1976. At the same time total gas production under the scheme has had to be related to a realistic long-term level of oil production.

A processing centre at Shedgum and a large fractionation plant at Juaymah in the Eastern Province seems likely to be completed in 1981, two years behind the original schedule. Completion of the remainder of the project, including the building of another fractionation plant at Yanbu linked by pipe line to the eastern oil fields, has been put back by at least five years.

Petrochemical delays These postponements have meant lengthy delays for some large industrial projects, in particular schemes for petrochemical plants. The building of at least five plants is being considered, three of which will probably be established in the industrial city of Jubail. These plants will be fed by the fractionation unit at Juaymah, so their completion will not be put off for too long. But a planned plant at Yanbu may now have to wait several years. The plants will probably all eventually be set up under 50–50 joint ventures between the Saudi Basic Industries Corporation (SABIC) and foreign companies, which will manage them and market their products.

As a result of the gas gathering scheme, NGL exports should increase considerably above the present capacity of around 360,000 barrels a day, with production being centred at plants like Ras Tanura, Berri and Juaymah. Two oil refineries at Jeddah and Riyadh, which aim to meet domestic demand, are being expanded to a total joint capacity of 325,000 b/d. Two large export refineries are planned at Jubail and Yanbu, to supplement the present 415,000 b/d refinery at Ras Tanura.

The Government has had plans to build two fertiliser plants. But these have been shelved mainly because of the poor market outlook. A plant, 51 per cent owned by the Saudi Arabian Fertiliser Company (SAFCO), has been running well below capacity. A scheme to make protein out of paraffin has also been put aside because of the uncertain market prospects.

Saudi Arabia's biggest non-oil based industrial project is a one million ton steel mill which SABIC is setting up in the new industrial complex at Jubail. The plant will use the direct reduction process to produce sponge iron, relying on natural gas for its energy source. In the initial years iron ore will be imported, but Saudi Arabia hopes eventually to mine enough ore of its own to meet the plant's needs. The bulk of the plant's output will supply various private-sector steel mills. Some of these are likely to be completed before the plant starts operating. Like the existing cold rolling mill in Jeddah, they will initially rely on imported sponge iron to make steel billets, iron sheets, reinforced bars and line pipe.

Private enterprise Private entrepreneurs have generally been keen to invest in industry, even though its future in the country is beset with uncertainties. One of the biggest of doubts has been over the availability of manpower, most of which in the industrial sector will have come from abroad. But the Government has helped to alleviate any fears by offering cheap finance for industrial investment through the Saudi Industrial Development Fund (SIDF). By February 1977 it had approved 175 loans for industrial projects worth over $400 million.

SIDF uses the Industrial Studies and Development Centre to judge the viability of schemes wanting loans. The Centre has produced feasibility studies on the development of individual industries. In the Eastern Province similar groundwork has been done by Aramco's Local Industries Development Centre which was established about 30 years ago. Its objective has been to help the establishment of manufacturing units which would be able to serve the country's oil industry.

Many new medium-sized industrial projects are likely to be centred on three existing industrial zones at Jeddah, Riyadh and Dammam and two new industrial estates planned for Mecca and Buraida. But a large number of smaller industries will be established in the industrial complexes of Jubail and Yarbu where they will act as ancillaries to the country's heavy industrial plants.

So far the private sector has concentrated mainly on the manufacture of building materials. So many companies are producing cement blocks and tiles that the Government has refused to grant any more manufacturing licences for these products until 1980. Private firms have also been active in the manufacture of metal products, mainly for the construction industry, and of processed foods and beverages. Some of the larger private industrial projects include cement plants, a heavy lorry assembly plant, and a unit for making asbestos cement pipes.

Agriculture

Saudi Arabia eventually hopes to be self-sufficient in most foods. But progress towards this aim has been slower than expected. The annual growth rate of agricultural production during the period of the 1970–75 Plan fell one per cent short of its target of 4.6 per cent. At the same time imports of cereals, vegetables and fruits have more than tripled in recent years, and some meat imports have more than doubled. During 1976/77 the Government allocated nearly SR 1,000 million ($2,800 million) for food subsidies.

Under the present Five-Year Plan nearly SR 4,000 million ($1,100 million) has been set aside for agriculture which is less than one per cent of total allocation. But substantial sums are also being spent on schemes for the exploitation of water resources from which agriculture will benefit. Generally by 1980 agricultural production is expected to show considerable improvements and in some sectors output is expected to be surprisingly high for such an arid country.

Production successes Experimental farms in Saudi Arabia have over the last few years achieved some significant successes. Cattle and poultry have been thriving on desert farms, producing milk and eggs for the local market, and sheep have been bred on artificial meadows on the edge of the Empty Quarter. But the more impressive achievements have been among the Saudi smallholders who have been steadily pushing up their output. There have been increases in key crops like wheat, maize, barley, citrus and alfalfa. During 1974-75 wheat output was more than doubled to 150,840 tons and now looks likely to reach its 1980 target of 250,000. This increase has been attributed partly to availability of wheat subsidies and to the introduction of the higher-yield *Mexipak* wheat. The country is at present nearing self-sufficiency in most vegetables, except potatoes, and in many varieties of fruit.

Some of the biggest increases in output have been in the Asir region in the southwest of the country which has the most fertile land. The area is on the edge of the monsoon belt and as a result has the country's highest rainfall. Asir accounts for most of the wheat, maize and sorghum production. Mecca province is also an important agricultural area, producing over 13 per cent of the nation's total output.

Saudi farmers are well supported by the Government. They can obtain cheap loans from the state-owned Agricultural Bank and receive subsidies ranging from 30 to 50 per cent for the purchase of farm machinery, fertilisers and animal feeds. Food is also subsidised at the retail level.

The Government is also embarking on large irrigation schemes which could more than double the amount of irrigated water to 2,500 million cubic metres by the 1980s. Large numbers of foreign experts have been brought in to plan irrigation projects, mainly in the southwest and eastern parts of the country. In some cases farms may have to be merged into larger units to make the projects viable.

But the Government's efforts may not eventually be enough to stop people leaving the land for the thriving cities. Rural depopulation is one of the major barriers to the success of the country's agricultural development programme. Urban wealth is not necessarily accompanied by rural prosperity and the more the cities outstretch the countryside the larger the rural exodus becomes. Perhaps the future of Saudi agriculture will hinge on the speed with which the Government can provide in rural areas basic utilities and health and educational facilities comparable with those in the cities.

Banking and Finance

The Saudi Arabian Monetary Agency is the Kingdom's central bank in all but name. It was established in 1952 and owes its present form to the Banking Control Law of 1966. The Saudi Arabian riyal is linked to the International Monetary Fund's Special Drawing Right, the rate for which is calculated daily by the Fund on the basis of a weighted average of rates for the sixteen major currencies. This system has been followed since 15 March 1975, when, instead of a direct link with the US dollar, the daily riyal-dollar rate began to be fixed on the basis of the daily dollar-SDR rate announced by the IMF. The daily rate is liable to alteration only if there is a significant change in the dollar-SDR rate.

There are two Saudi commercial banks, The National Commercial Bank, established in 1938, and the more recent Riyadh Bank, both with 27 branches. The Arab Bank, based in Jordan, has six branches, the Banque du Caire three and the Banque du Liban et d'Outre-Mer has a single office in Jeddah. Of foreign, and non-Arab institutions, General Bank of the Netherlands and the British Bank of the Middle East both have three branches, in Jeddah, Dammam, and Al-Khobar. There are five other foreign banks with one or two branches. The First National City Bank of New York has a branch in Riyadh.

SAMA handles Saudi Arabia's enormous surplus funds, the exact size of which is uncertain. At the end of 1976 the Agency put its international reserves at around $27,000 million with its total foreign investments an estimated $25,000 million. The Agency's deposits are placed in banks included on its own Approved List. This is thought to number at least 50. But the list is considered to be an informal document for the guidance of SAMA staff and is likely to be changed frequently in line with conditions on the international financial market.

Most SAMA deposits used to be short-term. But in recent years the agency has started to switch to long-term maturities.

437

P

It has also started to invest large sums in fixed-interest securities, in particular US Treasury bills and bonds. Occasionally it has ventured into the equity market. But generally SAMA follows a conservative investment policy, aimed at avoiding radical innovations and helping to give stability to the international financial market.

Restrictions on banks Within Saudi Arabia itself, SAMA has kept a relatively tight hold over the country's banks. The number of banks in the country is still comparatively small for a country of such oil wealth. In money terms Saudi Arabia has the biggest banking system in the Arabian Peninsula. Besides keeping down the number of banks, SAMA has also restricted the amount of loans they can make to domestic borrowers. Sometimes banks have channelled loans through banks in neighbouring Gulf countries, in particular Bahrain which has become an offshore banking centre.

Most of these external transactions have been carried out by foreign banks in Saudi Arabia. As a result SAMA has stepped up its Saudisation programme under which Saudis are given a majority share in foreign banks. Several have agreed to Saudisation because in return SAMA has decided to relax its ban on the opening of branches outside Jeddah.

Most loans from banks to Saudi Arabia are used to finance imports, commercial transactions and small contracting operations. But the banks have now become involved more in long-term lending, though in this field they are unable yet to compete with the low-interest loans provided by the Government's development funds.

They have also started to supply international loans in Saudi riyals. By early 1977 at least four riyal bond issues had been managed by the National Commercial Bank for state organisations in Morocco, Algeria and Spain. Several riyal loans had been made to banks in other Gulf states, especially offshore banks in Bahrain. The gradual internationalisation of the riyal from which the Saudi banks are now benefitting is reflected in the emergence of a market in the currency in London, and Frankfurt as well as Bahrain.

But despite the growing international prestige of the riyal, Saudi Arabia has been slow to create its own capital market.

The new riyal bonds have failed to find many domestic buyers and the National Commercial Bank has been keeping most of them on its own books. The bank has found it easier to sell Eurobonds locally.

The country's equity share market should however grow fairly rapidly over the next few years. By the end of 1976 there were only about 20 shares quoted but this number is likely to start to increase. The Saudisation of the foreign banks should give a big boost to equity trading. But it could be several years before the country has its own stock exchange, like that in neighbouring Kuwait.

Social Services

About 25 years ago education in Saudi Arabia consisted of memorising extracts of the Koran and a few basic mathematical skills taught by a village elder. Now over a million students, three quarters of them primary school children, are receiving a reasonably modern education. Over 20,000 pupils are studying at Saudi universities. Nonetheless only two thirds of boys and one third of girls are enrolled at primary school level.

Education has become a top priority. Under the Five Year Plan education has been allocated $21,400 million, or 14 per cent of the total. In recent budgets, the allocation has tended to be around 10 per cent of the total, and in 1976/77 nearly $4,000 million was devoted to education.

The Saudi Government has set a target of nearly 24,000 new classrooms by 1980 or an average of 90 to 100 new ones a week. This objective is unlikely to be reached because like the rest of the economy education has been affected by bottlenecks in the country's infrastructure and shortages of manpower. Over half the primary school teachers and about 85 per cent of secondary school teachers are from abroad, most of them being Egyptian or Palestinian. There are not even enough foreign teachers to meet demand and classes as a result tend to be overcrowded.

In its drive towards universal education, particularly at secondary level, the Government has had to face the problem of a high drop-out rate. Despite being paid for going to school, many secondary students do not want to continue their schooling when they can virtually pick up any job they wish outside. So far few students have graduated from technical or commercial secondary schools. With some courses students cannot be found to fill the vacancies. Sometimes it is the fault of the Government's own departments. Ministries are so desperate for Saudi staff that they offer to send students abroad to study on condition they return to take a job with them. Over 4,000 students are at present studying abroad, most of them in the US.

Administrative delays The education sector has tended to be hampered by a cumbersome decision-making process. The Ministry of Higher Education was recently formed to take charge of higher education institutions. But the prestigious University of Petroleum and Minerals at Dhahran has remained under the control of the Ministry of Petroleum & Minerals. All education of females is run by the separate Directorate of Girls Education which ensures that there are strictly separate facilities for boy and girl pupils.

The existence of many different authorities has also tended to cause administrative delays in the field of health care. Health facilities are run by the Ministry of Health, Ministry of Higher Education, the Ministry of Interior and the Ministry of Defence and Aviation. Each health service run by the various ministries tend to want its own special units. There is no lack of funds for buying equipment and machines but there is a desperate shortage of trained manpower to run them.

Under the Five Year Plan a total of SR 17,300 million has been allocated to health care. By early 1977 there were 62 hospitals with a total of 7,300 beds, 215 clinics or dispensaries and 372 health centres. There were also several hospitals for the defence and security forces. All these facilities were staffed by about 2,500 doctors and over 4,000 nurses. However, more medical staff are needed to ease the present heavy workload on doctors and nurses. All hospitals in the country are providing care and treatment for more patients than they were originally designed for.

There are plans for seven more 300-bed hospitals and three new 300-bed specialist hospitals. Because of the high demand the hospitals' capacity may be increased to 500 beds. The Government also wants to encourage the private sector to build hospitals and clinics and has offered to provide loans for private projects. The number of clinics/dispensaries will be raised to over 400 by 1980 and a system of mobile clinics may be introduced. In an effort to increase the local supply of medical staff Western hospital management firms are training Saudi nurses and the intake of Saudi Arabia's medical schools is being increased.

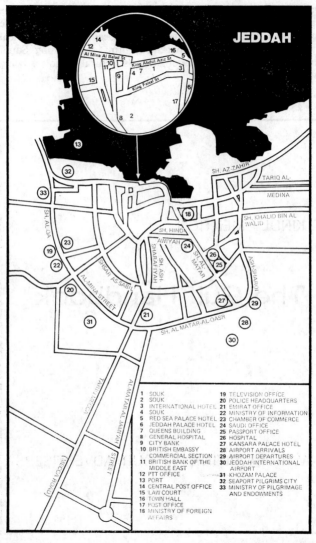

JEDDAH

1	SOUK	19 TELEVISION OFFICE
2	SOUK	20 POLICE HEADQUARTERS
3	INTERNATIONAL HOTEL	21 EMIRAT OFFICE
4	SOUK	22 MINISTRY OF INFORMATION
5	RED SEA PALACE HOTEL	23 CHAMBER OF COMMERCE
6	JEDDAH PALACE HOTEL	24 SAUDI OFFICE
7	QUEENS BUILDING	25 PASSPORT OFFICE
8	GENERAL HOSPITAL	26 HOSPITAL
9	CITY BANK	27 KANSARA PALACE HOTEL
10	BRITISH EMBASSY	28 AIRPORT ARRIVALS
	COMMERCIAL SECTION	29 AIRPORT DEPARTURES
11	BRITISH BANK OF THE	30 JEDDAH INTERNATIONAL
	MIDDLE EAST	AIRPORT
12	PTT OFFICE	31 KHOZAM PALACE
13	PORT	32 SEAPORT PILGRIMS CITY
14	CENTRAL POST OFFICE	33 MINISTRY OF PILGRIMAGE
15	LAW COURT	AND ENDOWMENTS
16	TOWN HALL	
17	POST OFFICE	
18	MINISTRY OF FOREIGN	
	AFFAIRS	

GUIDE

JEDDAH On the eve of the Arab Revolt against the Turks in 1917, T. E. Lawrence walked amid the lovely coral-ragged and wooden latticed Turkish buildings of Jeddah. The summer air stifled him. "It was not burning hot," he wrote, "but held a moisture and great age and exhaustion such as seemed to belong to no other place." The atmosphere was "oppressive, deadly". Today the weather is unchanged. The crumbling buildings of the Ottoman era are disappearing. But Jeddah still remains the Port of Mecca—the *qibla* or focus-point of Islam—and owes its cosmopolitan, sophisticated atmosphere to its 13 centuries as a gateway for the millions of pilgrims who each year make the *haj*, or pilgrimage, to Mecca.

For a long time lack of drinking water prevented the city expanding. It only began to grow about 30 years ago when Ibn Saud set up a water supply system. The real development of modern Jeddah began in 1950 when its great walls were pulled down. Now Jeddah is the busiest city and port in the kingdom, and because of its cosmopolitan history is the nearest in spirit to the culture of the West. The influx of Western expatriates and the luxuries of Western life over the past few years has not had the same shock effect in Jeddah as in Riyadh. The people of Jeddah are descended from many races of people who have settled in the city over the centuries. They are more worldly than the Nejdis further east. As the old gives way rapidly to the new, about the only sufferers are the fine old Ottoman buildings which are daily being swept away by the bulldozer.

The ornate wood-wrought balconies, casements, latticework balustrades and lattice screens of the old buildings could make a fine contrast to the sweeping lines of the city's modern architecture if only the Saudis would allow them to be preserved. Meanwhile the ones still left standing sit in the shadow of skyscrapers like the gleaming, curvilinear Queen's Building, which dominates the city business centre from the middle of King Abdul Aziz Street. From its top floor can be seen other new tall buildings rising up and present-day Jeddah taking shape amid the numerous construction sites.

To Western expatriate workers Jeddah is probably the most pleasant of all the Saudi cities because it has the best recreational and leisure facilities. Life in Jeddah can be sophisticated and elegant. There are good restaurants serving a variety of national foods. The quality of housing is better than in Riyadh and most villas in the fashionable residential area off the Medina Road have large patios and flourishing gardens. The shops are well stocked and even the furniture stores sell the latest Western designs. The intrusion of Western cultural interests is apparent in the setting up of European-style antique shops. Despite its obvious limitations social life can be rich and varied.

Above all, Jeddah has fascinating surroundings. Where else in the world is there the choice of spending the weekend by the sea or exploring the deep desert and mountains? On Fridays most people go to beaches like Obhor Creek, 30 miles north of Jeddah. For scuba diving and snorkeling, the Red Sea can be a paradise. A few yards out, the corals are full of dazzling shoals of colourful fish. Sometimes even a baby shark will dash among them. The more adventurous underwater swimmers go into the Creek to where the sea-bed shelf suddenly drops three hundred feet.

While Western influences begin to take a tight grip on Jeddah, the old culture struggles to remain intact. New restaurants try to emulate the chic eating places of Europe rather than reflect the heritage of the area. Even the thobes sold in the covered souk are now made of nylon and the incense burners are plastic rather than wood and brass. At the same time a mercenary spirit has penetrated the fabric of life. The taxi driver who boasts his purity during a journey may ask treble the proper fare at the end.

Hotels

Kandara Palace Hotel, Shara al-Matar. P.O.B. 473. Tel: 23155/25700. Telex: 40095. Considered to be Jeddah's best equipped hotel. Located conveniently close to the airport. 220 rooms (to be extended to 400 rooms). Also has suites and villas. Single person (double room) SR 225, two people SR 270. Suites from about SR 450. Villas from SR 600. 15 per cent service charge. Restaurant (lunch/dinner from SR 35). Tea garden. Swimming pool. Bookshop. Barbershop.

Jeddah Palace Hotel, opposite Foreign Affairs Ministry. P.O.B. 473. Tel: 32387/32255. Telex: 40095. In mid-1977 all rooms had been taken over by Saudia airline for its staff. When the hotel reopens, its prices will be similar to those of the Kandara Palace. 15 per cent service charge. Restaurant. Swimming pool.

Al-Attas and Al-Attas Oasis Hotels, off Shara al-Matar. P.O.B. 1789/1299. Tel: 20211/20400/40158. Telex: 40158. Two adjacent hotels under the same management. 212 rooms. Single room SR 150, single person (double room) SR 188, two people SR 225. 15 per cent service charge. Restaurant (lunch/dinner from around SR 30). Coffee shop. Swimming pool.

Riyadh Hotel. Tel: 33944/33950. Telex: 40154. 40 rooms. Single person SR 200, two people SR 240. 15 per cent service charge. Restaurant (lunch/dinner from SR 25). Shops.

Red Sea Palace Hotel, top of King Abdul Aziz Street. P.O.B. 824. Tel: 28555/28950/28787. Telex: 40014. Overlooks the Red Sea. 103 rooms and seven suites (large extension being built). Single person SR 200 (including meals). 15 per cent service charge. Restaurant, with patio facing sea. Shop.

Jeddah Airport Hotel, Shara al-Matar. Tel: 33155/33489. 51 double rooms and 18 suites. Single person SR 200 (including meals), two people SR 380. 15 per cent service charge. Restaurant.

Taj Palace Hotel, Shara al-Matar. Tel: 21288/21479. Most of its 50 rooms leased to a company. When fully reopened, prices around SR 180 (single person), SR 290 (two people). Restaurant (lunch/dinner SR 30).

Ar-Rehab, Shara al-Jadid. Tel: 32216/32302. Telex: 40091. 88 rooms. Single person SR 170, two people SR 220. 10 per cent service charge. Roof restaurant.

Atlas, Shara al-Jadid. Tel: 23361. 59 rooms. Single room SR 150, double SR 250. Willing to put extra beds in rooms. 10 per cent service charge. Restaurant (lunch/dinner from SR 25).

Asia, King Abdul Aziz Street. Tel: 25111/26218. 120 rooms. Single room SR 140, double SR 210. 15 per cent service charge. Restaurant (lunch/dinner from SR 25). Conference hall.

Medina, Shara al-Jadid. Tel: 32650. 45 rooms. Single person SR 120, two people SR 150. 10 per cent service charge. Restaurant (lunch/dinner from SR 20).

Khayyam, King Faisal Street. P.O.B. 6113. Tel: 33560/29893. Newly built hotel, just opened. Single person SR 126, two people SR 150. Restaurant.

Amin, King Abdul Aziz Street. P.O.B. 3785. Tel: 33191. 59 rooms. Single person SR 120. 10 per cent service charge. No restaurant.

International Hotel, top of King Abdul Aziz Street. P.O.B. 1700. Tel: 29022/29814. Telex: 40116. 80 rooms and 10 suites. Single room SR 80, single person (double room) SR 100, two people SR 120. 10 per cent service charge. Top floor restaurant (lunch/dinner from SR 20).

445

Bahauddin Hotel, Shara al-Jadid. 50 rooms taken over by airline company. When reopened prices should be around SR 150 for single person. Restaurant.

New Bahauddin, Shara al-Jadid. Tel: 23511. Telex: 40174. Single person SR 100, two people SR 160.

Al-Andolus, Shara al-Jadid. Tel: 34493. 20 rooms. Single person SR 70, two people SR 90.

Obhor Creek Hotel, Obhor Creek. One of two hotels 30 miles out of Jeddah. Close to beach. 38 rooms. Two people from SR 220. Restaurant (lunch/dinner from SR 20). 400-seat cinema. Swimming and water skiing.

Al-Attas Holiday Beach Hotel, Obhor Creek. Tel: 26444. 38 rooms and two villas with swimming pools. Single person SR 160, two people SR 180. 15 per cent service charge. Villas from around SR 2000. 15 per cent service charge. Restaurant. Cinema.

Al-Aziziah Palace Hotel, Taif. P.O.B. 17. Tel: 21666. Telex: 45010 (Jeddah). A good hotel which can be a useful last resort when hotels in Jeddah are fully booked. 28 rooms. Single room around SR 220, double SR 270. 15 per cent service charge. Restaurant (lunch/dinner around SR 30).

Several new hotels are being built in Jeddah and its surroundings, including a large *Sheraton Hotel*. Obhor Creek is likely to have considerably more hotels.

Restaurants

Kaymak Glace, Tariq al-Medina (near Foreign Affairs Ministry). Lebanese cuisine. Ice cream parlour. Meal for single person around SR 30.

Castello, off Shara Khalid Bin-Walid. Italian food.

American Style, off Palestine Road. Good grilled steak.

Topkapi, Shara Khalid Bin-Walid. Mainly Turkish food.

Spinzers, off Tariq al-Medina. Indian/Pakistani cuisine. Single person SR 20–30.

Shalimar, behind Jeddah Shopping Centre. Indian food.

Shangi-la, behind Jeddah Shopping Centre. Chinese cuisine. Take-away service.

Koreana, Shara Al-Sharafiyah (close to airport). Korean food.

Indian Restaurant, near Jeddah Shopping Centre. Tandoori food.

Queen's Building Restaurant, King Abdul Aziz Street. Located on the top floor with good view of city. European food.

International Hotel Restaurant, top of King Abdul Aziz Street. Enclosed roof garden with fine views.

448

Al-Attas Oasis Hotel Restaurant, off Shara Al-Matar. European food. Roof garden overlooking city.

The Black Tent, four miles out on the Medina road. Traditional Arab food served in a bedouin tent. Hubble-bubble pipe smoking and camel riding afterwards.

Kilo Ten Garden, six miles out on the Mecca road. Arabian dishes served in traditional style.

Airport Located close to the centre of the city. The airport buildings open out onto Airport Square, one of the city's busiest precincts. A new international airport which is reputedly going to be the world's biggest, is being built north of the city, scheduled for completion in 1979. So the present airport is only temporary. The departure and arrival lounges are large, but functional with minimal facilities. No duty-free shops, restaurants or even refreshment bars.

Taxis Official notices outside the airport and in the business sector say taxi fares are SR 4 for journeys inside the city centre and SR 7 to the outskirts. In fact taxi drivers charge at least 50 per cent more than this. Drivers demand around SR 6–7 for short trips and a minimum SR 10 for longer journeys. Taxis outside the hotels cost well above the norm. Taxis cannot be phoned, only hailed. Fares should be arranged beforehand with the driver.

Car hire firms *Arabian Car Rental*, Airport Square (opposite Kandara Palace Hotel). P.O.B. 5241. Tel: 33965. Telex: 33965. *Avis Rent-a-Car*, Shara Khalid Bin-Walid. P.O.B. 1271. Tel: 52930. Telex: 40029. *Sahary Rent-a-Car*, Tariq Mecca. Tel: 20400. Agents for Godfrey Davis.

Daily rates vary from SR 70 to SR 200 for a self-drive car and SR 120 to SR 500 for a chauffeur-driven car, depending on the size of the model. The first 62 miles are usually free after which an additional charge of around half a riyal for $\frac{5}{8}$ mile is added.

Travel Agencies *Attar Agencies*, Bab Sherif (close to British Bank of the Middle East). Tel: 23937. *Areen Travel Agency*, Tariq al-Medina. Tel: 33125/33126. *Aoueini Travel Agency*, Bab Sherif. Tel: 22882.

Airline offices Head Office: *Saudia*, Shara al-Matar. Tel: 25222.

Sales offices: *KLM*, King Abdul Aziz Street. Tel: 24684/25505. *Alitalia*, King Abdul Aziz Street. Tel: 25238/22107. *Air France*, Aoueini Travel Agency, Bab Sherif. Tel: 22882/32468. *British Airways*. Tel: 22937/22986. *Egyptair*, King Abdul Aziz Street. Tel.: 21144. *Iran Air*, King Abdul Aziz Street. Tel: 21172.

Korean Airlines. Tel: 25612. *Kuwait Air*, Binzagar Street. Tel: 28349. *Lufthansa*, King Abdul Aziz Street, Tel: 23324. *MEA*, Jeddah Palace Hotel. Tel: 21141/21933. *Olympic Airways*. Tel: 22228. *Pan Am*, King

Abdul Aziz Street. Tel: 31151/23731. *Alia*, near Mughrabi Building, Binzagar Street. Tel: 33414/21321.

Saudia, Ali Reza Building, King Abdul Aziz Street. Tel: 23222 (Switchboard) / 21222, 21433 (Reservations) / 26210 (Traffic) / 21111 (Information)/21666 (Confirmation). *Sudan Airways*, Bab Mecca. Tel: 23142. *Syrian Arab Airlines*, King Abdul Aziz Street. Tel: 25612. *Tunis Air*, Binzagar Street. Tel: 22448/22474. *TWA*, Queen's Building, King Abdul Aziz Street. Tel: 22228. *Yemen Air*, Binzagar Street. Tel: 33169.

Shipping agencies *Alatas Agencies*, Prince Abdulla al-Faisal Building. P.O.B. 4. Tel: 28333/28529. Telex: 40009. *Arabian Establishment for Trade*, King Abdul Aziz Street. P.O.B. 832. Tel: 24879/22808. Telex: 41038. *Ali Reza Shipping Co.*, King Abdul Aziz Street. Tel: 23629. *Orri Navigation*, Pier Road. Tel: 33144.

Post Office The main post office is off the lower end of King Abdul Aziz Street. It is advisable to buy stamps in bulk because the counter service can be chaotic. An airmail letter to Europe costs about SR 1 and usually takes 4–5 days. But the postal system is generally unreliable.

Telephone International calls have to be booked at least half-an-hour beforehand. Local calls can be difficult but links with Riyadh by direct dialling are generally good. The telephone directory tends to be out-of-date and copies are scarce.

Useful phone nos. For emergency numbers see *General Information* (Telecommunications). Other numbers: *Police* (for accidents)—32101. *Telephone services*—23795. *Long distance supervisor*—63670.

Telex Some hotels have telexes. There is a public telex at the PTT Office close to the main post office at the top of Port Road. It is a temporary building due to be replaced soon. A 60-word telex to Europe costs around SR 20.

Shops Jeddah's largest supermarket is the *Jeddah Shopping Centre* on the corner of Medina Road and Palestine Road. The adjacent *Al-Mukhtar's* supermarket is also popular.

Queen's Building has a variety of shops, some of which sell jewellery and craftwork. Among the city's art dealers are the *Fleming Gallery* on the first floor. *Albul Hassan* on the Medina Road specialises in oriental antiquities. There is a row of shops in Airport Square, selling antiques and carpets.

Souks There is a large modern covered souk off King Abdul Aziz Street. Most of the goods are imported with a particular emphasis on textiles. But like pre-Islamic times, frankincense is on sale with ornate incense burners.

Social clubs   Social clubs used by expatriates are attached to companies or embassies. American companies, like Raytheon and Lockheed, have particularly large clubs with good facilities. Visitors are usually welcome as long as they are accompanied by members.

Leisure sport   Obhor Creek, 30 miles north of the city, is rapidly becoming Jeddah's pleasure resort. It has good facilities for swimming, water skiing, fishing and sailing. The *Red Sea Sailing Club* has premises on the south side of the Creek. The Red Sea is unrivalled for its deep sea fishing and underwater swimming among the corals. Camping trips into the desert are popular but can be highly dangerous unless carefully planned. Otherwise most sporting/leisure facilities are only available at private clubs, most of them run by companies. The *Dunes Club* on the American Embassy compound has squash and tennis courts and a nine-hole golf course. The British Embassy also has squash and tennis courts, and a swimming club. Some hotels open their swimming pools to non-residents on payment of a fee.

Bookshops   The city has few shops selling foreign newspapers, periodicals or books. The *Kandara Palace Hotel* has a small bookshop.

Hospitals   The best hospitals for emergency treatment are the *Jeddah Clinic*, Shara Al-Matar (Tel: 27715) and the *Lebanese Hospital*, Medina Road (Tel: 52944), which has a 24-hour emergency service.

Pharmacies   *Mohammed Tamer Pharmacy*, King Abdul Aziz Street, Tel: 23982/22313. *Salehiya Pharmacy*, Shara Al-Matar. Tel: 24860. *Batarjee*, Bab Mecca. Tel: 23515/23259. *Mandial Pharmacy*, Medina Road. Tel: 29081.

Banks   Head offices: *Saudi Arabian Monetary Agency*, Airport Road. P.O.B. 394. Tel: 31122/31306. Telex: 40011/40094. *Al-Jazira Bank*, Kaki Building, Airport Road. P.O.B. 6277. Tel: 32888. Telex: 40036. *National Commercial Bank*, King Abdul Aziz Street, P.O.B. 3555. Tel: 23794. Telex: 40102/40086. *Riyadh Bank*. P.O.B. 1047. Tel: 32416. Telex: 40006/40232. *Saudi Banking Investment Corporation*, Queen's Building, King Abdul Aziz Street. P.O.B. 5577. Tel: 32000. Telex: 40156. *Islamic Development Bank*. P.O.B. 5925. Tel: 33994. Telex 40137.

   Main offices: *Algemene Bank Nederland*, King Abdul Aziz Street. P.O.B. 67. Tel: 21077/21078. Telex: 201012. *Arab Bank*, P.O.B. 344. Tel: 22896/23579. Telex: 40099. *Bank of Credit and Commerce International*. P.O.B. 5443. Tel: 33190/21550. Telex: 40183. *Bank Melli Iran*. P.O.B. 1686. King Abdul Aziz Street. Tel: 31687. Telex: 40188. *Banque du Caire*, King Abdul Aziz Street. Tel: 23266/23473. *Banque du Liban et d'Outre Mer*, Kabel Street. P.O.B. 482. Tel: 23285. *British Bank of the Middle East*, King Abdul Aziz Street. P.O.B. 109. Tel: 42868. Telex: 67007. *Banque de L'Indochine et de Suez*, King

Abdul Aziz Street. P.O.B. 1. Tel: 23344. Telex: 40168. *Citibank*, King Abdul Aziz Street. P.O.B. 490. Tel: 24155/24011. Telex: 40108.

Ministries/Government departments *Ministry of Foreign Affairs*, off lower end of Tariq al-Medina. Telex: 40104. *Directorate General of Mineral Resources*. P.O.B. 345. Tel: 33133. *Ministry of Commerce*, Jeddah Branch. Mecca Road. Tel: 23400. *Directorate General of Zakat and Income Tax*, Jeddah Branch. Airport Road. *Customs Department*, Jeddah Branch. Tel: 22100. *Passport and Nationality Directorate*, Jeddah Branch. Airport Road. Tel: 22100.

Embassies *Afghanistan*, Kilometre 3, Medina Road, Al-Kadesiah Street. Tel: 53142. *Algeria*, Medina Road, Ahmad Shawki Street. Tel: 53202. *Argentina*, Villa Bakr Khomais, (south of British Embassy). Tel: 52666. *Australia*, off Al-Hamra Road, Ruwais. P.O.B. 4876. Tel: 51303/52329. *Austria*, Medina Road, Kilometre 4 (opposite King Saud Mosque). Tel: 52548. Commercial office, Sharbatly Building, 4th Floor, Apartment No. 61. Tel: 26622/20134. *Bahrain*, Al-Ruwais (near the Old Royal Palace). Tel: 51905.

Belgium, Medina Road, Kilometre 2, Shakeeb Amawi Building. Tel: 53196. *Brazil*, Villa No. 1, west of Medina Road (east of Qasr al-Hamra). Tel: 54574. *Cameroun*, Villa Abdul Aziz Jokhdar Kandara, Al-Madik Street (adjoining Airport Street). Tel: 28260. *Canada*, 6th Floor, Commercial & Residential Centre, King Abdul Aziz Street. Tel: 34598/34111. *Denmark*, Commercial & Residential Centre, King Abdul Aziz Street. Tel: 33044. *Egypt*, Airport Street, Sharafia. Tel: 21011/21200.

Ethiopia, Sons of Amar Mansour Building, Mohammed Abdul Wahhab Street, Baghdadiyah. Tel: 23013. *Finland*, Villa Zogheibi, Ministry of Defence Office Street, Sharafiyah. Tel: 53192/54177. *France*, Shaikh Mohammed bin Abdul Wahhab Street. Tel: 21233/21447. *Gabon*, Khalid bin-Walid Street, Sharafia. Tel: 53497. *Gambia*, Villa Jamil Mustapha Nazir, Sharafiyah. Tel: 53292/52528. *West Germany*, Medina Road, Mustafa Ashoor Building. Tel: 53545/53344.

Ghana, Medina Road, Kilometre 4 (off Palestine Road). Tel: 52779. *Greece*, Kandara Palace Hotel, Villa 13. Tel: 34370. *Guinea*, 11 Abou Feras Street, Ruwais. Tel: 53718. *India*, Building of Shaikh Mohamed Ibrahim Masoud, near Baghdadiyah, Medina Road. Tel: 21602. *Indonesia*, Villa Abdul Malik bin Ibrahim, Gabali Street No. 9, Baghdadiyah, 21681, 21497. *Iran*, Medina Road, Abu al-Tayeb Street. Tel: 53145/51424/53143.

Iraq, Medina Road, Kilometre 5. Tel: 52498/52949. *Italy*, Ahmed Abdullah Amoudi Building, Sharafiyah. Tel: 21451/21452. *Japan*, Palestine Road. Tel: 42402/52405. *Jordan*, Khozam Palace, Sea Port Road. Tel: 23341/23022. *South Korea*, North Hamra Palace. Tel:

53218/51700. *Kuwait*, 17 Ali Bin Abi Taleb Street, Sharafiyah. Tel: 53163/53237.

Lebanon, Villa Bokhan, Kilometre 3, Medina Road. Tel: 52488/ 52696. *Libya*, Olayan al-Hashidi Building, Medina Road, Kilometre 5, (near Prince Khalid al-Faisal Palace). Tel: 51273. *Malaysia*, Shuhada Street, Kilometre 3, Medina Road. Tel: 52371/53866. Commercial Section: Flat 511 /512, 5th Floor, Commercial and Residential Centre, King Abdul Aziz Street. Tel: 24481. *Mauritania*, Villa Misfer, Kilometre 3, South Airport Road Fence, University Street, Mecca Road. Tel: 28171. *Morocco*, Medina Road, Al-Hamra Street (behind King Saud Mosque). Tel: 52568. *Netherlands*, Kilometre 1, Medina Road. Tel: 53611/53612.

Niger, Villa al-Shaikh Mohammed Ibrahim Masoud, Palestine Street (near American Embassy). Tel: 51551. *Nigeria*, Sayed Abdullah Abbas Sharbatly Building, Baghdadiyah (near Ministry of Foreign Affairs). Tel: 32533/32835. *Oman*, Medina Road, Ruwais, Kilometre 2 (opposite American Cultural Centre). Tel: 53618. *Pakistan*, 92 Sea Port Road (opposite Qasr Khozam). Tel: 27333/27569. *Philippines*, Kilometre 5, Medina Road (near the Villa of Prince Muhsin bin Abdul Aziz). Tel: 53343/53255/53266. *Qatar*, Medina Road (north of Ministry of Communications Office). Tel: 52538/53973.

Senegal, Medina Road (behind Telephone Building). Tel: 54465. *Somalia*, Kilometre 2, Medina Road, Tel: 51495/53025. *Spain*, Tunsi Building, Mecca Road, Kilometre 4. Tel: 23226. *Sudan*, Medina Road. Tel: 20560/33682. *Sweden*, Baghdadiah (corner of Medina Road and Sharafiyah Airport Street). Tel: 21416/21417. *Switzerland*, off Medina Road, Kilometre 2. Tel: 51387. *Syria*, Al-Huda Street, Al-Sharafiyah. Tel: 51049. *Thailand*, Madaris Street, Baghdadiyah (near the Office of Royal Protocol). Tel: 31344. *Tunisia*, Badanah Street, Mecca Road, Kilometre 3. Tel: 32133/33574. *Turkey*, Al-Musaidiya Street, Medina Road, Kilometre 7. Tel: 54873.

Uganda, Medina Road, Khalid bin-Walid Street, Sharafiyah, Tel: 52386. *United Arab Emirates*, Osman bin-Affan Street, Sharafiyah. Tel: 53770/54067. *United Kingdom*, Ruwais, Tel: 52544/52628/52768/ 52849/52974. Commercial Section: Dutch Bank Building, 4th Floor. Tel: 27122/27406. *United States*, Palestine Road, Ruwais. Tel: 52188/ 53299/52589/53410/54110. Commercial Centre: Jeddah Palace Hotel, Tel: 24226/32949/51694/54291.

Venezuela, Hamra Palace Street. Tel: 51124. *North Yemen*, Airport Street. Tel: 24291/25540. *Zaire*, Tel: 52977. *Taiwan*, Villa Amir Mansour, Mohammed Abdul Wahhab Street, Baghdadiah. Tel: 29147/22605/33997. Commercial Office: 503–504 Maghraby Building, Al-Jadid Street. Tel: 32860. *Chad*, Medina Road, Kilometre 5 (behind Telephone Building). Tel: 53662.

Newspapers/periodicals *Arab News*, Arab News Building, off Shara-fiah. P.O.B. 4556. Tel: 34962/28708. Telex 40045. English-language daily. *Saudi Gazette*, Al-Mina Street. P.O.B. 5576. English-language. *Replica*, P.O.B. 2043. English-language press review in newsletter format. *Al-Medinah*, Abdullah Suleiman Street. P.O.B. 807. Arabic. Circulation around 20,000. *Al-Ukadh*, Mina Street. P.O.B. 1408. Arabic 15,000 circ. *Al-Bilad*, Al-Bilad Publishing Corporation, King Abdul Aziz Street. Arabic. 5,000 circ.

Periodicals: *Saudi Business*, Arab News Building, off Sharafiah. P.O.B. 4556. Tel: 34962/28708. Telex: 40045. English-language business weekly. *Saudi Economic Survey*. P.O.B. 1982. English-language economic news weekly.

Media Both Jeddah's English-language dailies, *Arab News* and *Saudi Gazette*, give a good coverage of international news from the wires of news agencies. All Saudi news tends to be economic. Both local TV and radio stations have programmes in English, including news bulletins.

Useful addresses *Chamber of Commerce & Industry*, Prince Mansoor Building, Kabel Street. P.O.B. 1264. Tel: 31059/23535/3635. *Director*, Jeddah Customs. Tel: 31748. *Jeddah Port Customs*. Tel: 31222.

RIYADH In few cities of the world can the contrast between 20th century progress and a traditional, isolated culture be seen more clearly than in Saudi Arabia's capital Riyadh. The recent development boom, as reflected in massive building schemes, huge American cars, and shops flowing with luxury Western goods, lives side by side with the puritan traditions resurrected by the 18th century crusading armies of the Najdi warrior Ibn Saud, in alliance with the religious reformer Abdel-Wahhab. Unlike Jeddah, where pilgrims from many countries have settled for centuries, Riyadh until comparatively recently was as isolated as Tibet. It stood as a long-lasting symbol of desert life, of generations of pitiless living conditions. Today, changes in Riyadh are so swift that the visitor returning after a few years' absence can scarcely recognise it.

The city's tall, elegant water tower, its most prominent modern landmark, stands over a group of clay forts, a preserved micro-cosm of what Riyadh looked like until the old city walls were demolished a few decades ago. Also preserved as an item of cultural heritage is the Masmak Fort, which Ibn Saud the Great stormed with 10 men in 1901, toppling the regime of the rival Rashidi clan. Masmak Fort stands off Thimairi Street, which leads into Dira (or Safa) Square—an open space, dominated by the Ministry of Justice, which serves both as a car park and Riyadh's execution ground. Left of Thimairi Street are the gold and silver souks, and the bedouin souk where the stalls are piled with jambias, dillis (Turkish coffee pots), houdajs and wooden well wheels.

The city's two main streets are Batha Street, which accommodates the big company offices, banks and the main souk, and Al-Wazir Street, Riyadh's main shopping thoroughfare. Here the daily symbol of Saudi Arabia's cultural schizophrenia is the *muttawas*, the bearded religious policemen in thobes, gutras and henna who march down the street at prayer times waving sticks to force the shops to close.

The poorer section of the community lives in the heart of Riyadh, while the better-off reside in quiet suburbs with supermarkets and criss-crossing streets that have no names. Malaaz, bordered by Siteen Street, is the best-known residential area. Unlike in Jeddah, there are few gardens. It is almost as though the builders had constructed the houses so quickly that they forgot urban man's yearning for the soil.

Riyadh's major drawback is its limited social amenities. Almost all facilities for Western-style entertainment exist only within the compounds of large foreign companies. However quickly Riyadh develops, the prohibitive restrictions of Wahhabism prevent the official establishment of cinemas or discotheques.

The city's attractions are its dry, healthy climate and grand, abstract scenery. Even in the month of August the heat is tolerable. A few hours drive from the city, along desert tracks, are the wadis, sharp-edged escarpments, and bedouin camps where Saudis indulge in horse and camel racing, falconry and prolific feasting. King Khaled has a camp a few miles from Riyadh. It is no different from any other bedouin camp, except for the presence of a radio lorry enabling the King and Crown Prince Fahd to keep in touch with the outside world.

Hotels

Inter-Continental, Shara Maazar. P.O.B. 3636. Tel: 34500. Telex: 20076. Considered to be one of the best hotels in Saudi Arabia. 197 rooms

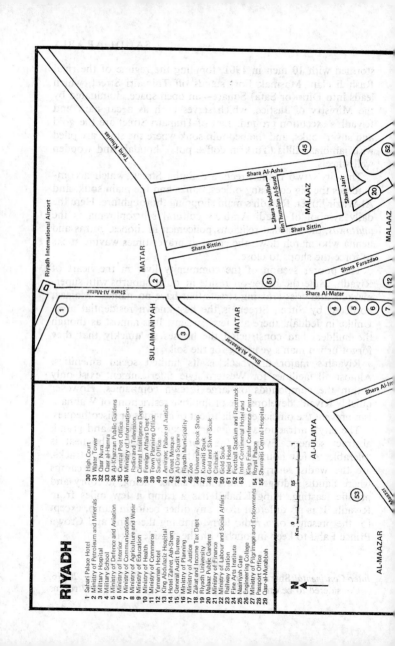

RIYADH

1 Sahari Palace Hotel
2 Ministry of Petroleum and Minerals
3 Military Hospital
4 Military School
5 Ministry of Defence and Aviation
6 Ministry of Interior
7 Ministry of Communications
8 Ministry of Agriculture and Water
9 Ministry of Education
10 Ministry of Health
11 Ministry of Commerce
12 Yamanah Hotel
13 King Abdulaziz Hospital
14 Hotel Zahret Ash-Sharq
15 General Audit Bureau
16 Ministry of Planning
17 Ministry of Justice
18 Zakat and Income Tax Dept
19 Riyadh University
20 Malaaz Public Gardens
21 Ministry of Finance
22 Ministry of Labour and Social Affairs
23 Railway Station
24 Fine Arts Institute
25 Nasiriyah Gate
26 Engineering College
27 Ministry of Pilgrimage and Endowments
28 Passport Office
29 Qasr-al-Murabbah
30 High Court
31 Water Tower
32 Shumra
33 Qasr al-Hamra
34 Al-Khazzan Public Gardens
35 Central Post Office
36 Ministry of Information:
   Radio and Television
37 Central Intelligence Dept
38 Foreign Affairs Dept
39 Town Planning Office
40 Saudi Office
41 Amirate; Palace of Justice
42 Great Mosque
43 Al Deira Square
44 Riyadh Municipality
45 Zoo
46 University Book Shop
47 Kuwaiti Souk
48 Gold and Silver Souk
49 Citibank
50 Gold Souk
51 Nejd Hotel
52 Football Stadium and Racetrack
53 Inter-Continental Hotel and
   King Faisal Conference Centre
54 Royal Palace
55 Shumaisi Central Hospital

Shara Al-Asha
Shara Abdallah BinThunaian Al-Saud
Shara Jarir
MALAAZ
Shara Sittin
Shara Sittin
MATAR
Shara Farazdao
Shara Al-Matar
MALAAZ
Tarig Khurar
Riyadh International Airport
Shara Al-Matar
SULAIMANIYAH
MATAR
Shara Al-Maazar
Shara Al-Im
AL-ULAIYA
AL-MAAZAR
Matar

Km.   0   05   1

N

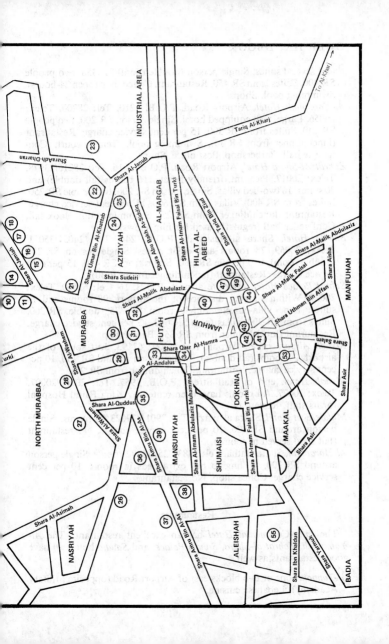

and several suites. Single person (double room) SR 350, two people SR 400. Suites from SR 450. Restaurant. Coffee shop (open 24-hours). Swimming pool. Shops.

Al-Yamamah Hotel, Airport Road. P.O.B. 1210. Tel: 28200. Telex: 20056. Large, well-equipped hotel. Single person SR 200, two people SR 240. Suites from SR 300. 15 per cent service charge. Restaurant (lunch/dinner from SR 30). Swimming pool. Tennis court. Conference hall. Barbershop. Post office. Shops.

Zahrat Al-Sharq Hotel, Airport Road. P.O.B. 3616. Tel: 28216/23978. Telex: 20017. Pleasant, friendly hotel. 116 rooms (all double) and 30 suites. 16 two-bed villas. Single person SR 200, two people SR 250. Suites from SR 400. Villas from SR 600. 15 per cent service charge. Restaurant (lunch/dinner from SR 25). Swimming pool. Bookstall. Conference hall (regularly used for film shows).

Saudia Hotel, Shara al-Nasiriyah. P.O.B. 244. Tel: 24051/35051 Telex: 20069. 78 rooms and eight suites. Single person SR 225 (double room), two people SR 280. Suites from SR 450. 15 per cent service charge. Restaurant (lunch/dinner from SR 30).

Sahari Palace Hotel, opposite airport. P.O.B. 16. Tel: 61500. Telex: 20027. Within walking distance of the airport. 98 rooms and 10 suites. Nine villa-chalets. Single room SR 225, double SR 260. Suites from SR 300, villas from SR 600. 15 per cent service charge. Restaurant (lunch/dinner from SR 35). Barbershop.

Riyadh Airport Hotel, Airport Road. Tel: 62193. Just south of the airport. 29 rooms (all double). Single person around SR 150. 10 per cent service charge. Restaurant (lunch/dinner from SR 25).

Riyadh Hotel, end of Rail Street. P.O.B. 1957. Tel: 20006/20007. Telex: 20077. All rooms have been rented by King Faisal Hospital for its staff. Restaurant.

Middle East Hotel, Shara al-Wazir. Tel: 29011/29023. 27 rooms. Single person around SR 100. 10 per cent service charge. No restaurant (but food served in rooms).

Al-Haramain, Shara Batha. Tel: 23831/25738. 72 rooms. Single person around SR 100. Willing to put extra beds in rooms. 10 per cent service charge. Coffee shop. No restaurant.

Restaurants

The *Inter-Continental Hotel* has an excellent restaurant. The *Al-Yamamah*, *Zahrat al-Sharq*, *Sahari Palace*, and *Saudia* hotels all have good restaurants as well.

Al-Tannour, one or two blocks east of Airport Road (opposite Military Academy). Lebanese cuisine.

Green Valley Restaurant, Airport Road (above Spinney's supermarket). International food. Single person around SR 30 (15 per cent service charge). Tea rooms.

Shangri-La, one block east of Airport Road. Tel: 62431. Chinese food.

Sindbad Restaurant, Shara al-Jamaa. Tel: 26557. Steak dishes.

Semiramis Restaurant, Shara al-Wazir. Tel: 23841. Lebanese specialities.

Airport Though relatively small, Riyadh's airport is one of the smartest in the Gulf. Neat, marble-floored terminal building. Refreshment bar, bank, and information desk.

Taxis Fix the fare with the driver beforehand. The official standard rate is SR 4. But short trips cost at least SR 7 and usually around SR 10. Drivers charge at least SR 15 for longer journeys.

Care hire firms *Sahary-Rent-a-Car*. Tel: 34500 (extension 5). Rates are much the same as those in Jeddah.

Travel agencies *Areen Travel*, Prince Mashaal Building, Batha Street. Tel: 28876/27685. *Saddick & Mohammed Attar*, Batha Street. Tel: 27690. *Saudi Travel and Tourist Agency*, Al-Sulaiman Building, Batha Street. Tel: 20251.

Airline offices *Saudia*, Batha Street (sales offices). Reservations—Tel: 23171/27332. Airport enquiries—Tel: 61400. *Air France*, c/o Areen Travel, Prince Mashaal Building, Batha Street. Tel: 28876. *British Airways*, Saddick & Mohammed Attar Co., Batha Street. Tel: 27690. *Gulf Air*, Saudi Travel and Tourist Agency. Tel: 22820. *Japan Air Lines*, Saudi Travel and Tourist Agency, Al-Sulaiman Building, Batha Street. P.O.B. 3519. Tel: 20251. *KLM*, Areen Travel Bureau, Airport Road, Al-Batha. Tel: 27685. *Lufthansa*, Al-Wazir Street. P.O.B. 2068. Tel: 24201. *Middle East Airlines*, Ghazi I. Shaker & Bros., Al-Toubaishi Building, Al-Batha Quarters. Tel: 25409.

Post Office The *Central Post Office* is on the corner of Shara al-Nasriyah and Shara Amru bin al-As. There are also several post collection boxes scattered round the city.

Telephone Telecommunications are reasonably good from Riyadh. International calls can be made without much delay. The local system is usually reliable and links with Jeddah and Dammam/Al-Khobar are good.

Useful phone nos. Emergency numbers for the whole of Saudi Arabia are listed in *General Information* (see Telecommunications). Other numbers: *Airport Information*—61400. *Trunk Call Controllers*—20094/2703.

Telex Most of the large hotels have telexes. Telexes can also be sent from the *Central Post Office* (see above).

Shops Two of the best supermarkets in Riyadh are *Spinney's* (Tel: 28493) and *Al-Mukhtar's*, which are adjacent to each other in the lower end of Airport Road.

Souks The city's main market is the Batha souk on Batha Street. Most stores sell imported products, but some have an interesting variety of locally-made leather goods. Nearby are a gold and silver, and a pottery souk, also some stores selling hubble-bubbles.

Social clubs All social clubs used by expatriates are linked to companies or embassies. Most welcome expatriate visitors as long as they are accompanied by a member.

Leisure/sport There are few leisure facilities but they are being expanded, particularly with spectator sports. The *Malaaz Stadium* in the east side of the city holds weekly horse and camel races during the cooler months usually on Monday afternoons, and a soccer match every Friday. Soccer is fast becoming Saudi Arabia's major sport and most international matches are played in the stadium.

Large Western companies, like the *British Aircraft Corporation* (*BAC*), have squash and tennis courts and swimming pools. Hotels with swimming pools usually allow non-residents to use them. One of the most popular outdoor activities is riding. There are at least two riding clubs in the city with fairly large stables.

For the more adventurous expatriates, desert trips are a favourite pastime. Camping and picnicking in the desert can be an exciting way to spend a weekend. But the desert can be very dangerous. It is always advisable to go with a party of at least two vehicles including someone who knows the desert well.

Riyadh has a good zoo which has a collection of gazelles and oryx which are rapidly becoming extinct in the desert. It is open on alternate days for men and women. Some hotels, like the *Zahret al-Sharq* and *Saudia*, put on film shows each night which are open to non-residents.

Bookshops The larger hotels have small bookstalls. But otherwise foreign books and magazines are difficult to buy.

Hospitals The *King Faisal Specialist Hospital*, one of the world's most well equipped hospitals, only treats referral cases. Emergency treatment can be obtained at the *National Hospital*, Siteen Street (Tel: 61211) or the *Obeid Hospital*, Farazdaq Street (Tel: 62695).

Pharmacies *Khayam Pharmacy*, Al-Wazir Street. Tel: 27250. *Al-Batafji*, Al-Wazir Street. Tel: 22043. *Tamer Pharmacy*, Al-Wazir

Street. Tel: 24646. Both the *National* and *Obeid* hospitals (see above) have pharmacies.

Banks Commercial banks: *Banque du Caire.* Tel: 28003/2003. *Riyadh Bank.* Tel: 24011/24511/25688. *Citibank.* P.O.B. 833. Tel: 24000. Telex: 20020. *Arab Bank.* Tel: 2411/24855. *National Commercial Bank.* Tel: 24044/25081. *Al-Jazira Bank,* Kazzan Street.

Other banks (financial institutions): *Saudi Arabian Agricultural Bank,* Omar bin al-Khattab Street. Tel: 23934/23911. *Saudi Credit Bank.* Tel: 29625. *The General Investment Fund,* Airport Road. Tel: 27000. *Real Estate Development Fund,* Airport Road. Tel: 33500. *Saudi Industrial Development Fund,* Al-Washam Street. P.O.B. 4143. Tel: 33703/33710/33830. Telex: 20065. *Saudi Development Fund.* P.O.B. 5711. Tel: 38268/38218.

Ministries/Government departments Ministries: *Commerce,* Airport Road. Tel: 23400. Telex: 20057. *Communications,* Airport Road. Telex: 20020. *Defence,* Airport Road. Telex: 20071. *Finance,* Airport Road. Telex: 20021. *Industry and Electricity,* Airport Road. *Information,* Shara Amru bin al-As. Telex: 20040. *Interior,* Airport Road. Telex: 20063. *Labour and Social Affairs,* Omar Ibn al-Khattab Road. Tel: 27100. Telex 20043. *Petroleum and Mineral Resources,* Airport Road. Tel: 61133. *Planning,* Shara al-Jamiah. Telex: 20075.

Government departments: *Directorate General of Zakat and Income Tax,* University Street. Tel. 33892. *Customs Department Headquarters,* Al-Washem Street. Tel: 23655. Also Airport Road. Tel: 61997. *Industrial Studies and Development Centre (ISDIC),* Airport Road. P.O.B. 1267. Tel: 20900. *Passport and Nationality Directorate,* Al-Washem Street. Tel. 20077. *Petromin,* Airport Road. Tel: 61133. Telex: 20058. *Saudi Government Railroad Organisation,* Omar Ibn al-Khattab Street. Tel: 24660.

Newspapers/periodicals

Dailies: *Al-Jazirah,* Municipality Building, Shara al-Nasiriyah. P.O.B. 354. Arabic. 15,000 circulation. *Al-Riyadh,* Yamamah Press Organisation, Dughaither Building. P.O.B. 851. Arabic. 10,000 circ.

Periodicals: *Al-Yamamah,* Yamamah Press Organisation, Dughaither Building. P.O.B. 851. Arabic weekly magazine. 1,000 circ. *Al-Dawa.* Arabic weekly. *Al-Mujtama,* Municipality Building, Shara, Al-Nasiriyah. P.O.B. 354.

Media Saudi Arabia's two English language dailies, *Arab News* and *Saudi Gazette* which are published in Jeddah, both circulate in Riyadh. The local radio and TV has programmes and news bulletins in English.

Useful addresses *Chamber of Commerce & Industry,* Khazan Street. P.O.B. 596. Tel: 22600/22700.

DHAHRAN/DAMMAM/AL-KHOBAR These three towns in the Eastern Province make up a triangular area which owes its vital importance almost entirely to the oil industry. There was hardly a building at Dhahran 40 years ago when the Arabian American Oil Company (Aramco) decided to set up its compound there soon after it discovered oil nearby. Dammam was a small fishing village and Al-Khobar a scattering of mud huts with a dhow harbour. Oil wealth has transformed Dammam and Al-Khobar into commercial and industrial centres and Dhahran into the operational capital of the country's immense oil industry. The area was the first to absorb an influx of Western expatriates and as a result it is more Westernised than any other in Saudi Arabia. Western influences are today the norm in this part of the Eastern Province. The *muttawas* (religious police) are rarely seen on the streets and many Arab women go round unveiled.

It is almost a misnomer to call **Dhahran** a town. It is more a collection of modern bungalows, laid out in a neat pattern more perfect than any American suburb. Though the great majority of Aramco's workers are Saudi, Dhahran has all the features of American life. There are soda-fountain bars, supermarkets and fashionable social and sporting clubs. But all these facilities are reserved generally for Aramco employees. Dhahran still remains very much a company compound. But it does also have the area's international airport and the University of Petroleum and Minerals, both of which are among the finest examples of modern architecture in the Gulf.

When the rains pour down between November and February, large pools of water form on the streets of **Al-Khobar.** People walk about in wellingtons, which is a strange sight in a desert country. Like Dammam, Al-Khobar was built so quickly and with such lack of planning that the need for proper drainage was forgotten. The romance of the small dhow port has disappeared, to be replaced by a mass of box houses and rows of little shops. It has become nonetheless a busy town of around 60,000 people acting as the commercial centre of the area. Its shops are better

Key to Dammam map on page 463. 1. Palace; 2. Pump Station; 3. Material Stores; 4. Covered Bazaar; 5. City Park; 6. Meat, Fish, Vegetables; 7. Suq al-Hareem; 8. Taxi, Bus Station; 9. Railway Station; 10. Post Office; 11. RR Radio; 12. Ministry of Education; 13. Ministry of Labour; 14. Taxi Stand; 15. Traffic Office.

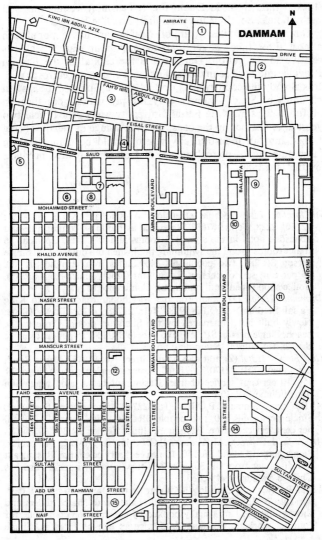

stocked than those in Dammam. It has more restaurants and better hotels. South of the town are some fine beaches.

Dammam, 12 miles north of Al-Khobar, has a population almost three times larger than its neighbour. But it lacks its relative sophistication. Dammam is the capital of the Eastern Province and has become one of its main industrial centres as well. It is already the country's major port on the Gulf and the eastern terminus of Saudi Arabia's only railway which goes through Hofuf to Riyadh. King Faisal University was opened there two years ago. Further up the coast the little village of **Jubail** is being turned into an industrial city which should be manufacturing large amounts of petrochemicals and other oil-related products by the late 1980s.

Hotels

Al-Gosaibi, Talal Avenue extension, Al-Khobar. P.O.B. 51. Tel: 42160/42228. Telex: 67008. Regarded as the most comfortable and luxurious hotel in the area. 171 rooms and 18 suites. Opens up 36 chalet rooms round the swimming pool when the hotel is full. Single person SR 280, two people SR 340. Suites from around SR 400. 15 per cent service charge. Restaurant (lunch/dinner from SR 35). Coffee shop (open until midnight). Conference room.

Dammam Hotel, Dammam (on the Al-Khobar road, close to King Faisal Stadium). P.O.B. 1928. Tel: 21738/21926. Telex: 60108. Newly built hotel, managed by the Sheraton group. Close to the beach. Single person SR 250, two people SR 300. 15 per cent service charge. Restaurant. Swimming pool.

Gulf Flower Hotel (Zahrat al-Khalij), Street No. 9, Al-Khobar Road, Dammam. Tel: 22170/23691. 63 rooms. Single person around SR 150. 10 per cent service charge. Restaurant has a good reputation (lunch/dinner SR 20).

Al-Dossary, Dammam. P.O.B. 5. Tel: 22740. 45 rooms and five suites. Single person SR 150, two people SR 210. Suites from SR 250. 10 per cent service charge. Restaurant (lunch/dinner SR 30).

Al-Khaja, 1st Street, Al-Khobar. P.O.B. 45. Tel: 43122. 142 rooms. Single person around SR 150. 10 per cent service charge. Restaurant (lunch/dinner from SR 30). Coffee shop (open 24 hours). Also has Chinese restaurant attached.

Motel Rezayat, just outside Al-Khobar on the Dammam road. P.O.B. 90. Tel: 702156. Telex: 67006. 260 chalets with shared toilets and shower units. All are usually booked by construction companies for contract workers. But sometimes visitors can be fitted in. Single person around SR 200 (meals included). Self-service restaurant (open only at fixed times). Swimming pool.

Al-Manara Hotel, Dammam. P.O.B. 6. Tel: 24066. 30 rooms. Single person around SR 150. 10 per cent service charge. Restaurant (lunch/dinner from SR 25).

Al-Haramain, Shara al-Malik, Dammam. Tel: 26421/26423. 45 rooms. Single person from around SR 120. No service charge. Roof restaurant (lunch/dinner from SR 20). Has two nearby smaller and cheaper hotels under the same management.

Al-Jabr Hotel, Shara Malik Khalid, Al-Khobar. Tel: 41348/41349. 30 rooms. Single person around SR 120.

Several new hotels are being built in the area, including the *International Airport Hotel*, close to Dhahran Airport, and an *Inter-Continental*.

Restaurants

The *Al-Gosaibi*, *Dammam* and *Gulf Flower* hotels have restaurants with good reputations. The *Al-Gosaibi* serves both Middle Eastern and European dishes. The *Al-Khaja Hotel*, Al-Khobar, has a Chinese restaurant (*Shangri-La*).

Maxim's, Abdul Aziz Boulevard, Al-Khobar. Tel: 42311. High class food. Mainly French cuisine. Set lunches for SR 25–35.

Yildizlar, Prince Khalid Street, Al-Khobar. Tel: 44637. International cuisine. Dinner for single person around SR 20. The *Al-Khobar Restaurant* on the floor below serves Arab food.

Arirang, Al-Ghatani Building, Dhahran Road, Al-Khobar. Korean/Chinese/Japanese dishes.

Airport Dhahran international airport has a remarkable looking terminal which must be one of the more impressive examples of modern architecture in the Gulf. Its tall pointed arches give it an authentic Arab appearance. But the excellence of the design is not quite matched by the facilities, which are limited. Dining room with adjacent refreshment bar, post office, bank, public telephones and small duty-free shop in departure lounge.

Taxis Taxis can be hailed but most tend to run between taxi stations. The Al-Khobar station is by the fountain on the waterfront and in Dammam there are stations in Mohammad Street and 19th Street. For trips between the two towns, a single or private taxi costs between SR 15–20. A shared taxi costs SR 2. Between Al-Khobar and Dhahran the charge is usually SR 5 for a single taxi and between Dhahran and

Dammam SR 10–15. Trips within towns generally cost around SR 5 for a single taxi. Drivers will try to overcharge visitors, particularly for trips between the two main towns, so fix the fare beforehand.

Car hire firms *Mahrus Rent-a-Car*, Al-Khobar. Tel: 44390/44642. *Codeco*, Al-Khobar. Tel: 42120. Rates will tend to be slightly higher than those in Riyadh and Jeddah.

Travel agencies *Kanoo Travel*, Prince Khalid Street, Al-Khobar. *Orient Travel & Tours*, Prince Khalid Street, Al-Khobar. *Saudi Travel & Tourist Agency*, Prince Khalid Street, Al-Khobar. Tel: 5137.

Airlines Many airline bookings and reservations are handled by the *International Travel Agency*, Dhahran Airport. Bookings—tel: 42000/ 41699/41697. Enquiries—5284/41931. Some airlines use other travel agencies to handle their sales.
  Saudia, Al-Khobar—tel: 42000/42103. Dammam—tel: 2333. *Gulf Air*—tel: 44342/41930/41931. *Air France*—tel: 3284. *PIA*—tel: 24432/ 34514. *Swissair*—tel: 2303. *KLM*—tel: 4462/2655/2656. *TMA*—tel: 3146. *Pan Am*—tel: 5289/5290. *MEA*—tel: 2365. *Lufthansa*—tel: 4274/4273. *Syrian Airlines*—tel: 5137. *Kuwait Airways*—tel: 42102. *Olympic Airways:*—tel: 44416.

Shipping agencies *United Shipping & Marine Services*, Dammam. P.O.B. 242. Tel: 21142/21311. Telex: 60029. *Middle East Shipping Agencies*, Dammam. P.O.B. 142. Tel: 26582/26644. Telex: 60052. *Yousuf Bin Ahmad Kanoo*, Seaport Road, Dammam. P.O.B. 37. Tel: 23011. Telex: 60011. *Ahmad Hamad Al-Gosaibi*, Al-Khobar. P.O.B. 106. Tel: 42666/42865/42867.

Post Office In Dammam the main post office is in 19th Street and in Al-Khobar in King Faisal Street.

Telephone International calls usually connected without much trouble. Difficult calls will be handled more quickly if made from the main Dammam post office which has the central exchange.

Useful phone nos. Emergency numbers for the whole of Saudi Arabia are listed in *General Information* (see Telecommunications). Other numbers: *Police* (Dammam)—22440. *Police* (Al-Khobar)—42290. *Telephone maintenance*—21206. *Customs*—3176/3119.

Telex Most hotels have telex facilities. Telexes can usually also be sent from the main post offices in Al-Khobar and Dammam.

Shops Al-Khobar has better shops than Dammam. One of the biggest stores in the area is the *Dhahran Shopping Centre*, Dhahran (on the Al-Khobar road). Some shops in the old back streets of Dammam sell traditional craftwork and other souvenirs.

Souks The area's main souks are in Dammam. Some good bargains can be found in the gold souk off Mohammad Street.

Leisure sport Aramco provides extensive recreational facilities for its employees. Visitors can sometimes use them if accompanied by an Aramco worker. Other local companies have tennis courts, swimming pools and private beaches, which visitors known to employees can also use.

There are many good beaches south of Al-Khobar which are popular for swimming, fishing, water skiing and sailing. A private beach club at Al-Zaziah has cabanas, a restaurant and other facilities. Some hotels run swimming pool clubs, and put on regular film shows which are open to non-residents.

Bookshops Al-Khobar has a number of shops selling foreign books, magazines and newspapers. There are two in Prince Mohammad Street—*Modern Adabuya Bookshop* and *International Bookshop*.

Hospitals *Central Hospital*—tel: 22640. *Al-Salama Hospital*, Al-Khobar—tel: 41011. *Al-Sharq Hospital*—tel: 43355.

Pharmacies *Al-Batorji National Pharmacy*, Al-Khobar. Tel: 41607. *Al-Safa*, Al-Khobar. Tel: 41615.

Banks *United Bank*, Dammam. P.O.B. 619. Tel: 24705/24540. Telex 60014. *Banque du Caire*, Anur Saud Street, Al-Khobar. Tel: 41560. *British Bank of the Middle East*, branches both in Dammam and Al-Khobar. Tel: 42868. *Riyadh Bank*, Al-Khobar. Tel: 41244. *National Commercial Bank*, Prince Khalid Street, Al-Khobar. Tel: 41446. *Banque de L'Indochine et de Suez*, Prince Nasir and 1st Street, Al-Khobar. *Algemene Bank Nederland*, Prince Nasir Street, Al-Khobar. Tel: 42544. *Arab Bank*, Al-Khobar. Tel: 43488. Also branch in Dammam.

Ministries/Government departments *Ministry of Commerce*, Dammam Branch. Tel: 21451. *Directorate General of Zakat and Income Tax*, Dammam Branch. Main Road. Tel: 22979. *Customs Department*, Dammam Branch, King Abdul Aziz Port. Tel: 23373. *Passport and Nationality Directorate*, Dammam Branch, Main Road. Tel: 22830. *Saudi Government Railroad Organisation*, Dammam Branch, Railroad Station. Tel: 21000.

Newspapers/periodicals *Al-Khalij al-Arabi*, Al-Khobar, Arabic weekly newspaper. *Akhbar al-Dhahran*, Dhahran. Arabic weekly. *Arabian Sun*, Dhahran. English weekly published by Aramco. *Al-Yawm*, Damman. P.O.B. 565. Arabic periodical.

467

Media Aramco has its own all-English TV and radio station. The radio station broadcasts throughout the day and evening and the TV usually transmits continuous programmes between 3–10 p.m.

Useful address   *Chamber of Commerce & Industry*, Dammam. P.O.B. 719. Tel: 21134.

ABHA/KHAMIS MUSHAYT

Abha, 60 miles from the Red Sea, is the capital of Asir Province. It has a pleasant temperate climate and the Governor of the Province, Prince Khaled, aims to make it a holiday resort for expatriates working in Saudi Arabia. A tourist village is planned and at least one luxury hotel is being built to supplement the town's two existing hotels. Abha lies on a plain 7,000 feet above sea level, surrounded like Rome by seven hills. Its Turkish fort looks down on green valleys where farmers have cultivated elaborate terraced plots. Until the 1920s this part of Asir Province was part of the Yemen and the town still shows Yemeni characteristics today. The town's water supply comes from a nearby dam which is one of the largest in the country.

Khamis Mushayt, 17 miles from Abha, is a small town which has a large population of expatriate workers. Many are employees for the British Aircraft Corporation which is doing work for the Saudi Arabian air force. The town's social and entertainment facilities are restricted to company compounds. It provides a good base for trips into the surrounding mountains where villagers wear bright clothes and tilted straw hats and the women are unveiled. The mountain people are very hospitable, offering visitors tea and coffee and greeting them with a kiss on the hands. One of the more remarkable villages is Habal which is perched on a knoll jutting out of a cliff face. The villagers pull themselves up and down with long ropes to reach the plain above.

Hotels

Aseer Hotel, Shara Taif. Tel: 6126. 16 rooms. Single person around SR 100. 15 per cent service charge. Restaurant (lunch/dinner around SR 20).

Abha Hotel, Shara al-Am. Tel: 6234. 20 rooms. Single person SR 50–70. 10 per cent service charge. Restaurant.

New Abha Hotel, Khamis Mushayt Road. Still under construction. 180 rooms. Restaurant. Swimming pool.

Airport   The area has been served by an airport at Khamis Mushayt. But a new airport is opening at Hillah, about half way between the two towns.

Souks   The area's souks have weekly "market days". Abha's is on Tuesday and Wednesday and Khamis Mushayt's on Thursday. On these days vendors from the surrounding mountains will descend on the towns, marking out their sales plots with handwoven blankets. The women from a mixture of tribes wear a variety of colourful, stylish clothing and the souks become transformed for the day. A wide selection of local craftwork is on sale. Huge gourds grown on vines have been hollowed out to be sold as milk jugs. Dresses are made on the spot, selling for SR 120 each. Large Yemeni-style silver necklaces can be bought for as little as SR 50.

GENERAL INFORMATION

How to get there   BY AIR (outside Gulf): Saudi Arabia has 20 airports of which Jeddah, Riyadh and Dhahran are the major ones. Of these **Jeddah** is the busiest. It has good direct connections with Europe, the Indian sub-continent and other Middle East centres outside the Gulf. Daily flights leave London for Jeddah, sometimes more than twice a day. There are five or six flights a week from Athens, Frankfurt and Paris and frequent connections from Amsterdam, Geneva, Rome and Zurich. There are daily flights from Beirut, Cairo (up to four a day), Khartoum, Sanaa (about three a day) and Taiz. Several flights a week also go to Jeddah from Aden, Amman, Casablanca, Damascus and Tripoli. A weekly service also connects the city with Addis Ababa, Algiers, Asmara, Istanbul, Larnaca and Port Sudan. Daily flights leave from Karachi and there are also regular connections from Bombay, Hong Kong, Jakarta, Seoul and Singapore.

   Dhahran also has daily flights from London and two to three flights a week from Amsterdam, Athens, Frankfurt, Paris, Brussels and Rome. There are daily flights from Beirut and several flights a week from Amman, Cairo, Damascus, Sanaa and Taiz. There is a daily service from Karachi and weekly flights from Bombay, Colombo and Delhi. **Riyadh** has several weekly flights from London and flights at least once a week from Geneva, Paris and Rome. There is a regular service from Amman, Cairo, Damascus, Sanaa and Aden, and about five flights a week from Karachi.

   BY AIR (inter-Gulf): There are daily flights between **Jeddah** and Bahrain and several flights a week from Dubai and Kuwait. There are also weekly connections from Abu Dhabi, Baghdad, Muscat and Tehran. At least four flights a day go to Bahrain from **Dhahran,** which is also served by several flights a week from Abu Dhabi, Dubai, Doha, Kuwait and Shiraz. There are also weekly flights from Baghdad, Muscat and Sharjah. **Riyadh** has virtually a daily service from Bahrain and regular connections from Kuwait, Dubai and Shiraz. There are also weekly flights from Abu Dhabi, Baghdad, and Doha.

BY AIR (domestic): Saudi Arabia has a reasonably efficient domestic air network operated by *Saudia*, the national airline. Besides Jeddah, Riyadh and Dhahran, there are airports at Turaif, Gurayat, Jouf, Badana, Rafha, Qaisumah, Gassim, Hail, Tabuk, Wedjh, Medina, Taif, Bisha, Abha, Gizan, Najran and Sharourah. The busiest route is between Jeddah, Riyadh and Dhahran. Up to a dozen flights a day connect Jeddah with Riyadh and Riyadh with Dhahran. There are usually three to four flights a day each way between Jeddah and Dhahran. On Jeddah–Riyadh flights passengers used to have to queue for tickets at a Saudia sales office, then queue again for a boarding pass at the airport the day before the flights. But since mid-1977 Saudi has counted the ticket as a boarding pass and allocated seats on a first-come first-served basis just before the flights leave. So passengers are advised to turn up at the airport well before their flight time to assure themselves of a seat. The same system is being introduced on the Riyadh–Dhahran route. Most of the country's other airports are connected by daily flights with Jeddah, Riyadh and Dhahran.

BY RAIL: Saudi Arabia has the only passenger railway line among Gulf Arab states outside Iraq. It runs between Riyadh and Dammam. There are two trains going each way every day, usually one in the morning and the other in the afternoon. During the 7–8 hour trip the train goes over the Dahna sands. A first class ticket costs SR 40 and a second class SR 30.

Visas Saudi Arabia refuses admission and transit to holders of Israeli passports, holders of passports valid for Israel and containing a visa (either valid or expired) or any indication that the passenger has been in Israel, and Jewish passengers. Passports are required by all except Muslim pilgrims holding pilgrim passes, tickets and other documents for their onward or return journey and entering the country via Jeddah or Dhahran. Visas are necessary for all except nationals of Saudi Arabia, Bahrain, Kuwait, Oman, Qatar or United Arab Emirates and passengers holding a letter of confirmation from Aramco. Transit visas are not required by passengers proceeding to a third country and having a confirmed ticket to a third country. They should leave by the next connecting flight and are not allowed to leave the airport.

Language The official language is Arabic. English is widely spoken among business circles.

Hours of business Banks: 08.30–12.00 and 17.00–19.00 Saturday to Wednesday, and 08.30–11.30 Thursday.

Government departments: 07.30–2.30 Saturday to Wednesday. Thursday and Friday are official holidays.

Companies and shops: There are no standard hours, only approximate. Jeddah, 09.00–13.30 and 16.30–20.00 (Ramadan—20.00–01.00). Riyadh, 08.30–12.00 and 16.30–19.30 (Ramadan—19.30–22.30). Eastern Province, 07.30–12.00 and 14.30–17.00 (Ramadan—19.00–23.00). Dhahran (Aramco), 07.00–11.30 and 13.00 –16.30 (closed Thursdays and Fridays).

Public holidays The weekly holiday is Friday, although many retail shops remain open on that day. The following public holidays are observed when all government and business offices are closed.

				1977/78
Id al-Adha (5 days)	...	...	...	from 22 November
Id al-Fitr (end of				
Ramadan, 6–8 days) ...	...	...	...	from 3 September 1978

The dates of the Muslim feasts are only approximate as they depend upon the physical sightings of the moon; they fall 10 to 12 days earlier in each Christian year. It is advisable to avoid both these holidays by several days before and after. Most offices close two days before Id al-Fitr actually begins.

Calendar Saudi Arabia follows the Islamic or Hijra calendar which dates from the Prophet Mohammed's flight from Mecca to Medina in A.D. 622. The lunar-based Hijra calendar is divided into a 12-month, 354-day year, which advances 11 days each year in comparison with the Gregorian calendar. The Hijra year 1398 begins on 11 December 1977 and ends on 29 November 1978.

Time GMT + 3.

Religion No religious practices other than Muslim ones are allowed.

Electric current The country is aiming towards a standardised 60 cycles, 220–127 volts throughout.

Health International certificates against smallpox are required by all visitors. Cholera immunisation is necessary if arriving within five days after leaving or transiting countries any parts of which are infected. Passengers arriving from an infected area are not allowed to bring in any cooked or raw foodstuff. Cholera vaccination is required by all visitors arriving from any countries parts of which are infected. A certificate of vaccination must show a single dose has been administered not less than one week and not more than six months prior to arrival in Saudi Arabia. A valid certificate of yellow fever immunisation is required if arriving within six days after leaving or transiting infected or endemic areas. Persons without valid smallpox, cholera or yellow fever certificates—if required—will be vaccinated on arrival. But if they come from an infected area they are subject to quarantine. Risks of malaria exist all year except in Al-Hasa, Arar, Jauf, Quraiya (Gurayyat), Riyadh, Tabuk, Taif and urban areas of Jeddah, Mecca, Medina and Qatif. Visitors going to risk areas should take preventive measures.

Water The standard of drinking water varies throughout the country. In many places it is still advisable not to drink from the tap. Even in big cities where the water comes from desalination plants, the poor distribution system still makes the water unsafe.

Post Air mail letters take four to six days to reach Europe and slightly longer to North America. Surface mail can be very slow with parcels taking up to six months to arrive. The post service tends to be unreliable and delays even with air mail are frequent.

Telecommunications Direct telephone links have now been established between Jeddah, Riyadh and the Dammam/Al-Khobar area. The country's telephone network now covers most major towns. and the system is now being extended to remoter areas. From the three main centres international communications are good.

The same service and emergency numbers are used throughout the country. *Trunk calls* 90. *International calls* 91. *Trunk complaints* 92. *Traffic accidents* 93. *Telephone faults* 94. *Telephone information* 95. *Ambulance* 97. *Fire brigade* 98. *Police* 99. Long distance code numbers: *Riyadh* 011. *Jeddah* 021. *Dammam/Al-Khobar* 031.

Currency The unit of currency is the Saudi Riyal (SR). The SR is sub-divided into 100 halalah. The following denominations are in circulations:

Notes: 1, 5, 10, 50 and 100 SR
Coins: 5, 10, 25, and 50 halalah.

The SR is also still sub-divided into 20 quirsh and there are 1, 2, and 4 quirsh coins in circulation. These are likely to be withdrawn.

Currency regulations There are no restrictions on the import or export of currency.

472

Customs regulations   Visitors are allowed to bring in 600 cigarettes or 100 cigars or 500 grammes of tobacco, and a "reasonable" amount of perfume. The import of alcohol is strictly prohibited and visitors are strongly advised not to attempt to bring any in because penalties are heavy. The import of pig meat and its by-products is also forbidden. Pornographic material of any kind is also completely barred.

Alcohol   The Saudi Government prohibits the drinking of alcohol. Visitors are advised to be very careful about this ban because offenders are liable to extremely severe penalties.

Useful advice   During the cooler months, medium to lightweight suits are recommended. In Riyadh where the temperature can sometimes drop to freezing point during winter nights an overcoat is a useful precaution. During the spring and summer lightweight clothes should be worn, and at most times an open-necked shirt will cause no offence. But jackets are usually worn on formal occasions and visitors calling on government officials should wear a suit and tie.

Saudi Arabia is a harsh place for women. They are expected to dress with extreme modesty. Shapeless ankle-length skirts with long sleeves are safest. Some expatriate women even wear the veil in public just to avoid trouble.

The Saudis are devout Muslims, praying five times a day when the muezzin's call comes over the loudspeakers. Praying is a time of quiet and privacy which foreigners are expected to respect.

Religious occasions tend to disrupt business life. The annual *Haj* (pilgrimage) and the fortnight either side of it in October/November can be a difficult time for visits. Airline seats tend to be fully booked and hotels in Jeddah will have few vacancies. Another period to avoid is the final 10 days of the fasting month of Ramadan and the 10-day period following it, when many businessmen and government officials take a holiday. Business activity tends to slow down during Ramadan with businessmen only being available for a short time in the day around noon and working for four to five hours in the evening.

Further reading   *Saudi Arabia*. Chase World Information Series. New York. 1976. *Saudi Arabia: Business Opportunities*. Metra Consulting Group, London. 1975.
At the Drop of a Veil, by Marianne Alireza. Boston. 1971. *Saudi Arabia*, by H. St John Philby. Arno Press, New York, 1972. *Saudi Arabia in the Nineteenth Century*, by Richard Winder. St Martin's Press. 1965. *Travels in Arabia Deserta*, by Charles Doughty. Jonathan Cape. 1964 *The Arab of the Desert: A Glimpse into Badawin Life in Kuwait and Saudi Arabia*, by Harold Dickson. Allen and Unwin. 1959. *Narrative of a Year's Journey through Central and Eastern Arabia (1862–1863)*, by

William Palgrave. Gregg International Publishers, England. 1969.
Arabian Sands, by Wilfrid Thesiger. Longmans. 1964.

Government

Head of State	King Khaled Ibn-Abdel-Aziz
Prime Minister	King Khaled Ibn-Abdel-Aziz
First Deputy Premier ...	Prince Fahd Ibn-Abdel-Aziz
Second Deputy Premier and Commander of the National Guard	Prince Abdullah Ibn-Abdel-Aziz
Defence & Aviation	Prince Sultan Ibn-Abdel-Aziz
Finance & Economy	Mohammad Ali Aba al-Khail
Petroleum & Minerals ...	Ahmad Zaki Yamani
Foreign Affairs	Prince Saud al-Faisal
Interior	Prince Nayef Ibn-Abdel-Aziz
Labour & Social Affairs ...	Ibrahim Ibn-Abdullah al-Anqari
Information	Mohammad Abdou Yamani
Industry & Electricity ...	Ghazi Abdel-Rahman al-Qusaibi
Commerce	Sulaiman Abdel-Aziz al-Salim
Public Works & Housing ...	Prince Moutib Ibn-Abdel-Aziz
Municipal & Rural Affairs ...	Prince Majid Ibn-Abdel-Aziz
Higher Education	Hasan Bin-Abdullah al-Shaikh
Justice	Ibrahim Ibn-Mohammad Ibn-Ibrahim al-Shaikh
Communications	Hussain Ibrahim al-Mansouri
Education	Abdel-Aziz al-Abdullah al-Khuwaiter
Planning	Hisham Nazer
Pilgrimage Affairs & Waqfs	Abdel-Wahhab Ahmad Abdel-Wasi
Agriculture & Water ...	Abdel-Rahman Ibn-Abdel-Aziz Ibn-Hasan Shaikh
Health	Hussain Abdel-Razzaq al-Jazari
Posts, Telegraphs & Telecommunications	Alawi Darwish Kayyal
Ministers of State	Mohammad Ibrahim Masud
	Abdullah Mohammad al-Omran
	Mohammad Abdel-Latif al-Milhim

UNITED ARAB EMIRATES

THE PRESIDENT OF THE UNITED ARAB EMIRATES

THE PRESIDENT OF THE UNITED ARAB EMIRATES

Shaikh Zayed bin Sultan al-Nahyan

Shaikh Zayed became President of the United Arab Emirates with its formation on 2 December 1971. He had been President of the earlier Federation of Arab Emirates from 1969. Shaikh Zayed was born in 1918, the grandson of Shaikh Zayed bin Khalifa—also known as Zayed the Great—who ruled Abu Dhabi from 1855 to 1909 and is the fourth son of Shaikh Sultan, who ruled from 1922 to 1926. Shaikh Zayed himself was acclaimed Ruler of Abu Dhabi in August 1966 following the abdication of his brother Shaikh Shakbut who had ruled from 1928. Shaikh Zayed is the leader of the Al Bu Falah branch of the Beni Yas tribe which has ruled in Abu Dhabi for over two centuries. Shaikh Zayed was Governor of the Eastern Province of Abu Dhabi from 1946 until his accession to the Shaikhdom.

United Arab Emirates

Area   32,280 square miles
Population   652,936 (1976 official figure)
Individual Emirates   Abu Dhabi 235,662; Dubai 206,861; Sharjah 88,188; Ras al-Khaimah 57,282; Fujairah 26,498; Ajman 21,566; Umm al-Qaiwain 16,879
Gross National Product $6,870 million (1975 estimate)
GNP per caput $10,480

GEOGRAPHY

The United Arab Emirates, approximately 32,280 square miles in area, stretches along the southern shore of the Gulf from the base of the Qatar Peninsula in the west to Oman and the Musandam Peninsula in the east. It lies approximately between latitude 22° 50′ and 26° north and 51° and 56° 25′ east.

Six of the emirates are coastal settlements on the Gulf. Abu Dhabi is by far the largest with 26,000 square miles of territory, though most of this is barren desert. The others have inland enclaves surrounded by one or more of the other emirates. Fujairah, the seventh emirate, is on the Batinah coast of the Gulf of Oman.

The emirates have 400 miles of coast line, 60 miles of which is on the Gulf of Oman. The Gulf coast consists mainly of *sabkha* or salt-marshes which in the summer become a white, flat expanse sometimes used by cars as an alternative to the roads. But

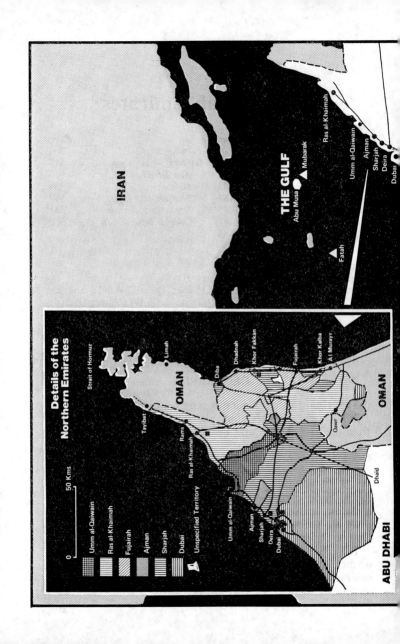

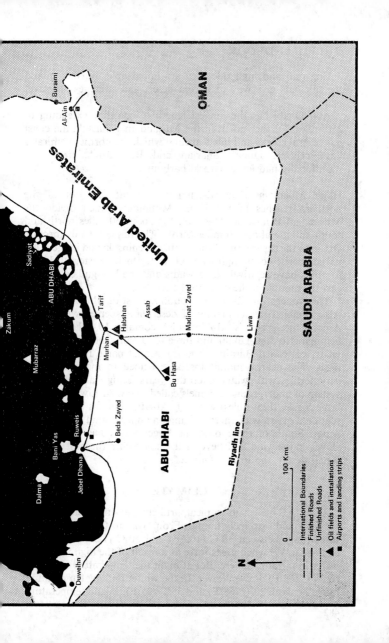

OMAN

United Arab Emirates

Buraimi

Al-Ain

SAUDI ARABIA

Zakum

Sadiyat

ABU DHABI

Tarif

Mubarraz

Habshan

Assab

Murban

Madinat Zayed

Dalma

Bani Yas

Bu Hasa

Jebel Dhana

Ruweis

Beda Zayed

Liwa

ABU DHABI

Duweihn

Riyadh line

0   100 Kms

——— International Boundaries
——— Finished Roads
········· Unfinished Roads
▲ Oil fields and installations
■ Airports and landing strips

N

during rain and high tide they are impassable. Further inland the salt flats give way to barren desert and stretches of gravel plain.

Abu Dhabi has the longest length of coastline extending to 250 miles. Further north in the Musandam Peninsula the coast has several creeks and inlets around which the northern emirates have centres. Dubai, Sharjah and Ras al-Khaimah have traditionally had large natural harbours.

Hajar Mountains Ras al-Khaimah lies at the foot of the northern reaches of the Hajar Mountains which divide the Musandam Peninsula. They run for about 50 miles north and south and are about 20 miles across. The range extends through Oman to the eastern tip of the Arabian Peninsula and in the UAE its peaks rise to as high as 8,000 feet. On its western side the foothills have relatively long wadis and shallow gullies. On the east the mountains lie close to the sea.

The western interior of the country, most of which comprises Abu Dhabi, consists mainly of desert interspersed with oases. Among the largest is Al-Ain which contains 10 villages, seven belonging to Abu Dhabi and three to Oman. One of the Omani villages is called Buraimi—the traditional name for the whole oasis. The nearby mountains have helped to make the oasis very fertile, with water over the years being harnessed by a system of underground channels called *falajs*. Al-Liwa is another large oasis, 125 miles west of Al-Ain, but its villages are scattered over a wider area, relying on underground reservoirs of water. South of these oases lie huge sand dunes which shift slowly in the wind and beyond them stretches the vast Rub al-Khali desert, the Empty Quarter.

CLIMATE

The UAE has a sub-tropical, arid climate. In the summer it is very hot and extremely humid. From May to October temperatures range between 38°C (100°F) and 50°C (122°F). Humidity can rise to 97° when mists form as a result of the high volume of water in the atmosphere. But at night the temperature may drop to 20°C (68°F) or even lower. In the winter midday temperatures range between 20°C (68°F) and 35°C (95°F). Inland temperatures tend to be higher during the day in the summer but lower during the night and humidity is generally lower.

The north *shamal* wind cools the atmosphere in the summer. But it is frequently laden with dust and sand and sometimes the air becomes so hazy that the sun is reduced to a pale disc. A south-easterly wind between May and October also helps to reduce the harsh heat. Rainfall is infrequent and irregular throughout most of the country. Rain comes mainly in the winter and rarely exceeds five inches a year in most places and may be as low as one inch or less. But the rainfall is higher in the mountain regions. As a result the land round Ras al-Khaimah and the narrow coastal plain on the Gulf of Oman is relatively fertile.

PLANTS AND WILDLIFE

Natural vegetation is sparse in most areas because of low rainfall and lack of underground water. The exceptions are the oases and land close to the Hajar range where waters from the mountains help vegetation to flourish. Abu Dhabi has also launched a programme of afforestation in parts of the desert which could attract rain, leading to the growth of wild plants.

Nonetheless, the desert has many plants which have adapted themselves to the arid conditions. Perennials and cactus type plants have various means of protecting themselves against loss of water, even during long periods of drought. Seeds of annuals can lie dormant for years and then suddenly germinate after a downpour. In a matter of weeks they grow to maturity and flower, shedding new seeds for the next rainfall. Other plants have long roots which reach down to underground water, while some stretch out their roots close to the surface to absorb as much surface water as possible.

Wildlife in the emirates has suffered from indiscriminate hunting and some fairly common species are now rare. The only existing oryx in the country are now in Al-Ain Zoo. The gazelle is extremely rare. The desert fox roams in some isolated parts and rodents like the jerboa (desert rat) can be seen occasionally.

Bird population As in other countries in the Gulf, the UAE's bird population has been increased by the developments of new farms and the growing of private and public gardens. Many more

483

migrant birds now stop in the green areas of the country. Tropical birds like bee eaters are a feature of the northern emirates. On the coast waders, gulls and cormorants are common. Sea eagles are sometimes seen hunting for fish. Inland the pools of the oases are inhabited by various water birds and ducks.

Hawking is still popular in the country, so young hawks are in demand for training. The Bedouin are highly skilled at training and are able to complete the job in a few weeks. Hawks are considered close personal possessions and their keepers tend to carry them everywhere they go. The most common prey for hawking is the lesser bustard (*habara*) which feeds off desert vegetation. But their numbers are fast declining and often hawk owners have to go abroad for hunting trips.

In the northern emirates fishing has long been a main source of income, particularly on the Gulf of Oman coast. The most common fish are tuna, bonitos, anchovy, jacks, and sardines. Sharks are frequently caught off the Gulf shores. Closer inshore shrimps are numerous and on some beaches crabs are a frequent sight. Green turtles use the shores of Ras al-Khaimah and Dubai as breeding grounds. The females travel long distances to lay their eggs in the same spot where they were born. They then return to the sea, leaving the eggs to hatch on their own and the young turtles to their own devices. As a result the eggs are often robbed by marauding animals and humans and only a few baby turtles survive the attacks of preying birds.

COMMUNICATIONS

Around a decade ago the UAE had virtually no asphalt roads. Now the country is reasonably well supplied with them. A coastal road links the six emirates on the Gulf. In parts it is dual carriageway and there are plans to convert the entire length into four lanes. A four-lane carriageway runs between Abu Dhabi and Al-Ain. With the completion of a road across the Hajar Mountains, Fujairah and the natural harbour of Khor Fakkan are connected with the rest of the country and the whole of the UAE is linked up with Oman's road system. A 290-mile road is being built through the west of Abu Dhabi into Qatar so that the country can be joined with the Trans-Arabian highway and have an overland route to Europe. Road building programmes in urban areas have helped to ease traffic, particularly in Dubai where there used to be only one bridge connecting the two main centres of Dubai town and Deira. Now both are linked by a second bridge and an underground tunnel.

There are four international airports—at Abu Dhabi, Dubai, Sharjah and Ras al-Khaimah. The busiest are at Abu Dhabi and Dubai where there are regular flights to Europe, the Indian sub-continent, the Far East and the main cities of the Middle East. The airports at Abu Dhabi, Dubai and Sharjah are being expanded because of increased traffic. Ras al-Khaimah's airport was opened in 1976.

In the last few years the UAE has embarked on a massive port building programme in a bid to end port congestion. But so many new berths are planned or are being constructed that soon the country may have more than it needs. Both Abu Dhabi and Dubai have large ports both of which are being expanded, and both emirates are planning second ports. Sharjah has a modern port and is due to open a second one on the Gulf of Oman coast at Khor Fakkan. Ras al-Khaimah has an artificial port and a second harbour at Khor Khowair. New ports are scheduled for completion at Ajman and Umm al-Qaiwain.

In 1976 six of the emirates decided to integrate their telephone systems under one organisation which now runs a total of around 40,000 lines. But Ras al-Khaimah decided to keep its system separate. Connections with the international circuit are maintained through earth satellites in Abu Dhabi, Dubai and Ras al-Khaimah.

SOCIAL BACKGROUND

An official census in the UAE in 1976 recorded a total population of 655,937. On the basis of an estimated annual growth rate of 19 per cent produced mainly by immigration, the total should now be nearing 800,000. About two-thirds of the population live in Abu Dhabi and Dubai, the majority of them in the urban centres of both emirates.

In most of the emirates the indigenous Arab population is in a minority. In Abu Dhabi it may be as low as 20 per cent or less. In addition to the local Arabs, there are Omani, Baluchi, Indian and Iranian communities—mostly in Dubai—which have been living in the area for many years. In the beginning of this century for example Dubai received a large influx of people of mixed Arab and Iranian stock who had moved across from the Iranian shores of the Gulf.

The last decade of oil wealth and all the development that has accompanied it has brought in a massive wave of foreign migrant workers. Rapid economic expansion has created a large number of jobs. With British and American companies playing a major part in the exploitation of oil in the UAE, large expatriate communities from the UK and the US are now living in Abu Dhabi and Dubai with smaller numbers in the other emirates. Europeans and Americans also work in banks and other businesses, as well as in hospitals, schools and government services. The British especially have set up their own schools, churches and social facilities.

A large number of teaching, hospital, middle-management and administrative posts have been filled by Egyptians, Jordanians, Lebanese, Syrians, and Palestinians. There has also been a big influx of workers from India and Pakistan, many of whom have found work on major construction projects. The opportunities for jobs for unskilled workers from the Indian sub-continent, where wages are low and unemployment high, is so great that illegal immigration is common. Boatloads of Indians or Pakistanis are thought to have been smuggled into the country.

Social change Most of the indigenous population of the emirates are Sunni Muslims who have been strongly influenced by the Wahhabism of neighbouring Saudi Arabia. But sudden economic growth has placed the innate conservatism of the UAE people under tremendous pressure. Traditionally the population of most of the emirates has been fishermen or pearl divers on the coast and nomads or oasis farmers inland. Most of the people are now wage-earners or are involved in their own businesses within the equivalent of a modern welfare state. In Abu Dhabi in particular many of the Bedouin nomads have been persuaded to live in permanent settlements. As a result the traditional tribal life which has prevailed for centuries is fast disappearing.

Nonetheless many social customs are still intact. Men continue to dress in the traditional white cotton robe and white head covering. Women are kept in seclusion, wearing the *burka* (head mask) and *abaya* (black clothing) in public. Though free education is available to all girls, some families have been reluctant to allow them to go to school. Women are discouraged from taking jobs though there are plenty of opportunities for them to work.

THE CONSTITUTION

The UAE's constitution makes provision for the following federal authorities: the President and Vice-President, the Supreme Council, the Council of Ministers, the National Assembly, and the Judiciary. The Supreme Council is composed of the rulers of the seven emirates and has responsibility for general policy on all matters and for the ratification of federal laws. Decisions on matters of substance require the support of five members who must include the Rulers of Abu Dhabi and Dubai. The President and Vice-President are elected for five years and may be re-elected at the end of their terms of office.

The Council of Ministers has executive authority, initiates laws and implements them, and is collectively responsible to the Supreme Council. The Prime Minister is appointed by the President, after consultation with his fellow members of the Supreme Council. The President also appoints the individual ministers, on the advice of the Prime Minister. Ministerial posts are shared between the Emirates with Abu Dhabi holding the largest number. The federal government's jurisdiction covers foreign affairs, education, health, public works, justice and communications.

The role of the National Assembly, which began its first full session in November 1972, is to discuss and, if necessary, propose amendments to federal laws presented to it by the Council of Ministers, before they are submitted for ratification by the Supreme Council. The National Assembly also has wide powers to debate other matters of public interest. Its 40 members are chosen, for two-year terms, by each emirate in the manner best suited to it. Abu Dhabi and Dubai are represented by eight members each, Sharjah and Ras al-Khaimah by six members each, and Ajman, Fujairah and Umm al-Qaiwain by four members each.

The Judiciary under the constitution consists of a Supreme Court and Primary Tribunals. The Supreme Court has a president and not more than five members, appointed by presidential decree after the approval of the Supreme Council. The Judiciary only has jurisdiction over matters assigned to it in the constitution, the local judicial authorities in each of the emirates retaining responsibility in other matters.

Emirate government None of the seven emirates themselves have a written constitution, and within each one all power rests in the ruler. He has ultimate legislative, executive and judicial power, though over the last few years some delegation of responsibilities has taken place. His political supremacy is based on personal and tribal loyalty without any reliance on state or administrative institutions. As a result the concept of state, as embodied in the federation, has been largely alien to the people of the emirates and is one of the major reasons why it has been slow to take a hold on the area.

Abu Dhabi however has taken steps to institutionalise power and Shaikh Zayed has said he wants to give his people opportunities to participate directly in national affairs. Since 1971 the emirate has had a Council of Ministers, now called an Executive Council, which dictates economic, social and political policy subject to the ruler's approval. Half the members of the council come from outside the ruling family. There is also a consultative assembly of 40 members, all appointed by the ruler, none of whom are members of the ruling family. The assembly has the right to make recommendations on draft laws to the Executive Council, helping to develop a consensus on legislative changes.

HISTORY

The early history of the area which now makes up the United Arab Emirates is still shrouded in some mystery. Archaeologists who first started digging in the UAE in the late 1950s have yet to piece together a comprehensive ancient history. But so far their discoveries show that since the earliest times thriving communities have been living in various parts of the country.

Indus Valley links Some archaeological sites have been tentatively dated back as far as 5000 B.C. Certain discoveries show that the area had trading links with Mesopotamia and the Indus

Valley and that it might have at least served as a staging post for trade between the two civilisations. Remains of decorated pottery unearthed at Umm al-Nar, an island lying close to Abu Dhabi city, are similar to finds in Baluchistan and the Sind and Indus Valleys. Copper fish hooks and pins date the Umm al-Nar remains to the Copper Age civilisation of the Indus Valley of about 2300 B.C. Relics of a settlement dug up at Hilli near Buraimi which have been dated to late in the third millenium also indicate that at the time the people probably had closer connections with the Indian sub-continent than Mesopotamia. The inhabitants of Hilli were wealthy enough to employ crafts-men, who were capable of cutting stones in geometric patterns. The erotic and extravagant nature of some of the carvings have been linked to the artistic styles then prevalent in the Indus Valley.

Excavations at Hilli and nearby Al-Ain have provided evidence that a stable and sophisticated society flourished in the vicinity for a period of at least 2,000 years. A group of Danish archaeologists have been speculating about the possi-bility that the UAE could have been the location of the missing land of Magan—the source of Mesopotamia's copper during the bronze age. But a capital of Magan has yet to be found as well as evidence of its copper mines and trading routes with Meso-potamia, the Indus Valley and Dilmun (ancient Bahrain, which acted as an entrepôt for the region).

The Greeks appear to have settled briefly in the northern section of the UAE when they took over parts of the Gulf shortly after the death of Alexander the Great at the end of the fourth century B.C. Hellenistic relics have been found at Mileiha and Umm al-Qaiwain, indicating that the Greeks took advantage of the shelter of the deep creeks which existed at the time on the coast. Evidence indicates that Ras al-Khaimah could have then been a busy sea port. Later it possibly had some connection with the kingdom of Sheba in Yemen in the early years A.D. and may have been used as a watering-place for ships transporting incense from the southern Arabian Peninsula.

The arrival of Islam Islam came to the area during the Muslim expansion across the Arabian Peninsula soon after the death of the Prophet Mohammad in 632 A.D. At this time the country appears to have consisted of a network of permanent settlements inherited from its early history. Arab historians in the eighth century mention Ras al-Khaimah (then called Julfar) as being a port used as a staging point by Muslim armies. The caliphs of Baghdad later used it as a base for their attacks on Oman.

By the 10th century the port became an outlet for trade from Al-Ain and for a while the northern parts of the Emirates came under the control of the Hawala tribe whose domain stretched into Oman. But the tribe lost its command of the area at the beginning of the 16th century when the Gulf first came under the orbit of spreading European power.

To European traders the Gulf was then attaining increasing importance because it provided a vital link between the sea route to India and the Far East and the overland route to Europe via Basra. The first Europeans to invade the Gulf were the Portuguese. They took Ras al-Khaimah and rebuilt its fort in 1631. But they soon began to lose their hold to the French, Dutch and British, all of whom were struggling for control of the region.

By the middle of the 18th century the British emerged with practically unchallenged supremacy among the European powers in the Gulf. At the same time the Hawala inhabitants of the north had begun to form a distinct group, called the Qawasim. For a while they became the indigenous dominant force in the territory as rulers of Sharjah and Ras al-Khaimah. They built up large fleets and became relatively wealthy traders and seafarers. By the beginning of the 19th century the Qawasim fleet comprised 63 large vessels and over 800 smaller ships, manned by 19,000 men.

Abu Dhabi established Meanwhile in the west an offshoot of the Bani Yas tribe, Al Bu Falah, had settled on the island of Abu Dhabi in the 1760s. The Bani Yas had originally come to Al-Liwa oasis after migrating from the Nejd, probably at the beginning of the 17th century. The Al Bu Falah went to the coast in the summer for fishing and pearling but when they discovered sweet water in Abu Dhabi they decided to set up a permanent settlement there. Soon they were growing prosperous from fish, pearls and dates and, backed by the loyalty of the rest of the Bani Yas tribe, they were within a short time competing with the Qawasim for command of the region.

But first the Qawasim were intent on fighting the British, who were determined to rule the seas in the Gulf. There were inevitable clashes with Qawasim and British boats. The British called it piracy and the area was known as the Pirate Coast with Qawasim becoming a dreaded word among British sailors. But the Qasimi shaikh who ruled the Qawasim claimed they were merely defending their own territorial integrity against an invading force. The Qawasim, for example, tried to levy tolls on foreign ships passing through the vital Straits of Hormuz which the British considered to be an act of piracy but which the Qasimi family regarded as an exercise of legitimate rights within Qawasim waters.

The British were also concerned about the growing influence of the Wahhabis of central Arabia on the area which they saw as a threat to their own power in the lower Gulf. The Wahhabis had established a garrison in Buraimi in 1795 which was used as a base for incursions into Oman. They also entered into a religious and political alliance with the Qawasim and both the British and Omanis suspected that they were encouraging the Qawasim to attack their vessels. Wahhabi pillaging provoked the Bani Yas to join forces with Muscat for their own protection. Soon the two turned against the Qawasim and in 1814 a joint force killed 300 Qawasim and captured 400 head of cattle.

British attack Ras al-Khaimah Eventually in September, 1809, the British decided to launch a major attack against the Qawasim stronghold at Ras al-Khaimah. A force of 1,000 British and 1,000 Indian troops supported by artillery set sail from Bombay in 16 ships, including four Royal Navy frigates. Later the detachment was joined by reinforcements provided by the Sultan of Muscat. The troops landed under the cover of ships' guns and destroyed as many boats and houses as they could. The Qawasim had fled to the hills and there was not even a Qasimi chief available to acknowledge the town's submission.

Ten years later in December 1819 the British sent a larger force to Ras al-Khaimah under the command of Major-General Sir William Grant Keir. Three thousand troops, 1,600 of them British, in 12 ships, were joined by three Muscati warships. A Muscati army was also sent overland to cut off any Qawasim retreat. But this time the Qawasim stayed to fight. At first they put up a stout resistance, killing or wounding 200 of the invaders. But soon the British artillery barrage became too much for them and after the Ras al-Khaimah fort fell, defenders and inhabitants were allowed to flee unmolested into the hills. The fort was demolished and the British set about bringing the whole area under formal submission.

In 1820 all the tribal chiefs of the area signed a treaty with Britain at which they agreed to stop all acts of piracy and give freedom to all shipping in the Gulf. A naval force remained stationed at Ras al-Khaimah to show that the British intended to enforce the treaty. But it soon withdrew to the island of Qishim on the northern Gulf coast which became a naval base for British operations in the region. Within a few years it became clear that the shaikhs were only prepared to obey the treaty to an extent necessary to avoid British retaliation.

Abu Dhabi domination However, the British presence was enough to give the colonial power a certain grip on the region. The Qawasim command of the seas was curtailed and soon the northern tribe was being overshadowed by the growing strength of Abu Dhabi. As early as 1823 the British Resident in the Gulf commented that Shaikh Tahnun of Abu Dhabi has 'influence and power (which) greatly exceeded any other chief on the coast'. At the time of Tahnun's death in 1833 Abu Dhabi town was estimated to have had 1,200 inhabitants with its ruler an acknowledged leader of 2,400 Bani Yas and 5,000 Manasir tribesmen in the Dhafrah interior of the emirate. The Abu Dhabi fleet had 300 craft and in the summer inland tribes joined the people of the town to provide a pearling crew of 2,500 men.

But the apparent unity of the Bani Yas under Al Bu Falah leadership then took a blow when a section called the Al Bu Falasah broke away after a dispute within the ruling family and moved out of Abu Dhabi to Dubai. Around 800 Al Bu Falasah kinsmen took over Dubai which had been controlled by Abu Dhabi and set up an independent principality. The shaikh of Sharjah took advantage of the rift to launch a series of joint attacks with Dubai against Abu Dhabi. Eventually Shaikh Khalifa of Abu Dhabi sued for peace and renounced all claims on Dubai which came for a while under Sharjah's protection.

Maritime truce   Continued strife among rival tribes prompted the British to intervene in 1835 to arrange a maritime truce between the shaikhs during the pearling seasons. The British believed that relative peace might return once pearling—the main resource of the area—could resume without being interrupted by petty wars. The truce was renewed annually and in May 1853 a Treaty of Maritime Peace in Perpetuity was concluded. It was signed by the shaikhs of Sharjah, Abu Dhabi, Dubai, Ajman, and Umm al, Qaiwain and as a result the region became known as the Trucial Coast.

The peace was enforced by the British Government in India. But Britain refrained from interfering in the activities of the shaikhs on land, to emphasise that she was only interested in the control of the sea. At no time did she hold sovereign rights over any of the Trucial States, even though in 1892 she became responsible for their external affairs. The conduct of internal affairs was left entirely in the shaikhs' hands.

Nonetheless Britain did not merely concern itself with keeping control of shipping in the Gulf. For example, under pressure from religious and radical groups at home it imposed a ban on the slave trade in the region. In 1839 the shaikhs agreed to prohibit slave trading by vessels under their control. But this had little effect and the trade continued unabated. In 1847 and 1856 Britian concluded two more anti-slavery agreements which proved far more effective and by the 1860s slave trading had begun to disappear in the Gulf.

British influence grows   The British also wielded considerable influence over the leaders of the area. In 1869 Shaikh Zayed of Abu Dhabi, then the dominant personality in the Trucial States, wrote to the British Resident: 'I am quite at your orders in everything and hope you will send me directions. I do not wish to consult any other. I feel satisfied you will see me cared for.' Soon afterwards, with obvious British approval, Zayed struck up an alliance with Muscat, Britain's traditional ally. Muscat agreed that Abu Dhabi should be entrusted with the defence of the hotly disputed oasis of Buraimi from which the Saudi Wahhabis had just been expelled.

After a short period of comparative peace, the Trucial States now went through two decades of petty wars. On the death of the

Shaikh of Sharjah in 1866, his domains were divided amongst his four sons into Sharjah, Ras al-Khaimah, Dibba and Kalba. This led to a series of conflicts in the Musandam Peninsula. At the same time Dubai, which was beginning to emerge as the commercial centre of the area, began to stir up trouble over debtors who were seeking sanctuary with rival shaikhdoms. In 1879 the British Resident, Colonel E. C. Ross, intervened to prevent further conflict over the issue of runaway debtors. Six shaikhdoms agreed to a British proposal providing for the return of fleeing debtors.

Britain then became alarmed about overtures being made to some Trucial States by other powers, notably Persia and France. As a result in March, 1892, she entered into separate but identical treaties with each Trucial ruler under which they bound themselves and their heirs to recognise Britain's special position in the Gulf to the exclusion of all others. They agreed not to cede, mortgage or dispose of parts of their territories to anyone except the British Government, nor to enter into any relationship with any other foreign government without British consent. In return Britain offered very little except protection. For the next 70 years Britian's grip on the area was at its strongest.

Abu Dhabi's decline Abu Dhabi's strong influence on the Trucial Coast and beyond was underlined by the British Royal Navy in 1900 when it drew up a list of the number of salutes the various Gulf shaikhs should receive. The shaikh of Abu Dhabi was to be given five, the same as the rulers of Bahrein and Kuwait. The other shaikhs of the Trucial States were to receive three each. But within a few years Abu Dhabi's power began to decline, mainly for economic reasons. The slide in influence was also accelerated by the death in 1909 of Shaikh Zayed the Great who had ruled the emirate for 54 years, showing considerable drive and political skill.

Shaikh Zayed died a natural death which was an achievement in itself. But his next three successors all met violent deaths. In 1922 Shaikh Hamdan was shot in the back by his brother, Sultan, while attending dinner at his home. Three years later Sultan was also shot in the back by his brother, Saqr, while climbing the stairs of his palace to pray at sunset. And in 1927 Saqr was shot by a Manasit tribesman.

By now Abu Dhabi's status had reached a new ebb. The pearling industry went into a slump in the 1920s when the Japanese began to flood the market with cultured pearls. But it suffered a mortal blow in the '30s when world recession snuffed out demand for luxury items like natural pearls in the West. Abu Dhabi became virtually poverty stricken. At the same time the emirate's rulers began to lose their sway over the tribes of the interior who began to switch their allegiance to the Saudis, now beginning to spread their influence again in the area.

Economic depression   The disintegration of the pearling industry also had a severe effect on some of the other Trucial States, as well as the rest of the Gulf. In 1925 the total catch by Arab states in the Gulf was valued at around $15 million (one-fifth of which went to Abu Dhabi). By 1946 the total value of pearling had tumbled to a mere $250,000.

However, some states were able to benefit from this economic depression. Dubai was able to take advantage of it to strengthen her hold as a commercial centre and entrepôt. This trading supremacy was obtained to some extent at the expense of Sharjah which allowed its port to silt up. But Sharjah was able to balance this loss by being chosen in 1932 as a stop-over point for flights to India and the Far East by Imperial Airways (now British Airways).

Oil discoveries   The area was rescued from penury by the discovery of oil. Some concessions were granted in the late '30s providing a small revenue for the rulers. But serious exploration did not start until after the Second World War. Oil was first struck in Abu Dhabi in the '50s, and soon afterwards in Dubai. In Abu Dhabi the oil at first made little difference. Shaikh Shakhbut was reluctant to spend any of it but after he was deposed in 1966 and replaced by his more progressive brother Shaikh Zayed, the emirate began to boom. Oil revenues rose from $54 million in 1967 to around $460 million in 1972 and its population soared from 17,000 to 70,000 in six years.

Dubai's oil revenue was augmented by rapidly rising income from trade. In particular it was earning huge sums by 'smuggling' gold into India where the rich were hoarding the metal as a protection against inflation. By 1970, 250 tons of gold a year were passing through Dubai, giving the emirate annual earnings of around $200 million. The effects of the growing prosperity of Abu Dhabi and Dubai gradually filtered through into the poorer neighbouring emirates of Ras al-Khaimah, Umm al-Qaiwain, Ajman and Fujairah. In 1972 oil was discovered off Sharjah which became the third emirate to benefit directly from oil wealth.

Meanwhile the British had been preparing to withdraw from the Trucial States and the rest of the Gulf. For a while during the 50s and 60s the British presence in the States actually increased. In 1952 they set up a Trucial States Council through which the shaikhs could work out a common administrative policy with the aim of setting up a federation. They also established a defence force called the Trucial Oman Levies (later changed to Trucial Oman Scouts). A large military base was built at Sharjah with the objective of replacing Aden as Britain's main defence headquarters in the Middle East. A British court was even created with jurisdiction over all British and non-Muslim subjects. But it soon became apparent that the British Government had neither the political will nor economic capacity to maintain its influence in the area.

British pull out In 1968 the British announced that they would be pulling out in 1971 and the next three years were taken up with difficult negotiations over the formation of a federation and the ending of disputes over ill-defined boundaries. Differences between Qatar, Abu Dhabi and Dubai over boundaries were settled early in 1970. But Saudi Arabia objected that its claim to certain parts of Abu Dhabi territory had not been taken into account. Later in the year King Faisal of Saudi Arabia demanded a plebiscite be held in the Buraimi district, now ruled mostly by Abu Dhabi, and quarrels between both parties over boundaries were not really finally resolved until 1974. Sharjah and Iran clashed over rival claims to Abu Musa island which had oil but in 1971 both agreed to share the revenue from oil production on the island.

The first talks on the creation of a federation began in 1968 when Abu Dhabi and Dubai agreed to form a union covering foreign affairs, defence and social services. The other Trucial States and Bahrain and Qatar were invited to join the union.

497

The leaders of the nine states formed themselves into a Supreme Council of Rulers later in the year and set up a working committee to draft a constitution. But big differences quickly became apparent and within a year the Supreme Council had reached stalemate. Bahrain with 40 per cent of the population of the area wanted a similar proportion of the seats on the ruling body of the proposed union. Qatar also had some big objections to the suggested federation and by 1970 it became obvious that both states would go their own way as independent countries.

Federation created   The other seven emirates then came under strong international pressure to iron out their differences. Kuwait and Saudi Arabia sent high-powered missions and the British special envoy to the Gulf, Sir William Luce, did some hectic lobbying among the rulers. Shaikh Zayed of Abu Dhabi emerged as a standard bearer for federation, declaring that his emirate was willing to unite with any state that was willing. Finally in July 1971 six emirates—Abu Dhabi, Dubai, Sharjah, Ajman, Fujairah and Umm al-Qaiwain—announced the formation of the United Arab Emirates. The new country became fully independent in December after Britain terminated all existing treaties with the Trucial States. Ras al-Khaimah hesitated for a while before joining the federation in 1972.

For the first few years the federation was a loosely knit state. Most of the emirates maintained separate defence forces. Abu Dhabi financed all the federal budget and the jurisdiction of certain federal ministries was mainly confined to Abu Dhabi itself, where the federal government was based. After the oil price rise of 1973, the UAE gave generous loans to developing countries, rising to $1,250 million in two years, but nearly all this money came from Abu Dhabi.

In external affairs the UAE became a strong backer of the Arab cause. It gave substantial support to the Arab forces in the October war of 1973 and participated fully in the oil embargo which followed it. The UAE was the first state to ban oil exports to the United States. It also gave large sums to the Arab 'front line' states, especially Egypt.

Recent Events

The federation of emirates which makes up the UAE has been achieving gradual progress towards greater unity. In May

1975 the seven rulers decided at a session of the Supreme Council to support in principle further centralisation measures. In November of the same year Sharjah placed its defence and security forces under federal command. It also abolished its flag in favour of the federal tricolour, a move which was immediately followed by Fujairah and Abu Dhabi. In May 1976 the other emirates with defence forces also agreed to merge them under a single federal command.

Despite these achievements the federalists still had to overcome obstacles in the advance to further unity. The emirates could not agree on the introduction of a permanent constitution which would have considerably strengthened the UAE and the country's interim constitution, maintaining the *status quo*, was extended for a further five years in November 1976. A border dispute caused a rift between Dubai and Sharjah in the summer of 1976 and attempts to mediate by UAE President Shaikh Zayed were unsuccessful. This so distressed Shaikh Zayed, who has been the driving force behind the federation, that he announced that he was resigning as president. He withdrew his resignation after receiving assurances from the other emirates that the federal government's authority would be strengthened.

Each emirate however has continued to pursue its own economic development. In some cases individual emirates have refused to take part in joint schemes. Ras al-Khaimah declined to join the federal telecommunications company, Emirtel, when it was set up in 1976, and in April 1977 emphasised its desire for independence by opening its own earth satellite station. But the UAE government machinery has been strengthened by the emergence of technocrats such as the new Minister of Planning, Said al-Ghobash, who is likely to give priority to economic planning on a federal scale.

ECONOMY

The United Arab Emirates has not only faced the ordinary problems of economic development but also the extra difficulty of trying to co-ordinate the economies of its seven members. Each emirate is intent on establishing an economic infrastructure which will give it independence within the union. Most are building ports and international airports and Abu Dhabi and

Dubai are setting up new industries which will compete against each other. At present the country lacks national economic objectives and the notion of planning on a federal scale is at an embryonic stage.

The country's oil exports have provided huge funds for development, though the bulk of them is concentrated in the hands of the two richest emirates, Abu Dhabi and Dubai. But the UAE's restricted natural resources has left it with few options in industrial development. Many new industries must be oil- or gas-related. Most, even if they are capital-intensive, are going to have to rely on imported labour. UAE nationals only constitute about 25 per cent of the 656,000 inhabitants and with a per caput income of $10,480 most locals have little need to take on menial jobs.

The main economic power in the UAE is Abu Dhabi, which earns the majority of the country's oil revenues and uses its money to keep the federation together. It has been paying the federal budget and, despite exerting pressure in 1976 on the other emirates to make a contribution, provided 98 per cent of the 1977 federal budget of $3,300 million. This was more than a three-fold increase over the 1976 federal budget of $1,077 million. But the 1977 total also included the budgets of Abu Dhabi's health, education and information departments which were transferred to the federal account. With these excluded the increase was a more modest $564 million.

Oil and Gas

The UAE's three oil producers—Abu Dhabi, Dubai and Sharjah—produced an average of 1.9 million barrels a day (b/d) in 1976. In 1978 Ras al-Khaimah expects to become the UAE's fourth oil exporter, though on a small scale. Altogether the country is thought to have oil reserves of 35,500 million barrels, the majority of them in Abu Dhabi.

Abu Dhabi's total oil revenues in 1976 officially amounted to around $5,000 million but this is thought to be an underestimate. Some estimates put them as high as $6,500 million. The emirate sided with Saudi Arabia at the OPEC conference at Doha in December 1976 and opted for a five per cent increase in oil prices while the other member states increased theirs by 10 per

R

cent. Sharjah and Dubai reluctantly agreed with Abu Dhabi's decision. In July, 1977, the price was raised another five per cent in order to restore OPEC unity. So Abu Dhabi's unofficial oil revenues should top $7,000 million in 1977.

Abu Dhabi output Abu Dhabi has two major oil companies. The Abu Dhabi Petroleum Company (ADPC) which controls most of the onshore production, and Abu Dhabi Marine Areas Operating Company (ADMA–OPCO) which controls most offshore production. ADPC is 60 per cent owned by the state firm Abu Dhabi National Oil Company (ADNOC). The remaining 40 per cent is held by a consortium consisting of British Petroleum (BP), Shell, Compagnie Français des Petroles (CFP–Total), Exxon, Mobil and Partex. ADNOC also has a 60 per cent share in ADMA–OPCO with the remainder taken by BP, CFP–Total, and the Japan Oil Development Company (Jodco). The Abu Dhabi Government has said that it has no immediate interest in a 100-per-cent takeover of the two companies. There are also two small offshore operators—Abu Dhabi Oil Company, owned entirely by Japanese interests and Al-Bukoush Company, which is 51 per cent controlled by CFP–Total.

ADPC has been working to a production ceiling of just over one million b/d, ADMA–OPCO to 550,000 b/d and the two smaller offshore operators to a combined total of 110,000 b/d. CFP–Total is at present involved in developing the offshore Upper Zakum Field for ADNOC with the aim to increasing Abu Dhabi's total oil output to two million b/d.

The emirate's offshore fields require massive amounts of water injection to bring the oil to the surface. This raises production costs to around $1 a barrel offshore while production of onshore oil is considerably cheaper at $0.30 a barrel. ADMA–OPCO now has the world's biggest offshore sea water injection system. Sea water is processed by chemical treatment, and then filtered and de-oxygenised to minimise its corrosive effects. The water-injection platform above the main Umm Shaif reservoir has an initial capacity of 500,000 b/d.

ADNOC's brief is to develop and control all oil and oil-related industries and it is involved in a number of projects both inside and outside the UAE. One of its main activities is marketing oil. In 1977 it was expecting to sell 60 per cent of its share of output. All the foreign equity holders in the two main oil companies, except Exxon, have signed buy-back contracts with the state firm. In the first half of 1977 ADNOC was disposing of an average of 870,000 b/d, the largest recipients being BP, CFP–Total, Amerada Hess and Gulf Oil of the US.

Dubai takeover In 1975 Shaikh Rashid of Dubai surprised Western oil companies by negotiating a 100-per-cent takeover of its oil industry, ahead of other Gulf countries. But Dubai Petroleum Company, a wholly-owned subsidiary of Continental Oil (Conoco) of the US, has remained the operator of the emirate's offshore Fatah fields. In 1976 Dubai earned an estimated $1,300 million from an average production of 320,000 b/d. The fields are believed to have enough reserves to last at least 15 years. But there may be other oil fields under Dubai's waters whose commercial potential has yet to be assessed. Dubai's oil is produced 58 miles offshore. So oil is stored underwater in *khazzans*—200 feet-high containers which each hold 500,000 barrels.

Sharjah's oil output averages about 37,000 b/d and comes from the Mubarak field which is operated by a US consortium managed by Buttes Gas & Oil Company. The field is shared 50–50 with Iran and Sharjah in turn has to share its revenue with Umm al-Qaiwain whose waters also cover part of the field. In 1975 Sharjah earned $35 million from the Mubarak output.

Ras al-Khaimah expects to become an oil exporter in June 1978. An American-European consortium has found oil about 15 miles east of Sharjah's Mubarak field. The first oil producing well tested at 4,000 b/d and it has been hoped that two other test wells would show that the emirate could go ahead with commercial production, though on a modest scale. Oil exploration has been taking place offshore from Fujairah and Umm al-Qaiwain claims that recent drilling has revealed large gas reserves. Ajman is the only emirate which appears to have little hope of finding either oil or gas.

Gas exploitation Both Abu Dhabi and Dubai have ambitious plans to exploit their gas reserves. Abu Dhabi is already exporting liquefied natural gas (LNG) and natural gas liquids from a large gas liquefaction plant on Das island. The plant, which came on stream in March, 1977, is run by the Abu Dhabi Gas Liquefaction Company (ADGLC), in which ADNOC has a 51 per cent stake with the remainder taken by BP, CFP–Total, Mitsui & Company and Bridgestone Liquefied Gas Company of Japan. When fully operational the plant will process 550 million cubic feet of gas a day. This will provide 2.2 million tons of LNG a year and one million tons of propane and butane and 220,000 tons each of pentanes and sulphur. The whole output is going to one client—Tokyo Electric Power Company, which is paying around $1 million a day for it.

Onshore, ADNOC decided in 1976 to go it alone with a $1,200 million scheme to harness and process gas reserves. The state firm's Western partners in ADPC pulled out of the project after a disagreement over costs. In the spring of 1977 Bechtel of the US was awarded a $400 million contract to set up two natural gas processing plants and Fluor Middle East won a $250 million contract for a plant to produce 500 million cubic feet of feed gas a day. The whole scheme will also include an export terminal and a pipeline from the onshore fields to Ruweis, 120 miles west of Abu Dhabi where the processing plants will be built. The project forms the basis of an ambitious plan to build an industrial complex at Ruweis.

In Dubai, Sunningdale Oils of Canada is the main contractor for a $250 million natural gas plant which is being constructed in the emirate's industrial zone of Jebel Ali, 15 miles outside Dubai city. The plant will provide gas for industries at Jebel Ali and will also export 370,000 tons a year of propane, 260,000 tons of butane and 2.3 million barrels of condensate. C. Itoh of Japan has already agreed to buy 60 per cent of the output.

Industry

Most large industrial projects in the UAE are inevitably oil- or gas-related and even schemes not involving hydrocarbons are relying on gas as a source of energy. Also all new industries will have to depend on immigrants for labour. Nonetheless the country hopes to establish a diverse industrial base before the UAE's oil reserves begin to run out.

Abu Dhabi has the most grandiose industrial plans, which are centred around the development programme of its state oil firm

ADNOC. The company already runs a 15,000 b/d refinery at Umm al-Nar Island which was opened in 1976 to meet local needs. Its capacity may be expanded so that it can serve the whole UAE market, and there are plans for a 120,000 b/d export refinery. ADNOC also has a controlling interest in the large gas processing plant on Das Island which is Abu Dhabi's biggest industrial project so far.

Ruweis complex But the emirate's industrialisation strategy rests on processing gas onshore, the plans for which are under the control of ADNOC. The gas will be the main source of energy and feedstock for a giant industrial complex at Ruweis. Besides two natural gas processing plants for which contracts were signed in early 1977 (see above), ADNOC is considering a fertiliser plant, iron and steel works, and petrochemicals complex. The fertiliser plant will have an annual capacity of 500,000 tons of ammonia, and 33,000 tons of urea. The iron and steel plant will produce 800,000 tons a year of sponge iron. The petrochemicals complex was in mid-1977 still at the feasibility stage.

The Abu Dhabi Government has also drawn up various plans for medium-sized industries in the emirate. These include glass and ceramics factories, an oil products plant, cable and electric wire plants, sheet metal plants and food factories. Other projects also include a cement factory at Al-Ain, a liquefied petroleum gas (LPG) extracting and bottling plant outside Abu Dhabi city, a steel rolling plant and flour mill and brick works.

Dubai's plans Dubai also has ambitious industrialisation plans and like Abu Dhabi it is setting up a large industrial zone which will contain the emirate's large industrial projects. Jebel Ali will have a population of 400,000 and will be served by a 74-berth industrial port. It will cover an area 13 miles long, between Dubai city and the Abu Dhabi border.

The natural gas plant being set up by Sunningdale Oils of Canada at Jebel Ali (see above) will provide the energy for an aluminium smelter which by 1981 will be producing 135,000 tons a year with output eventually reaching as high as 180,000 tons a year. The Dubai government will buy 20 per cent of the output for local consumption by light ancillary industries. The remainder will be exported, probably to other countries in the Gulf. The $612 million plant will be 80 per cent owned by the Government with the remaining shares owned by US, Japanese and local interests. The main contractor is British Smelter Constructions. A power and desalination plant is also being constructed to serve the plant.

Jebel Ali will also have a $350 million steel mill which by mid-1977 was still in the design stage. C. Itoh of Japan has been designing a 150,000 barrel-a-day refinery which is likely to be a joint venture between the Government and foreign interests. There are also plans for a cable manufacturing plant, and a steel fabrication complex which will be under total private ownership.

Drydock scheme   The largest project in Dubai outside Jebel Ali is a drydock which is due for completion by February 1979. It is being built by a joint British venture between Taylor Woodrow and Costain. It will have three docks which will be able to handle tankers of 350,000 dwt, 500,000 dwt and if necessary one million dwt. It will be linked to a ship repair yard at Jebel Ali capable of taking vessels of up to 30,000 tons. Dubai is also setting up a large cement plant with a capacity of 1,500 tons a hour which is due for completion in April 1978.

Sharjah is making a big effort to attract foreign industrialists by keeping red tape to a minimum. It has set up a National Industries & Development Company (NIDC) with the aim of promoting industrial projects in the emirate. NIDC has already set up a cement works with a capacity of 700 tons a day and a rope and a paper bag factory. The emirate also has a factory for plastic pipes, several paint plants, a perfume bottling plant, several steel products companies and a ready-mixed concrete producer.

Of the northern emirates, Ras al-Khaimah has the most industry. Its cement plant, with a 700 ton-a-day capacity, has been so successful that two 700-ton extensions are being built. The emirate has good raw materials for cement production. It also has some fine stone quarries for aggregate. Stone is being quarried by a Korean company for a port in Abu Dhabi and stone is also being exported to Saudi Arabia for a new port at Jubail. An asbestos cement works is being set up at Umm al-Qaiwain. Ajman, the UAE's smallest emirate, has plans to attract light industries. A small drydock is being built in the emirate by a Japanese concern.

Infrastructure development

In the rush for modern amenities, there has been a lot of duplication of facilities in the UAE. The country has four international airports and is building more. Within a short time it could have more port berths than in the whole of Saudi Arabia. In April 1977 Ras al-Khaimah became the third emirate to have an earth satellite.

One new amenity of which the country cannot build too many are roads. The UAE's road building programme has done much to bring the federation together. The recent completion of a road from the Gulf coast through the Hajar mountains to the Gulf of Oman gave Fujairah, the only emirate without a Gulf coastline, a direct link with the rest of the federation. A circular road going up the Gulf of Oman coast and back through the Hajar mountains has yet to be completed. Also a road going through western Abu Dhabi into Qatar, which will give the country a direct overland connection with Europe, was not finished by mid-1977.

Construction boom Over the last few years Abu Dhabi has been the centre of the most construction activity. Abu Dhabi city, now a modern metropolis, is only about seven years old, having been built virtually from scratch. The National Bank of Abu Dhabi has financed the construction of 270 buildings alone, costing a total of $217 million. Most of the medium-sized buildings have been constructed by Lebanese, Egyptian and Syrian contractors while the prestige quality structures have been reserved for large Western building companies which can offer the latest techniques and designs. But one of the emirate's biggest building schemes—the $225 million Zayed Sports City—is being constructed by a Lebanese firm.

Abu Dhabi is spending a lot of money on extending and building ports. A $17 million 10-berth extension to Mina Zayed has recently been completed and the inner port is having an additional 13 berths. A new outer harbour with 34 berths is being built with the contract for the first phase being awarded to the South Korean contractor, Dong Ah, which has also been constructing a ¾-mile bridge linking Abu Dhabi island with the mainland. Abu Dhabi also plans to build an industrial port to serve its industrial zone at Ruweis. The emirate is establishing a second international airport on the mainland 15 miles from Abu Dhabi City and there are plans for a civil airport at Al-Ain.

Dubai's biggest prestige building scheme has been the 39-storey Dubai International Trade and Exhibition Centre which has been constructed by Bernard Sunley of the UK. The project, which includes a 335-room hotel, is the biggest of its kind in the Middle East. The centre was scheduled to open at the beginning of September, 1977. A 22-berth extension to the emirate's Mina Rashid is being built at a cost of $200 million, with the first five berths due to come into operation in 1979. The 15-berth port has been experiencing considerable congestion which has not helped Dubai's important re-export trade. The extension will be complemented by the building of a 74-berth port at Dubai's industrial zone at Jebel Ali. Its first five berths are due to be completed in 1978. Dubai also plans to build a second airport, able to take 2,000 passengers an hour.

Trans-shipment Sharjah has been experiencing a small boom in office and residential buildings and rows of large tower blocks are transforming the landscape in Sharjah town. The emirate also aims to become a trans-shipment centre and a specialist in the handling of container ships. When the new Mina Khaled in Sharjah town is fully operational it will have a container roll-on, roll-off terminal and other facilities to achieve a rapid cargo throughput. A container port is being built at Khor Fakkan on the Gulf of Oman coast, due for completion in July 1978. Sharjah hopes that the port will attract substantial business from shippers who want to avoid sending large vessels into the Gulf. The port will be served by a trucking system which will take goods overland to the Gulf coast. In early 1977 Sharjah opened an international airport.

Ras al-Khaimah is building a six-berth port which will have facilities for container ships. In 1976 the emirate opened an international airport which has been slow to attract both passenger and cargo traffic. Umm al-Qaiwain is also extending its harbour and Fujairah has been considering building an international airport.

Agriculture and Fisheries

In 1973 only 50 square miles, less than 0.16 per cent of the state's total area, was under cultivation in the UAE and since then total farming land has not increased significantly. Only five per cent of land in the UAE is thought to be cultivable. Nonetheless efforts are being made to develop agriculture, with self-sufficiency in food as the ultimate aim. Few agricultural programmes have to face such harsh conditions. From May to October the climate is very hot and there is no rain. In winter it is relatively mild but the rainfall is minimal and unreliable except in the emirate of Ras al-Khaimah where the rainfall is above the average. Water is at a premium and underground supplies often have a high mineral content.

The UAE Ministry of Agriculture & Fisheries calculates that a total area of 37,065 acres is under cultivation, divided into 7,756 farms. Some of these are thought to be unproductive for most of the year. Total vegetable production has been estimated at 55,000 tons a year. The ministry has been spending a relatively large amount of money on boosting agriculture in the northern emirates. In 1977 the ministry was allotted $14.6 million by the federal budget, part of which was likely to be spent on a survey of water and soil resources.

The hostile conditions have forced the country to investigate new farming techniques, in particular controlled-environment cultivation. New techniques in arid zone agriculture are being pioneered and of outstanding interest is the project on the island of Sadiyat in controlled environmental farming, run by the Abu Dhabi Arid Lands Research Centre. It is an integrated complex for the generation of electricity, the desalination of sea water and the production of vegetables. The desalinated water irrigates vegetables planted inside air-inflated polythene greenhouses in which atmospheric conditions are closely controlled. On Sadiyat, five acres have been producing a ton of vegetables a day. A similar commercial project, comprising 15 acres of 'plastic farm', has been set up at Mazaid, in the desert about 125 miles from the Abu Dhabi coastline. It is run by Compagnie Française des

Petroles (CFP–Total) which claims to be making a profit out of sales of vegetables grown in greenhouses and outdoors.

Near Al-Ain, another experiment, under Japanese control, has involved the establishment of a pilot plot of about one acre, with a one-eighth of an inch thick film of asphalt laid to a depth of 24 to 35 inches under the ground. The film prevents the precious irrigation water seeping away and protects the farm soil from the infiltration of saline water.

Cattle farm More conventional research dates back to 1955 when the Agricultural Trials Station was established at Digdagga in Ras al-Khaimah. Good arable land can be found in this emirate combined with ample supplies of water, either from its relatively plentiful rainfall or underground sources. The Agricultural Trials Station is now one of the most advanced research units in the UAE with almost 400 acres under experimental cultivation. A large selection of fruits and vegetables is grown as well as alfalfa for animal fodder. At Meleiha, another experimental unit has become a model of modern irrigation methods. In addition, in Ras al-Khaimah, experimental cross-breeding with a large herd of Friesian cattle, derived from British stock, has been producing good results.

Al-Ain is also an important centre of agricultural research. In 1968, the first experimental farm was established—a 200-acre development and educational project. Now, over 1,200 acres come within the scope of the project with related village developments. Wheat is being grown on 160 hectares which in 1976 produced 300–350 kilos from 1,000 square metre plots. The good results came from crossing Palestinian seed with Pakistan varieties with the aim of creating strains suited to the arid and saline soil. There are also plans for a large poultry farm and a dairy farm at Al-Ain.

Recently perhaps the most ambitious of all projects has been to transform selected areas of the Abu Dhabi emirate from sandy, wind-blown desert into green forest. The aim is to improve the climate, reduce the severity of dust storms and combat soil erosion as well as to enjoy the obvious aesthetic benefits. Water is scarce but maximum use is made of available supplies by an ingenious 'trickle irrigation' system which controls the amount of water fed to each tree and overcomes the problems of evaporation and salt concentration experienced with conventional methods. Already over 1,700 acres have been planted along the route from Abu Dhabi to Al-Ain. A British firm has been also involved in tree planting projects in Dubai and Sharjah.

Industrial fishing Fishing has been a traditional source of income in the UAE and still remains the main livelihood of many nationals in the northern emirates. They are being helped to raise their earnings by cheap federal loans for the purchase of modern vessels and equipment. With fish commanding a relatively high price on the local market, small-scale fishing can still be relatively profitable. But the biggest economic potential is in industrial fishing which is already taking place in the northern emirates, arousing concern that uncontrolled large-scale operations may lead to a rapid depletion of the rich fishing grounds off the Gulf coast.

The first industrial fishing scheme was set up by the Ras al-Khaimah Fish Company using a Norwegian firm as consultants. Its plant is processing about 250 tons of fish a day, producing a maximum of 50 tons of fishmeal a day. Fishmeal fetches a high price on the world market so the output is exported to the other Gulf countries and Taiwan. The factory needs 500 kilos of fish, mainly mackerel and sardine, to produce 100 kilos of meal which has a 65 per cent protein content.

The Ajman government is setting up a much larger project in a joint venture with a Peruvian company. It will have a fish meal plant with a capacity of 60 tons an hour, with an estimated maximum catch of 400,000 tons a year. But initially the catch, which will be brought in by 12 vessels, is expected to be lower than this. The UN Food & Agriculture Organisation (FAO) at present estimates that only 250,000 tons of fish can be taken from the Gulf without depleting resources.

Trade

Oil is the major and only significant export from the UAE. Some food, live animals, fish meal, skins and hides are exported but in 1976 non-oil exports only amounted to $1.1 million. Re-exports, however, remain an important part of Dubai's economy, making up about 30 per cent of the emirate's imports.

Even before its oil revenues started, Dubai was a prosperous trading centre and entrepôt port, and its re-exports are estimated to have risen five-fold to $420 million in 1971–75.

Following the boost in oil revenues, and the country's accelerated development, imports doubled between 1973 and 1974, from $836 million to $1,637 million. By 1976 they had more than doubled again to $3,400 million. Nearly all the country's requirements have to be imported, including food, consumer goods, capital equipment and construction materials. Significantly the largest items on the import bill are manufactures, machinery and transport equipment. Imports of capital goods have been increasing more quickly than consumer products and in 1976 made up 44 per cent of the total, compared with only 26 per cent in 1970. Consumer goods amounted to 43 per cent of 1976 imports, 10 per cent of which was food.

In 1976 Abu Dhabi's imports rose by only six per cent from $949 million in the previous year to $1,000 million. The small increase is due to a levelling off of imports of oil-field and construction equipment and materials. The UK remained the emirate's principal supplier taking 18 per cent of the market. Dubai's imports grew by 35 per cent in the same year to $2,400 million. This figure might have been even higher but for congestion at Port Rashid.

Banking and Finance

The quadrupling of oil prices in 1973–74, and the corresponding increase in oil revenues, stimulated a rapid increase in the number of banks operating in the UAE to handle the enormous influx of funds. In early 1973 there were 20 commercial banks, of which six were locally incorporated and 14 were foreign. There were a few branches in the other emirates but most of them were concentrated in Dubai, Abu Dhabi and Sharjah. By March 1975, the number had increased to 39 commercial banks, 11 locally incorporated and 28 foreign, with a total of 255 licensed offices, of which 159 were already operating. There was by then a forward exchange market and both Abu Dhabi and Dubai had clearing house facilities. In mid-1977 there were 419 branches of 55 fully-licensed commercial banks, two restricted licence banks (RLBs) and two merchant banks.

The mushrooming banking system have been under the control of the UAE Currency Board, established in May, 1973. The Board has many, though not all, of the powers of a central bank and one of its principal functions has been to promote a sound financial system. At the instigation of the Board, there is now a unified banks' association in place of two independent ones. The Board has used a number of regulations for the conduct of banking business. These include the fixing of the maximum interest rates on local currency deposits and the best buying and selling rates for foreign currencies.

Bank upheaval The banking system went through an upheaval in the first half of 1977. In January there was a run on the dirham, two banks failed in May and the Currency Board's British managing-director, Ronald Scott, resigned. He was replaced by a triumvirate of three top UAE specialists in public finance. The two failed banks were Janata Bank, owned by the Central Bank of Bangladesh, and the Ajman Arab Bank, which had been locally incorporated in Ajman. Both were suspended from the clearing house system. The Currency Board has since raised the amounts banks have to deposit with the board and imposed a tighter ratio of the bank's own funds to liabilities.

Despite this temporary crisis, the UAE government believes that the country's banking system is basically sound. The plethora of banks can give a misleading impression of uncontrolled growth. But in fact about a dozen banks, mainly those which have been well established in the country, handle two thirds of all deposits. Commercial banking is also heavily concentrated in Dubai where, being the country's trading centre, about 50 per cent of credit goes on trade (by contrast 60 per cent of credit in Abu Dhabi goes on property and construction). Many of the new banks, which have set up business in the country, have also been playing a large part in the commercial development of the country.

Tentative steps have been taken to make the UAE a regional financial centre, rivalling the offshore banking operations in Bahrain. The Currency Board has announced that it intends to license 12 restricted licence banks (RLBs), possibly with the aim of forming the nucleus of an offshore banking system. But by mid-1977 only two RLBs were doing business in the country—

Amex of the US and Banca Commerciale Italiana. Development of RLBs may have been delayed by disagreements over their financial status. Dubai, for example, was opposed to giving them any tax exemption. Nonetheless the beginnings of a capital market have begun to emerge. Twelve dirham loans have been issued, two of them large ones.

Public finance Outside the commercial banking sector, the UAE has several public financial institutions. The UAE Development Bank, based at Abu Dhabi, aims to stimulate industrial development in the private sector by providing cheap loans and, if necessary, taking an equity share in projects. The bank has taken equity participation in 32 industrial schemes, including a furniture factory and an asbestos cement plant. The bank is able to borrow government funds at two per cent interest and also to borrow at market rates.

The Abu Dhabi Fund for Arab Economic Development (ADFAED) is the country's main institutional outlet for foreign aid, which all comes from Abu Dhabi. The emirate has been allocating nearly 30 per cent of its income to aid, the majority of which has gone to the Arab frontline states, particularly Egypt. ADFAED handles the project side of the aid programme. By September, 1976, the Fund's total loan commitments had reached $415 million though only $44.5 million had been disbursed. Much of this money was going to non-Arab Third World countries.

The Abu Dhabi Investment Authority (ADIA) handles Abu Dhabi's large oil surpluses. In mid-1977 it had about $4,500 million on its books, of which $2,500 million was already invested, and $1,000 million was in cash. Another $1,000 million made up the 60 per cent of the emirate's 1976 budget left unspent. ADIA's investments abroad are distributed in equities, US bonds and real estate. It has also created a merchant bank, the Abu Dhabi Investment Company (ADIC), in which it has a 60 per cent share. It acts as an investment company for both ADIA and the Ruler's office, handling some of his private portfolios.

UNIFORM WITH THIS VOLUME:
THE SOUTH AMERICAN HANDBOOK

Social Services

The UAE allocates more to education than on any other single item—as much as $150 million in 1976. But it is estimated that only about 20 per cent of this sum was actually spent. The Ministry of Education is also the biggest employer with a payroll of 10,800.

Little more than twenty years ago there was not a single school in the territory that is now the UAE. The first school opened in Sharjah in 1953. It provided free education for 450 boys between the ages of six and 17. Then, lack of finance was a limiting factor, but neighbourly assistance, particularly from Kuwait, enabled more schools to be built. Apart from Abu Dhabi, which was then developing its own system, there were 35 schools in 1967 catering for more than 10,500 boys and girls.

A law of 1971, the year of the UAE's formation, made primary education compulsory for all children over the age of six. Union of the emirates has given a great stimulus to education and by 1976 there were 110 schools, as well as teacher training centres, technical and trade schools, and business and post-secondary study courses. Altogether there were 90,000 students in 1976, some of them adult illiterates.

Drop-out rate   One of the major problems has been the high drop-out rate among pupils, despite payments by the Government to parents for sending their children to school. In 1976 the number of 11-year-old pupils totalled 6,059, but by 14 this had dropped to 3,779 and by 18 to 1,069. There were 1,300 men and 270 women studying at universities abroad. Of the total number of students UAE nationals are estimated to make up only half.

Health has been given a high priority by the UAE Government and allocations in the annual budget have risen fortyfold to $80 million between 1972–76. There is now a free medical service throughout the country, with hospitals in all the major centres of population and clinics in most small towns and rural areas.

Standards vary and one of the most efficient hospitals now in operation is the Rashid Hospital in Dubai with 400 beds, offering both in-patient and out-patient treatment in medicine, surgery, obstetrics, orthopaedics and intensive care. Two 320-bed hospitals are being built at Abu Dhabi City and a 510-bed hospital is being constructed at Al-Ain. In Abu Dhabi the establishment of first-class hospitals is now a priority. A new maternity hospital has recently opened in Abu Dhabi City, to be managed by Allied Medical of the UK. This firm is also managing Shajah's new 100-bed Al-Qasimi hospital. There are plans for a 90-bed hospital at Umm al-Qaiwain and 250-bed hospitals in Ras al-Khaimah and Fujairah.

GUIDE

ABU DHABI Abu Dhabi is the wealthiest and largest of the UAE's seven emirates. Politically also it is the major force in the federation. Its ruler, UAE President Shaikh Zayed, was the main strength behind moves to bring the state into being in 1971 and has done the most since to keep it together. Some of the other emirates harbour fears that Abu Dhabi aims to take control of the whole country but this anxiety is inconsistent with Shaikh Zayed's deep belief in federalism.

Abu Dhabi's wealth comes solely from oil and gas. Its oil reserves are estimated to be at least 30,000 million barrels and its gas reserve to be around 33,000 million barrels (oil equivalent). Large expanses of its territory still remain unexplored so its hydrocarbon reserves are likely to be much higher. At present Abu Dhabi earns five times more from oil and gas than Dubai, the second richest emirate in the UAE. This gap in earnings is likely to widen, giving it even more economic power within the federation. But so far Abu Dhabi's oil revenues have been to some extent a unifying factor. They have been financing most of the UAE federal budget which for the poorer northern emirates is the main source of development funds. Without Abu Dhabi money these emirates would have been still without roads, schools, hospitals and electricity.

Oil has brought about a remarkable transformation in Abu Dhabi itself. In the early 1960s the emirate's capital was a small collection of barasti huts surrounding the ruler's palace, and a few mosques. Since then it has been transformed into one of the most modern of the lower Gulf's cities. Out of a few years of frenetic building activity has emerged a spacious metropolis of wide boulevards lined with rows of tall office and apartment blocks. A lot of the architecture is functional but there is enough original design to give the city a character of its own. The grass, flowers and bushes on the roundabouts and central reservations of the dual carriageways, watered continually at great expense, offset the sandy colours of the tall buildings. They also belie Abu Dhabi's image as a stark, desert country.

Virtually nothing remains of old Abu Dhabi except the ruler's

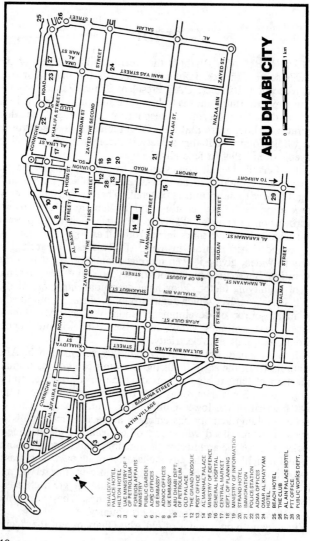

ABU DHABI CITY

0 — 1 km

1 KHALIDIYA
  PALACE HOTEL
2 HILTON HOTEL
3 UAE MINISTRY OF
  OF PETROLEUM
4 FOREIGN AFFAIRS
  MINISTRY
5 PUBLIC GARDEN
6 ADCO OFFICES
7 UK EMBASSY
8 ADNOC OFFICES
9 UK EMBASSY
10 ABU DHABI DEPT.
  OF PETROLEUM
11 OLD PALACE
12 THE GRAND MOSQUE
13 POST OFFICE
14 AL MANHAL PALACE
15 MINISTRY OF DEFENCE
16 GENERAL HOSPITAL
17 CENTRAL MARKET
18 DEPT. OF PLANNING
19 MINISTRY OF INFORMATION
20 STRAND HOTEL
21 IMMIGRATION
22 POLICE STATION
23 ADMA OFFICES
24 AL KHAYYAM
  HOTEL
25 BEACH HOTEL
26 THE CLUB
27 AL AIN PALACE HOTEL
28 PTT OFFICE
29 PUBLIC WORKS DEPT.

Old Palace. The capital's impoverished past has disappeared without trace amid a mass of contemporary architecture. One of the few imposing buildings of traditional design is the Great Mosque on Airport Road which was completed in 1970. The Old Palace itself, which lies in the centre of town, dates back to 1793. Shaikh Zayed himself lives in the Manhal Palace in Manhal Street, which was also built in 1970.

A big influx of expatriate workers has left the city with a major housing problem. Though a large number of houses and apartments are being built, the construction industry cannot keep up with the demand for homes. The resulting shortage has been exploited by building speculators who have been buying up land with bank loans and recouping their capital outlay within three years. A three-bedroom flat has been fetching rents of between Dh 65,000–85,000 a year and a small villa Dh 110,000–120,000, all payable two years in advance. But the developers have been concerned with the top end of the market where the customers are mainly North American and European expatriates. At the bottom where there is little money to be made housing for the Baluchi and Iranian labourers and Indian clerks has been neglected. Many have been left to look after their own needs. As a result enclaves of shanty homes have risen up on the wasteland between the huge office buildings, somewhat tainting Abu Dhabi's wealthy aura.

To the east of Abu Dhabi city is the emirate's port, Mina Zayed. This is being expanded and a new port is being constructed on adjacent reclaimed land. By the early 1980s the two ports together will have a total of nearly 60 berths. But unlike in neighbouring Dubai, Abu Dhabi is keeping its main industrial development well away from its capital city. Industrialisation will be centred at Ruweis near the Jebel Dhanna oil terminal, 125 miles west of the city. Projects planned include an oil refinery, and gas liquefaction, fertiliser, petrochemical and steel plants.

Archaeologists have discovered the remains of ancient graves on the small island of Umm al-Nar, near the Muqta Bridge beyond Abu Dhabi Airport. Excavations revealed a number of burial mounds of a unique type. In addition, jars and vases have been found. The archaeologists dated the early inhabitants of Umm al-Nar to about the middle of the third millennium BC.

Hotels

Hilton, end of Corniche (three miles outside city). P.O.B. 877. Tel: 61900. Telex: 2212 AH. Considered to be Abu Dhabi's best hotel, but expensive and out of town. 186 rooms, plus 21 cabanas (round the swimming pool). Single room Dh 275 (excluding breakfast), double Dh 385. 15 per cent service charge. Restaurant serves Oriental/European food (breakfast Dh 25, lunch and dinner Dh 100). Dancing in evenings. Coffee shop. Disco (entry Dh 10). Bars. Swimming pool, tennis courts, bowling alley. Film shows with buffet supper on Tuesday evenings at swimming pool (Dh 50). Conference facilities.

Ramada Inn Hotel, one mile from airport. P.O.B. 77260. Tel: 77260. Telex: 2904 AH. Abu Dhabi's newest hotel, aims to rival Hilton. 200 rooms. Single room Dh 245 (excluding breakfast), double Dh 330. 15 per cent service charge. Restaurant with dancing in evenings (breakfast Dh 20, lunch and dinner Dh 70). Coffee shop. Bars. Swimming pool. Conference room.

Al-Ain Palace Hotel, Corniche. P.O.B. 33. Tel: 22377. Telex: 2227 AH. More centrally located than other higher class hotels. Reputation for friendly atmosphere and good service. 104 rooms and 16 apartments. Single room Dh 230 with meals, double Dh 320. Apartments Dh 400 (full board). Restaurant (breakfast Dh 15, lunch and dinner Dh 40). Bar. Swimming pool. Conference room.

Khalidiya Palace Hotel, end of Corniche (beyond Hilton). P.O.B. 4010. Tel: 62470. Telex: 2506 AH. Lacks atmosphere. 131 rooms. Single room Dh 220 (excluding breakfast), double Dh 300. 15 per cent service charge. Large restaurant overlooking sea (breakfast Dh 15, lunch Dh 40, dinner Dh 50). Daily buffet at lunch time (Dh 55). Bar. Swimming pool. Conference room.

Omar Khayam, Shaikh Zayed Street. P.O.B. 123. Tel: 22101. Telex: 2520 AH. Conveniently located but of medium standard. 126 rooms. Single room Dh 220 (including breakfast), double Dh 330. 15 per cent service charge. Restaurant (breakfast Dh 10, lunch and dinner Dh 30). Bar.

Zakher, Umm al-Nar Street. P.O.B. 41940. Tel: 41940. Telex: 2392 AH. Central but only of average standard. 66 rooms. Single room Dh 180 (including breakfast), double Dh 230. 15 per cent service charge. Restaurant (breakfast Dh 10, lunch Dh 28, dinner Dh 30). Bar.

Strand, Airport Road. P.O.B. 821. Tel: 41100. One of Abu Dhabi's oldest hotels but of declining quality. 65 rooms. Single room Dh 150, double Dh 200. 10 per cent service charge. Restaurant (breakfast Dh 10, lunch Dh 25, dinner Dh 25). Bar.

Balbek, Airport Road (just beyond Strand Hotel). P.O.B. 365. Tel: 41677. A refuge for those who forgot to book. 45 rooms. Single room Dh 140, double Dh 160. No service charge, Restaurant (breakfast Dh 10, lunch Dh 13, dinner Dh 15).

A *Meridien* hotel should be completed in late 1978. Work has recently started on a *Sheraton* hotel.

Restaurants

The Hilton, Ramada Inn, Khalidiya Palace, Al-Ain Palace and Omar Khayam hotels all have good restaurants of which the Hilton's *Pearl Restaurant* is considered to be the best.

The Club, near the port. Tel: 22788. Restricted to members only but guests are admitted with members (entry Dh 15 for lunch, Dh 20 for dinner). Lunch Dh 25–30 (single person), dinner Dh 40. Licensed.

Capri, just off the Corniche (near Golden Fish restaurant). Tel: 61282. French bistro-style with plenty of atmosphere. Fairly expensive. Unlicensed.

Mandarin, Shaikh Zayed Street. Tel: 61361. Mainly Chinese cuisine. Quick service. Single person Dh 40–50. Take-away.

Golden Fish Restaurant, Corniche. Tel: 61091. Large and usually crowded. European/Lebanese food. Dh 40 for single person. Unlicensed.

Seaside Restaurant, Corniche. Tel: 45644. Overlooks sea. Varied menu. Single person Dh 25–30. Unlicensed.

Al-Kasr, Airport Road. Tel: 23351. Lebanese cuisine. Single person Dh 30. Unlicensed.

Pizzaria, Shaikh Hamdan Street. Large pizza costs around Dh 18.

Night clubs

Ewan Super Night Club, Corniche. Tel: 41184. Very expensive. Entrance Dh 40. Restaurant. Bar open 10 p.m.–4 a.m. Cabaret with orchestra begins at 10 p.m., floorshow at 12.30 a.m. Hostess drinks service—cocktail Dh 30, whisky (bottle) Dh 280, wine/champagne (bottle) Dh 150, beer/whisky (glass) Dh 15.

Airport 12 miles from the city centre. Average facilities—restaurant, bank, post office. No duty-free shop. Small departure lounge with cramped seating. A new international airport, nine miles from Muqta Bridge, due for completion in 1980.

Buses An irregular bus service operates within the city with a flat rate fare of 25 fils. There is a regular bus service to Al-Ain (single fare Dh 3). But no buses operate between Dubai and Abu Dhabi. The bus station is at the junction of Airport Road and the Corniche.

Taxis The introduction of taxi metres in mid-1977 is likely to mean a gradual increase in the city's fares, which have remained unchanged for two years making them among the cheapest in the lower Gulf. The usual fare for journeys within the centre of town have been Dh 2.50, to the outskirts (in particular Port Road and Batin) Dh 3, and to and from the airport Dh 20–25. At night fares go up, particularly to and from the airport. Late-arrivals may have to pay up to Dh 40 into town. Taxis waiting outside hotels usually charge above the norm. Most taxi drivers are expatriates who do not know the city well. Directions are by landmark. It is best to know exactly where you are going beforehand.

Fares to Dubai are between Dh 150–200 for single or "engaged" taxi, about Dh 30 for shared taxi. To Al-Ain Dh 150 single, Dh 30 shared. The taxi rank for long-distance journeys is opposite the gates of the British Embassy, near the Old Palace.

Car Hire *Avis Rent-a-Car*, Corniche. P.O.B. 3237. Tel: 23760. Telex: 2669 AH. Offices at Hilton Hotel (Tel: 62805) and Ramada Inn Hotel (Tel: 77260, ext. 131). Minimum rate for saloon car (self-drive) Dh 120 for 24 hours, plus 50 fils per kilometer over 100 kms. Weekly rate Dh 770. Chauffeur-driven car Dh 110 minimum for eight hours. Avis is allowed to issue temporary drivers licences for holders of International Licenses.

Abdullah al-Sheibani. P.O.B. 334. Tel: 41610. Minimum charge (self-drive) Dh 90 for 24 hours, plus 50 fils per kilometre.

Travel agencies

Omeir Travel Agency, Omeir bin Youssef Bldg., Shaikh Hamdan Street (opposite Old Souk). P.O.B. 267. Tel: 41328/41662. General sales agents for Alitalia, British Airways, Qantas, Alia and Singapore Airlines.

Gulf Express Travel, Al-Otaiba Bldg., Shaikh Hamdan Street. P.O.B. 2007. Tel: 41707/43012.

Gulf Travel & Services Bureau, Masaood Building, Shaikh Hamdan Street. P.O.B. 806. Tel: 41233. General sales agents for Air France, Egyptair, Lufthansa, Sabena.

Salem Travel Agency, Umm al-Nar Street. P.O.B. 346. Tel: 41821/ 41822. General sales agents for Pan Am, Syrian Arab Airlines, Ethiopian Airlines, Tunis Air, Thai International, SAS Scandinavian Airlines.

Abu Dhabi Travel Bureau, Shaikh Hamdan Street. P.O.B. 278. Tel: 44524. General sales agents for Air India, Iran Air, Iraqi Airways, KLM, Saudia.

Sultan bin Youssef & Sons, Shaikh Hamdan Street. P.O.B. 698. Tel: 43229. Agents for Pakistan International Airlines.
Ajnahah (WINGS) Travel Agency, Shaikh Hamdan Street. P.O.B. 742. Tel: 23590.

Airline Offices *Gulf Air*, Omeir Travel Agency, Shaikh Hamdan Street (opposite old souk). P.O.B. 573. Manager U.A.E. tel: 41143/ 43371. Tickets & Reservations tel: 41662. Flight Enquiries tel: 77329/ 77277 Ext. 259/260. *Air France*, G.S.A. Gulf Travel & Services Bureau, 1st floor Masaood Building, Hamdan Street. P.O.B. 806. Tel: 45743. *Air India*, G.S.A. Abu Dhabi Travel Bureau, 2nd floor Abu Dhabi Travel Bureau Building. P.O.B. 278. Tel: 41578/41197. ALIA, G.S.A. Omeir Travel Agency, Hamdan Street. P.O.B. 416. Tel: 43415.
Alitalia, Omeir Travel Agency, Hamdan Street. P.O.B. 267. Tel: 41662. *Bangladesh Biman*, G.S.A. Al-Rumaithi Co., Sheikh Khalifa Street. P.O.B. 4356. Tel: 42190. *British Airways*, G.S.A. Omeir Travel Agency, Hamdan Street. P.O.B. 267. Tel: 41663. *Egyptair*, G.S.A. Gulf Travel & Services Bureau, Masaood Building, Hamdan Street. P.O.B. 8060. Tel: 41233. *Ethiopian Airlines*, G.S.A. Salem Travel Agency, Umm al-Nar Street. P.O.B. 346. Tel: 41821.
Iran Air, Abu Dhabi Travel Bureau, Abu Dhabi Travel Bureau Building, Hamdan Street. P.O.B. 278. Tel: 41578. *Iraqi Airways*, G.S.A. Abu Dhabi Travel Bureau, Abu Dhabi Travel Bureau Building, Hamdan Street. P.O.B. 278. Tel: 41578/44817. *KLM*, G.S.A. Abu Dhabi Travel Bureau, Abu Dhabi Travel Bureau Building, Hamdan Street. P.O.B. 278. Tel: 41578. *Kuwait Airways*, Rashid Aweidah Building, Hamdan Street. P.O.B. 278 Reservations tel: 44524. Airport Flight Enquiries tel: 77431. *Lufthansa*, G.S.A. Gulf Travel & Services Bureau, Masaood Building, Hamdan Street. P.O.B. 8060. Tel: 41233.
Middle East Airlines, Abdul Jalil Bldg., Hamdan Street. P.O.B. 355. Reservations tel: 41210. Office tel: 41220. *Pakistan International Airlines*, G.S.A. Sultan bin-Youssef & Sons, Hamdan Street. P.O.B. 698. Tel: 43229. *Pan Am*, G.S.A. Salem Travel Agency, Umm al-Nar Street. P.O.B. 346. Tel: 41821. *Qantas*, G.S.A. Omeir Travel Agency, Hamdan Street. P.O.B. 267. Tel: 41662. *Sabena*, G.S.A. Gulf Travel & Services Bureau, Masaood Building, Hamdan Street. P.O.B. 806. Tel: 41233.
SAS Scandinavian Airlines, G.S.A. Salem Travel Agency, Umm al-Nar Street. P.O.B. 346. Tel: 41821. *Saudia*, G.S.A. Abu Dhabi Travel Bureau, Abu Dhabi Travel Bureau Building, Hamdan Street. P.O.B. 278. Tel: 41578. *Singapore Airlines*, G.S.A. Omeir Travel Agency, Hamdan Street. P.O.B. 267. Tel: 41662/41328. *Syrian Arab Airlines*, G.S.A. Salem Travel Agency, Umm al-Nar Street. P.O.B. 346. Tel: 41821.

Swissair, G.S.A. Abdul Jalil Travel, Abdul Jalil Building, Hamdan Street. P.O.B. 279. Tel: 41210. *Thai International*, G.S.A. Salem Travel Agency, Umm al-Nar Street. P.O.B. 346. Tel: 41821. *Tunis Air*, G.S.A. Salem Travel Agency, Umm al-Nar Street. P.O.B. 346. Tel: 41821. *Yemen Airways*, Abu Dhabi Travel Bureau Building, Hamdan Street. P.O.B. 266. Tel: 41578.

Shipping agencies *Gray Mackenzie & Co*. Corniche. P.O.B. 247. Tel: 23131. Telex: 2245 AH. *Yusuf bin-Ahmed Kanoo*, Shaikh Zayed Street. P.O.B. 245. Tel: 44444. Telex: 2282 AH. *Abu Dhabi Commercial Agencies*, Hamdan Street. P.O.B. 693. Tel: 22309. Telex: 2702.
Abu Dhabi Services Office, 1st floor Wimpey Bar building, Hamdan Street. P.O.B. 746. Tel: 41379. Telex: 2406. *Intergulf Marine & Services*, 3rd floor Bank Melli Iran Building, Shaikh Khalifa Street. P.O.B. 514. Tel: 43739. Telex: 2374. *ITMS Agencies Services Ltd.*, Hamdan Street. P.O.B. 4141. Tel: 45351. Telex: 2492. *National Maritime & Air Co.*, Shaikh Khalifa Street. P.O.B. 2775. Tel: 44766. *Rais Hassan Saadi & Co.*, Shaikh Khalifa Street, P.O.B. 465. Tel: 22929. Telex: 2744.

Post Offices The main post office is in Airport Road, with a branch office in Shaikh Hamdan Street. Opening hours: 8–1 p.m., 4–6 p.m. (closed Friday).

Telephones Local calls are free. Lines to Dubai, Al-Ain and Sharjah are often congested. International calls have to be booked by visitors, though subscribers can dial direct to Europe.

Useful phone nos. *Emergency*—44663. *Ambulance*—198. *Fire*—22777. *Police*—199. *Telephone operator*—100. *Directory and dialling code enquiries*—45145. *Enquiries* (General enquiries and enquiries about calls already booked)—42410. *Fault reports*—41960. *Telex*—41007. *International and Trunk call bookings*—41910. *Telegram enquiries*—43250. *Airport enquiries/reservations* (after hours)—77329/77277.

Telex Most hotels have telex facilities. There is public telex service at the Emirtel office in Airport Road (adjacent to the main post office).

Shops Supermarkets: *Spinney's*, just off the Corniche. Tel: 61969. Flies in fresh fruit and vegetables from Britain. *Abelas*, near Spinney's. Tel: 41051. *Abbas Ismail & Sons*, Bani Yas Street (near Omar Khayam Hotel). Tel: 41314/23604. Liquor stores: *African & Eastern* (Near East) *Ltd.*, Shaikh Zayed Street. Tel: 41416. *Gray Mackenzie & Co.*, Corniche. Tel: 23131. Alcohol only sold to residents with special permits. Films: *Jashanmal & Sons*, Corniche. Tel: 45316. *Deans Trading Establishment*, Shaikh Zayed Street. Tel: 62625. Souvenirs:

The Antique Shop, Shaikh Zayed Street (corner Airport Road). Interesting collection of copper, brass and Yemeni jewellery but expensive. *The Art Shoppe*, Hamdan Street (near Algemene Bank). Sells original paintings and other art work.

Souks The city has two souks, on either side of Shaikh Khalifa Street. Sells mostly modern imported goods. Jewellery is reasonably priced.

Social clubs *The Club*, located on the eastern outskirts. Abu Dhabi's main social club, with membership of 2,500. Temporary membership of three months is available to leave replacements and visitors related to a member. Guests admitted with member (entry Dh 15 during day, Dh 20 at night), but are prohibited at weekends and during public holidays. Facilities: swimming pool, squash, badminton and tennis courts, beach, sailing section, bar, restaurant, library. Film shows twice a week.

Tourist Club. Government sponsored. Guests admitted (entry Dh 10). Tennis courts, bowling alley, beach, slipway for boats. Restaurant. Unlicensed.

Golf Club. Moving to new club house and course after its former premises were closed down in spring 1977. No temporary membership but visitors accompanied by members are admitted (charge Dh 10).

Rugby Club. Small unlicensed club house. Members hold barbecues, darts nights and other social functions.

Leisure/sport Most recreational facilities in Abu Dhabi are provided by social clubs. The Corniche beach is good for swimming, though it sometimes gets crowded. Women on their own are advised not to use it. There are two attractive parks in the city, one in the centre and the other near the airport. Several of the city's cinemas frequently show English-language films.

For local Arabs the favourite traditional pastimes are hawking and camel racing. Hawking is a winter sport, involving long trips into the desert. Camel racing is also restricted to the cooler months.

Book shops *Jashanmal & Sons*, Corniche. P.O.B. 316. Tel: 45316. Wide selection of foreign books, paperbacks, foreign newspapers and magazines.

The Family Bookshop, Shaikh Zayed Street. P.O.B. 956. Tel: 45702. Has the largest variety of books and the most reasonably priced.

The Department Store, near the British Embassy. Has a wide variety of books in different languages, particularly English, French and German, together with newspapers and periodicals.

Hospitals *General Hospital*, Airport Road (near Ministry of Defence). Tel: 41630. Outpatients department. Adequate for minor operations but serious cases should be sent to Dubai. A new hospital is due to be completed in 1978.

Pharmacies *Fahimi Clinic*, Independence Street, extension of Sh. Khalifa Street. P.O.B. 144. Tel: 42654. Offering a complete range of medicines, cosmetics and perfumes. Also stocks hospital equipment, medical instruments, baby food, toiletries etc.
Modern Pharmacy, Hamdan Street. P.O.B. 289. Tel: 43746.
Union Pharmacy, Hamdan Street. P.O.B. 945. Tel: 42420.
The names of pharmacies open all night are announced by the Ministry of Health on the television every evening.

Banks Head office: *U.A.E. Currency Board*, P.O.B. 854. Tel: 43728. Telex: 2330/2396. In June 1977 the main office moved to a building opposite the Fahimi Clinic on Shaikh Khalifa Street. A new building is under construction not far from the Hilton Hotel which will house the entire Currency Board.
Commercial banks (main offices): *National Bank of Abu Dhabi*, Shaikh Khalifa Street. P.O.B. 4. Tel: 43262. *Algemene Bank Nederland, N.V.*, Hamdan Street. P.O.B. 2720. Tel: 45400. *Arab Bank for Investment & Foreign Trade*, Shaikh Khalifa Street. P.O.B. 2484. Tel: 42082. *Arab Bank Ltd.*, Shaikh Khalifa Street. P.O.B. 875. Tel: 41131. *Bank of Baroda*, Shaikh Khalifa Street, P.O.B. 2303. Tel: 44220. *Bank of Credit & Commerce International S.A.*, Shaikh Khalifa Street. P.O.B. 2622. Tel: 44622. *Bank Melli Iran*, Shaikh Khalifa Street. P.O.B. 2656. Tel: 45802. *Bank of Oman*, Shaikh Khalifa Street. P.O.B. 858. Tel: 43693. *Bank Saderat Iran*, Shaikh Khalifa Street. P.O.B. 700. Tel: 43159. *Banca Italiana Commerciale*, Airport Road. Tel: 24330. *Banque de Paris et des Pays Bas*, Airport Road. P.O.B. 2742. Tel: 43560. *Banque du Caire*, Shaikh Khalifa Street. P.O.B. 533. Tel: 43036. *Barclays Bank International*, Corniche. P.O.B. 2734. Tel: 45313. *British Bank of the Middle East*, Corniche. P.O.B. 242. Tel: 43080. *Chartered Bank*, Corniche. P.O.B. 240. Tel: 43077. *Commercial Bank of Dubai*, Shaikh Khalifa Street. P.O.B. 2466. Tel: 45701. *Distributors Co-operative Credit Bank Iran*, P.O.B. 888. Tel: 41358. *Emirates Commercial Bank*, Tahnun Building. P.O.B. 939. Tel: 45865. *First National Bank of Chicago*, Shaikh Khalifa Street. P.O.B. 2747. Tel: 23750. *Citibank*, Shaikh Khalifa Street. P.O.B. 999. Tel: 41410. *Grindlays Bank Ltd.*, Corniche. P.O.B. 241. Tel: 43076. *Federal Commercial Bank*, Shaikh Khalifa Street. Tel: 24920. *Habib Bank A.G. Zurich*, Hamdan Street. P.O.B. 2681. Tel: 22838. *Habib Bank Ltd.*, Hamdan Street. P.O.B. 897. Tel: 41618. *Janata Bank*, Corniche. P.O.B. 2630. Tel: 44542. *Khalij Commercial Bank*, Hamdan Street. P.O.B.

2832. Tel: 45820. *U.A.E. Development Bank*, Airport Road. P.O.B. 901. Tel: 44982. *National Bank of Dubai*, Shaikh Khalifa Street. P.O.B. 386. Tel: 41611. *Toronto Dominion Bank*, Shaikh Khalifa Street. P.O.B. 2664. Tel: 45500. *United Bank Ltd.*, Corniche. P.O.B. 237. Tel: 41397. *United International Bank Ltd.*, Hamdan Street. P.O.B. 2533. Tel: 43232.

Ministries/Government departments Abu Dhabi Government Departments: *Customs*. P.O.B. 255. Tel: 22278. *Finance*. P.O.B. 246. Tel: 61400. Telex: 2221. *Municipality*. P.O.B. 263. Tel: 43161. Telex: 2001. *Organisation & Management*. P.O.B. 371. Tel: 41690. *Petroleum*. P.O.B. 9. Tel: 41230. Telex: 2273. *Planning*. P.O.B. 12. Tel: 44595. *Ports*. P'O.B. 422. Tel: 24534. Telex: 2731.

Mina Zayed. P.O.B. 422. Tel: 22835. Telex: 2731. *Public Works*. P.O.B. 3. Tel: 41720. Telex: 2663. *Purchasing*. P.O.B. 838. Tel: 41490. Telex: 2314. *Social Services*. P.O.B. 2460. Tel: 43790. *Town Planning*. P.O.B. 862. Tel: 43160. *Water & Electricity*. P.O.B. 219. Tel: 22191. Telex: 2369. *National Consultative Council*. P.O.B. 933. Tel: 43175.

UAE (Federal) Ministries/departments: *Presidential Court*. P.O.B. 280. Tel: 42361. *Ministry of Agriculture & Fisheries*. P.O.B. 213. Tel: 62782. *Ministry of Communication*. P.O.B. 900. Tel: 62900. Telex: 2668. *Posts*. P.O.B. 300. Tel: 42411. Telex: 2131. *Ministry of Defence*. P.O.B. 907. Tel: 41931. *Ministry of Economy & Commerce*. P.O.B. 901. Tel: 62520. Telex: 2897. *Israel Boycott Office*. P.O.B. 694. Tel: 41970. *Ministry of Education*. P.O.B. 295. Tel: 41850. Telex: 2581.

Ministry of Electricity & Water. P.O.B. 629. Tel: 41998. *Ministry of Finance & Industry*. P.O.B. 433. Tel: 41030. Telex: 2937. *Ministry of Foreign Affairs*. P.O.B. 1. Tel: 62000. Telex: 2214. *Ministry of Housing*. P.O.B. 878. Tel: 41300. *Ministry of Information & Culture*. P.O.B. 17. Tel: 41480. Telex: 2283. *Ministry of Interior*. P.O.B. 398. Tel: 44111. Telex: 2398. *Naturalization & Immigration Administration*. P.O.B. 228. Tel: 41280. *Ministry of Islamic Affairs & Awqaf*. P.O.B. 2272. Tel: 44359.

Ministry of Justice. P.O.B. 753. Tel: 62490. *Ministry of Labour*. P.O.B. 809. Tel: 62890. *Ministry of Petroleum & Mineral Resources*. P.O.B. 59. Tel: 62333. Telex: 2544. *Ministry of Planning*. P.O.B. 904. Tel: 62270. Telex: 2920. *Ministry of Public Works*. P.O.B. 88. Tel: 41720. *Ministry of Social Affairs*. P.O.B. 261. Tel: 41580. *Ministry of State for Cabinet Affairs*. P.O.B. 899. Tel: 61555.

Civil Service Commission. P.O.B. 2350. Tel: 41020. *Ministry of Youth & Sports*. P.O.B. 539. Tel: 44200. *State Ministry of Supreme Cabinet Affairs*. P.O.B. 545. Tel: 43921. *Federal National Council*. P.O.B. 836. Tel: 42774. *U.A.E. Currency Board*. P.O.B. 854. Tel: 43728. Telex: 2330/2396.

Embassies *Bangladesh*, Saeed bin-Ahmed al-Otaiba Building, Airport Road. P.O.B. 2504. Tel: 44247. *Britain*, Corniche. P.O.B. 248. The Commercial Section is in Hamdan Street. Tel: (Embassy) 41305; (Commercial Section) 43035. *Egypt*, Shaikh Khalifa bin-Mohd Building, Hamdan Street. P.O.B. 4026. Tel: 22950. *France* (Commercial Section), Shaikh Khalifa Street. P.O.B. 4036. Tel: 44256. *Gabon*, Shaikh Zayed Street. P.O.B. 2653. Tel: 22893. *India*, Manahal Street. P.O.B. 4090. Tel: 63170. *Iraq*, P.O.B. 4030. Tel: 42326. *Japan*, Mana Al-Otaiba Building, Corniche. P.O.B. 2430. Tel: 44696.

Jordan, Shaikh Zayed Building No. 3, Shaikh Khalifa Street. P.O.B. 4024. Tel: 42740. *Kuwait*, Corniche. P.O.B. 926. Tel: 61340. *Lebanon*, Shaikh Zayed Building No. 3, Shaikh Khalifa Street. P.O.B. 4023. Tel: 42792. *Libya*, Shaikh Khalifa Street. P.O.B. 2091. Tel: 42750. *Mauritania*, P.O.B. 2714. Tel: 62431. *Morocco*. P.O.B. 4066. Tel: 45863. *Pakistan*, Harib bin-Sultan Building (2nd floor), Hamdan Street. P.O.B. 846. Tel: 42631. *Saudi Arabia*, P.O.B. 4057. Tel: 45867.

Somalia, Airport Road. P.O.B. 4155. Tel: 43812. *Sudan*, Hamdan Street. P.O.B. 4027. Tel: 22750. *Syria*, P.O.B. 4011. Tel: 42786. *Tunisia*, P.O.B. 2592. Tel: 43853. *U.S.A.*, Corniche. P.O.B. 4009. Tel: 61534. *West Germany*, Hamdan Street. P.O.B. 2591. Tel: 43359. *Yemen (North)*, 1st floor Shaikh Khalifa bin-Mohd Building, Hamdan Street. P.O.B. 2095. Tel: 22800. *Zaire*, 1st floor Al-Fardan Building, Hamdan Street. P.O.B. 2592. Tel: 45260.

Belgium, P.O.B. 3686. Tel: 24090. Telex: 286.

Newspapers/periodicals *Al-Ittihad*. Arabic Daily published by the Ministry of Information and Culture. P.O.B. 17. *Emirates News*. English Daily. Published by the Ministry of Information and Culture. P.O.B. 17. *Abu Dhabi Chamber of Commerce Review*. Arabic Monthly issued by Abu Dhabi Chamber of Commerce and Industry. P.O.B. 662. *Al-Dhafra*. Arabic Weekly. P.O.B. 4288. *Al-Wihda*. Arabic Daily. P.O.B. 4234. *U.A.E. and Abu Dhabi Official Gazette*. Arabic. P.O.B. 899.

Al-Fajr. Arabic Daily. *Al-Ayyam*. Arabic Bi-monthly. *Sawt al-Umma*. Arabic Weekly. *Al-Wathiba*. Arabic Daily. *Diri al-Watan*. Arabic Monthly published by the Ministry of Defence. *Al-Shurta*. Arabic Monthly published by the Ministry of Interior. *Akhbar al-Petrol wa al-Sinad*. Arabic Monthly published by the Ministry of Petroleum. *Al-Adala*. Arabic. Quarterly published by the Ministry of Justice. *Mahar al-Islam*. Arabic Monthly published by the Ministry of Islamic Affairs.

Media Abu Dhabi has an English-language semi-official daily, *Emirates News*, published by the U.A.E. Government. The English-language *Gulf Weekly Mirror*, printed in Bahrain, publishes a special lower Gulf edition with news from Abu Dhabi. Local radio and TV carry English-language programmes and news bulletins.

Major companies Industrial/trading firms: *Gray Mackenzie & Co. Ltd.* P.O.B. 247. Tel: 23131. Insurance brokers, clearing agents, marine craft operators, travel, commercial trading.

Yusuf bin-Ahmed Kanoo. P.O.B. 245. Tel: 44444.

African Eastern (Near East) Ltd. P.O.B. 49. Tel: 43258. Air Conditioning, office equipment and agents. Liquor retailers.

Mohammed bin-Masaood & Sons. P.O.B. 322. Tel: 41370. Shipping, marine services, Abu Dhabi Aluminium Factory, agents, engineering and contracting.

Galadari Brothers. P.O.B. 4069. Tel: 43314. Agents.

Omeir bin-Youssef. P.O.B. 267. Tel: 4337. General motor agents.

Spinney's (1948) Ltd. P.O.B. 243. Tel: 45670.

A. A. Zayani & Sons. P.O.B. 281. Tel: 22368. Agents, office furniture.

Alawi Trading Company. P.O.B. 983. Tel: 22485. Agents.

National Shipping Gulf Agency Co. (Abu Dhabi) Ltd. P.O.B. 377. Tel: 43008. Shipping agency, packing, clearing and forwarding agents, marine services.

Al-Saad General Trading & Cont. Co. P.O.B. 184. Tel: 22594. Steel works, fabrication and construction.

Insurance Companies:

Northern Assurance Co. Ltd. P.O.B. 865. Tel: 42223.

Royal Insurance Co. Ltd. P.O.B. 1076. Tel: 42746.

American Life Insurance Co. P.O.B. 970. Tel: 43420.

Abu Dhabi National Insurance Co. P.O.B. 839. Tel: 43171.

Gulf Insurance Co. P.O.B. 2514. Tel: 44380.

Yusuf bin-Ahmed Kanoo. P.O.B. 245. Tel: 44444.

Accountants:

Whinney Murray & Co. P.O.B. 136. Tel: 41609.

Peat Marwick Taseer Hadi & Co. P.O.B. 4313. Tel: 43318.

Coopers & Lybrand. P.O.B. 990. Tel: 41058.

Oil Companies:

AbuDhabi Marine Areas Operating Company (ADMA-OPCO). P.O.B. 303. Tel: 43900.

Abu Dhabi National Oil Co. (ADNOC). P.O.B. 898. Tel: 45600.

Abu Dhabi Petroleum Company (ADPC). P.O.B. 270. Tel: 61506.

Abu Dhabi Gas Liquefaction Co. (ADGLC). P.O.B. 3475. Tel: 41622.

Useful addresses

Abu Dhabi Chamber of Commerce. P.O.B. 662. Tel: 41880.

Al-Ain Al-Ain is a 100-mile drive across the desert from Abu Dhabi, along an asphalted dual-carriageway. Near the town, the sand changes from yellow to an ochre pink amid high dunes over which camels roam freely.

Before becoming Ruler in 1966, Sheikh Zayed was responsible for running the affairs of the Eastern Province of Abu Dhabi, which includes Al-Ain, promoting development in Al-Ain town and the surrounding villages. Water distribution for agriculture was improved, the main source of water in the area coming underground from the neighbouring mountains in the Oman. New underground canals were built and old ones repaired.

Al-Ain is remarkable for its greenery. All central reservations and roundabouts are covered with grass. Some roundabouts are a profusion of flowers and shrubs. The town is considerably smaller than Abu Dhabi city but it is growing fast. The main street through the centre has recently been widened, pavements are being built and new shops are being opened.

Among buildings of interest is the Muatarad Mosque, with three gold-painted onion domes offset by twin minarets. The Crown Prince's palace lies on the left-hand side of the main road, close to a mosque with a golden ball topping the minaret. Across the desert stands the fortress of Al-Ain erected by Shaikh bin-Zayed in 1910 but recently restored. The original mud-walled bastion is closed. Behind is the Department of Tourism and Archaeology and a museum, opened in November 1971. It has exhibits showing aspects of Bedouin life and items of archaeological interest, like pottery, bronze and brass as well as paintings and stone engravings. Included in the collection are discoveries from Umm al-Nar, Hilli and Jabal Hafit.

The Hafit mountain slopes near the Al-Ain oasis have been a focus of archaeological investigation. In 1963 a low grave mound was found on the plain, some distance from the oasis and hundreds of potsherds of a similar type to those found on Umm al-Nar island were discovered. Recent investigations of the grave-mounds on the slopes of Jebel Hafit have uncovered Jamdat Nasr pottery from Mesopotamia in about 3,000 BC. Similar burial places were found at **Hilli,** one of the nine villages in the Buraimi Oasis. One tomb at Hilli has been completely reconstructed and flanking the sides of the openings can be seen stone carved figures of animals and people, dating back approximately to 2,700 BC. The most recent and exciting find was at Quattarah, a village near Hilli. A rectangular stone structure was uncovered by a farmer and it is probable that it is another tomb. A set of beads, a small bull with a spiky ridged back and other ornaments in pure gold were also found.

Hotels

Al-Ain Hilton. P.O.B. 1333. Tel: 41410. Telex: 2417. Attractively designed with luxurious atmosphere. 100 rooms. Single room Dh 200, double Dh 300. 15 per cent service charge. Restaurant (breakfast Dh 20, lunch Dh 90, dinner Dh 100). Coffee shop. Swimming pool (open to non-residents with a charge). Tennis courts. Conference facilities.

Restaurants Some small restaurants serve Lebanese food. There is also a *Wimpey Bar* and *Kentucky Fried Chicken.*

Taxis The usual fare for a short journey in the town is around Dh 3. A shared taxi to Abu Dhabi city costs about Dh 30. A single ("engaged") one about Dh 150.

Buses Buses run regularly to Abu Dhabi (Dh 3 for single fare).

Travel agencies *Ilyas Travel Agency.* P.O.B. 1448. *Al-Ain Express Travels.* P.O.B. 1127. Tel: 41747. *Al-Otaiba Travel Bureau.* P.O.B. 1358. Tel: 41497.

Useful phone nos. *Ministry of Information & Culture*—41595. *Fire*—41222. *Police*—41222.

Souks The town has a large covered vegetable souk. Buraimi, seven miles over the border in Oman, has a more traditional souk.

Leisure/sports Al-Ain has a camel race course where racing takes place regularly in the cooler months. The town also has a large zoo, one of the biggest in the lower Gulf.

Book shops *Jashanmals & Sons.* Tel: 41307. Sells English-language newspapers/periodicals.

Hospital *Al-Ain Hospital.* Tel: 41230. Equipped to perform emergency operations. A new hospital is being built.

DUBAI Often referred to as 'The Hong Kong of The Gulf', Dubai has a history that goes back further than most of the lower Gulf cities. At one time two 'ruling families' were at war fighting across the Creek which today divides Dubai city into two distinct areas, Dubai and Deira. Now, however, it is united under the rulership of Shaikh Rashid bin-Said al-Maktoum, and shows every sign of the boom which has hit the Gulf.

Dubai is probably one of the few centres in the Gulf where people do not talk or seem to worry about the day the oil runs out. Probably because by the time it does, they will not need to. It is a city that has been built on a tradition of trading. But the Dubai Government is trying to give the emirate a more broadly-based mixed economy and are pushing ahead with an industrialisation programme. Oil revenues, which started coming in 1969, are making ambitious projects possible in the shortest time but Dubai has not relied on oil alone. Its growth had begun, to some extent, before the days of oil revenues. It is now phenomenal. At one time a road on the outskirts of the city can have an uninterrupted view of the desert. A few months later the same road is a dual carriageway, lined with showrooms, villas or tower blocks. The tower blocks are no longer three- and four-storey buildings. They are now rising to 20 and even 30 storeys high. By 1979 Dubai's International Trade and Exhibition Centre with 39 floors should be completed. The list of new projects in hand, let alone those on the drawing board, seems endless. One of the largest projects within the present city boundary is the construction of a new development area on reclaimed land on the Dubai corniche, which will accommodate 80,000 people. The area will have the largest private enterprise building complex ever to be constructed in the UAE. It will include a 475-room hotel and 400 apartments with a revolving restaurant on top of 29 storeys.

But despite the pressures of sudden change Dubai has managed to retain something of the atmosphere of its past. The souks have not been pulled down yet and look much like they did in the years when Dubai was a gold smuggling centre and an emporium for all sorts of oriental merchandise. There are still bargains to be found among the little jewellery shops in the dark passageways of Deira souk. Skyscraper buildings are going up on all sides of the Creek, but the waterway has kept its charm. Its quays are lined with large dhows from other Gulf ports unloading and picking up cargoes. Despite the building of a bridge and tunnel, the motorised *abra* (small open-topped boat) remains the main form of transport. During the rush hour there is a constant stream of abras going from one bank to the other. But one prominent feature of the past has been fast disappearing. Air conditioners have made redundant the tall wind vents which sat like massive chimneys on the tops of most Dubai houses. Now few remain. No doubt in time most relics of old Dubai will fade into oblivion.

Modern progress has helped to make Dubai a much more pleasant place to live in. Communications are among the best in the region. Power cuts are now infrequent. Water is drinkable from the tap. The streets are relatively clean and the refuse collection system is good. Traffic congestion has been eased by the building of a tunnel under the Creek and a new bridge and by-pass. Rents, however, continue to climb to excessive levels. Three-bedroom apartments in Deira can cost between Dh 60,000 and Dh 80,000 a year and rents for villas can go over Dh 120,000. The Dubai Government is trying to relieve the housing shortage by building large blocks of flats and villas for rents ranging from Dh 15,000 to Dh 20,000. But these will still be insufficient to meet the demand for homes.

The emirate's expansion is not being restricted to the city of Dubai. At Jebel Ali, fourteen miles from the present city centre, a new city is being constructed. Not only will it have the largest port in the Middle East and Dubai's second airport, but already a large amount of private industry is being sited there. Primarily, it will be an industrial city. A 74-berth port will serve an aluminium smelter, a gas liquefaction plant, oil refinery, steel mill and extrusion plant. By turning Jebel Ali into a manufacturing centre the Dubai Government aims to add a flourishing industrial element to Dubai's trading economy. Jebel Ali will in time become Dubai's industrial suburb as it merges gradually with the main city.

Hotels

Inter-Continental, facing onto the Creek (Deira side). P.O.B. 476. Tel: 27171. Telex: 5779. One of the best equipped hotels in the lower Gulf. 331 rooms and 39 suites. Two-tier price system—moderate and maximum. Single room Dh 210 (mod.), Dh 260 (max.). Double Dh 280 (mod.), Dh 330 (max.). Suites from Dh 650. Breakfast Dh 18

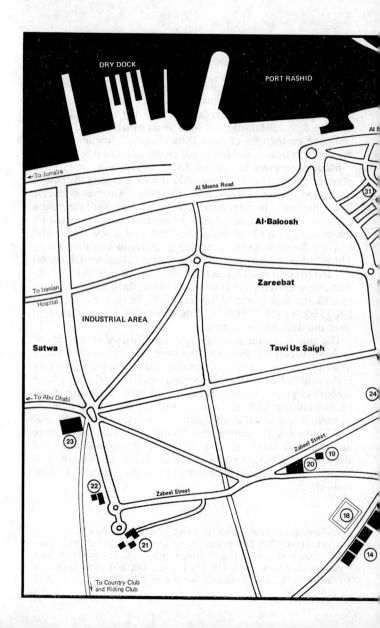

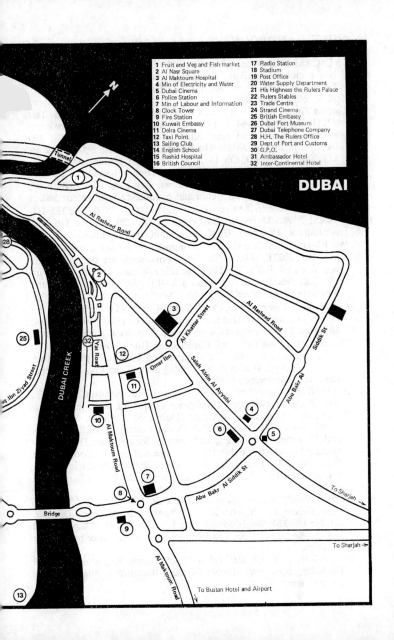

DUBAI

1 Fruit and Veg and Fish market
2 Al Nasr Square
3 Al Maktoum Hospital
4 Min of Electricity and Water
5 Dubai Cinema
6 Police Station
7 Min of Labour and Information
8 Clock Tower
9 Fire Station
10 Kuwait Embassy
11 Deira Cinema
12 Taxi Point
13 Sailing Club
14 English School
15 Rashid Hospital
16 British Council
17 Radio Station
18 Stadium
19 Post Office
20 Water Supply Department
21 His Highness the Rulers Palace
22 Rulers Stables
23 Trade Centre
24 Strand Cinema
25 British Embassy
26 Dubai Fort Museum
27 Dubai Telephone Company
28 H.H. The Rulers Office
29 Dept of Port and Customs
30 G.P.O.
31 Ambassador Hotel
32 Inter-Continental Hotel

(English). Restaurant (*Panorama*). Coffee shop (open 24 hours). Night club. Two bars. Swimming pool. Tennis courts. Shops. Newsagent. Doctor on 24-hour call. Conference facilities for 500. Banqueting for 400.

Carlton Tower, facing onto the Creek (Deira side). P.O.B. 1955. Tel: 27111. Telex: 6328/6410. 152 rooms and 18 suites. Two-tier price system—seafront and rear. Single room Dh 250 (rear)/Dh 300 (seafront), double Dh 350/Dh 400. Suites from Dh 600. Breakfast Dh 20–25 (English), Dh 18–20 (Continental). Three restaurants— *Le Grenier* (Lebanese cuisine), *Butterfly* (International), *La Cascade Gourmet*. Coffee Shop (open 24 hours). Two bars. Swimming pool. Shops. Newsagent. Conference and banqueting facilities for 500.

Oasis Hotel, close to the Creek (Deira side). P.O.B. 1556. Tel: 25252/4. Telex: 5494. 37 rooms. Single room Dh 220, double Dh 280. Restaurant. Two bars. Conference/banqueting facilities.

Bon Vivant (Flotel), on the Creek (opposite *Inter-Continental*). P.O.B. 436. Tel: 20271. Telex: 6400. 180 rooms (some are suites). Rooms cost from Dh 160 to Dh 240 (depending on deck level), suites from Dh 320. Restaurant (set menu Dh 40). Night club. Two bars. Swimming pool. Shop. Conference/banqueting facilities.

International Trade Centre Hotel, Trade Centre. To be managed by Hilton International. Due to be opened end of 1977. 350 rooms and 16 suites. Two restaurants. Coffee shop. Two bars. Swimming pool.

Sheraton Hotel, on the Creek (Deira side). Due to open April, 1978. 280 rooms and 58 suites. Restaurant. Coffee shop. Nightclub. Bar. Swimming pool. Health club. Bowling alley. Tennis courts. Shops. Ballroom. Conference facilities.

Astoria Hotel. Opened mid-1977. 108 rooms. Restaurant. Coffee shop. Bar. Shops. Newsagent. Conference/banqueting facilities.

Ambassador Hotel, close to Creek (Dubai side). P.O.B. 3226. Tel: 31000. Telex: 5467. One of Dubai's older quality hotels. 81 rooms and 18 suites or de luxe double rooms. Single room Dh 180 (including breakfast), double Dh 320, suite and de luxe double room from Dh 390. Restaurant (set menu Dh 40). Nightclub (with restaurant). Two bars. Swimming pool. Conference/banqueting facilities.

Airlines Hotel, close to *Oasis Hotel*. P.O.B. 736. Tel: 31555. Telex: (c/o *Ambassador Hotel*): 5467. 43 rooms. Single room Dh 180, double Dh 320. Single/double suite Dh 220/Dh 340. All prices full board. Restaurant. Bar. Swimming pool. Conference/banqueting facilities.

Jumairah Hotel. P.O.B. 403. Tel: 41526. 65 rooms. Single room Dh 180 (including breakfast), double Dh 320. Restaurant. Nightclub (*La Fiesta*). Bar.

Bustan, P.O.B. 1533. Tel: 21261. Telex: 5460. On the outskirts, but frequent transport provided into town and back. 36 rooms and two suites. Single room Dh 175 (including breakfast), Dh 215 (full board). Double Dh 260 (including breakfast), double Dh 350 (full board). Suites from Dh 325. Restaurant (set menu Dh 35). Nightclub. Three bars. Swimming pool. Conference facilities.

Claridge Hotel. P.O.B. 1833. Tel: 22018/27141. Telex: 5875. 112 rooms and four suites. Single room (including breakfast) Dh 160, double Dh 240. Suite from Dh 400. Restaurant (Dh 30 single person). Coffee shop (open 24 hours). Bar. Shop. Conference/banqueting facilities.

Apollo Hotel. P.O.B. 736. Tel: 32728. Telex (c/o *Ambassador Hotel*): 5467. 25 rooms, Single room Dh 160 (full board), double Dh 300. Restaurant. Bar.

Bristol, P.O.B. 1471. Tel: 24171. Telex: 5732. 34 rooms. Single room Dh 120, double from Dh 180. Breakfast Dh 10. Three restaurants (Continental/Chinese/Japanese). Bar.

Annexe Hotel, adjacent to *Ambassador Hotel*. P.O.B. 736. Tel: 31185. Telex (c/o *Ambassador Hotel*): 5467. 38 rooms. Single room Dh 120 (including breakfast), double Dh 220. Restaurant. Bar.

Phoenicia Hotel, Al-Nasr Square. P.O.B. 4467. Tel: 27191. Telex: 5853. Single room Dh 200, double Dh 250, suite Dh 500. Breakfast Dh 10 (English), Dh 15 (continental). Restaurant. Bar.

Restaurants

HOTEL RESTAURANTS

Panorama, Inter-Continental. Tel: 27171. International cuisine. Main course prices from Dh 35. Occasional cabaret spots.

Le Grenier, Carlton Tower. Tel: 27111. Lebanese cuisine. Main course prices from Dh 20. Music.

Butterfly, Carlton Tower. Tel: 27111. International/French cuisine. Main course prices from Dh 20.

Palm Restaurant, Bon Vivant Flotel. Tel: 20271. International cuisine. Set menu Dh 40. Main course prices from Dh 25.

OTHER RESTAURANTS

Mandarin, P.O.B. 228. Tel: 33272. Chinese cuisine. Pleasant surroundings. Dh 35 basic meal.

Rose & Crown, close to Oasis Hotel. P.O.B. 275. Tel: 26739. French cuisine. Main course prices from Dh 30. Quality of food tends to vary. Two bars.

Safari Club, P.O.B. 1582. Tel: 25552. International cuisine. Main course prices from Dh 35. Cover charge Dh 6 (Thursdays Dh 10).

Golden Dragon, P.O.B. 2044. Tel: 35517/31340. Chinese cuisine.

Dh 55 for basic meal including beverages. Plush but informal atmosphere. Take-away service.

Chalet Suisse. P.O.B. 3621. Tel: 22392. International cuisine. Prices from Dh 25 (Dh 35 for steak). Good reputation. Pleasant atmosphere.

Sahara, P.O.B. 4126. Tel: 21518. International cuisine. Main course prices from Dh 25. Cover charge Dh 7.50. Expensive and noisy.

Pizza-Vino, opposite Oasis Hotel. P.O.B. c/o 1582. Tel: 24884. Pizzas and wine only. Prices from Dh 10. Good for quick meal in nice surroundings.

N.B. All restaurants add between 15–20 per cent to bill for service charge and municipality tax.

Nightclubs

Panorama Lounge, Inter-Continental Hotel. Tel: 27171. Open until 2 a.m. Live music and disco.

Le Grenier Disco Club, Carlton Tower Hotel. Tel: 27111. Open until 2 a.m.

Falcon Night Club, Bon Vivant Flotel. Tel: 20271. Open until 2.30 a.m. Variety of music and shows. No food.

Venus Room, Ambassador Hotel. Tel: 31000. Open until midnight. Music/cabaret. Food prices from Dh 25.

La Fiesta Night Club, Jumairah Hotel. Tel: 41526. Open to 3 a.m. Cover charge Dh 20. Music/cabaret. Food prices from Dh 15.

Bustan Night Club, Bustan Hotel. Tel: 21261. Open until 3 a.m. Music until 2 a.m. Cover charge Dh 5. Food prices from Dh 25.

Sahara. Tel: 21518. Open until 3 a.m. Cover charge Dh 15 (Dh 7.50 if eating). Music by pop group. Food prices from Dh 25.

Safari Club. Tel: 25552. Open until 3.30 a.m. Cover charge Dh 6 (Thursdays Dh 10). Music/entertainment till 3 a.m.

Airport   Regarded as one of the best and most modern airports in the Gulf. Ten minutes from Dubai's city centre. A duty free shopping centre includes a bank, newsagent, camera shops, tobacconist, and parfumerie. A wide variety of watches and gifts are also on sale. The airport has its own restaurant but service is poor.

Buses   The Municipality operates a city bus service but it is only used by locals and manual workers. Not recommended for the visitor.

Abras   These are small boats which cross the Creek between Dubai and Deira. There are both motorised and rowing abras which in the summer are covered with shades. An abra trip is an experience which should not be missed. Fares differ at the various staging points but for a trip directly across the creek, sharing the boat with other passengers, the fare is 10 fils on the motorised abras and 25 fils for the longer journey from the heart of Deira to the Dubai side souk. Rowing abras usually cost Dh 2–3 per person. If an abra crossing is made by only one person the fare should be pre-arranged—usually about Dh 4–5. Some abra operators will give half hour pleasure trips on the creek for Dh 15–20. They provide a spectacular view of the city and of the dhows moored alongside the Creek.

Taxis More efficient and cleaner than in many Arabian cities but nevertheless a visitor should be cautious about fares. Always fix them with the driver beforehand. If possible check with your hotel reception before making a journey to get an idea of what you should pay. Likewise, at the airport check with an airline desk. Taxis at the airport are regularly known to charge Dh 30 for the ten minute trip to Dubai's Inter-Continental Hotel. It should be a maximum of Dh 20. Taxis at hotel ranks usually charge more than taxis hailed in the street. Most short journeys cost between Dh 3–5. Shared taxis about Dh 1. Single taxis usually charge at least Dh 10 for a trip over the Creek.

Long-distance taxis have a station opposite the Deira Cinema. For trips to Ras al-Khaimah they charge Dh 100–120 for a single or "engaged" taxi, Dh 12 for a shared one (Dh 24 for the front passenger seat). An "engaged" taxi to Sharjah costs around Dh 12, Dh 2 shared. To Abu Dhabi the "engaged" fare is between Dh 150–200 depending on the type of taxi, shared around Dh 30. Tipping taxis above the fares they charge is not necessary although in mid-1977 there was talk of introducing taxi metres in which case a tip may be necessary.

Car hire firms *Dubai Rent-a-Car.* Tel: 28886. *Gulf Rent-a-Car.* Tel: 25545. *Jumairah Rent-a-Car.* Tel: 34934. *National Rent-a-Car.* Tel: 24647.

Daily rates average about Dh 120 for a medium-size four-door saloon. Visitors should note it is *not* permitted to drive on an international driving licence. A temporary licence must be obtained from the Dubai Police traffic department. This will be issued to anyone with a full valid licence from their home country, provided they pass an eye test.

Travel agents *Dubai National Air Travel Agency* (DNATA). P.O.B. 1515. Tel: 22151. *Oman Travel Agency.* P.O.B. 690. Tel: 22798. *Algaith and Almoosa Travel Agency.* P.O.B. 1810. Tel: 22371. *Al-Naboodah Travel Agency.* P.O.B. 1200. Tel: 22522.

Airline offices Most airline offices are in the DNATA building behind the Phoenicia Hotel (Al-Nasr Square).

Air France, P.O.B. 1200. Tel: 22522. *Air India,* P.O.B. 1701. Tel: 23717. *Alia,* P.O.B. 1515. Tel: 26806. *British Airways,* P.O.B. 1989.

Tel: 24644. *Egyptair*, P.O.B. 1515. Tel: 80754. *Gulf Air*, P.O.B. 595. Tel: 22151. *Iran Air*, P.O.B. 4389. Tel: 22698. *Iraqi Airways*, P.O.B. 5067. Tel: 25482.

KLM, P.O.B. 1696. Tel: 21533. *Kuwait Airways*, P.O.B. 1984. Tel: 22151. *MEA*, P.O.B. 1515. Tel: 21888. *Pakistan International Airlines*, P.O.B. 1878. Tel: 22036. *Saudia*, P.O.B. 1810. Tel: 22371. *Scandinavian Airlines*, P.O.B. 1515. Tel: 28916. *Singapore Airlines*, P.O.B. 3358. Tel: 20647. *Syrian Arab Airlines*, P.O.B. 1810. Tel: 22371. *Trans Mediterranean*, P.O.B. 1778. Tel: 22167. *TWA*, P.O.B. 1810. Tel: 22371.

Shipping agencies *YBA Kanoo*. P.O.B. 290. Tel: 32525. *Gulf Agency Company*. P.O.B. 2404. Tel: 31300. *Gulf Shipping Company*. P.O.B. 2578. Tel: 31151. *Gray Mackenzie and Company*. P.O.B. 70. Tel: 21221. *General Shipping*. P.O.B. 1034. Tel: 31181. *Interstate Shipping S.A.* P.O.B. 2404. Tel: 31324.

Post offices Opening hours: 8.00 a.m.–1.00 p.m. and 4.00 p.m.–6.00 p.m. Closed Thursday afternoon and Friday. *Central Post Office*. Tel: 32900. *Deira branch*. Tel: 21952. *Riqa branch*. Tel: 21863. *Satwa branch*. Tel: 40364.

Telephones There are no public telephone booths in the streets. But all local telephone calls are free, shops and most hotels will allow anyone to use their telephones.

International calls can be made from either hotels or from the Emirates Telecommunications Corporation (Emirtel) offices on either Dubai side or Deira (near the Ambassador Hotel on Dubai side and near the Sheraton Hotel on Deira side). Dubai has an excellent internal and external telephone service. All telephone directories are in English as well as Arabic. A useful hint to the visitor who does not know his way around Dubai is to remember that the telephone number can give him an approximate location of the person he is calling. All numbers beginning with the digit '2' are on the Deira side of the creek, all beginning with '3' are on the Dubai side, '4' Jumaira, '7' Zabeel area, '5' dry-dock area, '6' Sharjah road area, '8' temporary numbers (usually in Deira).

Useful phone nos. *Police*—21111. *Fire*—22222. *Rashid Hospital*—71111. *Al-Maktoum Hospital*—21211. *Ministry of Information*—25433. *Airport* —24222 (Flight enquiries—24680). *Immigration Department*—22501. *EMIRTEL*—26111 (Dubai-side branch office—31371).

Cables/telexes Most hotels have telex machines for the use of visitors. Calls and cables can also be sent from the Emirtel offices (see **Telephones**).

Shops Opening hours 9.00 a.m.–1.00 p.m. and 4.00 p.m.–8.00 p.m. daily, except Friday. *Al-Nasr Novelty Stores.* Tel: 61622. On the Dubai Sharjah road. A department store selling virtually everything from knives and forks to sailing dinghies. Specialising in gift items. *Arts and Gems* (Deira). Tel: 24937. Luxury gifts and clothing. *Khalid* (Deira). Tel: 22326. Specialists in silverware, jewellery and crystal glass. *Jashanmal and Sons* (Dubai-side). Tel: 31735. Department store specialising in items for the home, shoes, cosmetics and electrical goods.

Souks The best time to go shopping in the souks is between about 5.00–7.00 p.m. when they are at their busiest. The atmosphere gives a true feeling of what souk shopping is all about. There are three main souks in Dubai—two of which are on the Deira side of the creek, the general souk and the gold souk.

The gold souk is some distance from most hotels so it would be advisable to take a taxi. If you decide to walk ask for the Al-Ras fishmarket. The beginning of the gold souk is only about 200 yards from the fishmarket and extends for about a quarter of a mile. The gold is no longer cheap but good craftmanship is still evident in ornate pieces.

The general souk in Deira is nearer the city centre. Again it is better to ask for directions locally. Here the traders are selling everything from cans of paint to dried tobacco and cloth. On the Dubai side of the creek the general souk consists largely of shops selling electrical appliances, cameras, radios and an assortment of general goods imported from all corners of the globe.

Leisure and sports clubs/social centres None of the social centres or clubs in Dubai have any specific temporary membership for visitors, although many of them will often welcome a visitor as the guest of a member.

Dubai Country Club. Tel: 70182. Swimming, squash, tennis, golf, and darts. Film nights, discotheques and a restaurant. *Lions Club.* Tel: 31934. Meets every second Thursday of the month at 1.30 p.m. at the Ambassador Hotel. *Dubai Round Table.* Meets every first and third Tuesday of the month at the Oasis Hotel at 8.00 p.m. Round Tablers from other countries always made welcome. *Dubai Polo Club.* Games usually played every Friday at grounds adjacent to the Dubai Country Club. Spectators welcome. Opportunities for games for experienced polo players. *Dubai Rugby Club.* Games played most Friday afternoons in the winter months at ground near Dubai Country Club. Followed in the evening by a social night at clubhouse. Spectators and anyone wanting a game welcome. *British Sub Aqua Club.* Has a clubhouse in Ajman but meetings are frequently held in Dubai. Dives often held on the UAE's east coast on Fridays. For further information telephone John Lewis 32015.

Newsagents/bookshops There are numerous newsagents and bookshops throughout the city. Those with the widest stock include: *Jashanmal and Sons.* Tel: 31735. *Malik Newsagents.* Tel: 24449. *National Newsagents.* Tel: 26441. *Inter-Continental Hotel Bookshop.* Tel: 27171.

Hospitals Dubai has two relatively good general hospitals—*Rashid* (Tel: 71111) and *Al-Maktoum* (Tel: 21211).

Pharmacies For late night opening consult local press. *International Pharmacy.* Tel: 21397. *Shareeb Pharmacy.* Tel: 21612. *Al-Faraki Pharmacy.* Tel: 25844. *National Pharmacy.* Tel: 32813.

Banks *Al-Ahli Bank.* P.O.B. 1719. Tel: 24175. *Algemene Bank Nederland.* P.O.B. 2567. Tel: 33335. *Arab African Bank.* P.O.B. 1049. Tel: 21245. *Arab Bank.* P.O.B. 3285. Tel: 31612. *Bank Melli Iran.* P.O.B. 1894. Tel: 21130. *Bank of Baroda.* P.O.B. 3162. Tel: 31955. *Bank of Credit & Commerce International S.A.* P.O.B. 5032. Tel: 20281. *Bank of Oman.* P.O.B. 2111. Tel: 21924.

Bank Omran. P.O.B. 19. Tel: 31855. *Bank Saderat Iran.* P.O.B. 4182. Tel: 31620. *Banque de L'Indochine et de Suez.* P.O.B. 4005. Tel: 25280/25289. *Banque de Paris et des Pays Bas.* P.O.B. 1944. Tel: 26243. *Banque du Caire S.A.E.* P.O.B. 150. Tel: 25175. *Banque du Liban et D'Outre Mer.* P.O.B. 4370. Tel: 26017. *Banque Libanaise Pour Le Commerce S.A.* P.O.B. 4207. Tel: 22291. *Barclays Bank International.* P.O.B. 1891. Tel: 26158.

British Bank of the Middle East. P.O.B. 66. Tel: 32000. *Chartered Bank.* P.O.B. 999. Tel: 31515. *Chemical Bank.* P.O.B. 4619. Tel: 25279. *Commercial Bank of Dubai.* P.O.B. 1709. Tel: 22101. *Dubai Bank.* P.O.B. 2445. Tel: 21201. *Dubai Islamic Bank.* P.O.B. 553. Tel: 29861. *First National Bank of Chicago.* P.O.B. 1655. Tel: 26161/5. *Citibank.* P.O.B. 749. Tel: 32100.

Gillett Bros. Discount Co. P.O.B. 5476. Tel: 24008. *Grindlays Bank.* P.O.B. 4166. Tel: 26991/3. *Habib Bank A.G. Zurich.* P.O.B. 3306. Tel: 26027. *Habib Bank.* P.O.B. 888. Tel: 25171. *Middle East Bank.* P.O.B. 5547. Tel: 28871/2. *National Bank of Abu Dhabi.* P.O.B. 4436. Tel: 26141. *National Bank of Dubai.* P.O.B. 777. Tel: 22241. *National Bank of the Middle East.* P.O.B. 152. Tel: 28873. *The Royal Bank of Canada.* P.O.B. 3614. Tel: 25536.

Toronto Dominion Bank. P.O.B. 2510. Tel: 33340. *UAE Bank for Development.* P.O.B. 2449. Tel: 22987. *UAE Development Bank.* P.O.B. 5022. Tel: 29800. *United Bank.* P.O.B. 1000. Tel: 22347/27033/22576.

545

T

will you help us?

We do all we can to get our facts right in *The Gulf Handbook*. Each chapter will be thoroughly revised year by year by people living in each country. When revision is not enough whole sections will be rewritten. But the territory covered by the Handbook is enormous. New hotels and restaurants are springing up all the time. A new cabaret is born, a street is renamed. Names and addresses of good hotels and restaurants for businessmen are always very welcome.

Due possibly to a recent visit, you may have information more up-to-date than ours, or perhaps a suggestion for information to be included in future editions. Please write and tell us about it; your letters will be most welcome.

—**Thank you**

Trade & Travel Publications Ltd
Middle East Economic Digest Ltd
The Mendip Press, Parsonage Lane,
Westgate St., Bath BA1 1EN England

Dubai Ministries/Government departments *Dept. of Health & Medical Services.* P.O.B. 4545. Tel: 70261. *Health.* P.O.B. 1853. Tel: 23583. *Dept. of Information.* P.O.B. 1420. Tel: 25236. *Finance & Industry.* P.O.B. 1565. Tel: 25579. *Economy & Commerce.* Tel: 07–6234 (Res). *Immigration & Resident Permit Dept.* P.O.B. 4333. Tel: 29728. *Dept. of Ports & Boundaries.* P.O.B. 5024. Tel: 26271/3. *Defence.* P.O.B. 2838. Tel: 32330.

Education. P.O.B. 3962. Tel: 22943. *Communications.* P.O.B. 1131. Tel: 23797. *Public Works.* P.O.B. 1828. Tel: 24261/9. *Information & Tourism.* P.O.B. 5010. Tel: 25433. *Labour & Work.* P.O.B. 4409. Tel: 23141. *Agriculture & Fisheries.* P.O.B. 1509. Tel: 24136/9. *Electricity & Water.* Tel: 24276/9. *Housing & Town Planning.* P.O.B. 1617. Tel: 28919.

Justice. P.O.B. 1682. Tel: 21959. *Social Affairs.* P.O.B. 5025. Tel: 26181/5. *Awqaf & Islamic Affairs.* Tel: 26741. *Youth & Sport.* P.O.B. 1671. Tel: 25633. *Cabinet Affairs (Protocol Dept.).* P.O.B. 2604. Tel: 31086. *State Ministry of Cabinet Affairs.* P.O.B. 899. Tel: 29360. *Petroleum & Mineral Resources.* P.O.B. 9. Tel: 24949.

Embassies *Britain.* P.O.B. 65. Tel: 31071. Telex: 5426. *Kuwait.* P.O.B. 806. Tel: 21341. *India (Consulate).* P.O.B. 737. Tel: 32656. *Iran (Consulate).* P.O.B. 2832. Tel: 31157. *Pakistan (Consulate).* P.O.B. 340. Tel: 31412. *Saudi Arabian Misson.* P.O.B. 806. Tel: 22163. *U.S.A..* P.O.B. 5343. Tel: 29007.

Newspapers/periodicals

Gulf Weekly Mirror. English. P.O.B. 290. Tel: 33417. Telex: 5950. Weekly newspaper covering the Gulf. Printed in Bahrain but carries lot of news from Dubai. Large local business news section.

Emirates News. English. Published in Abu Dhabi. P.O.B. 791 Abu Dhabi. Tel (Abu Dhabi): 41480. Daily newspaper, semi-official. Covers world news from the wires of Reuter, AP and UPI and a small amount of local Government news.

Al-Ittihad. Arabic. Semi-official Government daily newspaper published in Abu Dhabi. P.O.B. 791 Abu Dhabi. Tel (Abu Dhabi): 41480. World and local government news in Arabic.

Al-Akhbar Dubai. Arabic. Semi-official weekly magazine published in Arabic with features and news mostly about Dubai and the Arab world.

The Recorder. English. P.O.B. 597, Sharjah. Tel (Sharjah): 22139. World news from the wires of Reuter, published daily and useful for accommodation advertisements.

Al-Jundi. Arabic Monthly. P.O.B. 2838. *Al Amm.* Arabic Monthly. *Dubai external Trade Statistics.* English Monthly. P.O.B. 516. *Dubai official Gazette.* Arabic-English published quarterly or as necessary. *Dubai Chamber of Commerce Review.* Arabic-English Monthly.

Radio/T.V. *Dubai Colour Television and Dubai Broadcasting.* P.O.B. 1695. Tel: 70255. Television programmes, some in English, between about 6.30 p.m. and midnight. New all-English channel with English news and programmes due to be put on air late 1977.

Adjacent radio station broadcasts continuous music from 7.30 a.m. to midnight in stereo on FM band with short world newscasts at 7.30 a.m., 2.30 p.m., and 8.30 p.m. in English. Stock exchange reports broadcast in English at 2.45 p.m.

Churches *Holy Trinity Church.* Minister—Rev. P. Sturdy. Tel: 70247. Children's service Saturday at 5.00 p.m. Holy Communion at 8.00 a.m. and 7.45 p.m. Interdenominational service at 7.00 p.m. Sunday. *Church of S. India* (Mr. T. Koshy). Tel: 34409. Meets at Holy Trinity Church Friday at 7.00 p.m. *Dubai Christian Assembly.* Tel: 31965. Prayer meeting Tuesday at 7.00 p.m. Gospel meeting on Friday at 7.00 p.m. and worship meeting on Sunday at 7.00 p.m.

Marthoma Christians (Father Varky). Tel: 31113. Meets Thursday at Holy Trinity Church at 7.30 p.m. *Evangelical Christian Church of Dubai.* Meetings at Jumairah American School Sunday and Wednesday at 7.00 p.m. *St Thomas's Evangelical Christian Church of India.* Meetings held at Dubai Christian Assembly Hall Thursday at 7.00 p.m. *Indian Pentecostal Church of God.* Tel: 35364/61640.

Useful Addresses/Major Companies:
Dubai Chamber of Commerce and Industry. P.O.B. 1457. Tel: 21327.
Merrill Lynch (stockbrokers). P.O.B. 3911. Tel: 25261/4.
Sir William Halcrow and Partners (consultants to the Government). P.O.B. 360. Tel: 70380.
Government Statistics Office. P.O.B. 516. Tel: 31074.
Bernard Sunley and Sons. Tel: 70080.
Al-Futtaim/Wimpey. P.O.B. 152. Tel: 22123.
McDermott. P.O.B.3098. Tel: 27131.
Dubai Petroleum Company. P.O.B. 2222. Tel: 22141.
Oilfields Supply Center. P.O.B. 1518. Tel: 26171.
Costain/Taylor Woodrow. Tel: 50551. Poste Restante.
Balfour Beatty. Tel: 20033.
Ballantyne and Miller (Lawyers). P.O.B. 5000. Tel: 28563.
Neil McNeill (Lawyer). P.O.B. 2510. Tel: 22727/23758.
British Smelter Constructions. P.O.B. 245. Tel: 27595 (Deira), 41942 (Jebel Ali).
Galadari Brothers. P.O.B. 22. Tel: 23296/7.
Galadari Cementation Construction. P.O.B. 2050. Tel: 23296/7.

SHARJAH Just 15 minutes from Dubai by road, Sharjah is like its neighbour a rapidly expanding emirate. Its relatively small oil income puts it bottom of the Middle East oil league, below Bahrain. So it has had to use a different formula to speed up its growth—in effect a lack of red tape. The Sharjah Government has made it as easy as possible for companies to open in the emirate using Sharjah's advantageous geographical position. As a relatively recent developer, it has had the advantage of being able to learn from the mistakes of other emirates.

Sharjah has many new hotels. Communications are good. The new international airport is one of the most sophisticated and up-to-date in the Gulf. But, with the exception of freight, it will probably be some time before it is served by many international airlines. It is only half an hour's drive from the bustling Dubai international airport, open long before Sharjah's International shipping companies use Sharjah's port for an increasing amount of container cargo. But despite the influx of imported goods Sharjah remains a poor shopping centre. Most small shops hold only limited stocks, with many being subsidiaries of shops in Dubai.

Sharjah is in fact being developed in the shadow of Dubai. The emirate is providing facilities and services supplementary to those in Dubai. Investment money from other parts of the Gulf is financing the building of tall apartment blocks which will house people working in Dubai. Big, luxurious hotels are being constructed to accommodate visitors whose main business will be in Dubai. In many respects Sharjah looks destined to become a residential suburb to its richer neighbour. Nonetheless its economy should have a base broad enough to guarantee it a certain independence.

The emirate's Gulf-of-Oman coast has, for example, great potential. The sleepy town of Khor Fakkan will soon be transformed into a busy port which will save ships from going through the Hormuz Straits to unload cargo. On either side of the town are long, sandy beaches which have become a weekend playground for people on the UAE west coast. One of the big attractions is underwater swimming among the coral reefs. This coastline is fast becoming the leisure centre of the UAE.

GULF HANDBOOK

1 SHARJAH CARLTON
2 MERIDIEN HOTEL
3 OLD PORT
4 LAYYAH
5 LAYYAH WHARF
6 TOWN WHARF
7 SUQ WHARF
8 LAYYAH SPIT
9 FISH WHARF
10 ZEHRA SQUARE
11 ZEHRA SCHOOL
12 SHARJAH SPORTS CENTRE
13 OLD AIRPORT
14 ARABIAN CLUB
15 NEW TRAFFIC OFFICE
16 NEW PALACE
17 OLD PALACE
18 MINA KHALID
19 AL-QASSIMI HOSPITAL

SHARJAH

Hotels

Sharjah Carlton, Al-Khan area (on western outskirts). P.O.B. 1198. Tel: 23711. Telex: 8012. Large, plush hotel adjacent to the beach. 175 rooms and 16 suites. Single room Dh 240, double Dh 375, suite Dh 720. Restaurant (set menu Dh 36). Nightclub. Coffee shop (open 24 hours). Three bars. Swimming pool. Shops. Newsagent. Conference facilities for 120, banqueting for 700.

Sheba Hotel, opposite old airport. P.O.B. 486. Tel: 22554/22522. Telex: 8053. Sharjah's first hotel. Still maintains a good standard. 60 rooms. Single Dh 130, double Dh 200. Breakfast (continental) Dh 15. Restaurant (Dh 35 basic meal). Two bars. Conference facilities for 50 people, banqueting for 300.

Novotel. P.O.B. 6015. Tel: 56566. Telex: 8213. Opened in spring, 1977. 159 rooms and four suites. Single Dh 220, double Dh 295, suites from Dh 550. Breakfast Dh 20 (English), Dh 12 (continental). Restaurant (set menu Dh 50). Coffee shop. Two bars. Swimming pool. Shop/newsagent. Conference and banqueting facilities for 150 people. Free bus service into Dubai.

Meridien, adjacent to Sharjah Carlton. Tel: 56126. Scheduled to be opened latter half of 1977. 230 rooms and six suites. Two Restaurants (French/Arab cuisine). Coffee shop. Bar. Swimming pool. Private beach. Shops. Bank.

Summerland Motel. P.O.B. 1083. Tel: 24321. Telex: 8079. Consists of 32 suites of two rooms each. Most are permanently booked by companies. Single bed Dh 250, double Dh 300. Restaurant (*Al-Tannur*—set menu Dh 36). Bar. Conference facilities.

Grand Flotel, on Khalid Lagoon. P.O.B. 5019. Tel: 57192. Telex: 8251. Converted cruise liner opened mid-1977. 200 rooms and eight suites. Single room Dh 150 (inside), Dh 175 (outside). Double Dh 225. Suite from Dh 300. Breakfast Dh 15. Restaurant (*Captain's Table*). Nightclub (*The Anchorage*). Coffee shop/grill lounge. Two bars. Swimming pool. In-house TV. Cinema. Badminton courts. Shops.

Sands Motel. P.O.B. 5165. Tel: 56475. 36 rooms. Single room Dh 600 per week (including breakfast), double Dh 800, three beds Dh 1000. Restaurant (*The Cellar*). Two bars. Shop. Newsagent.

Holiday Inn Hotel, P.O.B. 88. Tel. 357357. Telex: 8305. 14 storey building, due for completion by end 1977. Overlooking lagoon. 250 rooms. Restaurant on the rooftop. Bars. Coffee shop.

Several new hotels are planned or under construction in Sharjah. They include an *Inter-Continental* (close to the old airport), *Gulf* and a *Carlton Tower*. A hotel, to be managed by Trust Houses Forte of Britain, is planned for Khor Fakkan on the Gulf of Oman coast.

Restaurants

Novotel Hotel Restaurant. Tel: 56566. Mainly French cuisine. Main course prices from Dh 25. Set menu Dh 50. Music. Five per cent municipality tax.

Carlton Hotel Restaurant. Tel: 23711. International/Lebanese cuisine. A la carte prices from Dh 15. Set menu Dh 36.

Al-Tannur Restaurant, Summerland Motel. Tel: 24321. Oriental/ European cuisine. Main course from Dh 25. Set menu Dh 36. Music till 1 a.m.

Captain's Table, Grand Flotel. Tel: 57192. French/Arab cuisine. Main course from Dh 38. Open till 3 a.m.

The Cellar, Sands Motel. Tel: 56475. International cuisine. Main course from Dh 20. Music till midnight.

Night clubs

The Anchorage, Grand Flotel. Tel: 57192. No food. Cover charge Dh 15.

Beachcomber Night Club, Carlton Hotel. Open till 2.30 a.m. International cuisine. Main course from Dh 25. Music/cabaret till 2.30 a.m. Cover charge Dh 10.

Airport Five miles from city centre. A new airport, officially opened at beginning of 1977 but still served by few international airlines. Only 30 minutes by car from Dubai airport. Managed by the German Frankfurt Airport Authority. Good passenger facilities. Transport by private car or taxi. No airport buses. Duty free shops.

Taxis Standard of taxis and taxi driving in Sharjah is poor. Fix the fare with the driver beforehand. There is no official scale of fares and it is advisable to ask your hotel reception for an approximate guide. A short journey in the city usually costs about Dh 2–3. The fare from the city centre to the Sharjah Carlton Hotel is a minimum Dh 10. A single or 'engaged' taxi to Dubai costs Dh 12, shared about Dh 2. The Dubai taxi stand is near the Grand Flotel.

Travel Agencies *Gray Mackenzie & Co.* Tel: 22340. *Kanoo Travel Agency.* Tel: 22436. *Orient Travel & Tourist Agency.* Tel: 22776. *Sharjah National Travel & Tourist Agency.* Tel: 22054. *Oman Travel Agency.* Tel: 22326.

Shipping agents *Arabian Mercantile & Maritime Co.* Tel: 23547. *Gray Mackenzie & Co.* Tel: 22340. *Gulf Agency Co. (Sharjah).* Tel: 22163. *Helmico Trading & Shipping Co.* Tel: 23873. *Sharjah Shipping Co.* Tel: 23166.

Airline offices *Air Ceylon*. Tel: 24251. *Gulf Air*. Tel: 22436. *Air Intergulf*. Tel: 24741. *Yemen Airways*. Tel: 24301 (airport). *Huns Air*. Tel: 24301 (airport).

Car hire Hotels have car hire facilities. *Worldwide Rent-a-Car*. Tel: 25547. Rates are much the same as those in Abu Dhabi and Dubai.

Post Office The main post office is in Al-Roba Street. (Tel: 22428).

Telephone/telex services The Emirates Telecommunications Authority (Emirtel) offers excellent telephone and telex facilities from Sharjah to other world centres. There is automatic telex dialling to most countries and automatic trunk telephone dialling to most Gulf countries and Europe. Telephones are in extremely short supply. Many offices either do not have one or have less lines than they want. Internal telephone calls in the city are free. International calls should be made from your hotel or alternatively from the Emirtel offices (Tel: 25111).

Useful phone nos. *Police*—22211. *Fire*—22411. *Al-Qassimi Hospital*—24211. *Municipality*—22254. *Airport*—24301. *Post Office*—22428. *Telephone Company* (Emirtel)—25111. *Telephone enquiries*—18. *Ambulance*—22111.

Gift shops *Jashanmal & Sons*. Tel: 22412. *Salman Poor Alawazi*. Tel: 23389. *Eastern Star Novelties*. Tel: 22190.

Souks Sharjah has an excellent souk often regarded by expatriates as being one of the cheapest and best in the UAE. Gold and silver items abound. One souk trader well worth visiting is "Cheeky" who makes solid silver dhows.

In late 1977 the souk is due to be rehoused in a new ornate complex being built on the road into Sharjah from Dubai.

Social Clubs The new *Beach Club* on the Ajman road, due to be opened before the end of 1977, aims to provide Sharjah with its first large social club. Otherwise there are several small clubs: *Al-Orooba Club*. Tel: 22856. *Egyptian Club*. Tel: 23579. *National Arts Club*. Tel: 23176. *Sharjah Club*. Tel: 22272. *UAE Flying Club*. Tel: 22774. *Women's Guild of the Chaplaincy of Dubai & Sharjah*. Tel: Dubai 29440/40885. *Sharjah Contracts Club*. (Folk Singing). Tel: 22471. *Dubai & Sharjah Singers*. Tel: Dubai 41019.

Hospitals Sharjah's main hospital is the 100-bed Al-Qassimi (Tel: 24211), opened at the end of 1976. It is managed by a British company and staffed by British doctors and nurses.

Pharmacies *Alsaaf Pharmacy*. Tel: 23566. *Al-Orooba Pharmacy*. Tel: 23355. *Ibn Sina Pharmacy*. Tel: 22435. *National Pharmacy*. Tel: 22339. *Modern Pharmacy*. Tel: 22082. *Najm Pharmacy*. Tel: 23641. *Sharjah Pharmaceutical House*. Tel: 22850.

Banks *Algemene Bank Nederland.* P.O.B. 1971. Tel: 25161/24561. *Arab Bank.* P.O.B. 130. Tel: 22333. *Bank Melli Iran.* P.O.B. 459. Tel: 22510. *Bank of Credit & Commerce International S.A.* P.O.B. 713. Tel: 22983. *Bank Saderat Iran.* P.O.B. 316. Tel: 22470. *Bank of Sharjah.* P.O.B. 1394. Tel: 23521. *Banque du Caire.* P.O.B. 254. Tel: 22021. *Banque Libanaise pour le Commerce S.A.* P.O.B. 854. Tel: 25161/24561. *British Bank of the Middle East.* P.O.B. 25. Tel: 22755. *Chartered Bank.* P.O.B. 5. Tel: 22247. *Commercial Bank of Dubai.* P.O.B. 677. Tel: 22520. *Citibank.* P.O.B. 346. Tel: 22533. *Grindlays Bank.* P.O.B. 357. Tel: 22471/23471. *Habib Bank A.G. Zurich.* P.O.B. 1166. Tel: 22442. *National Bank of Abu Dhabi.* P.O.B. 1109. Tel: 22601. *National Bank of Sharjah.* P.O.B. 4. Tel: 25521. *United Bank.* P.O.B. 669. Tel: 22666.

Sharjah Ministries/Government departments *Communications.* Tel: 22426 (General Manager's residence). *Social & Labour Affairs.* Tel 22136. *Planning.* Tel: 22704/5. *Agriculture & Fisheries.* Tel: 22759 (Agricultural Advisor). *Education.* Tel: 22623. *Information.* Tel: 22010. *Health.* Tel: 22303/4. *Interior.* Tel: 22205. *Immigration & Naturalisation Dept.* Tel: 22417.

Media The only newspaper with offices in Sharjah is the *Recorder Daily Bulletin* which gives a very brief account of world news from the wires of Reuters news agency. The English-language *Gulf Weekly Mirror* circulates in Sharjah (offices in Dubai), as well as the Arabic daily *Al-Ittihad* and the English-language Government paper *Emirates News* (both published in Abu Dhabi). There is no television station, although Dubai and UAE television are received clearly. But there is a radio station, broadcasting music and occasional news bulletins.

Useful addresses/major companies
Abdul Rahman Mohamed Bukhatir. P.O.B. 88. Tel: 22770.
ADRECO. P.O.B. 682. Tel: 23019.
Archosi. P.O.B. 1465. Tel: 23237.
Brown, Crozier and Wyatt. P.O.B. 2034. Tel: 25365.
Chamber of Commerce. P.O.B. 580. Tel: 22464.
Cenforce Gulf. P.O.B. 1880. Tel: 25221.
Eastern Contracting. P.O.B. 1596. Tel: 23489.
Kennedy and Donkin. P.O.B. 1817. Tel: 24446.
Mothercat. P.O.B. 121. Tel: 22496.
Professional Group Australia. P.O.B. 1176. Tel: 23671.
Roughton and Partners. P.O.B. 1782. Tel: 24436.
Six Construct. P.O.B. 1472. Tel: 23453.
Tarmac International. P.O.B. 1499. Tel: 22071.
Westminster Dredging. P.O.B. 1168. Tel: 23473.
White, Young, and Partners. P.O.B. 1219. Tel: 23913.

THE NORTHERN EMIRATES In the northern emirates of Ajman, Umm al-Qaiwain, Ras al-Khaimah and—on the east coast—Fujairah, life styles have changed most in recent years. Where a year or two ago there were sandy tracks there are now roads, and where there used to be traditional barasti huts there are now neat rows of air-conditioned houses. The towns have kept a good deal of their character. Long-eared goats, thriving on an ever-increasing number of cardboard boxes and gaily coloured wrappers of imported American and European food-stuffs, still roam the streets. There are still fishermen fishing and farmers farming. But both the economy and life style is rapidly changing. Finance for development has largely come from the federal purse, but recently Ras al-Khaimah and Umm al-Qaiwain have found oil or gas.

Ras al-Khaimah Ras al-Khaimah, the most northerly emirate, retains its position as supplier of 50 per cent of fresh food in the UAE and potentially could supply all the country's needs. Agriculture and fishing still employs or supports about three-quarters of the 58,000 population. Seeds, fertiliser and insecticides are made available to local farmers at 50 per cent of cost by the Ministry of Agriculture and services such as ploughing, spraying and mechanical repairs are free. Digdagga has an experimental research station and a herd of English Friesian cattle.

Ras al-Khaimah now has its own international airport, its own earth satellite station, and an eight-berth port is under construction. The Union Cement Company has been near to doubling its 700 tons per day output and Ras al-Khaimah's sulphur-free rock from the mountains is in great demand by the construction industry throughout the UAE. The American company, McDermott, is rolling more than 6,000 feet of pipe a month for export around the Gulf and Middle East from its recently-established pipe factory. A fishmeal and fish oil processing plant is being built by a Norwegian firm.

Ras al-Khaimah town is divided into two parts, one called Ras al-Khaimah and the other Al-Nakheel. Both sit either side of the entrance to a lagoon much of which is now reclaimed land. Al-Nakheel is at the northern end, standing closest to the Hajar mountains which rise up above the town. The emirate's capital still lacks any large prestigious modern buildings. When they come, they are likely to be built on the Ras al-Khaimah side which appears to have the most room for development.

Hotels

Ras al-Khaimah Hotel, on the outskirts of town. P.O.B. 56. Tel: 28251. Telex: 9113. Fine view from rooms. Built on hill overlooking lagoon with Hajar mountains behind. 108 rooms. High proportion taken by ship crews (Ras al-Khaimah is a crew transfer point). Single room Dh 220, double Dh 300. Restaurant (breakfast Dh 15, lunch and dinner Dh 33). Bar. Swimming pool. Hotel's casino closed in mid-1977 but may be turned into nightclub.

Ibn Majid, on western outskirts of Ras al-Khaimah side. P.O.B. 351. Tel: 28429. Due to open early 1978. Restaurant.

Restaurants

Picnic, on Oman Road. Lebanese/European cuisine. Single person Dh 25.

Indian Restaurant, behind Shell filling station, Ras al-Khaimah side. Take-away service.

Middle East Restaurant, behind Shell filling station, Ras al-Khaimah side. Good *shahwarma*.

Airport Nine miles from Ras al-Khaimah hotel. Opened in 1976. Though of international standard, it is underused, with only a few flights a week. Temporary terminal.

Taxis Fares are arranged with the driver beforehand. Usual fare for short journey is Dh 3–5. Between Ras al-Khaimah and Al-Nakheel it is around Dh 10.

Single or 'engaged' taxis to Dubai cost between Dh 100–120, depending on type of car. At night, passengers are liable to pay up to Dh 200. Shared taxis cost Dh 12 or Dh 24 for the whole front passenger seat. Fares to Sharjah are slightly cheaper. The Dubai/Sharjah taxi stand is about a mile out of the Ras al-Khaimah side. Taxis charge Dh 5 to and from the stand.

Abras The two sides of town are connected by abras (small taxi-boats). The staging point at Al-Nakheel is at the end of the port jetty. A shared abra costs 25 fils and an 'engaged' one about Dh 2.

Car Hire *Ras al-Khaimah Hire Care.* P.O.B. 311. Tel: 29357. Daily rates (24 hours) range from Dh 90 to Dh 170. Ras al-Khaimah authorities accept international driver's licences for visiting drivers. But drivers travelling outside the emirate will need a temporary Ras al-Khaimah licence. This is issued by the local police on presentation of a home licence, passport and two photos.

Travel agencies *Ras al-Khaimah Travel Agency*, close to Cinema Roundabout, Al-Nakheel. Tel: 21536.

Airline offices *Gulf Air* (representative office). Tel: 29523.

Shipping agencies *Gray Mackenzie & Co.*, Tel: 21655.

Post Office Main post office is on Ras al-Khaimah side close to Borsley Building. A new central office is being built. The Al-Nakheel branch is near Gray Mackenzie liquor store.

Telephones The emirate has its own earth satellite, opened in spring 1977, which is run by *Ras al-Khaimah Telecommunications Authority*. International calls are often quicker than calls to other emirates. The local system is reasonably efficient.

Useful phone nos. *Ambulance*—21251. *Police*—29351. *Operator*—10. *International phone calls*—15. *Enquiries*—18. *Speaking clock*—141. *Telegrammes*—13.

Telex Telexes can be sent from the offices of *Ras al-Khaimah Telecommunications Authority* at Al-Nakheel, beyond Cinema roundabout.

Shops *Spinney's* have a small supermarket on the Oman road (Tel: 21317). There is a little antiques shop, adjacent to Habib Bank on the Ras al-Khaimah side.

Souk There is no central souk, only small fish and vegetable markets.

Leisure/sport Leisure activities are restricted. The area is good for swimming and fishing, particularly deep sea fishing. Boats can be hired from local fishermen. There is a small expatriate sailing club. In the cooler months, camel races are held a few miles out of town in the early morning. But only a few privileged locals know when they are taking place.

Book shops *Jashanmals & Sons*, on Oman road. Tel: 28132. Sells foreign newspapers, magazines and a few books.

Hospitals There are two hospitals—*Al Nakheel Hospital* and *Kuwait Hospital*. But their facilities are limited and visitors are advised to go to Dubai or Sharjah for treatment.

Pharmacies *New Alshifa Pharmacy*, Tel: 21327 (Ras al-Khaimah side), 21727 (Al-Nakheel).

Banks Head office: *Bank of Arab Coast*. P.O.B. 342. Tel: 28190. Main offices: *The Arab Bank*. P.O.B. 20. Tel: 21238. *Bank of Oman*. P.O.B. 499. Tel: 21621. *British Bank of the Middle East*. P.O.B. 9. Tel: 28214. *Commercial Bank of Dubai*. Tel: 28447. *Grindlays Bank*, Sabah Street. P.O.B. 225. Tel: 28452/8453. *Habib Bank*. P.O.B. 205. Tel: 21549. *Rafidain Bank*. P.O.B. 273. *United Bank*. P.O.B. 182. Tel: 28109.

Ministries/Government departments *Ruler's office*. P.O.B. 1. Tel: 29433. *Ruler's Secretary*. Tel: 29350. *Ruler's Adviser and Director of Petroleum Affairs*. Tel: 21530. *Technical Adviser*. Tel: 29421. *Ministry of Information*. Tel: 28138. *Ras al-Khaimah Municipality*. Tel: 28422.

Media Ras al-Khaimah TV mainly shows American films and TV programmes. The local radio station broadcasts English news bulletins. The Emirate has few publications of its own. *Ras al-Khaimah Magazine* is a bi-monthly published by the Department of Information. The Chamber of Commerce puts out a quarterly in Arabic.

Major companies Cement/aggregate: *Union Cement*. P.O.B. 170. Tel: 21556. *Ras al-Khaimah Rock Company*. Tel: 28236. *Raymond International*, Khor Khweir. Traders/contractors: *Al-Nahda Trading & Construction*. P.O.B. 446. Tel: 29200. *United Developing Enterprise Co.*. P.O.B. 309. Tel: 28268. Telex: 9118. *Union Construction Co*. Tel: 28227. *Archicat*. P.O.B. 530. Tel: 21656. *Al-Burj Enterprise Co*. P.O.B. 121. Tel: 29310. *Al-Futtaim*. Tel: 22442. Insurance: *Ras al-Khaimah National Insurance Co*. P.O.B. 506. Telex: 9116.

Useful addresses *Ras al-Khaimah Chamber of Commerce*, adjacent to Borsley Building, Ras al-Khaimah side. Tel: 212348.

Ajman Geographically surrounded by Sharjah, this emirate has been developing quickly over the last two years. Its creek is being dredged and the draining walls extended under a federal project. The shipyard of Ajman Heavy Industries, a joint venture between the Ajman Government and six Japanese concerns, builds and repairs boats of up to 7,000 or 8,000 tons which previously had to go to Bandar Abbas for maintenance. The town itself has been comparatively slow to develop as a commercial centre. Ajman's own bank—The Ajman Arab Bank which was the first drive-in bank in the emirates—was forced to close down temporarily in mid-1977 when the UAE Currency Board imposed restrictions on loan deposit ratios.

Two companies are exploring Ajman's vast resources of high grade marble and one of the largest fishmeal plants in the UAE is to be situated in the emirate.

A detailed future town plan has been drawn up, featuring two industrial areas. One of Ajman's most recent successful products has been mineral water. A bottling plant has been set up in Masfut—one of Ajman's two inland dependencies—to produce 50,000 bottles of mineral water a day for local consumption and export to other parts of the Gulf.

Ajman's population of 22,000 is being gradually swelled by expatriate workers with jobs in Dubai and Sharjah who have set up home in the emirate. They have been attracted by the comparatively low rents still being charged by Ajman landlords. As a result an increasing number of modern villas and apartments are appearing on the periphery of Ajman town. However, for the present the emirate has no hotels.

Useful phone nos. *Municipality*—4331. *Hospital*—4235. *Fire*—4254. *Police*—4254.

Banks Head office: *Ajman Arab Bank*. P.O.B. 414. Tel: 22818/22951. Telex: 9510. Main offices: *Arab Bank*. P.O.B. 17. Tel: 4431. *Bank of Credit & Commerce International SA*. P.O.B. 146. Tel: 4313. *Bank of Oman*, P.O.B. 11. Tel: 4440. *Bank Saderat Iran*. P.O.B. 16. Tel: 4232. *British Bank of the Middle East*. P.O.B. 260. Tel: 4843. *Habib Bank*. P.O.B. 14. Tel: 4350. *United Bank*. P.O.B. 15. Tel: 4229.

Umm al-Qaiwain Umm al-Qaiwain's 17,000 population is mainly dependent on fishing for its income. It receives subsidies from the UAE Ministry of Agriculture & Fisheries which provides credit facilities and technical services. But the emirate may soon become much less reliant on its traditional source of income because relatively large amounts of natural gas have been found in Umm al-Qaiwain. There could, however, be a long delay before this potential wealth is fully exploited. For the moment development projects remain limited. The creek is being turned into a small cargo port and a 300-ton-a-day fish oil factory has been designed by Norconsult of Norway. Two hotels are planned, one of which will be in the dependency of Falaj al-Mu'alla. Offshore, a nearby island provides a sanctuary for a bird colony and has attracted a number of ornithologists, while onshore there is a popular weekend water-skiing and sailing club.

Restaurant

Umm al-Qaiwain Casino, on the outskirts of Umm al-Qaiwain town. Not a place for gambling but a good Lebanese restaurant, located on the beach. Popular with people from Dubai and Sharjah on Fridays. Licensed.

Useful phone nos. *Municipality*—6245. *Hospital*—6352. *Fire*—6250. *Police*—6250.

Banks *Bank of Credit and Commerce International SA.* P.O.B. 49. Tel: 6451. *Habib Bank.* P.O.B. 32. Tel: 6350. *National Bank of Dubai.* Tel: 6251. *United Bank Limited.* Tel: 6238.

Fujairah The UAE's only emirate whose land is confined to the Gulf of Oman coast. It is only relatively recently that it has become linked with the outside world. Until a new asphalt road through the Hajar mountains was completed two years ago, Fujairah suffered from isolation. It was a good two-hour journey through wadis and along winding mountain tracks to Fujairah town. Now the emirate's 27,000 population is beginning to see the first benefits of modern development. Plans have been drawn up for a new harbour, hotels and industrial plants. Like Sharjah, which also has territory on the east coast, Fujairah should profit handsomely from the coast's immense potential for leisure facilities.

Hotels

Fujairah Beach Motel, on the northern outskirts of Fujairah town. P.O.B. 283. Tel: 552. Telex: 9013. Fujairah's first and so far only quality hotel. Lebanese management. 30 rooms. Single room Dh 200, double Dh 300. 15 per cent service charge. Restaurant (special Friday *maza* lunch for Dh 35). Bar. Swimming pool.

A hotel, to be managed by *Hilton International,* is being built in Fujairah. Due for completion sometime in 1978.

Useful phone nos. *Ministry of Information and Culture*—317. *Municipality*—33. *Hospital*—30. *Fire*—24. *Police*—24.

Hospital There is a small hospital in Fujairah town (Tel: 30).

Banks *British Bank of the Middle East.* Tel: 221. *United Bank.* Tel: 231. *Bank Saderat Iran.* Tel:241. *National Bank of Abu Dhabi.* Tel: 345.

GENERAL INFORMATION

How to get there BY AIR (from outside Gulf): The United Arab Emirates has four international airports at Abu Dhabi, Dubai, Sharjah and Ras al-Khaimah. But the country is almost entirely served by Abu Dhabi and Dubai airports, of which Dubai has the best connections.

From Europe there are daily flights from London and Paris to **Dubai.** Flights between London and Dubai can average about three a day. There are also flights five or six days a week to and from Amsterdam and Athens, and several flights a week between Dubai and Brussels, Rome, Frankfurt and Zurich. There are flights at least two days a week to and from New York—the only direct connection with North America. Otherwise most travellers from there go via London or Amsterdam.

Dubai also has good connections with Middle East centres outside the Gulf. There are several flights a week to and from Amman, Cairo, Damascus and Larnaca. There is a daily service between Beirut and Dubai.

From the Indian sub-continent there is a daily service from Karachi and Bombay with at times several flights a day. There are flights six days a week to and from Singapore. Flights go at least once a week each way between Dubai and Bangkok, Colombo, Dacca, Delhi, Kuala Lumpur, Manila and Tokyo. There are also flights at least two days a week to and from Melbourne and Sydney.

Flights to **Abu Dhabi** from London leave on average twice a day. There are also flights several days a week from Paris and Amsterdam and a less frequent weekly service from Brussels, Frankfurt, Zurich, Rome and Copenhagen. There are no direct connections from North America.

There is a daily service between Beirut and Abu Dhabi and flights several days a week to and from Amman, Cairo, Damascus and Sanaa. Abu Dhabi is also connected by at least one flight a week from Addis Ababa, Khartoum, Istanbul, Taiz, Tunis and Mogadishu.

Flights go several days a week from Karachi and Bombay to Abu Dhabi and there is a flight at least once a week from Bangkok, Manila, Singapore, Rawalpindi, Kuala Lumpur and Dacca.

Sharjah has only one service from Europe—a weekly flight from Zurich. Weekly flights connect Sharjah with Cairo, Sanaa and Taiz. There are also two flights a week from Colombo. Two flights a week go between **Ras al-Khaimah** and Beirut and there are weekly flights to there from Damascus and Bombay.

INTER-GULF/DOMESTIC SERVICES Most inter-Gulf and domestic flights are operated in the United Arab Emirates by *Gulf Air*, which is partly owned by Abu Dhabi. Both Abu Dhabi and Dubai are connected with Bahrain by a service averaging about four flights a day. Dubai also has a daily service running to and from Bandar Abbas and Muscat. It has flights going five to six days a week to Shiraz, Kuwait and Baghdad, and a slightly less frequent service to Dhahran and Jeddah. There are two flights a week between Dubai and Riyadh. An average of three flights a day go between Abu Dhabi and Doha and there are each-way flights four to six days a week between Abu Dhabi and Kuwait, Muscat, and Dhahran. There are less frequent flights to and from Jeddah, Riyadh, Bandar Abbas, Shiraz and Baghdad. Ras al-Khaimah has weekly flights to and from Kuwait and Doha.

In the United Arab Emirates itself, *Gulf Air* runs a daily service between Abu Dhabi and Dubai (with usually two to three flights each way a day). There are also flights six days a week between Abu Dhabi and Sharjah.

BY SEA A regular passenger liner service runs from Dubai to Bombay and Basra. There are also passenger facilities on cargo ships sailing to the UAE from the US, the Far East, Australia and Europe.

Visas All visitors require visas except nationals of the UAE, Bahrain, Iran, Kuwait, Oman, Qatar and Saudi Arabia. Applications for visas from UAE embassies should be sent well in advance of departure and usually must be accompanied by a letter from the visitor's company.

Visas valid for 30 days may be obtained for a sponsored visit. The sponsor must be a UAE resident who can obtain the visa from immigration departments. A 96-hour transit visa may be issued on arrival at Dubai and Sharjah airports provided the visitor holds a ticket with a reserved seat for an onward or return journey. In Abu Dhabi this transit visa is issued only to people who can provide a guarantee from a known person of their departure. Otherwise they will be asked to deposit their passport at the airport immigration office.

Language Arabic, but English widely spoken.

Hours of business Government offices work in the winter from 0800–1400 Saturday to Wednesday, 0800–1200 Thursday; in the summer 0700–1300 Saturday to Wednesday, 0700–1100 Thursday. Closed Friday.

Banks open 0800 to midday Saturday to Wednesday and 0800 to 1100 on Thursday. Closed Friday.

General office hours differ from office to office but usually 0800 to 1300 and 1600 to 1800 Saturday to Wednesday and 0800 to 1300 only on Thursdays. In the summer some companies start an hour earlier and work a shorter afternoon.

Shops usually remain open to 2000 but close between 1300 and 1600 Saturday to Thursday. Some shops are open for limited hours on a Friday morning.

Public holidays

Id al-Adha	*21 November
UAE National Day	2/3 December
New Year (Hijra)	*12 December
New Year	1 January 1978
Birth of the Prophet	*25 February
Night of Ascension	* 3 July
Ascension Day	6 August
Id al-Fitr	3–6 September

* Subject to lunar reckonings.

Time GMT + 4.

Electric current 220/240 volts. The standard fitting is for 15 amp 3-pin square plugs.

Health All visitors must have an international certificate of smallpox vaccination. Cholera vaccination is recommended for all passengers. In Abu Dhabi it is required for anyone arriving within six days from Lebanon, Saudi Arabia, Syria and North Yemen. Infants under one year of age are exempt. Yellow fever immunization is necessary for those arriving within six days from an infected area. All visitors are advised to take preventive medicine against malaria which is endemic in all areas.

Water Dubai's water is fresh and not desalinated. It can be drunk freely although visitors would be advised to drink bottled mineral water if only staying for a short time. Local water can initially cause a slight stomach upset for anyone not used to drinking it. In Abu Dhabi most expatriates boil and filter their water, particularly in the summer months.

Post Overseas air mail tends to be more reliable than local mail. An airmail letter to Europe takes three to five days on average. An airmail letter costs 90 fils to Western Europe and Dh 1.40 to North America. Local mail between emirates can take up to two weeks to arrive. Overseas surface mail is highly unreliable with parcels taking up to a year.

Telecommunications With at least three earth satellite stations in the country, international links are generally good. Calls to other Gulf countries can be made direct and subscribers can dial direct to Europe as well. Local calls, particularly between each emirate, can be difficult. During peak office hours calls can take a long time to come through. There is frequent congestion on lines linking Abu Dhabi, Dubai, Sharjah and Al-Ain.

Currency The UAE Dirham equals 100 fils. Coins: 5, 10, 25, 50 fils and Dh 1. Notes: Dh 1 (presently being replaced by Dh 1 coin), Dh 5, Dh 10, Dh 50, Dh 100, and Dh 1,000. Visitors are advised not to exchange foreign money in hotels. A better rate of exchange will be given in banks or in the souk.

Currency Regulations There are no regulations governing the movement of currency in or out of the country.

Customs regulations Visitors are allowed to bring in 200 cigarettes or half pound of tobacco and a 'reasonable amount' of perfume. The import of narcotics, wines and spirits and natural or cultured unstrung pearls is prohibited.

Customs officers will usually look for drugs, goods banned under the Arab Boycott (which include certain items of toiletry, perfumes and records and cassettes produced on certain labels), and pornographic and semi-pornographic material. Publications like *Playboy* are not permitted.

Local dishes There is no really "local" speciality although the local *hamour* fish is highly recommended.

Alcohol Non-Muslims can buy alcohol in hotel bars and restaurants without restriction, though in Abu Dhabi the authorities are clamping down on drinking in restaurants.

In Dubai a special licence has to be granted by the Dubai Police to purchase alcohol in one of the half dozen or so shops that sell it. Prices in hotels and restaurants average about Dh 7–8 for a canned beer or a small whiskey.

In Abu Dhabi there are only two retail outlets for the purchase of alcohol for home consumption—*Gray Mackenzie & Co.* on the Corniche, and *African & Eastern (Near East)* on Shaikh Zayed Street. Buyers must hold a drinking permit which is issued only to people with a residence visa. The price of a standard bottle of whisky is Dh 20, gin Dh 16 and a crate of beer Dh 50.

Useful advice Visitors should bring a good supply of shirts and underwear because of the high humidity and temperatures. In the winter it is advisable to bring some warm clothing because temperatures drop considerably, particularly at night.

Businessmen are expected to wear suits when attending meetings, particularly with government officials. But generally office staff rarely wear suits.

Practically all the hotels, restaurants and clubs have fairly steep service charges added to the bill and, therefore, tips are not generally required. Nor is it necessary to tip the taxi drivers.

Further Reading

The UAE, Sixth Anniversary. Published December 1977. Available from UAE Embassies.

Dubai, Pearl of the Gulf. Issued by Department of Information, Dubai Municipality.

The United Arab Emirates. By Michael Tomkinson. London, 1975.

Arab States of the Lower Gulf. By John Duke Anthony. The Middle East Institute, Washington DC, USA, 1975.

The United Arab Emirates (An Economic & Social Survey). By F. G. Fenelon. Longman 1973.

Abu Dhabi, Birth of an Oil Sheikhdom. By Clarence C. Mann. Beirut. 1969.

Arabian Sands. By Wilfred Thesiger. Longman 1959.

Supreme Council

President	Shaikh Zayed bin-Sultan al-Nahyan (Ruler of Abu Dhabi)
Vice-President	Shaikh Rashid bin-Said al-Maktoum (Ruler of Dubai)
Members	Shaikh Sultan bin-Mohammad al-Qasimi (Ruler of Sharjah)
	Shaikh Saqr bin-Mohammad al-Qasimi (Ruler of Ras al-Khaimah)
	Shaikh Ahmad bin-Rashid al-Mualla (Ruler of Umm al-Qaiwain)
	Shaikh Hamad bin-Mohammad al-Sharqi (Ruler of Fujairah)
	Shaikh Rashid bin-Humaid al-Nuaimi (Ruler of Ajman)

UAE Government

Prime Minister	Shaikh Maktoum bin-Rashid al-Maktoum
Deputy Prime Minister ...	Shaikh Hamdan bin-Mohammad al-Nahyan
Finance & Industry	Shaikh Hamdan bin-Rashid al-Maktoum
Interior	Shaikh Mubarak bin-Mohammad al-Nahyan

Defence	Shaikh Mohammad bin-Rashid al-Maktoum
Foreign Affairs	Ahmad Khalifah al-Suwaidi
Economy & Trade	Shaikh Sultan bin-Ahmad al-Mualla
Information	Shaikh Ahmad bin-Hamed
Communications	Mohammad Said al-Mualla
Public Works & Housing ...	Mohammad Khalifah al-Kindi
Education, Youth & Sport ...	Abdullah Omran Taryam
Petroleum & Mineral Resources	Manaa bin-Said al-Otaibah
Electricity & Water Resources	Thani bin-Isa Bin-Harib
Justice, Islamic Affairs & Awqaf	Mohammad Abdel-Rahman al-Bakr
Health	Khalfan al-Roumi
Fishery Resources	Said al-Raqbani
Planning	Said al-Ghobash
Labour & Social Affairs ...	Abdullah al-Mazrui
Minister of State without Portfolio	Shaikh Ahmad Bin-Sultan al-Qasimi
Minister of State for Cabinet Affairs	Said al-Ghaith
Minister of State for Supreme Council Affairs	Shaikh Abdel-Aziz al-Qasimi
Minister of State for Foreign Affairs	Saif bin-Said al-Ghobash*
Minister of State for Interior Affairs	Hamuda Bin-Ali
Speaker of Federal National Council	Taryam Omram Taryam
Attorney General	Khalifah al Muheiri

*Assassinated late October 1977.

Currency Guide

The list below of the currencies and exchange rates is given for your guidance only. The rates given have been rounded; they applied in early September 1977.

	$ =	£ =	DM =	SF =	FF =	Yen =
Bahrain Dinar (BD)	0.3958	0.6887	0.1702	0.1638	0.08063	0.001481
Egypt Pound (£E) official	0.3940	0.6855	0.1705	0.1635	0.0805	0.001455
Pound (£E) parallel market	0.6975	1.2145	0.3020	0.2900	0.1425	0.002580
Iran Rial (IR)	70.71	123.0580	30.4120	29.2790	14.4070	0.2647
Iraq Dinar (ID)	0.2899	0.5127				
Kuwait Dinar (KD)	0.2869	0.4993	0.1234	0.1188	0.05846	0.001074
Lebanon Pound (£Leb)	3.1125	5.4112	1.3312	1.2915	0.6347	0.01165
Oman Riyal (RO)	0.3455	0.6013	0.1486	0.1430	0.0704	0.001294
Qatar Riyal (QR)	3.9505	6.8750	1.6350	1.6160	0.8049	0.01462
Saudi Arabia Riyal (SR)	3.5297	6.1427	1.5181	1.4615	0.7191	0.01321
United Arab Emirates Dirham (Dh)	3.8996	6.7864	1.6772	1.6147	0.7945	0.01460
US $ rate		1.7403	2.3330	2.4300	4.9180	266.75

Index to Advertisers

Index to Places